Fifth Edition

Child, Family, School, Community
Socialization and Support

Fifth Edition

Child, Family, School, Community
Socialization and Support

Roberta M. Berns

Saddleback College
University of California, Irvine

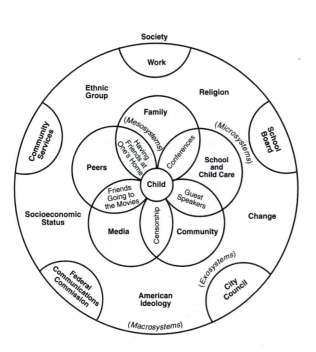

WADSWORTH

THOMSON LEARNING

Australia • Canada • Mexico • Singapore • Spain • United Kingdom • United States

WADSWORTH

THOMSON LEARNING

Publisher   Earl McPeek
Developmental Editor   Tracy Napper
Project Editor   Claudia Gravier
Art Director   Carol Kincaid

Printed in the United States of America
1 2 3 4 5 6 7 05 04 03

For more information about our products,
contact us at:
Thomson Learning Academic Resource Center
1-800-423-0563

For permission to use material from this text,
contact us by:
Phone: 1-800-730-2214   **Fax:** 1-800-730-2215
Web: http://www.thomsonrights.com

Library of Congress Catalog Card Number:
00-101061

ISBN: 0-15-507410-5

Production Manager   Christopher Wilkins
Compositor   Clarinda
Printer   R.R. Donnelley, Willard

Asia
Thomson Learning
60 Albert Street, #15-01
Albert Complex
Singapore 189969

Australia
Nelson Thomson Learning
102 Dodds Street
South Melbourne, Victoria 3205
Australia

Canada
Nelson Thomson Learning
1120 Birchmount Road
Toronto, Ontario M1K 5G4
Canada

Europe/Middle East/Africa
Thomson Learning
Berkshire House
168-173 High Holborn
London WC1 V7AA
United Kingdom

Latin America
Thomson Learning
Seneca, 53
Colonia Polanco
11560 Mexico D.F.
Mexico

Spain
Paraninfo Thomson Learning
Calle/Magallanes, 25
28015 Madrid, Spain

PREFACE

PURPOSE

I wrote *Child, Family, School, Community* to reconfirm and document the most basic theory of relationships known to humankind—that people need people to survive. Children need supportive adults as well as other children; adults need a supportive community including other adults; and children are the core of society, nurtured by it and for it. The first edition of *Child, Family, Community* focused on the child socialization process. The second edition added information about how societal support can empower children and their families. The third edition featured ethnic diversity's influence in socialization. The fourth edition expanded the title and emphasized the role of school and child care as socializing agents in a changing society and embraced the concept of inclusion (that all children should have equal access to appropriate educational opportunities). This edition emphasizes the bi-directionality of interactions between the child and various socialization agents, illustrating the child's role in his or her own socialization. It also includes more information on links between various ecosystems and how they affect the child.

AUDIENCE

Child, Family, School, Community is for anyone who deals with children—parents, teachers, and professionals in human services, home economics, public health, psychology, and social work. It is an introductory text for the combination of disciplines that most affect a child's development. It can be used for both lower and upper division courses, such as child and community relationships and child socialization. I have used it at the community college as well as at the university by varying the type and depth of assignment.

DISTINGUISHING FEATURES

Child, Family, School, Community is distinctive because of its comprehensive coverage. It integrates the contexts in which a child develops, the relationships of the people in them, and the interactions that take place within and between contexts. It also addresses the need for parents and professionals who work with children to enable all children to adapt optimally to a changing world.

The title of the book indicates that when one is concerned about children's development one must also be concerned with the contexts in which children develop. For example, the teacher is concerned with children's families because when children come to school, they bring with them their attitudes toward learning, experiences in dealing with others, and self-concepts, all of which germinated in the family. To enhance a child's development, the teacher must work with the child's family and communicate goals, be supportive of the family's values, and enlist the family's cooperation for providing optimal learning experiences.

The professional is concerned with the child's family because when the child has a problem, whether it be emotional, intellectual, social, or physical, the professional must work with the family to determine the cause, to develop a treatment plan, and to evaluate the results.

Parents, teachers, and professionals are concerned with communities (including the peer group, media, and neighborhood) because communities make certain decisions that affect children. For example, a community shows its support for children in the way that it allocates its tax money for schools, services, libraries, and safety. A community also shows support for children via its business policies, such as maternal or paternal leave, flextime, and child care.

THEMES AND PEDAGOGY

To provide an optimal environment for children's growth and development parents need knowledge and skills, as well as support. To get or give support (psychological, financial, medical, or political), one must understand the roles of people and environments in the lives of children. Thus, I have analyzed the socialization influences of the family, child care, the school, the peer group, the mass media, and the community on children's development. I have explained how the interactions of these agents with the child (including the child's contribution to his or her own development) and with each other contribute to the outcomes of socialization—values, morals, attitudes, motives, self-control, gender roles, and self-esteem. I also have illustrated how maltreated, disabled, and ethnically diverse children can be empowered by special socialization supports.

I have organized classic research as well as contemporary studies on children, families, schools, and communities according to the ecological approach to enable the student to understand the many settings and interactions influencing development. The ecology of human development encompasses the disciplines of biology, psychology, sociology, anthropology, and education as they affect the person in society.

Whenever one analyzes something, one takes it apart and evaluates its components. Occasionally, in the process, one loses sight of the whole. I have tried to avoid this by including chapter outlines, prologues as advance organizers (classic stories compared to modern ones with questions to stimulate critical thinking about the chapter), case studies, examples, epilogues as conclusions to the prologues, and summaries. I have also included applications and activities in each chapter to enable the student to experience the relationship between theory and practice. For further study, Internet sites and book resources are listed.

Because our society is changing so rapidly, a major concern of parents, professionals, and politicians is how to socialize children for an unknown future? What skills can we impart? What knowledge should we teach? What traditions do we keep? In addition to including ways in which children are socialized, I have incorporated the theme "children, change, challenge, and choice" to address this concern.

"Children and change" refers to children growing up in a changing world and the impact of change on their socialization. This focuses on how can children be empowered to use their abilities to function optimally in society as well as to contribute to society's well being and perpetuation.

"Children and challenge" calls on adults to contribute to the optimal development of all children.

"Children and choice" refers to one of the basic principles of our society— pluralism. The book describes various ways of accomplishing goals. It stresses value clarification that supports making responsible choices among alternatives.

NEW TOPICS AND ANCILLARIES

Some current topics covered in the book are socially toxic communities, ethnically diverse socialization, collaborative caregiving, bullies and victims, gangs, preventing violence, and development of self-control and emotional regulation.

Ancillaries include a student study guide, instructor's manual, and a Web site.

SOCIALIZATION AND SUPPORTIVE INFLUENCES

The seeds for this book were probably sown about forty years ago. I was a freshman in the College of Human Ecology at Cornell University taking a child development course taught by Dr. Urie Bronfenbrenner. Today Dr. Bronfenbrenner, professor of psychology, human development, and family studies, is most well known for his research on children and families in various settings as well as for his advocacy of government and business policies to support families.

To sum up Dr. Bronfrenbrenner's philosophy:

(1) A child needs the enduring, irrational involvement of one or more adults in care and joint activity with the child, and (2) for one or more adults to provide such care and involvement, required are public policies and practices that provide opportunity, status, resources, encouragement, examples, and, above all, time for parenthood, primarily by parents, but also by other adults in the child's environment, both within and outside the home.

Dr. Bronfenbrenner's enthusiasm for children and families, his dynamic lecture style, and his probing questions regarding the current state of human development research, as well as public policy, provided me with an analytic perspective to examine whatever else I read or heard thereafter.

The seeds for this book could not have flowered had it not been for the care their host (the author) received in her growth and development. My family, my teachers, my friends, the neighborhood in which I grew, and my experiences growing up all contributed to this book. Even as I reached adulthood, the seeds for this book are still being nurtured along by others—my husband (Michael), my children (Gregory and Tamara) and their spouses (Kathleen and Alexander), my grandchild (Helen), my friends, my neighbors, my students, and my colleagues.

As flowers grow, to maintain their shape and stimulate new growth they must be pruned and fertilized. I would like to thank my reviewers of all editions and editors for for their valuable input in this process. Specific thanks to the reviewers of this edition: Deborah Davis, Chaffey College; Nancy Fowell, University of Wisconsin, Whitewater; Beulah Hirschlein, Oklahoma State University; Al Lorenz, Glendale Community College; Charles Snow, East Carolina University; and Ruth Thomas, University of Minnesota, Twin Cities.

For the fruit of the harvest, this fifth edition, I would like to thank my editor, Tracy Napper, for plowing this version with me. Also many thanks to the rest of the book team at Harcourt: Claudia Gravier, project editor; Christopher Wilkins, production manager; and Carol Kincaid, art director.

Roberta M. Berns
May 2000

CONTENTS

Chapter 11: Implicit Socialization Outcomes . . 475

Chapter 12: Explicit Socialization Outcomes . . 529

I dedicate this book to significant people in my life:

My Children—Gregory and Tamara

(Their spouses—Kathleen and Alexander,

my grandchild—Helen)

My Family—husband, Michael,
brother, parents, and grandparents

My School—Cornell University (Dr. Urie Bronfenbrenner), Saddleback College, and
University of California, Irvine (my colleagues and students)

My Community—New York (past) and California (present)

•

Roberta M. Berns

"*The more things change, the more they remain the same.*"

— *Alphonse Karr*

Chapter 1

ECOLOGY OF THE CHILD

Prologue

FROM MYSTICAL MYTH TO TECHNOLOGICAL TRAGEDY

Times may change, but human nature endures. The dream to be able to fly is as old as humankind.

In Greek mythology, a skillful inventor, named Daedalus, was summoned to the island of Crete by King Minos to trap the Minotaur, a half-man and half-bull-like creature. Daedalus brought his son, Icarus, to help him execute his design. To contain the beast, they built a labyrinth—a maze so confusing that when one entered he or she could not escape. So clever was the project, that King Minos decided to retain Daedalus and Icarus so that he could use their talents in other ways. Wanting to return home, Daedalus began to plan an escape. He collected feathers and fastened them with twine and wax to some gently curving twigs. After observing how birds fly and practicing with the wings fastened to their shoulders, Daedalus and Icarus prepared for their flight home to Greece. When the weather was just right for their journey, Daedalus instructed his son "to fly a middle course"—warning him not to fly so low as to make the feathers heavy from the moisture of the sea, or so high as to cause the wax to melt from the heat of the sun.

The joy of flying completely captured the mind of Icarus; the temptation to reach heaven was too great for so immature a child. In spite of his father's shouts, Icarus soared higher and higher. Soon his feathers began to fall out, and realizing his mistake too late, he tumbled downward into the sea. After much searching, Daedalus found the body of his dead child and carried it back to Greece. He hung up his wings forever.

In contemporary California, a 7-year-old child, Jessica Dubroff, also tried to fulfill her dreams of flying. She wanted to be the youngest person to fly across the continental United States. Her father invested in flying lessons and hired a single-engine Cessna to "be her wings." Jessica's flight was closely followed by the media and so was witnessed by many via television. Jessica, her father, and the flight instructor exalted in the first leg of the journey. Excitement and overconfidence overtook reason and contributed to the decision to make the second leg of the journey even though weather conditions were not optimal. As the plane descended, the wind and rain proved too great to overcome; the plane took a nose dive and crashed on a suburban highway.

Although the motives for Icarus' and Jessica's flights differed, his being escape and hers being fame, the cause of death was the same—self-exaltation—both were overconfident and impressed with their ability to fly. While Icarus had the voice of reason from his father to guide him away from such childhood fantasies (even though he ignored it), Jessica did not. ◼

- *What is society's concept of "childhood" in terms of abilities, needs, and responsibilities?*
- *How do technology and media influence the concept of childhood?*
- *Should children be pushed to compete with adult records of achievement?*
- *Should children be permitted to follow their dreams without adult guidance and limits? What is parental responsibility?*

ECOLOGY, CHANGE, AND CHILDREN

E**cology** is the science of interrelationships between organisms and their environments; for humans, it involves the consequent psychological, social, and cultural processes that develop over time (Bronfenbrenner & Morris, 1998). Environmental, or societal change, influenced by such forces as demographics, economics, politics, and technology, presents challenges to human adaptation. The purpose of this book is to examine how growing up in a changing world affects the development of children via socialization. Children are socialized and supported by their families, schools, and communities. Children perpetuate the present into the future. Families, schools, communities, and society as a whole accept responsibility for ensuring children's well being by providing a safe and healthy environment in which to live as well as by investing in children's education.

Issues facing children and families will be presented for critical analyses at the beginning of each chapter in a prologue and revisited at the end of each chapter in an epilogue.

Ecological Trends

As society undergoes change, trends such as the following continue to challenge families', schools', and communities' commitment to children's needs:

- Family size is shrinking.
- The United States is a highly mobile society, and few children spend their entire childhood in one residence.
- The proportion of children with mothers in the labor force has grown dramatically.
- The number of homeless families with children has increased.
- The proportion of children living with both biological parents has declined while the fraction living with single-parent families has grown. The number of children who experience divorce and remarriage has risen. The effects of divorce on children are often long-lasting.
- The number of children who are abused or neglected has increased.
- Children are more likely than other age groups to live in poverty. Children under age 6 living in a female-householder family are particularly at risk. African American and Hispanic American children are more likely to be living in poverty than Anglo children. Poor children are more likely to have health problems and physical or mental disabilities.
- The number of children who have no health insurance has increased.
- The suicide rate for adolescents is increasing.
- Violent crime in communities has exploded in the past decade, with much of it involving teenagers. Poverty, intolerance, drugs, and family violence are contributors.

- The recognition and responsiveness to the range of individual differences among children of the same age has increased.
- There is wider acknowledgment of cultural diversity.
- Children with disabilities must be included in programs for all children.

Sources: Children's Defense Fund (1998). *The state of America's children yearbook 1998.* Washington, D.C.: Author; and Elkind, D. (1998) *Reinventing childhood: Raising and educating children in a changing world.* Rosemont, NJ: Modern Learning Press.

SOCIETY, CHANGE, AND CHALLENGE

With change comes challenge. As Mahatma Gandhi said, "The future will depend on what we do with the present." To understand the world our children will inhabit in the twenty-first century, significant worldwide changes cited by various futurists will be examined.

CHANGE AND SOCIETAL TRENDS

According to John Naisbitt (Naisbitt, 1994; Naisbitt & Auberdene, 1990), the major global trend is interconnectedness. This is evidenced by more economic cooperation among nations. For example, cotton may be grown in the United States, the fabric woven in Chile, the clothing assembled in Thailand, and the final product marketed in the United States. Former communist countries are adopting democratic policies and are competing economically via free enterprise. They are becoming globally interconnected by entering into trade agreements with other countries. Technological advances in communication media have facilitated interconnectedness among nations—satellites have enabled countries across the Pacific and Atlantic oceans to receive American television signals. Anyone any place in the world owning a video recorder has access to information that exists on videotape; interconnecting telephone and computers across the world as well as facsimile machines are fostering instant communication. Political leaders of nations have connected to work on agreements to reduce arms. There is the recognition among most developed countries that war is an obsolete way of solving problems, and there is a global concern for world humanity and human survival, as was exemplified by the United Nations Security Council's creation of an international tribunal to prosecute those responsible for war crimes. Naisbitt (1994) predicts that economic survival and competition in a world market will influence individual societies' decisions regarding political, technical, economical, and social changes. Will societies aim toward accumulating individual wealth, or will they cooperate to reduce world poverty, improve world health, and promote the Earth's environment? These are the challenges facing us today that will affect our children in the future.

One of the immediate consequences of economic, technical, and political inter-connectedness for children is that they will have to be able to think: to apply, analyze, synthesize, and evaluate information, not just regurgitate facts (Fiske, 1992). The ability to think and use knowledge becomes critical in a world plugged into machines and bombarded with information and choices (Postman, 1992).

Children will be influenced by how traditional power structures in governments, banks, businesses, labor unions, and medicine deal with the new realities in economics, health care, communications, media, transportation, education, and ecology. Futurist Alvin Toffler (1990) and Naisbitt (1994) describe a world plugged into information via telecommunications; power is directly linked to knowledge, and knowledge has become central to economic development. Thus, the control of knowledge has the potential for changing traditional power structures. For example, on a global level, access to information gave the people in communist countries the power to demand democratic reforms. The communist structure in Eastern European countries has crumbled. In the United States, for example, the access to knowledge has changed the doctor–patient relationship. Power has shifted from the doctors (who possessed most of the medical knowledge) to the patients and the insurance companies; doctors practicing inappropriately are likely to be sued by their patients, and what doctors may be paid for their services is often determined by what insurance companies deem equitable (managed care). The access to knowledge has also changed the traditional power structure between politician and constituent in that people don't have to depend on their representatives to propose a law; they can gather enough voter signatures and have an initiative put on the ballot. Still another example is the changed relationship between educators and the public in that parents serve on school boards that make decisions regarding schools, and educators must be accountable for children's learning. Thus, the more knowledgeable more and more people become, the less likely it is for power to remain in the hands of the few at the head of an organization.

Some of the ways our society is coping with the increasing link between knowledge and power are described by social scientist Peter Drucker (1992), and by Naisbitt in *Megatrends 2000* (Naisbitt & Auberdene, 1990), which discusses ten major social, economic, political, and technical changes that helped shape our society from the 1980s to the 1990s, and will influence the future. These trends represent indirect effects on children. Naisbitt's synthesis was based on over twelve years of monitoring and analyzing what had been reported in 6,000 local newspapers in cities and towns all over the United States.

Megatrends for the Millennium

1. Our society is still basically industrial, but our economy is based more on the creation and distribution of information than on goods.

2. As technology increases, humans compensate by finding ways to interact with one another.

3. Our national economy is no longer self-sufficient; it is increasingly dependent upon the world economy.

4. We are restructuring from a society run by short-term considerations to one that looks to long-term considerations.

As technology increases, humans compensate by finding ways to interact as exemplified by beepers and cellular phones.

5. We are going from centralization to decentralization; we have learned to achieve results from the bottom up.

6. We are relying less on institutions for help and more on ourselves.

7. We are going from a representative democracy to a participatory democracy.

8. We are giving up dependency on hierarchal structures in favor of informal networks.

9. More U.S. citizens are living in the South and West, leaving behind the old industrial cities of the North.

10. From a limited range of personal choices (either/or) we are expanding into a range of multiple options.

Industrial Society to Information Society

The U.S. economy is no longer based on agriculture or manufacturing, but on information (Postman, 1992). The information society began around 1956–1957. In 1956 the transatlantic phone service was inaugurated; and for the first time in U.S. history, white-collar workers in technical, managerial, and clerical positions outnumbered blue-collar workers. Thus more people worked with information than with products. In 1957 access to information became global. *Sputnik* was launched by the Soviet Union; the technology to communicate via satellites was introduced. Since then, computers, telephones, and cable television have hastened the development of the information society.

The type of society we live in is reflected by the type of work done by adults. In 1950 only about 17% of the workers had jobs dealing with information. In the 1980s the figure was over 77% and included programmers, teachers, clerks, secretaries, health personnel, accountants, stockbrokers, managers, insurance agents, administrators, lawyers, bankers, and technicians (Cetron, 1988; Levine & Levine, 1996). Today, virtually every job relies on information whether it is for keeping records, for predicting sales, or for surveillance. Thus, in an information society, the major resource is knowledge. Consequently, the value of basic reading, writing, and computational skills, as well as the ability to think and to learn, becomes crucial in terms of socialization. Managing information, evaluating it, and using it appropriately also becomes crucial.

In the past, crucial skills may have been hunting ability, farming ability, or business ability. Toffler (1980) explains the changes in abilities valued at a particular time in history as being influenced by waves of economic and social change that affected socialization. The rise of agriculture was the first wave of change (about 8000 B.C. until about 1700 A.D.). Before that, most humans lived in small, migratory groups and survived by hunting, gathering, fishing, or herding. Thus the ability to hunt as well as be self-reliant and adapt to different situations was crucial to survival. The development of agriculture brought with it a more stable way of life. Humans no longer had to depend on what nature had to offer; they could grow their own food on a piece of land season after season. Families were larger, often including several generations, all of whom contributed to the family's welfare. As agriculture became the way of life, the ability to farm as well as be deferent to one's elders and be responsible to one's family became crucial to survival.

Gradually, villages sprang up in agricultural areas. Small businesses grew, too. Humans began to have some choice in how they would live. They could farm or they could work in the villages, performing a trade such as shoemaking or tailoring.

The second wave of change came from the urbanization of Europe through the Industrial Revolution (from about 1700 until 1955). The growth of factories provided all kinds of jobs for people—in textiles, food processing, transportation, engineering, building, and so forth. People had to be educated for such a way of life. They could no longer be adequately socialized by their families or as apprentices to tradespeople. They had to attend school in order to learn the skills necessary to survive in an industrial society. They had to learn to communicate—to speak, read, and write. They had to learn to compute—basic arithmetic skills necessary to function in a money-based economy. And they had to learn appropriate attitudes so they could "fit" in the industrial system. For example, according to Toffler (1980, p. 382):

> The coming of the Second Wave . . . was accompanied by the spread of the **Protestant Ethic** with its emphasis on thrift, unremitting toil, and the deferral of gratification — traits which channeled enormous energies into the task of economic development. The Second Wave also brought changes in objectivity–subjectivity, individualism, attitudes toward authority, and the ability to think abstractly, to empathize and to imagine.

Thus, the ability to work hard, be thrifty, and compete became crucial to survival (*see* Table 1.1).

Table 1.1	**Relationship of Socialization to Change**	
	SOCIETAL CHARACTERISTICS	**SOCIALIZATION SKILLS**
	Hunting, Gathering, Fishing, Herding	Self-Reliance Independence Adaptability Ability to Survive
FIRST WAVE OF CHANGE:	Agriculture	Farming Ability Physical Strength Self-Sufficiency Deference to Elders Responsibility for 　Family Members
SECOND WAVE OF CHANGE:	Manufacturing	Trade or Craft Education Thrift Hard Work Deferral of Gratification Ability to Fit Into 　an Organization
THIRD WAVE OF CHANGE:	Information	Knowledge High-Technology Skills Adaptability Acceptance of Responsibility Working Well With Others Problem-Solving Ability

As the second wave progressed, work in the factories and offices became more specialized and more repetitive. Employers wanted workers who were obedient and cooperative. Thus, the ability to conform to the requirements of the organization became crucial to survival. William Whyte, in his classic book *The Organization Man* (1957, pp. 7–8), describes the similarity of traits among the corporation man at DuPont, the seminary student in the church hierarchy, the doctor in the corporate clinic, the physics Ph.D. in the government laboratory, the engineer at Lockheed, and the young lawyer in a firm on Wall Street. Whyte calls these similar traits "The Social Ethic": "Man exists as a unit of society. Of himself, he is isolated, meaningless; only as he collaborates with others does he become worthwhile, for by sublimating himself in the group, he helps produce a whole that is greater than the sum of its parts."

The third wave of change (about 1955) was the development of high technology (innovations in science applied to industry)—the computer, telecommunications satellites, facsimile machines, space travel, the jet, and the birth control pill. The third wave has shown that white-collar and service workers outnumber blue-collar workers for the first time. As the velocity of the second wave of change exceeded that of the first wave, so the velocity of this third wave of change is already surpassing that of the second wave. For example, the speed of communication, transportation, and computation and the amount of power available to us since 1945 has increased by a billion times over all the rest of human history. For another example, the U.S. Bureau of Labor Statistics (1999) projects service-producing industries (health business, social services, engineering, and management and related services) will account for virtually all job growth. Only construction will add jobs in the goods-producing sector, offsetting declines in manufacturing and mining.

As the Third Wave cuts across our society, work grows less, not more, repetitive. It becomes less fragmented, with each person doing a somewhat larger, rather than smaller task. Flextime and self-pacing replace the old need for mass synchronization of behavior. Workers are forced to cope with more frequent changes in their tasks as well as a blinding succession of personnel transfers, product changes, and reorganizations.

What Third Wave employers increasingly need, therefore, are men and women who accept responsibility, who understand how their work dovetails with that of others, who can handle ever larger tasks, who adapt swiftly to changed circumstances, and who are sensitively tuned in to the people around them (Toffler, 1980, p. 385).

Thus one challenge presented by societal change is how to foster cooperation and sensitivity to others. There are ways in which the peer group can do this. Another challenge is how to foster prosocial behaviors, such as responsibility and cooperation. As shall be seen, research on the development of such behaviors has found that certain parenting styles, opportunities for role taking, and experiences that involve assuming responsibility contribute to the development of prosocial behavior.

Because, "as we move from an industrial to an information society, we will use our brain power to create instead of our physical power, and the technology of the day will extend and enhance our mental ability" (Naisbitt, 1982, p. 249), a third challenge presented by societal change becomes the need for tomorrow's citizens to access available information quickly, be effective problem solvers, and be able to make decisions and create solutions (Toffler, 1990). Not only must today's graduates know how to read, compute, and communicate; they must also know history so they can have a perspective

Assembly line workers must be socialized to conform to certain standards of productivity.

on political, economic, and social issues; they must be culturally literate so they can interact globally, and they must understand basic science so they can make informed decisions about the application of technology to space exploration, nuclear power, computers, and medicine.

Organizational Goals to Individual Goals

The Organization Man (Whyte, 1957) describes the decade of the growth of the bureaucracy of the organization (the corporation, the government, the university, the labor union, and the charitable organization). During the 1960s and 1970s, products were mass marketed, and high technology was spreading from workplaces to schools to health-care systems to homes. The organization and its values were engulfing our way of life.

The organization's main principle is that the needs of the group supersede those of the individual. Thus the organization man's attention is dominated by problems of collective work. The way of life of the organization involves group pressure, anonymity of achievement, and the obstruction of individual creativity. The group becomes the source of creativity and gives meaning to people's need to belong.

What eventually happens, however, is that as the organization gets larger, its division of labor becomes more complex and the sum of uncaring relationships increases, especially with computer technology (Dreman, 1997; Postman, 1992). The organization group, then, no longer becomes a source of creativity and no longer provides meaning for people's need to belong. As bureaucracy increases, certain human attributes, such as pride and responsibility decline, while alienation and self-interest grow (Rothman, 1996).

Most work settings, government agencies, schools, traditional religious institutions, and community services are large organizations. In order to perform efficiently, they operate with formal rules governing relationships and responsibilities, which foster strict neutral feelings among those involved in the organization. Frequently, individual rights must be subordinated for the greater benefit of the organization. Thus, individuals may often feel powerless to make a contribution to the organization and feel uncared for when they have a problem.

Ironically, people generally respond to high technology by seeking more humanistic responses. As technology increases, people look for ways to interact and fulfill the basic human need to belong (Dreman, 1997; Naisbitt, 1994). For example, as childbirth became more and more technical—mothers gave birth in hospitals; they were medicated to avoid pain; babies were whisked away immediately after birth to be cleansed, measured, weighed, and tested; bottle feeding consisting of special formulas was encouraged; fathers were not allowed in labor or delivery rooms—people began to demand more humanistic, natural methods of childbirth, such as no medication, mothers holding babies and nursing them after birth, fathers present at birth, and more births at home.

That values in the workplace are different today (more individual and less organizational emphasis) from those in the second wave of change has been documented by various surveys (Etzioni, 1993; Plummer, 1989), illustrating a decrease in the number of U.S. citizens who believe "hard work always pays off" and are motivated by strict work guidelines and clear tasks. Today, an increasing number of workers reflect a pursuit of self-interest rather than communal or organizational values (Etzioni, 1993). Motivation, as such, is exhibited in wanting more meaning and self-esteem from their work as well as demanding more rights from employers for personal happiness. The workplace has become a significant source of self-esteem.

The third wave of change rewards workers who are "proactive," who exercise direction, who demand their work be worthy of their talents and be socially responsible, whereas the second wave rewarded workers who were obedient and cooperative, trusting their welfare to the authority in charge. To illustrate, the best-selling book *In Search of Excellence,* by Thomas J. Peters and Robert H. Waterman, Jr. (1982), describes some basic principles used by the best-run U.S. companies. One principle, for example, is the creation in *all* employees of the awareness that their best efforts are essential to the success of the company and that their efforts will be rewarded. Another involves breaking up the large organization into smaller groups and encouraging autonomy and competitiveness within the groups, while keeping the administrative layers simple and lean.

What Peters and Waterman continually observed in the excellent companies they studied was extraordinary energy exerted above and beyond the call of duty on the part of the workers. Why? The authors concluded that when workers are treated humanistically, feel they are cared for, and are given even a modicum of control over their destiny, they are motivated to excel. In other words, workers do their best work when they are treated as human beings who count rather than as cogs in a piece of machinery who can easily be replaced.

Schools as well as businesses illustrate the movement from organizational goals to more human ones. As computer literacy is becoming required in schools, so is value education and the demand for moral education (Berreth & Berman, 1997; Martin, 1995). Perhaps our increased dealings with machines have resulted in the removal of an important external control on our consciences, other people, who ensured that the morals inculcated by our families when we were children remained with us as adults. Interacting with people is a built-in check on appropriate behavior. If you do not behave appropriately, others will not interact with you—they will not play with you; they will not do you favors; they will not help you; they will not do business with you. While a computer can facilitate interaction with others, it is impersonal, facial expressions, eye contact, body language are missing. As will be discussed later in the book, it has been shown that antisocial behavior is related to disturbed human connections. The widespread use of computers in banks, businesses, and government agencies has corresponded to the rise in crimes involving the computer—for example, illegal transferring of funds from banks, stealing information by breaking the code to gain access to a program, or entering a program to alter or sabotage information. Thus schools must emphasize the importance of human values and connections along with computer education.

National Economy to World Economy

All the countries of the world are growing increasingly interdependent. Two inventions have contributed to making the world a global economic village: the jet airplane and the communications satellite. Two needs have contributed to the development of a world economy: the need to find new sources of natural resources (especially energy) and the need to find cheaper sources of labor:

> What we have seen in the past 25 years is an extraordinary globalization of production based not merely on the export of raw materials or finished manufactured goods from one country to another, but on the organization of production across national lines.

The transnational corporation may do research in one country, manufacture components in another, assemble them in a third, sell the manufactured goods in a fourth, deposit its surplus funds in a fifth, and so on. It may have operating affiliates in dozens of countries. The size, importance and political power of this new player in the global game has skyrocketed since the mid-1950's (Toffler, 1980, p. 318).

An example of shared production between countries is the manufacturing of baseball mitts. The cowhide comes from the United States, is shipped to Brazil to be tanned, and then to Japan to be made into a baseball mitt.

There has also been a rapid proliferation of transnational trade unions and of religious, cultural, scientific, sports, and ethnic movements that flow across national lines (for example, International Red Cross, Oceania Football Confederation, International Federation of Women Lawyers). Literally thousands of transnational meetings, conferences, and symposia bring members of such groups into contact with one another. Telecommunications enable members to interact anytime, anywhere.

We live in the most interdependent society the world has ever experienced. The more complex and technological the world becomes, the more each of us is dependent upon thousands of persons whom we do not know and have never seen. Thus understanding human beings and their interactions is a necessity in a world where we are thoroughly dependent upon other people. The challenge, then, is to socialize children to be cooperative and develop attitudes that accept human diversity.

Short-Term to Long-Term Considerations

In a rapidly changing society, we must be alert to changes, be able to anticipate their impact, and be responsive. We must be willing to reconceptualize what we are currently doing. For example, the current system of education is a relatively short-term way of approaching the concept of learning. Reconceptualizing on a long-term basis would be lifetime education coinciding with lifetime employment. The long-range perspective may mean that education should be of a generalist nature rather than specific, for if one becomes too specialized one may soon become obsolete.

Certain abilities are needed if society looks to long-term considerations: the ability to delay gratification, the ability to plan, the ability to be flexible, and the ability to make decisions. How these abilities can be fostered is a challenge to parents, teachers, and other significant socializing agents.

That society is looking toward long-term rather than short-term considerations is evidenced by the approaches currently being used with children who have special socialization needs. For example, in the past, children who were abused were removed from their homes, and their parents were put in jail. The approach was to protect the children and punish the parents. Since this approach did not remedy the problem, a more long-term approach has been instigated. Basically, it involves repairing the parent–child relationship via education and counseling so that future abuse is prevented and the family can remain intact whenever possible.

Involvement in concern for the environment by government, business, and individuals is probably the most concrete example of a long-term consideration. Such environmental concern can be seen in the banning of harmful chemicals in products, carpooling incentives, and recycling.

Centralization to Decentralization

Centralization during the second wave of change was exhibited in the growth of mass media. People generally watched the same television programs and read the same magazines because there were few choices. Consequently, there tended to be a growth of "mass minds"—similar values and attitudes. Some of the evidences of decentralization are deregularization by government of industry, local involvement in politics, local control of education, the increase in the number of people moving to small towns, and the "demassification" of the media:

> Before the advent of mass media, a first-wave child growing up in a slowly changing village built his or her model of reality out of images received from a tiny handful of sources—the teacher, the priest, the chief or official and, above all, the family (Toffler, 1980, pp. 151–157).

> The Second Wave multiplied the number of channels from which the individual grew his or her picture of reality. The child no longer received imagery from nature or people alone but from newspapers, mass magazines, radio, and later on, from television (Toffler, 1980, p. 157).

The third wave has brought with it "demassified media." Newspapers have been losing their readers as a result of competition from mini-circulation weeklies that serve specific neighborhoods and communities. Major mass magazine circulation has also declined, and there has been an explosion of mini-magazines aimed at small, special-interest, regional, and local markets. The number of radio stations has increased, and so has the diversity of offerings. The choice of programs on television has also increased due to satellites and various cable channels as well as the availability of home video recorders. The number of radios and televisions per household multiplied. Movies and movie theaters abound.

Decentralization, then, involves more freedom of choice, but also more responsibility. Responsibility entails becoming informed regarding what alternatives exist and the consequences of making various choices. This is a difficult challenge because it first requires one to become a wise information consumer. While local control of education means that schools can be more responsive to community needs, it also means elected school board members have the responsibility of evaluating local goals with those of the state and federal government for learning.

Institutional Help to Self-Help

> For decades, institutions such as the government, the medical establishment, the corporation, and the school system were America's buffers against life's hard realities—the needs for food, housing, health care, education—as well as its mysteries—birth, illness, death. Slowly we are beginning to wean ourselves off our collective institutional dependence, learning to trust and rely only on ourselves. . . . In a sense, we have come full circle. We are reclaiming America's traditional sense of self-reliance after four decades of trusting institutional help (Naisbitt, 1982, p. 131).

An example of institutional help for low-income citizens is the welfare-to-work grant program (Personal Responsibility and Work Opportunity Act of 1995) offering training, counseling, and child care to welfare recipients to enable them to provide for themselves.

An example of self-help is the Neighborhood Watch Program in many communities. Neighbors "watch out" for each other's welfare by reporting suspicious activity to the police.

> Self-help means community groups acting to prevent crime, to strengthen neighborhoods, to salvage food for the elderly, and to rebuild homes, without government assistance or at least with local control over government help. Medically, self-help is taking responsibility for health habits, environment, and lifestyle, and is demanding to be treated holistically (Naisbitt, 1982, p. 133).

It is families reclaiming their responsibility for education and care of the elderly and disabled:

> Self-help is the blossoming of America's entrepreneurial movement, which rejects large corporations in favor of self-employment and small business. In the schools, it is increasing parental activism along with questioning of the public school system—and in some cases the rejecting of it for private schools or (more radically) home education (Naisbitt, 1982, p. 133).

It is government reducing financial support for health and welfare programs to children and families by requiring people to take "personal responsibility" for their problems.

The numerous choices of videos available for every audience contributes to the "demassification" of media.

It is privatization of certain public functions. For example, some cities provide a trash pick-up; others require citizens to pay a delegated independent contractor for the service.

Representative Democracy to Participatory Democracy

Citizens, workers, and consumers are demanding and getting a greater voice in government, education, business, and the marketplace: "Citizens and educators are recognizing that improvement in the education of children and community support for education occur only when the consumer has a strong, honest part in setting policy and making decisions" (Suchara, 1982, p. 130). Examples of participatory democracy, or advocacy, can be found in many communities whose citizens are concerned about education or growth in their neighborhoods. They have been playing a participatory role in government by writing letters to their legislatures, inviting their representatives to meetings and voicing their desires, running for office, and getting community support to put initiatives on the ballot.

People whose lives are affected by a decision feel they should be part of the process of arriving at that decision, whether in a marriage, in the family, in friendships, at work, or in community organizations: "People must feel that they have 'ownership' in a decision if they are to support it with any enthusiasm" (Naisbitt, 1982, p. 188).

Thus, the challenge such societal change provides is for people to learn how to participate in a group—how to communicate, how to cooperate, and how to be assertive. As will be seen, these skills can be fostered by certain parenting and leadership styles, as well as by certain peer group experiences.

Hierarchies to Networking

Hierarchies are groups of persons arranged in order of rank. Networks are groups of people of equal rank who share ideas, information, and resources. Networks exist to foster self-help; to exchange information; to change society; to improve productivity, work, and life; and to share resources. They transmit information in a way that is quicker, more humanistic, and more energy-efficient than any other existing process (Naisbitt, 1994; Toffler, 1994).

Networking provides social contacts similar to those people had in the past with relatives, neighborhoods, churches, and long-term friendships. These traditional relationships have weakened with urbanization and geographic mobility. Networks satisfy people's need to belong and their need for support. The network model of organization and communication "has its roots in the natural, egalitarian and spontaneous formation of groups among like-minded people. Networks restructure the power and communication flow within an organization from vertical to horizontal" (Naisbitt, 1982, p. 251).

An example of networking is the formation in many communities of groups of parents who share a goal. For instance, Parents Who Care is an organization of parents who share concern for the health and well-being of youth and who want to prevent alcohol and drug dependence. These groups work cooperatively in their own communities. They provide resources such as films, speakers, reading lists, and names of counseling agencies for parents and youths regarding questions and/or specific problems. They also provide a positive support group for people in the community. Other examples of networks are organizations such as Parents Anonymous, the National Depressive and Manic Depressive Association, and the National Association for the Advancement of Colored People.

On a global level, telecommunications has made global networking a reality and has contributed to the formation of new strategic alliances among nations (Naisbitt, 1994). On a personal level, e-mail has enabled people with similar interests and concerns to join "chat groups." Pagers and cellular phones enable people to connect with one another.

Movement from North to South and East to West

That we live in a mobile, changing society is illustrated by the shift in U.S. demographics; more people live in the South and West than in the North and East (Adler & Adler, 1998; U.S. Bureau of the Census, 1990). This shift was not just in population but in wealth and economic activity as well (Francese, 1995). To illustrate,

> The public sector is hurt: people leave school systems, sewer systems, streets, hospitals, and other public infrastructures already in place in the Northeast, and move to high growth areas that are already strained by ballooning growth and that must duplicate the public infrastructures of schools, transportation, sewage, and hospitals at a great expense, while the snow belt loses the tax base to preserve its infrastructure . . . (Naisbitt, 1982, p. 221).

> For the skilled and the mobile, and especially for the young, these cities represent the promise of continued growth and prosperity. But what are the prospects if you are unemployed in the North? What it boils down to is the need to change or adapt . . . acquiring skills in an industry operating in your area (Naisbitt, 1982, p. 228).

This shift implies that the challenge of socializing for the future should be to encourage adaptability, or effective ways of dealing with the environment, specifically adaptability to new settings, new roles, and new experiences. For example, some cities are undergoing "urban redevelopment" with the help of public funds to attract people and business. The suburbs are facing problems such as traffic, crowding, and crime that previously only characterized cities. The means of acquiring adaptability is really the subject of this book—how children are socialized to function effectively in a changing society.

Either/Or to Multiple Options

There has been a movement from mass production to mass customization. Computers and scanners enable companies to offer many choices and track consumer selections for future availability. The multiple options available to us today, compared to the past, can be illustrated in any supermarket, clothing store, or automobile dealership. When I was growing up, telephones were all black, sheets were white, the only kind of pizza available was cheese, ice cream came in five flavors, and the only pain reliever available over the counter was aspirin. Today, telephones come in all colors, shapes, and sizes; sheets can be matched to the decor of your bedroom; pizza is available with

Today's consumer has many choices.

practically anything on it; ice cream flavors are infinite; and the number of available pain-reliever combinations is overwhelming. Multiple options cater to individuality, but making the choices requires thought and consumes time.

Instead of the traditional nuclear family with Dad as the breadwinner and Mom as the housekeeper and caretaker of the children (now only a small minority of U.S. families fit this pattern), we are seeing many postmodern variations, such as single-parent families, stepparent families, childless families, and dual-earner families. Other multiple options are exemplified by the decline of gender-bound, or sex-stereotyped, jobs and by the acceptance of ethnic diversity in terms of language, customs, and behavior. Although flexibility in human relations is positive, it creates a need for new standards and patterns of behavior.

The availability of multiple options for the consumer, in the job market, and in lifestyles may have contributed to the confusion characteristic of many of today's adolescents when faced with making commitments. Without adult guidance in decision-making skills, without standards, and without experience, young people may cope with too many choices by avoidance, either via irresponsibility or abuse of alcohol or drugs (Elkind, 1994; Hewlett & West, 1998; Newcomb & Bentler, 1989).

CHANGE AND THE CONCEPT OF CHILDHOOD

One of the challenges brought on by change is the concept society has of childhood. We assume childhood to be a special period of time when we are cared for, taught, and protected because we are not mature enough to do these things for ourselves. Does the period of childhood change—lengthen or shorten—when society changes?

Sometimes parents are more eager for their child to participate in sports than is the child.

Before the Renaissance (fourteenth through sixteenth centuries) there was no concept of childhood; there was only infancy and adulthood. If a child lived beyond age 7, the child was treated like a miniature adult (Aries, 1962). There was no distinction in the clothing worn by children and adults. Children were treated harshly, not lovingly. They were expected to work and were included in all adult activities, even drinking and partying. Seven-year-olds could even be punished the same way adults were (put in jail or hanged) for a crime such as pilfering.

With the development of the printing press in the middle of the fifteenth century came the attitude that one could not become an adult unless he or she could read (Postman, 1985, 1992). In the sixteenth century, this came to mean that schools were created so that children could be taught to read. Because school was designed for the preparation of a literate adult, a concept of childhood emerged: children came to be perceived not as "miniature adults" but as "unformed adults" (Postman, 1985). The concept of childhood as we know it evolved over the following three centuries. It came to be regarded as the bridge between infancy—total dependence—and adulthood—total independence.

As society became more complex, the need for an education preparatory to adulthood became more apparent. For example, one consequence of the Industrial Revolution (eighteenth–twentieth centuries) was the passage by many Western countries of compulsory education laws. Children *had* to attend school to prepare themselves to be functioning members of society.

The need for protecting children also became more apparent. Another consequence of the change that took place during the Industrial Revolution was the recognition of children's rights. Prior to the nineteenth century, children could be exploited to work in factories for long hours under harsh conditions. The nineteenth and twentieth centuries saw the passage of labor laws that limited the age at which children could be employed and the conditions under which they could work. Thus, from the Renaissance until today, the span of childhood has lengthened and, gradually, the special needs of children have been recognized.

Today, however, a common concern revolves around the loss of childhood (Elkind, 1988, 1994; Garbarino, 1986; Weissbourd, 1996), implying "Where has it gone?" Gone are many of the physical consequences of growing up in a changing society—toiling in the sweatshops, trekking five miles to school, dying from influenza—but equally true are the psychological consequences ushered in: pressure to achieve, stress, substance abuse, violence, eating disorders, teen pregnancies, depression, and suicide (Children's Defense Fund, 1998; Elkind, 1994).

The childhood that had evolved from the time of the Renaissance—a romanticized time of fantasy, play, freedom from responsibility, and freedom to develop at one's own pace—has now been reversed into a time of reality, work, and hurrying to develop to fit the pace of societal change. The time of childhood is once again shortening.

Children today must cope with a world in which both parents work, drugs are readily available, and sex and violence are only as far away as the television set (Children's Defense Fund, 1998; Elkind, 1994; Weissbourd, 1996). Children are regarded as consumers. From the numerous ads for toys, food, and clothing, you would think children were the ones who had the purchasing power. Sports are rarely played for amusement as they were a generation ago; learning specific skills and how to compete have become goals. Soccer, football, and Little League games are now analyzed and even commercialized, just like professional sports. The video camera has enabled games to be rehashed the next day and the next, instead of being tossed aside in the name of fun. Teams are often funded by businesses for uniforms, equipment, and travel in return for advertising.

The age of protection for children has been undermined by societal pressures on parents. Today's children are increasingly thrust into independence and self-reliance before they have the skills and ability to cope (Elkind, 1994; Garbarino, 1995a; Weissbourd, 1996). Some consequences are the rise in psychosomatic ailments such as stomachaches, headaches, wheezing, dizziness, and chest pains among school-age children and the rise in emotional problems such as depression, substance abuse, eating disorders, and suicide among adolescents (Hewlett & West, 1998; Zill & Schoenbom, 1990).

What can we do to cope with these consequences of change? Can we meet the challenge?

We need to understand the process of **socialization**—the process by which human beings, beginning at birth, acquire the skills to function as social beings and participants in society. We also need to understand the impact of change on socialization. Finally, we need to be able to make choices that will support and prepare today's children for tomorrow's challenges.

SOCIALIZATION, CHANGE, AND CHALLENGE

Children are socialized by many people in society—parents, siblings, grandparents, aunts, uncles, cousins, friends, teachers, coaches, and role models on television, in the movies, and in books. These agents of socialization employ many techniques, which will be discussed, to influence children to behave, think, and feel according to what is considered worthy.

What all these agents believe is worthy is an outcome of their own socialization—their own values, morals, attitudes, and self-concepts. Also, children play a role in their own socialization. A child's behavior may stimulate other people to behave in certain ways. For example, a defiant child is more likely to elicit stricter discipline than a child who usually complies with adult requests and apologizes for misconduct. The environment also has its part in the process. The environment is that which the child experiences—the setting, the roles, and the interactions. For example, a child growing up in a large family on a farm has different socialization experiences from a child growing up in a single-parent family in the city. As children grow, they encounter different environments.

Socialization is a very complex process, indeed. The more technological and diverse the society, the more children have to learn in order to adapt effectively, the more socializing agents and experiences contribute to the process, and the more time the socialization process takes. For example, as Asian, European, and Latin American countries compete with the United States in world trade, American children who learn languages other than English will be advantaged when they enter the business world. As society changes, more and more challenges are posed to the socializing agents because there are more choices to be made. Once again, should childhood be compressed to accommodate all the opportunities that exist, or should socializing agents evaluate and select what is to be learned?

When societal change occurs as, for example, rapid technological and scientific advances, mobility, and economic fluctuations, socializing agents are affected. Adults are affected directly by the uncertainty that change produces, as well as by the new opportunities and challenges it presents. Economic fluctuations affect job security and can have a major negative impact on family finances. However, sometimes such stresses uncover positive strengths in the family members—for example, spousal emotional support and children's cooperation. How adults cope with societal change indirectly affects children. Two parents in the workforce usually require child care and family time becomes the "second shift" (Hochschild, 1990). Parents learn to perform several tasks simultaneously. New technology helps (talking on a speaker phone while folding clothes). However, while doing multitasks may be more efficient, it may also contribute to lack of attentiveness.

One result of societal change is seen in goals of child rearing and education. Psychologist David Elkind (1987a, 1994) sees today's parents as being very concerned with developing the intellectual abilities of their children. This concern is evidenced by the growth of preschools and kindergartens with academic programs, the development of infant stimulation programs such as "Mommy and Me" classes, the availability of "how-to" books on teaching your baby to read, do math, and be brighter, as well as the proliferation of computer software for children. The concern is also evidenced by the pressure on elementary schools to emphasize formal instruction involving passive listening and memorization rather than a *developmentally appropriate* curriculum, which involves knowledge of children's normal growth patterns and individual differences. For example, preschool children are exposed to active, hands-on, age-appropriate, meaningful experiences.

As a consequence of this parental concern with nourishing the intellect, children are under pressure to become "intellectually independent" and "intellectually successful" at an early age. This is measured by test scores, performance in various activities such as athletics and music, and being accepted by certain prestigious schools (even preschools!). Elkind (1988) cited an example of this push for having superkids. A mother complained to her son's first-grade teacher, "How is he going to get into M.I.T. if you only give him a 'satisfactory'!" Elkind believes such a push for excellence is causing an increase in stress symptoms in children.

> Carol's parents were very proud of their daughter. Considered a "gifted" student, she did very well in school while juggling a full schedule that included ice skating, gymnastics, and piano lessons. At age 10, Carol won her elementary school's outstanding student award, placed first in an ice-skating competition, and gave a solo piano recital. At age 13, she was selected as a candidate for admission to a prestigious private girls' high school. Two days before the scheduled entrance exam, Carol took an overdose of sleeping pills.
>
> Why did Carol choose suicide? Other adolescents face varying degrees of pressure and stress, yet develop coping strategies. Was it her family situation? friends? school? community? or a combination of these complex relationships?

That children are pressured to know more than their parents is really not a new phenomenon; it is part of evolution or societal change. As new knowledge is discovered, it is the children who learn it in school. For example, many schools are now training children to be computer literate. There is likely to be tension in the parent–child relationship in cases where children can figure things out more efficiently with computers than their parents can with traditional paper-and-pencil methods. As another example, children of immigrants learn to be Americanized in school whereas their parents may cling to the attitudes and behavior patterns learned in their countries of origin. Thus, societal change can produce family tensions; it can also produce challenges. To reduce tension in the parent–child relationship resulting from an imbalance of knowledge, parents can be challenged to become knowledgeable in the very activities their children are pursuing. For example, parents can share activities; they can provide the opportunity for children to teach them; they can read books, talk to experts, and request adult education courses (for example, on how to use a computer); and they can volunteer to help in the classroom in order to learn along with their children. There needs to be a distinction between encouraging and motivating children to succeed and pressuring them with inappropriate expectations. Schools can also be challenged to involve parents more in their children's learning. Parent involvement in school will be discussed later.

Another result of societal change, according to Elkind (1994), has been a shift in the value of the child's place in the family. There has been a move away from child-centeredness. Traditionally, parents sacrificed for their children—their energy and resources went to their children. They may have saved money for their children's college education instead of buying a new car. Today, however, some parents see their needs and rights as being at least equal to their children's, rather than subordinate.

Elkind sees this trend evidenced in the pressure placed on children to attain emotional independence at an early age. For example, "latchkey" children (so-called because they usually carry their own keys) let themselves into their homes after school and often have to be responsible for younger siblings as well as for themselves. Even though they are independent for part of the day, many are fearful of staying alone. Some are resentful that they cannot play with their friends, for many latchkey children are not permitted to let anyone into the home for safety reasons. Most spend their time watching television. What sorts of adults will these "independent" children become?

SOCIALIZATION AND CHILD DEVELOPMENT

Socialization is complex; it involves many variable experiences, interactions, and environments that affect children's development. Analyzing the variables involved in the socialization process can help people deal with change. Understanding how the "input"—socialization interactions in various settings and situations—affects the "output" of socialization—values, morals, attitudes, behavior, self-control, gender roles, and self-concept—enables us to manipulate that input to induce the desired output.

A simplified example of this kind of manipulation is described in a classic book, *Walden Two* by B. F. Skinner (1948). *Walden Two* is a utopian community founded on behavioral principles. To teach self-control, young children (age 3 to 4) are given lollipops dipped in sugar at the beginning of the day, to be eaten later, provided that they have not been licked. There are practice sessions in which the children are urged to examine their own behavior in the following situations: when the lollipops are concealed, when the children are distracted from thinking about the candy by playing a game, and when the lollipops are in sight. Thus, when the children are given the lollipops again for a real exercise in self-control, they have at their disposal some adaptive behaviors to use (put them out of sight, keep busy) to help them avoid the temptation.

Another example of how input can be employed to affect output is Sherif's (1956) classic Robber's Cave experiment, in which manipulation of the environment was used, first to bring about antisocial behavior (hostility) between two groups of young boys, and then to reverse that pattern. How was this done? To produce friction, competitive tournaments were held—baseball, tug-of-war, touch football, and so on. Frustration led to name-calling, raids, and aggressive behavior. To eliminate this friction, the counselors rigged a series of crises that forced all the boys to work together in order to solve the problem. Once, the water line was deliberately broken, and another time the camp

Children are socialized for societal change, as exemplified by this child who is doing her homework on the computer.

truck broke down just as it was going to town for food. Thus antisocial behavior gave way to prosocial behavior when a compelling goal for all concerned had to be achieved. Anti- and prosocial behavior will be discussed in more detail later in the book.

The above examples are illustrations of intentional socialization, that which is done on purpose. In reality, all of us have unique biological characteristics and therefore come into the world with different "wiring," which will cause each of us to perceive and interact with the world differently. A muscular, coordinated child will tend to be attracted to sports, while a frail, timid child will tend to avoid competitive activities. Thus, children play a role in their own socialization (Scarr, 1992), which sometimes makes intentional socialization difficult. In contrast to the scientifically shaped utopian society described in *Walden Two* or the manipulated situation in the Robber's Cave experiment, in reality each human being is exposed to many different environments in which many different interactions and experiences, both intentional and unintentional, take place. Therefore, individuals reflect both their biological characteristics and their socialization experiences (Bugental & Goodenow, 1998). As the child changes, so must the process of socialization; socialization is not static; it is transactional and bidirectional (Sameroff, 1987). Ideally, as children develop, control over their behavior gradually shifts from the adult to the child. More specifically, infant, and toddlers require much adult direction. Preschoolers are developmentally capable of directing some of their activities and are exhibiting some self-control of their behavior. School-agers can direct most of their activities with adult support and some direction. Adolescents who have been socialized by nurturant adults exhibit much self-control and self-directed behavior.

Some of the effects of various socialization experiences, interactions, and environments will be examined in later chapters when such questions as these are discussed: What are the effects of divorce on the child? What are the impacts of both parents working outside the home? Is child care helpful or harmful? What type of schooling will raise the academic achievement of students? How influential are friends? Should children participate in organized sports? How does the media influence child development? Should children with disabilities be included in the mainstream? Should ethnically diverse children be Americanized, or should societal institutions be modified to meet their special or unique needs?

EXAMINING SOCIALIZATION IN AN ECOLOGICAL CONTEXT

Developmental psychologist Urie Bronfenbrenner (1979, 1989, 1995; Bronfenbrenner & Morris, 1998) believes that the social context of individual interactions and experiences determines the degree to which individuals can develop their abilities and realize their potentials. His conceptual model (*see* Figure 1.1) for studying humans in their various social environments—the ecology of human development—allows for a systematic study of interactions including the child's role in his or her development over time, and serves as a guide for future research on the very complicated process of socialization.

Ecology, as we said at the beginning of the chapter, studies interrelationships between humans and their environments, including the consequent psychological, social, and cultural processes over time. According to Bronfenbrenner's bioecological theory, there are four basic structures—the *microsystem,* the *mesosystem,* the *exosystem,* and the *macrosystem*—in which relationships and interactions take place to form patterns

Figure 1.1   An Ecological Model of Human Development

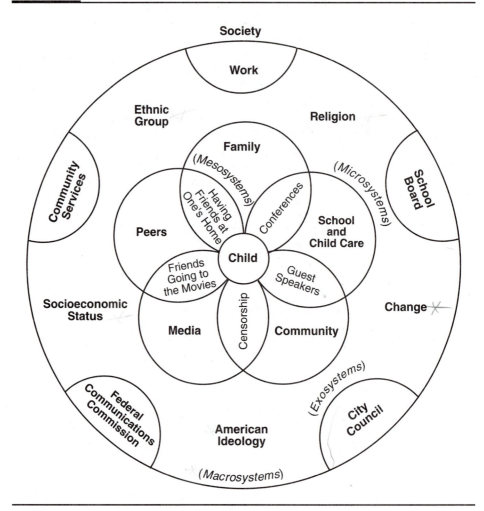

Source: Based on concepts from U. Bronfenbrenner (1989). Ecological systems theory. In R. Vasta (Ed.), *Annals of Child Development* (Vol. 6). Greenwich, CT: JAI Press.

that affect human development. Such a conceptual framework enables us to study the child and his or her family, school, and community as dynamic evolving systems that are influenced by change (*chronosystems*), as in economics, politics, and globalism. A computer analogy might be hypertext and links on the Internet. Sites are always changing, new links via hypertext are always forming, and what information you glean from one site affects the information that you can obtain from another.

MICROSYSTEMS

The first basic structure, the **microsystem** ("micro" meaning small) refers to the activities and relationships with significant others experienced by a developing person in a particular small setting such as family, school, peer group, or community.

The *family* is the setting that provides nurturance, affection, and a variety of opportunities. It is the primary socializer of the child in that it has the most significant impact on the child's development. According to James Garbarino (1992), the child who is not adequately nurtured or loved, such as one who grows up in an abrasive or dysfunctional family, may have developmental problems. Also, children who do not have sufficient opportunities to manipulate objects, to model desirable behaviors, to initiate activity, and to be exposed to a language-rich environment will be at a disadvantage when they reach school. This early disadvantage will persist and even worsen as the child progresses through school, unless intervention, such as provided by some quality child-care programs, can modify the opportunities at home and in school.

The *school* is the microsystem in which children formally learn about their society. The school teaches reading, writing, arithmetic, history, science, and so on. Teachers encourage the development of various skills and behaviors by being role models and by providing motivation for children to succeed in learning.

The *peer group* is the setting in which children are generally unsupervised by adults, thereby gaining experience in independence. In the peer group, children get a sense of who they are and what they can do by comparison with others. Peers provide companionship and support as well as learning experiences in cooperation and role taking.

The *community,* or neighborhood on a smaller scale, is the main microsystem in which children learn by doing. The facilities available to children determine what real experiences they will have. Is there a library? Are stores and workplaces nearby where children can observe people at work? Are the people with whom children interact in the community similar or diverse? Are the people in the community advocates for children? These questions relate to the significance of the community as a socializer.

The *media,* exemplified by television, movies, videos, books, magazines, music, and computers, is not regarded as a microsystem by Bronfenbrenner because it is not a small, interactive setting for reciprocal interaction. However, I consider it as significant a socializer as the microsystems described above because it presents a setting in which a child can view the whole world—past, present, and future, places and things, roles and relationships, attitudes and values. Television and movies also provide models for behavior. In addition, because computers are interactive and can be combined with any media, they provide potentials for relationships (e-mail, for example).

The child's development is affected in each of the aforementioned settings not only by the child's relationships with others in the family, school, peer group, or community, but also by interactions between members of the particular microsystem. For example, the father's relationship with the mother affects her treatment of the child. If the father is emotionally supportive of the mother, she has been found to be more involved and have more positive interactions with the child (Cox, Owen, Henderson, & Margand, 1992). For another example, a child's classroom performance varies as a function of whether or not the teacher taught the child's older sibling and how well that sibling performed (Seaver, 1973). A teacher who taught a high-achieving older sibling tended to have high expectations for the younger sibling. The younger sibling, then, was more likely to perform as expected.

MESOSYSTEMS

The second basic structure, the **mesosystem** ("meso" meaning intermediate), consists of linkages and interrelationships between two or more of a developing person's microsystems, such as the family and the school, or the family and the peer group.

The impact of mesosystems on the child depends on the number and quality of interrelationships. Bronfenbrenner (1979) uses the example of the child who goes to school alone on the first day. This means that there is only a single link between home and school—the child. Where there is little linkage between home and school "in terms of values, experiences, objects, and behavioral style," there also tends to be little academic achievement for the child. In contrast, where all these links are strong, there is likely to be academic competence. To illustrate, a longitudinal study following adolescents from their last year of middle school through their first year of high school found a relationship between academic performance and the joint effects of family and school (Epstein, 1983). When the style of family interaction was similar to the school's, in that both settings encouraged child participation, academic performance was enhanced (Ginsburg & Bronstein, 1993). Thus, the more numerous the qualitative links or interrelationships between the child's microsystems, the more impact they have on socialization. Mesosystems, then, provide support for activities going on in microsystems. For example, when parents invite a child's friends to their home, or when parents encourage their child to join a certain club, team, or youth group, the socialization impact of the peers is enhanced through parental approval.

Another example of mesosystem impact occurs when a community censors the movies that can be shown in local theaters; the impact of the media as a socializing agent is then reduced because of lack of sponsorship. However, censorship may actually motivate some individuals to see a movie, thereby increasing its influence.

Exosystems

The third basic structure, the **exosystem** ("exo" meaning outside), refers to settings in which children are not active participants, but which affect them in one of their microsystems—for example, parents' jobs, the city council, parental social support networks. The effects of exosystems on the child are indirect via the microsystems. To illustrate, when parents work in settings that demand conformity rather than self-direction, they reflect this orientation in their parenting styles in that they tend to be more controlling than democratic. Thus the child's socialization is impacted. When the city planning commission approves a freeway through a neighborhood or an air traffic pattern over a school, children's socialization is impacted in that the noise interferes with learning. Studies (for example, Melson, Ladd, & Hsu, 1993) have shown a positive relationship between parents who have friends, relatives, and neighbors who help them in their parenting role and children's competence.

Macrosystems

The fourth basic structure, the **macrosystem** ("macro" meaning large), consists of the developing person's society and subculture to which the developing person belongs, with particular reference to the belief systems, lifestyles, patterns of social interaction, and life changes. Examples of macrosystems include the United States, the middle or lower class, Hispanic or Asian ancestry, Catholicism or Judaism, urban or rural areas. Macrosystems are viewed as patterns, or sets of instructions, for exosystems, mesosystems, and microsystems. Democracy is the basic belief system of the United States and so is considered a macrosystem. Democratic ideology affects the world of work, an exosystem—for example, employers cannot discriminate in hiring. Democratic ideology affects how schools communicate with families; school–family interaction is a mesosystem—for example, schools must inform parents of policies, and parents have the right to question those policies. Democratic ideology also affects what is taught in schools, a microsystem—for example, children must learn the principles upon which the United States was founded.

Although someone may live in the United States and subscribe to its basic belief system of democracy and, consequently, be influenced by that macrosystem, that person may also be part of other macrosystems such as his or her ethnic group. **Ethnicity** refers to an attribute of membership in a group in which members identify themselves by national origin, culture, race, or religion. Because the United States is becoming more and more ethnically diverse, we need to understand some basic effects of various macrosystems. More details on specific ethnic groups will be discussed throughout the book.

According to cultural anthropologist Edward T. Hall (1964, 1966, 1976, 1988), people from different macrosystems, or cultures, view the world differently, unaware that there are alternative ways of perceiving, believing, behaving, and judging. Particularly significant are the unconscious assumptions people make about personal space, time, interpersonal relations, and ways of knowing. These assumptions can interfere with communication, a point upon which Hall focuses to illustrate differences as well as similarities among cultures.

Hall classifies macrosystems as being *low* or *high* context. Generally, **low-context** macrosystems are characterized by rationality, practicality, competition, individuality, and progress; **high-context** macrosystems are characterized by intuitiveness, emotionality, cooperation, group identity, and tradition (*see* Table 1.2).

In a *low-context macrosystem* such as Anglo-American, urban, middle class, meaning from a communication is gleaned from the verbal message itself—a spoken explanation, a written letter, or a computer printout. *What* is said is often more important than *who* said it. For example, employees in government, business, or education routinely communicate by phone or memorandum without ever meeting the other individuals involved. In a *high-context macrosystem,* on the other hand, such as Native American, Hispanic American, Asian American, or rural United States, meaning from a communication is gleaned from the setting in which the communication takes place. For example, a Spanish-speaking person can communicate familiarity by whether he or she uses the formal or informal word for "you." A person raised in traditional Japanese culture can communicate degree of respect by how deeply he or she bows.

In general, people in *low-context macrosystems* tend to try to control nature (for example, irrigating desert areas) and have more fragmented social relations in that they may behave one way toward friends, another way toward business colleagues, and yet another way toward neighbors. Members of *high-context macrosystems* tend to live in harmony with nature and with other humans who are part of their social network. Whereas individuals in *low-context macrosystems* usually develop an identity based on their personal efforts and achievements, people in *high-context macrosystems* tend to gain their identity through group associations (lineage, place of work, organizations). Members of *low-context cultures* expect personal freedom, openness, and individual choice. Members of *high-context cultures* are less open to strangers, make distinctions between insiders and outsiders, and are more likely to follow traditional role expectations.

Table 1.2   World Views

	Low-Context Macrosystems	**High-Context Macrosystems**
General Characteristics	Rationality	Intuitiveness
	Practicality	Emotionality
	Competition	Cooperation
	Individuality	Group identity
	Progress	Tradition
Significant Values	Emphasis on concrete evidence and facts	Emphasis on feelings
	Efficient use of time	Build solid relationships through human interaction
	Achievement	Character
	Personal freedom	Group welfare
	Humans can control nature and influence the future	Nature and the future are governed by a power higher than human
	Change is good	Stability is good

- *What if these views represented two individuals wanting to marry?*
- *What if one view represented a teacher's and the other a student's?*
- *What if one view represented an employer's and the other an employee's?*

Both low- and high-context macrosystems illustrate adaptiveness for human survival: *low-context cultures* provide ways of adapting, changing, and using new knowledge that can benefit society, and *high-context cultures* provide a strong human support network that helps guard against the alienation of a technological society. Different parenting styles influence the child's degree of interdependence on others and curiosity to explore new things.

To illustrate, on a recent day-long cruise to see the glaciers in Alaska, I had the opportunity to observe the contrast in parenting styles in a high- and low-context family. The high-context family consisted of a mother and father, a baby (about 10-months-old), and a grandmother and grandfather. The baby was continually held and played with by one of the adults. She was kissed and jiggled and spoken to. There were no toys to amuse her. When it was lunchtime, the mother, after distributing the food she had brought to the adults, took some food from her plate, mashed it between her fingers, and put it in the baby's mouth. After lunch the grandmother and grandfather took turns rocking the baby to sleep. The baby never cried the whole day. The care she received fostered a sense of *interdependence*.

In contrast, the low-context family, consisting of a mother, father, and a baby (about 15-months-old), had brought a sack of toys for the baby to play with while the parents enjoyed the sites through a nearby window. After a while, the baby began to fuss; the father picked him up and brought him to the boat's window pointing out seals and birds and glaciers. Later, when the baby tired of his toys, the mother held his hands and walked him around the deck. The baby was given crackers and a bottle to soothe him when he cried. The care he received fostered a sense of *independence*.

Changes in a macrosystem can result in changes in exosystems, mesosystems, and microsystems. A very thorough, longitudinal study of 167 California children born in 1920–1929 illustrating the effects of such changes was done by sociologist Glen Elder (1974, 1979, 1998) and his colleagues (Elder & Hareven, 1993; Elder, Van Nguyen, & Casper, 1985). They compared the life-course development of children whose families had experienced a change in their socioeconomic status due to the Great Depression and those who had not. The immediate exosystem effect was loss of a job. This in turn caused emotional distress, which was experienced in the home and affected the children (effect on a microsystem). There were also secondary exosystem effects: families hit by the Depression exhibited a loss of status of the father in the eyes of the children and an increase in the importance of the mother. The affected father's parenting behavior became more rejecting, especially toward adolescent girls. Children, especially boys, from affected families expressed a stronger identification with the peer group. Children from affected families participated more in domestic roles and outside jobs, with girls being more likely to do the former and boys the latter.

The fact that longitudinal data were available over a period of more than sixty years gave Elder the opportunity to assess the impact of childhood experience, within and outside the family, on behavior in later life. He found that the long-term consequences of the Depression turned out to vary according to the age of the child at the time. On the one hand, children who were *preadolescents* when their families suffered economic loss, compared to those of the same socioeconomic status from families who did not suffer economically, did less well in school, showed less stable and less successful work histories, and exhibited more emotional and social difficulties, even in adulthood. Such adverse effects have later been explained (Conger et al., 1994) as due to the impact of economic hardship on the quality of parenting and hence psychological well-being of children.

On the other hand, those who were *teenagers* when the Depression hit their families did better in school, were more likely to go to college, had happier marriages, exhibited more successful work careers, and in general were more satisfied with life than youngsters of the same socioeconomic status who were not affected by the Depression. These favorable outcomes were more pronounced for teenagers from middle-socioeconomic-status backgrounds but were also evident among their lower-status counterparts.

Interestingly, adults whose families escaped economic ruin turned out to be less successful, both educationally and vocationally, than those whose families were deprived. Why was this so? According to Elder (1974):

It seems that a childhood which shelters the young from the hardships of life consequently fails to develop or test adaptive capacities which are called upon in life crises. To engage and manage real-life (though not excessive) problems in childhood and adolescence is to participate in a sort of apprenticeship for adult life. Preparedness has been identified repeatedly as a key factor in the adaptive potential and psychological health of persons in novel situations (pp. 249–250).

Thus a major consequence of the Depression was that economic loss changed the relation of children to the family and the adult world by involving them in work that was necessary for the welfare of others. This early involvement contributed to deprived children's socialization for adulthood. Elder hypothesized that the loss of economic security forced the family to mobilize its human resources. Everyone had to take on new responsibilities.

With regard to the effect of today's abundance on the socialization of our youth, Elder (1974) expressed the following concern:

> Since the Depression and especially World War II various developments have conspired to isolate the young from challenging situations in which they could make valuable contributions to family and community welfare. Prosperity, population, concentration, industrial growth with its capital-intensive formula, and educational upgrading have led to an extension of the dependency years and increasing segregation of the young from the routine experiences of adults. In this consumption-oriented society, urban middle-class families have little use for the productive hands of offspring, and the same applies to community institutions. . . .
>
> This society of abundance can and even must support "a large quota of nonproductive members," as it is presently organized, but should it tolerate the costs, especially among the young; the costs of not feeling needed, of being denied the challenge and rewards which come from meaningful contributions to a common endeavor (pp. 291–293)?

Low-context cultures value cultivating the land, whereas high-context cultures value living in harmony with it.

Elder's challenge calls for the need to bring adults back into the lives of children and children back into the lives of adults.

Elder's study shows how ecological change can have varying impacts on a child's socialization depending on other variables, such as the age and gender of the child, the existing family relationships, and the socioeconomic status of the family prior to the change, thereby illustrating the multiplicity of variables interacting to affect socialization.

MICRO-, MESO-, EXO-, MACROSYSTEM INTERACTION

The influences of the significant socializing agents—family, school, peer group, media, and community *(microsystems)*—on the child are examined separately in this book, pointing out the numerous variables affecting socialization: the various interactions that take place between the socializing agents *(mesosystems);* those settings in which the child is not directly involved that each socializing agent experiences *(exosystems);* and the total contexts where the socializing occurs *(macrosystems),* as shown in Figure 1.1.

To illustrate the complex interaction of the systems involved in socialization is the finding that academic performance is affected by whether or not a child's mother is employed and whether the employment is full- or part-time. The impact of the mother's employment depends on why she went to work, as well as the father's attitude and role in the family, the child's age and temperament, and whether or not the mother is satisfied (which may depend on company policies of sick leave, flextime, and child care) (Hoffman, 1989).

Since socialization must pass on the cultural heritage to the next generation while also enabling that generation to become competent adults in society, every socializing agent engages in preparing children for both stability and change. It is paradoxical that training for stability, which is implemented by passing on the cultural heritage and the status quo to children, involves making children's behavior somewhat predictable and conforming; but preparation for change, which includes enabling children to become competent for a future society, very likely involves disrupting some stable patterns and encouraging new ways of thinking and behaving. The challenge, then, of successful socialization in today's society is to rear children to maintain certain values, morals, attitudes, behaviors, and roles, while being adaptable to change, so that they will become responsible, caring, competent human beings.

What is it that makes some people responsible for their actions and others not? Does the answer lie in the way they were socialized—did the responsible individuals become that way because their parents were loving and these individuals grew up wanting to please them? Or is that these individuals were punished from a very early age when they did not behave responsibly (for example, did not call to say they would be home late)? Or were they trusted to take on tasks involving responsibility, such as babysitting, gardening, money management, and so on, at an early age and expected to take the consequences for their mistakes (not being hired again as a sitter or a gardener) as well as the rewards for their successes (more jobs, higher pay)? Did they have responsible adults to emulate, or did they spend most of their time with friends or watching television? Did their teachers have certain standards and demand responsibility (for example, home-work to be turned in on time or not accepted), or were the standards and evaluation procedures vague?

Julie, an attractive young lady about 20 years of age, came to me with tears in her eyes after the semester was over, requesting to take my child development course again. When asked why, she broke down and sobbed, "I got an *F*. . . . I got *B*s on all the exams, but I didn't do the observations. I guess I didn't organize my time responsibly." I could understand her tears. She was an attentive student who contributed to class discussions and, judging by her test scores, studied the material. What I couldn't understand was why she didn't take the time to do the required observations, which represented 40% of her grade, when she very well knew the consequences. (My grading policy is written on the course syllabus, which everyone is given, and it is discussed several times.)

As a college professor who interacts with hundreds of students each year, I am continually plagued with the question of why some students responsibly prepare for examinations, complete their assignments, and turn in papers on time, while other students do not. The latter group are generally nice people who are usually attentive in class, yet when they get their final grades, they show astonishment and come to me to request a reprieve, a chance to repeat the course with the promise of completing the required work.

The dilemma exemplified in the box relates to influences of microsystems and mesosystems on socialization. What about influences of exosystems and macrosystems?

We live in a society where the lines of responsibility are often fuzzy. Years ago, if I got sick, I was responsible for paying the doctor. Today it is primarily my insurance company's responsibility (my employee benefits include health coverage). Years ago, when a carpenter was hired to build some cabinets, the carpenter took responsibility for the quality of materials and work. Today, because of diversification and specialization, it is rare for one person to be responsible for a whole job—there is the bank that may loan money for the materials, the lumberyard that supplies the materials, and the delivery trucks that bring the materials to the lumberyard and to the customer. If a job is not completed on time, perhaps it is due to the bank taking longer than expected to approve the loan, or the lumberyard ordering the wrong materials, or the delivery trucks not operating because of a union strike. Who is really responsible?

Years ago, if you did not pay your bills on time, you had to face people—people at the bank or at the store or at the telephone company, for example. Since face-to-face encounters usually cause some embarrassment, most people try to avoid them. Thus a motivating factor causing people to pay their bills on time was the avoidance of shame-producing situations. Today, a computer handles the billing; generally, the people to whom you may owe money are not even aware of it. People do not have to face computers, however, and worry about their reputations in town if they should default on a payment.

Do the technological advances in society, then, lessen responsibility? How are children affected by such advances? Children experience toys that do not work as they were advertised, textbooks that do not arrive on time, adults who abdicate responsibility (do not pay child support, become substance abusers, or simply do not care). So children who may be reared to be responsible—by their families, their religion, their culture, their school—are still exposed to many situations in which irresponsibility exists. Some situations even seem to reward irresponsibility. For example, people who default on their bills may be able to get a loan to pay them, as well as being able to deduct from their taxes the interest on certain loans. As one can see, the outcomes of socialization influenced by microsystems and mesosystems are extremely complicated, and they become even more so when the effects on a child's exosystems and macrosystems are also considered.

A CONSEQUENCE OF CHANGE: SOCIAL TOXICITY

As has been discussed, the future is shaped by the present. Social trends affect macrosystems and exosystems, which in turn affect microsystems and mesosystems. Accompanying these changing trends are positive and negative consequences, some dangerous to children's development.

The report, *America's Children: Key National Indicators of Well-Being, 1998* (Federal Interagency Forum on Child & Family Statistics, 1998), is a governmental effort to monitor the overall status of the nation's children. Indicators measured are economic security, health, behavioral and social environment, and education.

- Economic security indicators—document poverty and income among children and the basic necessities, such as housing, food, health care.
- Health indicators—document physical health and well being of children including immunizations and probability, at varying ages, to die.
- Behavior and social environment indicators—document the number of youths who are engaged in illegal, dangerous, or high-risk behaviors such as smoking, drinking alcohol, using drugs, committing violent crimes.
- Education indicators—document success in educating the nation's children, including preschool, reading, overall achievement, completion of high school and college.

James Garbarino, professor and author of *Raising Children in a Socially Toxic Environment* (1995), believes violence, drugs, uncaring communities, poverty, abusive families and custody battles are poisoning children's lives and are responsible for the less-than-optimal well-being of America's children. As pollution toxified our physical environment, our social environment is being toxified by the breakdown of family and community support systems resulting in alienation, depression, vengeance, and/or paranoia.

Garbarino (1995) says society must revise its conception of childhood; childhood should be viewed as "the social space in which to lay the foundation for the best that human development has to offer" (p. 12). All children should "be shielded from the direct demands of adult economic, political, and sexual forces" (p. 8). Children have a right to be protected from poverty. They have a right to be protected from excessive consumerism and commercial advertising that preys upon their immaturity. They have a right to be protected by laws against situations deemed harmful.

Garbarino discusses what can be done to strengthen children's "social space":

- Children need stability; government and business must therefore have policies that are supportive of families, such as personal leaves.
- Children need security; law enforcement policies must therefore ensure that their physical and social environments are safe from violence.
- Children need affirmation and acceptance; they must therefore have opportunities to spend time with caring adults who enable them to be part of the larger community and who give them a sense of values and spirituality.

Joy Osofsky (1997) agrees citing "evidence that many adolescents and young adults who first become delinquent and later develop into criminals were exposed earlier in their lives to much violence, disorganized families, poor education, and limited opportunities" (p. 5). She asserts the need to make a commitment to changing media values communicated to children, providing economic opportunities and other options for youth, and applying stricter gun control.

That growing up today is more difficult than it was a generation ago is documented by Sylvia Ann Hewlett, economist, and Cornel West, professor, in their book, *The War Against Parents* (1998). Hewlett and West show how government, business, and media have waged a silent war against parents. Families' roles of commitment and care have been negatively impacted by government taxes and housing policies, corporate profits and greed, media degradation. Parents need support from the macrosystem and exosystems to do their job. Hewlett and West call for parents to advocate a Parents' Bill of Rights (pp. 231–232). Parents are entitled to:

1. Time for their children (paid parenting leave).
2. Economic security (a living wage, job opportunities, tax relief).
3. A pro-family electoral and legal system.
4. A supportive external environment (violence-free and drug-free neighborhoods, quality child care, family health benefits).
5. Honor and dignity (an index of family well being needs to be developed and parents should be afforded certain privileges, like those granted to senior citizens).

Epilogue

Child socialization outcomes are dependent upon contexts of development. Change in one context affects changes in other contexts. A change over time is society's concept of childhood. This concept is influenced by macrosystems such as history, politics, economics, culture. Seven-year-old Jessica could fly a plane because the technology was available at that time in history. There were no laws limiting her aeronautical activities. Her parents could afford to give her flying lessons. Her culture encouraged achievement, competition, and winning. The media "feeds on" reporting new records and champions. Jessica's parents believed love was exhibited by supporting their child's dreams without constraints. ■

SUMMARY

Ecology involves studying humans in their physical, social, and cultural environments, all of which are affected by societal change. The purpose of this book is to examine how growing up in a changing world affects the development of children via socialization, the process by which individuals are enabled to participate in society.

Ten major trends in which society has been moving and their potential impact on socialization are discussed: (1) industrial society to information society; (2) organizational goals to individual goals; (3) national economy to world economy; (4) short-term considerations to long-term considerations; (5) centralization to decentralization; (6) institutional help to self-help; (7) representative democracy to participatory democracy; (8) hierarchies to networking; (9) movement from North to South and East to West; (10) either/or to multiple options.

One of the challenges brought on by change is the concept society has of childhood. The period of protection for children has gone from being short during the Renaissance to long during the Industrial Revolution. As societal pressures increase, many fear that the concept of childhood will be compressed.

When societal change occurs, the agents who socialize children are affected and children bear the consequences. The agents of socialization are the family, the school, the peer group, the media, and the community. These agents employ different socialization techniques. Children play a transactional role in their own socialization, too. The "output" of socialization (values, morals, attitudes, behavior, self-control, gender roles, self-concept) is affected by the "input," which can be intentional or unintentional.

Socialization is examined in an ecological context. Bronfenbrenner's model of human ecology consists of four basic structures (the microsystem, the mesosystem, the exosystem, and the macrosystem) in which relationships and interactions take place.

The microsystem is the immediate small setting where the child is at a particular time. The mesosystem consists of the interrelationships intermediate between two or more of a person's microsystems. The exosystem refers to outside settings in which children do not actually participate, but which affect them in one of their microsystems. The macrosystem refers to the larger society and its ideology in which a child grows up. Macrosystems can be classified as high context or low context, each type having different influences on a person's perspectives on the world.

Effects of change in the macrosystem on exosystems, mesosystems, and microsystems are exemplified by Elder's study comparing families who were deprived during the Depression and those who were not. A major influence for children growing up in deprived families was their involvement in the adult world of work necessary for the welfare of others. The long-term consequences of the Depression were found to depend on the gender and age of the child, the existing family relationships, and the socioeconomic status of the family at the time when economic hardship hit.

The interaction of micro-, meso-, exo-, and macrosystems make socialization very complex. The challenge is to pass on the cultural heritage to the next generation while also enabling that generation to deal with change.

Accompanying societal change are consequences. Children are exposed to an increasingly socially toxic environment. Children need to be shielded from adult economic, political, and sexual forces. Parents need support from government and business to fulfill their commitment and caring roles.

ACTIVITY

Purpose: To understand the impact of change on microsystems and mesosystems.

1. Describe one to three changes you observed:
   - in your family as you grew up
   - in your school
   - in your peer group
   - in the media—television or books
   - in your community

2. Pick one change for each microsystem and discuss:
   - why you think it occurred
   - how it impacted you
   - what impact it had on the other microsystems, if any

3. Cite at least one example of each of the ten megatrends discussed in this chapter from the media (TV, movies, books, or magazines).

RESOURCES

Fed World Information Network
http://www.fedworld.gov

U.S. Bureau of Labor Statistics
http://www.bls.gov

Library of Congress State and Local Government Resource Page
http://lcweb.loc.gov/global/state/

Yale Bush Center in Child Development and Social Policy
http://pantheon.cis.yale.edu/

U.S. Bureau of the Census
http://www.census.gov/

RELATED READINGS

Aries, P. (1962). *Centuries of childhood: A social history of family life.* New York: Knopf.

Bronfenbrenner, U. (1979). *The ecology of human development.* Cambridge, MA: Harvard University Press.

Cleverly, J., & Philips, D. C. (1986). *Visions of childhood: Influential models from Locke to Spock.* New York: Teachers College Press.

Drueker, P. (1992). *The age of discontinuity: Guidelines to our changing society.* New Brunswick, NJ: Transaction Publishers.

Elder, G. H. Jr., Modell, J., & Parke, R. D. (1993). *Children in time and place.* New York: Cambridge University Press.

Elkind, D. (1988). *The hurried child: Growing up too fast too soon* (rev. ed.). Reading, MA: Addison-Wesley.

Erikson, E. (1963). *Childhood and society.* New York: Norton.

Gans, H. J. (1999). *Popular culture and high culture: An analysis and evaluation of taste.* New York: Basic Books.

Garbarino, J. (1995). *Raising children in a socially toxic environment.* San Francisco: Jossey-Bass.

Garbarino, J. (1992). *Children and families in the social environment* (2nd ed.). New York: Aldine de Gruyter.

Hewlett, S. A. & West, C. (1998). *The war against parents.* Boston: Houghton Mifflin.

Moen, P., Elder, G. H. Jr., & Luscher, K. (Eds.). (1995). *Examining lives in context: Perspectives on the ecology of human development.* Washington, DC: American Psychological Association.

Naisbitt, J., & Auberdene, P. (1990). *Megatrends 2000.* New York: William Morrison.

Postman, N. (1992). *Technopoly: The surrender of culture to technology.* New York: Vintage.

Skinner, B. F. (1948). *Walden two.* New York: Macmillan.

Toffler, A. (1980). *The third wave.* New York: Bantam.

"The childhood shows the man, as morning shows the day."

— *John Milton*

UNDERSTANDING SOCIALIZATION

Prologue

A FATEFUL FAIRYTALE

The Adventures of Pinocchio, *by Carlo Collodi (1972 [1882]), is a classic story illustrating the trials and tribulations of a little boy growing up and the agents who contribute to his socialization.*

Gepetto, a woodcarver, wants a son very much, so he carves a little boy out of a block of wood and names him Pinocchio. While Gepetto sleeps, the Blue Fairy appears and gives the wooden boy life.

The Blue Fairy tells Pinocchio that if he wants to become a real boy, he must prove himself to be brave, truthful, and unselfish: "Be a good son to Gepetto—make him proud of you! Then, some day, you will wake up and find yourself a real boy."

However, the Blue Fairy warns Pinocchio that the world is full of temptations and that he must learn to choose between right and wrong in order to become human. Pinocchio asks how he will know the difference. The Blue Fairy explains he must rely on his own conscience to tell him. Pinocchio, who does not know what a conscience is, remains perplexed. Fortunately, a little cricket, Jiminy Cricket, who had been observing the whole scene, volunteers to serve as Pinocchio's conscience. The Blue Fairy leaves Pinocchio in Jiminy Cricket's hands, asking him to give Pinocchio the benefit of his advice and experience.

The story of Pinocchio tells of his adventures and inability to resist temptation. One time he starts off to school, but sells his books in order to go to a marionette show. Another time he wanders off and meets with thieves, who steal his money and try to kill him. He is saved by the Blue Fairy who then puts a spell on him that makes his nose grow long every time he tells a lie—which is supposed to remind Pinocchio not to do wrong. Eventually, however, Pinocchio succumbs to the temptation of going off to Playland where boys can be lazy and play all day. There he finds out that laziness can last for just so long. Good-for-nothing boys end up making jackasses of themselves. Without Jiminy Cricket, who helps his escape from Playland before it is too late, Pinocchio would have turned completely into a jackass.

Full of remorse, Pinocchio searches for Gepetto, only to find out that the woodcarver has been swallowed by a whale, and the boy goes to sea to save him. Pinocchio vows to work hard at his studies to become someone of whom Gepetto can be proud. Because Pinocchio has risked his life, thereby demonstrating braveness and unselfishness, the Blue Fairy turns him into a real boy. Thus Pinocchio finally becomes socialized into the human race. ■

- *Why did Pinocchio give up the pleasures and irresponsibilities of play for the hard work and responsibilities of school?*
- *What motivated his desire to care for others, rather than himself?*
- *Was the change in his behavior due to his love for Gepetto? the fear of punishment? the desire to be rewarded by the Blue Fairy? Did he learn from his experiences?*

The story of Pinocchio's struggle to become a real boy parallels any child's struggle to become socialized, hence its timelessness. The Blue Fairy's warnings are like those of any parent. Jiminy Cricket's advice is like that of a teacher. Pinocchio's adventures with the lazy boys are like those with one's peer group. Finally, Pinocchio's triumph of learning the difference between good and evil represents the significant outcome of socialization—a conscience.

This chapter explores the process of socialization, its aims or goals, its agents, and its methods; outcomes of socialization will be discussed in detail later.

SOCIALIZATION

Socialization is the process by which individuals acquire the knowledge, skills, and character traits that enable them to participate as effective members of groups and society (Brim, 1966).

- Socialization is what every parent does—"Help your brother button his jacket." "We use tissues, not our sleeves, to wipe our noses."

- Socialization is what every teacher does—"Study your spelling words tonight." "In our country we have the freedom to worship as we choose."

- Socialization is what every religion does—"Honor your father and mother." "Do not steal."

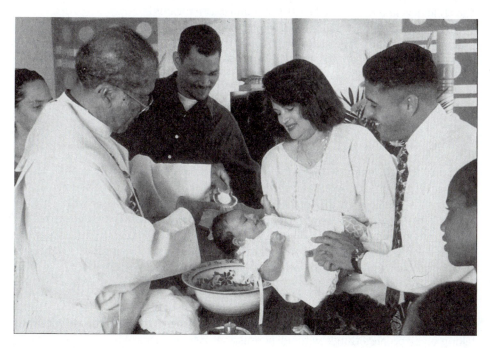

Babies are born into a culture.

- Socialization is what every employer does—"Part of your job is to open the store at eight o'clock and put the merchandise on the tables." "Your request must be in writing."
- Socialization is what every government does through its laws and system of punishment for violations.
- Socialization is also what friends do when they accept or reject you on the basis of whether or not you conform to their values.

The concept of socialization, including parenting or child rearing, social development, and education, really goes back in time as far as human life: "Train up a child in the way he should go: and when he is old, he will not depart from it" (Proverbs 22:6). Many forces in society contribute to children's development—as do the children themselves.

SOCIALIZATION AS A UNIQUE HUMAN PROCESS

Most social scientists agree that socialization is unique to human beings. Over 60 years ago George Mead (1934) wrote that it is language that sharply separates humans from other animals, that language makes ideas and communication of these ideas possible, and that language also makes it possible to replace action with thoughts, and then use thoughts to transform behavior. A little boy who breaks his mother's favorite vase and encounters her anger understands her threat the next day when she says, "If you don't hold your glass with both hands, it might fall and break, and then I will be very angry." The child now knows very well what *break* and *angry* mean.

Language enables humans to develop *mind,* the ability to reason, and *self,* one's characteristic pattern of behavior. It is reason and behavior that enable us to internalize the attitudes of others. *Internalization* is the process by which externally controlled behavior shifts to internally, or self-controlled, behavior. Self-controlled behavior and emotional regulation in humans motivates social control and the development of a society in which people want others with whom they interact to behave as appropriately as they do.

> Erin's thought one day was to try out Mom's makeup. In the process, the eyeshadow got on her fingers, and she wiped it on her shorts. She then sat down on Mom's bed to look in the mirror, leaving a smudge of blue shadow where her bottom touched. She soon got bored with this activity, wiped her moist, red mouth on Mom's yellow towel, and went outside to play. Fifteen minutes later, tears were streaming down Erin's cheeks as Mom pointed to the trail of evidence while scolding her for taking other people's things without permission.

Erin's thoughts led to behavior that brought out her mother's attitude regarding taking other people's things without permission. Her mother's expression of this attitude to Erin will lead to Erin's internalization of self-control. If other children, too, learn to internalize this control, a human society is possible.

Figure 2.1   An Ecological Model of Human Development

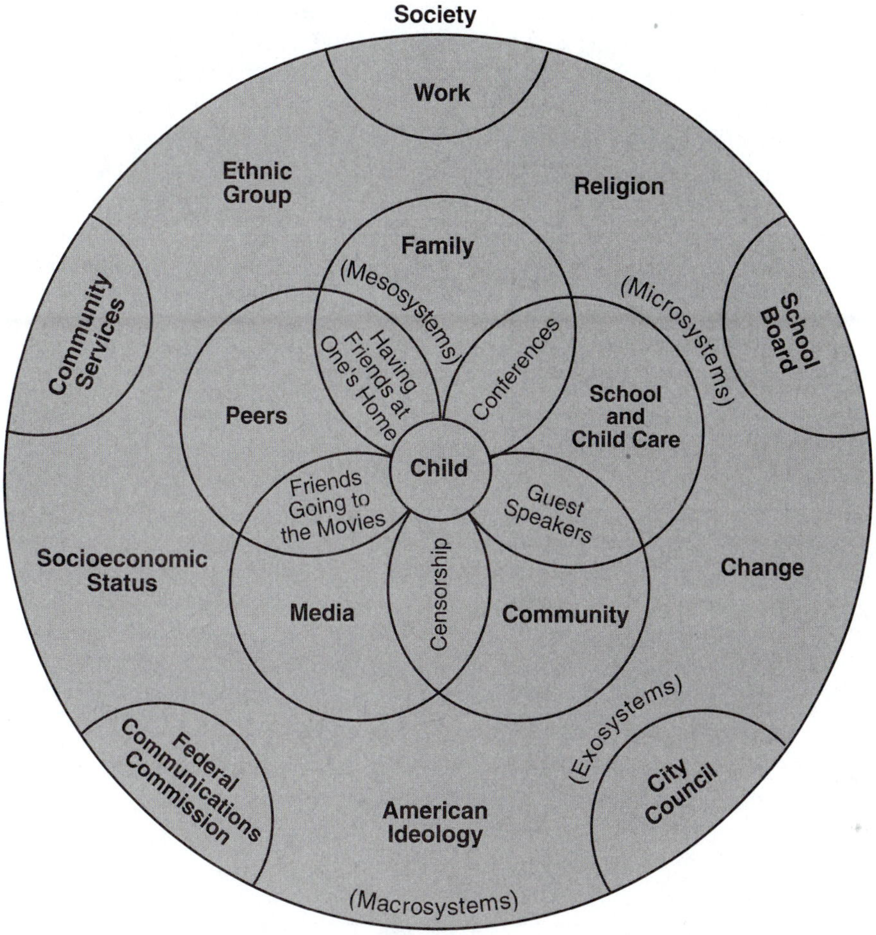

Socialization involves the interactions between the child and micro-, meso-, exo-, and macrosystems.

Socialization begins at birth and continues throughout life. Newborn human biological organisms with inherited characteristics come into the world with certain needs, which change as they develop. They are given names, which indicates that they are members of society. They are clothed in the manner appropriate to the society into which they are born. In the United States they are diapered, dressed in stretch suits, and kept in cribs. In certain African societies they are swaddled and put on their mothers' backs. The way their parents respond to their cries, the way their parents speak to them, the way their parents organize their rooms, the toys their parents buy for them, the people their parents allow them to spend time with (babysitter, relatives, and so on) all contribute to infants' socialization and consequent development.

Children play a role in their own socialization. As most parents will tell you, children are sometimes the ones responsible for how they are treated by others. You know if you smile, you are more likely to get a smile back than if you frown. The way you socialize children is often influenced by their reaction to you. For example, I needed only to look sternly at my son or speak in an assertive tone, and he would comply with what was asked of him. My daughter, however, would need to experience consequences (usually several times)—being sent to her room, withdrawal of privileges, having to do extra chores—before she would comply with my rules. Thus, not only do children actively contribute to interactions but, in so doing, they affect their own developmental outcomes transforming themselves in the process and influencing how others reciprocate (Bugental & Goodnow, 1998) (*see* Figure 2.2).

Research supports what parents have known for centuries: babies are born with different **temperaments** (Buss & Plomin, 1975; Chess & Thomas, 1987; Kagan, 1994; Thomas, Chess, & Birch, 1970). That is, they respond differently physiologically to various experiences. This is evident soon after birth in the individual differences in activity level, distractibility, adaptability to new situations, mood, and so on. How caregivers respond to their children's temperaments influences the socialization process. If there is a "goodness of fit" between the child's temperament and his or her caregivers, then socialization is likely to proceed smoothly (Chess & Thomas, 1987). For example, if the child does not adapt easily to new situations (is a "slow-to-warm-up" child), and the caregivers understand this and are patient (not pushing the child, yet encouraging him or her to get used to new things slowly), then socialization is likely to be smooth.

Figure 2.2   How Children Affect Their Own Developmental Outcomes

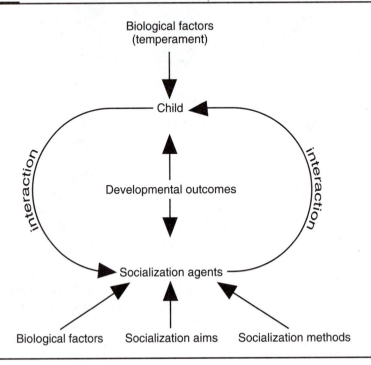

If, on the other hand, the fit between the child's temperament and the caregivers' is poor, socialization is likely to be rough. For example, if the child is very active, responds intensely to people and things, and is moody (a difficult child), and the caregivers force him or her to sit still, punish him or her for crying or being frightened, and demand a smile much of the time, then socialization may turn out to be a battleground of wills.

As infants become children, adolescents, and then adults, they interact with more people and have more experiences. In so doing, they acquire skills, knowledge, attitudes, values, motives, habits, beliefs, interests, morals, and ideals. You may learn to read from your first-grade teacher. You may learn to appreciate music from an uncle who takes you to concerts. You may learn about sportsmanship from your coach and about love from the girl or boy down the street.

Thus, from the point of view of society, individuals are socialized to fit into an organized way of life. And from a personal point of view, socialization has enabled them to discover theirselves—their potentialities for personal growth and fulfillment. By going to school, children not only gain knowledge; they also find out in what subjects they do best. As members of a peer group, they not only learn to cooperate; they find out whether they are leaders or followers. Over time, children choose and are exposed to different environments that impact their development (Bronfenbrenner & Morris, 1998).

INTENTIONAL AND UNINTENTIONAL SOCIALIZATION

Much socialization is intentional. When an adult tells a 6-year-old to share a toy with a 4-year-old sibling, that is intentional socialization. Or when an adult reminds a 10-year-old to write a thank-you note to Grandma, that too is intentional socialization. Thus, when adults have certain values that they consistently convey explicitly to the child, and when they back these up with approval for compliance and consequences for noncompliance, this conveyance is referred to as *intentional socialization.*

Much of socialization, however, takes place spontaneously during human interaction, without the deliberate intent to impart knowledge or values. *Unintentional socialization* may be the product of involvement in human interaction or observation of interaction. For example, a 4-year-old approaches two teachers conversing and excitedly says, "Miss Jones, Miss Jones, look!" One teacher says, "Sally, don't interrupt; we're talking." Later that morning Sally and her friend Tanya are busily playing with Legos. Sally is explaining and demonstrating to Tanya how to fit the pieces together. Miss Jones comes to the housekeeping corner and interrupts with, "Girls, please stop what you're doing and come see what Rene has brought to school."

It is very likely that the message Sally received from the morning's interactions was that it is not OK to interrupt adults, but it is OK for adults to interrupt children.

Another example of unintentional socialization is the mother who has told her daughter that alcohol and drugs are damaging to her physical and mental health. Yet when the daughter describes a party she went to where there was beer and drugs, and the mother indicates her fascination with the party's events by her attentive expression and her questions, what message is the daughter really receiving (especially if the mother herself uses alcohol or drugs, and her daughter sees this)?

In sum, children respond to and learn from experiences of emotion, body language, and other cues as well as verbal statements. These are all constructed, interpreted, and transformed to influence future behavior.

AIMS OF SOCIALIZATION

Socialization enables children to learn what they need to know in order to be integrated into the society in which they live. It also enables children to develop their potentialities and form satisfying relationships. Socialization aims to develop a self-concept, enable self-control, empower achievement, acquire appropriate social roles, and implement developmental skills.

DEVELOP A SELF-CONCEPT

Charles Cooley (1964), considered to be one of the founders of sociology, observed that through the experiences of interacting with others, children begin to distinguish themselves from others. Children call themselves "I" or "me"—"I hungry" "Me do it." As they begin to act independently, they gradually become aware that others are evaluating them, saying "Good boy/girl" or "No, don't do that." Thus their behavior is being judged according to certain rules and standards. These rules and standards must be learned and understood before the individual is capable of self-evaluation. As children gradually learn these criteria, each develops a self-concept; this concept reflects the attitudes of others and is termed "the looking-glass self." Mead (1934) referred to this gradually maturing way of looking at the self as "the generalized other." When children refer to themselves as "shy" or "hardworking," they have incorporated the standards of others into the description.

Thus, a self-concept develops when the attitudes and expectations of others with whom one interacts are incorporated into one's personality, making it possible to regulate one's behavior accordingly.

Psychologist Erik Erikson (1963, 1980) has explained the personality development of individuals as the outcome of their interactions in their social environment. He identified eight critical stages of psychosocial development in a human's life that impact the self-concept: *Trust versus Mistrust, Autonomy versus Shame and Doubt, Initiative versus Guilt, Industry versus Inferiority, Identity versus Identity Diffusion, Intimacy versus Isolation, Generativity versus Self-Absorption,* and *Integrity versus Despair* (*see* Table 2.1 for a chronological diagram of the eight stages).

Infancy: Trust versus Mistrust (Birth to Age 1)

The first "task" of infants is to develop the "cornerstone of a healthy personality," a basic sense of trust in themselves and of the people in their environment. The quality and consistency of care the infant receives determines the successful outcome of this stage. A child whose basic needs for nourishment and physical contact are met will develop a sense of trust. This sense of trust lays a foundation for a positive self-concept. A child whose care is negligent or inconsistent will develop a sense of mistrust, which may persist throughout life and result in a negative self-concept. Some mistrust, however is healthy in that it can guard against danger and manipulation. Contemporary research shows a positive relationship between parental nurturance and self-worth (Harter, 1998; Hopkins & Klein, 1994).

Table 2.1	Erikson's Stages of Psychosocial Development

Erikson's Eight Stages of Psychosocial Development (represented as dimensions). Note that an individual's development could be described as being at any point on the horizontal dimension lines, rather than at one extreme or the other. The importance of interactions with one's social environment in the development of a self-concept is indicated by the socializing agents that are most significant at various stages.

Infancy — Trust ————— Mistrust
Family

Early Childhood — Autonomy ————— Shame/Doubt
Family

Play Age — Initiative ————— Guilt
Family   School (Child Care)

School Age — Industry ————— Inferiority
Family   Peers   School   Community

Adolescence — Identity ————— Identity Diffusion
Family   Peers   School   Community

Young Adulthood — Intimacy ————— Isolation
Family   Peers   Community

Adulthood — Generativity ————— Self-Absorption
Family   Peers   Community

Senescence — Integrity ————— Despair
Family   Peers

Early Childhood: Autonomy versus Shame and Doubt (Age 2 to 3)

Physical and cognitive maturation enables children to behave autonomously—to walk without help, feed themselves, get things off the shelf, assert themselves verbally. If children are allowed to be self-sufficient according to ability, the outcome of this stage will be a feeling of autonomy. If children are deprived of the opportunity to develop a will, if they are continually being corrected or reprimanded, later they may feel shame when being assertive and self-doubt when being independent. However, some shame is healthy in that it can prevent certain socially unacceptable behaviors such as picking one's nose in public.

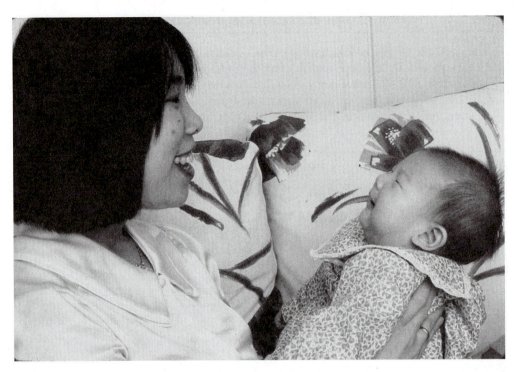

Mother–child interaction is the basis for attachment and sense of trust.

Play Age: Initiative versus Guilt (Age 3 to 5)

Children's increasing ability to communicate and to imagine leads them to initiate many activities. If they are allowed to create their own games and fantasies, to ask questions, to use certain objects (a hammer and wood, for example) with supervision, then the outcome of this stage will be a feeling of initiative. If they are made to feel that they are "bad" for trying new things and "pests" for asking questions, they may carry a sense of guilt throughout life. Probably the reason "Pinocchio" has remained a favorite story is that, like all children, Pinocchio was continually learning which activities he initiated were OK and which ones were not. Thus, some guilt is healthy in that it can control misbehavior.

School Age: Industry versus Inferiority (Age 6 to Puberty)

During school age, while learning to accept instruction and to win recognition by showing effort and by producing "things," the child is developing the capacity to enjoy work. The outcome of this stage for children who do not receive recognition for their efforts, or who do not experience any success, may be a feeling of incompetency and inferiority. Children who are praised for their efforts will be motivated to achieve, whereas children who are ignored or rebuked may give up and exhibit helplessness. Yet, some feelings of inferiority are healthy in that they can prevent the child from feeling invincible and taking dangerous risks.

A sense of initiative is influenced by having opportunities to produce things.

Adolescence: Identity versus Identity Diffusion (Puberty to Age 18)

With rapid growth and sexual maturity, the young person begins to question people, things, values, and attitudes previously relied on and to struggle through the crises of earlier stages all over again. The developmental task during adolescence, then, is to integrate earlier childhood identifications with biological and social changes occurring during this time. The danger in this stage is that while young people are trying out many roles, which is a normal process, they may be unable to choose an identity or make a commitment, and so will not know who they are or what they may become (identity diffusion). Since adolescence is a time for exploration, some diffusion is healthy in that it can allow for learning what is suitable and what is not for an individual.

Young Adulthood: Intimacy versus Isolation (Age 18 to Middle Adulthood)

Individuals who have succeeded in establishing an identity are now able to establish intimacy with themselves and with others, in both friendship and love. The danger here is that those who fear losing their identity in an intimate relationship with another may develop a sense of isolation. Some isolation is healthy, however, in that it can enable one to learn about oneself and provide time for individual pursuits.

Adulthood: Generativity versus Self-Absorption (Middle Adulthood to Late Adulthood)

From the development of intimate relationships comes generativity, the interest in establishing and guiding the next generation. This interest can be manifested by becoming a parent or by being involved with the development of young people through teaching, church, Scouts, and so on, as well as productivity and creativity in one's work. There is the possibility in this stage that the lack of generativity may result in self-absorption, which may show up as depression, hypochondria, substance abuse, or promiscuity. Yet, some self-absorption is healthy in that it can lead to creativity and the development of hobbies.

Senescence: Integrity versus Despair (Late Adulthood to Death)

The individual who has achieved an identity, who has developed a satisfying intimacy with others, who has adapted to the joys and frustrations of guiding the next generation, reaches the end of life with a certain ego integrity or positive self-concept—an acceptance of responsibility for what one's own life is and was and where it fits in the continuum of life. For those who have not achieved that integrity, this stage may produce despair or an extremely negative self-concept.

Despairing individuals tend to be in ill health, abuse drugs and/or alcohol, or commit suicide. They may become burdens to their families physically, financially, or psychologically. On the other hand, individuals with senses of integrity are likely to have friends, be active (physically and mentally), and look at life positively even though they know that death is imminent. Exemplifying an integral self-concept, or sense of integrity, can be summed up in what Rose Kennedy, who lived to be 104, said before she died. "I find it interesting to reflect on what has made my life, even with its moments of pain, an essentially happy one; I have come to the conclusion that the most important element in human life is faith" (Goldman, 1994, p. 20). Probably the only despair that is healthy is that which leads to change or greater appreciation of life.

ENABLE SELF-CONTROL

Self-control includes the ability to regulate one's emotions and behavior. This can be interpreted as routing our feelings through our brains before acting on them according to the situation. Regulated behavior often involves postponing or modifying immediate gratification for the sake of a future goal. This implies being able to tolerate frustration. For example, you curb your urge to spank a child who has just thrown a plate of food on the floor in a tantrum because you want to set an example of how to deal with frustration. When you are trying to maintain your weight, you postpone satisfying those hunger pangs until mealtime. You postpone sexual intercourse until marriage because of your religious or personal goals. Even though you hate to wake up early, you set your alarm in order to be at work on time because your supervisor depends on you.

Early relationships, especially attachment to parents, play a significant role in the development of emotional regulation (Bridges & Golnick, 1995) and "emotional intelligence" (Goleman, 1995). As the child progresses from infancy to childhood, emotional and behavioral regulation gradually shifts from external socializing agents to internal, self-induced mechanisms (Eisenberg, 1998). Caregivers provide children with information (body language, facial expressions, verbal instructions and explanations) to help children deal with situations. As children develop cognitively and have more real experiences; they learn how to interpret events; how to express emotions appropriately; strategies for coping with disappointment, frustration, rejection, anger, and so on.

EMPOWER ACHIEVEMENT

Socialization furnishes goals for what you are going to be when you become an adult—a teacher, a police officer, a business executive. These goals provide the rationale for going to school, getting along with others, following rules, and so on. In other words, socialization gives meaning or purpose to adulthood and to the long process a child has to go through to get there. In order for Pinocchio to become a real boy, he had to go to school as well as learn right from wrong.

Significant adults and peers influence one's motivation to succeed. For example, adults who know enough about the child to provide the appropriate challenge at the "right" time with the "right" amount of support are likely to produce highly competent and motivated children (Eccles, Wigfield, & Schiefele, 1998).

ACQUIRE APPROPRIATE SOCIAL ROLES

In order to be part of a group, one has to have a function that complements the group. For example, in a group of employees, the supervisor's function or role is to lead the employees; in a family group, the parents' role is to nurture the child; in a peer group, the role of friends is to provide emotional support. We have many social roles throughout life, some of which occur simultaneously, and we must assume the appropriate behavior for each at the appropriate time. I am a wife, a parent, a child, a teacher, and a friend—all at the same time. As a wife, I am a confidante; as a parent, I am nurturant; as a child, I am submissive; as a teacher, I am a facilitator; as a friend, I am emotionally supportive.

Gender is a social role, too, in that boys and girls learn gender-appropriate behavior from significant members of their society (Ruble & Martin, 1998).

IMPLEMENT DEVELOPMENTAL SKILLS

Socialization aims to provide developmental social, emotional, and cognitive skills to children so that they can function successfully in society. Social skills may require learning how to obtain information from other people, using the telephone, conducting business negotiations, and the like. Emotional skills may involve controlling aggressive impulses, learning to deal with frustration by substituting another goal for one that is blocked, or being able to compensate for mistakes. Cognitive skills may involve reading, mathematics, writing, problem-solving, geography, history, and science.

Psychologist Robert Havighurst (1972) examined how society's expectations with regard to certain behavioral skills change according to the maturation of the individual, using the term *developmental task* to explain this aspect of socialization. "A **developmental task** is midway between an individual need and a societal demand." According to Havighurst, the developmental tasks of life are those things one must learn if one is to get along well in society. As we grow, we develop physically, intellectually, and socially. Our physical development will enable us to walk, control our bladders, and use a pencil. Our intellectual development will enable us to learn to read, do arithmetic, and solve problems. Our social development will enable us to cooperate, empathize, and interact with others. And our emotional development will enable us to regulate our impulses and express our feelings. Developmental tasks categorized according to societal demands for certain behaviors are listed below; how they change for the individual from birth to death can be found in table A-1 in the Appendix.

1. Achieving an appropriate dependence/independence pattern.
2. Achieving an appropriate giving–receiving pattern of affection.
3. Relating to changing social groups.
4. Developing a conscience.
5. Learning one's psychosociobiological role.
6. Accepting and adjusting to a changing body.
7. Managing a changing body and learning new behavioral patterns.
8. Learning to understand and control the physical world.
9. Developing an appropriate symbol system and conceptual abilities.
10. Relating oneself to the cosmos.

As we develop in these dimensions, we face new expectations from significant socializing agents in the surrounding society. We are expected to learn to walk, talk, use the toilet, and dress ourselves. We are expected to read, write, add, and subtract. We are expected to share, develop a conscience, and achieve an appropriate gender role. We are expected to love other people and be responsible for our actions.

Thus developmental tasks arise from societal pressures on individuals according to their development: "If the task is not achieved at the proper time, it will not be achieved well, and failure in this task will cause partial or complete failure in the achievement of other tasks yet to come" (Havighurst, 1972, p. 3). If children do not have experiences in language, such as being spoken to and making sounds during the critical stage of language development (first year), their ability to communicate will be handicapped for the remainder of their lives. A child who is not socialized to develop a conscience may engage in delinquent behavior in adolescence. A child who does not have experiences receiving and giving affection may not succeed in a marriage or family relationship.

Those who do not succeed in a developmental task face the disapproval of others because they have not behaved as expected. As a reminder of the Blue Fairy's disapproval, Pinocchio's nose grew long whenever he did not tell the truth.

Developmental tasks differ from society to society, and each group in a society has its own developmental definitions and expectations. For example, a common

Achieving the developmental task of independence—"I can walk all by myself!"

developmental milestone for Anglo, middle-class infants is to "sleep through the night." This expectation is usually fulfilled by about age 4 to 6 months and is often facilitated by parents feeding the baby just before they go to sleep and/or by playing with the baby and putting him or her to sleep for the night as late as possible. However, in many other ethnic groups where the infant sleeps with the mother and nurses on demand, "sleeping through the night" is not pushed as a developmental milestone.

Diversity in developmental definitions and expectations may account for some of the social adjustment problems in school among children from minority ethnic or cultural groups. For example, the developmental task for achieving an appropriate dependence/independence pattern may be interpreted differently by various groups. Most middle-class American mothers, as well as American teachers, expect children to be independent of adults by school age in that they can take care of personal needs and learn on their own with some directions. Japanese mothers, on the other hand, expect some of their child's dependency needs to be transferred to the teacher when the child goes to school, and Japanese mothers generally remain very involved in their child's learning throughout school. Hispanic and Hawaiian mothers expect their child's dependency needs to be transferred to older siblings, and interdependence, rather than independence, is encouraged. Thus, Japanese, Hispanic, Hawaiian, and children from other *high-context* cultures may experience conflicts between developmental skills taught by their families and those taught in American schools (Bennett, 1995).

Every individual in a society (along with his or her genetic traits) is the outcome of the process of socialization. The success of this outcome in terms of society's expectations will depend on a series of interactions with significant socializing agents, such as parents, teachers, peers, and media, that constitute the community in which this individual lives. Figure 2.3 illustrates the processes and outcomes of socialization.

AGENTS OF SOCIALIZATION

The generalized community is made up of many groups that play a part in socializing an individual. These groups or agents of socialization exert their influence in different ways and at different times.

Figure 2.3   The Processes and Outcomes of Socialization

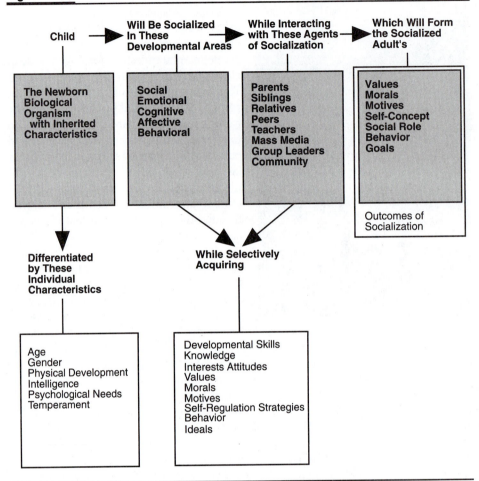

Source: Adapted from E. B. McNeil (1969, p. 5). *Human Socialization*. Belmont, CA: Brooks/Cole.

In the early years the family assumes the primary role of nurturing the child. As the child gets older, the peer group becomes a primary source of support. In primitive societies training for competency occurs in the family in the form of learning to hunt or to build a shelter, whereas in industrial societies it occurs in the school in the form of learning to read, write, compute, master science or geography, and so forth.

Each agent has its own functions in socialization. Sometimes the agents complement each other; sometimes they contradict each other. The value of getting along with others is usually taught in the family, the school, the church, the peer group, and perhaps in the media, with the agents complementing each other. The value of academic achievement, however, may be supported by some families and the school, but scorned by the peer group—an example of contradiction among the agents of socialization. The media and the peer group may support sexual experimentation, while the family and church condemn it.

FAMILY

The family is the child's introduction to society and has, therefore, borne the major responsibility for socializing the child. The family into which a child is born places the child in a community and in a society; newborns begin their social lives by acquiring the status their families have, which influences their opportunities. For example, children in low-income families not only have fewer material things, they also have less opportunity to develop their abilities. Since they cannot compete with others of their age who have more things and more opportunities, lower-status children are likely to believe they have little control over the future and, therefore, try less hard in school, accomplishing less.

The family also passes on its socioeconomic status through its ability to afford higher education for its children. Middle- and upper-status children are more likely to go to college after high school, whereas lower-status children are more likely to go to work. And those who have not achieved in high school, perhaps from lack of motivation, have fewer job opportunities. Educational level, then, is a strong determinant of future occupation and income.

The family exposes the child to certain cultural experiences available in the society— perhaps religious instruction, Scouts, music lessons, Little League, soccer, and so on. Parents buy certain toys for their children, arrange certain activities together such as games, outings, and vacations. These depend to a large extent on socioeconomic status.

The family functions as a system of interaction, and the way it conducts personal relationships has a very powerful effect on the psychosocial development of children. Through various interactions with family members, such as siblings, grandparents, and other relatives, the child develops patterns for establishing relationships with others.

Socializing Agents and Their Messages: The Reality

Typical American children start the day with some instructions and expectations from their parents about finishing breakfast, setting an after-school schedule, cleaning their rooms, and so on. A few additional remarks may be added by older siblings regarding the condition of the bathroom when they went to use it.

On the way to school the bus driver may refuse to allow loud talking or changing seats once the bus has begun moving. At school, one teacher may stress independence and competition, and another may emphasize cooperation and dependence on the group. After school, teachers may assume different roles, perhaps as coaches or club leaders. The team or the club members may value the best athlete or the one who sells the most raffle tickets, but in the classroom setting they may dislike the one who gets the best grades or reads the most books.

Back at home, the television sends messages via the various programs. One day a child may watch *Barney and Friends* and feel empathic and altruistic. Another day the child may watch *Batman, Superman,* or *Power Rangers* and come away feeling aggressive.

In reality, children receive many demands from socializing agents as well as conflicting messages.

These patterns are expressed and further developed in relationships with peers, authority figures, co-workers, and ultimately a spouse and children.

> Marie, the oldest of three children, was responsible for helping her mother care for her younger siblings. She often had to play a game with her younger sister while her mother nursed the baby, or she had to watch the baby while her mother drove her sister to preschool. In her relations with her friends, Marie was the one always saying, "Let's play this" or "Let's play that" or "This is the way you're supposed to draw a house (or dog or cat)." In school she was often appointed to be a monitor. As an adult, Marie got a managerial position in her office.

"The family into which a child is born is the child's first reference group, the first group whose values, norms, and practices one refers to in evaluating one's behavior" (Elkin & Handel, 1989, p. 143). For example, there is now evidence that marital conflict and distress are related to children's difficulties with peers (Rubin, Bukowski, & Parker, 1998). For another example, it has been found that children of employed mothers from kindergarten age through adulthood have less restricted views of gender roles (Ellis, 1994; Hoffman, 1989). In passing on values, expectations, and practices, families also pass on to children certain behavior patterns toward others. These behavior patterns vary by ethnicity (Greenfield & Suzuki, 1998; Rotherdam & Phinney, 1987).

Dimensions of Ethnic Behavior Patterns

1. Group versus individual orientation. At one extreme of this dimension is orientation toward the group as exhibited by some ethnic families, such as Japanese, Hawaiian, Mexican, and Middle Eastern, who emphasize affiliation, cooperation, and interpersonal relations. At the other extreme of this dimension is individual orientation, which is exhibited by many middle-class American and Western European families, who focus more on individual accomplishment, competition, and independence from the group. One's orientation on this dimension becomes significant in a situation where one has to choose between obligation to one's family or to one's personal ambitions, such as keeping a job to remain geographically close to kin rather than relocating to earn more money or prestige.

2. Active versus passive coping style. An active coping style is associated with "doing" and "getting things done" rather than on "being" or "becoming," as characterized by a passive coping style. An active coping style also involves a future time orientation where time moves quickly and a perception that one can control and change the environment, rather than the passive coping style belief that all events are determined by fate and are, therefore, inevitable. Hispanic Americans are less active in orientation than are Anglo Americans (Bennett, 1995). One's orientation on this dimension becomes significant in motivating families to seek social services, such as psychological, when problems occur.

3. Submissive versus egalitarian attitude toward authority.   This dimension can be observed in children as to whether they regard their parents and teachers as clear authority figures whom they respect and obey without question, or rather see them as more nearly equal figures with whom they may disagree and question. Young Mexican American and Asian American children are generally more obedient, respectful, and accepting of authority than are Anglo American children (Bennett, 1995). One's orientation on this dimension becomes significant in such situations as workplaces that reward assertiveness.

4. Open/expressive versus restrained/private communication style.   African American children are more openly and freely expressive, both positively and negatively, in a wide variety of situations (Bennett, 1995) than are Anglo Americans who, in turn, are more direct and open in social interactions than are Asian Americans who tend to be more polite and ritualistic (Bennett, 1995). One's orientation on this dimension becomes significant in communicating with those whose orientation differs.

In Chapter 1, socialization outcomes of different world views were discussed. Likewise, these examples of behavior patterns from diverse ethnic groups passed on by families are important, as will be seen throughout the book, especially when they differ from the standards socialized by the school.

According to extensive cross-cultural research done by Kagicibasi (1996), family behavioral patterns and consequent socialization practices can basically be categorized as *interdependent* (family loyalty, intergenerational dependency, control, obedience are stressed) and *independent* (individual achievement, separateness of generations, egalitarianism, consensus are stressed). A child brought up with *interdependent* values would <u>give</u> his or her parent money if needed; a child brought up with *independent* values might <u>lend</u> the parent money, perhaps even charging interest.

Many immigrants have brought their cultural behavior patterns to the United States. The following is an excerpt from a family analysis done by a college student from a Persian Jewish family in Los Angeles (cited in Greenfield & Suzuki, 1998, p. 1081):

Being a first generation immigrant I have had to deal with . . . adjusting a collectivistic upbringing to an environment of individualism. In my home my parents and family coming from a country and culture . . . [with] beliefs of family as the central and dominant unit in life, endeavored to instill in us a sense of family in the collectivistic sense.

We were brought up in a home where the "we" consciousness was stressed, rather than the "I" consciousness. We were taught that our behavior not only had implications for . . . ourselves but also for the rest of the family, for example, if I stayed out late at night, not only would I be taking the chance of getting robbed, raped, and/or murdered (implications of that experience for me), but also my younger brother and sister who looked up to me would also be jeopardized (implications of my actions for others). . . .

We were also taught to be responsible not only for ourselves, but also responsible for every other family member; thereby sharing the responsibility for both good and bad outcomes and playing a major part in each other's lives. For example, if my brother did bad in school, I was also responsible because as his older sister I was responsible to help him and take care of him and teach him right from wrong. I was, to an extent, as responsible for his actions as he, and my parents were (Yafai, 1992, p. 3).

SCHOOL AND CHILD CARE

The school acts as an agent of society in that it is organized to perpetuate that society's knowledge, skills, customs, and beliefs. The school's part in the transmission of culture is continually under debate because expanding knowledge and technology make it impossible to transmit everything. Thus difficult choices have to be made as to what is most important—with consequent conflicting opinions. All education springs from some image of the future.

Socializing children for a society of rapid change is a continual challenge. In such changing conditions, when educators become unsure of what is right for the next generation to learn in order to be adequately prepared for the future, the trend becomes education for adaptability. What is education for adaptability? Is it teaching basic skills or problem solving? Is it an individual or group enterprise? Computers can enable individualized learning; cooperative activities can enable group learning. Schools must choose how to balance them. While schools must encourage the creative capacities of the young to adapt to a changing physical and social environment, they still have the task of maintaining the status quo and ensuring cultural continuity. Ideally, the school must act as an agent to foster respect and adherence to the existing social order of society, but reality proves this is not a constant.

Education professor John Goodlad (1984) studied documents related to the purposes of schooling spanning 300 years of U.S. history. He found four broad categories of goals: academic (reading, writing, arithmetic); vocational (preparation for world of work); social and civic (preparation to participate in a democracy); and personal (develop individual talent and self-expression).

The social order of society is communicated to the child largely in the classroom—a setting in which children are evaluated by the teacher's comments, report cards, marks on papers, charts, classmates' judgments, and self-judgments. "Who can help Sally with that problem?" "Who has read the most books?" "Only papers with the best handwriting will be displayed for parents' night." Evaluation contributes to socialization in that the norms and standards of society are learned via the criteria of the evaluation. The self-concept emerges from how well the child meets the expectations of others, the evaluators (Brophy, 1986; Harter, 1998).

The political ideology of society is communicated to the child via textbooks and how subjects are taught. How

Some children have been taught to lower their eyes and bow their heads as a sign of respect when spoken to by an adult.

is the classroom setting organized? Do students compete with one another participating in discussion, or do they pursue activities independently?

Socialization outcomes in teacher-centered and learner-centered classrooms are different (Linney & Seidman, 1989). Teacher- and learner-centered classrooms will be discussed in more detail later in the book. The teacher in the school also contributes to the socialization process by serving as a model for children to imitate (Brophy, 1992). Teachers who are involved in their subject matter tend to have active, curious students who want to learn.

Child care has become an important socialization agent due to societal changes. The specific effects of care from one other than a parent are controversial due to many variables (Belsky & Rovine, 1988; Clark-Stewart, 1987). Specifics will be discussed in a later chapter.

PEERS

The peer group comprises individuals who are of approximately the same age and social status and who have common interests. Experiences in child-care facilities can expose children to peer relations months after birth. However, reciprocal interactions in the peer group don't usually begin until about age 3, when the child starts to understand the views of others and, therefore, is able to cooperate, share, and take turns. Cognitively, the child is beginning to move away from **egocentrism,** the characteristic of being able to look at the world only from one's own point of view. As the child matures and develops new interests, his or her peer groups change. Some may be based on proximity, such as the children in the neighborhood or the classroom, or interest, such as those on the soccer team or in Scouts.

> The peer group gives children experience in egalitarian types of relationships. In this group they engage in a process of give-and-take not ordinarily possible in their relationships with adults. . . . In the peer group they gain their first substantial experience of equality. Children entering a peer group are interested in the companionship, attention, and good will of the group (particularly of the members of the group who are significant for them), and the group is in a position to satisfy this interest. For behaving in the appropriate or valued manner, the group rewards its members by bestowing attention, approval, or leadership or by giving permission to participate or to employ certain symbols. For behaving otherwise, the peer group punishes by disdain, ostracism, or other expressions of disapproval (Elkin & Handel, 1989, p. 184).

Thus children come to look at themselves from the point of view of the group. The peer group rewards sociability, or getting along, and rejects deviations, such as eccentricity, aggression, and showing off. The child learns to obey the "rules of the game" and how to assume the various roles required in the game, such as batter, pitcher, or catcher. The peer group exerts control by simply refusing to include those who do not conform to its values or rules.

An example of the power of peer group pressure is the classical children's story by Hans Christian Andersen of "The Emperor's New Clothes." The emperor, who was very vain about his clothes, bought some cloth that—according to the merchants who sold it—was visible only to those not worthy of their positions in life. He proudly wore his new outfit made of this unique cloth in a parade before the entire town. No one dared admit to others that the emperor really hadn't any clothes on, for fear of being judged unworthy. It took the astonished cry of an innocent child to make everyone realize the truth.

The peer group functions as a socializing agent in that it provides information about the world and oneself from a perspective other than that of one's own family (Hartup, 1983; Rubin, Bukowski, & Parker, 1998). From the peer group children receive feedback about their abilities. Through interaction with their equals, people find out whether they are better than, the same as, or worse than their friends in sports, dating, grades, and so on. Within the peer group the child can experiment with various roles—leader, follower, clown, troublemaker, or peacemaker—and discover how the others react.

Peers also serve as a support group for the expression of values and attitudes (Hartup, 1983). Members often discuss situations with parents, siblings, and teachers. Beyond that, friends may offer sympathy and/or advice in handling problems. That children spend an increasing amount of time with their peers was illustrated in a study of children ages 2 to 12 (Ellis, Rogoff, & Cromer, 1981). It was observed that by age 8, children were interacting six times more with other children than with adults. The peer group, then, as an agent of socialization exerts a strong influence on the ideas and behavior of those who need social approval and fear rejection.

MEDIA

Mass media includes newspapers, magazines, books, radio, television, videos, movies, computers, and other means of communication that reach large audiences via an impersonal medium between the sender and the receiver. Unlike other agents of socialization, the mass media do not ordinarily directly involve personal interactions; the interactions are of a more technical nature. The mass media must, however, be considered socializing agents, because they reveal many aspects of the society and elicit cognitive processes in children that affect their understanding of the real world (Huston & Wright, 1998). Newspapers report such items as the current baseball scores or government policy; magazines illustrate the latest fashions or suggest things to do with free time in the summer; radio stations play popular songs; books discuss such issues as sex and drugs; television gives glimpses of hospitals, courtrooms, or family situations. Television, videos, and movies also show relationships between people in various settings so that children are provided with images or patterns of how to behave or interact in similar situations.

Television and books provide information about society. Through them viewers and readers come to learn about parts of the world they might not otherwise encounter or experience. Television and books take you under the sea, to outer space, to the jungles, to other times, and to other countries.

Television and books provide role models—the hero, the villain, the detective, the doctor, the lawyer, the mother, and the father. They reflect social attitudes—beliefs about political issues, such as war or taxes; and social issues, such as abortion or child abuse, occupations, sex, and minority groups.

Children, because of cognitive immaturity, are of special concern regarding media influence (Huston, Zillman, & Bryant, 1994). They process the content they see and hear and transform it into something meaningful to them, which may or may not be accurate or desirable. One concern is that young children may come to think of all people in a group as having the same characteristics as the people in that group presented on TV or in books, and this may influence their attitudes. For example, on the majority of television shows and movies, the white male is portrayed as dominant, brave, powerful, and competent (Comstock & Paik, 1991; Huston & Wright, 1998; Isaacs, 1999). This is true in textbooks as well. This is especially true for children who do not have the real experience to evaluate the attitude portrayed.

Another concern is children's susceptibility to advertising (Condry, 1989; Huston & Wright, 1998). Many children demand parents buy products and toys seen on TV. Children often imitate well-known media characters. For example, the Mighty Morphin Power Rangers have invaded preschools and schools not only in the increase in violent behavior among children, but in the toys, clothing, and supplies marketed (Levin & Carlsson-Paige, 1995). Commercialism is implemented in children's sports and schools, as well as on TV.

With the introduction of new technology to mass media, such as modems, and compact discs, children can play a greater role in their own socialization. They can, for example, access any information that is on the Internet (unless the computer has software to block access, like some parents have done to prevent their children from connecting to pornographic networks). They also have more opportunities to interact with media independent from adult mediation (many households have more than one TV).

COMMUNITY

The term **community** is derived from the Latin word for fellowship. It refers to the affective relationships expected among closely knit groups of people having common interests. It also refers to people living in a particular geographical area who are bound together politically and economically. The function of the community, then, is to provide a sense of belonging, friendship, and socialization of children (Etzioni, 1993). Many sociologists and psychologists are concerned with the erosion of community ties as we move toward the future (Garbarino, 1992; Schorr, 1997). The factors contributing to this erosion, such as fear of violence, technology, "busyness," as well as coping strategies will be discussed later.

The size, population, and mobility pattern of a community determine the pattern of human interaction. In a town with a small and stable population of a few thousand, most people know each other, in contrast to a large, more mobile town of many thousands. Small-town interaction involves more intimate details of people's lives than does large-town interaction. In a small town, people see each other in many settings—at the store, school, movies, and church. In a large town, relationships are more fragmented—it is unlikely that one would just by chance see a friend at a restaurant, simply because there are so many restaurants available to dine at in a large town. Similarly, a large town provides more activities than does a small town. Thus, one's interactions focus on the community groups to which one belongs—Scouts, Little League, the "Y," the church, and so on.

One function of such community agencies as those mentioned above is to give children different perspectives on life—to broaden their range of experience and give them new statuses or roles. In this respect, community agencies and organizations contribute to the socialization of children. In Scouting, for example, children learn about various occupational roles through a badge program. The Scout is supervised by a designated community "sponsor"—perhaps by a veterinarian, in performing various tasks such as caring for an animal. A church youth group might participate in a project of visiting people in a home for the elderly on a regular basis. Community libraries open the world of reading to children; museums open the worlds of art, science, geography, zoology, and so on.

Neighborhoods are often stratified by economic status (Levine & Levine, 1996)—the lower-economic-status families may live in less desirable sections, whereas the upper-economic-status families may live in large homes surrounded by green lawns or in apartments with doormen. The location of these neighborhoods in the larger community influences interaction patterns. If children from different neighborhoods attend a particular school, or share community services such as recreation and library, all the children have an opportunity to interact with many diverse individuals. On the other hand, if the neighborhoods are segregated, each having its own school and recreational facilities, the children generally interact with those like themselves.

People in the neighborhood, the adults and the older children, are the ones with whom the young child interacts and "probably stand second only to parents in terms of their power to influence the child's behavior" (Bronfenbrenner, 1979, p. 161; Schorr, 1997). The adults in the neighborhood are role models. They may be carpenters, engineers, entrepreneurs, teachers, or recreation leaders. The older children are models of behavior and interaction. Children often learn games and cues about getting along with certain people from older children: "Mrs. Grady is an old grouch; she won't give your ball back if it goes in her yard."

A community can have an *informal social support system* of the family—relatives, friends, neighbors who can be counted on to help in a crisis. For example, when Mrs. Cooper went to the hospital, her mother-in-law came to care for the children, and the neighbors took turns cooking meals and doing errands for the family. A community can also have a more *formal social support system,* such as institutionalized child care, Big Brothers/Big Sisters, Meals on Wheels, and Parents without Partners. These formal support systems can be funded by tax dollars, donations, or membership fees.

Formal support systems in a community usually emerge through the

Communities provide various perspectives and interactions for children.

process of advocacy. *Advocacy* means speaking or writing in support of something—for example, setting goals on behalf of children and seeing that politicians or governmental agencies implement them. It is a long and arduous process, however, to go from goals to laws. Thus, if community members want to improve opportunities for their children, they must get involved in politics. Politics begins locally, in one's own community. If community members want their children to have "the right to full opportunity for play and recreation," they can communicate this desire to their city council members and follow through by examining how their local tax dollars are distributed. For example, one city doubled the money previously budgeted for programs such as child care, youth activities, senior citizens' food, and a shelter for victims of domestic violence. Most of the money had been previously allocated to street repair.

METHODS OF SOCIALIZATION

Since socialization is the process by which people learn the ways of a given society so that they can function effectively within it, how are these ways transmitted to the child? (*See* Table 2.2.)

AFFECTIVE METHODS (EFFECT EMERGES FROM FEELING)

Affective refers to feelings or emotions, such as love, anger, fear, disgust. Affective mechanisms include responses to others, feelings about self, feelings about others, expression of emotions. Affect emerges from person-to-person interaction, which leads to attachment. The socialization of the child, whether intentional or unintentional, is accomplished through person-to-person interaction. When people are attached to one another, they interact often; thus attachment and interaction are bidirectional (Thompson, 1998).

Attachment is an "affectional tie that one person forms to another specific person, binding them together in space and enduring over time" (Ainsworth, 1973, p. 1). Socialization begins with personal attachment (Elkin & Handel, 1989). The human infant is born helpless, requiring care. In the process of caring for the infant, the parents or caregivers hold, play with, and talk to the infant. They respond to the feelings in them evoked by the child. This sensitive, responsive caregiving is the foundation for social interaction, and it is this interaction that contributes to many socialization outcomes for the child (Bowlby, 1988; Thompson, 1998).

Infants who are responded to when they cry, who are fed, held, and spoken to, will develop a *secure attachment* and a sense of trust toward the world. On the other hand, infants who receive minimal or inconsistent care will develop an *insecure attachment* and a sense of mistrust (Erikson, 1963). Our first human relationship, then, provides the basis for our later expectations regarding other relationships.

An outcome of attachment, other than feelings of trust or mistrust for future social interactions, is the feeling of competence. Paradoxically, the more securely attached children are to a nurturing adult, the safer they feel to explore the environment. On the other hand, the more insecurely attached they are, the less likely they are to leave their caregivers and try out new things (Ainsworth, 1973). Follow-up observations in

Table 2.2	Methods of Socialization

AFFECTIVE (effect emerges from feeling)
    attachment

OPERANT (effect emerges from acting)
    reinforcement
    extinction
    punishment
    feedback
    learning by doing

OBSERVATIONAL (effect emerges from imitating)
    modeling

COGNITIVE (effect emerges from information processing)
    instruction
    setting standards
    reasoning

SOCIOCULTURAL (effect emerges from conforming)
    group pressure
    tradition
    rituals
    symbols

APPRENTICESHIP (effect emerges from guided participation)
    structuring
    collaborating
    transferring

preschool showed that infants who were judged to be securely attached at age 1.5 years were more enthusiastic, sympathetic to others, cooperative, independent, and competent than those who displayed insecure attachment at that age (Sroufe, 1978). Several studies have found insecurely attached children to exhibit disruptive, hostile, or aggressive behavior in preschool (Sroufe, 1996; Waters et al., 1993). Attachment to the primary caregiver is the first of many important emotional relationships with significant others that the child will form in the future. These significant others may include relatives, teachers, friends, and coaches. Because each of these others is unique and because each situation the child encounters with these others is unique, each will contribute in a different way to the child's socialization.

David Elkind (1981b, pp. 20–24) discusses the importance of attachment in determining how children learn: "In children's early years, adults predigest experience for them much as mothers predigest food to provide milk for their babies." Adults, then, communicate to children their own learning experiences. The adults are mediators. Elkind cites an example of a teacher who always had children around her when she used various art materials. She showed them different ways paper could be folded and how to use a brush, and she joyfully produced new colors when she mixed the paints. The children acquired not only the ability to fold paper, make brush strokes, or mix paint; they also acquired an attitude of appreciation, enjoyment, and respect for art materials. This kind of learning is referred to by Elkind as the acquisition of mediating structures. Personal attachment to adults enables children to abstract mediating structures from them.

An example of mediating structures is described by Reuveen Feurstein (1980). In comparing children who immigrated to Israel from Yemen and Morocco, Feurstein found that even though both groups of children attended school in Israel, the Yemenite children were better learners than the Moroccan children. Case histories of the children revealed that as part of their religious training, the Yemenite children had studied with their fathers. Feurstein called this kind of interaction a "mediated learning experience," in which the adult provides the mechanisms for the acquisition of learning. Thus, by becoming attached to an adult who enjoys learning, the child's attitude toward future learning is acquired.

When the child is attached to a caregiver, socialization takes place in many ways. Some of these result from the child's action (an *operant method*); some of them result from the child's imitating (an *observational method*); some of them result from the child's information processing (a *cognitive method*); some of them result from the child's cultural traditions (a *sociocultural method*); and some of them result from guided participation (an *apprenticeship method*).

OPERANT METHODS (EFFECT EMERGES FROM ACTING)

Operant refers to producing an effect. When one's behavior is followed by a favorable outcome (reinforcement), the probability of that behavior occurring again is increased. When one's behavior has no favorable outcome (for example, it does not get attention; it is ignored) or has an unfavorable outcome (punishment), the probability of that behavior occurring again is decreased. Operant methods take into account the participatory role of individuals in their own socialization.

There are several socialization techniques that can be used to increase desired behavior.

Reinforcement

Reinforcement is an object or event that is presented following a behavior and that serves to increase the likelihood that the behavior will occur again. Reinforcement can be *positive* (reward given for desired behavior)—examples are food, physical contact, praise. Reinforcement can also be *negative*. **Negative reinforcement** is the termination of an unpleasant condition following a desired response—for example, allowing children to come out of their rooms when they stop a temper tantrum, or stopping a spanking when the child apologizes.

When one desires to reinforce a behavior that is complex, involving many steps, such as writing the alphabet, shaping can be used. **Shaping** is the systematic immediate reinforcement of successive approximations of the desired behavior until the desired behavior occurs and is maintained. Writing the alphabet involves holding a pencil and copying lines and circles in a specific way on a piece of paper. The lines and circles must be a certain size and a certain distance from one another. At a child's first attempt, the teacher may reward a line of any size that resembles the letter. Then the teacher may reward only straight lines, then straight lines of a certain size, and so on, until the child reaches the desired level of performance. Shaping is an effective socializing mechanism to teach various skills.

The following is a summary of conditions under which reinforcement can be effective as a socializing technique (Martin & Pear, 1996):

- The desired behavior must first be exhibited before it can be reinforced. In training a child to defecate in the toilet, the caregiver must put the child on the seat and wait for the behavior to occur before reinforcing it. The main unresolved question accompanying the technique of positive reinforcement is: How do you get children to make the desired response in the first place so that they can be rewarded?

- The desired behavior must be reinforced immediately the first time it occurs. If you want children to verbalize their requests rather than point to or grunt for desired objects, you must reward them when they say, for example, "Juice."

- Initially, the desired behavior must be reinforced each time it is exhibited. Every time children verbalize their requests they should get what is asked for. Every time children defecate in the toilet, they should be rewarded.

- When the newly acquired behavior is being performed relatively frequently, reinforcement can then become intermittent. Reward or praise can be given every few times the behavior is performed or it can be given every few days instead of every time. "I'm glad you're asking for what you want." "I'm proud you're using the toilet now."

- Since the long-range goal is self-reward, subjective reinforcers, such as privileges and praise, should be used in conjunction with objective reinforcers, such as food, toys, or money.

There are several problems in using reinforcement as a socializing technique, other than having to wait for the desired behavior to occur: (1) Individuals respond differently to reinforcers. For some children, a toy is an effective reinforcer; for others, adult approval is more effective. It is sometimes difficult to find the best one. (2) The child may become bored with the reinforcer, so its effectiveness diminishes. (3) Being human, it is difficult for adults to constantly reward children's desired behavior, even during the initial stages. If parents want to train a child to urinate in the toilet, they must be present as well as ready to put the child on the toilet at certain intervals. They also must wait patiently for the desired behavior to occur. (4) Adults sometimes unintentionally reinforce the very behaviors they want to eliminate. When children who have been toilet trained begin to urinate in their pants again, perhaps because they see their baby brother or sister do it, and the mother says, "I thought you were a big boy (girl)," it is highly likely that the undesired behavior will occur again because negative attention is better than no attention. (5) While the goal is for the child to internally regulate his or her behavior, reinforcement is externally regulated and may reduce the motivation for self-control.

There are also socialization techniques that can decrease or eliminate undesired behavior, such as extinction, punishment, feedback, and learning by doing.

Extinction

If reinforcement increases the likelihood of a response occurring again, then the removal of the reinforcement should decrease and eventually eliminate, or extinguish, the likelihood of the repetition of the response. **Extinction** is the gradual disappearance of a learned behavior, due to the removal of the reinforcement. For example, to extinguish the habit of nail biting, a father decides to ignore his daughter every time she bites her nails, instead of nagging her to stop, as he used to do. Thus he removes the previous reinforcement of attention. When she does not bite her nails for a 10-minute stretch, however, he praises her. Gradually the interval between nail-biting episodes becomes longer and longer, with the father giving praise every half-hour for not nail biting, but still ignoring his daughter when she does bite her nails.

Extinction must be used in conjunction with reinforcement to be effective as a socializing method. Annoying behaviors such as tantrums, dawdling, and tattling respond well, but more complex or deep-seated behaviors such as aggression, stealing, and overeating do not.

"Time-out" is a type of extinction where all reinforcement is removed. Usually, the child spends a specified amount of time in his or her room, or in a corner, or in any place where behavior can be ignored. "Time-out" can give a child time and space to better manage emotions and behavior. Reasons for the "time-out" should be given so the child can employ them for self-control in the future.

Punishment

According to David Ausubel (1957), it is impossible to guide behavior effectively using only positive reinforcement and extinction; children cannot learn what is not approved or tolerated simply by making a reverse generalization from the approval they receive for acceptable behavior. Children have to be enabled to process what they are *not* supposed to do, as well as what they *are*. Thus nonhostile punishment or constructive responses designed to correct misbehavior can have an informative effect.

Punishment consists of physically or psychologically painful stimuli or the temporary withdrawal of pleasant stimuli when undesirable behavior occurs. A physically painful stimulus might be a spanking; a psychologically painful stimulus might be a scolding; withdrawal of a pleasant stimulus might be removing a privilege such as TV. Punishment has been used as an intervention technique to discourage undesirable behavior. It is probably most valuable when a child's behavior must be stopped quickly for safety reasons. A 2-year-old who runs out into the street is more likely to be stopped from doing it in the future by a quick swat on the rear end than by a reward for staying on the sidewalk. A 2-year-old also can't really understand the logical reasons for not running into the street. Thus a more concrete physical reminder may be necessary.

For punishing to be useful as an effective socializing technique, the following summary applies (Martin & Pear, 1996):

- *Timing*—The closer the punishment is to the behavior, the more effective it will be.
- *Reasoning*—Punishment accompanied by an explanation is more effective than punishment alone. "We do not play in the street because cars might hurt us."

- *Consistency*—If children are consistently punished for repeating a behavior, they are more likely to stop it than if they are sometimes punished, sometimes ignored, and sometimes rewarded. Aggression is an example of a behavior sometimes handled inconsistently. It may be punished at home or at school when the child is caught, yet may be rewarded in the peer group.
- *Attachment to the person doing the punishing*—The more nurturant the relationship between the punisher and the punishee, the more effective the punishment. A child whose parent denies a privilege for undesired behavior, such as coming home late, is less likely to repeat that behavior than if an acquaintance, such as a babysitter, administers the punishment.

The use of punishment as an effective technique in modifying behavior has been criticized for the following reasons (Martin & Pear, 1996):

- Punishment may stop the undesirable behavior immediately, but by itself does not indicate appropriate or desired behavior.
- Punishment may merely slow the rate at which the undesirable behavior is emitted, rather than eliminate it entirely. Or it may change the form in which the undesirable behavior is emitted. People who stop smoking often report they begin eating more. Children who are punished for physical aggression may engage in verbal aggression ("I hate you." "You big doody head.").
- Punishment by an adult may have an undesirable modeling effect on the child. Parents who abuse their children are likely to have been abused by their parents.
- The emotional side effects of punishment (fear, embarrassment, low self-esteem, and tenseness) may be psychologically more damaging than the original behavior.

In sum, punishment can function as a socializing technique when used appropriately (Martin & Pear, 1996). It can provide an opportunity to reestablish attachment or affection following emotional release; it can provide vicarious learning by observation of others being punished; it can reduce guilt in that it can provide an opportunity to correct the misbehavior; and when combined with reasoning, it can enable the internalization of moral standards. Thus, when using punishment, be aware of the negative, as well as the positive, consequences for the child.

Exemplifying Effective Uses of Punishment

When a group of 10-year-old boys wrote on the wall of their camp cabin, their counselor required them to spend the afternoon scrubbing walls instead of going swimming. This type of punishment is referred to as a "logical consequence"—one that is arranged by the parent or another adult and that is logically related to the misbehavior (Dreikurs & Grey, 1968). For a logical consequence to be effective, however, it must make sense to the child. For example, Todd continually left his clothes around his room after repeatedly being told to put them in the hamper. His mother finally said, "Clothes that do not get picked up do not get washed." Todd still did not pick up his clothes. Finally, when Todd wanted to wear his favorite shirt and realized it was not washed because he had not put it in the hamper, the consequence became effective—he picked up his clothes.

Feedback

Feedback is evaluative information, both positive and negative, about one's behavior. It can take the form of an approving nod, a questioning look, a comment, further instructions, or a reminder. Feedback provides knowledge of results and how to improve them, which has been shown to be important to learning (Bangert-Drowns et al., 1991).

An example of a classical feedback experiment illustrates the value of knowing the results while learning a simple skill (Baker & Young, 1960). The task to be learned was to reproduce on paper the length of a 4-inch piece of wood. The subjects were blindfolded. However, they could feel the piece of wood. One group of subjects was told after each performance whether they were within .20 inch of the correct length. The other group received no feedback. When both groups were tested, the group receiving feedback consistently improved, whereas the group receiving no knowledge of results made no consistent progress. When the feedback was stopped, that group's accuracy dropped abruptly.

This experiment demonstrated that in order to increase accuracy of performance, individuals must change incorrect responses. In this case, unless the individuals were made fully aware of their incorrect behavior, change was unlikely to occur.

A summary of the effects of feedback on performance is summarized as follows (Good & Brophy, 1986):

- Feedback generally increases motivation.
- Feedback usually improves subsequent performance.
- Generally, the more specific the knowledge of performance, the more rapidly performance improves.
- Feedback given punctually is usually more effective than that given long after a task has been completed.
- Noticeable decreases in feedback often result in a marked decline in performance.
- When knowledge of results is not provided, individuals tend to develop substitutes. For example, they may compare their performance to that of peers to determine whether it is better or worse.

Feedback, then, is an important socializing mechanism. It provides children with information on how they are measuring up to standards of behavior and performance: "Susie, your letters need to go on the line. I've circled your best one; make five more just like it." "Jack, that frown on your face is most unpleasant; what is your problem?"

"Garth, next time you have a friend over, say 'Thank you for coming.'" "Terry, that outfit looks very good on you."

Learning by Doing

Sometimes socialization occurs through experiencing and interacting. As an ancient Chinese proverb says, "I hear and I forget, I see and I remember, I do and I understand." Psychologist Jean Piaget (1952), known for his developmental theory of cognitive development, states that children learn through their own activity. Likewise, psychologist Jerome Bruner (1981) believes children learn through discovery. Learning is a slow process of construction and transformation of experience into meaning. Learning to ride a bicycle is an example of learning by doing. It involves experimenting and discovering how to shift your weight while pedaling, holding on, and watching where you are going, all at the same time.

Offering developmentally appropriate choices, meaningful activities that create opportunities for children to succeed, enables children to learn by doing because they can experience what works and what doesn't. For example, evidence from studies on children supports the relationship between learning by doing and successful problem-solving. In one study (Smith & Dutton, 1979), a group of children was given the opportunity to play with materials involved in a problem. Another group received instruction on how to solve the problem, but was not given the opportunity to play with the materials. The group that played with the materials ended up solving the problem as easily as the children who had had instruction. On a more complex problem requiring innovative thinking, the group that had the opportunity to play with the materials did better in solving the problem than the group that had received instruction. Thus, as Piaget and Bruner said, experience leads to discovering ways to tackle problems. Learning by doing, then, transforms the individual in some way, affecting future development.

The computer is an interactive tool that provides opportunities for experiential learning—problem-solving, creativity, simulations, and personal tutoring (Lepper & Gurtner, 1989). It also is capable of supporting many different learning styles while enabling the user to learn how to learn (Papert, 1993), an example of transformation. Everytime I get new software for my computer, I learn how to use it by doing it; seeing what works and what doesn't.

Problem-solving can involve interacting with others. Most interactional skills are learned by doing. When one smiles and says "Hi," one usually gets a positive response. When one sulks after losing a game, one may not be invited to play again (Dana learned that Tania would come to her house if she let Tania play on her swing

This child is learning to rollerblade by doing it.

set. Bobby learned that if he hit Matt, Matt would tattle, whereas Chuck would not), another example of transformation.

When children play, they are learning by doing (Hughes, 1995). They are being socialized in that they are practicing physical, intellectual, and social skills: physical skills such as climbing, jumping, writing, cutting; intellectual skills such as remembering, reasoning, making decisions, solving problems; social skills such as communicating, sharing, cooperating, competing, having empathy. For example, as children experiment with different behaviors and social roles, they are finding out what it feels like to be Mom, or baby brother; they are experiencing what it is like to wash the car, or to play doctor; they are feeling the joy of approval and the despair of disapproval. They are constructing views of the world that will influence future thinking and behavior.

OBSERVATIONAL METHODS (EFFECT EMERGES FROM IMITATING)

Six-year-old Vicky went on her first boat ride in her uncle's new boat. She watches the waves ripple on the lake, as her uncle joyfully demonstrated the power of his boat's new motor to her parents. When they docked, Vicky's uncle tied up the boat. The next day Vicky could not wait to go for another ride. She besieged her uncle with questions while motoring around the lake, and when they pulled up to the dock, to her uncle's amazement Vicky jumped out, grabbed the rope, and tied up the boat.

Vicky's behavior, her attitude about boating, and her performance in tying up the boat illustrate socialization via observational learning, or modeling.

Modeling

Modeling is a form of imitative learning that occurs by observing another person (the model) perform a behavior and experience its consequence. It enables us to learn appropriate social behavior, attitudes, and emotions vicariously or secondhand. The models can be parents, siblings, relatives, friends, teachers, coaches, or television characters. Jerome Kagan (1971, 1984) explains how the child assumes complex patterns of behavior through identification with a model:

> Identification is, in fact, the belief of a person that some attributes of a model (for example, parents, siblings, relatives, peers, and fictional figures) are also possessed by the person. A boy who realizes that he and his father share the same name, notes that they have similar facial features, and is told by relatives that they both have lively tempers, develops a belief that he is similar to his father. When this belief in similarity is accompanied by vicarious emotional experiences in the child that are appropriate to the model, we say that the child has an identification with the model (Kagan, 1971, p. 57).

Modeling is a significant socializing method. As children mature, they acquire a wide range of behaviors through modeling from parents, siblings, teachers, and friends, which become part of their repertoire for future interactions.

Modeling (observational learning) involves the ability to abstract information from what is observed, store it in memory, make generalizations and rules about behavior, retrieve the appropriate information, and act it out at the appropriate time. Thus modeling enables one to develop new ways of behaving in situations not previously experienced. Vicky, for example, "knew" how to tie up the boat without having previously tried it or been instructed on how to do it. However, the probability that children will imitate a model is a function of their (1) attention, (2) level of cognitive development, (3) retention, (4) type of activity being observed, (5) motivation, (6) ability to reproduce the behavior, and (7) repertoire of alternative behaviors (Bandura, 1989; Bandura, Ross, & Ross, 1963a).

Many ethnic groups, especially high-context cultures such as Native Americans, emphasize observation and modeling as socialization methods. These methods enable children to participate in chores alongside adults or older siblings according to their developmental abilities. For example, in some African tribes girls as young as age 3 are given their own hoes to work in the gardens with their mothers and older sisters (Whiting & Edwards, 1988).

Various factors affect the extent to which children will imitate modeled behavior. Models who are perceived as similar (physically and/or psychologically) to the observer are likely to be identified with and imitated: "I have yellow hair, just like Mommy." "You have a strong will just like your grandfather." Models who are perceived as nurturant are more likely to be identified with and imitated: "My daddy always brings me presents when he comes back from a trip." "My coach always has time to listen to me." Models who are perceived as powerful or prestigious are more likely to be identified with and imitated (Bandura et al., 1963a): "My grandmother won first prize in the fair for her chocolate cake!" "My teacher is the smartest person in the whole world!"

Children's behavior is also influenced by whether the model with whom they identify is punished or reinforced. It has been demonstrated that children who see a model being punished for aggressive behavior are less likely to imitate that behavior than children who see a model being rewarded or experiencing no consequences (Bandura, 1965).

Television provides an excellent example of a context in which observational learning and consequent modeling take place. There is much evidence that children learn both prosocial and antisocial behavior by watching TV (Comstock & Paik, 1991; Pearl, 1982). For example, children who watched an episode of *Lassie* wherein the master risks his life to rescue Lassie's puppy were more helpful in a task following the show (Sprafkin, Liebert, & Poulos, 1975). For another example, studies of preschool children showed that there was a relationship between violent television viewing and aggressive behavior during free play at preschool (Levin & Carlsson-Paige, 1995; Singer & Singer, 1980).

The reason for the likelihood of televised behavior being modeled, whether it be prosocial or antisocial, is that children observe someone being rewarded for an act. Prosocial behavior on TV is generally reinforced by the person getting lots of attention or becoming a hero. Antisocial behavior is generally reinforced on TV by the person "getting away with it" or getting a desired object.

COGNITIVE METHODS (EFFECT EMERGES FROM INFORMATION PROCESSING)

Socialization techniques using cognitive methods involve those that specifically focus on how an individual processes information, or how the individual abstracts meaning from experiences. Strategies used by socialization agents are instruction, setting standards, and reasoning.

Instruction

Instruction provides knowledge and information and is a useful socializing mechanism. For instruction to be effective, however, the child must be able to understand the language used as well as remember what was said. In other words, instruction must provide specific information at a child's level. "Bring me your shoes" would be appropriate for a 2-year-old. "Get your jacket out of the closet, turn out the pockets, and bring it to me" would not. Even a 2-year-old who knows what a jacket is will probably forget the second part of the instruction ("turn out the pockets") because a child at that age simply cannot remember to do three things at once.

"Instructions" conjures up the image of the piece of paper that comes at the bottom of the box with 20 bicycle parts. Instructions usually communicate how to do something, but they also communicate directions or orders. "Don't sit on the coffee table, sit on the chair."

"Greg [age 9], please clean up your room," says Mom.

An hour later, Mom goes into Greg's room and observes that his bedspread is rumpled, books are on his desk, and his model airplanes are strewn among his shoes on the floor of his closet.

Mom yells, "I told you to clean up your room!"

Greg replies, "But I did; I put all my books and toys away."

And that he had.

The problem here is that the instructions are not specific enough for Greg. (If the instructions for putting the bicycle together were as vague as Mom's, the parts would still be in the box.) Mom probably has an image of a clean room that includes an unrumpled bed, books on the bookshelf, and toys on the appropriate closet shelf. Greg's image of a clean room, on the other hand, may simply include space to walk and lie down. Thus, Mom's instructions, to be effective, must say, "Greg, please clean your room—straighten your bedspread, put your books on the shelf, and your toys in your closet on the shelf." If Greg were younger—for example, age 4—he might answer, "But I don't know how to straighten my bed." Then Mom would know what parts of the instructions could and could not be followed independently. Thus, for instructions to be effective, they must be understood. To be understood, the instructor must be willing to rephrase, to demonstrate, and to repeat. Exemplary coaching techniques involving instruction, explanations, practice, and feedback were employed successfully with preschool and school-age children to enable them to make friends (Mize & Ladd, 1990; Oden & Asher, 1977).

Setting Standards

A **standard** is a level of attainment or a grade of excellence regarded as a goal or measure of adequacy. When parents set standards for children, they are telling children what they should do: "You are three years old now; I want you to dress yourself." "I expect only *A*s and *B*s on your report card." Setting standards provides children with advance notice of what is expected or not expected of them, thus helping them become socialized. The laws of a country, the licensing requirements for driving, and the rules in a city for building are all examples of set standards. A contract, or written agreement, specifying goals for learning or behavioral expectations can be a vehicle by which standards are communicated.

Standards are set by many socializing agents. In *Are You There, God? It's Me, Margaret* by Judy Blume (1970), to be a member of the secret sixth-grade club, you had to wear a bra, tell when you got your period, and keep a Boy Book (a list of boys you liked). The standards are set in this example by a peer group. Standards are also set by teachers. Some accept only good handwriting and perfect spelling on papers to be graded. Others may set standards regarding content and creativity. Good and Brophy (1991) noted that teachers demanded better performances from high-achieving students—for example, teachers were less likely to accept an inadequate answer from them than from low-achieving students. Standards are set by coaches: "You will do ten sit-ups every day, get eight hours of sleep a night, and eat a balanced diet." Thus setting standards is a recurring method of socialization throughout life.

Reasoning

Reasoning is giving explanations or causes, for an act. The purpose of giving reasons in the process of socialization is to enable the child to draw conclusions when encountering similar situations.

When a teacher says to a preschool child who has just spit on another child, "Keep your spit in your mouth; spitting spreads germs and is rude. How would you like that?" that teacher is using reason to influence the child's behavior.

The problem with giving reasons is that children may not understand the words used (for example, "spreads germs," "is rude"), and often they are not able to generalize a reason to another situation. Because, according to Piaget (1974), children under age 3 are generally **egocentric,** thereby lacking the cognitive ability to take another's point of view and consequently believing that everyone looks at things similarly to them, the child in the above example can't mentally take the view of the child who has been spat upon and so doesn't relate to the teacher's reasons.

Some children under age 3 do react to others' emotions with altruistic behavior. **Altruism** refers to actions that are intended to aid or benefit another person or group of people without the actor's anticipation of external rewards. Such actions often entail some cost, self-sacrifice, or risk on the part of the actor. A team of researchers (Radke-Yarrow & Zahn-Waxler, 1986; Radke-Yarrow, Zahn-Waxler, & Chapman, 1983; Zahn-Waxler, Radke-Yarrow, & King, 1979) interviewed mothers of 15- and 20-month-old children. The mothers were trained to observe and report incidents of their children's altruism when others were distressed, such as efforts at reparation when someone was hurt, trying to comfort a victim, offering a toy, or going to find someone else to help. The researchers found that the way the mother interacted with her child when another was in distress was clearly related to her child's degree of altruism. The mothers of highly altruistic children did not simply offer cognitive reasoning of the other's distress; they reacted emotionally, sometimes quite strongly, and stated forcefully that socially responsible behavior was expected, such as "You made Shawna cry; you must never bite." Consequently, for children under age 3, if reasoning is to be used as a socializing technique, it must be combined with other methods—for example, an emotional reaction—to be effective.

An older child between age 4 and 7, who is moving away from egocentrism, may be able to understand how another person feels or views things, but may not be able to generalize the reason to another situation, because at this age a child's ability to reason is **transductive** (connecting one particular idea to another particular idea based on appearance rather than logic) as opposed to **inductive** (connecting a particular idea to a more general idea based on similarities) or **deductive** (connecting a general idea to a particular idea based on similarities and differences). The following are illustrations of the different types of reasoning:

- *Transductive reasoning*—"Kyle has red hair and hits me, therefore all boys with red hair hit."
- *Inductive reasoning*—"I can't hit Kyle; therefore, I can't hit any other children."
- *Deductive reasoning*—"I can't hit other children; therefore, I can't hit Kyle."

Around age 7, children begin to think less intuitively and more concretely (Piaget, 1954); that is, they can understand reasons if they are associated with real, concrete events, objects, or people. The 7-year-old understands when told "You must not hit people with blocks because it hurts very much; look how Kyle is crying," because 7-year-olds can *see* that hitting Kyle with a block caused Kyle to cry. Children who think concretely, however, cannot yet reason in terms of abstract principles; they cannot yet understand "The law punishes people who hit." Since they cannot visualize it, the law is an abstraction of which they as yet have no concept.

Around age 11 or 12, children begin to think less concretely and more abstractly. They are able to perform formal, or logical, operations (as are involved in science); they are capable of rational thought (Inhelder & Piaget, 1958). They can think in terms of past, present, and future and can deal with hypothetical problems: "If everyone went around hitting everyone else whenever angry, then the world would end up in a war."

Reasoning as a socializing mechanism is most effective when children exhibit the ability to think logically and flexibly. This occurs after age 11 or 12, as the child enters adolescence. At this stage, reasoning ability allows for adaptation to whatever problem is presented, thus enabling adolescents to benefit and learn from concepts imparted to them as young children. Reasoning is used more often as a socializing method in ethnic groups that value verbal skills, abstract thought, assertiveness, and self-reliance (Kagan et al., 1986).

Baumrind (1971a, b, 1989) distinguishes parents who are willing to offer reasons behind the directives issued (**authoritative** parents) from parents who do not offer directives at all and rely upon manipulation to obtain compliance (**permissive** parents), and from parents who expect the child to accept their word as right and final without verbal give and take (**authoritarian** parents). According to Baumrind, the authoritative approach may best enable children to conform to social standards with minimal jeopardy to "individual autonomy or self-assertiveness." In one study, preschool children from authoritative homes were consistently and significantly more competent than other children (Baumrind, 1989). In another study (Elder, 1963), it was shown that seventh- to twelfth-graders were more likely to model themselves after their parents if their parents explained the reasons behind their decisions and restrictions.

Thus, it would seem that even though reasoning as a socializing mechanism is not as effective for young children as it is for adolescents, the continual use of reasoning by the parents is habit-forming. Children who are habitually given reasons for directives benefit more and more from reasoning as they mature in terms of being more and more able to rationalize and guide their own behavior (Hoffman, 1988).

Sociocultural Methods (Effect Emerges from Conforming)

Culture involves learned behavior, including knowledge, beliefs, art, morals, law, customs, and traditions, that is characteristic of the social environment in which an individual grows up. The sociocultural expectations of those around an individual continually influence that individual's behavior and ensure conformity to established precedents. Some of the socializing techniques by which sociocultural expectations influence behavior are group pressure, tradition, rituals, and symbols.

Group Pressure

Group pressure is a cultural method because it involves conforming to certain norms. Communities comprise social groups—family, neighborhood, church, peers, club, and school. The groups to which one belongs influence one's behavior. Because humans have a need to affiliate with other humans and because social approval determines whether or not one is accepted by the group, humans will tend to conform to the group's expectations (group pressure).

In a classic study by Asch (1958), male subjects were asked to judge the length of lines. In each experimental session, there was only one actual subject, while the others had been previously coached to express certain opinions. Thus, the real subject often faced a situation where his eyes told him one line was the longest, while the others in the group all said another line was the longest. Several of the subjects consistently yielded to the pressure of the group, even though the group's opinion was erroneous. Later interviews with those who conformed to the majority opinion explained that they thought something was wrong with their eyesight and that the majority were probably correct.

In a similar experiment by other researchers (Hamm & Hoving, 1969), children age 7, 10, and 13 were asked to judge how far a light moved—a perceptually ambiguous task. Before the subjects made their decisions, however, two other children gave their answers. Just as Asch discovered, many of the subjects patterned their answers on the group estimates.

Individuals are influenced by group pressure because they desire social identity, social approval, and/or because they believe the group's opinions are probably correct (Bugental & Goodnow, 1998). The influence of the social group varies according to (Hartup, 1983):

1. *Attraction to the group.* The more people want to belong to a group, the more likely they will be to conform to group pressure. In elementary school and junior high school, attraction to the group becomes very important. Children of this age may have the same hairstyles, wear the same kind of shoes, and even talk alike.

2. *Acceptance by the group.* The role or status a person has—leader versus follower—in a group affects the degree of influence. A follower is more subject to group pressure than is a leader. It was found that boys who were anxious, dependent, and not sure where they stood in the group were more susceptible to group influence (Harrison, Serafica, & McAdoo, 1984).

3. *Type of group.* The degree of influence a group has depends on the affective relationships between the members. Groups in which the ties are very close, such as family or friends, exert a stronger influence than groups in which the affective ties are more distant, such as Scouts or Little League.

When individuals are influenced by group pressure because they believe the group's opinions are probably correct, it is usually because they lack confidence in their own judgment. For example, if you like a movie and later find out everyone else dislikes it, or if you have a certain political opinion and find out the rest of the group believes differently, you might begin to question your own judgment.

Children generally lacking the experience and knowledge to have faith in their own judgment are more likely to succumb to group pressure, especially if the group is older, because they are more likely to trust the group's opinion.

Certain ethnic groups, such as Japanese, who value a sense of dependence on the group and community emphasize group pressure ("What will other people think?") as a socializing technique to control nonconforming behavior and foster achievement (Stevenson & Lee, 1990).

Tradition

Tradition is the handing down of customs, stories, beliefs, and so on from generation to generation. In an ethnic group, tradition refers to all the knowledge, beliefs, customs, and skills that are part of that ethnic group's heritage. In religion, tradition refers to the unwritten religious code handed down from Moses, Jesus and the Apostles, or Mohammed. In a family, tradition is implemented in the way it celebrates holidays and tells stories. The stories that families tell represent perspectives on events and relationships that are passed on from one generation to the next. These stories give meaning to the family (Fiese et al., 1999).

Since tradition represents humans' ways of having solved certain problems in the past, through socialization the offspring of each generation receive a "design for living" from their ancestors—how to get shelter, how to get along with one another, how to dress, how to feed oneself, and so on. Traditional beliefs, attitudes, and values are also transmitted from one generation to another—the belief in God, the attitude that children should be protected, the value of hard work.

Tradition is a sociocultural method of socialization in that it sets the pattern for the way one satisfies basic biological needs—eating, sleeping, elimination, or sexual behavior. Some ethnic groups traditionally eat with chopsticks, others with forks and knives. Some ethnic groups sleep on the ground, others in beds. Some cultures eliminate outdoors; others have enclosed toilets. Some ethnic groups have premarital sexual taboos; others do not.

Tradition also sets the patterns by which people interact with one another. Social interaction refers to who does what in the society (roles) and how it is done (behavior). In some ethnic groups it is traditional for the women to do the cooking; in other ethnic groups the men do it. In some ethnic groups the elderly are considered the wisest and are revered; in other ethnic groups they are considered obsolete and useless. In some ethnic groups a price is fixed in advance for an exchange in the marketplace; in other ethnic groups the exchange is accomplished by an agreed-upon price only after a certain amount of bargaining. In some ethnic groups people greet one another by surnames; in other ethnic groups first names are used.

Traditions become unquestioned ways of doing things that stay with us, even though we may forget the reasons behind them:

> A bride served baked ham, and her husband asked why she cut the ends off. "Well, that's the way Mother always did it," she replied.

Traditions help remind us of socialized values such as this celebration of independence.

The next time his mother-in-law stopped by, he asked her why she cut the ends off the ham. "That's the way my mother did it," she replied.

And when Grandma visited, she too was asked why she sliced the ends off. She said, "That's the only way I could get it into the pan" (James & Jongeward, 1971, p. 97).

Rituals

Rituals connect us with our past, define our present, and give us a future direction (Black & Roberts, 1992). A **ritual** is a set form or system, a ceremonial observance of a prescribed rule or custom. The symbols or symbolic actions embrace meaning that cannot always be easily expressed in words. Some familiar examples of rituals are the baptism or naming ceremony; the communion, signifying the acceptance of the church's beliefs; the bar or bas mitzvah, signifying the age of responsibility; graduation, signifying an accomplishment; and the Navajo ritual called *Blessing Way*, signifying "for good hope." Rituals not only serve as a socialization function, but as a protective one for the child as well, because they provide stability; something the child can "count on" in spite of change (Parke & Buriel, 1998).

The ritualization of behavior is a way of creating respect for traditions. A ritual evokes appropriate feelings. The ritual of saying the Pledge of Allegiance evokes feelings of loyalty and reaffirms national identity. The ritual of saying grace evokes feelings of humility and thankfulness. The ritual of marriage signifies faithfulness and procreation.

The ritual also functions to signify changes in people's status as they move through the cycle of life. These rituals are called **rites of passage.** The most common rite of passage occurs at puberty to acknowledge passage from the state of childhood to adulthood and celebrate the transformation. Some rites involve a circumcision ceremony, as in some African or Australian tribes; some involve parties, such as a debutante ball; some involve the recitation of knowledge, as in the bar mitzvah. The ritual serves as a mechanism of socialization in that it announces to the rest of society that a certain individual has a new position and will fill a new role in the society, and it makes the individual aware of the new status and its accompanying roles and responsibilities.

Symbols

Symbols are acts or objects that have come to be generally accepted as standing for or representing something else (Vander Zanden, 1993), especially something abstract: the dove is a symbol of peace, the cross is a symbol of Christ's death, and the circle is a symbol of the Great Spirit.

Symbols are a powerful code or shorthand for representing and dealing with aspects of the world (Hewitt, 1994). The significance of symbols as socializing mechanisms lies in the attitudes they conjure up and the accompanying behavior they stimulate. A crown conjures up the image of authority and all the attitudes associated with it. The resultant behavior would be respect and obedience. A country's flag conjures up feelings of patriotism. A salute might be the socialized behavior. Certain ways of dressing may serve as symbols of status and roles in society. A uniform may indicate a police officer; a BMW may symbolize wealth; a sarong may symbolize virginity. Symbols, then, as socializing mechanisms, serve as cues to behavior.

According to anthropology professor Leslie White (1960, p. 73)

All culture (civilization) depends upon the symbol. It was the exercise of the symbolic faculty that brought culture into existence and it is the use of symbols that makes the perpetuation of culture possible. Without the symbol there would be no culture, and man would be merely an animal, not a human being.

The symbol to which White is referring is language. Language makes it possible to replace behavior with ideas and to communicate these ideas to the next generation.

APPRENTICESHIP METHODS (EFFECT EMERGES FROM GUIDED PARTICIPATION)

Barbara Rogoff (1990) believes all the methods of socialization discussed thus far are imparted in the child's macrosystem via various apprenticeships. In other words, the child, or novice, is guided to participate in various social activities by someone who has more expertise. This person could be a parent, a sibling, a relative, a teacher, a peer, a coach, and so forth.

To illustrate how apprenticeship as a socializing method works, we look at how children learn to feed themselves. First, the child is totally dependent on his or her mother for nourishment. As the child matures physically and cognitively, he or she observes others feeding themselves and wants to try the activity independently. The mother, or caregiver, *structures* the feeding activities according to the capability of the child—at first providing soft food the child can grasp with his or her fingers, such as fruit or crackers. Then the caregiver might give the child a utensil, such as a spoon or cup or pair of chopsticks, at first guiding it into the child's mouth until the child can do it himself or herself with support when needed. Thus, the caregiver and the child participate or *collaborate* in the activity together. When the child exhibits appropriate mastery, the caregiver *transfers* the responsibility for independent feeding to the child.

In sum, apprenticeship as a method of socialization progresses from the expert structuring activities for the novice according to ability, to collaborating in joint activities so that support can be provided when needed, to transferring responsibility for the management of the activity when the activity is appropriately mastered.

The ages at which these progressions in apprenticeship take place vary according to the macrosystem in which the child grows up. For example, in Anglo American ethnic groups, self-feeding (drinking from a cup and using a spoon or fork) is expected by age 2, whereas in some Asian American ethnic groups, the child is breast-fed until age 2 (and in some groups, age 4), thereby extending the apprenticeship progression from dependence to independence.

Epilogue

Socialization of the child is multifaceted with the parents as managers. Socialization methods work differently according to the person implementing them, the situation, and the child to whom they are directed.

Pinocchio was influenced by Gepetto, Jiminy Cricket, the Blue Fairy, and others. Gepetto provided love and acceptance, Jiminy Cricket provided instructions, feedback, support, and encouragement. The Blue Fairy provided standards and rewards. The others provided experiences for learning by doing. After experiencing many consequences, both positive and negative; Pinocchio adopts Gepetto's values to be "good" and is rewarded by turning into a "real boy." ■

SUMMARY

Socialization is the process by which individuals acquire the knowledge, skills, and character traits that enable them to participate as more or less effective members of groups and society.

The concept of socialization goes back in time as far as human life. Most social scientists agree that socialization is unique to humans due to our capacity for language. Language enables us to communicate ideas and replace action with thought and then use thought to transform behavior. Self-control comes from the internalization of thoughts.

Socialization begins at birth and continues throughout life. Children play a role in their own socialization. Socialization may be intentional or unintentional. It occurs through human interaction, and so is bidirectional, resulting in transformations in the individual.

Socialization enables children to develop their potentialities and form satisfying relationships.

Socialization aims to develop a self-concept. Erikson's eight stages of psychosocial development are discussed: Trust versus Mistrust, Autonomy versus Shame and Doubt, Initiative versus Guilt, Industry versus Inferiority, Identity versus Identity Diffusion, Intimacy versus Isolation, Generativity versus Self-Absorption, and Integrity versus Despair.

Socialization aims to enable self-control and empower achievement. It teaches appropriate social roles and developmental skills (social, emotional, cognitive). A developmental task is "midway between an individual need and a societal demand." Developmental tasks differ from society to society.

Every individual in society is the outcome of the socialization process. The success of this outcome in terms of society's expectations depends on a series of interactions with significant socializing agents that are components of the community in which the individual lives.

The significant agents of socialization discussed in this chapter are the family, the school, the peer group, the media, and the community.

The family is the child's introduction to society and has, therefore, borne major responsibility for socializing the child. The family is a system of interaction. The relationships have a powerful effect on the psychosocial development of children. The family is the child's first reference group for values.

The school acts as an agent of society in that it is organized to perpetuate that society's knowledge, skills, customs, and beliefs. It also acts as an agent to foster respect for and adherence to the existing social order while educating for adaptability.

Child care has become an important socialization agent due to societal changes as seen in amount of time spent on the child being cared for by individuals outside the family.

The peer group gives children experience in egalitarian types of relationships. Children learn to look at themselves from the group's point of view. Peers also serve as a support group for the expression of values and attitudes. They exert a strong influence on those who need social identity and approval.

The media, unlike other agents of socialization, do not directly involve personal interaction. The media are also considered to be socializers, however, because they teach many of the ways of the society. For example, television, videos, and movies show relationships of people in various settings, so children are provided with patterns of how to behave. Books provide information about the world that the child might not otherwise experience. Computers connect the child to history, current events, games. Children process media information constructing meaning and transforming it to behavior.

The community provides a sense of belonging and friendship. The population distribution of a community affects the interactions a child will have. The type of agencies, such as the Scouts, the "Y," and Little League, that a community provides affects the experiences a child has while growing up. The services a community provides, such as libraries, museums, and cultural events, affect which parts of society are opened to the child. Communities can be support systems for families. Advocacy is the process by which this occurs.

Since socialization is the process by which individuals learn the ways of a given society so that they can function effectively within it, the following are methods by which these ways are transmitted: affective methods (attachment), operant methods (reinforcement, extinction, punishment, feedback, learning by doing), observational methods (modeling), cognitive methods (instruction, setting standards, reasoning), sociocultural methods (group pressure, tradition, rituals, symbols), and apprenticeship methods (structuring, collaborating, transferring).

ACTIVITY

Purpose: To understand the impact of agents of socialization on development.

1. Name the three most important things you learned from your parents while growing up.

2. Name three people other than your parents who had a major influence on you as a child or adolescent.

3. Describe each one's influence, using specific examples.

4. What methods of socialization did your parents and the significant others in your life use?

5. Whom are you influencing in ways similar to the ones you have described?

6. What are your aims and methods of socialization?

RESOURCES

American Academy of Child &
Adolescent Psychiatry
http://www.aacap.org

National Academy for Child
Development
http://www.nacd.org/

American Academy of Pediatrics
http://www.aap.org

RELATED READINGS

Bandura, A. (1986). *Social foundations of thought and action: A social cognitive theory.* Englewood Cliffs, NJ: Prentice-Hall.

Best, R. (1983). *We've all got scars: What boys and girls learn in elementary school.* Bloomington: Indiana University Press.

Bowlby, J. (1988). *A secure base: Parent–child attachment and healthy human development.* New York: Basic Books.

Bronfenbrenner, U. (1970). *Two worlds of childhood.* New York: Russell Sage.

Chess, S., & Thomas, A. (1987). *Know your child.* New York: Basic Books.

Coleman, J. S. (1961). *The adolescent society.* Glencoe, IL: Free Press.

Dreikurs, R., & Grey, L. (1968). *A new approach to discipline: Logical consequences.* New York: Hawthorn.

Dunn, J. (1985). *Sisters and brothers.* Cambridge, MA: Harvard University Press.

Erikson, E. (1963). *Childhood and society.* New York: Norton.

Golding, W. (1954). *Lord of the flies.* New York: Putnam.

Goleman, D. (1995). *Emotional intelligence.* New York: Bantam.

Milgram, J. I., & Sciarra, D. J. (Eds.). (1974). *Childhood revisited.* New York: Macmillan.

Rogoff, B. (1990). *Apprenticeship in thinking: Cognitive development in social context.* New York: Oxford University Press.

Weissbourd, R. (1996). *The vulnerable child.* Reading, MA: Addison-Wesley.

"My soul knows that I am part of the
human race, . . . as my spirit is part of
my nation. In my very own self, I am part
of my family."

— *D. H. Lawrence*

Chapter 3

ECOLOGY OF THE FAMILY

Prologue

ROMANCE VERSUS REALITY

William Shakespeare's classical story, Romeo and Juliet, embraces the theme of romantic love's fragility against life's harsh realities.

Set in the Middle Ages when family ties were binding, Romeo, a Montague, attends a ball given by the Capulets, arch enemies of his family. He meets and falls in love with Juliet, daughter of the house. The lovers have to resort to secret meetings. Their passionate relationship is interrupted when Romeo is banished from his town of Verona because he becomes involved in a street fight between members of the Montague and Capulet families. Meanwhile, Juliet, against her will, has been betrothed to Paris to strengthen the Capulet house. To avoid an obligatory marriage to a man she doesn't love, Juliet takes a sleeping potion to bring on a semblance of her death. Romeo, without knowing the truth, rushes home to Verona where he drinks poison at Juliet's tomb. When Juliet awakens and sees her lover dead by her side, passionately, she stabs herself.

Throughout history and across cultures, marriage was based on connecting families for practical purposes—politics, economics, religious beliefs. This was reality. The result was the formation of a new family with significant extended ties. Romantic love was not a factor in the choice of a mate. It was believed that if the backgrounds of the couples were well suited, love would follow.

Modern, especially American, cultures expect marriage to be based on romantic love. If the macrosystem backgrounds (culture, religion, economics, politics, education) of the lovers are not compatible, "love will conquer all," and differences in values and behavior will be resolved. On this premise, a new family is formed.

Tradition influenced the selection of a bride from the royal class for Prince Charles, heir to the throne of England. Princess Diana may have married Prince Charles for love, but Charles married her to give his family and country royal offspring.

The divorce of Charles and Diana was a break in tradition. It signified a change from duty (obligation and commitment to others)—what is best for the country?—to freedom (obligation and commitment to self)—what is best for me?

That Diana was killed in a car crash with her lover is an ironic twist. Unlike Romeo and Juliet, they did not have to die to be together; British society had evolved to accept love unions outside of royal class boundaries. Charles' brother, Prince Edward, was allowed to marry a commoner.

- What are the consequences (positive and negative) of subscribing to a value of obligation to the self (choosing a mate attractive to the individual) on one end of the spectrum to obligation to others (choosing a mate approved of by one's family and society), on the other end of the spectrum?
- Who has the most "at stake" in the marriage—adults or children?
- How are one's views on love and marriage related to the family system (structure, functions, relationships)? how one copes with change? and how one's children are socialized?

FAMILY SYSTEMS

This chapter provides an understanding of what a family is, what a family does, how different families respond to change, and how different families cope with external forces. Family Systems' Theory views the family as a whole—its structure and organizational patterns and how individual members interact with one another—its functions (Parke & Buriel, 1998).

In Chapters 1 and 2, the aims, challenges, and consequences of socialization were discussed and the agents of socialization identified. Here the family, the primary agent of socialization, is explored. A family is a microsystem. The classic definition of a family, according to sociologist George Murdock (1962, p. 19), is "a social group characterized by common residence, economic cooperation, and reproduction. It includes adults of both

Figure 3.1   An Ecological Model of Human Development

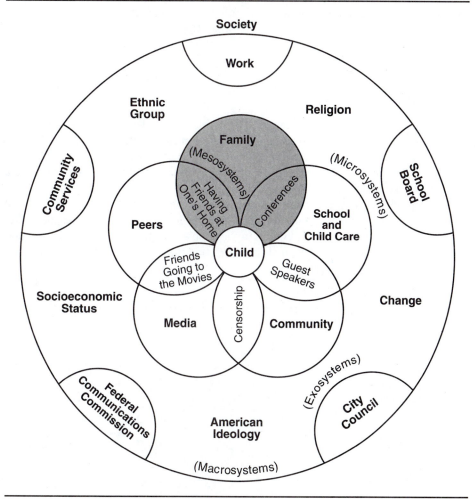

The family is a primary influence on the child's development.

sexes, at least two of whom maintain a socially approved sexual relationship, and one or more children, own or adopted, of the sexually cohabitating adults."

How many people do you know who fit into the classic definition of a family? Today, there are more relationships that do *not* conform to Murdock's definition than who do, illustrating the impact of societal change on the family system's form and function.

To accommodate changes in family patterns, the U.S. Bureau of the Census defines a family as "two or more persons related by birth, marriage, or adoption, who reside together." Thus, a family can be two or more adult siblings living together, a parent and child or children, or two adults who are related by marriage, but have no children, in addition to adults who adopt a child.

Some states and cities have legally recognized certain unrelated people in caring relationships who live together in a household as a "family" (Skolnick, 1991). These laws pertaining to "domestic partnerships" may help gay couples, foster parents, and step-families have rights and privileges in health insurance, hospital visiting prerogatives, bereavement leave, and annuity and pension benefits (J. Seligman, 1990).

It is important to understand the changes in the concept of family because these changes affect the functions that families perform, the roles its members play, and the relationships its members have with one another, thereby affecting the socialization of children.

Basic Structures

Families are organized in different ways around the world. A family consisting of a husband and wife and their children is called a **nuclear family.** For the children, such a family is the **family of orientation,** which means the family into which one is born. For the parents, the nuclear family is the **family of procreation,** that which develops when one marries and has children (*see* Figure 3.2).

The significance of the nuclear family is that it is the main source of children and so provides the basis for the perpetuation of the society. Most societies assign responsibility for the care and socialization of children to the couple who produces them and sanction the sexual union of a male and a female by law or tradition—in our society, by legal mar-

Figure 3.2　Nuclear Family

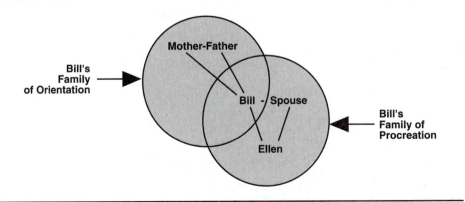

riage. The purpose of the institution of marriage is not only to legalize sexual union but also to fix the obligation toward children who result from that sexual union. In the nuclear family, the wife and husband depend upon each other for companionship and the children depend on their parents for affection and socialization.

The extended family pattern consists of relatives of the nuclear family who are emotionally, and perhaps economically, dependent upon each other. They may, or may not, live nearby (*see* Figure 3.3).

In some cultures or ethnic groups, such as Native Americans, Asian Americans, and Italian Americans, great emphasis is placed on the extended family (obligation to family supersedes obligation to the self). In these ethnic groups, tradition has dictated certain obligations and responsibilities to various members of the extended family—for example, who socializes the children? who decides how the family resources are allocated? who cares for the needy family members? Some cultures emphasize the mother's side of the family as having the responsibility for socialization, authority, and resources. These families are known as **matriarchal**. A contemporary example would be the royal family in Great Britain headed by Queen Elizabeth II. Other cultures emphasize the father's relatives as having the responsibility for care of the family's members, authority, and resources. These families are known as **patriarchal.** This organizational pattern is much more common in the world than is the matriarchal. Examples of patriarchal families can be found in the Bible as well as in movies about the "Mafia," such as the *Godfather* series.

In the United States, both sides of the extended family are generally regarded as equal, or **egalitarian.** Your mother's parents have as much legal authority and responsibility over you as do your father's parents. That is, if something happened to your parents and they could no longer care for you, both sets of grandparents would have equal claim to your custody.

Because we live in an egalitarian society, whose parents' house you go to for holidays after you are married sometimes has to be negotiated. In traditional societies, the rules are set; in modern ones like ours, the rules are ever changing.

Figure 3.3   Extended Family

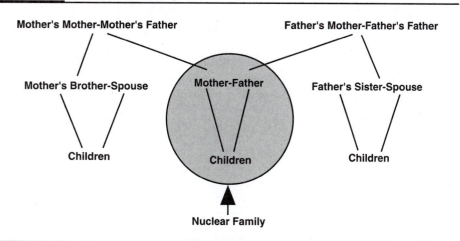

Regardless of whether your extended family is matriarchal, patriarchal, or egalitarian, its main function is support—the relatives you go to when you need help or when you have joys to share. Since, in today's society, many families do not have an extended family for support (for a variety of reasons: moving, divorce, remarriage, death), the people they turn to for help might be friends, neighbors, co-workers, or children's teachers. These people assume some of the support functions of the extended family and become one's personal network (Dean, 1984). It has been shown that people who have no such personal network have to rely on the formal network of society—professionals or government agencies—for their support (Garbarino 1992). Support services provided by the formal network are influenced by politics, economics, culture, and technology. For example, federally funded preschool Head Start was launched by the Democrats and reduced by the Republicans. The American cultural norm of working for a living influenced the change in welfare support. Technology such as telecommuting can influence family members' time together (*see* Figure 3.4).

Figure 3.4 Sources of Family Support

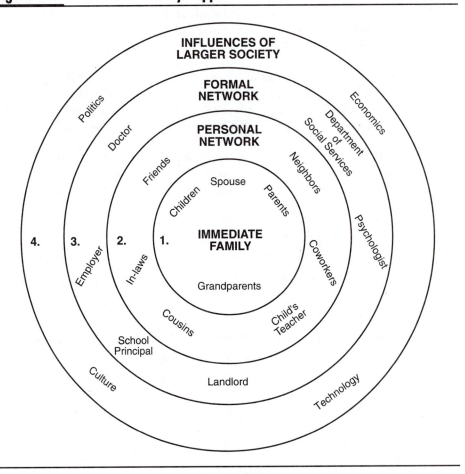

Source: Adapted from C. Dean's visualization of U. Bronfenbrenner's concepts, in Parental empowerment through family resource programs. *Human Ecology Forum*, 1984, *14*(1)18.

BASIC FUNCTIONS

To understand the significance of a family, we look at the basic functions it performs. In general, the family performs certain functions that enable society to survive, although these functions may vary widely. Family functioning may be viewed on a continuum with "healthy," or functional, on one end and "unhealthy," or dysfunctional, at the other keeping in mind that no family is "healthy" all the time. Economic, health, and social stresses can upset some or all of the following functions:

- *Reproduction*. The family ensures that the society's population will be maintained; that is, a sufficient number of children will be born and cared for to replace the members who die.

- *Socialization/Education*. The family ensures that the society's values, beliefs, attitudes, knowledge, skills, and techniques will be transmitted to the young.

- *Assignment of social roles*. The family provides an identity for its offspring (racial, ethnic, religious, socioeconomic, and gender roles). An identity involves behavior and obligations. For example, a Jewish person may not eat pork and may feel obliged to give to charity. A Chinese person may eat with chopsticks and defer to the authority of his or her elders. A person born into a high socioeconomic status may have to choose a spouse from a similar familial background. In some families, girls are socialized to do housework and be caregivers whereas boys are socialized to be breadwinners.

- *Economic support*. The family provides shelter, nourishment, and protection. In some families, all members except very young children contribute to the economic function by producing goods. In other families, one or both parents earn the money that pays for goods the entire family consumes.

- *Emotional support*. The family provides the child's first experience in social interaction. This interaction is intimate, nurturing, and enduring, thus providing emotional security for the child. The family cares for its members when they are ill, hurting, or old.

CHANGES IN THE FAMILY

Throughout history, families have been changing in the ways they execute their various functions, including economic, socialization/education, nurturance/support, reproductive, and the assignment of social roles.

ECONOMIC FUNCTION

Until the eighteenth century, most American families were extended. They owned and occupied farms and plantations that were self-sufficient in that they produced most of what the families needed. They built their own houses, grew their own food, and made their own furniture and clothing. Things the family needed but did not produce were usually obtained through barter.

Early-American farm life required everyone's participation for family survival.

These early-American families were economic units in which all members, young and old, played important productive roles in the household. Thus children were essential to the prosperity of the family. The boys helped cultivate the land and harvest crops, while the girls helped cook, sew, weave, and care for domestic animals and younger children.

Not only were these early families economic units, they were the main source of education and religious training for children (Keniston, 1977). Boys learned their roles from their fathers; girls learned their roles from their mothers. Reading was done from the Bible. Families were also totally responsible for supporting their members—economically, physically, and emotionally. When parents became too old to work, children took care of them. When family members became ill, the family nursed them. In times of stress the family provided the strength to endure.

By the nineteenth century, there were noticeable changes in the structure and functions of the family. In Europe, technical advances, such as the mechanization of the textile industry, the harnessing of steam power, and the establishment of a factory system, had revolutionized the economy. What had been essentially an agrarian system became an industrial system by the middle of the nineteenth century. The impact on the family was tremendous. The agrarian extended family pattern that had endured for 5,000 years changed to an urban nuclear family pattern in a relatively few years (Saxton, 1983).

The agrarian family was generally patriarchal. In most European countries, there existed a tradition of **primogeniture,** the right of the eldest son to inherit his father's estate. After the father died, the eldest son took over the farm and was responsible for caring for the members of his family who had to defer to his authority. The purpose of primogeniture was to keep the family's property intact. Younger brothers (sisters usually left when they married) could stay on the farm, work, and be cared for. Until industrialization provided an alternative means for them to earn a living, they often had no choice.

In countries where inheritance laws required equality among the children in that the family property was divided when the parents died, industrialization often started as domestic or cottage industry, so called because work took place in the home. When the inherited farm was divided among the children, each portion was too small to be profitable. For the adult children, cottage industries provided ways to supplement their inheritance.

The change from an agrarian to an industrial system occurred in America many years later. During the nineteenth century, farm families had begun raising crops to sell and using the proceeds to buy goods produced by others. Thus families gradually became less and less self-sufficient. As industries grew in America, family members began to work for wages in factories and businesses. Money, then, became the link between work and family.

SOCIALIZATION/EDUCATION FUNCTION

By the late nineteenth and early twentieth centuries, women and children were also seeking employment outside the home, and the family could no longer be totally responsible for their children's education. Gradually, schools took over this function.

The public, or "common school," emerged in the middle of the nineteenth century under the leadership of Horace Mann. The main rationale for compulsory, free public education was that families could no longer educate their children for a productive role in the increasingly complicated U.S. economy. Schools were expected to teach good work habits and basic skills, and form good character. Today, many states require that schools teach such topics as sex education, substance abuse prevention, and vocational training, things previously assumed to be the domain of the family.

NURTURANCE/SUPPORT FUNCTION

The family's role in providing care for the sick has diminished, as has its economic and educational self-sufficiency. In the nineteenth century health care as we know it today did not exist. There were no preventive inoculations (except for smallpox in the latter part of the century), no clinics, few hospitals, few medications, and doctors were few and far between. The sick were cared for by their families, as were the elderly. Today, families rely on the medical profession to provide health care, including immunization, diagnosis and treatment of illnesses, and surgery. Families also rely on community services to provide day care and transportation for the elderly, due to increases in dual-career homes and family mobility, which often results in great physical distances between generations.

REPRODUCTIVE FUNCTION: FAMILY SIZE

As families depended less upon agriculture as an economic base, household size declined. There were fewer parents, siblings, and boarders living with couples (Korbin, 1978). Thus the number of adults available in the house to care for children decreased. Also, whereas in the past families had many children hoping some would survive, advances in medicine to decrease infant mortality, and the availability of birth control impacted family size. With the home no longer the workplace, there were fewer responsibilities for children and less need for them to contribute to the maintenance of the family. Thus large families became liabilities rather than assets. There has been a sharp decline in fertility rate and average number of children born per family. For example, the birthrate (number of births per thousand population) was 25.0 in 1955, 16.7 in 1990, and 14.7 in 1998 (National Center for Health Statistics, 1998).

ASSIGNMENT OF SOCIAL ROLES

Social roles within the family are defined by which members perform what jobs, as well as the distribution of authority.

Wife/Mother

When the family was self-sufficient, the wife's role consisted of being responsible for the preparation of food, the making of clothes, the care of children, the management of the house, the care of the animals, and the cultivation of the gardens. Her husband had the authority in the family. When the economy changed and the farms started to sell produce and animal products, the men took over the responsibilities of making contacts for sales and transporting the goods; the woman's role diminished.

Industrialization provided an opportunity for the expansion of women's roles, but few jobs were open to women initially. In the nineteenth and early twentieth centuries in the United States, women were usually employed only as seamstresses, laundresses, maids, cooks, housekeepers, governesses, teachers, and nurses. Not until World War I did this pattern change. Today, over half of the mothers with children under age 18 are employed. They work to support their families if they are family heads, or to contribute to the family income, or for fulfillment.

Husband/Father

Traditionally, a man was responsible for economically supporting his wife and children; a wife was responsible for maintaining the household. This division of labor between husband and wife affected their parental roles (Mintz, 1998). In colonial families, children learned appropriate gender roles from both father and mother since there was no sharp split between work and home. In nineteenth-century families, however, mothers assumed more child rearing tasks because fathers worked in industry and were away from home much of the time.

Now, according to research (Parke 1995; Tamis-LeMonda & Cabrera, 1999) on fathers' involvement in child rearing, the role of *father* is being redefined by technological and ideological changes in our society. In many families men are assuming more household and child-care responsibilities. This is especially true in families where the mother is employed. It is also true in cases where the parents are divorced where the father has custody or partial custody of the children. Today, many fathers are active participants in the socialization of their children. For example, fathers are attending childbirth and parenting classes along with their wives. Many hospitals permit the father to be present at the delivery. It is no longer uncommon to see fathers in the grocery store with young children, taking their children out in the stroller, or dropping them off at child care. Some fathers are raising children as single parents. While father-involvement in parenting is generally positive for children, some children experience adverse effects from inconsistent, unstable support (Tamis-LeMonda & Cabrera, 1999). The macrosystem has to implement policies that enable fathers to contribute to the healthy development of their children.

Children

Currently, the home economy of preindustrial times has practically disappeared (although the computer has enabled many people to connect to their work from home). Most adult family members work for pay outside the home, and children rarely work at all. Work and family life are separate entities. Families have become consumption units rather than production units. Children used to be an economic asset in that they contributed to the family by doing chores or contributing wages earned outside the family. Now they have become an economic liability in that they not only have to be sheltered, clothed, and fed until age 18, they have to be educated as well. In dual-earner families, the cost of child care must be added to the economic liability. Not only are children expensive to raise, most cannot be counted on to provide economic support when their parents reach old age.

Authority Patterns/Role Expectations

Authority patterns in the family can be traced back in time. In Western history, the biblical family pattern is described as patriarchal and extended. Abraham, Isaac, and Jacob had several wives who, along with their children, constituted their families.

In ancient Rome, absolute authority, *patria potestas (paternal power),* was given to the father over his children. The father was guardian over his sons as long as he lived, and even had the right to kill them. When the sons married, they lived with their families in the father's household, forming an extended family. Families, to continue their lineage, arranged marriages for their sons with women of equal status. Marriage was monogamous, the commitment was to one person at a time (usually for life).

Roman family law influenced all parts of the Roman Empire and was incorporated by many of the new emerging nations during the Middle Ages. For example, the power of the father, the dowry, the lower status of women, and the extended family were Roman-influenced characteristics of the medieval family in Mediterranean countries.

Even in America, these patterns were evident during colonial times. In traditional agricultural families, men, women, and children knew what was expected of them; roles were rigid and based on custom. A woman had to be a good cook, since her family depended on her food preparation for survival. A man had to be a hard, steady worker, for his family's survival depended on his ability to farm. Children learned their appropriate social roles very early—obedience and responsibility were the norm. Since practically all families were agricultural, the role expectations for children were agreed upon by the entire community. The father was responsible for the education of his children, and there were no competing socialization agents. Morals were taught and modeled; there was no questioning or discussion about what was right or wrong.

In contemporary families, however, the roles of family members are more complex and flexible because they are based on change. First, children rarely see their fathers or mothers at work outside the home. In fact, they rarely see anyone at work other than those with whom they come in contact in their daily lives, such as teachers, doctors, or store personnel. Consequently, they do not know what is expected of them as adults. They have to piece together information from what they observe, what they read about, and what they see on TV.

Second, role expectations for males and females are not agreed upon by the community. In one family the woman may be expected to stay home and care for the children and the house while the husband earns money to support the family. In another family the woman may be expected to contribute to the family income by working outside the home, and the husband may be expected to help with child care and household duties.

Third, the contemporary family is nuclear. Gone are the models and social pressures of extended family members who reinforced socialization. Gone, too, in most contemporary families, is the unquestioning acceptance of the father as patriarch. With the pressure for women's rights has come an awareness of the need for equality between males and females. Unlike women in traditional families, contemporary women have legal rights equal to men's; for example, women may own property after they are married, and have the right to equal educational opportunities. Thus women have the education and the legal right to participate in family decision making. Unlike traditional families, where decisions were handed down from the father, contemporary families more than likely have discussions before reaching decisions.

Because little choice was available to traditional families, discussion and decision making based on alternatives were unnecessary. Traditional families had to survive. They had to have shelter, clothing, and enough food to eat. The food that was served was that which was available or was in season. If they were hungry, people could not afford the luxury of disliking peas, for example.

Most contemporary U.S. families have adequate shelter, clothing, and food. In fact, most have the economic ability to choose among what is available in houses, home furnishings and decorations, clothing, and food. Home appliances have changed the chores done in the home. Refrigerators and freezers have eliminated the need to preserve food by canning and drying. Automatic washers and dryers have eliminated the hours at the washboard and clothesline. Vacuum cleaners reduce the workload of cleaning. Convenience-food items available in the store today practically eliminate the need to cook, especially if one has access to a microwave oven.

Children in traditional families were given responsibility early. They knew that their contribution to the functioning of the family was necessary. Traditional parents did not have to consult books on how to raise a responsible child. Many contemporary families have to "find" chores for their children to perform to teach them responsibility.

Traditional families were large. Children had many companions and role models in their siblings. In contrast, most contemporary families are small; children look to their peers for companionship and various socializing agents for role models.

MEETING THE CHALLENGE OF CHANGE: FAMILY EMPOWERMENT

The functions that the traditional family performed, such as health care, formal education, and elderly care, have gradually been taken over by institutions outside the family. What functions, then, are left to the contemporary family? Children still are born to and cared for by families. Families still provide economic and emotional support for their members. Families still provide identities for their members. And the family is still the primary socializing agent for children.

Since many significant agents other than the family, such as school, peers, media, and community, contribute to the socialization of the child, the family has changed from an economic unit to a management unit. Parents must choose quality day care for their children, if necessary; consult with teachers; find good health care; know who their children's friends are; monitor the television programs their children watch, the movies they see, and the books they read; and know of available community services.

Families need to become **empowered** or enabled to have control over resources affecting them. That is, to be an effective management unit, they have to have access to knowledge and skills that enhance their ability to influence their personal lives and the community in which they live (Vanderslice, 1984). Empowerment is a process that evolves from analyzing one's own strengths and resources, becoming educated in skills one is lacking, and participating in the community. Social policy enacted in the 1990s began to reflect the concept of empowerment in that government funding to families is tied to becoming self-reliant rather than dependent. For example, the government imposed a time limit and funded training programs as incentives for people receiving welfare to get jobs.

CONSEQUENCES OF CHANGE ON FAMILIES AND CHILDREN

"Families are not static but dynamic and are continuously confronted by challenges, changes, and opportunities" (Parke & Buriel, 1998, p. 511). While some families can develop coping styles to adapt to changes and remain healthy and functional, others may become victims of the consequences of change. They may experience stress, dissolution, or an unanticipated lifestyle. They are at risk for becoming unhealthy, or dysfunctional. Various family ecologies such as stress, transitions in family ties, and dual-earner families will be examined.

STRESS

STRESS is a concept from physics that refers to physical forces and the ability to withstand strain. Dr. Hans Seyle applied the concept to refer to the human ability to adjust to danger signals. He was interested in the biochemical changes that occur when an individual reacts to stress. He defined stress as "the nonspecific response of the body to any demand" (Seyle, 1956, p. 54). Others have expanded the definition to include any demand that exceeds the person's ability to cope (Honig, 1986).

There are *physical stressors* such as disease, overexertion, allergies, and abuse. There are *sociocultural stressors* such as crowding, traffic, noise, bureaucracies, crime, and change. And there are *psychological stressors* such as personal reactions to real or imagined threats and reactions to real or imagined pressure to achieve (Kuczen, 1987).

Stress is not new. In hunting-and-gathering societies, the fear of not finding food or shelter was a stressor. In agricultural societies, the unpredictability of the weather was a stressor. In industrial societies, working long hours was, and still is, a stressor. In information societies, information overload and excessive choice are stressors. One must make decisions in areas in which one has little or no expertise, and often facts and opinion are blurred. Children today face many of the same stressors of growing up that children a generation ago faced: separation anxiety, sibling rivalry, coping with school, peer pressure, being independent. However, children today also face stressors that were practically nonexistent a generation ago (Elkind, 1994; Hewlett & West, 1998). For example, the escalation of violence in families and communities and the bombardment of consumerism into homes, schools, extracurricular activities, as well as in the media.

> When I went trick-or-treating on Halloween, I never worried about being kidnapped or finding a razor blade in my candy. I knew if I got sick at school the nurse would call my mother, and she would come and get me. Today, many schools do not have nurses, neither can mothers leave their jobs to pick up sick children. I rode the buses and subways while growing up, whereas my children fear gangs and weapons. Newspapers consisted of news stories with few advertisements; today it is the reverse.

One reason why children face more stressors today is that the traditional protectiveness or "buffering" function of the family is not there for them in many cases (Elkind, 1994; Hewlett & West, 1998). For many children family life has become less stable and less predictable, primarily because of the doubling of the divorce rate since 1965 (Footlick, 1990; Whitehead, 1996). Currently, more than a third of children are living with a single parent due to divorce (U.S. Bureau of the Census, 1998). Children who witness their family being dissolved face stressors of fear of abandonment, loss of love, and loss of self-esteem (Furstenburg & Cherlin, 1991). Changes in child-care arrangements, whether due to family transitions or caregiver turnover, can cause similar stress in children.

Another stress is that family life has become fragmented. People are pressured by occupational and community demands for their time. Pagers, cellular phones, and e-mail have all contributed to merging the boundaries between family and other commitments. Thus time for family is jeopardized.

The danger of fragmented family life can be compounded when both parents are employed. The husband works, the wife works, and the children go to school. If working hours are staggered, the family may not eat together. Chores have to be done after work. If children have after-school activities, they have to be coordinated with the parents' already busy schedules. Then there are meetings—school, work, and community meetings. So hardly any time is left for communication or shared leisure. Needless to say, this causes stress. And what happens when one parent is transferred to another city or state and the other parent's job doesn't allow for similar mobility? For single parents, the danger of fragmentation is even greater.

Children in single-parent families or in families where both parents work may have to adapt to the stress of separation earlier and for longer periods of time than do children in families where one parent is home. They may also have to assume more responsibility at an earlier age, such as caring for self or siblings after school, doing household chores, getting homework done without help, and so on (Elkind, 1994), which may be beneficial from some, but harmful to others.

For many children, their families' goal orientation is the stressor. Families are pushing children to achieve at early ages. This can be seen in the demand for structured academic programs in kindergarten, and even preschool, for reading and math (Elkind, 1987b). It can also be seen in the participation in community activities: soccer, Little League, gymnastics, music lessons, and so on. When the child has no time to play—to choose activities and playmates, to imagine, to dream—the child experiences stress in having to always perform or always produce.

These children have to cope with the disastrous physical and psychological effects of a flood that swept their community.

Finally, for many children and families unrealistic expectations of family life are the stressors. Due to the diminished opportunities for real experiences with family relationships, people tend to get their views of what a family should be from the media. Perceived reality affects beliefs, expectations, and consequent emotions (Condry, 1989). Although there is no clear scientific data regarding the media's influence on expectations of family life, the media industry has little doubt about its impact, as measured by TV show ratings such as *The Cosby Show* and *Seventh Heaven* (Skill, 1994).

The idealistic family has strong roots in our culture, as evidenced by the media. According to Dolores Curran (1985, p. 8), author of *Stress and the Healthy Family*, stress is "acknowledged and even expected" as part of one's work, but it is "demeaned and denounced" as part of one's family: "Families aren't supposed to be places of stress; they are supposed to be places of peace and harmony in which we recoup from the pressures of the outside world and gather energy to put back into our jobs." These unrealistic expectations of family life produce great guilt in parents who live with everyday family stresses.

Family stress affects all the individual members of the family. An ill child, unexpected company, a perfectionist mother, and a workaholic father are all examples of common stressors that can disrupt harmony in the home. We somehow have the expectation that families should be able to cope with these common stressors, whereas we expect families to exhibit problems when they go through major stressors such as divorce, single parenting, remarriage, bereavement, income change, and substance abuse. However, Curran (1985) and others (Olson, 1997) have found family stressors to include:

1. Economics
2. Children's behavior
3. Insufficient couple time
4. Lack of shared responsibility in the family
5. Communicating with children
6. Insufficient "me" time
7. Guilt for not accomplishing more
8. Spousal relationship
9. Insufficient family play time
10. Overscheduled family calendar

How families cope with stress can be assessed by how they solve problems, how they communicate, adapt to change, their social supports, their spiritual beliefs, their self-esteem and personal adjustment, and absence of pathology, deviance, or drug use (Curran, 1983; Olson, 1997; Stinnett & Defrain, 1985).

The studies have shown that functional families that are resilient to stress are more likely to exhibit certain key characteristics—behaviors and values—than are families that are at risk for dysfunction when stressed. The strength of each characteristic and the combination of characteristics, as well as how they are demonstrated, may vary from one family to another and may be influenced by ethnic orientation. But, in general, the total picture of functional families is as follows:

- *Display of love and acceptance*. Members of strong families show their love and appreciation for one another. This acceptance and warmth is expressed spontaneously—physically (smile, touch, hug) or verbally ("I love you," "You're a good son/daughter"). Family members cooperate rather than compete with one another.

- *Communicativeness*. Family members are spontaneous, honest, open, and receptive to one another. This means expressing negative as well as positive feelings. Conflicts are faced and handled, rather than repressed into resentment. However, some ethnic groups such as Asians believe it is better not to express negative feelings in order to avoid conflicts.

- *Cohesiveness*. Family members enjoy spending time together. Sharing chores, resources, and recreational activities is felt to be important. There is also respect, however, for individual differences, autonomy, and independence. It is common in Anglo families for members to engage in individual as well as family pursuits, whereas this is not necessarily the pattern among other ethnic groups.

- *Communication of values and standards*. Parents in strong families have definite and clear values and make them known to their children. These values and standards are discussed and practiced. There is also tolerance and respect for individual differences. Parents are models as well as teachers.

- *Ability to cope effectively with problems*. Stress and crises are faced optimistically with the purpose of finding solutions. Alternatives are explored, and family members are mutually supportive.

The challenge of adapting to the impact of societal change on the family can probably be best met by looking at the characteristics of functional or successful families as models to emulate, rather than clinging to some family pattern that worked in the past (Coontz, 1997).

The family is a dynamic social system that, as has been discussed, has functions, roles, and authority patterns. The way the system operates and adapts to change affects the relationships within it. Having just explored how stress in general affects the family as a system, specific stressors will be analyzed as to how each affects the functions, roles, authority patterns, and consequently the relationships within families.

TRANSITIONS IN FAMILY TIES

While families are always in a process of transition (marriage, childbirth, death), certain events affect the socialization of children more than others. These are divorce, single parenting, and stepparenting.

Changes in family ties are documented by the increase in divorce and in the proportion of children living with only one parent. According to the U.S. Bureau of the Census (1998) and the National Center for Health Statistics (1997), the divorce rate was 25% of the population in 1966, 53% in 1979, and 47% in 1990. The number of children living with one parent (divorced or never married) in 1998 was 28%.

Parental divorce is not a singular event but rather represents a series of stressful experiences for the entire family that begins with marital conflict before the actual separation and includes many adjustments afterward. Families must often cope with "the diminution of family resources, assumption of new roles and responsibilities, establishment of new patterns of interaction, reorganization of routines . . . , and the introduction of new relationships into the existing family" (Hetherington & Camara, 1984, p. 398). More specifically, parents in conflictual marriages are less able to help their children regulate emotions and behavior, as well as self-soothe their own stress (Wilson & Gottman, 1995).

Even though the divorce rates have risen in the 1990s, so have the remarriages (U.S. Bureau of the Census, 1998). Married adults comprise 56 percent of all American adults. When a divorced person remarries, the children gain a stepparent. With the stepparent come additional kinship relationships. New roles and obligations not dependent on custom and tradition have to be formed.

Divorce and the Family

The fragmentation of the family, its diminished functions, unrealistic expectations, role changes, the economic state of society, stress, and changes in the law have all been blamed for divorce.

Traditional divorce law permitted divorce only if one spouse committed such serious marital misconduct as adultery, cruelty, or desertion. Traditional divorce proceedings involved the determination of who was guilty and who was innocent. Child custody arrangements and financial settlements were intended to reward the innocent party and punish the guilty one. Divorce cases were often costly financially and emotionally—to both parents and children. Criticisms of existing laws led to the passage of no-fault divorce laws. These laws do away with assigning blame and allow divorces on the basis of "irreconcilable differences" or "marital breakdown." Thus the new laws tried to reflect how marriages really deteriorate. Unintentionally, however, the no-fault divorce laws have turned out to be very harmful to women and children, especially economically.

Lenore Weitzman (1985), in her book *The Divorce Revolution*, documents that while divorce usually improves the economic position of husbands, it seriously reduces that of women and children who remain with their mother in more than 90% of the cases. Thus the husband's standard of living improves by 42% after the divorce, while the wife's declines by 73%. The framers of the new laws, who were preoccupied with the defects of the traditional laws, did not consider that the old laws did offer protection to women and children. A woman, deemed to be the innocent party, wouldn't have to agree to a divorce unless her husband, deemed to be the guilty party, provided adequate support for her and the children. Further, judges would often divide property in accordance with family need. The mother and children retained the family home and enough support to avoid sudden poverty (Skolnick, 1987).

Today, in most states, the family's assets are divided equally between the spouses, but according to Weitzman (1985), the man ends up getting half while the woman must share her half with the children because she, generally, is the custodial parent. Often the family home must be sold in order to divide the couple's tangible assets. The husband and wife usually retain each of their intangible assets such as education, career, future earning power, pension(s), and insurance. Thus, today's divorce laws have had a tremendous influence on how the family is able to adjust to inevitable changes accompanying dissolution of a marriage.

Divorce has certain consequences on family functioning and the socialization of children: barring external social support, the effect of divorce on the custodial parent is that the responsibilities double. The single parent is responsible for financial support, child care, and home maintenance. Because the parent is under great stress, parenting diminishes (Emery, 1988; Goodman, Emery, & Haugaard, 1998). The effects on the children may be increased responsibility for them, less time available to spend with the parent to receive love and security, and the lack of two role models of different genders.

To assess the effect of divorce, one must examine how all the various members of the family deal with the transition, reestablish their role obligations to one another, and perform such functions as the following (Hetherington & Clingempeel, 1992; Hetherington, Stanley-Hagan, & Anderson, 1989):

- *Economic functions*. The family must obtain enough money to provide for the support of its members.
- *Authority*. Power for decision making within the family must be allocated.
- *Domestic responsibilities*. The physical and emotional well-being of the children must be provided for, and the residence must be maintained.
- *Support*. Caring and involvement toward one another provide the emotional support necessary for family survival.

The ability of the divorcing family to carry on its former functions is affected not only by the coping skills of its members, but also by macrosystem forces. These forces include economic disparity for females, societal attitudes regarding the ideal two-parent family, and available informal or formal support services (Coontz, 1997; Hetherington, 1989).

Women, regardless of marital status, do not earn income on the same scale as men. Although men are legally required to support their children following divorce, and in some cases their wives too, evidence shows that the majority of men do not continue to provide support, even though the court orders them to do so (Children's Defense Fund, 1998). Thus a woman who heads a family must turn to her own family of orientation or the public welfare system for economic assistance. Evidence shows that children who live in mother-only families have almost a 1 in 2 chance of being in poverty, in contrast to a less than 1 in 10 chance for children living with two parents (U.S. Bureau of the Census, 1998).

The effects of the change in the economic status of the family resulting from divorce means not only a change in family consumption habits, but often a change in housing (Weitzman, 1985). Moving in itself constitutes stress to the family; for one thing, former neighborhood supports are no longer available; for another, maintaining two households is costly when a parent lives in one place but must contribute to another.

Divorce affects the distribution of authority within the family. Prior to the divorce the father may have had more authority because, traditionally, he had been regarded as the primary breadwinner, or authority may have been shared by both parents. After the divorce, however, the custodial parent assumes the day-to-day authority over the children, and the noncustodial parent becomes restricted to areas spelled out in the divorce agreement. Hetherington and Clingempeel (1992) found that both fathers' and mothers' authority over children, as indicated by their parenting practices, tended to deteriorate

These children are sharing domestic responsibilities.

in the first two years following the divorce. There was less consistency, control, and affection.

Divorce affects the distribution of the domestic functions of the family. Prior to the divorce, both parents performed chores related to family functioning. If the mother was not employed, it was likely that she was primarily responsible for household duties and child care, while the father was earning the money. After the divorce, the mother is more likely to have custody of the children (Hetherington & Clingempeel, 1992). Generally, she has to find work outside the home because of the father's reduction in his economic contribution to her and the children. In addition, she has to find someone to care for the children. The father has to assume the domestic duties associated with his separate household or else hire someone to clean, cook, shop, and do laundry.

In families where the mother was employed prior to the divorce, perhaps the father shared domestic responsibilities with her, so after the divorce she has to assume his chores as well.

Hetherington, Cox, and Cox (1982) found that the families of divorced mothers who had custody of their children were less likely to eat dinner together or play together than intact families. Divorced mothers were less likely to read aloud to their children when putting them to bed, and their children had more erratic bedtimes. Also, the households of divorced mothers and fathers were more disorganized than were nondivorced households.

The isolation of the nuclear family from relatives compounds the dilemma of the burdens thrust upon the single-parent family—relatives cannot be called upon for help with child care, household duties, or emotional support. Since emotional support is one of the functions of the family, and divorce removes one adult from the context, the remaining adult no longer has someone with whom to share the burdens and joys of child rearing. Neither is there someone with whom to share the daily decision making and to provide needed psychological support.

Effects of Divorce on Children

According to the National Center for Health Statistics (1997), almost one out of two marriages ends in divorce. Most divorces occur within the first 10 years for both first marriages and remarriages. The number of children under 18 whose parents divorce is about 17%. Children experience a deep sense of loss, develop divided loyalties, and feel helpless against forces beyond their control.

Parental divorce involves a series of stressful interactions between children and their environment as the family restructures. However, not all children react to divorce in the same way (Sandler, Tein, & West, 1994). Children's reactions depend on the various personalities involved, coping skills, and the parents' relations with their children (Cowan, Powell, & Cowan, 1998). Reactions also depend on such factors as age and gender, how much family disharmony existed prior to the divorce, and how available other people are for emotional support (Hetherington, Stanley-Hagan, & Anderson, 1989). Studies by Hetherington (1988, 1989) show that during and after parental divorce, children often exhibit marked changes in behavior, such as acting out, particularly in school. An analysis of academic achievement of high school students showed that those from divorced families had significantly lower achievement levels than those from intact families (Cherian, 1989).

Wallerstein and Kelly (1980) found that divorce affected the self-concept of the preschool child. In particular, the child's views of the dependability and predictability of relationships were disrupted. Some children blamed themselves for the break-up. For example, one 5-year-old child said, "If only I didn't whine like Daddy said, he wouldn't have left me." Even a year later, in a follow-up study, almost half of the children in the sample still displayed heightened anxiety and aggression. These authors also found that school-age children responded to divorce with sadness, fear, feelings of deprivation, and some anger (Wallerstein, Corbin, & Lewis, 1988; Wallerstein & Kelly, 1980). They, like the preschool children, were still struggling, after a year, with the changes in their lives. School-age children had difficulty focusing their attention on school-related tasks.

In various studies done by Hetherington and Clingempeel (1992), young children of divorce were found to be more dependent, aggressive, whiny, demanding, unaffectionate, and disobedient in behavior than children from intact families. They feared abandonment, loss of love, and bodily harm. The behavior and fears expressed were, in part, due to the parents' preoccupation with their own needs, as well as the ensuing role conflicts. When compared to parents of intact families, divorced parents of preschoolers were less consistent in their discipline and less nurturant. Also, communication was not as effective, and fewer demands for mature behavior were made of the children.

Adolescents, unlike younger children, feel little sense of blame for the separation of their parents, but they feel resentment. They are often pawns for each parent's bid for loyalty: "She tells me terrible things about my dad; when I'm with him, he tells me terrible things about her." They are also still burdened by the painful memories of the divorce 10 years later (Wallerstein, Corbin, & Lewis, 1988).

Whether the child is a boy or girl influences the impact of the divorce. Research shows boys are harder hit. Hetherington (1988), and her colleagues (1989), in explaining this, hold that boys receive less support from their mothers, teachers, and peers than girls. Girls tend to cry and whine to vent their sadness—and it gets them help. Boys, on the other hand, may bully other children and cry only when hit back.

According to Lamb (1997), the father's role in the socialization of children is very important. He not only models and teaches gender roles, he also models and teaches other values and morals. As children grow, society is interpreted to them by each parent. Children from a single-parent family lack the live-in, gender role model of the parent, usually the father, who has left.

Children involved in custody battles are the most torn by divorce. To avoid this win/lose situation, some parents are turning to joint custody, sharing responsibility for their children. The effects of various custody arrangements are discussed later.

Although divorce is upsetting to everyone involved, it is probably worse for a child to live in an embattled household. For parents, divorce is a very stressful time, and feelings of depression, loss of self-esteem, and helplessness interfere with parenting abilities. Parents must find support outside the family to bolster their confidence in themselves and ability to parent. They must tell the child that even though they are divorcing each other, they are not divorcing the child.

A serious long-range effect of divorce is the removal of marriage models. Unrealistic expectations of future mates occur. Children may grow up idealizing the absent parent. Ideals are wishes for perfection; they are untempered by reality. For example, a child growing up in a two-parent home may experience Daddy's illnesses (Daddy needs to be cared for, too), disagreements (that may or may not be worked out), and physical affection from both parents. The child growing up in a single-parent home may fantasize situations and relationships regarding the missing parent; reality, inevitably brings disappointment.

Single-Parent Mothers

In the United States, the percentage of children living with a single parent has more than doubled since 1970. Single mothers raising children outnumbered single fathers raising children by 2 to 1 (U.S. Bureau of the Census, 1998).

Single parenthood can occur through death, divorce, desertion, births outside marriage, adoption without marriage, or even artificial insemination. Some people believe that having a husband is no longer a prerequisite for raising children.

Female heads of households often have to work outside the home, as well as care for the children and maintain the household. They are likely to depend on other caregivers. Frequently, female-headed families are poor, or at least a drop in the family's standard of living occurs if the woman was previously married. Thus single-parent mothers experience economic as well as emotional and physical strain (Hetherington & Clingempeel, 1989).

Generally, preadolescent boys show more intense and enduring problems in response to their parents' divorce than do girls. Two years after the divorce many boys have trouble concentrating, so they do poorly on intelligence tests and have difficulty with math. Also, they interact aggressively with their mothers, their teachers, and boys their own age. Monitoring of boys was lower in divorced nonremarried households and the boys engaged in more antisocial behavior (Hetherington, 1993; Hetherington & Clingempeel, 1992). Although preadolescent girls seem to adjust to the divorce within two to three years, evidence has accumulated showing problems related to feminine gender role development emerging at adolescence. Problems in heterosexual relationships, precocious sexual activity, and confrontational exchanges with the mother are examples (Hetherington, 1993; Hetherington & Clingempeel, 1992).

If the father is absent and if, consequently, the father–daughter relationship is halted, then two possible patterns of difficulties in heterosexual relationships can occur. One is passiveness, withdrawal, and shyness with males. The other is aggressiveness, overt activeness, and flirtatiousness (Hetherington, 1972). During the teen years, girls of divorce may show increased conflict with their mothers, increased noncompliance, and problems in sexual behavior, including pregnancy (Chase-Lansdale & Hetherington, 1990). Studies (Coontz, 1997; Miller, Forehand, & Kotchick, 1999) that control for family process (monitoring, communication) have found that single parenthood is *not* related to early teen sexual behavior, but *rules* about dating are; ethnicity was not influential. Apparently, it is harder to establish and enforce such rules when one parents alone, without support.

In sum, the effect of the father's absence on boys and girls depends on the age of the child at the time of separation from the father, how long the father is absent, the quality of the mother–father relationship before separation, the availability of substitute appropriate male models, and the emotional state of the mother during and after the separation (Biller, 1993; Wallerstein & Kelly, 1988).

Single-Parent Fathers

Because children under age 18 are much more likely to be living with their mothers than with their fathers, little research has been done on children being raised by single-parent fathers, and most studies have involved school-age children. Until recently, custody of the children of divorcing parents was usually automatically awarded to the mother. Now, however, many courts are taking into consideration the actual needs of the children involved when custody is awarded, and more fathers are getting custody.

Another reason that little research has been done on children being raised by single-parent fathers is that fathers with custody, more than mothers, use additional caregivers, such as babysitters, friends, relatives, and daycare centers. Thus children growing up in single-father homes have interactions with female role models, which makes it difficult to research the effect on children of the absence of their mothers. Father-custody children have more contact with their mothers than mother-custody children have with their fathers (Parke & Buriel, 1998; Santrock & Warshak, 1979).

Studies done by Santrock and Warshak (1979) and Eliot (1982) compared families in which the mother was awarded custody, families in which the father was awarded custody, and two-parent families. They found that girls who live with their fathers and boys who live with their mothers are less well adjusted than those who live with the same-gender parent. Boys who live with their fathers are less demanding, more mature, independent, sociable, and have higher self-esteem than girls in father-custody situations. Likewise, girls who live with their mothers are less demanding, more mature, independent, sociable, and have higher self-esteem than boys in mother-custody situations. However, another study (Downey & Powell, 1993) of 400 eighth-grade boys and girls failed to find any evidence that boys and girls benefit significantly from living with their same-sex parent.

Problems for fathers raising children are similar to those of mothers. In general, fathers find it difficult to obtain child-care help (day care, after-school care, housekeepers). Sometimes day-care centers' hours do not coincide with work hours, and the cost of a housekeeper is prohibitive. There is also role overload in having to work, care for children, and maintain the house. Social life suffers.

A common problem among fathers is that they receive little preparation for home-making and parenting. Buying groceries, mending, ironing, doing dishes, and keeping the house clean are difficult adjustments. Many fathers have little knowledge regarding the normal developmental stages of children or about parenting (Biller, 1993). While fathers' *economic* responsibility for their children has been the focus of public policy and consequent legislation, fathers' *emotional* responsibility has been ignored until recently (Amato, 1998). Fathers are now being included in prenatal, preschool, and elementary school programs.

Joint Custody

Joint custody is a modern-day solution to the quandary facing many judges: Which adult claimant should be given custody of a child? It also provides the rationale for father–mother involvement in child rearing which enables the child to relate to both male and female role models (Biller, 1993). A concern expressed by Mary Ann Mason (1998) in her book *Custody Wars*, is that the legal shift to "equal treatment" of men and women has translated into parents' rights taking precedence over children's needs.

Joint legal custody divides decision-making authority for the child between the divorced parents. Typical areas requiring decisions include discipline, education, medical care, and religious upbringing. Sometimes physical custody is divided as well. For example, a child may spend weekdays with one parent and weekends and holidays with the other, or six months with one and six months with the other.

Recommendations for Community Support of Single Parents

- Extend availability of day-care facilities to evening hours.
- Form babysitting cooperatives in neighborhoods or places of employment.
- Make transportation available for children to and from day care to parent's home or work.
- Provide classes on single parenthood and opportunities for support groups.
- Provide "Big Sister" programs (for girls from mother-absent homes) as well as "Big Brother" programs (for boys from father-absent homes).

As the number of divorces has climbed, so has the number of states giving legal sanction to some form of joint custody. As a result, some nuclear families split by divorce are evolving into a new form, called the **binuclear family,** in which the children are part of two homes and two family groups. Binuclear families are not limited to joint custody cases, but parents without custody tend to become less involved in the child's life.

Joint custody has as many negatives as positives, depending upon the individuals and situations involved. The main advantage is that it requires that the parents' top priority be the child. Parents have to set aside their differences and make decisions based on the child's welfare, not their own (Bowman & Ahrons, 1985). Joint custody is more apt to encourage continued child-support payments and mutual sharing of parental responsibilities (Steinman, Zemmelman, & Knoblauch, 1985). However, usually the parents are divorcing because they can no longer communicate or cooperate with one another. So, in reality, what may happen is that parents divide authority; the joint-custody child, then, instead of having two decision-making parents, ends up having none because the parents can't agree. Lack of consensus or inconsistency is confusing to a child and may undermine discipline.

If the divorce was bitter, then the increased communication between the parents, as required by joint custody, is likely to become more hostile, thereby exposing the children to even more conflict and psychological damage (Johnston, Kline, & Tschann, 1989). Another problem occurs when parents use the child to communicate messages between them (Furstenburg & Cherlin, 1991): "Tell your father to send the check, or he won't get to see you next weekend," and to inform each parent of the other's activities (Parke & Buriel, 1998).

While joint custody gives the child access to both parents, thereby avoiding the feeling of being abandoned by the noncustodial parent, some children, especially younger ones, are actually harmed by the inevitable continual separation and reattachment. Preschool children have a very difficult time understanding why everyone can't live in the same house and "Why, if Mommy loves me and Daddy loves me, don't they love each other anymore?" School-age children express confusion and anxiety over their schedules, anxiety that spills over into school performance and relationships with friends (Francke, 1983). For example, a 6-year-old became obsessed with carrying his backpack everywhere because he was afraid of leaving his homework at one parent's house while he stayed at the other's. An 11-year-old girl felt that she could never be anyone's "best" friend because she didn't stay in one house long enough. To her, being a best friend meant being around all the time.

Among the unanswered questions about joint custody is: What happens over time? Children grow and change. Parents remarry, take new jobs, or relocate. What works today may not work tomorrow.

Grandparents Raising Grandchildren

About 6% of children under age 18 are cared for by their grandparents. This represents a 76% increase from 1970 (U.S. Bureau of the Census, 1998). Some reasons are that the child's parents are deceased, the child was abandoned, or the court granted legal custody to the grandparent(s) because the parents were deemed unfit to nurture and support. Substance abuse, teen pregnancy, divorce, physical and mental illness, abuse, neglect, and incarceration are reasons cited (U.S. Bureau of the Census, 1998). Many custodial grandparents do not fit the stereotype of senior citizens enjoying retirement activities (Smith, Dannison, & Vach-Hasse, 1998). Their median age is 53 and some have to care for their own parents in addition to their grandchildren. The constant challenge leaves many grandparents physically, emotionally, and financially drained. Parenting grandparents are becoming increasingly more common and, consequently, new research is needed.

The challenges faced by parenting grandparents are changes in relationships with their spouse and other family members, financial stress, possible feelings of uncertainty,

Many grandparents today are raising their grandchildren. This grandfather shares his love of fishing with his granddaughter.

isolation, anger, grief, fear, and worries about health or death (deToledo & Brown, 1995; Minkler & Roe, 1993).

The challenges faced by children being raised by grandparents are to develop a sense of belonging and stability amid the transition from their own homes. Common feelings are grief, fear, anger, guilt, and embarrassment. Sometimes these feelings are exhibited in such "acting-out" behaviors as physical or verbal aggression, regression to immature behavior (crying, whining, bed-wetting), manipulation, withdrawal, and hyperactivity (deToledo & Brown, 1995; Minkler & Roe, 1993).

Stepparents

Due to the changing nature of families, as well as budgetary constraints, the U.S. Bureau of the Census no longer provides statistics on the number of children residing in stepfamilies. However, according to projections based on earlier data, reveal that one out of three Americans is now a stepparent, a stepchild, a stepsibling, or a cohabiting member of a stepfamily (Larson, 1992; Stepfamily Association of America, 1999).

Because of the increase in the number of stepfamilies, the concept of family needs reexamining, according to the Stepfamily Association of America: "All kinds of institutions from schools to hospitals to the courts will have to adapt to the special needs of stepfamilies" (Kantrowitz & Wingert, 1990, p. 77). Most societal institutions have policies based on intact families. Although they may be full-time parents to their spouses' kids, stepparents, in many cases, have no legal rights. For example, if a child needs emergency surgery, hospitals almost always require the consent of a biological parent or legal guardian.

Not only do the legal issues represent special problems for the stepfamily, so do the psychosocial issues. Each family member has experienced the trauma of divorce or death or separation from a parent or spouse. When a new family is formed, new problems are likely to arise. The impact of remarriage on a family is second only to the crisis of divorce (Hetherington & Clingempeel, 1992).

The stepfamily is also called the "blended family." The interactions are similar to those in any family; they are sometimes tainted with anger, jealousy, value conflicts, guilt, and unrealistic expectations. One of the most common unrealistic expectations is the belief in instant love. Stepfamily relationships are, generally, instant; they do not evolve as they do in a family of orientation, where a child is born and grows.

Children in a stepfamily may feel abandoned by the parent with whom they have formed a close bond after the divorce. Having to live with new rules and values, while still trying to deal with the old rules and values from both parents, places an enormous burden on the child. Also, the stepfamily often adds more children to the household. This involves adjustments in relating to new siblings. Thus, when families blend, the members are very much affected. In the early months of remarriage, there is likely to be less family cohesion, more poorly defined family roles and relationships, poorer family communication, less effective problem resolution, less consistency in setting rules, less effective disciplining, and less emotional responsiveness. Both stepmothers and stepfathers take a considerably less active role in parenting than do custodial parents (Bray, 1988). Even after two years, disengagement is the most common parenting style (Hetherington, Stanley-Hagan, & Anderson, 1989). Stepfamilies also may suffer from lack of external support, fueled by a history of media myths—the "wicked stepmother," the "molesting stepfather" (Rutter, 1994).

In general, families in which the custodial father remarries and a stepmother joins the family experience more resistance and poorer adjustment for children than do families in which the custodial mother remarries and a stepfather joins the family (Hetherington, Stanley-Hagan, & Anderson, 1989). The introduction of a stepparent may also strain the child's relationship with the noncustodial parent. Remarriage often presents children with loyalty dilemmas that they are too inexperienced to solve (Francke, 1983). If they like the stepparent, is that disloyal to their noncustodial parent? Or worse, will they lose the love of their biological parent? Does the noncustodial parent compete with the stepparent for the child's loyalty by buying the child things or by "putting the stepparent down"? Does the child view the stepparent as usurping the biological parent's role? ("She wants us to call her 'Mother.' I won't," said a 10-year-old girl. "He can't tell me what to do; he's not my real father," said a 7-year-old boy.)

Families in which both parents bring children from a previous marriage are associated with the highest level of behavior problems (Santrock & Sitterle, 1987). The addition of instant siblings to the family constellation is both bewildering and taxing to the children (Francke, 1983; Rutter, 1994). For example, overnight the birth-order hierarchy may shift. The child who has been the oldest may inherit an older brother; the child who has been the youngest may inherit a baby sister. Children often compete for attention, especially with the biological parent. Children who have differing histories of upbringing must now live under the same roof with new sets of rules. For example, children who were given choices at mealtime must now adapt to having to eat everything that is put on their plates, or "no dessert." A child who has had to make his or her bed and clean his or her room now has to share a room with a child who has never had those responsibilities.

At least half of children living in stepfamilies are likely to face an additional strain—the birth of a half-sibling to their biological parent and the new spouse (Kantrowitz & Wingert, 1990). Not only is there yet another threat to securing parental love, but common sibling rivalry is intensified by half- versus full-blooded relationships (Francke, 1983; Rutter, 1994).

The complications in roles and relationships faced by the stepparents are evidenced by the increased risk of divorce among remarriages, especially those with children from a previous marriage (Emery, 1988). Whereas about 50% of first marriages end in divorce, for second marriages the estimated divorce rate is 60% (Kantrowitz & Wingert, 1990). Divorce is most likely to occur in remarried families during the first five years, the time in which the new stepfamily is trying to restructure and "refunctionalize" (Parke & Buriel, 1998). Although after five years, stepfamilies are as stable as intact families of the same duration (Rutter, 1994).

Of course, not all stepchildren have behavioral or emotional problems. Studies have indicated that younger children and older adolescents are most likely to accept a stepparent, whereas preadolescent and early adolescent children from about age 9 to 15 do the poorest (Hetherington & Clingempeel, 1992; Hetherington, Stanley-Hagan, & Anderson, 1989). In the first two years following remarriage, conflict between mothers and daughters was found to be high. Hostility, coercion, and demandingness were exhibited toward both mother and stepfather. Interestingly, while boys exhibit more antisocial behavior following divorce, two years after remarriage their behavior was no different from that of boys from nondivorced families (Hetherington, 1989). It may be that for girls, a stepfather is an intrusion on the relationship with the mother, whereas for boys the stepfather is a support and a role model. The six-year follow-up of one ongoing study of stepfamilies found that where the stepparent was firm, but warm, and where the children's natural parents maintained close relationships with them, the children were functioning better than those in either single-parent families or conflict-ridden intact families (Hetherington, 1989).

In sum, the effect of remarriage on the child depends on several factors (Hetherington & Clingempeel, 1992; Hetherington, Stanley-Hagan, & Anderson, 1989; Stinnett & Birdsong, 1978):

- Which additional stressors (moving, finances, stepsiblings) are present
- Age, developmental status, and gender of the child
- Quality of the child's relationship with both biological parents (custodial and noncustodial)
- Quality of the child's relationship with the stepparent and siblings
- Temperament, personality, and emotional stability of the child and the parents
- Availability of parent substitutes or other social supports for the child
- Parenting styles of biological and stepparents

A majority of all divorced adults remarry within a few years to form a stepfamily (Stepfamily Association of America, 1999). A positive consequence for children who have seen the disruption of adult relationships, either through death or divorce, can then have the opportunity of seeing a couple working together in a constructive way. Communicating and allowing feelings to be vented, perhaps in family meetings or in private discussions with each parent, can help blended-family members adjust to one another and form positive relationships. Knowing what the pitfalls are can help stepparents deal with them when they arise. Counseling and/or self-help support groups, such as the Stepfamily Association, can be very beneficial.

Homosexual Families

Homosexual families are becoming more visible in society today (Goodman, Emery, & Haugaard, 1998). Most common are two lesbian women living together raising children from one or both of their previous relationships with men. There are also lesbian relationships in which one of the women becomes artificially inseminated or adopts a child as well as two gay men living together with custody of own or adopted children.

Attitudes about homosexuals generally stem from one's personal feelings about one's own sexuality. These attitudes include fear, disgust, indifference, and acceptance (Brown & Zimmer, 1986). Because of abounding negative attitudes, many homosexuals, especially those raising children, hide their relationships (Kantrowitz, 1996). Children of homosexuals who are open about their relationship face being teased by other children (Gollnick & Chinn, 1998)—"Why do you have two mommies?", "Your dad is a ——."

Many issues faced by homosexual families are similar to those faced by divorced, stepparent, and various custodial arrangements. Overriding these, however, is how the homosexual family manages the stigmatized attitude of society. Society does not legally sanction homosexual marriages or families. Some cities and businesses, however, have implemented policies for domestic partners because generally housing, insurance benefits, emergency room visits, and school permission forms exclude the homosexual partner.

The initial reactions of children of gay and lesbian parents to learning their parents' homosexuality are confusion, lack of understanding, worry, shame, disbelief, anger, and guilt (Harris & Turner, 1986). Children in homosexual homes may be afraid to bring friends home or become involved in school activities because contact with others threatens exposure (Ross, 1988).

Homosexual parents may also cope by being secretive (pretending to be heterosexual). Being open about their homosexuality renders them vulnerable to discrimination and ostracism. However, being secret, although arguably adaptive, is accompanied by the consequences of self-betrayal and disconnectedness from social support (Ross, 1988). New associations must be continually monitored regarding the safety of disclosure. Many homosexual parents fear they will lose custody of their children if their sexual preference is known (Kantrowitz, 1996).

Research on children living with homosexual parents and their partners has focused on three fearful attitudes society in general possesses: that the children will become homosexual, that they will be sexually molested, that there will be psychological damage due to the stigma of being raised by homosexuals. According to Goodman, Emery & Haugaard (1998), research has shown no higher incidence of homosexuality among children raised by homosexuals than by heterosexuals, neither have there been any reported incidences of sexual abuse; also, children reared by homosexuals are not necessarily more psychologically troubled than children reared by heterosexuals.

However, as children approach adolescence and become concerned about their identities and sexual orientation, any family deviations from the norm among their peers can be magnified. The normal developmental changes that occur during adolescence, coupled with the problem of having to cope with a stigmatized parent, can multiply the potential problems facing the adolescent and his or her family (Ross, 1988).

Variables affecting the adolescent's perception of the situation include his or her relationship with the biological parents, the partner, and friends; level of acceptance in the community; and self-confidence. The adolescent who is struggling to achieve an identity and sexual orientation may feel the need to prove he or she is not homosexual by engaging in sexual acts with the opposite sex. He or she may become panicked by his or her own homosexual feelings, which are common in adolescence, yet potentially more threatening to one being raised by homosexuals (Ross, 1988).

DUAL-EARNER FAMILIES

American society has a deep-seated view that a woman's role is in the home (Brazelton, 1989; Hochschild, 1989). She should be there for her children; if she is not, they will suffer in some way. This biased attitude has contributed to society's reluctance to give employed women the support they need, especially in the area of child care, including parental leave and services.

About two-thirds of mothers with children younger than age 6 work outside the home. Labor force participation roles for these mothers have increased about 50% since 1975 (Children's Defense Fund, 1998).

Mother employment almost always improves the economic well-being of families with children, and often it is the difference between whether or not they can make ends meet. To the extent that mothers' working keeps children out of poverty and ensures that their basic material needs are met, it has important benefits (National Commission on Children, 1991). Other benefits of dual-earner families besides increased family income include personal stimulation for the mother (if she enjoys her job), a closer relationship between father and children (due to his increased participation in family matters), and greater sense of responsibility for the children.

The main socialization effect of dual-earner families is the quality of care for the children. (Outcomes of different child-care arrangements will be discussed in Chapter 5.) Other dual-earner family liabilities include "role overload," resulting from the increased responsibilities of the parents and the sacrifice of social relationships. Most employed mothers have less time to spend with their children. They also no longer have time to visit relatives and friends, or be part of community and school organizations.

Hoffman's review (1989) of the research on maternal employment reveals that a variety of effects, depending on individual factors, result when a mother is employed outside the home. In general, Hoffman concludes that such mothers provide different role models than mothers who remain at home. She also found that employment affects the mother's emotional state—sometimes providing satisfactions, sometimes role strain, and sometimes guilt—and this, in turn, influences the mother–child interaction. When the mother is satisfied with her career and does not feel guilty about working, relations with children are similar to those of nonemployed mothers who are content with their homemaking role.

Some individual factors influencing the impact of a mother's employment are the age, gender, and temperament of the child; the socioeconomic status of the family; the quality of the parents' marriage; the mother's satisfaction with her job; the father's satisfaction with his job; and the father's involvement with the children and support of the mother.

One finding that has occurred frequently in various studies is that children of employed mothers, from kindergarten age through adulthood, have less stereotyped views of gender roles (Parke & Buriel, 1998). This is influenced by the mother's discussion of her work, as well as the father's participation in household tasks and child care.

There is some evidence that employed mothers use different child-rearing practices than do nonemployed mothers. Generally, employed mothers are more authoritative, or democratic, in that there is discussion about expectations and responsibilities (Greenberger & Goldberg, 1989). This parenting style will be discussed in more detail in Chapter 4.

Preschool boys have been found to be more sensitive to the type of care they receive, apparently needing a caregiver who is "tuned in" to their needs (Baydar & Brooks-Gunn, 1991). Therefore, boys exhibit more negative behavior such as crying, noncompliance, and aggressiveness when their mothers are employed, especially full-time.

School-age and adolescent children of employed mothers have been found to be better adjusted socially, get along better with their families and friends, and feel better about themselves than do middle-years' children of mothers who stay at home (Hoffman, 1989). Perhaps this is because employed mothers, out of necessity, are likely to grant their children greater independence when they exhibit readiness in addition to giving them more household responsibilities (Hoffman, 1989). Adolescent daughters of working women have been found to be more outgoing, independent, and motivated, and they score higher academically than daughters of homemakers (Hoffman, 1984). Perhaps this is because of the role model presented by the employed mother in addition to being given encouragement to achieve.

Longitudinal studies on intact, middle-class families found that maternal employment status per se was not significantly related to children's development. Children from infancy to adolescence whose mothers were employed or nonemployed developed similarly in cognitive development, language development, social maturity, emotional expressiveness, behavioral adjustment, school motivation, and gender-role development (Gottfried & Gottfried, 1988). The reason that maternal employment alone is not significantly related to child outcomes is that many other factors in the child's ecology, as were mentioned before, affect development (Parke & Buriel, 1998).

The trend today is toward dual-earner families. The impact of this trend on the family really depends on the coping strategies of the particular family: What are the parents' attitudes toward each other's jobs, as well as their own? How are work and family life coordinated? Who cares for the children, and what kind of care are they receiving? Who does the household chores? How are unexpected problems (machine breakdowns, illness) handled? How flexible is each parent's work schedule?

Coping Strategies for Dual-Earner Families

- Working parents should think of themselves as household managers who delegate and supervise rather than do.
- Working parents need to determine their priorities as well as what is really essential—clothes ironed or a game played with the children.
- Working parents need to set aside routine "quality" time for each other and the children. For each other, uninterrupted time away from household

and child-care duties will do. For children, any activity that raises the child's self-esteem is quality time—for example, talking about their day, reading to them, or playing a game with them.

- Working parents need time alone, time to pursue an interest, time to refresh their energies.

- Working parents should learn to say "no" sometimes. When invited somewhere or asked to help on a committee, they might respond, "Let me check and get back to you." This response gives them time to evaluate the invitation and see if it fits in with other commitments to family members.

- Working parents should advocate family-responsive corporate policies such as leaves, flexible work hours, job sharing, child-care support, and seminars dealing with work/family issues (Galinsky, 1986).

All the changes and consequences of change on families and children are influenced by macrosystems, such as socioeconomic status, ethnic orientation, and religious orientation.

MACROSYSTEM INFLUENCES ON FAMILIES AND SOCIALIZATION

Specific effects of macrosystems (socioeconomic status, ethnic orientation, and religious orientation) and how they influence socialization are examined to better understand how larger contexts can impact how family systems operate.

SOCIOECONOMIC STATUS

All societies have their own ways of ranking people, and they differ in the criteria used for placing people in certain classes or statuses. Some societies stratify members by **ascribed status;** that is, family lineage, gender, birth order, or skin color determines a person's class. For example, in the British royal family marriages can occur only with members of the nobility, and the first-born son is automatically heir to the throne.

Other societies stratify members according to **achieved status;** that is, education, occupation, income, and/or place of residence determine an individual's class. The United States exemplifies a society in which status can be attained by achievement—Abraham Lincoln, the sixteenth president of the United States, was the son of a farmer. Academic achievement, trade skills, and athletic talent enable some lower-class youths to attain high status.

Traditional societies, those that rely on customs handed down from past generations as ways to behave, tend toward ascribed status for stratification; **modern societies,** those that look to the present for ways to behave and are thus responsive to change, tend toward achievement status. Stratification is based on the importance of individuals' contributions to a particular society's ability to function. For example, one person makes

This child learns the tradition of weaving as her mother supervises and provides help when necessary.

jewelry; another sells shoes; another is a doctor. Jewelry may be important to those who can afford it; shoes may be necessary for everyone in cold climates; a doctor contributes to the well-being of everyone in the society. Thus people in societies are not equally dependent on one another; some people are therefore more important to society than others and so are ranked higher in terms of social class or status. How a society stratifies or ranks people in social classes is shown by income earned and prestige acquired. In the United States, doctors are ranked high, whereas salespeople are ranked low.

It is more difficult for people to change their rank, or social class, in societies using ascribed criteria than in societies using achievement criteria. In societies using ascribed criteria, however, it is possible for achievements to change a person's ranking. For example, a person born into a lower-class family could become a soldier or a priest and thereby attain higher status. On the other hand, in societies using achievement criteria, individuals' ascribed criteria (conditions of birth) affect their status. For example, those born into the upper class will receive a head start on achievement due to their families' ability to educate them, live in certain neighborhoods, and buy certain material things.

When statuses are ascribed, the roles are set in tradition. In other words, when one is born into a certain status, children are socialized primarily by modeling their elders and being instructed in the traditional ways. When statuses are achieved, however, as is the case in modern societies undergoing change, "the established system for assigning individuals to recognized statuses may break down. Wholly new statuses may come into existence" (Inkeles, 1969, p. 616). Thus what happens in societies that stratify by achievement is that members may find themselves inadequately socialized to play the roles of the statuses they seek or have been assigned. For example, farmers who want to be competitive and profitable have to seek more technical knowledge than that which was learned from their parents. Society, then, has to compensate for this inadequate socialization by the family and rely on other institutions such as the school or business to prepare individuals for their new roles. Farmers may take such courses as plant pathology, genetics, animal husbandry, and economics.

According to sociologist William Goode (1982), it is the family, not merely the individual that is ranked in society's class structure. This is an illustration of the macrosystem's influence on a child's development in that the social class and status of the family help determine an individual's opportunities for education and occupation, as well as for social interaction. The members of the community in which the family lives, the children's friends, and the guests invited to the home generally come from the same social class. Even though U.S. citizens play down the existence of social classes, social scientists recognize that different groups in our society possess unequal amounts of money, prestige, influence, and "life chances" (Levine & Levine, 1996). Despite its egalitarian principles, the United States has been widening the gap between the rich and poor (Ramsey, 1998).

Social class membership begins exerting its influence before birth and continues until death. Health care and diet of the mother affect the birth of the child. The incidence of birth defects is higher in the lower classes than in the middle and upper classes. Economic pressure and lack of opportunities affect the mental health of the lower-class family, as well as determine socialization practices (Parke & Buriel, 1998). Lower-socioeconomic status parents have been found to be more dominant, controlling, and punitive than higher-socioeconomic status parents, who have been found to be more verbal, democratic, and use various techniques. Economics, or lack of money, prevents lower-social-class parents from using an allowance as a reward. Lower-class children cannot be sent to their rooms as a punishment, because there may be no room they can call their own to which they can be sent. Neither can lower-class children have privileges removed for noncompliance, such as going to the movies, because they do not have those opportunities anyway. Thus lower-class families frequently use physical punishment as a socializing technique, whereas middle- and upper-class families have more options available (Hart & Risley, 1995).

Socioeconomic classes can be described in terms of averages. They differ, on *average*, by income, occupation, housing, education, social interaction, and values. It is these defining criteria that influence socialization. Sociologists vary in the way they see the social structure in the United States. Some sociologists believe that while differences in rank exist, true class lines cannot be drawn, since the United States is an open society with much mobility up and down and numerous informal social interactions.

Class Descriptions

The following descriptions apply to the majority of people in a given socioeconomic class, but not to every person in the class (Levine & Levine, 1996).

Upper Class.   In general, upper-class families have inherited their wealth and have a family tradition of social prominence that extends back several generations. Much emphasis is placed on the extended family, which is often either patriarchal or matriarchal.

Figure 3.5   Social-Class Structure in the United States

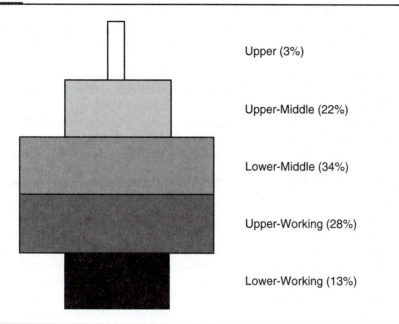

Upper (3%)

Upper-Middle (22%)

Lower-Middle (34%)

Upper-Working (28%)

Lower-Working (13%)

Source: D. U. Levine and R. F. Levine (1996, p. 7). *Society and Education* (9th ed.). Needham, MA: Allyn and Bacon.

Many upper-class families believe proper rearing is more important in order to fulfill adult roles than is formal schooling. If children do go to school to train for an occupation, it must be a high-status one such as medicine, law, or business. Upper-class children generally attend private schools and prestigious private colleges.

Middle Class.   In general, middle-class families have earned their status by achievement (education and/or hard work): "It is not who you are, but what you are." Much emphasis is placed on the nuclear family even though ties are still maintained, often loosely, to the extended family. These families tend to be egalitarian.

A high value is placed on achievement, respectability, and harmonious interpersonal relationships within the family. Education and the ability to get along with others are considered essential to adult success.

The upper-middle class generally includes business executives and professional people.

The lower-middle class generally includes salespeople, small businessowners, contractors, craftspeople, and farmers.

Lower Class.   In general, lower-class families are composed of semiskilled and unskilled workers. Much emphasis is placed on the extended family; close ties with relatives are maintained. Patriarchal patterns are more common (except where the father is absent), as is the distinction between male and female roles.

Many lower-class families emphasize respect for elders and the importance of survival. These families are most affected by economic fluctuations. Many experience being in debt, being laid off, and/or being on welfare. Often, children must help the family rather than further their own education. Some don't complete high school.

Historically, the lower class includes the newest immigrants to the United States who are willing to work at menial jobs while learning the ways of American society.

Underclass.   In recent years, many social scientists have begun to identify another class: the underclass. This class differs from the others in its degree of hopelessness for upward mobility. People in the underclass are stuck at the bottom of the social structure and perceive themselves as having little chance of ever escaping from a pervasively poverty-ridden environment (Wilson, 1987). The underclass is composed of many faces: female-headed families; street-living homeless alcoholics, drug users, and the mentally ill who have been "deinstitutionalized"; the destitute elderly, illegal aliens, rural families from economically depressed areas; and any other group who, for whatever reason, cannot get an adequate education, job, or housing. The underclass, in essence, represents a contradiction to the concept that social mobility is available to anyone in America who is willing to work hard enough for it. Unfortunately, because of the hopelessness of getting out of such extreme poverty, the underclass has become a culture of illegitimacy, drugs, and crime, as well as joblessness. How the underclass developed and what should be done about it remain debated issues among social scientists and public policymakers. The problems for underclass children include exposure to drugs and AIDS, child abuse, poor housing or homelessness, insufficient health care, inferior education, insufficient child-care programs and other community services, welfare dependency, and crime (Levine & Levine, 1996).

Families that have many responsibilities without adequate resources negatively impact the present and future opportunities for their children.

Influence of Socioeconomic Status on Socialization

Children from the lower class are often identified in school as slow learners, aggressors, and truants. Studies comparing the relative intelligence of children of high- and low-socioeconomic status show that those from high-status homes score higher on IQ tests and achievement tests than do children from low-status homes (Patterson, Kupersmidt, & Vaden, 1990). The differences are more marked in later childhood and adolescence than in infancy (Levine & Levine, 1996).

Various theories have been advanced to explain this contrast in intelligence. One of these has to do with heredity—intelligence is inherited, and brighter persons achieve higher statuses (Jensen, 1969, 1988). Another theory stresses environment—the limited resources of lower-status families prevent them from providing intellectual stimulation, especially verbal, for their children. Recent brain research concludes the influence of environmental stimulation and stressors during infancy to be significant and long lasting for cognitive development (Young, 1994). Evidence shows that if special schooling is provided, especially in the preschool years, the IQ scores of lower-status children improve (Bereiter & Engelmann, 1966; Spitz, 1992). A third theory is that of the self-fulfilling prophecy. It is felt that IQ tests are biased toward the middle class, so lower-class children, who have a different set of experiences, do not score as well. Their scores cause teachers to have low expectations: "Since Johnny has a low IQ, I won't give him as many math pages as the others." Thus, Johnny does not learn as much as the others, and his intellectual potential decreases (Brophy & Good, 1986).

The belief that improving the environment of lower-class children could reduce the difference in achievement levels between the classes led to the War on Poverty in the 1960s. Under the leadership of President Lyndon Johnson, many governmental programs were instituted, including "compensatory education." Compensatory education included hiring remedial reading specialists, counselors, and truant officers. Head Start was launched for preschool children considered to be disadvantaged—programs that provided various learning experiences to enable children to be more successful when they entered elementary school. These included language experiences and abstract thinking skills because it was realized that there are significant social-class differences in the use of language and concept development (Levine & Levine, 1996).

The structure and syntax of language used by the upper-middle class is far more complex than that used by the lower class (Bernstein, 1961). Use of complex language indicates a more abstract, as opposed to concrete, perception of reality. Bernstein (1961) uses the following example to illustrate this concept: "I'd rather you made less noise, dear" might be what a middle-class mother would say to her boisterous child, whereas "Shut up!" might be what a lower-class mother would say. Thus the middle-class child learns the abstract meanings of words like *rather* and *less;* the lower-class child gets a simple, concrete message, directly to the point.

Other experiences provided for Head Start children are opportunities to be successful and to be rewarded for this success. It has been shown that the socializing technique of reinforcement or reward for desired behavior given by significant people in a child's life is very effective in motivating the child to repeat the behavior. Middle-class parents reward children, especially sons, for ambition, high levels of aspiration, and long-range goals. To achieve one's ambitions and long-range goals, one must defer gratification. Generally, middle-class children learn from their parents to defer gratification ("Save for a rainy day" "Study hard now so you'll be able to get a good job in the future"), whereas lower-class children do not.

Middle-class parents train their children to be achievement-oriented. Self-discipline, initiative, responsibility, academic achievement, and restraint of aggression are encouraged. Lower-class parents, on the other hand, focus on the behavior rather than the attitudes or motivation of the child. Perhaps this is because they tend to view the world in terms of concrete events and practical outcomes. Faced with the realities of substandard housing, overcrowded neighborhoods, and inadequate services from public institutions, the lower classes' apparent lack of achievement motivation reflects a profound lack of trust in the social system that has excluded them from its benefits (Wilson, 1987).

Various studies (Dodge, Pettit, & Bates, 1994; Levine & Levine, 1996) have examined the relationship between lower-social-class socialization and achievement as well as behavior. Levels of achievement depend on what people feel can be attained. More important than achievement to those struggling to survive is security. Toughness in boys is admired as an ability to get ahead of other people; intellectualism is regarded as unmasculine. Students grouped according to their abilities tend to reinforce each other's attitudes and behavior. Living for the present is the norm, perhaps because opportunities to "live it up" are so rare. Skills in budgeting time and money tend to be lacking.

In upper-class families the child is generally regarded as the carrier of the family's name, its heritage, and its status. The family is able to bear the maximum costs of child rearing (material goods, private schooling, setting up in business or career). Children are expected to meet family standards for behavior and for educational and vocational attainment. Socializing children in upper-class families to be responsible and to achieve is a challenge when such children already "have everything." Pressures to conform to family standards come not only from the nuclear family, but from the extended family (even the dead relatives) as well: "What would Grandfather Smith say?"

Whereas relatives play a large role in the socialization of upper-class children to conform to family standards, middle-class children are reared more by their families of orientation; relatives are expected not to interfere. Lower-class children and their parents rely on their kin for support, mostly emotional, rather than for the intentional purpose of socialization, even though much unintentional socialization does take place through the social interactions occurring between relatives. The reason for this networking is to reduce insecurity and to develop a defense against criticism from society. Besides relying on relatives, lower-class families tend to adapt to their lifestyle by relying on fate and luck; belief in such factors as causes of their destiny helps to relieve their feelings of responsibility for their poverty (Elkin & Handel, 1989).

Lower-class families, in rearing their children, put emphasis on not being a nuisance. Physical punishment is the form of discipline most likely to be used. Children must be trained to adjust to the conditions of many people occupying the same small space. They are also taught early to assume responsibility for doing chores around the home, caring for smaller children, and running errands. Middle-class families are more likely to use reasoning and nonphysical forms of discipline (Maccoby, 1980; Parke & Buriel, 1998). They emphasize conformity to "what people will say" or "how it would look." Children are taught early to look toward the future. ("Eat your vegetables so you'll grow big and strong." "When you can use the potty, you'll be able to wear big-boy pants like Daddy instead of diapers.")

Lower-class families are so burdened with survival in the present that it is difficult for them to socialize their children to delay gratification or be oriented to the future, as our society's education system is structured. They have inadequate resources, such as income, education, and good jobs, to meet their needs in life. They are plagued with sickness, injuries, and entanglements with the law, and lack the money, knowledge, and access to support services to cope with these problems. The pessimistic view that "things will turn out as badly as they generally have in the past" pervades their lives. Their relatively low level of skill makes them easily replaceable in their jobs. Since they have previously experienced little success in shaping their lives, they expect nothing else in the future (Levine & Levine, 1996).

However, generalizations about the influence of socioeconomic status on socialization do not always apply.

In her book, *Common Purpose*, Lisbeth Schorr (1997) describes support programs that have strengthened families and neighborhoods in the United States. For example, a program called Youth Build, begun in Harlem, New York, recruited adolescents from poor families to build and renovate low-cost housing. The youth are trained by journeymen in construction skills and the personal habits and qualities that contractors seek in entry-level workers. They also attend school and are trained in leadership skills that, together with job skills, will help them rebuild their own lives and provide them with the prospect of moving out of the lower class. What makes Youth Build successful is the caring support and commitment of its staff, as well as the sense of family and community among its members. They help each other and execute consequences for disruptive behavior, absences, and substance abuse. Building something tangible and useful in one's own neighborhood provides a sense of pride and respect which, in turn, leads to a sense of personal responsibility for life's outcomes.

Implications of Socioeconomic Status for Professionals: The Challenge

Professionals whose experiences have been typically middle class must understand the differences in various social class behavior and motivations if they are to work effectively with children from all socioeconomic statuses.

The ability to delay gratification is a middle-class value; immediate gratification is the norm among the lower class. Professionals can provide children feedback on their behavior with cues or specific instructions, and tangible, immediate rewards, such as small tokens (stickers, toys), rather than giving hypothetical reasons—for example, "You must do well in school so that you'll get a good job" or "You must take turns on the slide so the others will be your friends."

When a teacher tells a 5-year-old child not to hit "because it hurts" and the 5-year-old replies, "That's why I hit him," the teacher needs to learn that some lower-class values include "Stand up for yourself," "Fight for your territory," and "Don't ask for help." That teacher cannot rely on reasoning in this case to modify the child's aggressive behavior. A more effective socializing technique in this case might be setting standards with reinforcement for compliance and consequences for noncompliance. In other words, the teacher would tell all the children the standard or expectations in advance, as well as the consequences for deviation. ("We use our words to tell someone our angry feelings" "When I hear words, I will give you a sticker." "We do not hit anyone. If you hit someone, you get a warning; if you hit someone again, you will have to sit in the hall outside the room for five minutes.")

For professionals who work with groups outside their own class experience, the challenge is not to make everyone into upper- or middle-class people, but rather to downplay those aspects of class socialization that hamper personality development (limited language, experiences, and cognitive stimulation) and enhance those aspects of class socialization that make the individual a unique, contributing member of society (helpfulness of kin, responsibilites given to children, ability to cope with adversity).

ETHNIC ORIENTATION

Ethnicity, as discussed earlier, is an attribute of membership in a group in which members continue to identify themselves by national origin, race, or religion. Ethnic distinction can be based on physical and/or cultural attributes. Physical attributes include such things as skin color, body build, and facial features. Cultural attributes include a shared history, language, traditions, rituals, customs, beliefs, attitudes, and values. Ethnic orientation, then, constitutes a macrosystem.

Ethnic groups differ in the way they deal with basic questions of living (Harrison, Wilson, Pine, Chan, & Buriel, 1990). The basic need to eat is universal, but the kind of food one eats and how one eats it are determined by the ethnic group to which one belongs. The basic need of shelter is also universal, but the types of dress and housing depend on the particular culture. Ethnic groups also differ in child-rearing practices—in their methods of socialization of the child. Another variable introduced into families ecologies is the immigration history—which family members came to the United States and when? Which have adopted American values for child rearing, which maintain those of their culture, and which are bicultural (Parke & Buriel, 1998)?

Because children are socialized by various methods of communication and interaction, examining differences in the way parents relate to children provides insight into general socialization outcomes according to ethnic orientation (Greenfield & Suzuki, 1998). For example, a study that compared American and Japanese mother–infant interaction found that American mothers interacted more vocally with their infants than did Japanese mothers. In contrast, Japanese mothers exhibited more body contact with their infants and, in so doing, soothed them into physical quiescence. A comparison of the infants revealed that American infants were more vocal, more active, and more explorative of their environments than were the Japanese infants, who were more passive (Caudill, 1988; Caudill & Weinstein, 1969).

Parents socialize children to encourage the development of those qualities and attributes required for their expected adult roles in their particular society or according to their specific ethnic orientation. To illustrate, in a classic study, Barry, Child, and Bacon (1959) evaluated 104 societies to find out whether the child-rearing practices of parents in industrialized societies, such as the United States, differed from those of parents in agricultural societies, such as India. They found that parents in industrialized societies socialized children for achievement and independence, whereas parents in agricultural societies socialized children for obedience and responsibility. In a recently study examining attitudes toward family obligations, it was found that Asian and Latin American adolescents possessed stronger values and greater expectations regarding their duty to respect and assist their families than their peers with European backgrounds. These differences were large and consistent across socioeconomic status and gender (Fuligni, Tseng, & Lam, 1999).

Another socialization outcome affected by ethnic orientation is the way in which children learn to adapt to their environment. One way of adapting is to be actively independent and struggle to master problems and challenges; another is to be passively obedient, cooperative with others, and accept environmental stresses rather than change them. Socialization outcomes for children are implemented by sleeping arrangements; feeding practices; parenting styles; peer, school, and community experiences, which vary by culture (Greenfield & Suzuki, 1998). For example, an important socialization outcome generally valued by American parents is to guide children to learn to make their own decisions and establish separate individual existences. Children are taught to assert themselves and stand up for their own rights. In contrast, Japanese parents generally value self-control, compliance to adult authority, and cooperation. Children are taught to depend on parents, defer to elders, and sacrifice personal goals for those of the family.

There are many ethnic groups in the United States, and not all have the same status and power as the majority group (white, Anglo Saxon, Protestant), even though equality is an American value. These other ethnic groups are commonly referred to as "minorities," even though, in reality, these groups will soon outnumber Anglo Americans. Being socialized in a family of a different orientation from that of the school, which represents the majority orientation, can be problematic for the child. Table 3.1 outlines some areas of diverse socialization patterns, keeping in mind there is variation within groups. Implications of ethnic orientation for professionals working with children will be discussed later.

Ethnic Norms

Part of one's ethnic orientation involves **norms,** the rules, patterns, or standards that express cultural values and reflect how individuals are supposed to behave. Some dimensions of differing ethnic behavioral patterns were introduced in Chapter 2. This discussion examines ethnic or cultural norms from the perspective of variations in human ways of surviving. In the 1960s, Florence Kluckhohn (1961; Kluckhohn & Strodbeck, 1961) developed a way of analyzing the seemingly limitless variety of cultural lifestyles. She suggested that there are five basic questions that humans in all places and circumstances must answer. These questions greatly help our understanding of ethnic diversity and socialization:

1. *How do humans relate to each other?* Are relationships basically individualistic, where importance is placed on what one accomplishes and on personal rights and freedom? Or is importance placed on belonging to a group (family, peers, community)? The American norm generally, as exemplified by the Bill of Rights, is personal freedom, whereas the Japanese norm generally, as exemplified by family loyalty, is commitment to the group.

2. *What is the significant time dimension?* Is it past, present, or future? Some cultures associate time with religious beliefs; for example, Hispanics generally live each day as it comes, believing that God will provide for the future. Other

Table 3.1	Some Areas of Diverse Socialization Patterns in the U.S.	
SOCIALIZATION AREAS	**MAJORITY ETHNIC ORIENTATION**	**MINORITY ETHNIC ORIENTATION**
Interpersonal relationships	Competition and individual accomplishment; take risks; active learning style	Cooperation and group accomplishment; save face; passive learning style
Orientation toward time	Plan for the future, work and save now for a better future for yourself; efficiency, punctuality, time should not be "wasted"	Focus on the present, trust that the future will be provided for; units of time are undifferentiated; value the past, tradition, and ancestors
Valued person	Busy, materialistic, practical, assertive	Relaxed, spiritual, emotional, quiet
Relationship of humanity to nature	Control nature, use science and technology to "improve" nature	One with nature, respect and live with nature; belief in fate
Most cherished values	Independence, individual freedom, achievement	Dependence, loyalty to the group and tradition

Sources: Kluckhohn (1961), Maehr (1974), and Thiederman (1991).

cultures, such as American and European, generally associate time with progress, and therefore generally plan for the future, even though it may require sacrifice in the present. Still others view the concept of time as subordinate to activities and interactions instead of dominating them. For example, African Americans generally approximate when an event will start or end (the party takes place when everyone gets there), while Anglos generally tend to put events on a precise schedule (the party takes place from 8:00 to 12:00).

3. *What is the valued personality type?* Is it simply "being"? Is it "being in becoming"? Or is it "doing"? Asians generally believe that a person "is being in becoming" in that one's deeds in this life determine the quality of one's next life. Anglos stress generally "doing" to enhance the quality of one's present life.

4. *What is the relationship of humans to nature?* Are humans subjugated to nature? Are humans seen as existing in nature? Do humans have power over nature? Western cultures generally assume nature can be controlled. Examples are our use of pesticides, irrigation, and various technologies that make farming more efficient. Other cultures, such as Native American, however, are generally taught that land and all that grows is only lent to be cared for and shared, not exploited.

5. *What are the innate predispositions of humans?* Are they evil? Neither good nor bad? Good? If one believes humans are essentially bad, one assumes the child's will must be broken and tends to use punitive and controlling measures to

The physical closeness between father and child is important to foster attachment and interdependence.

socialize the child, as was done by Calvinist and Puritan parents, for example. If one believes humans are neither good nor bad, one assumes the child can be molded and shaped by experiences provided by the adult. This philosophy was advocated by British philosopher, John Locke (1632–1704). If one believes humans are essentially good, one assumes the child will seek out appropriate experiences and develop accordingly. Jean Jacques Rousseau (1712–1778), a French philosopher, advocated such a belief.

RELIGIOUS ORIENTATION

Religion is a "unified system of beliefs and practices relative to sacred things, uniting into a single moral community all those who adhere to those beliefs and practices" (Durkheim, 1947, p. 47). Understanding some basic purposes of religion also helps us be more sensitive to diversity.

Over 85% of the population in the United States and Canada identify with one of five major faiths: Protestant (58%), Catholic (25%), Jewish (2%), Latter-Day Saints (2%), and Orthodox (1%) (Gollnick & Chinn, 1998). While these religious groups share the same Old Testament heritage, their interpretations and beliefs differ. Other major world religions found in the United States include Islam, Buddhism, and Hinduism.

Religion is a macrosystem in that it influences patterns of gender roles, sexual behavior, marriage, divorce, birthrates, morals, attitudes, and child rearing. It also may affect one's dress, dietary habits including alcohol consumption, health care, and social interactions including ethics (Gollnick & Chinn, 1998).

At birth, children are inducted into their family's religion, often in a public naming ceremony. The family's religious beliefs determine what is selected from the environment to transmit to the child. The family also interprets and evaluates what is transmitted. For example, Roman Catholics believe in strict obedience to authority and do not believe in divorce or birth control. Thus children from Roman Catholic families are brought up to obey their parents and the church. They are also reared to believe in the sanctity of marriage and to believe that sex is for producing children.

Not only does religion influence families and their socialization of children, but it influences the community as well, in respect to values and behavior. The most dominant religious group in the United States (Protestants) has undoubtedly influenced the political and economic foundations of our country (Weber, 1930). The **Protestant Ethic** is a religiously derived value system that defines the ideal person as individualistic, thrifty, self-sacrificing, efficient in use of time, strong in personal responsibility, and committed to productivity. By following this value system, believers feel one can reach salvation. An example of the Protestant Ethic's influence on politics is welfare reform—laws passed to require welfare recipients to work after a certain amount of time receiving government assistance. Some religious groups get members elected to government offices and school boards to influence policies, such as abortion laws, school prayer, and evolution curriculum.

Functions of Religion

Generally, religion provides people with "a way of facing the problems of ultimate and unavoidable frustration, of 'evil,' and the generalized problem of meaning in some non-empirical sense, of finding some ultimate why" (Williams, 1960b, p. 327).

A Bar Mitzvah celebrates this 13-year-old boy's studies of Jewish history, culture, and prayer.

Every religion includes some beliefs that are shared by all its adherents. For example, Judaism teaches that a "good life" can be led only in a community; good Jews must always view their actions in terms of their effect on others. They believe in responsibility for others and regard charity as a virtue. Muslims give a percentage of their annual income to the poor. The ultimate goal of Buddhism is to be fully in the world and relate compassionately to others.

Most religions provide an ideology that enables individuals to comprehend events that happen to them; death, illness, financial crises, and injustices all make sense if these are seen as part of a divine plan. Religion helps fill the gap between scientific and technical knowledge and the unknown.

Religious beliefs and practices help individuals accept and cope with crises without overwhelming psychological costs. For example, prayer helps people feel that they are "doing something" to meet the crisis. If the crisis is resolved, the individual's faith in prayer is confirmed. If the crisis is not resolved, the individual can explain the outcome as part of God's plan. Thus one can avoid feeling that life's catastrophes are senseless.

Most religions have beliefs about death. Some preach hell for those who transgress in life on Earth and heaven for those who lead a good life. The hope of a blissful immortality makes the death of a loved one more tolerable and the thought of one's own death less terrifying.

Religion helps people establish an identity and gives meaning to their lives. Many religious activities reflect pride and celebration. Religious rituals symbolize faith, honor God, or serve to remind members of the group of their religious responsibilities. Rituals may include observing holidays, saying prayers, tithing, handling sacred objects, wearing certain clothing, and eating certain food (or fasting). For example, Holy Communion commemorates the climactic meal of Jesus' life and his sacrifice for humankind. In partaking of the holy bread and wine, the communicant partakes of Christ.

Carl Jung (1938) wrote that religion provides individuals who have a strong commitment to traditional norms and values with moral strength and behavioral stability. In other words, religious people are more likely to comply with societal norms, especially if they believe those norms are divinely sanctioned. They look upon social deviance as a form of religious deviance. This was confirmed via research (Gorsuch, 1976; Hassett, 1981) showing that moral behavior was consistently related to religious commitment.

How has your ethnic and religious heritage influenced your values, morals, attitudes, and behavior?

Epilogue

There are many types of family systems that are subsystems of larger contexts, or macrosystems, including history, politics, economics, and culture. Macrosystem values, such as obligation to self or others, affects family functions.

Changes in the family system affect child outcomes, which are bidirectional. Families can meet the challenge of adapting to societal change through love and acceptance, communicativeness, cohesiveness, communication of values and standards, and the ability to cope with problems.

SUMMARY

The family is viewed as a system affected by external and internal factors. The classic definition of the family is "a social group characterized by common residence, economic cooperation, and reproduction. It includes adults of both sexes, at least two of whom maintain a socially approved sexual relationship and one or more children, biological or adopted, of the sexually cohabiting adults." The current definition of the family is "any two or more related persons by birth, marriage, or adoption who reside together." Thus the concept of family has changed.

The basic structures of a family are the nuclear and the extended family. A nuclear family consists of husband, wife, and children. An extended family consists of kin related to the nuclear family, who are emotionally, and perhaps economically, dependent upon each other. Extended families can be matriarchal, patriarchal, or egalitarian.

In general, the family's basic functions are reproduction, socialization/education, assignment of social roles, economic support, and nurturance/emotional support. Functional families maintain resilience and adaptability; dysfunctional families are at risk for break up or problems.

Families have changed in their economic function, their socialization/educational function, and their nurturance/support function.

The demography of the family has changed from past generations. Not as many people reside in the household, and families are producing fewer children.

The roles of women, men, and children have changed in the family. Authority patterns in the family have changed, too. Traditionally, families were patriarchal; the father was the recognized legal authority. Today, families are egalitarian. Single-parent families headed by the mother are matriarchal. Single-parent families headed by the father are patriarchal.

The functions remaining for the contemporary U.S. family are economic support, socialization/education, nurturance/support, and assignment of social roles. Other agents in society have taken over some of the previous family responsibilities, such as economic production, formal education, and health/elderly care. The contemporary family functions as a managerial unit rather than as a self-sufficient production unit. To be effective management units, families need to be empowered, enabled to have control over resources affecting them.

Family changes affect children. One impact of change is stress, which can come from loss of stability, fragmentation, role overload, and unrealistic expectations of family life.

Evidence of the impact of family change on children is the increase in the number of divorces. The proportion of children living with one parent has increased as well. All children do not react to divorce the same way—personalities involved, coping skills, parents' relations with their children, age and gender of the child, and availability of others for support are all factors that influence the reaction to the divorce. Divorce affects the custodial parent, too—responsibilities double, and stress increases. Joint-custody arrangements may give the children access to both parents, but may also cause confusion.

Grandparent custody is another arrangement affecting children, especially in regard to their sense of belonging and stability. Community support is beneficial.

Another evidence of the impact of family change is the increase in the number of remarriages. The impact of remarriage on a family is stressful. Children in a stepfamily have to form new relationships and accept new rules and new values, while still having to deal with the old relationships, rules, and values. Reestablishing an effective functioning family system is a challenge.

Homosexual families, on the increase, can influence children if they become concerned about their identities. How the community responds is also a factor in a child's development.

Still, other evidence of the impact of family change is the increase in the number of mothers employed outside the home. The age, gender, and temperament of the child, the socioeconomic status of the family, the quality of the parental marriage, the mother's satisfaction with her job, the father's satisfaction with his job, and the father's involvement with the children as well as availability of quality child care are factors determining the effects of maternal employment.

Certain characteristics of families influence socialization—socioeconomic status, ethnic orientation, and religious orientation.

Most societies are stratified. In traditional societies, status is usually ascribed; in modern societies, status is usually achieved. One's status or social class influences how one is socialized. The different socioeconomic classes rear children differently; academic performance and behavior are affected.

Ethnicity involves identification with a group based on national origin, race, or religion. Ethnic attributes can be physical, cultural, or both. Members of an ethnic group share a history, language, and set of traditions, rituals, customs, beliefs, attitudes, and values.

People with diverse ethnic orientations differ in the ways they deal with basic questions of living, which affects socialization and consequent behavior patterns.

Religion is a unified system of beliefs and practices relative to sacred things, uniting into a single moral community all those who adhere to those beliefs and practices. At birth, children are inducted into their family's religion, which influences the family's socialization practices. Religion provides an ideology that enables individuals to comprehend events that happen to them and gives them an identity and a support system for traditional norms and values.

ACTIVITY

Purpose: To understand the influence of certain family characteristics on socialization and development.

1. Of what socioeconomic status was your family of orientation? Upon what criteria did you base your answer?

2. List the values, beliefs, or attitudes supported by your ethnic group.

3. List the values, beliefs, or attitudes supported by your religion.

4. What were some stresses your family of orientation experienced, and how did your family cope?

5. What were three socialization goals communicated by your family of orientation? (Were they successful or unssucessful?)

6. List three goals you have for yourself.

7. List three goals you have for your family of procreation.

8. Is there any connection between your family of orientation's socialization goals and your goals for your family of procreation?

RESOURCES

National Parent Information
Network/ERIC
http://www.ericpsed.uiuc.edu/npin/
npinhome.htm/

Stepfamily Association of America
http://www.stepfam.org/

U.S. Department of Labor
http://www.dol.gov

Families and Work Institute
http://www.familiesandworkinst.org/

RELATED READINGS

Arms, K. G., Davidson, J. K., & Moore, N. B. (1992). *Cultural diversity and families*. Dubuque, IA: Brown & Benchmark.

Barnett, R. C., & Rivers, C. (1996). *She works; he works*. Cambridge, MA: Harvard University Press.

Blankenhorn, D. (1995). *Fatherless America*. New York: Basic Books.

Bria, G. (1998). *The art of family: Rituals, imagination, and everyday spirituality*. New York: Dell.

Coleman, M., & Ganong, L. (1994). *Remarried family relationships*. Newbury Park, CA: Sage.

Coontz, S. (1997). *The way we really are: Coming to terms with America's changing families*. New York: Basic Books.

Cummings, E. M., & Davies, P. (1994). *Children and marital conflict. The impact of family dispute and resolution*. New York: Guilford Press.

Elkind, D. (1994). *Ties that stress: The new family imbalance*. Cambridge, MA: Harvard University Press.

Francke, L. B. (1983). *Growing up divorced*. New York: Fawcett Crest.

Furstenberg, F. F., & Cherlin, A. J. (1991). *Divided families: What happens to children when parents part*. Cambridge, MA: Harvard University Press.

Gilbert, D., & Kahn, J. A. (1987). *The American class structure: A new synthesis* (3rd ed.). Chicago: Dorsey Press.

Griswold, R. L. (1994). *Fatherhood in America: A history.* New York: Basic Books.

Hareven, T. (1999). *Families, history, and social change: Life course and cross-cultural perspectives*. Boulder, CO: Westview Press.

Hetherington, E. M. (Ed.). (1999). *Coping with divorce, single parenting, and remarriage: A risk and resiliency perspective*. Mahwah, NJ: Erlbaum.

Kornhaber, K., & Forsythe, K. (1995). *Grandparent power: How to strengthen the vital connection among grandparents, parents, and children*. New York: Crown.

Lerner, J. (1994). *Working women and their families*. Newbury Park, CA: Sage.

Martin, A. (1993). *Lesbian and gay parenting handbook: Creating and raising our families*. New York: HarperCollins.

Mason, M. A. (1998). *The custody wars: Why children are losing the legal battle—and what we can do about it*. New York: Basic Books.

McAdoo, H. P. (Ed.). (1993). *Family ethnicity: Strength in diversity*. Newbury Park, CA: Sage.

Stinnett, N., & Defrain, J. (1985). *Secrets of strong families*. Boston: Little, Brown.

Visher, E., & Visher, J. (1979). *Stepfamilies: A guide to working with stepparents and stepchildren*. New York: Brunner/Mazel.

Wallerstein, J. S., & Kelly, J. B. (1996). *Surviving the breakup*. New York: Basic Books.

Whitehead, B. F. (1996). *The divorce culture: Rethinking our commitments to marriage and family*. New York: Vintage Books.

Wilson, J. (1978). *Religion in American society: The effective presence*. Englewood Cliffs, NJ: Prentice-Hall.

"You are the bows from which your children as living arrows are sent forth."

— *Kahlil Gibran*

ECOLOGY OF PARENTING

Prologue

MATERIALISTIC MAYHEM

An ancient Greek myth tells of a very rich king whose name was Midas. He was fonder of gold than of anything else in the whole world, except perhaps his young golden-haired daughter, Marygold. As a parent, he thought the best thing he could do for his beloved child would be to bequeath her the largest pile of yellow glistening coins that had ever been heaped together since time began. Whenever he saw the gold-tinted clouds of a sunset, or yellow dandelions in the fields, or orange roses growing in his garden, he wished they would turn into gold coins.

He became so obsessed with his desire to possess gold that he forgot the reason why he wanted it was to show his love for his daughter concretely. One day while he was in his treasure room admiring his gold collection, a stranger dressed all in white appeared.

"You are indeed a wealthy man, King Midas," observed the stranger.

"Yes," said the king, "but think how much more gold is out there in the world."

"Are you not satisfied?" asked the stranger.

"No, of course not. I often lie awake at night planning of new ways to get more gold. Sometimes I even wish that everything I touch would turn to gold."

"Do you really wish that, King Midas?"

"Yes, nothing would make me happier."

"Then you shall have your wish. Tomorrow when the sun rises, you shall have the golden touch," proclaimed the stranger. And with that, he vanished.

Midas thought he had dreamed the whole encounter, but went to sleep that night hoping it was true. When he awoke the next morning and touched his slippers, they turned to gold! Excitedly, he began touching things in his room; they all turned to gold.

He looked out the window at the garden where his daughter Marygold loved to play and ran outside to touch all the flowers. "Won't Marygold be happy," he thought. When Marygold saw the garden, she cried. "I won't be able to smell the flowers anymore; I won't be able to play in the garden, either!"

Not knowing how to comfort her, King Midas ordered breakfast be served. However, as soon as Midas's lips touched the food, it turned to gold. He sputtered and spat. Marygold, thinking her father had burned his mouth, went to hug him, but alas, as her arms went about his chest, she, too, turned to gold.

King Midas began to sob; his beloved daughter was now a statue who couldn't laugh, or play, or kiss him. He had robbed her of her essence.

The stranger appeared again and asked, "Are you happy now King Midas?"

"How can I be happy? I am miserable. I can't eat, I can't smell, I can't touch my daughter . . ."

"But you have the Golden Touch . . ."

"Please give me back my little Marygold and I'll give up all the gold I have. I've lost all that was worth having."

"You have become wise," said the stranger. "Go plunge in the river and take from it water to sprinkle on whatever you wish to transform."

Midas learned that being the best parent to his daughter did not mean giving her all the gold in the world. Such materialism only served to turn her into a material being herself; and statues have no spirit.

Centuries later, other parents thought they were doing the best for their daughter by encouraging her to compete for materialistic things. As Midas collected gold for his daughter, John and Patricia Ramsey collected competitive opportunities for theirs. Jon Benet Ramsey, age 6, was a beauty pageant star. The parenting style of her parents came to the attention of the media in 1996 because their daughter was found murdered in their Colorado home on Christmas morning.

Photos of Jon Benet in her beauty pageant attire and makeup led the public to believe her parents had created a seductress, but did her parents kill her? If so, why? If not, who did? That Jon Benet was part of the adult world of vanity, competition, and consumerism leads one to suspect some malicious motive.

Even if the Ramseys did not kill their daughter, many say they killed her childhood. Did they push on her their values of fame and fortune as King Midas did to Marygold? Was their parenting style pressured by a society that values appearances and material wealth? Unfortunately, unlike Midas, they did not get the chance to reevaluate. ■

- *Where do we get our values and information about how we should parent?*
- *What is a "good" parent (in terms of society, the child, the self)?*

PARENTING

As a complement to Chapter 3, this chapter explores a major task of families, which is the physical protection, emotional nurturing, and socialization of children—commonly referred to as parenting. Parenting is a relationship that unfolds over time (Bornstein, 1995).

Parenting, according to developmental psychologist Jerome Kagan (1975), means implementing a series of decisions about the socialization of your children—what you do to enable them to become responsible, contributing members of society, as well as what you do when they cry, are aggressive, lie, or do not do well in school. Parents sometimes find these decisions overwhelming. One of the reasons parenting can be confusing is that there is little consensus in the United States today as to what children should be like when they grow up or what you do to get them there. Another reason parenting is confusing is that it is *bidirectional* and *dynamic*—an adult's behavior toward a child is often a reaction to that child's behavior, changing with time (Lerner, 1998). Thus, by influencing adults, children influence their own development. Causes for behavior are viewed from a circular rather than a linear perspective (Cowan, Powell, & Cowan, 1998). The concept of the bidirectionality of parenting is exemplified throughout the chapter.

While *parenthood* is universal, *parenting* is highly variable among societies. We will examine how parenting styles in the United States have evolved and compare them to parenting styles in other cultures.

Figure 4.1   An Ecological Model of Human Development

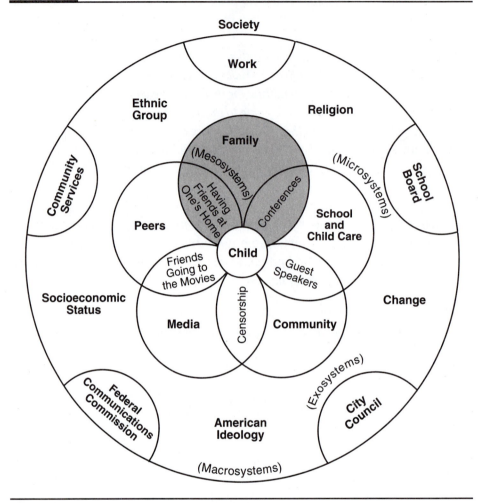

Parenting is the means by which the family socializes the child.

PARENTING AND TRADITION

Fifty years ago, parenting decisions were easier to make because it was assumed that one's main purpose in life was to serve God by being faithful and following the teachings of one's religion. Children were constantly exhorted to overcome their base natures in order to please God (Spock, 1968).

In some countries one's purpose in life was held to be to serve one's country—for example, in France under Napoleon Bonaparte and in Germany under Hitler. This still holds true today in China! Parents and teachers are expected to agree with the country's leaders about what values and attitudes to instill in children.

In other places in the world it is assumed that children are born and raised to serve the purposes of the family—for example, in rural India: Children are trained to work at jobs considered of value to their particular family; children defer to their elders and marriages are often arranged for the benefit of the family.

In the United States few children are brought up to believe that their principal destiny is to serve their family, their country, or God. American children are generally given the feeling that they are free to set their own goals in life. However, ethnic groups in the United States that subscribe to the value of interdependence bring up their children to be obligated to their families (Fuligni, Tseng, & Lam, 1999). Political ideology influences parenting styles in that children must be raised to function as citizens. Most traditional societies subscribe to an aristocratic political ideology. In an **autocracy** one person has unlimited power over others. Many modern societies subscribe to a democratic political ideology. In a **democracy,** those ruled have power equal to those who rule; the principle is equality of rights. In an autocracy relationships between people are understood in terms of a pecking order. The autocratic traditional family system follows the order. The father is the authority who has power over the mother and the children. Women and children have few rights. In a democracy, relationships between people are based on consensus and compromise. The democratic modern family system considers the rights of all members.

PARENTING AND CHANGE

As U.S. society has undergone social and economic change, people have questioned the inadequate implementation of democratic ideals written in the Constitution, particularly those regarding equality. In the 1960s, people were especially concerned with unfair opportunities for ethnic minorities and women. As a result, the Civil Rights Act of 1964 was passed, which required that ethnic minorities and women be treated equally in housing, education, and employment. Similar legislation was extended to individuals with disabilities in 1990. Such legislation has had beneficial economic effects in terms of opportunities to earn a living, as well as beneficial psychological effects on minorities' self-concept.

The notion that unlimited authority is no longer appropriate in U.S. society, because it is incongruent with democracy, has filtered down to children. Parents find it difficult to raise children by the "do it because I said so" method. Also, children learn democratic ideals in school and from the media, so they are not willing to be ruled autocratically. Appropriate child rearing in a democratic society becomes a challenge, especially for parents who were raised autocratically.

Parenting today raises new questions that previous generations seldom had to face. Should we have children? How many and how far apart? Abort the unexpected or the imperfect? Should we be strict or permissive? Should we stress competitiveness or cooperation? What activities should be encouraged? Because society is changing so rapidly and because of new advancements in science and technology, parents cannot look to experience for answers as their parents could.

Several social scientists (Bronfenbrenner, 1986; Hewlett & West, 1998) are concerned that a number of developments—many themselves beneficent—have conspired to isolate the family and to reduce drastically the number of relatives, neighbors, and other caring adults who used to share in the socialization of American children. Among the most significant forces are occupational mobility, the breakdown of neighborhoods, the separation of residential from business areas, consolidated school districts, separate patterns of social life for different age groups, and the delegation of child care to outside institutions. What today's parents lack is a support system.

Because of the nature of today's rapidly changing society, parents spend less time with their children. A majority of mothers hold jobs outside the home. Fathers often must travel in connection with their work and are away for days or even weeks at a time. Parents may have meetings to attend in the evenings and social engagements on the weekends. Various studies found that lack of time together is perceived as the greatest threat to the family (Hochschild, 1997; Leach, 1994).

Due to the changing nature of society and its pressures on the ability of the family to function optimally, parenting today has become a "journey without a road map."

PARENTING AS AN EVOLVING SYSTEM

Parenting involves a continuous process of interaction that affects both the parents and the children. When one becomes a parent, one rediscovers some of one's own experiences in childhood and adolescence—for example, making snowmen, playing hopscotch, playing hide-and-seek, and running through the sprinklers on a hot day. When one becomes a parent, one's experience is expanded. Not only do children have a unique way of looking at the world (for example, they believe the moon follows them at night when they go for a ride in the car, that dreams come through the window when they are sleeping, and that you can walk on clouds); they also open new doors for parents. My son became interested in astronomy and opened up a world of telescopes, stars, planets, and galaxies to our family. My daughter became interested in running and opened up a world of track-and-field events to us. When children bring their work home from school, new information, ideas, and values are shared with their parents.

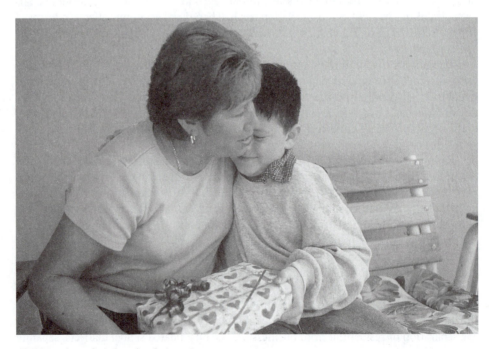

Children show their love by their actions.

Like a game involving strategies and counterstrategies, parenting requires continual adaptation to children's changing capacities. As children grow, parents need to adapt to the increased amount of time they are awake. As children learn to walk, parents need to set limits for their safety. When the child goes to school, decisions have to be made about achievement, friends, television, activities outside of school, and so on. When the child approaches adolescence, parenting involves determining which decisions are to remain the parents' and which are to be assumed by the adolescent.

Parenting is time-consuming and difficult; it is also joyful and satisfying. Children are loving, open, and curious. What could be more gratifying than the first handmade card your child gives you that says "I luv u," or when your grown up-child asks for your advice?

MACROSYSTEM INFLUENCES ON PARENTING IN THE UNITED STATES

The purpose of examining the macrosystem influences on parenting is to provide an understanding of historical, cultural, political, and economic values, that indirectly, have contributed to U.S. children's socialization and development.

HISTORY

Prior to the eighteenth century, it was not uncommon for children to be considered significant only if they contributed to their elders' welfare; no thought was given to their individual needs. If parents could not afford to care for them, they could be abandoned. Parenting was adult-centered.

Beginning in the eighteenth century, there was some improvement in the way children were treated. Contributing to this reform was the reexamination of the writings of Locke, Rousseau, and Pestalozzi, who all advocated **humanism,** a system of beliefs concerned with the interests and ideals of humans rather than those of the natural or spiritual world (Berger, 1995). Specifically, British philosopher John Locke's (1632–1704) best-known concept was that a newborn's mind is a blank slate **(tabula rasa)** and that all thought develops from experience. Children are neither innately good nor innately bad. The influence of this concept on contemporary parenting has been to encourage parents and teachers to mold children's minds by providing them with optimal experiences.

During the eighteenth century in colonial America, children were needed to do the endless chores. The father was the primary authority. Children were to be seen and not heard; immediate obedience was expected. Discipline was strict; those who disobeyed were believed to be wicked and sinful and were severely punished. Tradition and religion influenced child-rearing practices: "He that spareth his rod, hateth his son: but he that loveth him chasteneth him betimes" (Proverbs, 13:24). "Train up a child in the way he should go: and when he is old, he will not depart from it" (Proverbs 22:6). There was also much emphasis on manners and courtesy (Berger, 1995). Early Americans viewed early childhood "as a negative period of life, a sort of necessary evil full of idle deviltry and cantankerous mischief; the child survived it and his parents endured it as best they could until late adolescence, when life hesitatingly began" (Bossard & Boll, 1954, p. 526). Childhood was regarded as a foundation period of great importance, a period of bending the twig to affect the shape of the future tree.

Parenting has also been influenced by French philosopher Jean Jacques Rousseau (1712–1778), who believed children are innately good and need freedom to grow because an insensitive caregiver might otherwise corrupt them. Rousseau's writings influenced Johann Pestalozzi (1746–1827), who emphasized the importance of the mother as the child's first teacher. The mother is more likely than other adults to be sensitive to her child's needs. That the mother was most important in the upbringing of the child was corroborated by Robert Sunley's (1955) analysis of child-rearing literature from nineteenth-century magazines, books, and journals.

Another influence on contemporary attitudes about child development and parenting was psychologist G. Stanley Hall (1846–1924) who, like Rousseau, believed that young children are innately good and will grow naturally to be self-controlled adults, if not overdirected (Berger, 1995). This idea influenced many contemporary attitudes on child development and parenting. Parenting was becoming child-centered. Unlike the traditional emphasis on the needs of the parent, contemporary ideas of child rearing place paramount importance on the individual needs and welfare of the child. However, parents still directed the child-rearing practices.

Although at the end of the nineteenth century, parenting literature was espousing love and affection for children in order to mold their characters, at the beginning of the twentieth century, the discipline method advocated to mold character involved rewards and punishment. *Infant Care*, published in 1914 by the Children's Bureau, recommended strict child rearing. For example, thumb-sucking and masturbation were believed to damage the child permanently (Wolfenstein, 1953). At the beginning of the twentieth century, the parenting literature advocated rigid scheduling of infants. Mothers were told to expect obedience, ignore temper tantrums, and restrict physical handling of their children (Stendler, 1950).

In the 1920s, the influences of John B. Watson's theory of **behaviorism,** which holds that only observable behavior is valid data for psychology, and Sigmund Freud's theory of personality development, which dealt with nonobservable (unconscious) forces in the mind, began to appear in books and magazines. Watson's theoretical view defined learning as a change in the way one responds to a particular situation: behavior that is reinforced or rewarded will be repeated; behavior that is not reinforced will be extinguished or eliminated. Both Watson and Freud believed in the importance of the early years in setting the stage for later development. Watson believed in the importance of firmness early in a child's life, because behavior is conditioned by specific stimuli; if parents give in to bad behavior, that bad behavior persists. Thus good habits must be conditioned from the beginning. Freud believed that harmful early experiences can harm children's development (especially when these are buried in the unconscious mind); that **fixations,** or arrested development, can occur at any time in life; and that children's growing personalities must therefore not be repressed, or else children will be inevitably marked as adults. The scientific methods described by Watson gave credibility to behaviorism. Freud's writings regarding the need to express—rather than repress—emotions were also extremely influential.

In the 1940s, mothers were told that children should be fed when hungry and be toilet trained when they developed physical control. This was very different from the rigid scheduling of feeding and toilet training previously advocated. Even handling of

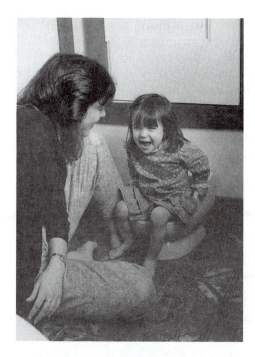

Behavior, like using the toilet, that is reinforced will be repeated.

genitals was considered natural, whereas years before parents were warned to take every precaution to prevent it (Wolfenstein, 1953). Benjamin Spock, in the 1946 edition of *The Common Sense Book of Baby and Child Care,* advised parents to enjoy their children and their roles as parents. He advocated self-regulation by the child rather than strict scheduling by the parents. Spock wanted to encourage parents to have a greater understanding of children and to be more flexible in directing their upbringing. He based his recommendations on the writings of educators such as John Dewey (who believed children should learn by doing) and psychoanalysts such as Sigmund Freud (who believed children's psychological development occurred in natural stages and that healthy outcomes were influenced by parents).

Bigner (1979) analyzed the child-rearing literature in several women's magazines from 1950 to 1970. He found that in the early 1950s physical punishment, spanking, was condoned, but by the end of that decade it was discouraged on the ground that physical punishment does no more than show a child that a parent can hit. Most articles encouraged self-regulation by the child. Parents were advised to hold, love, and enjoy their children and to emphasize the importance of children feeling loved. Parents were also urged to recognize individual differences, to realize that development is natural, for maturation cannot be pushed. Arnold Gesell's (Gesell & Ilg, 1943) extensive work influenced this view. He published norms, or average standards, of child development based on observations of children of all ages, and concluded that the patterns for healthy growth were biologically programmed within the child and that if the parents would relax, growth would occur naturally.

Toward the end of the 1950s, after the Soviet Union's successful launching of the first satellite into space, the concern for intellectual development in children became urgent. Jean Piaget's theories on cognitive development were of interest to professionals working with children. He emphasized that knowledge comes from acting in one's environment. Thus the importance of giving children a stimulating environment and many experiences was reinforced.

The movement from a *parent-centered* approach to child rearing, with its strict discipline, to a more *child-centered* approach, with more flexibility, is partially the result of parents turning to the mass media, which publicized scientific and humanitarian views on child rearing. It is interesting to note that Spock revised the 1946 edition of his book on child care, which advocated a child-centered approach, to reflect a change in his attitude. The 1957 edition read, "nowadays there seems to be more chance of a conscientious parent's getting into trouble with permissiveness than with strictness" (Spock, 1957). Spock realized the consequences of parents focusing exclusively on what children need from them, rather than what the community will need from children when they grow up. Even though Spock continued to maintain his belief that children's needs should be attended to, subsequent editions of his book addressed the rights of parents—children need to feel loved, yet parents have the right to demand certain standards of behavior (Spock, 1968, 1985).

In sum, the trend in parenting attitudes in the United States over time has swung from *parent-centeredness* to *child-centeredness* to more of a *balanced* approach.

CULTURE

Like historical events, the culture or ethnic group one grows up in has indirect effects on parenting attitudes and consequent parenting styles (Parke & Buriel, 1998). To illustrate, Garcia-Coll (1990) reviewed the literature on cultural beliefs and care-giving practices and concluded that parenting goals and techniques depend to some extent on the nature of the tasks that adults are expected to perform or competencies that adults are supposed to possess in a given population. For example, in the United States adults are expected to read, write, compute, and be economically self-sufficient. American children are thus expected to achieve in school, are given an allowance to learn the value of money, and are pressured to get a job at least by the time they finish their schooling. In the Fiji Islands, however, adults are expected to farm, fish, and be able to make economic exchanges with relatives on the bigger islands (West, 1988). Fijian children are thus expected to relate to others in the community, to learn to help adults work, and to share resources.

LeVine (1977, 1988) proposes that there are universal parenting goals. They involve

1. ensuring physical health and survival,
2. developing behavioral capacities for economic self-maintenance, and
3. instilling behavioral capacities for maximizing cultural values, such as morality, prestige, and achievement.

However, cultures vary on the importance they place on these goals as well as how they implement them. Also, if one goal is threatened, it becomes the foremost concern and overrides the need to implement the others. To illustrate, if a society has a high rate of infant mortality, parents will concentrate more on the goal of physical health and survival; the pursuit of learning to participate economically and learning cultural values will be postponed until a later age, when the child's survival is relatively certain. Societies with bare resources for subsistence place emphasis on training children in skills that will be economically advantageous in adulthood, thereby minimizing survival risks. Once society has tested and adopted various methods for survival, these methods become part of the folk tradition and get passed on to children.

How various cultures prioritize these universal parenting goals may explain differences in maternal behavior toward infants (Richman, LeVine, New, & Howrigan, 1988). For example, the Gusii of Kenya prioritize the parenting goal of physical health and survival. They interpret holding the child as a form of protection from physical hazards such as cooking fires and domestic animals, and have no alternatives like cradle boards, playpens, or infant seats. The Gusii mothers also soothe their infants through rapid physical comforting when they cry. This close physical contact enables the mother to know when her baby is becoming sick as opposed to being hungry or temporarily distressed because a sick baby will not be comforted by physical contact or food.

For another example, American mothers prioritize the parenting goal of developing capacities for economic self-maintenance. They verbalize with and gaze at their infants more frequently than do the Gusii. This reflects the belief that infants can communicate socially. By the time the American infant can walk, holding declines rapidly; infant seats, playpens, and high chairs are used to protect the locomotive infant from harm. This reduction in human physical contact reflects the value Americans put on separateness and independence.

POLITICAL/SOCIOECONOMIC SYSTEM

Cultural anthropologists Beatrice Whiting and John Whiting (1975) wanted to see the relationship between the political/socioeconomic system of the society, the structure of the family, and parenting styles. Did the way the society governed and supported itself to survive relate to the way it reared its children?

The Whitings classified the socioeconomic system as simple or complex. Simple societies had economies based on subsistence gardening. Roles for men, women, and children were clearly defined, and emphasis was placed on cooperation in order to survive. Complex societies, on the other hand, had economies based on occupational specialization. There was a class system and centralized government, and competition was emphasized. Family structure was classified as extended or nuclear, depending on whether there were specified relations with kin or whether the family was free to do "its own thing."

The Whitings observed the behavior of 134 children between the ages of 3 and 11 in Kenya, the Philippines, Mexico (representing simple socioeconomic systems); and Okinawa, India, and the United States (representing complex socioeconomic systems). The categories of social behavior that were found in the children of all six cultures, in varying degrees, included nurturance, responsibility, dependence, dominance, sociability, intimacy, authoritarianism, and aggressiveness. Since some of these categories consistently occurred together in the six cultures, they were organized into two dimensions in order to investigate the effect of culture on the social behavior of children. One dimension of behavioral categories was *nurturant–responsible* (offered help, offered support, suggested responsibility) versus *dependent–dominant* (sought help, sought attention, sought dominance). The other dimension was *sociable–intimate* (acted sociably, teased sociably, touched) versus *authoritarian–aggressive* (reprimanded, assaulted).

The societies having a relatively simple socioeconomic structure with little or no occupational specialization, no class or caste system, a localized, kin-based political structure, and no professional priesthood had children who were more *nurturant–responsible* and less *dependent–dominant*. The societies having a more complex socioeconomic structure, characterized by occupational specialization, social stratification, a central government, and a priesthood, had children who scored low on *nurturance–responsibility* but high on *dependence–dominance*.

The children of societies whose family structure was nuclear and egalitarian scored high on *sociability–intimacy* and low on *authoritarianism–aggressiveness*. The children of societies whose family structure was based on the extended family and was patriarchal scored high on *authoritarianism–aggressiveness* and low on *sociability–intimacy* (*see* Figure 4.2).

> Formulas for appropriate adult social behavior dictated by the socioeconomic and family system are embedded in the value system of the culture. Nurturance and responsibility, success, authority, and casual intimacy are types of behavior that are differentially preferred by different cultures. These values are apparently transmitted to the children before the age of six (Whiting & Whiting, 1975, pp. 178–179).

Thus the social behavior of the children of each culture type was found to be compatible with the adult role requirements of the society. In societies based on a simple socioeconomic structure, reciprocity among kin and neighbors is essential. People offer help and support to one another; dominance and attention-seeking are frowned upon. In societies based on a more complex socioeconomic structure, dominance and attention-seeking are behaviors that may enhance a person's chance to rise in social status; help and support of others are regarded as counterproductive.

In societies having a patrilineal, extended family system, the male head of the family must exercise authority over the family members. He must be able to express aggression when necessary, a skill learned in reprimanding younger siblings during childhood. In societies having a nuclear, neolocal (newlyweds set up a new place or residence)

Figure 4.2   Relationship between Sociocultural Characteristics and Socialized Behavior

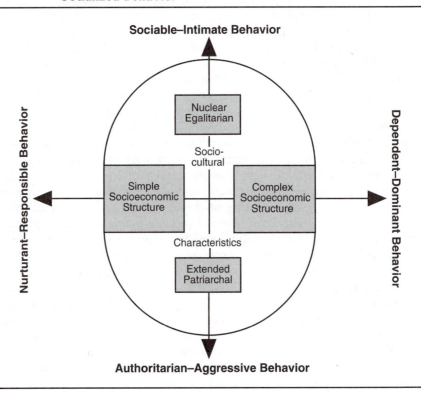

In some cultures, children are given important responsibilities that contribute to the welfare of the family.

family system, authoritarianism and aggressiveness are not as necessary as sociability and intimacy.

Whiting and Edwards (1988) examined the ideologies of six cultures in regard to expectations of children by age and gender. The social behavior of girls and boys age 2 to 10 who lived in communities in India, Okinawa, the Philippines, Mexico, Kenya, and the United States was investigated: With whom did the children interact? Did they go to school, or did they have responsibilities at home? What activities occupied their time—caring for siblings, doing errands, or playing?

It was discovered that different societies varied their expectations of behavior according to age. In some societies, 6-year-olds were expected to learn the ways of their ideology by taking on household responsibilities and caring for younger siblings, whereas in others, 6-year-olds were expected to go to school. Different societies also varied their expectations of behavior according to gender. Some societies had different ideologies for boys and girls, and assigned children to settings or activities accordingly. Boys were allowed more autonomy and expected to exhibit more dominant behavior with others; girls were kept in close proximity and expected to engage in more nurturing activities with younger siblings.

PARENTAL SOCIOECONOMIC STATUS

A family's socioeconomic status is based on the parents' income, occupation, and education. In general, parents of a high-socioeconomic status have high incomes, highly respected occupations, and are well educated; parents of a low-socioeconomic status have low incomes, unskilled or semiskilled jobs, and are poorly educated; parents of a middle socioeconomic status have medium incomes, business or professional occupations, and a good education. It must be remembered that not all families can be classified according to the criteria discussed here; some parents are very well educated and have very low incomes (graduate students, for example), and some parents have very high incomes and are not well educated (some businesspersons, for example). Also, there is as much variation within socioeconomic status groups as between them. For example, in a study of lower-class, blue-collar families, LeMasters (1988) found that fathers had different ideas about raising their children, especially their sons, than did the mothers. According to the blue-collar fathers in the study, to become a "man" a boy has to learn to fight, to defend himself, and to give back at least as much punishment as he takes. If a boy doesn't learn this, he will be weak and tend to be "victimized" all his life, not only by men, but also by women. The blue-collar mothers in the study, on the other hand, were trying to raise their boys for family roles—to be more sensitive and cooperative rather than "macho."

The following descriptive (not evaluative) generalizations are made on the basis of many research studies that compare the parenting styles of families of high- and low-socioeconomic status (Hart & Risley, 1995; Hoff-Ginsberg & Tardiff, 1995; Parke & Buriel, 1998), keeping in mind variations exist within each class:

- Parents from low-socioeconomic statuses tend to emphasize obedience, respect, neatness, cleanliness, and staying out of trouble; whereas parents from high-socioeconomic statuses are more likely to emphasize happiness, creativity, ambition, independence, curiosity, and self-control.

- Parents from low-socioeconomic statuses tend to be more controlling, authoritarian, and arbitrary in their discipline and are apt to use physical punishment, whereas parents from high-socioeconomic statuses tend to be more democratic. They are more likely to use reason with their children and be receptive to their children's opinions.

- Parents from high-socioeconomic statuses tend to show more warmth and affection toward their children than parents from low-socioeconomic statuses.

- Parents from high-socioeconomic statuses talk to their children more, reason with them more, and use more complex language than do parents from low-socioeconomic statuses.

A major reason why parenting styles differ according to socioeconomic status is that families tend to adapt their interactional patterns to the level of stress they are experiencing. High-, as well as low-socioeconomic families experience stress, such as work problems, health problems, and relationship problems. However, low income and other stressors related to poverty (housing, unsafe neighborhoods, job turnover) influence parents' well-being, the tone of their marriage, and the quality of their relationship with their children (Cowan, Powell, & Cowan, 1998). According to several studies (Dodge, Pettit, & Bates, 1994; McLoyd, 1990), economic hardship experienced by lower-class families is associated with anxiety, depression, and irritability. This emotional stress increases the tendency of parents to be punitive, inconsistent, authoritarian, and generally nonsupportive of their children. The emotional strain encourages the parent to adopt parenting techniques, such as physical punishment and commanding without explanation, that require less time and effort than other methods, such as reasoning and negotiating. Expecting unquestioning obedience from children is more efficient than trying to meet the desires of all family members.

Parental Occupations

So far macrosystem influences, such as historical change, culture, and political and socioeconomic systems, on parenting styles have been discussed. Now an **exosystem** influence—the parents' work is examined. Complex societies in which there are many roles to perform have complex stratification systems, or many criteria upon which status is based, such as income, occupation, education, and place of residence. The more complex the society and the more roles that exist, the more complex the job of socialization becomes. When one performs a role, one takes on the behavioral expectations of that role through the process of socialization. For example, army officers will behave in an authoritarian manner, giving commands, whereas lawyers will use logic, reason, and explanation in performing their roles. Do the socialized role behaviors performed in one's occupation (the exosystem) carry over into parenting styles?

To find out, Miller and Swanson (1958) examined the child-rearing practices of American parents who had different occupational roles, which they classified as bureaucratic versus entrepreneurial. Bureaucratic occupations were characterized by a direct salary and relatively high job security—for example, civil service employees, public school teachers, military personnel, and some corporate employees. Entrepreneurial occupations were classified as those in which a person is self-employed or works on the basis of a direct commission—for example, physicians, owners of businesses, and certain salespeople such as real estate agents. Miller and Swanson found that bureaucratic families tended to stress egalitarian practices and to emphasize social adjustment or "getting along"; entrepreneurial families tended to emphasize independence training, mastery, and self-reliance. The entrepreneurial parents also tended to depend heavily on psychological techniques of discipline, such as "You've disappointed me with your behavior," rather than, "No television for the rest of the night for you."

Sociologist Melvin Kohn (1977) analyzed the ways in which middle-class occupations in general differ from lower-class occupations. Middle-class occupations typically require the individual to handle ideas and symbols, as well as be skilled in dealing with interpersonal relations, whereas lower-class occupations typically involve physical objects rather than symbols and do not involve as many interpersonal skills. Also, middle-class jobs often demand more self-direction in the prioritizing of job activities and in the selection of methods to get the job done than do lower-class jobs, which are more often routinized and subject to more strict supervision.

People who work in bureaucratic jobs, like those in a hospital, tend to incorporate the value of following the rules in their parenting styles.

Kohn's (Kohn, Naoi, Schoenbach, Schooler, & Slomezynski, 1990; Kohn, 1977) later research on differences in parent–child relationships in middle and lower classes indicated that lower-class parents were likely to judge their children's behavior in terms of its immediate consequences and its external characteristics, whereas middle-class parents were more concerned with their children's motives and the attitudes their behavior seemed to express. Kohn explained these differences as due to the different characteristics required in middle- and lower-class occupations.

Kohn (Kohn, 1977; Kohn, Naoi, Schoenbach, Schooler, & Slomczynski, 1990) demonstrated that middle-class parents were more likely than lower-class parents to want their children to be considerate of others, intellectually curious, responsible, and self-controlled; lower-class parents were more likely to want their children to have good manners, to do well in school, and to be obedient. Thus the middle-class parent tends to emphasize self-direction for the child, whereas the lower-class parent tends to emphasize conformity. Kohn also demonstrated that fathers whose jobs entail self-direction, who work with ideas instead of things, who are not closely supervised, and who face complexity on the job value self-direction in their children, whereas those whose work requires them to conform to close supervision and a highly structured work situation are more likely to want their children to conform. Bronfenbrenner (1979) and Crouter (Bronfenbrenner & Crouter, 1982; Crouter & McHale, 1993) say parents' workplaces affect their perceptions of life and the way they interact with family members. Therefore, parenting styles tend to be extensions of the modes of behavior that are functional for the parent. In dual-earner families, so prevalent today, it is possible for mothers and fathers, due to the nature of their jobs, to come to favor different parenting practices and these, in turn, may vary according to their children's gender (Crouter & McHale, 1993; Greenberger, O'Neil, & Nagel, 1994).

Thus, it is likely that the differences found in social class socialization practices are not only due to variations in physical resources, but also to the different types of adult models available to children for patterning behaviors, the differences in breadth and quality of learning experiences provided for the children, and the kind of child-rearing practices implemented by the parents. These differences manifest themselves in terms of lifestyles, values, attitudes, social roles, and skills.

PARENTING STYLES

Parenting style encompasses the emotional climate in which behaviors are expressed (Cowan, Powell, & Cowan, 1998). Thus parenting styles are usually classified as *warm* or *cold, responsive* (sensitive) or *nonresponsive* (insensitive). Behaviors expressed by parents are viewed by researchers in terms of *control* and *involvement* (or disengagement) (Maccoby & Martin, 1983).

BETWEEN PARENT AND CHILD

A microsystem effect on children is the parent–child relationship within the family. Research has shown parenting styles to have an impact on children's behavior, specifically self-control and prosocial behavior. **Self-control** refers to the ability to inhibit one's impulses, behavior, and/or emotions. **Prosocial behavior** refers to actions that benefit another. Also, researched are competence and achievement motivation. **Competence** involves behavior that is socially responsible, independent, friendly, cooperative, dominant, achievement-oriented, and purposeful. **Achievement motivation** refers to the tendency to approach challenging tasks with confidence of mastery.

Parenting styles are usually described in terms of major dimensions or degrees: **authoritative** (democratic), **authoritarian** (parent-centered), or **permissive** (child-centered). (Please see the appendix for more detailed definitions of the basic parenting styles.) It must be realized that parents are never simply one category or one extreme; they are often a mixture. Parenting is so complex that often such factors as the particular situation (including stress), the child's age, gender, birth order and siblings, the child's temperament (including how the child responds to parental demands), the parent's previous experience, and the parent's temperament influence parenting. In order to better understand the effects of parenting styles on children's behavior, researchers base their findings on the parenting styles observed most frequently in various situations.

Fostering Self-Control and Prosocial Behavior

Diana Baumrind (1966, 1967, 1971a, 1973) studied parenting practices by observing the behavior of preschool children. She rated their behavior according to degree of impetuosity, self-reliance, aggressiveness, withdrawal, and self-control.

The parents of groups of preschool children were observed and interviewed to determine how their parenting styles differed. Baumrind found that parents of the "competent," "contented" children were controlling and demanding as well as being warm, rational, and receptive to the child's communication. She labeled this combination of high control and positive encouragement of the child's autonomous and independent strivings "authoritative." Parents of the "withdrawn," "discontented" children were detached, controlling, and somewhat less warm than the other parents. Baumrind labeled this group "authoritarian." Parents of "immature," "impulsive" children were noncontrolling, nondemanding, and relatively warm. Baumrind labeled this group "permissive" (*see* Table 4.1).

Later studies (Brophy, 1989; Hart, DeWolf, & Burts, 1992) have supported Baumrind's findings that parenting style affects children's behavior. For example, children of authoritarian parents showed little independence and scored in the middle range on social responsibility. Children of permissive parents conspicuously lacked social responsibility and were not very independent. Children of authoritative parents were independent and socially responsible.

According to Baumrind, both the authoritarian and permissive parents in her studies had unrealistic beliefs about young children. Whereas the strict or authoritarian parents thought the child's behavior must be constrained, the permissive parents tended to look at the child's behavior as natural and refreshing. Neither group seemed to take into account the child's stage of development—for example, the desire in early childhood to model parental behavior or the inability in early childhood to reason when given a parental command. Thus Baumrind, and others (Steinberg, Mounts, Lamborn, & Dornbusch, 1994) endorsed the authoritative parenting style for adapting to the American values of independence, individualism, achievement, and self-control. Authoritative parents take into account their children's needs as well as their own before deciding how to deal with a situation. They exert control over their children's behavior when necessary, yet they respect their children's need to make their own decisions. Reasoning is used to

Table 4.1	Relationship of Parenting Styles to Children's Behavior	

PARENTING STYLE	**CHARACTERISTICS**	**CHILDREN'S BEHAVIOR**
Authoritative (democratic)	controlling but flexible demanding but rational warm receptive to child's communication values discipline, self-reliance, and uniqueness	self-reliant self-controlled explorative content cooperative
Authoritarian (adult-centered)	strict control (self-will curbed by punitive measures) evaluation of child's behavior and attitudes with absolute standard values obedience, respect for authority, and tradition	discontent aimless withdrawn fearful distrustful
Permissive (child-centered)	noncontrolling nondemanding acceptance of child's impulses consults with child on policies	least self-reliant impulsive aggressive least explorative least self-control

explain parenting policies, and communication from the children is encouraged. Children experience democracy at home.

While most earlier parenting research took place with young children, later studies that include adolescents in order to reveal the long-term effects of parenting styles have been implemented (Baumrind, 1991; Holmbeck, Paikoff, & Brooks-Gunn, 1995). Dornbusch and his colleagues (Dornbusch, Ritter, Herbert, Roberts, & Fraleigh, 1987) found that authoritative parenting is positively correlated with adolescent school performance, whereas authoritarian and permissive parenting are negatively so. Steinberg and his colleagues (Steinberg, Elman, & Mounts, 1989; Steinberg et al., 1994) confirmed the rela-

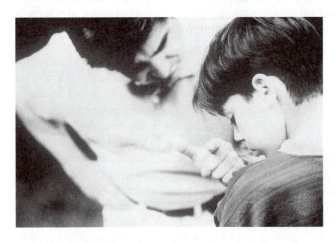

The scolding a child gets from a parent for wrongdoing exemplifies the authoritarian parenting style.

The verbal give-and-take discussion this mother and daughter are having exemplifies the authoritative parenting style.

tionship between authoritative parenting and academic performance. They explained it as being due to the effects of authoritativeness on the development of a healthy sense of autonomy and, more specifically, on the development of a healthy psychological orientation toward work. Thus, authoritative parenting influences not only how a child behaves in the early years, but also how a child deals with responsibility, as exhibited in adolescence.

Authoritative parenting is not the norm among various ethnic groups within the United States and other countries. More common is the authoritarian style utilized by Asian Americans, Hispanic Americans, and African Americans (Greenfield & Suzuki, 1998). Certain conditions, such as lack of social supports or living in dangerous neighborhoods may make strict discipline necessary to protect children from becoming involved in antisocial activities (Brody & Flor, 1998; Ogbu, 1994).

While authoritarian parenting is perceived by Americans and Europeans to be strict and regimented stressing adult domination, it is perceived by Chinese people to be a means of training (*chaio shun*) and governing (*guan*) children in an involved and physically close way (Chao, 1994). The Chinese concept of authoritarianism comes from the Confucian emphasis on hierarchical relationships and social order. Standards exist, not to dominate the child, but to preserve the integrity of the family unit and assure harmonious relations with others (Greenfield & Suzuki, 1998). Thus, Baumrind's definition of authoritarian parenting (*see* Appendix) and child development outcomes (discontent, withdrawal, distrust, lack of instrumental competence) do not always apply cross-culturally.

Fostering Competence and Achievement Motivation

In the 1960s the government was interested in funding projects that would help children learn. Burton White (1971) and his colleagues at Harvard (White & Watts, 1973) studied the relationship between parenting styles and the development of competence versus incompetence in preschoolers. First they had preschool teachers rate their children (*see* Table 4.2), ages 3 to 6, representing different socioeconomic statuses, as competent or incompetent.

Then to find out when the differences in competence appeared, the researchers went into the homes of the competent and incompetent children who had younger infant siblings, in order to observe the mother–child interaction from infancy to age 3.

No differences in competency were found among infants who were siblings of the competent and incompetent children. Yet by 10 months of age, differences in competency began to show up, and by age 2 and often as early as 18 months, children could be classified as competent or incompetent. What is so significant about the period of development between 10 and 18 months? This period is the time when children begin to talk, walk, explore, and assert themselves. It is during this time that the parenting style is revealed, a good example of the bidirectionality of the parent–child relationship.

How did the parenting styles differ? The mothers of the competent children designed a safe physical environment at home so their children could explore and discover things on their own. They also provided interesting things to manipulate. These could be pots and spoons as well as commercial toys. Surprisingly, these mothers spent no more than 10% of their time deliberately interacting with their children, yet they were always "on call" when needed. They made themselves available to share in their children's exciting discoveries, answer their children's questions, or help their children in an activity for a few minutes here and there while they went about their daily routines. They enjoyed their children and were patient, energetic, and tolerant of messes, accidents, and natural curiosity. They set limits on behavior and were firm and consistent in their discipline. The mothers of the competent children used distraction with infants under age 1; distraction and physical removal of either the child or the object from age 1 to 1.5; and distraction, physical distance, and firm words after age 1.5.

The mothers of the incompetent children were diverse. Some spent little time with their children; they were overwhelmed by their daily struggles, and their homes were disorganized. Others spent a great deal of time with their children. They

This young boy exhibits competence.

Table 4.2   The Harvard Preschool Project: Differences in Learning

COMPETENT CHILDREN	INCOMPETENT CHILDREN
• get attention in socially acceptable ways	• remain unnoticed or are disruptive
• use adults as resources	• need a lot of direction to complete a task
• get along well with others	• have difficulty getting along with others
• plan and carry out complicated tasks	• lack ability to anticipate consequences
• use and understand complex sentences	• have a simplistic vocabulary

were overprotective and pushed their children to learn. Still others provided for their children materially, such as giving them toys, but restricted their children's instinct to explore by ruling certain places and possessions out of bounds. The mothers of the incompetent children used playpens and gates extensively.

In sum, White's research has shown that human competence develops between 10 and 18 months, and it is the parenting style that fosters competence; parenting style includes arrangement of the environment, shared enthusiasm with the child, having a lot of energy, setting reasonable limits according to the child's developmental level, and being available as a resource when needed. According to Burton White (1975, p. 4), "The informal education that families provide for their children makes more of an impact on a child's total educational development than the formal educational system." Such an informal initial education is essentially enabling the child to "learn how to learn" (White, 1995). Research on school-age children confirms the connection between parenting style and competence in school (Grolnick & Ryan, 1989).

In order to assess the relationship of the environment provided by families to the intellectual development of the child specifically, Bettye Caldwell, Robert Bradley, and colleagues (Bradley, Caldwell, & Rock, 1990; Caldwell & Bradley, 1984) developed an assessment scale to determine the quality of the home environment for children under age 3. This scale, called HOME (Home Observation for the Measurement of the Environment), contained 45 items in six areas:

1. Emotional and verbal responsiveness of parent (parent responds to child's vocalizations with verbal response).

2. Avoidance of restriction and punishment (parent does not interfere with child's actions or prohibit him or her more than three times during the observation).

3. Organization of the physical and temporal environment (child's play environment is accessible to child and is safe).

4. Provision of appropriate play materials (child has toys that are safe, that are age-appropriate, and that stimulate play).

5. Parental interaction with the child (parent keeps child within visual range and looks at, touches, or talks to child frequently).

6. Opportunities for variety in daily stimulation (parent reads stories or plays games with child).

Studies following the relation between childrens' HOME scores for young preschoolers and IQ scores, as well as later academic achievement, showed a strong positive correlation (Bradley & Caldwell, 1984; Bradley, Caldwell, & Rock, 1990). Also as White's group discovered, the most critical time for influencing a child's intellectual development is the first two years of life.

Does the same relationship between home environment and children's intellectual development apply in other than Western cultures? To find out, Sigman and her colleagues (1988) observed the home interactions experienced by 110 Embu children age 15 to 30 months growing up in a rural Kenyan community. The results were similar to those of White and Watts as well as those of Bradley, Caldwell, and Rock. Children who were talked to frequently, whose vocalizations were responded to, and who engaged in sustained social interactions passed more items on the Bayley Mental Scale at 24 months and 30 months than those who did not receive such attention. Children who were carried a great deal between 15 and 30 months of age scored poorly. The researchers suggest that carrying a child after he or she can walk may restrict exploration of the environment.

CHILD, FAMILY, AND COMMUNITY LINKAGES

While parenting styles influence children, and children influence parenting styles, both parents and children interact in a family system that, by itself, has certain influential characteristics (size, for example). In turn, this family system, as has been discussed, is affected by historical, cultural, political, and economic characteristics. Thus, parenting, like any other influence on development, must be examined in its own context (Luster & Okagaki, 1993; Parke & Buriel, 1998; Sameroff, 1983). The contexts to be examined are certain characteristics of the child, the family, and the community.

Child's Characteristics

Some characteristics of the child that influence parenting style include age, temperament, gender, and presence of a disability.

Age. As the child gets older, parent–child interactions change. During infancy, parenting tasks are primarily feeding, changing, bathing, and comforting. As the child is awake more, play is added to the repertoire of activities. During the second year of life, physical and verbal restraint must be introduced for the child's safety. The child must be prevented from going into the street, from eating poisonous materials, from handling sharp objects, and so on.

During the preschool years, parenting techniques may expand to include reasoning, instruction, isolation ("time-out"), withdrawal of privileges (negative consequences), and reinforcement or rewards. As the children mature during school age, parents may encourage them to become more responsible for their behavior by allowing them to make certain decisions and to experience the positive as well as the negative consequences. For example, if a child requests a pet fish for his or her birthday, then the parents should allow the child to have the responsibility of feeding it. If a child chooses to bounce a ball off the side of the house and breaks a window accidentally, then the child should be given the responsibility of paying for the damage.

Parenting and Prevention of Adolescent Problem Behavior

Studies have shown that adolescents whose parents are warm, affectionate, and communicative toward them are less likely to abuse drugs or engage in delinquent acts or join gangs than children who do not have good parental relationships (Baumrind, 1991; Grotevant, 1998; Steinberg, Lamborn, Darling, Mounts, & Dornbusch, 1991).

Adolescence is a time when parent–child relations are tested. Many of the everyday demands of family life—doing one's assigned chores, being considerate of other members, communicating, adhering to standards (coming home on time, keeping appointments, writing thank-you notes, doing homework)—can become areas of conflict.

Psychiatrist Judith Brook (Brook & Cohen, 1990) has proposed a developmental model of adolescent substance abuse. They believe that the seeds for adolescent problem behavior can be sown during early childhood if parents don't provide adequate nurturance and families are conflict-ridden. Children growing up in such families fail to identify with parental attitudes, values, and behavior. As these children approach adolescence, they are immature in self-control and turn to peers for immediate gratification. They thus become susceptible to drug and alcohol abuse, especially if their friends do drugs and/or alcohol.

When parents react negatively to an adolescent's push for autonomy and become overly strict or overly permissive, the adolescent is more likely to rebel by exhibiting problem behavior (Patterson, DeBaryshe, & Ramsey, 1989).

The research also suggests that the effect of conflict between a child and one parent can be offset by a positive relationship with the other parent. Positive parent–child relationships can also negate the influence of a peer group that abuses drugs or alcohol and engages in delinquent behavior.

Thus parenting styles established in childhood impact adolescent problem behavior.

As children enter adolescence, parents may deal with potential conflicts by discussion, collaborative problem-solving, and compromise. My son neglected to clean his room. It was "a waste of time" to make his bed and put his things away, since he would just be using them again. Because I like order and neatness, his behavior caused me to nag. After discussing his reasons for not complying with my standards and my reasons for him to do so, we agreed on a compromise: the day I cleaned house, he was to tidy his room; other days, he could keep the door closed, but not locked.

Researchers (McNally, Eisenberg, & Harris, 1991; Parke & Buriel, 1998) have found that while specific parenting practices change according to the age of the child, basic parenting styles remain quite stable over time. For example, a parent might isolate a preschooler who is hitting a younger sibling until some self-control is established. That parent might use reasoning and/or withdrawal of privileges for a school-ager who fights. Parenting practices may also change according to the situation. For example, a parent who usually gives a child instruction on how to behave in advance, may resort to yelling when rushed. Thus, even though the methods may change, the goal of self-control and the emotional climate (*authoritarian, authoritative,* or *permissive*) of attaining that goal remains stable.

Temperament. Temperament is the combination of innate characteristics that determine an individual's sensitivity to various experiences and responsiveness to patterns of social interaction. It is a central aspect of an individual's personality, and has been shown to be stable over time. For example, Kagan and his colleagues (Kagan, Reznick, & Gibbons, 1989) have studied shyness and sociability. Children who were classified as shy, or inhibited, at age 21 months due to their timidness with unfamiliar people and their cautiousness in strange surroundings exhibited similar behavior when they were examined at age 7.5. Children who were rated as sociable, or uninhibited, as toddlers were talkative and outgoing with strange adults and peers in unfamiliar settings at age 7.5.

Temperament influences one's interactions with others, how infants respond to their caregivers, and how caregivers respond to children, thereby illustrating the concept of bidirectionality. Thus certain parenting styles may be elicited by a child's temperament (Sameroff, 1994). For example, a very active child may have to be told more than once to sit still at the table or may have to be removed from the table to eat alone, whereas a less active child may only have to be told "Sit still at the dinner table so the food won't spill off the plate." Some methods of child rearing may have to be modified to suit a child's temperament. A child who has irregular patterns of hunger and sleep would be better suited to a more flexible "demand" feeding schedule, whereas a child who exhibits regularity is more suited to feeding at scheduled intervals.

In a classic longitudinal study of 136 children from infancy to adolescence, Thomas, Chess, and Birch (1970; Chess & Thomas, 1987) nine temperamental characteristics were isolated. This model is still used by researchers today:

1. *Activity level:* the proportion of inactive periods to active ones.
2. *Rhythmicity:* regularity of hunger, excretion, sleep, and wakefulness.
3. *Distractibility:* the degree to which extraneous stimuli alter behavior.
4. *Approach/withdrawal:* the response to a new object or person.
5. *Adaptability:* the ease with which children adapt to their environments.
6. *Attention span and persistence:* the amount of time devoted to an activity and the effect of distraction on the activity.
7. *Intensity of reaction:* the energy of response, regardless of its quality or direction.
8. *Threshold of responsiveness:* the intensity of stimulation required to evoke a response.
9. *Quality of mood:* the amount of friendly, pleasant, joyful behavior, as contrasted with unpleasant, unfriendly behavior.

It was found (Chess & Thomas, 1987; Thomas & Chess, 1977) that the 136 behavioral profiles were clustered in three general types of temperament. "Easy" children displayed a positive mood and regularity in body function; they were adaptable and approachable, and their reactions were moderate or low in intensity. At the other extreme, "difficult" children were slow to adapt and tended to have intense reactions and negative moods; they withdrew in new situations and had irregular body functions. The group in the middle, the "slow to warm up" children, initially withdrew but slowly adapted to new situations; they had low activity levels and tended to respond with low intensity. These temperamental types could be recognized by the second or third month of life.

Although individual temperament seems to be established at birth, environmental factors play an important role in whether or not a person's style of behavior can be modified. Regarding this interplay of heredity and environment, if the two influences blend together well, one can expect healthy development of the child; if they are incompatible, behavioral problems are almost sure to ensue (Thomas & Chess, 1977, 1980).

Thomas and Chess recommend that parents adjust parenting styles to their offspring's temperament, although they emphasize that "a constructive approach by the parents to the child's temperament does not mean an acceptance or encouragement of all this youngster's behavior in all situations" (1977, p. 188). *Difficult* children need consistent, patient, and objective parents who can handle their instability. For example, instead of expecting very active, distractible children to concentrate for long periods of time on their homework, parents can reward them for shorter periods of work with pleasurable breaks in between, as long as the task is finished. *Slow to warm up* children do best with a moderate amount of encouragement coupled with patience; parents and teachers should let these children adjust to change at their own pace. *Easy* children tend to adapt well to various styles of child rearing. Thomas and Chess refer to the accommodation of parenting styles to children's temperaments as **"goodness-of-fit."**

Infant temperament determines what kinds of interactions parents and infants are most likely to find mutually rewarding. For example, *difficult* children are more likely to accept change and enjoy new experiences if their parents are accepting, encouraging, and patient, rather than critical, demanding, and impatient. Just because infants are born with certain temperaments does not preclude them from adapting to certain behaviors demanded of them; the key is how the parents do it.

The following explains how temperament mediates environmental input and individual responsiveness: first, temperament sets the tone for interaction. Children who are sociable will communicate a different mood when they encounter people than will children who are more reserved. Second, temperamental differences will determine the kinds of behaviors a child may initiate. Active children will experience more things because they are constantly doing and on the go. They will probably have more social interactions because of their activities. Their temperamental differences may either encourage or discourage the responses of others. Others may react positively or negatively to a child's exhibited temperament. For example, if a parent accepts a child's frequent emotional expressions of joy, sadness, or even anger, as normal behavior that parent is likely to reward those behaviors by being attentive. On the other hand, if a parent disapproves of overt displays of emotion, that parent is likely to punish those expressions by disapproval (Buss & Plomin, 1984).

Not only is a child's temperament influential, but the parents' temperament affects their parenting styles and how they respond to their child's behavior, as well (Lerner, 1993). An active parent may be impatient with an inactive infant; a sociable parent may feel rejected by a withdrawn child; a reserved parent may feel intimidated by an aggressive child. Thus, parents, due to their own temperaments, may encourage, ignore, or discourage certain exhibitions of their children's temperament (Buss & Plomin, 1984).

Gender. Parents provide different socializing environments for boys and girls (Ruble & Martin, 1998). They give them different names, different clothing, and different toys. Fathers, in particular, are more likely to act differently toward sons and daughters than are mothers (Fagot, 1995; Huston, 1983). Also, fathers tend to be more demanding of their children than are mothers (Doherty, Kouneski, & Erikson, 1998; Lamb, 1981). Parents of school-age children were interviewed regarding parenting techniques used with their sons and daughters. Parents reported being more punishing and less rewarding with same-gendered children. Parents of girls emphasized cooperation and politeness; parents of boys emphasized independent and self-reliant behaviors (Power, 1987).

The types of play activities that are encouraged differ for boys and girls. There is also some evidence that parents encourage girls to be more dependent, affectionate, and emotional than boys. In addition, as boys get older, they are permitted more freedom than girls—for example, they are allowed to be away from home without supervision more than girls are (Huston, 1983). Thus, the gender of the child elicits different parenting styles from the parent. Gender-role socialization will be discussed more specifically in Chapter 12.

Presence of a Disability. The presence of a disability in a child influences parenting styles. Parental reactions to the diagnosis vary enormously, including grief, depression, and/or guilt (Meadow-Orlans, 1995). The nature, onset, and severity of the disability as well as the availability of support systems are factors in how the parents cope.

Another common reaction when a child is identified as disabled is anger—anger with God, fate, society, professionals, oneself, the other parent, or even the child. In addition, parents may also experience frustration as they seek an accurate diagnosis or referral of a child who has a problem that is not so readily identifiable.

Society expects parents to love their children. When a parent experiences negative feelings at the birth of a child, that parent commonly feels guilt. Unable to accept feelings of rejection or hostility, parents may blame themselves for experiencing emotions unbefitting a good and loving parent, especially a parent of a child so in need of love and special care. Guilt may also be related to a parent's feeling that something he or she did, or failed to do, caused a child's disability.

Parenting is a difficult and complicated task. Parenting a child with a disability is even more so. Although most people will tolerate a 2-year-old's temper tantrum in a grocery store, they are apt to stare, or even make remarks, at a 10-year-old behaving in the same manner. Many parents have difficulty from time to time getting responsible babysitters, but parents of children with disabilities have even more. It is a challenge to change the diapers on a preadolescent, or care for a blind preschooler, or calm down a hyperactive child.

Not only is parenting a child with a disability more complicated and difficult, it is also more likely to cause major psychological stress in the parent, resulting in disturbed family interactions. According to Ann and H. Rutherford Turnbull (1986, 1997), the parents of children born with disabilities may lose self-esteem. This can be transmitted to the child as overprotection, rejection, or abuse. The child may experience ambivalence, sometimes feeling love and sometimes, anger. The frustrations of parenting a child with disabilities can tax anyone's patience. Parents worry about the care, the expense, and the future of their child. Some parents dedicate themselves totally to their child with dis-

Parenting a child with disabilities is a challenge.

abilities. This pattern can lead to marital conflicts, neglect of other children, and family disruption.

Children with disabilities also have some psychological hurdles to overcome. They must adapt to being different: "Why do I have to use crutches?" "Why am I this way and my brother isn't?" "Will I still have to use crutches when I grow up?" Children may feel guilty about the inconveniences they perceive themselves to have caused—the financial burden (for example, the cost of special equipment), the extra work and care, the inability to measure up to parental aspirations. The attention given children with disabilities may be resented by siblings, who may make these children feel guilty.

Siblings may also experience emotions such as sorrow, anger, and guilt. In addition, they may feel embarrassment and resentment and, as a result, not want to be identified as a relative of the child with disabilities. According to studies on siblings (Simeonsson & Bailey, 1986), the most central concern of siblings of children with disabilities is avoiding identification with them. In addition to being ashamed, siblings fear others questioning their normality; and they may wonder about themselves (Bernstein, 1984).

Siblings may also resent the amount of time and/or money directed toward a brother or sister with disabilities. They may feel deprived of attention or resources they want and feel they need. While sibling responses to having a brother or sister with disabilities may be negative in certain respects, positive reactions are common. These include increased maturity, compassion, tolerance for individual differences, patience, sense of responsibility, and greater appreciation for family and health (Heward, 1996).

Family Characteristics

Some characteristics of the family that influence parenting style are size (number of siblings), configuration (birth order, spacing, and gender of siblings), as well as parents' stage of life, marital quality, and abilities to cope with stress (Cowan, Powell, & Cowan, 1998).

Size (Number of Siblings).   Both parents and children are affected by the number of children in the family. The more children there are, the more interactions within the family, but there is likely to be less individual parent–child interaction. Children in large families may have many resources to draw on for company, playmates, and emotional security. They may also have increased responsibility in the form of chores or caring for younger siblings. Parents in larger families, especially those with limited living space and economic resources, generally tend to be more authoritarian, tend to be more likely to use physical punishment, and tend to be less likely to explain their rules than are the parents of smaller families. The emphasis is on the family as a whole rather than the individuals within (Bossard & Boll, 1956; Elder & Bowerman, 1963; Furman, 1995). However, it has also been found that effects of family size on parenting style is mediated by parental education, occupation, social class, intactness of the family, and ethnic orientation (Blake, 1989).

Configuration (Birth Order, Spacing, and Gender of Siblings).   Not only does the number of children in a family affect child-rearing practices, but the spacing and gender of the siblings also influence parent–child interactions. With the birth of each sibling comes different temperaments, different ages, and new relationships for parents to handle.

A number of studies (Furman, 1995; Sutton-Smith, 1982) have shown parenting practices of firstborn and later-born siblings to be different even when each was the same age. Firstborns received more attention, affection, and verbal stimulation than their later-born siblings. They also were disciplined more restrictively and were coerced more by their parents. More mature behavior was expected of them than of their siblings.

Findings have shown that mothers helped their firstborns in solving problems more frequently than they did their later-borns. And mothers of firstborns applied more pressure for achievement than they did on their later-borns (Zajonc, 1976).

It is much more difficult to predict the sibling effects on later-borns than firstborns because, with later-borns, there are more variables to take into account, such as number of siblings, the space between them, and the gender distribution. For example, the interactions of the youngest male born after two females differ from the interactions of the youngest male born after two males. The patterns change, too, if there are six years between siblings versus two years.

Judy Dunn (1988, 1992) has examined the socialization effects siblings have on each other. While most studies, some of which have been discussed, investigate bidirectional influences of siblings on parenting behavior and differential parenting on siblings, Dunn has added the perspective on social understanding to what goes on inside families. Siblings provide opportunities for cooperation, competition, empathy, aggression, leading, following, and so on. Older siblings function as tutors or supervisors of younger brothers or sisters (Parke & Buriel, 1998). Dunn has shown that from 18 months on, children understand how to hurt, comfort, and exacerbate a sibling's pain. They understand what is allowed or disapproved in their families. They even can anticipate responses of adults to their own and others' misbehavior as well as comment on and ask about the causes of others' actions and feelings. Dunn concludes that the ability to understand others and the social world is closely linked to the activities and relationships with siblings and parents.

What about only children? Are they more pressured to grow up or are they babied? Do they suffer socially and emotionally from not having sibling relationships that involve closeness, compromises, and conflicts?

Only children experience more parent–child interaction, and their relationships with their parents are reported to be more positive and affectionate than those of children with siblings (Falbo & Polit, 1986). In a study of 2-year-olds with an unfamiliar peer in a laboratory room, Snow, Jacklin, and Maccoby (1981) observed that only children were more advanced socially than children with siblings in that they showed more positive behavior as well as assertive–aggressive behavior. Secondborns showed the least. Only children have also been shown to perform better academically in school than children who have siblings (Falbo & Polit, 1986).

Thus it would seem that being an only child is not harmful to development; rather, it may be beneficial. There are disadvantages, however, such as too much pressure from parents to succeed, loneliness, or not having anyone to help care for aging parents.

Parents' Stage of Life. The need for parenting practices to change in response to children changing over time has already been discussed. According to Ellen Galinsky (1981), parents go through six stages of changes in their expectations and practices for children from infancy to adolescence: (1) image-making, (2) nurturing, (3) authority, (4) interpretive, (5) interdependent, and (6) departure. Parents, too, are in the process of development over time (Cowan, Powell, & Cowan, 1998). As they get older, parents have health concerns, career changes, responsibilities toward their parents, and so on.

A new area of research is the impact of parents' childhood and adulthood relationships with their parents on their parenting practices (Cowan, Powell, & Cowan, 1998). For example, mothers who reported having had an insecure childhood relationship with their parents have less effective parenting strategies with their preschool children than mothers who reported having had a secure relationship. Apparently, having a good "working" model to emulate influences parenting.

Marital Quality. Marital quality contributes to children's development in that the parents form a co-parenting alliance, cooperating with and supporting each other (Cowan, Powell, & Cowan, 1998). United parents are less subject to "manipulation" by their child. What child hasn't tried to get one parent to "give in" when the other parent has refused a request?

Research shows that children whose fathers are involved in their care do better socially and academically than children whose fathers play a marginal parenting role (Coontz, 1997). McHale (1995) found that marital distress observed in a two-way problem-solving discussion was associated with hostile–competitive co-parenting with sons, and differing levels of involvement with daughters.

Marital distress culminating in divorce imposes a major disruption in relationships among all members of the family. As was discussed in Chapter 3, divorce affects the parenting style of both the custodial and noncustodial parent, with the custodial parent (usually the mother) becoming more authoritarian and restrictive, and the noncustodial parent (usually the father) becoming more permissive and indulgent, at least initially. Such a major stress also affects children's behavior, with children becoming more aggressive, rebellious, and manipulative.

There is evidence that stressors outside the family, such as economics, work problems, illness, peer relationships, disrupt the parent–child relationship, thereby interfering with children's optimal development (Patterson & Capaldi, 1991). Conversely, the availability of social support has a buffering effect and lessens the strain (Cowan, Powell, & Cowan, 1998).

Abilities to Cope with Stress.   Parents who are tired, worried, or ill and those who feel they have lost control of their lives are likely to be impatient, lacking in understanding, and unwilling to reason with their children. To see whether and how stress affects child rearing, a stressful situation was created in which parents were observed interacting with their toddlers and preschool-age children. A laboratory playroom was equipped with play materials that were complex enough to require the children to request help. It was also equipped with such items as a breakable vase, a filled ashtray, and a stack of index cards. The parents were given mental tasks to perform, while the children played in the room. It was found that when the parents were preoccupied with their task, they became less responsive to their preschool children (less likely to play with them, talk to them, help them) and more interfering, critical, and authoritarian with their toddlers (Zussman, 1980).

What are the effects of real-life stress on parental interaction with children—for example, divorce, illness, death, abuse, or financial problems? A study (Patterson, 1982) obtained daily reports from a group of mothers concerning the occurrence of crises of varying magnitudes, including an unexpectedly large bill, a car breaking down, illness of a family member, and quarrels between spouses. The mothers were asked to include their moods. Family interactions were also observed. The number of crises experienced was found to be a positive prediction of maternal irritability. It was hypothesized that the more often a mother became irritable, the less likely she was to deal with family problem-solving, and that unsolved problems accumulate and lead to increased stress. Further, disrupted family interaction leads to an intolerant discipline style that in turn fosters antisocial behavior in the child (Patterson & Dishion, 1988).

Unemployment and consequent economic deprivation is another example of family tension. There is a considerable body of research showing an association between paternal job loss and intrafamily violence, such as wife-beating and child abuse (Hoffman, 1984; Luster & Okagaki, 1993). The possible explanations offered are the greater amount of time the father spends at home, which increases the possibility of conflict; a possible increase in the father's discipline role; a reaffirmation of the father's power in order to save face; and tension from diminished economic resources.

Finally, it has been shown that crises or stress do not always disrupt family functioning. The type of stressor, personalities, and relationships within the family, as well as the presence of social support networks outside the nuclear family, are influential factors (Cochran, 1993; Yogman & Brazelton, 1986).

Community Characteristics

The community is considered here to include social environments outside the family context of parenting. They can be supportive in that they help parents cope with stress (Crnic, & Acevedo, 1995). Relatives and friends are examples of informal supports; psychologists and employers are examples of formal supports. Each of these types of social support systems can provide instrumental physical and financial support, emotional support, informational support (Bugental & Goodnow, 1998). Formal support systems are discussed in Chapter 10.

ETHNICALLY DIVERSE PATTERNS OF PARENTING

Ethnic minorities, taken as a whole, constitute the fastest growing segment of the U.S. population (McAdoo, 1993). Such a demographic change impacts the way child socialization is viewed.

Various ethnic communities differ in certain child-rearing practices, for example, in the communication that takes place, how affection is displayed, how children's behavior is controlled, and what skills are emphasized. These differences are viewed as adaptive strategies to cope with the demands of various ecological contexts. Some generalizations on ethnic patterns of parenting follow (Garcia-Coll, Meyer, & Britton, 1995; Parke & Buriel, 1998). Assimilation into Anglo society affects the implementation of certain diverse practices.

Asian American

Asian American parents consider themselves responsible for teaching children appropriate behaviors. Children are nurtured in the early years closely by the mother. Parenting

Mother and son exhibit close physical contact and warm interaction.

of infants can generally be described as permissive—infants are seldom allowed to cry for prolonged periods before they are picked up; they are fed on demand; they are weaned at a later age than Anglos; the child is allowed to sleep with his or her parents; and toilet training is gradual. Verbal communication is relatively restrained compared to Anglos; rather, nonverbal communication, such as facial expressions and body language, is used. The child becomes dependent on the mother to satisfy his or her needs. This dependency, as well as the closeness, fosters in the child a sense of obligation, which is continually reinforced as the child grows older. Consequently, the mother is able to use shame and guilt to control behavior by appealing to this sense of duty when the child deviates from her expectations. Parents are generally not overtly affectionate with children, but show their love in indirect ways, such as by sacrificing their own needs for their children's. As children reach school age, they are subjected to stricter discipline and taught that their actions reflect no only on themselves but on their families. Fathers usually assume the role of disciplinarian.

Confucian principles generally are the foundation upon which Asian American family structure and roles are based. The structure is hierarchical with each member's role based on age and gender. Typically, Asian American families are patriarchal and members place family needs above individual needs. Children show obedience and loyalty to parents and are expected to take care of elderly parents (Bugental & Goodnow, 1998).

Native American

Native American families "may be characterized as a collective cooperative social network that extends from the mother and father union to the extended family and ultimately the community and tribe" (Bugental & Goodnow, 1998, p. 504). Children are socialized by the extended, as well as the nuclear, family. There are strong bonds of affection between family members. Children are taught to respect elders (age is a "badge of honor"—if you have grown old, you have done the right things). Traditionally, it is the old people who pass on the cultural heritage to the younger ones. Children are taught brotherhood, sharing, spirituality, and personal integrity. Respect is taught by examples as well as by instruction. Spirituality is taught via rites and rituals. Cooperation is highly valued—generally, there is no competition within the group, neither is there majority rule; rather, consensus is sought based on the needs of the group overriding the needs of the individual. Modesty and moderation are stressed—don't talk for the sake of talking; don't boast when one achieves; don't show emotions. Children are not expected to be perfect, only to do what they are capable of for their age. Therefore, failure is not a concept. The goal is to improve on one's past performance. Approval is indicated through a smile, a pleasant tone of voice, or a friendly pat. Children are corrected by the adult lowering his or her voice. Generally, there is no physical punishment, neither is there verbal praise. Frowning, ignoring, withdrawal of affection, and shaming are forms of social control, as is group pressure. Criticism of another is traditionally communicated indirectly through another family member, rather than directly.

Hispanic American

Hispanic American parents encourage children to identify with the family and community. Children are close to members of the extended, as well as the nuclear, family. This fosters a sense of obligation to the family. Respect for parents is emphasized, as is obedience and fear of authority. Generally, there is not much encouragement of curiosity or independence; rather, cooperation is taught. Children are socialized to be sensitive to the feelings and needs of others. Age and gender are important determinants of roles and status. Older children are given responsibility for socialization of younger ones. There is an emphasis on appropriate behavior and the honor of the family in the community. Children learn by observation, by doing, and by the reactions of others. Self-regulation occurs by building new behaviors onto old.

African American

African American families value close family ties and a strong sense of familial obligation. Children relate to many people of all ages in the household. Generally, there is more emphasis on interaction with people than with things. Body contact (embraces in greeting or to thank) is encouraged. Mothers are physically close to their infants, often sleeping with them. Babies are fed on demand rather than on a schedule. Mothers become involved early on in bowel and bladder training. Nonverbal communication with babies is common, such as caressing and rubbing their feet. Mothers communicate directions for household tasks with few words; the tasks are broken down into small units, with brief direction for each short task following completion of the previous one. This type of communication approximates the rhythm pattern in African American music. Mothers also will echo the child's words and tone of voice. For example, the child says, "I want an ice cream cone." Mother says, "I want an ice cream cone, too." This is a way of communicating to the child, that although each might want something, he or she can't have it.

Shirley Brice Heath (1989) observed communication styles in low-income African American families. She found that adults asked children different types of questions than typically heard in middle-class Anglo families. Anglo parents ask "knowledge training" questions, such as "What is this story about?" African American parents in Heath's sample asked only "real" questions; those to which they did not know the answer, such as, "What's in that box?" Often conversations were acted out and contained a lot of teasing.

APPROPRIATE PARENTING PRACTICES

Influences on parenting in general and specific parenting styles have been discussed so far. This section examines which parenting practices are appropriate for optimal child development, while the next discusses practices which are inappropriate, resulting in negative childhood outcomes.

Parental *values* and *attitudes* about what is important and appropriate are reflected in their parenting styles. Appropriate parenting practices are influenced by parents' *knowledge* and understanding of child development, including normal behavior for specific ages and how children process information differently as they mature. Appropriate parenting practices can also reflect a knowledge of socialization methods (described in Chapter 2). For example, when is it appropriate to use *guidance,* a preventative socialization method, and *discipline,* a corrective socialization method? (*see* Figure 4.3)

Understanding why children misbehave can help parents choose an effective method. Children sometimes misbehave because they are tired, hungry, uncomfortable,

Figure 4.3   Parental Practices: Guidance and Discipline

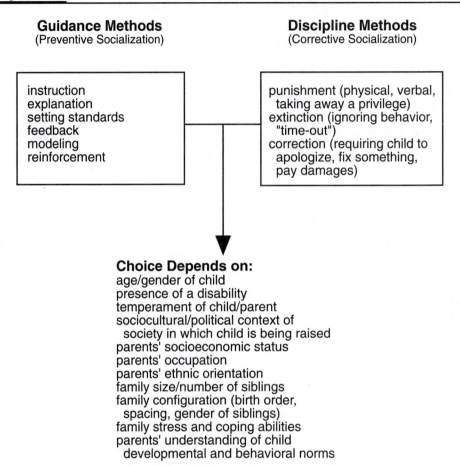

Guidance Methods
(Preventive Socialization)

Discipline Methods
(Corrective Socialization)

instruction
explanation
setting standards
feedback
modeling
reinforcement

punishment (physical, verbal,
    taking away a privilege)
extinction (ignoring behavior,
    "time-out")
correction (requiring child to
    apologize, fix something,
    pay damages)

Choice Depends on:
age/gender of child
presence of a disability
temperament of child/parent
sociocultural/political context of
    society in which child is being raised
parents' socioeconomic status
parents' occupation
parents' ethnic orientation
family size/number of siblings
family configuration (birth order,
    spacing, gender of siblings)
family stress and coping abilities
parents' understanding of child
    developmental and behavioral norms

or sick. Sometimes children don't understand what is expected of them or why they did something wrong. Children may react to parental demands with anger, such as when they are told they can't have the candy displayed at the supermarket. They may misbehave when they are fearful, such as when left in a new and strange place. They may be jealous when a new sibling arrives and misbehave to get attention. They may feel hurt or disappointed when an adult lets them down, such as not fulfilling a promise or when parents divorce, and react with revenge.

The neighborhood in which a family resides can influence parenting practices by the response to various neighborhood ecologies (Bugental & Goodnow, 1998), such as rural or urban, safe or unsafe. O'Neil and Parke (1997) found when parents perceived their neighborhoods to be dangerous and low in social control, they placed more restrictions on their children's activities. On the other hand, parents with neighbors who have similar values about child rearing don't have as much need for so many restrictions (Parke & Buriel, 1998).

INAPPROPRIATE PARENTING PRACTICES: CHILD MALTREATMENT

Maltreatment is defined as any intentional harm to or endangerment of a child. It includes unkindness, harshness, rejection, neglect, deprivation, abuse, and/or violence (Barnett, Manley, & Cicchetti, 1993). It is a broader term than abuse and neglect and can be viewed as a continuum with homicide at one extreme and parental force for disciplinary purposes at the other (Pagelow, 1982). Cultures differ in what constitutes maltreatment (Goodman, Emery, & Haugaard, 1998). However, it is generally agreed that maltreating parents fail to meet the physical or emotional needs of the developing child and, in many cases, the trust the child places in the parent is betrayed (Starr, 1990). Child maltreatment constitutes inappropriate parenting in that it may result in child maladaptation (Rogosch, Cicchetti, Shields, & Toth, 1995). Child maltreatment occurs in all economic, social, ethnic, and religious groups. Estimates of the number of children who are neglected, physically abused, sexually abused, or psychologically abused varies according to who is reporting; however, it is agreed that abuse and neglect are marks of risk for later development of aggressive behavior and emotional or psychological problems (Goodman, Emery, & Haugaard, 1998).

Research suggests that maltreatment during childhood has far-reaching consequences in adulthood (Cicchetti & Lynch, 1993; Starr, 1990) such as inability to trust, low self-esteem, depression, relationship problems, sexual problems, learning difficulties, eating disorders, and alcohol or drug problems. The lack of normal nurturing during childhood may result in the adult need to replace the missing love and security with externals, such as drugs, alcohol, food, material objects, sex, gambling, and relationships (Farmer, 1989).

> Ellen's addictions began when she was a teenager. "In high school, I used alcohol and drugs to numb myself just so I wouldn't have to feel anything," she states flatly. "I just couldn't deal with the pain, with the insanity of it all. I'd walk around all the time depressed" (Farmer, 1989, p. 7).

What can be done to help maltreated children? While parents in our society have the fundamental right to raise their children as they see fit, the Fourteenth Amendment of the United States Constitution, which states that *everyone* has equal protection under the law, warrants legal intervention when the safety of the child is in jeopardy. Intervention may involve filing criminal charges, referral to community agencies for counseling and treatment, and/or removal of the child from the care and custody of the parent, guardian, or caregiver. Every state has child protective laws with varying procedures.

DEFINING CHILD ABUSE AND NEGLECT

To better understand the forms child maltreatment may take, each is examined separately even though they may occur simultaneously. **Abuse** is defined as maltreatment, including physical abuse, sexual abuse, and psychological or emotional abuse. **Neglect** is defined as maltreatment involving abandonment, lack of supervision, improper feeding, lack of adequate medical or dental care, inappropriate dress, uncleanliness, and lack of safety.

Physical abuse is maltreatment involving deliberate harm to the child's body. This includes children who are intentionally bruised, wounded, or burned. Some physical abuse takes place under the guise of discipline. The places on children's bodies where they are wounded and the shape of the wound can give clues that indicate abuse rather than accident. While physical beating with a hand or an object such as a belt or hairbrush is the most common cause of physical abuse, other sources are kicking, shaking, choking, burning with cigarettes or scalding in hot water, freezing, and throwing the child around.

Physical abuse of children is more likely to occur in families where there is domestic violence—verbal conflict or physical aggression between partners (Dodge, Bates, & Petit, 1990; Straus, 1992). Research shows a direct relation between physical abuse, aggressive behavior in children, and juvenile deliquency in adolescents (Rogosch et al., 1995). This may be due, in part, to modeling and, in part, to deficient abilities to process social information (Dodge, Bates, & Petit, 1990). In other words, adolescents attribute hostile intentions to others, and they lack strategies to solve interpersonal problems.

The **sexual abuse** of a child occurs whenever any person forces, tricks, or threatens a child in order to have sexual contact with him or her. This contact can include such "nontouching" behaviors as an adult exposing himself or herself, or asking a child to look at pornographic material. It includes behaviors ranging from the sexual handling of a child (fondling), to actual genital contact, to intercourse, to violent rape. In all instances of child sexual abuse, the child is being used as an object to satisfy the adult's sexual needs or desires.

Children who are sexually abused often go through phases of (1) secrecy; (2) helplessness; (3) entrapment and accommodation; (4) delayed, conflicted, and unconvincing disclosure; and (5) retraction (Goodman, Emery, & Haugaard, 1998). These phases can be explained by realizing that the child is vulnerable to a more powerful and knowledgeable adult. The adult demands secrecy and threatens the child if he or she tells—"I'll take your cat away." "Your mom will spank you." Thus, to enable the child to share, one must ensure a supportive and nonpunitive response.

The most common forms of sexual abuse of children are fondling and oral stimulation. Physical injury is rare. The offender often uses bribery, manipulation to secrecy with threats, and psychological power over the child because most sexual abuse occurs with an adult the child knows and trusts (Finkelhor, 1984). Although some sexual abuse occurs between adult women and children, in a majority of cases it is the adult male who is the perpetrator of child sexual abuse. Both young girls and boys are victims.

Because children, by their very nature, are trusting and obedient, and because of their age and lack of experience as well as their dependence upon adults, they are vulnerable to incest and molestation. Most sexual assaults follow a gradually escalating pattern whereby the perpetrator first attempts to gain the child's trust and affection before attempting sexual contact (Koblinsky & Behana, 1984).

Child victims may experience guilt, anxiety, confusion, shame, embarrassment, fear, sadness, and a sense of being bad or dirty. Every child reacts differently. Some child victims do not understand that the abuse is "sexual" in nature; therefore they may find some elements of the abuse pleasant if the abuse was not forceful or scary.

The way certain adults view children provides a clue to why sexual abuse takes place. These adults feel children in their care are their property to do with as they wish. A great myth of child abuse is that the child wants sex (O'Brien, 1984). Child sexual abusers also exhibit characteristics of low self-esteem, poor impulse control, and childish emotional needs (Koblinksy & Behana, 1984). They themselves were likely to have been abused as children.

Incest deserves special attention. The closer the victim and offender are emotionally, the greater trauma the victim experiences. Ongoing incest, or sexual abuse by someone close to the family, can disrupt necessary psychological developmental tasks of a child. Victims may develop poor social skills with peers their own age, often feel unable to trust people—yet desperately want to trust—and may become depressed, suicidal, self-destructive, and confused about their sexuality. A high percentage of drug abusers, juvenile runaways, and prostitutes have been sexually abused as children.

Psychological or emotional abuse is maltreatment involving a destructive pattern of continued attack by an adult on a child's development of self and social competence, taking the forms of rejecting, isolating, terrorizing, ignoring, and corrupting (Garbarino, Guttman, & Seely, 1986). Psychological or emotional abuse can occur when parents are inconsistent in their talk, rules, or actions; when they have unrealistic expectations of their children; when they belittle and blame their children; when they do not take an interest in any of their children's activities; or when they do not ever praise their children. For example, a mother leaving a dance class with her sobbing 5-year-old daughter said, "Why can't you learn the positions like the others? You always embarrass me. Sometimes I can't believe you're really my daughter."

Parents who psychologically abuse their children are prompted not by the child's misbehavior, but by their own psychological problems. They are usually people who received inadequate love and nurturing from their own parents (Helfer & Kempe, 1989; Kempe & Kempe, 1978). Parents may use a steady stream of verbal abuse that discounts the child's achievements and blows out of proportion every sign of misbehavior. Words like *always, never,* and *should* imply that a child invariably fails to live up to a parent's expectations. Psychologically abusive parents may display irrational expectations so that normal behavior is seen as a deficiency on the part of the child and a failure on the part of the parent. For example, forgetting to give the parent change from lunch money may be viewed as stealing rather than a mistake.

Psychological abuse is also associated with physical and sexual abuse as well as is neglect. Exposure to domestice violence (to be discussed in more detail in Chapter 7), a form of psychological abuse, results in emotional, social, behavioral, and learning problems, too (Margolin, 1998; Straus, 1992).

Things Parents Should Never Do

- Never call children derogatory names.
- Never threaten to leave your child.
- Never say, "I wish you were never born!"
- Never sabotage the parenting efforts of your spouse.
- Never punish when you've lost control of yourself.
- Never expect a child to think, feel, or behave like an adult.

CAUSES OF CHILD MALTREATMENT

To understand the causes of child abuse and neglect, one has to not only examine the family interactions, but also the cultural attitudes sanctioning violence and aggression as well as the community support system (Rogosch, Cicchetti, Shields, & Toth, 1995).

Figure 4.4 provides a model to illustrate the interaction between child, family, community, and cultural factors involved in maltreatment. For example, some influences on child maltreatment include temperament of the child, marital distress, unemployment, and lack of community support, as well as cultural values, such as tolerance for violence and a view of the child as property (Belsky, 1993; Emery, 1989).

According to Cicchetti and Lynch (1993), risk and resilient factors must be weighed before predicting maltreatment. Risk factors include those that are *ongoing,* such as parental history of being abused; and *transient,* such as parent's loss of a job. Resilient factors include ongoing ones such as the child's easy temperament; and transient ones, such as an improvement in the family's financial status.

The Family and Maltreatment

As has been discussed, the process of parenting is very complex. It can be stressful and frustrating, as well as rewarding. Parenting involves the ability to continually give love, support, and guidance. Some individuals, because they themselves were never given love, support, or guidance, do not know how to give them to their own children.

Many abusers have a family history of being maltreated (Rogosch et al., 1995; Starr, 1990). When one is maltreated, one feels unworthy, inadequate, unacceptable. This results in low self-esteem. The next generation tends to model the parenting and attitudes to which it has been exposed. Thus, unless it can be broken, maltreatment becomes a self-perpetuating cycle.

When children grow up under negative conditions, are scapegoated, belittled, and under constant criticism, they cannot develop their full potential or grow to be competent adults. They live out all the negative feelings they have developed as a result of the self-image they have received from their parents or caretakers and are thus prone to character and behavior disorders, self-doubt, and internal anger.

When life's stresses are added to feelings of inadequacy and lack of parenting skills, child abuse and neglect may be the result. Families who have emotional problems, financial problems, stress, and lack of knowledge about child development, and who are immature, may neglect or abuse their children. Abusive parents lack understanding of child development and consequently often have unrealistic expectations. They expect their children to eat when they are fed, not to be messy, to be obedient, to be quiet, and to give love. When children do not behave like adults, the parents lash out at them because their inability to conform to their parents' expectations serves as a reminder of their own inferiority (Farmer, 1989). When parents were themselves abused as children, their ability to control their feelings, in addition to their perspective of parenting, is affected.

> Vicky was reported for child abuse. She had tied her 3-year-old son to the bed because, earlier that morning, he had gone to his friend's house and had not telephoned his mother to report his whereabouts. The little boy sobbed, "But Mommy, I forgot my number." Often, abusive parents believe that their child's behavior is deliberate and purposeful (Helfer & Kempe, 1989). "She spit up on my new blouse because she was mad at me," said a mother of her 1-month-old daughter. "He ran in the street just to frighten me," said a mother of her 2-year-old son.

Figure 4.4   An Interaction Model of Risk and Resilient Factors in Child Maltreatment

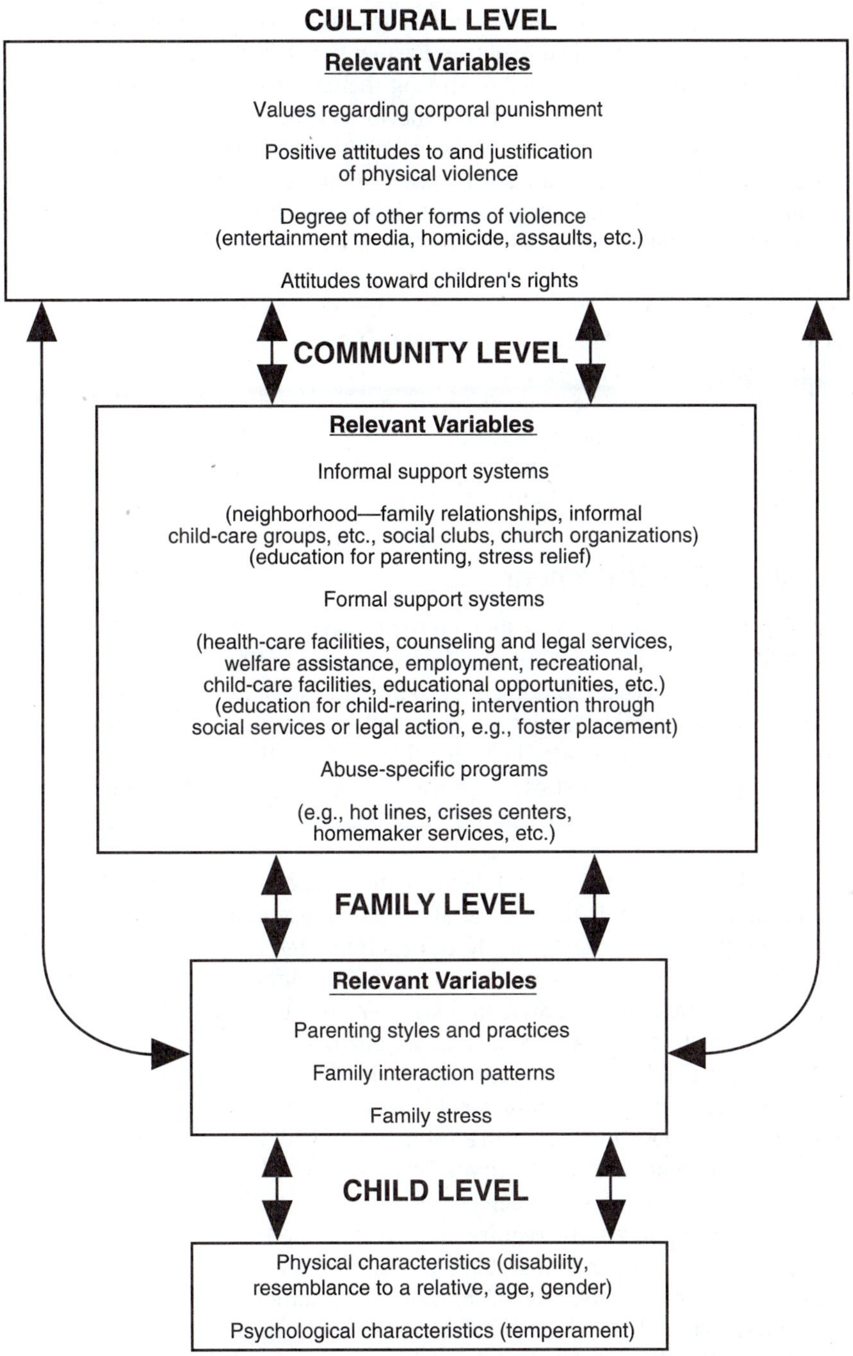

CULTURAL LEVEL

Relevant Variables

Values regarding corporal punishment

Positive attitudes to and justification
of physical violence

Degree of other forms of violence
(entertainment media, homicide, assaults, etc.)

Attitudes toward children's rights

COMMUNITY LEVEL

Relevant Variables

Informal support systems

(neighborhood—family relationships, informal
child-care groups, etc., social clubs, church organizations)
(education for parenting, stress relief)

Formal support systems

(health-care facilities, counseling and legal services,
welfare assistance, employment, recreational,
child-care facilities, educational opportunities, etc.)
(education for child-rearing, intervention through
social services or legal action, e.g., foster placement)

Abuse-specific programs

(e.g., hot lines, crises centers,
homemaker services, etc.)

FAMILY LEVEL

Relevant Variables

Parenting styles and practices

Family interaction patterns

Family stress

CHILD LEVEL

Physical characteristics (disability,
resemblance to a relative, age, gender)

Psychological characteristics (temperament)

Sources: Adapted from R. D. Parke and N. G. Lewis (1981). The family in context: A multilevel interactional analysis of child abuse. In R. Henderson (Ed.), *Parent-Child Interaction.* New York: Academic Press, p. 171; D. Cicchetti and M. Lynch (1993). Toward an ecological/transactional model of community violence and child maltreatment: Consequences for child development. *Psychiatry, 56,* 96–118.

Parents who abuse their children often have psychological problems. Depression and alcoholism have been linked to abuse (Farmer, 1989; Small, 1987). Abusive parents are emotionally immature and need nurturing themselves. Thus they look to the child to meet their needs (Farmer, 1989). This behavior is called "role reversal" and has been found to be the most commonly observed psychological characteristic in abusive parents (Farmer, 1989). Abusive parents, instead of seeing themselves as nurturers of the child, expect the child to meet their needs for love. When the child fails to meet this expectation, abuse results (Belsky, 1993). As one mother of a 3-week-old said, "When he cried all the time no matter what I did, that meant he didn't love me, so I hit him." These parents also lack appropriate knowledge of behavior management and developmental norms. Physical, or corporal, punishment is their only source of control.

Abusive parents often have a low threshold of stress and frustration (Farmer, 1989; Mitchel, 1987). There may be financial problems and marital discord; they may suffer from overload and lack support networks in the community (Belsky, 1993). Many of these parents are unprepared for possible financial indebtedness, the constant demands children make, and the responsibilities that keep them from other activities.

The Child and Maltreatment

Certain physical and psychological characteristics have been associated more often with abused children than with nonabused children (Belsky, 1993)—for example, behaviors such as crying, hyperactivity, and inability to give an acceptable response to the parent. Disabilities, such as mental retardation, were also found to be associated with abuse. Additionally, a child's appearance or behavior that reminds the parents of their own parents or of negative characteristics of themselves was found to contribute to a negative parent–child relationship. Such children may become scapegoats for buried negative feelings.

In sum, children who are more difficult than average to care for seem to be the subjects of more maltreatment (Rogosch et al., 1995). These children may be demanding, whiny, crying, stubborn, resistive, sickly, or negative. High rates of mistreatment of premature babies, as well as those with developmental difficulties, have been reported (Fontana, 1991). Such children are commonly sensitive to all stimuli; they are restless, distractible, prone to anoxia and colic, and are disorganized sleepers (Maidman, 1984). Not only do these children require more care than average, it is likely that their parents have received less support, encouragement, and advice in caring for them. Also, parents who don't have the opportunity to form an attachment with the child after birth (as in the case of premature babies or babies with medical problems who must remain in the hospital for a time) are at more risk for neglect or abuse (Kennell, Voos, & Klaus, 1976). The main reason is that children who require more than average nurturance, such as children who are premature, sickly, or colicky, tend to make their parents feel less successful.

When babies are irritable, difficult to soothe, and difficult to engage in eye contact, parents tend to blame themselves and may project such anger on the child or withdraw from relating to the child. Depending upon the parents' knowledge about child development and the parents' emotional needs, such child behaviors may weaken the initial attachment process.

An older child's reaction to discipline may in turn evoke harsher discipline, possibly culminating in abuse. Studies have shown that of the various responses children make to being disciplined (ignoring, pleading for another chance, apologizing, defiance), defiance is most likely to lead to harsher discipline (Patterson, DeBaryshe, & Ramsey, 1989).

The Community and Maltreatment

Researchers have reported that a significant characteristic of abusive families is their isolation from the rest of the community (Emery, 1989; Garbarino, 1977), and consequent lack of support. Frequently, there are no close relatives nearby, or they have few friends. Thus they have no one to turn to for guidance, comfort, or assistance when they need advice or have a problem. They have no one to relieve them of child-care responsibilities when they need to get away from the house occasionally.

The line between physical abuse and acceptable discipline sometimes depends on the interpreter. Society expects parents to socialize their children to behave acceptably, so to foster acceptable behavior, some parents use physical, or corporal, punishment. Although occasional spankings could not legally be classified as child abuse, parental use of corporal punishment as a means of dealing with behavioral problems may have future undesirable consequences, such as teaching the child to be aggressive to resolve conflicts. To help determine whether corporal punishment should be interpreted as abuse, James Garbarino has defined maltreatment as "acts of omission or commission by a parent or guardian that are judged by a mixture of community values and professional expertise to be inappropriate and damaging" (Garbarino & Gilliam, 1980, p. 7).

Poverty, unemployment, social isolation of families, transient lifestyle, lack of recognition of children's rights, cultural acceptance of corporal punishment, and limited help for families in crisis are environmental factors that correlate highly with abuse (Garbarino & Gilliam, 1980; Thompson, 1994). The most frequently reported environmental stressor for abusive and neglectful families is their lower socioeconomic status (McLoyd, 1998).

Epilogue

*P*arenting *occurs in context. It is affected by cultural, family, and personal values. It is also affected by knowledge of child development and socialization methods as to what is appropriate for different ages and situations. Midas's and the Ramseys' parenting styles were both influenced by their materialistic values. Apparently, neither Midas nor the Ramseys had knowledge of child development; although Midas eventually learned through his daughter.*

As children change, so does parenting. Parenting is bidirectional. To be an effective parent, supportive connections are necessary. ■

SUMMARY

Parenting means implementing a series of decisions about the socialization of a child. There is little consensus today in the United States about what children should be like when they grow up and what parents need to do to get them there.

In earlier times, children were regarded as existing solely for their contribution to their family's welfare. Parenting styles were strict. Contemporary ideas of parenting regard the child as an individual whose development must be nurtured and protected by the family. Parenting practices in the twentieth century were influenced by "experts." They ranged from strict to permissive to democratic.

Parenting is conducted within various macrosystems, such as the history, culture, the political/socioeconomic system. All cultures have parenting goals but vary in importance. The political and social ideologies of different societies translate into different expectations for children. Different economic systems have different family structures and different formulas for appropriate adult social behavior, which are transmitted to children.

The socioeconomic status of a family influences parenting style. It has been found that generally lower-socioeconomic status parents are more punitive, emphasizing obedience and higher-socioeconomic status parents use more reasoning, emphasizing independence and creativity.

Parental occupations influence parenting styles in that skills required at work tend to be emphasized at home.

Baumrind identified three dominant styles of parenting—*authoritarian* (adult-centered), *permissive* (child-centered), and *authoritative* (democratic). Children of authoritarian parents showed little independence and scored in the middle range on social responsibility. Children of permissive parents conspicuously lacked social responsibility and were not very independent. Children of authoritative parents were independent and socially responsible.

Competence develops between 10 and 18 months of age. Competence is fostered by the caregiving style, including the arrangement of the environment, sharing enthusiasm with a child, having a lot of energy, setting reasonable limits according to the child's developmental level, and being available as a resource when needed. A measurement of the quality of the home environment (HOME) correlated with IQ scores.

Parenting styles are influenced by characteristics of the child, such as child age, temperament, gender, and presence of a disability.

Parenting styles are also influenced by characteristics of the family, such as size (number of siblings), configuration (birth order, spacing, and gender of siblings), parents' stage of life, as well as abilities to cope with stress.

Appropriate parenting practices are influenced by parental understanding of developmental and behavioral norms for children as well as socialization techniques. Parents respond to their child's development by changing their expectations and parenting tasks, and so is bidirectional. Parents need to know when it is appropriate to use guidance and discipline. Guidance techniques are preventative, whereas disciplinary techniques are corrective.

Various ethnic communities differ in certain parenting styles and practices. Asian American, Native American, Hispanic American, and African American patterns of parenting differ in emphasis on the individual versus the group. Generally, American parents value self-reliance; Asian American parents value respect for elders; Native American parents value group harmony; Hispanic American parents value family loyalty; and African American parents value obedience.

Inappropriate parenting is maltreatment, which involves intentional harm to or endangerment of a child. It includes abuse and neglect. Maltreating parents fail to meet the physical or emotional needs of the developing child. Whether families succumb to maltreatment depends on ongoing and transient risk and resilient factors.

Children who are intentionally bruised, wounded, or burned are physically abused. Physical abuse is often related to domestic violence.

Children who are abandoned, lack supervision, do not receive proper nutrition, need medical or dental care, are frequently absent or late for school, do not have appropriate or sufficient clothing, are unclean, or live in unsafe or filthy homes are neglected.

The sexual abuse of a child occurs whenever any person forces, tricks, or threatens a child in order to have sexual contact with him or her.

Psychological or emotional abuse includes unreasonable demands put on a child that are beyond his or her capabilities and may include persistent teasing, belittling, or verbal attacks.

The parents in abusive families tend to have been abused as children. These parents also tend to have unmet emotional needs. They have unrealistic expectations for children and often lack knowledge of child development. In many cases, they believe that their children's behavior is deliberate and meant to hurt them. These parents also have very low self-esteem. Depression and alcoholism have been linked to abuse.

Abusive families tend to be isolated from the community in that they lack a supportive network of relatives and/or friends upon whom to rely when in need of help or support. They also have a low tolerance for handling stress, in addition to financial, emotional, and health problems. Corporal punishment is often their only means of dealing with misbehavior. There is a documented relationship between poverty and neglect.

Certain characteristics have been associated more with abused children than with nonabused children—such as crying, hyperactivity, disabilities, prematurity, negativism, and whininess.

ACTIVITY

Purpose: To examine your values relating to parenting.

A License for Parenting?

Write the appropriate requirements for a parenting license. Include (1) physical (health status, age, etc); (2) psychological (temperament, educational status, etc); (3) social (marital status, finances, etc) requiements; as well as (4) experience with children.

What Would You Do?

1. Three-year-old Charles spilled his milk all over the table and began to cry.

2. Just as you walk out of the grocery store, you notice your 5-year-old daughter eating a candy bar that you did not purchase.

3. Bill, age 10, has recently begun to ignore your requests to put his things away. He also has been "forgetting" to do his regular chores.

4. Your 8- and 10-year-old children have lately been arguing about everything. When they have nothing specific to argue about, like a toy, a game, or a television show, they tease each other.

5. Your 6-year-old daughter does not want to go to school. You talk to the teacher to find out what the problem is. The teacher says your daughter is shy and will not participate in class or interact with the other children.

6. Your 9-year-old son is watching the news on television and asks, "What does 'rape' mean?"

7. Your 2-year-old has been coming into your bedroom for the past three nights about 3:00 A.M.

8. Your 11-year-old daughter asks to spend the night at a school friend's house, and you have never met the friend's parents.

RESOURCES

National Center for Fathering
http://www.fathers.com

National Clearinghouse on Child Abuse and Neglect
http://www.calib.com/nccanch

National Parent Information Network
http://www.npin.org

STEP (Systematic Training for Effective Parenting)
http://www.agsnet.com/fast.asp

RELATED READINGS

Brazelton, T. B. (1992). *Touchpoints.* Reading, MA: Addison-Wesley.

Chess, S., & Thomas, A. (1987). *Know your child.* New York: Basic Books.

Cleverly, J., & Phillips, D. C. (1986). *Visions of childhood: Influential models from Locke to Spock* (rev. ed.). New York: Teachers College Press.

Dinkmeyer, D., & McKay, G. D. (1973). *Raising a responsible child: Practical steps to successful family relationships.* New York: Simon & Schuster.

Dodson, F. (1974). *How to father.* New York: New American Library.

Dodson, F. (1987). *How to single parent.* New York: Harper & Row.

Dreikurs, R. (1964). *Children: The challenge.* New York: Hawthorn.

Dunn, J. (1985). *Sisters and brothers.* Cambridge, MA: Harvard University Press.

Faber, A., & Mazlish, E. (1982). *How to talk so kids will listen and listen so kids will talk.* New York: Avon.

Faber, A., & Mazlish, E. (1988). *Siblings without rivalry.* New York: Avon.

Fontana, V. J. (1991). *Save the family, save the child: What we can do to help children at risk.* New York: Dutton.

Garbarino, J., Eckenrode, J., & Barry, F. D. (1997). *Understanding abusive families: An ecological approach to theory and practice.* New York: Jossey-Bass.

Ginott, H. (1965). *Between parent and child.* New York: Macmillan.

Gordon, T. (1991). *Discipline that works: Promoting self-discipline in children at home and at school.* New York: Plume.

Hart, B., & Risley, T. R. (1995). *Meaningful differences in the everyday experiences of young American children.* Baltimore: Brookes.

Hewlett, S. A., & West, C. (1998). *The war against parents: What we can do for America's beleaguered moms and dads.* Boston: Hougton Mifflin.

Ilg, F. L., Ames, L. B., & Baker, S. M. (1991). *Child behavior* (rev. ed.). New York: Harper & Row.

Konner, M. (1991). *Childhood: A multicultural view.* Boston: Little Brown.

McAdoo H. P. (Ed.). (1993). *Ethnic families: Strengths in diversity.* Newbury Park, CA: Sage.

Satir, V. (1988). *The new peoplemaking.* Mountain View, CA: Science and Behavior Books.

Snow, R. L. (1997). *Family abuse.* Boulder: Perseus.

Steinberg, L., & Levine, A. (1990). *You and your adolescent: A parent's guide for ages 10–20.* New York: Harper Perennial.

Straus, M., Gelles, R. J., & Steinmetz, S. K. (1980). *Behind closed doors: Violence in the American family.* Garden City, NY: Anchor Books.

Turecki, S., & Wernick, S. (1994). *Normal children have problems, too.* New York: Bantam Books.

White, B. L. (1995). *The new first three years of life.* New York: Simon & Schuster.

Wolin, S. J., & Wolin, S. (1993). *The resilient self.* New York: The Free Press.

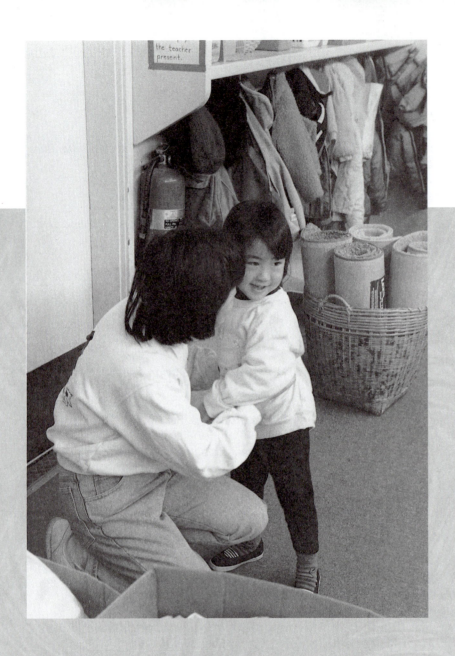

"I would be true, for there are those who trust me;
I would be pure, for there are those who care;
I would be strong, for there is much to suffer;
I would be brave, for there is much to dare."

— *Howard Arnold Walter*

Chapter 5

ECOLOGY OF CHILD CARE

Prologue

Child Care
What Is Quality Care?
History of Child Care

Correlates and Consequences of Child Care
Child Care and Social Development
Child Care and Cognitive Development
Child Care and the Community
Child Care, Challenge, and Choice

Child Care and Socialization
Socialization Effects of Different Preschool Programs
Socialization Effects of Child-Care Ideologies

Collaborative Caregiving
Caregivers and Child Protection
Epilogue
Summary
Activity
Resources
Related Readings

Prologue

COLLABORATIVE CAREGIVING

A classic caregiving story, Mary Poppins, by Mary Shepard and Pamela Travers, tells of the adventures Mary, the magical nanny shares with Jane and Michael Banks. Jane and Michael are the sullen, spoiled children of wealthy parents who have no clue as to how to raise them since they always have delegated the caregiving of their children to various nannies. Everything changes when Mary arrives: she is firm, strict, and demanding . . . but she is also loving and fun. After the children complete their schoolwork or chores, she takes them on fantastic adventures, like stepping into the drawings made with chalk on the sidewalk. She also does silly things with them, like having tea upside down on a ceiling. When Mary feels confident that Mr. and Mrs. Banks have absorbed the caregiving skills they need and that Jane and Michael have achieved some self-reliance, she leaves to become a nanny at another family's home.

Another, more realistic, caregiving story is of Helen Keller who was born in Alabama in 1880. She was a normal, healthy baby during early infancy. However, at 18 months of age, she became ill. This resulted in the loss of her sight and hearing. Her parents hired a teacher, Anne Sullivan, who after many attempts, finally reached Helen by having her put her hand under the water pump faucet and spelling "w-a-t-e-r" in her hand—the breakthrough of learning to sign in order to communicate. The understanding that everything had a name awakened Helen's curiosity and desire to learn. ■

- *Should parents seek caregiving help (full- or part-time, babysitter, nanny, day care)?*
- *How can parents and caregivers collaborate for optimal socialization and developmental outcomes?*

CHILD CARE

Child care, or as it is sometimes called, **day care,** refers to the care given to children by persons other than parents during the parts of the day when parents are absent. When mothers work outside the home, fathers are the single most important source of family-provided child care for preschoolers (O'Connell, 1993). When both parents are unavailable, the family must rely on nonparental caregivers. Child care can begin as early as birth and extend into the school years (after school and on vacations) until children are old enough to care for themselves. Most states have laws regarding the age children can legally be left unsupervised by an adult. Child care for school-age children (school-age child care) is sometimes referred to as **extended day care.**

The nurturing, or care of children today is for a significant part of the day, more likely to be provided by caregivers other than parents. Specifically, 13 million preschool children—including 6 million infants and toddlers—spend all or part of their day in a nonparental care setting. Millions of school-age children have no supervised care at all during times when school is closed (Children's Defense Fund, 1998). Because children are spending significant socialization time in nonparental care settings, and at very young ages, this chapter examines the influence of child-care settings on development.

The availability, affordability, and adequacy of child care has become an increasingly serious concern over the past 25 years. In the mid-1970s approximately 30% of mothers with children under age 6 were employed, as were more than 50% of mothers of school-age children. By the end of the 1990s, these percentages had grown to 65% and 77%, respectively (Children's Defense Fund, 1998). In the twenty-first century, these numbers will climb even further due to the rising cost of living that forces many parents to contribute to the family income jointly.

There are several different types of child care. A friend, relative, or sitter may come to the home and care for the child. The family may hire a nanny (someone who has received child-care training) to live in. Families may cooperate and provide care by taking turns. Independent caregivers may provide care for children in their homes (family day care). Parents may take children to a center for care during the day. Regardless of the type, quality child care involves certain basics: a caregiver who provides warm, loving care and guidance for the child and works with the family to ensure that the child develops in the best way possible; a setting (home or center) that keeps the child safe, secure, and healthy; and developmentally appropriate activities that help the child develop emotionally, socially, mentally, and physically (Clarke-Stewart, 1993). Many states require fingerprinting for caregivers so background checks can be made through the police department. The terms *nursery school, preschool, early childhood education,* and *child development program* are sometimes used to describe certain types of programs for young children. Because all care for children has an impact on their socialization or education, the terms *child care* or *day care* will be used to refer to nonparental caregiving.

Child care has been used during the latter part of the twentieth century for three basic purposes:

1. enrichment for middle-class preschoolers;
2. intervention to equalize learning opportunities for disadvantaged preschoolers (low income, minority status, disabled, abused); and
3. employability for parents.

Enrichment. The first cooperative nursery school was inaugurated at the University of Chicago in 1915. The purpose was to give the children of faculty wives opportunities to play in a supervised environment where they could develop impulse control, verbal skills, and knowledge about the world. Parent participation was required. Such nursery schools were popular with middle-class families from the 1930s to the 1960s. In the late 1960s, due to child development research and political pressure for the United States to keep pace with Russian scientific advances, a new purpose was incorporated into nursery school programs—to stimulate intellectual growth (Clarke-Stewart, 1993).

Intervention. In the 1960s, civil rights groups demanded equal opportunities in education, jobs, and housing. Thus, in 1964, the Economic Opportunity Act was passed to provide educational and social opportunities for children from low-income families. Preschool programs that would compensate for the perceived physical, social, and academic disadvantages of children who came from families of low-socioeconomic status, ethnic-minority status, or who were identified as disabled or abused were funded by tax dollars. The purpose of such intervention was to provide the children with skills they would be unlikely to get at home to enable them to succeed in school and avoid poverty in adulthood. Intervention programs are usually comprehensive in that they provide health and nutrition services, social services, and parental involvement. An example of a federally funded comprehensive preschool intervention program is Head Start. Its goal is to enable children from qualified families to enter school ready to learn. The rationale for such early intervention came from research concluding that early experiences stimulate intellectual development (Bloom, 1964; Hunt, 1961). Public money spent to enhance the early childhood years would be more beneficial than public money spent to correct a deficiency in the later childhood years.

In addition to child development research, the political climate in the 1960s was also part of the rationale for early intervention. President Lyndon Johnson felt that the only way to break the cycle of poverty was through education. Intervention programs seemed to be a solution that would equalize opportunities through education. Education would ultimately enable people to get jobs to support themselves, rather than depend on welfare.

Thus we see how science (the recognition of the importance of the early childhood years to development) and politics (equal educational opportunities lead to greater economic opportunities) were both involved in passing legislation and exemplify how exosystems influence children's development.

Employability.   Child-care services are used to enable women to seek job training and/or employment outside the home (Lamb, 1998). Economic necessity, due to the increase in the cost of living and the increase in single-parent families, has resulted in a growing reliance on nonparental care by many families in the United States (Hernandez, 1995). Recent welfare reforms to increase employability have been implemented. The 1996 welfare law allows recipients of Temporary Assistance to Needy Families (TANF) to collect federally funded benefits for a maximum of 60 months. States can modify requirements with state funds. Recipients of TANF must be engaged in work-related activities (training, job search, job) within their state's time limit. The immediate effect of the imposed time limit for welfare was to increase the demand for available, accessible, affordable child care.

WHAT IS QUALITY CARE?

Due to the patchwork of services that currently exists and the projected need for future child care, quality child care has become an issue of concern among working parents, professionals who deal with children, and legislators (Lamb, 1998; Whitebook, Howes, & Phillips, 1989).

Since "quality" tends to be a subjective evaluation of excellence, research has approached the problem of an objective definition by closely examining the many aspects, both physical and social, of the child-care setting. For example, the federal government initiated the National Day-Care Study (Ruopp, Travers, Glantz, & Coden, 1979) for the purpose of ultimately constructing national child-care standards. The task was to identify key child-care components that best predicted good outcomes for children and to develop cost estimates for offering those components within programs. The study found

Figure 5.1 An Ecological Model of Human Development

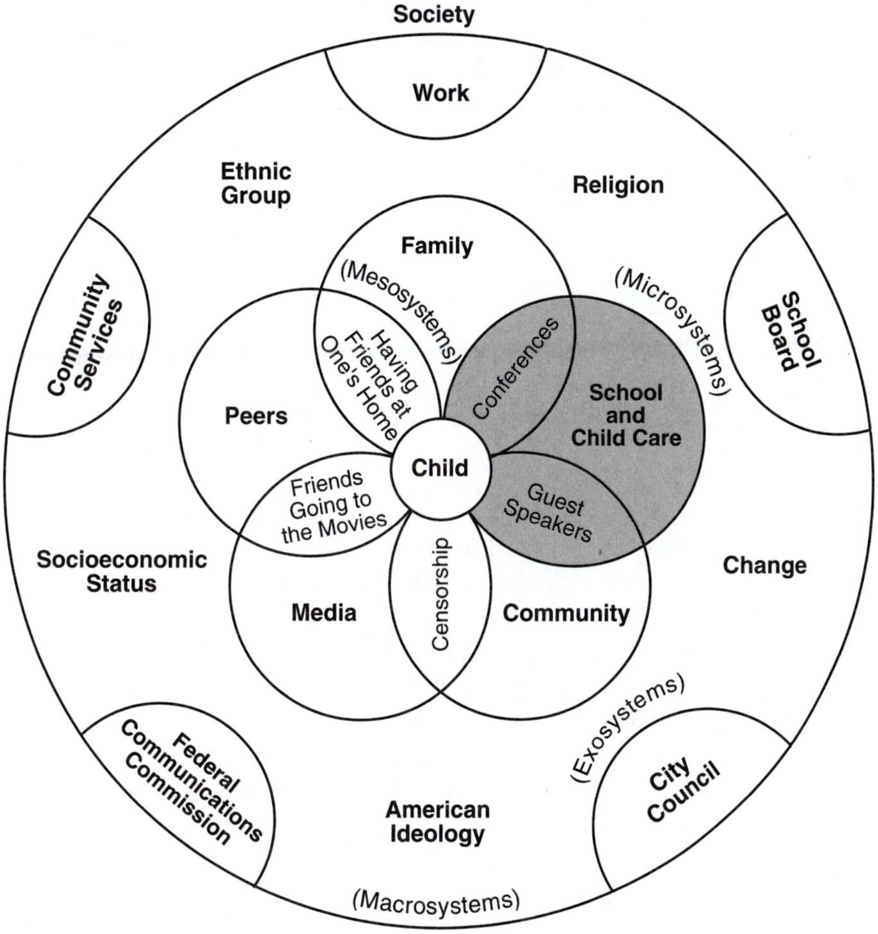

Child care is a significant influence on the child's development.

the components of child care that were the most significant predictors of positive class-room dynamics and child outcomes to:

- The size of the overall group
- The caregiver–child ratios
- Whether the caregiver had specialized training in child development or early childhood education

These findings show that in classrooms that had smaller groups and those where the teacher had specialized training, teachers could engage in more social interaction with children. Thus the children were more cooperative, more involved in tasks, more talkative, and more creative. They also made greater gains on cognitive tasks. These findings were confirmed in later studies (Hofferth, 1992; NICHD, 1996; Phillips, 1987).

"Quality" can mean different things to different people. Hence, some studies focus on objective features of child-care settings: child–staff ratios, physical space, teacher qualifications, staff training, wages, and safety. Other studies focus on subjective features: how caregivers interact with children and the experiences children have. Useful measures, such as the Early Childhood Environment Rating Scale (Harms & Clifford, 1980), are now available to assess quality.

An analysis of studies of child-care centers reveals that typical quality is considerably below what is considered good practice (Love, Schochet, & Meckstroth, 1996). For example, the Cost, Quality, and Child Outcomes Study (CQO, 1995) reported that in more than 400 centers studied in four states, only 8% of infant programs and 24% of preschool programs were of good or excellent quality. In 40% of infant programs and 10% of preschool programs, quality was rated as poor.

What factors contribute to less than optimal quality?

1. The education credentials of caregivers who work in child-care centers are often inadequate relative to the skills required. The National Institute of Child Health and Human Development (NICHD) Early Child Care Research (1996) found that only a third of infant child-care providers had any specialized training in child development, and only 18% had a bachelor's degree or higher.

2. Staff turnover is high, ranging from 25% to 50% each year. This means that children are continually adapting to new caregivers, and administrators are constantly training new staff (Whitebook, Howes, & Phillips, 1989).

3. Staff compensation, including wages and benefits, is exceptionally low. Child-care staff are among the lowest paid of all classes of workers in the United States. Worker compensation is significantly related to quality of care provided (Whitebook, Howes, & Phillips, 1989).

Over the past 15 years, a number of studies have examined the effects of varying levels of quality on children's behavior and development. Conclusions were similar in that a significant correlation exists between program quality and socialization outcomes for children (Frede, 1995). Outcomes related to quality include cooperative play, sociability, ability to resolve conflicts, self-control, and language and cognitive development.

While most studies on quality care have focused on effects on the child, a few have examined effects on parental sense of well-being because the emotional state of the parents influences choice of child care, satisfaction at work, and parenting (Phillips, 1992). For example, Mason and Duberstein (1992) have found that the objective factors of availability and affordability of care overshadow the subjective factor of quality in parental sense of well-being and, hence, choice of child care.

Advocacy for Quality Care

Since national standards for "quality" care do not exist, the National Association for the Education of Young Children (NAEYC), an organization of professionals involved in early childhood education, took on the task of setting its own criteria. A position statement on criteria for high-quality early-childhood programs was published in 1984. Briefly, a high-quality program is

> . . . one which meets the needs of and promotes the physical, social, emotional, and cognitive development of the children and adults—parents, staff, and administrators—who are involved in the program. Each day of a child's life is viewed as leading toward the growth and development of a healthy, intelligent, and contributing member of society (National Association for the Education of Young Children, 1984, p. 7).

Child-care programs that meet the criteria can voluntarily apply to the National Academy for Early Childhood Programs (a division of NAEYC) for accreditation, thereby receiving national recognition for high-quality standards and performance. Accreditation specifics will be exemplified later.

In 1986, NAEYC expanded its position on quality. With the proliferation of programs for young children and the introduction of large numbers of infants and toddlers into group care, NAEYC felt the need for a clear definition of *developmentally appropriate practice,* a term often used in the criteria for quality early-childhood programs. In response to the trend (seen in many programs) toward increasing emphasis on formal instruction in academic skills, NAEYC published specific guidelines for developmentally appropriate practices for programs servicing children from birth through age 8 (Bredekamp, 1986, 1993; Bredekamp & Copple, 1997). **Developmental appropriateness** involves knowledge of children's normal growth patterns and individual differences. Research in human development indicates that there are universal, predictable sequences

These preschool children are engaged in a developmentally appropriate activity with the support of their teacher.

of growth and change that occur in childhood, adolescence, and adulthood. These predictable changes occur in all domains of development—physical, emotional, social, and cognitive. Knowledge of typical development of children within the age span served by the program provides a framework from which caregivers provide the learning environment and plan appropriate experiences. Play is viewed as the primary indicator of children's development. Each child is viewed as a unique person with an individual pattern and timing of growth, as well as individual temperament, learning style, and family background. Both the program and interactions should be responsive to individual differences. Learning in a developmentally appropriate program emerges as a result of the interaction between the child's thoughts and experiences with materials and people. The curriculum should match the child's developing abilities while also challenging the child's interest and understanding (Bredekamp, 1986, 1993).

After much hard work, debate, and compromise involving numerous child-advocate organizations, a federal child-care bill was eventually passed in 1990. The bill included a Child Care and Development Block Grant to state governments, requiring them to designate a lead agency to direct their child-care programs, to set health and safety standards, and to allow eligible low-income families to choose any licensed child-care provider. In addition, the child-care bill included tax credits for working families with children if they have child-care expenses for one or more children under age 13 and pay for child care in order to work.

To address the concerns from parents about the ability to balance family and work responsibilities, the government passed the Family and Medical Leave Act (FMLA) in 1993. The FMLA requires all public employers and private employers with 50 or more workers to provide up to 12 weeks of unpaid leave per year to employees who need to care for a new child (own, adopted, or foster) or a seriously ill family member, or who themselves become seriously ill.

Accreditation of Child-Care Programs.   Voluntary systems exist nationally to establish higher quality standards than are required by law for both child-care centers and family day-care homes (Helburn & Howes, 1996).

1. *Child-Care Centers.* In 1984, the National Association for the Education of Young Children (NAEYC) developed an accreditation system for child-care centers involving self-evaluations by staff and parents. Professional validators from NAEYC conduct visits to determine whether or not standards have been met; if they have, the program is accredited for three years. Standards are designed for programs serving children from infancy through age 8 in centers caring for more than 10 children; school-age programs are eligible if a majority of children are 8-years-old or younger.

The standard criteria, based on research and professional consensus, include: staff qualifications and training; administration and staffing patterns (group size and adult–child ratios); physical environment; health and safety; and nutrition and food service. For example, for children age 0 to 12 months, the standard is ages 6 to 8 children per group with an adult–child ratio of 1:3 to 1:4; for children ages 4 to 5 years, the standard is 16 to 20 children per group with an adult–child ratio of 1:8 to 1:10.

2. *Family Day-Care Homes.* In 1988, the National Association for Family Day Care (now, the National Association for Family Child Care, or NAFCC) began a program for voluntary accreditation for family child-care homes. The process includes

self-evaluation as well as external validation of aspects of program operation: health and safety, nutrition, indoor and outdoor play environments, interactions, and professional responsibility. Continuing education for the caregiver, such as cardiopulmonary resuscitation (CPR), is also required.

3. *In-Home Care: Nannies.* The oldest professional nanny organization in the United States is the International Nanny Association (INA). It includes nannies, nanny employers, nanny placement agencies, and nanny educators. Since 1987, INA has worked to professionalize the nanny industry by maintaining high standards of conduct, respecting and supporting families in their task of nurturing children, and promoting continuing professional growth. Background checks, referrals, conferences, and newsletters are some of their services.

History of Child Care

The various child care contexts in which children have been cared for and the educational practices employed throughout history are examined here to better understand the impact of child care as a microsystem on socialization. Generally, child care and educational practices were affected by macrosystems: (1) historical events, such as war and the Depression; (2) political values, such as the responsibility to aid the poor and include the disabled; (3) technological change, such as pressure to impart academic skills to children as early as possible; and (4) sociocultural change, such as immigration and sensitivity to diversity.

Day care for children is not new, neither is it unique to the United States (Lamb, 1998). During the beginning of the nineteenth century, industrialization was accompanied by the growth of factories and cities. At the same time, the United States experienced a flood of immigrants who were fleeing the famine in Ireland and the revolution in Germany. Many of these immigrants settled in cities so they could work in the factories. Many of the women had to work to help their families survive. For example, the first day nursery in the United States was opened in 1838 by Mrs. Joseph Hale to provide care for the children of seamen's working wives and widows (Clarke-Stewart, 1993).

During the twentieth century, child care expanded. Generally, day care was set up in a converted home. Most child care could be classified as custodial; in other words, children's basic needs for food, shelter, sleep, and supervision were met. The caregivers cooked, cleaned, and washed clothes as well as watched the children. Some programs taught children cleanliness and manners, trying to instill obedience and a belief in hard work and punctuality. Some even hired kindergarten teachers to come in for a few hours each day to teach reading, spelling, sewing, and weaving. Others offered classes for the mothers in child rearing, English, cooking, and sewing as well as providing assistance with family problems (Clarke-Stewart, 1993). Thus the underlying philosophy of child care in the nineteenth and early twentieth centuries was that it existed to provide a support service for needy families.

In 1933, President Franklin Roosevelt initiated the Federal Economic Recovery Act and the Works Progress Administration (WPA) in order to alleviate effects of the Depression. Public funds became available for the first time to expand day care programs; jobs then became available for unemployed teachers, nurses, cooks, and janitors.

In 1938, when the WPA was dismissed, day nurseries declined until World War II. Then, with the massive mobilization of women into war-related industries, day care once again flourished to accommodate the children of women who were employed to assist in the war effort. Child-care centers were established with federal funds by the Lantham Act of 1942.

Even though the Lantham funds were withdrawn in 1946, child-care facilities continued to exist. Some were run by charitable organizations emphasizing social work and serving families with financial and other problems. Others were private, paid for by mothers who worked. Still others were set up for the purpose of enriching children's development (Clarke-Stewart, 1993).

As the twentieth century progressed, the American philosophy of child care evolved from a support service for needy families to a developmental service for all children. Child-care programs began to flourish in the United States in the 1960s. There were several reasons, among them a positive change in public attitude toward women who worked, the realization that provision of day care would allow more women to get off the welfare rolls, and research studies showing that children learned more rapidly during the early years of life. The 1960s saw public funds for preschool programs for poor children such as Head Start.

The 1971 White House Conference on Children pointed to the need for quality child care as the most serious problem confronting families and children. Unfortunately, as the twenty-first century begins, we still have no official national policy or federal standards aimed at establishing a system of child care that is of good quality. Child-care standards continue to vary widely from state to state and family to family. Why is this so?

One reason is that traditional views of parenting in this country have delegated the primary responsibility of child care to the family. Some people in government and business support the view of "individualism," that each should be able to care for its own without outside assistance (Schorr, 1997).

Another reason is the fear of government involvement in what is considered a basic personal right: to bring up one's children according to one's values, one's religion, and one's culture. Federal involvement in private matters is thought of by some as teetering on socialism. Is the underlying fear that if the government foots the bill for child care, then the government will call the shots?

In general, the federal government has not yet committed itself to implement child-care standards (except in programs where federal funds are involved). This means the task is left to the states, local communities, private enterprise, professional organizations, and the consumer (*see* Appendix: How to Choose a Good Early Childhood Program).

Since nonparental child care has become a fact of life, the question from the 1980s to 1990s, which was "Is day care helpful or harmful to children?", needs to be reframed to "What kind of child care is most supportive of children and families?"

There are a variety of opinions among professionals and laypeople on whether or not children should be enrolled in day care. There are also opinions on the age at which children should be enrolled and whether such care should be full- or part-time. There are even opinions on the types of program that should be offered. For example, some believe the preschool experience should focus on learning how to get along with others, exploring the environment, and dealing with feelings; others believe the preschool experience should focus on academic skills, such as reading and math. The debate goes on.

CORRELATES AND CONSEQUENCES OF CHILD CARE

Much of the early controversy regarding the effects of child care on the child's development was centered on the fear that separation from the mother, especially in infancy, would disrupt the natural mother–child bond of attachment and would result in psychological and social problems. Thus most of the original research studies examined the effects of separation on the child. It should be noted that the infant separation studies were done in residential institutions, rather than in child-care centers as we know them today. More recent studies have examined the overall effects of different child-care settings (home versus alternative) on children—for example, children's social relationships with other children, as well as their relationships with their mothers, and changes in their intellectual development. The most recent studies have used an ecological approach combining family factors and child-care factors (Clarke-Stewart, Allhusen, & Clements, 1995), as well as cultural factors (Lamb, 1998) that work together to affect children's development. It is now well accepted that "childrearing has become a collaborative endeavor with children moving back and forth . . . between their homes and child care" (Phillips & Howes, 1987, p. 9). The mesosystem links may be supportive, competitive, or neutral. Classical as well as modern studies will be examined.

CHILD CARE AND PSYCHOLOGICAL DEVELOPMENT

What is the effect of separating infants from their mothers? One of the first studies to report the detrimental effects of separating infants from their mothers was done by Rene Spitz in 1946. He compared the development of infants raised by caregivers in a foundling home (a home for illegitimate and abandoned babies) to infants raised by their mothers in a prison. Each caregiver in the foundling home was responsible for caring for at least eight infants. The mothers, who were all either mentally retarded or emotionally disturbed, were responsible for caring for their own infants in the prison. The infants raised in the foundling home had poor appetites and lacked interest in their surroundings; they exhibited severe depression, according to Spitz. As a result, they were retarded in their growth and mental development. The infants raised by their mothers in prison, on the other hand, developed normally. Even though the mothers in the prison were socially deviant, the one-on-one care and nurturance they gave their infants enabled the infants to exhibit normal development; whereas even though the caregivers in the institution were professionally trained, they had eight babies to nurture and probably could not establish emotional attachments with each one. Spitz supported "nature" care.

In 1952, John Bowlby (1966, 1969, 1973) wrote that maternal love and care are the most important influences on an infant's future development. He concluded, after reviewing studies on infants separated from their mothers, that any break in the early mother–child relationship could have severe emotional, social, and intellectual consequences. What Bowlby meant by "any break" was loss of mother in infancy due to death, or separation from mother because of hospitalization, employment, or other circumstances such as neglect—being physically present but emotionally absent. He went on to

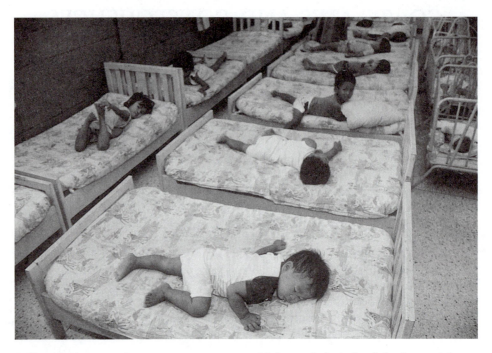

Babies who do not receive one-on-one care are at risk for psychological and developmental problems.

say that deprivation of the early mother–child relationship would cause the infant to become depressed, physically and mentally retarded, or delinquent. Bowlby, too, supported "nature" care.

A 30-year longitudinal study completed in 1966 by Harold Skeels demonstrated that it is the quality of care (nurture) that affects children's development, not the relationship of the (nature) person who provides it. Thus the care can come from someone other than the child's mother. Skeels studied 25 infants who were institutionalized because they were deemed mentally retarded. Of these, 13 were later transferred to the institution for retarded women, where the infants were "adopted" by small groups of residents, who lavished care and attention on them. The remaining 12 infants stayed where they were. After two years, the transfer group had gained an average of 28.5 points on an IQ test, but the control group had lost an average of 26.2 points.

Thirty years later, Skeels did a follow-up study on the original 25. He found that 11 out of the 13 who were transferred to the institution for retarded women had been adopted by families, 12 out of the 13 had achieved an education and become self-supporting adults with responsible jobs. Their own children had average IQs. As for the control group, 11 out of the 12 children survived. Four of these were in institutions, one was a vagrant, one was a gardener's assistant at an institution, three were dishwashers, one was a part-time worker in a cafeteria, and one was a domestic worker.

This study showed that children need care and nurturance to develop normally (in this respect, Skeels agrees with Spitz and Bowlby); that the care and nurturance can be provided by someone other than the mother (here Skeels disagrees with Spitz and Bowlby); and that infants who are initially deprived can grow up normally if intervention by a caring, nurturing person is provided (Spitz and Bowlby did not even consider this possibility). Skeels supported "nurture" care.

Skeels's study has implications for society. If deprivational effects caused by neglect in infancy can be reversed by intervention, then we can enable many children to grow up to be independent, self-sufficient, responsible adults who are assets to society rather than liabilities. There are still unresolved questions. Which children qualify for intervention? When do you intervene? What type of intervention is best? What kind of program do you provide and for how long? Is day care worth paying for? Does the government or some other agency have the right to intervene? Is society willing to pay the cost of intervention? These questions will be discussed in more detail later.

Selma Fraiberg (1977), a psychologist and author, defends mothering: The mother is the primary caretaker of the infant; good maternal care "is every child's birthright," so society's intervening role should be to help inadequate mothers improve their relationships with their infants, rather than subsidize alternatives to mothering, such as day care. Sandra Scarr (1984), another psychologist and author of *Mother Care/Other Care,* provides evidence that babies and young children can be successfully reared by qualified others.

What exactly is so special about the early mother–child relationship? During the first year of life children become attached to their primary caregivers, the persons who hold them, comfort them, feed them, and play with them. This caregiver is usually the mother, but it can be the father, grandparent, an older sibling, or another person not related to the child. Feelings of attachment distinguish this caregiver from others. When children are in strange situations or not feeling well, they want to be near the person they are attached to; no one else will do.

Researchers access the level of attachment to the mother by putting children in a strange or stressful situation; for instance, leaving them alone in a room with a stranger and observing their reactions to their mother's presence, her departure, and her return. An *insecure attachment* is usually indicated when the child clings to the mother when she leaves or cries hysterically until the mother returns. An insecure attachment is also usually indicated when the child ignores the mother when she leaves and avoids her when she returns, or when a child clings to the mother one moment and rejects her the next. A *secure attachment* is indicated when the child is able to leave the mother's side to explore the toys in the room—obviously, however, preferring the mother's company to the stranger's. When the mother leaves, the child shows concern or becomes mildly upset, but gets over it quickly. When she returns, the child greets her happily (Ainsworth, 1973, 1979; Ainsworth & Bell, 1970).

Jay Belsky (1988, 1992) shows that babies less than 1-year-old who receive nonmaternal care for more than 20 hours a week are at a greater risk of developing insecure relationships with their mothers; they are also at increased risk of emotional and behavioral problems in later childhood. Youngsters who have weak emotional ties to their mothers are more likely to be aggressive and disobedient as they grow older.

Others (Clarke-Stewart, 1988, 1992; Phillips & Howes, 1987) take issue with Belsky, saying the evidence is insufficient to support the claim that infants in full-time day care are at risk for emotional insecurity. That day care infants exhibit different attachment behaviors than home care infants may mean they have developed a coping style to adapt to the different people who care for them as well as the daily separations and reunions. In addition, the assessment of attachment procedures commonly used may not be an accurate way of comparing differences in attachment between infants reared in such diverse environments. Thus not all children who begin day care in infancy are insecurely attached, aggressive, or noncompliant, neither are they intellectually advanced. There are individual differences for day care children just as there are for children reared at home (Clarke-Stewart, 1989, 1992; Honig, 1993).

Finally, recent data on psychological functioning of children who have attended day care in infancy are confounded often by the child's temperament and gender, family socioeconomic status, marital status, parent–child relationships, number of hours daily in care, and quality of care (McCartney & Galanopoulos, 1988; NICHD, 1997; Phillips, 1992). According to Michael Lamb (1998) who reviewed the research, it now appears that day care in itself does not reliably affect mother–child attachment. Adverse effects occur only when poor quality day care concurs with such risky conditions as insensitive and unresponsive maternal behavior (NICHD, 1997). In sum, children in a quality child-care program, compared to children cared for at home attach to their mothers similarly.

Child Care and Social Development

Children in day care may be with peers from infancy. Infants stare at each other and touch each other. Toddlers may smile at each other, share toys, and fight over toys. Three-year-olds may play games, share, take turns, argue, and fight. Four-year-olds may, in addition, role play. ("Let's play house. You be the mommy, and I'll be the baby.")

Results of a substantial number of studies on the social development of preschool children conclude that children attending some form of child-care program interact more with peers positively and, often, negatively, and that they are less cooperative and responsive with adults than home-care children (Clarke-Stewart, Allhusen, & Clements, 1995; Field, Masi, Goldstein, & Perry, 1988; NICHD, 1998).

Specifically, children who have had experience in a child-care program seem to be more socially competent than those who have not had such an experience. They are more self-confident, more outgoing, and less fearful. They are also more assertive and more self-sufficient. They know more about the social world—gender roles, taking the perspective of others, solving problems regarding getting along with another child, and emotional labels ("cheater," "crybaby," "bully"). They are not only more socially competent, they have also been observed to be less polite, less respectful of others' rights, and less compliant with adult demands, as well as being more aggressive and hostile to others (Clarke-Stewart, 1989; Clarke-Stewart, Allhusen, & Clements, 1995; Lamb, 1998).

This child clings to his mother for an extra hug when left at child care because he is attached to her.

CHILD CARE AND COGNITIVE DEVELOPMENT

Generally, day care children's intellectual performance is higher than that of children from similar family backgrounds who do not attend a day care program. For example, it has been shown that children, especially from low-income families, who attend a quality preschool program for children age 2.5 to 5, even part-time, compared to children who do not, are more verbally expressive and more interactive with adults (Clarke-Stewart, 1993; Honig, 1990, 1993; Lazar, 1977). It has also been demonstrated that children who attend quality child-care programs are better able to meet the requirements in the primary grades of elementary school and function at an increased intellectual capacity during their initial years of schooling; IQ scores approached an increase of up to 10 points at the end of program implementation. Academic achievement in these children continues to be better through high school than those who did not attend a quality preschool (Karoly, 1998; Schwienhart & Weikart, 1993). Although longitudinal studies have shown the increase in low-income children's intelligence test scores were not permanent, there was a significant reduction in grade retention as well as the need to be placed in a special-education program (Karoly, 1998; Schweinhart & Weikart, 1993).

Intervention Programs

Most research on the effects of day care on children's cognitive development focuses on intervention programs, which provide compensation rather than enrichment per se, as do the traditional preschool programs. *Compensation* means making amends for what is lacking. Intervention programs attempt to make up for the perceived academic, physical, and social disadvantages of children who come from low-socioeconomic-status families or ethnic minority families, or are disabled, or have been abused. The purpose of intervention is to prevent, or compensate, for perceived disadvantages that impede achievement in U.S. public schools. Intervention preschool programs are usually comprehensive in that they provide health and nutrition services, social services, parental involvement, in addition to education. An example of such a comprehensive program is Head Start, a federally funded preschool intervention program for qualified families intended to enable children to enter school ready to learn.

Many types of intervention programs were implemented in the 1960s and 1970s, using different curriculum models (discussed later). While children enrolled in such programs fared better academically, socially, and emotionally than their nonparticipant counterparts (Karoly, 1998), the debate as to which type of intervention is best, for whom, for how long, and where (home or school) remains an issue (Beatty, 1995).

Even though there are many variations of intervention programs, most investigators concur that in order to enable the child to become a competent member of society, the child's family must be involved. Thus the best type of intervention (among government funded programs) is one that reinforces the strengths of the family as a child-rearing system—in that it enables the family to be the primary educator of its children, links the family to the formal educational system through involvement, and links the family to resources in the community so that the family can receive needed health and social services. These are known as family support programs. An example of such a

The father is influencing his daughters' competency and total educational development through his interest and involvement in their learning.

program is the Child and Family Resource Program (CFRP), which began in 1973 as part of Head Start. It enrolled qualified families of children from birth through age 8, rather than just the children. It provided diagnostic medical, dental, nutritional, and mental health services as well as treatment. It also provided prenatal care and education for pregnant mothers. It assisted parents in promoting the development of infants and toddlers, as well as providing preschool comprehensive Head Start services for children age 3 to 5. It eased the transition from preschool to elementary school and offered special development programs for children with disabilities. Finally, it provided services such as counseling, referrals to community agencies, family planning assistance, and help in dealing with emergencies or crises.

Family support programs exist today under the comprehensive Child Development Program (CCDP). These programs have shown more developmentally appropriate behavioral expectations for children by the mothers and more prosocial behavior exhibited by the children (Greenfield & Suzuki, 1998).

In sum, accurately predicting the socialization outcomes of intervention programs is difficult due to the numerous variables that must be taken into account, such as quality of the mother–infant relationship, socioeconomic status of the family, educational level of the parents, stress on the family, available family supports, temperament and gender of the child, spacing of the siblings, age at which the child enters the program and for how many hours per day, quality of the caregiver–infant relationship, and quality of the program (see Table 5.1).

Table 5.1	Variables Influencing Child-Care Socialization Outcomes

Child-Care Variables
  Type of care (in-home, family day care, center care)
  Type of program (compensatory, enrichment)
  Compensation of caregivers
  Stability of caregivers
  Adult–child ratio
  Quality of day care setting
  Sensitivity and responsivity of caregiver to child
  Caregiver education/training
  Part- or full-time day care

Family Variables
  Socioeconomic status
  Ethnicity
  Family structure (single, step, extended)
  Parental educational level
  Mother employed part- or full-time
  Mother's attitude toward work
  Mother's attitude toward child care
  Mother's sensitivity and responsiveness to child
  Roles and relationships between parents
  Father's involvement in child care
  Parenting styles
  Stress
  Availability of social supports in community

Child Variables
  Age at entry into day care
  Gender
  Health
  Temperament
  Security of attachment to mother

CHILD CARE AND THE COMMUNITY

Child care not only affects the child and the family, it impacts the community as well, exemplifying mesosystem linkages. Before examining the effects of child care on the community, it must be realized that it is often assumed that children in home settings are experiencing caregiving from one or more adults who are committed to meeting the child's needs and capable of supervising safe, developmentally appropriate activities. This assumption is invalid in many homes, as is illustrated by data from the U.S. Census Bureau (1998) indicating that about 5 million children age 5 to 14 are left alone to care for themselves outside of school hours, while their parents work. There is no exact number of children under age 5 who are left alone all day, but a significant number are cared for by a sibling under age 14. Children who are unsupervised by adults after school (sometimes referred to as "latchkey" children) are more likely to become involved in antisocial acts in their neighborhoods than children who attend an after-school program (Children's Defense Fund, 1998; Steinberg, 1986; Vandell & Su, 1999). Self-care, or "latchkey," children are discussed in Chapter 10.

Thus, when examining the effects of child care on the community, one must ask the question: How does day care affect those children whose families' other alternatives are no care or inadequate care? Only then can one make a responsible decision regarding the economic cost of child care to the community versus the social (and economic) costs to the community, resulting from inadequately socialized children who may need government social services, such as welfare, when they grow up.

The quality of family life in a community is often elevated by the provision of child care (Garbarino, 1992). For example, Garbarino and Kostelny (1992) found that support for child care in certain neighborhoods correlated significantly with a lower incidence of child abuse and neglect. Thus the effect of child care on the community was that it helped prevent child maltreatment and, in so doing, resulted in a reduced need for more costly government social services to protect at-risk children, such as foster care.

Finally, child care affects the economics of the community in that it enables adults to work. In some societies, the government totally supports via tax funds child care for such a purpose—for example, in China, France, and Belgium. Likewise, some American businesses have become involved in supporting child care to attract and keep their employees (Galinsky, 1986; Lamb, 1998). The question, "Is child care a public, private, or individual concern?" remains unresolved in the United States—who will pay?

If child-care needs in the United States are so great, why is cost such a problem? Child-care costs depend on the age of the child, whether the care is part- or full-time, and the type of care. Next to housing, food, and taxes, child care is parents' biggest expense.

The current official policy in the United States is that the government will pay for child care for disadvantaged families (defined by specific criteria) and will give tax credits to other families up to a maximum set by Congress. It is less costly for the government to fund child care for a child than it is to fund other services such as special education, welfare, or programs for juvenile delinquents. Government-subsidized child care enables the parents to work. Also, research shows that certain types of child care have the potential to break the cycle of poverty in which needy families find themselves (Lamb, 1998).

For example, Lynn Karoly and her colleagues (1998) examined nine early intervention programs including Ypsilanti, Michigan's Perry Preschool Project (Schweinhart & Weikart, 1993), begun in 1962, following 123 poor African American children for 25 years from age 3 or 4 to age 27. Compared to nonparticipating peers (children were randomly assigned to groups), children who had attended a "quality preschool" significantly outperformed those who had not. Specifically, the major findings of Karoly's review were the following:

- Gains in emotional or cognitive development for the child, typically in the short run, or improved parent–child relationships
- Improvements in educational process and outcomes for the child

- Increased economic self-sufficiency, initially for the parent and later for the child, through greater labor force participation, higher income, and lower welfare usage
- Reduced levels of criminal activity
- Improvements in health-related indicators, such as child abuse, maternal reproductive health, and maternal substance abuse

Thus, preschool, or child care as it has been referred to, does have lasting effects. It is beneficial for children because it starts them off on a more positive track. From the beginning, they experience greater success in school, which leads them to have pride in themselves. This reinforces them to become more committed to school and, in so doing, they are less disruptive. Preschool is beneficial for society because it is cost efficient, according to Schweinhart and Weikart (1993) and others (Karoly, 1998) due to the reduced need for special education and the lessened likelihood of dropping out of school and ending up on welfare or becoming delinquent (*see* Figure 5.2). In terms of tax dollars, child care appears to be worth the expense (Karoly, 1998; Schweinhart & Weikart, 1993).

CHILD CARE, CHALLENGE, AND CHOICE

The challenge of the future will be for communities to provide more choices in quality child-care services, due to the increased need. Availability, accessibility, and affordability

Figure 5.2   High/Scope Perry Preschool Project: Major Findings at Age 27

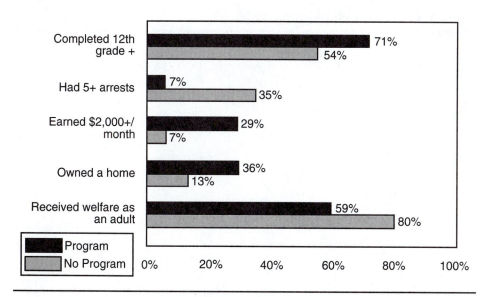

Source: L. J. Schweinhart and D. P. Weikart (1993). Success by empowerment: The High/Scope Perry Preschool Study through age 27. *Young Children, 49*(1), p. 54.

remain a problem (Children's Defense Fund, 1998). The types of child care most often used for infants and toddlers (younger than age 3) have been relatives, family day care homes (care in the home of a nonrelative), and centers. Preschoolers (child age 3 to 4) have been most frequently cared for in a child-care center and by relatives, whereas the most common types of care (excluding self-care) for school-age children have been family day care homes and relatives (*see* Figure 5.3). Among this usage, however, a most striking trend is the substantial growth in use of center-based care for all-age children, especially by full-time employed mothers (Hofferth, 1996; Willer, Hofferth, Kisker, Divine-Hawkins, Farquhar, & Glantz, 1991). If center-based care is the trend, how can such child-care options be increased?

One way is for the government to expand existing programs, such as Head Start, to include more children. Another way is for business to provide assistance in child care for its employees, such as parental leaves; flexible scheduling; providing a list of community resources for parents to choose from, known as "resource and referral"; providing start-up costs or contributions to a community child-care center in return for preferential admission for employees' children; providing financial assistance to pay for child care; and providing on-site child care. It has been found that employer-sponsored day care has several benefits: new employees are easier to recruit, employee absenteeism is lower, employees have a more positive attitude toward their work, and the job turnover rate of employees is lower (Galinsky, 1986, 1992). In addition, day care facilities located at a parent's place of work can provide a beneficial link between family and community for children. For example, parents can visit children during breaks, and children can learn about the work their parents do by touring the industry and meeting employees. Some of the innovations businesses have implemented to support family life are outlined in Table 5.2.

Figure 5.3   Who's Watching the Children?

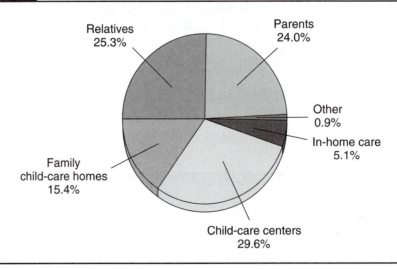

Source: Children's Defense Fund (1998). *The State of America's Children Yearbook, 1998.* Washington, DC: Author, p. 44.

Table 5.2   Exosystem Link: Business Support for Families

1. Child-care, elder-care, and ill-dependent assistance programs
2. National resource and referral service networks
3. Flextime programs to allow employees to adjust their workdays by as much as two hours in either direction
4. Extended leave-of-absence policies permitting up to a three-year break from full-time employment with part-time work in the second and third years
5. Work-at-home programs
6. Family-issues sensitivity training for managers and supervisors
7. School partnerships, including donations of equipment, time for employees to volunteer, or time for parent–teacher conferences
8. On-site employee-staffed child-care centers
9. Job-sharing programs
10. Parent education seminars

Still another way to increase child-care options is for the elementary school to extend its services to include children younger than age 5, as well as extend the hours it is normally in session. As was mentioned, a majority of school-age children whose parents are employed care for themselves before and after school. Other children may be cared

for by a neighbor. Still others may participate in a community program. Unsupervised children, contrary to popular belief, are not the most likely to be be found in impoverished, minority communities; rather, self-care is most common when mothers work full-time and parents are divorced or separated regardless of income (Lamb, 1998). Indeed, extended day care can be an effective link among child, family, and school as it complements, supports, and extends the school's educational purposes and supports the family in its education and nurturance of children. To illustrate, according to Schorr (1997), Edward Zigler, one of the founders of Head Start envisioned the schools of the twenty-first century to include full day care as well as being

Adult role models in an extended day care program can positively impact children's development.

the hub of social services for families. Bowling Park Elementary School in Norfolk, Virginia, is such a school. It includes infants and preschoolers and their parents, responding to family needs. A breakfast club where parents can discuss parenting, children's books, and so on, as well as adult education courses are offered. The concept is for children to feel connected to people who care.

Another extended day care program that is a cooperative community venture exists between the public school district in some cities and the YMCA. The school district provides several schools as sites for the program. The Y provides the trained recreational leaders and transportation—if an extended program is not available at their school, the children are bused to a nearby extended day care site after school. The male and female recreational leaders provide care that promotes the physical, social, emotional, and cognitive development of children. Games, crafts, and help with homework are some of the activities. An added bonus from this program for some children is the opportunity to develop a relationship with a male role model. Such opportunities are important for children living with single mothers.

Adult-supervised, extended day care is important in light of research that found both boys and girls in fifth through ninth grade to be more susceptible to peer pressure when they were in an after-school situation in which there was no consistent adult control (Lamb, 1998; Steinberg, 1986).

CHILD CARE AND SOCIALIZATION

As has been discussed, there are different types of child care: care provided by an individual in the child's own home (in-home care), care provided in someone else's home (family day care), and care provided in a center either part- or full-time (center-based care). *See* Table 5.3 for a summary of the socialization effects of types of child care. (Children who care for themselves, "latchkey children," are discussed in Chapter 10.)

There are also different educational practices, or curriculum models that are implemented in center-based care. A **curriculum** includes the goals and objectives of the program, the teacher's role, the equipment and materials, the space arrangement, the kinds of activities, and the way activities are scheduled.

SOCIALIZATION EFFECTS OF DIFFERENT PRESCHOOL PROGRAMS

Because many child-care programs, especially center-based ones, follow a curriculum, some examples are briefly described in this chapter, keeping in mind that some programs select only certain facets of the various curriculum models. A curriculum translates theories about learning into action; consequently, they have different socialization effects. Curricula can be generally categorized as **teacher-directed** (learning activities are planned by the teacher for all the children), or **learner-directed** (learning activities emerge from individual interest and teacher guidance). The curriculum models used in child-care programs that we will briefly discuss are the *cognitively oriented curriculum, direct instruction, Montessori,* and *developmental interaction.*

Table 5.3   Socialization and Types of Quality Child Care[a] for Young Children[b]

	IN-HOME CARE (PRIVATELY FUNDED OR VIA RELATIVE)	FAMILY DAY CARE (PRIVATELY FUNDED)	CENTER-BASED CARE (PRIVATELY AND PUBLICLY FUNDED)
Physical setting	adult-oriented (valuable and breakable items moved)	adult-oriented but some specific child materials and play areas	child-oriented (toys, educational materials, specific areas for play)
Caregiver special training	unlikely	some	more likely to have college courses related to and experience with children (especially in public centers)
Adult–child interaction	frequent and personal	close	mostly adult-directed and shared with other children
Activities	mostly unplanned (generally around housekeeping chores)	some planned	planned curricula (group and individual)
Peer interaction	little	varied	much
Developmental differences (based on a series of tests done in a laboratory playroom and observations at home)	scored lowest on assessments of cognitive ability, social understanding (taking another's perspective and empathy), cooperation, friendliness, and independence from mother	scored highest on assessments of friendliness; lowest on independence from mother	scored higher on assessments of cognitive ability, social understanding (taking another's perspective and empathy), cooperation, friendliness, and independence from mother
Socialization outcomes (interpretation of results)	one-to-one interaction and training by adult	experience in complex interactions with different age children	increase in social competence, maturity, intellectual development

Notes:

[a]These are general differences *between* types of care; there are also differences *within* each type of care (Clarke-Stewart, 1987; Clarke-Stewart, Allhusen, & Clements, 1995).

[b] Age 2 to 4.

Cognitively Oriented Curriculum

The **cognitively oriented curriculum,** developed by David Weikart and associates at the High/Scope Educational Research Foundation in Ypsilanti, Michigan, is an attempt to translate Jean Piaget's theory of cognitive development into an educational program. It blends the virtues of purposeful teaching with open-ended, child-initiated activities. It would be classified as "learner-directed."

Piaget believed that humans adapt mentally to their environments through their interactions or experiences with people, objects, and events. He viewed the child as an active learner who explores, experiments, and plans, thereby constructing knowledge. Learning, or mental adaptation to one's environment, occurs through **assimilation,** or incorporation, of experiences and **accommodation,** or reconciliation of differences, of experiences. An example of assimilation is seeing a bluebird for the first time. The experience is incorporated into one's mental concept of a bird. An example of accommodation is seeing a butterfly, calling it a bird, and being told it is not a bird but a butterfly. The experience adjusts the original mental concept of butterfly, resulting in accommodating the concept that all things that fly are not always birds. When one can assimilate *and* accommodate new information, one is in **equilibrium,** or balance, according to Piaget, thereby allowing the information to be incorporated. We continually assimilate and accommodate throughout our lives. However, we do not always reach equilibrium. When we cannot accommodate some new information at the time we encounter it, we reject it. To minimize rejection in a child's learning experiences, Piaget recommends that all new experiences be planned in such a way that a child can make a connection or relationship to previous experiences. The implications of this recommendation for education are significant. For example, if teachers can assess the cognitive structures of all children through parent conferences, observation, interviews, and tests, they can then select appropriate learning activities and tasks that will promote cognitive growth. Otherwise, if a child lacks the cognitive structure for a given task, the child will fail; the new information will be rejected because the child cannot accommodate it at that particular time. For example, 4-year-olds generally have a poor understanding of equality. Thus, trying to convince a preschooler that the piece of cake on his plate is the same size as his sister's, even though her plate is smaller, thereby making the cake on her plate look larger, will be useless.

In addition to experiences or interactions with people, objects, and events, motivation is also a factor in intellectual development. According to Piaget, all children mature in a certain order. At first, they understand their environment only through their senses and motor abilities that enable them to explore. He called this stage **sensorimotor.** It involves only understanding the here and now. As children develop language, they understand what words symbolize, but they think everyone understands things as they do. They can also consider only one characteristic of a thing at a time. Piaget called this stage **preoperational.** Children in this stage make judgments based only on how things appear. By the time children reach school age, their understanding of the world expands to incorporate concepts about time, equality, weight, distance, and so on, but their understanding is limited to concrete, or actual, things they can see or manipulate. Piaget called this stage **concrete operations.** Whereas children in this stage can apply logical, systematic principles to specific experiences, they still cannot distinguish assumptions or hypotheses from facts. It is not until adolescence that children come to understand abstract concepts such as government and are able to employ logical thinking. Piaget

This child is actively involved in constructing her own learning by doing a concrete task that expands her understanding of sorting and numbers, concepts involved in math.

called this stage **formal operations.** In this stage, children can think logically about hypotheses as well as concrete facts.

In the cognitively oriented curriculum, children are encouraged to become actively involved in constructing their own learning. The teacher observes the children individually, questions and evaluates them, in order to identify the developmental level. Knowing the developmental level enables the teacher to involve children in appropriate activities that they will be capable of accommodating. The teacher organizes the environment so that children can choose from an array of developmentally appropriate materials and activities. The teacher encourages goal-setting and problem-solving by asking the children to plan what they are going to do and how it is to be done. Meanwhile, the teacher is enabling the children to have key experiences that stimulate thinking processes, language development, and social development.

Thus the child learns to make decisions, to set goals, and to solve problems by finding alternatives to plans that did not work out as anticipated (Hohmann & Weikart, 1995). A preschool child's goal might be to build a road with blocks. A goal a third-grader might choose is to make a book of the planets, with descriptions and drawings.

In a cognitively oriented program, the children's emerging abilities are "broadened and strengthened" rather than "taught." In other words, once an ability is recognized by the teacher, it is nourished by the activities the teacher then provides. Children are not pushed to achieve at another developmental level. They also are not taught facts per se; they learn to think for themselves. Emphasis is placed on self-direction, rather than external reinforcement from others (as emphasized in behavioral programs). For example, a child may choose to make an airplane at the workbench. The teacher asks the child what materials are needed to carry out the project. When the airplane is complete, the teacher asks the child to tell how the airplane was made. A discussion about how airplanes fly might follow.

Direct Instruction Curriculum

The **direct instruction curriculum** is based on behaviorist principles of dividing learning tasks into small progressive segments and reinforcing mastery of them. It would be classified as "teacher-directed." Also known as academic preschool, the curriculum was initially developed at the University of Illinois by Carl Bereiter and Siegfried Engelmann. It was later elaborated by Engelmann and Wesley Becker at the University of Oregon. The program was based on the idea that waiting for children to become academically ready was not a very sound educational practice, especially for children from lower socioeconomic groups. The behaviorist theory of B. F. Skinner (1954) provides the foundation for the direct instruction curriculum. **Behaviorism** is the doctrine that observed behavior, rather than what exists in the mind, provides the only valid data for psychology.

Those who subscribe to behaviorism believe that it is possible to ensure learning and that the school can create readiness through behavioral principles of reinforcement and individualized instruction, whatever the IQ or background of the child. In the behavioral approach to education, learning is mastery of specific content. The content and sequence are determined by the teacher or the school—whoever is responsible for planning the curriculum. Learners receive immediate feedback for their responses. Incorrect responses require repetition of the task; correct responses are reinforced, and the learner progresses to the next task.

The Bereiter–Engelmann (1966) preschool program, which was specifically designed for children from low-income families, implements the behavioral approach to learning. Bereiter and Engelmann believe that children from low socioeconomic levels are behind in language development. This lag causes them to have difficulty understanding what is required of them in school. To catch up with their age-mates, they need intense instruction in structured, detailed, sequential skill building. Concepts are organized explicitly and concisely in presentation books for teacher use. All the teacher needs to do is teach the lessons exactly as they are presented in the book. The Bereiter–Engelmann program also prescribes classroom-management techniques, such as rewarding students for correct responses, instructional-pacing techniques (how much time to spend on a topic or with a child), and group management—for example, using hand signals to cue students to respond. The program is designed to foster IQ gain and improve achievement-test performance in the early school years (Horowitz & Paden, 1973).

A revised form of the Bereiter–Engelmann program for use in elementary schools is the Engelmann–Becker program. It stresses hard work, focused attention, and achievement in reading, language, and arithmetic. The direct instruction curriculum uses few of the play materials normally seen in many early childhood programs. The reason for this is to minimize environmental distractions that could tempt the children to leave the task at hand and explore. Children are expected to be quiet, respond to the teacher, and not interrupt or leave their seats without permission.

Montessori Curriculum

Dr. Maria Montessori was a physician in Italy at the turn of the century. She developed methods of working with *mentally retarded* children that were adapted for use with normal children in her *Casa del Bambini*. Her principles of education were described in a journal in the United States in 1909 and eventually became very popular in many parts of the world. Trainers were sent to her school to learn her methods and apply them in early childhood programs. However, philosophical differences in the United States prevented Montessori's curriculum from "taking off." In the 1960s, interest in the Montessori curriculum by parents and teachers was renewed.

Montessori (1967) believed that children should be respected and treated as individuals and that adults should not impose their ideas and wishes on them. Children must educate themselves. The Montessori curriculum is classified as "learner-directed."

Children naturally absorb knowledge just by living. However, there are sensitive periods when children absorb knowledge most easily. Thus the role of the adult should be to recognize these sensitive periods and prepare the children's environment for the optimum use of these periods of learning (Montessori, 1967). In order, then, for teachers to take advantage of these sensitive periods, they must be keen observers of children's behavior. They also have to know when to encourage the child, when to divert the child, and when to leave the child alone.

A **Montessori curriculum** involves children of different ages. The teacher, called a directress or director, prepares the classroom environment for the children so that the children can do things independently. Sometimes the younger children learn from the older ones. The teacher introduces materials to the children by demonstrating the correct way to use them. The children are then free to choose any materials they wish to work with. Children work on the floor or on child-sized furniture. The Montessori program provides material designed for exercises in daily living, sensory development, and academic development (Miller & Dyer, 1975). Exercises in daily living include gardening, setting the table, buttoning buttons, and folding clothes. Sensory development includes work with shapes, graduated cylinders, blocks, and puzzles. Academic materials include large letters, beads and rods for counting, and equipment for learning about size, weight, and volume. All the materials are designed in such a way that children can determine whether they have succeeded in using them properly. Reward for success or reprimand for failure is nonexistent in a Montessori school (unlike behavioral programs). Rather, each child is encouraged to persist as long as possible on a chosen task because each child is respected as a competent learner.

This activity exemplifies one typically found in a teacher-centered classroom, such as direct instruction.

The Montessori curriculum fosters reality training. For example, toys such as replicas of furniture or dress-ups are not included. Children use real things instead of play things and do real tasks, such as setting the table with real silverware and ironing with a real iron.

Only one of each type of equipment is provided in a Montessori classroom. A child must wait until the child using a particular piece of equipment is finished. The intent of this is to help children learn to respect the work of others and cope with the realities of life.

Developmental Interaction Curriculum

The Bank Street curriculum, developed by Elizabeth Gilkeson and associates at the Bank Street College of Education in New York City in 1919, focuses on the development of self-confidence, responsiveness, inventiveness, and productivity (Gilkeson & Bowman, 1976). It is classified as "learner-directed." The program is also referred to as the **developmental interaction curriculum** because it is individualized in relation to each child's stage of development, while providing many opportunities for children to interact and become involved with peers and adults. The curriculum was influenced by the writings of John Dewey (1944), who believed children are naturally curious and learn by exploring their environment; and Sigmund Freud (1938), who believed the interactions in the first five years of a child's life are significant in forming the child's personality.

The curriculum is designed to help children understand more fully what is already known to them. Learning is organized around children's own experience bases. Gradually, children's orbit of knowledge and understanding is enlarged by enabling children to explore in greater depth things already familiar to them. Teachers must continually assess children's progress in order to challenge children to experience new levels of complexity (a feature similar to the Montessori curriculum).

The classroom is arranged to include a variety of interest centers where children can pursue special projects, ample storage space for children to have easy access to materials, a quiet area for reading, and a library, musical instruments, and art materials. There are also places for the care of animals and plants.

All areas of the curriculum are integrated through the development of themes or units—for example, community helpers, animals, seeds, and so on. Concepts are built around the theme. For example, seeds grow into plants such as wheat; plants such as wheat are used to make ingredients for food such as flour; ingredients are combined and cooked to make food such as bread. Activities are built around the concepts. For example, seeds might be planted, and bread might be baked. The activities lead to other learning involvements. For example, cooking leads to math—measuring, counting, adding, weighing. Books may be read about seeds, a trip may be taken to a bakery, and so on. Motivation to learn comes from the pleasure inherent in the activities themselves; extrinsic rewards, such as praise or tokens commonly used in behavioral programs, are generally not used in the Bank Street curriculum to influence children's learning, choice of activities, or behavior. The teacher gains the children's cooperation by showing care, concern, and support.

The results of the study showed that children from the *teacher-directed programs* (where there was more drill, practice, direct praise for good work, and time spent in reading and math activities) scored higher on reading and math achievement tests. They also showed more persistence in the ability to do this kind of work. They took responsibility for their failures. Children from the *learner-directed programs* (where there were more varied materials, more opportunities for choice and exploration, and more interpersonal contact) scored higher on the nonverbal reasoning and problem-solving tasks. They also expressed responsibility for their successes. The children from these classrooms were involved in more cooperative work with other children and were more independent (Miller & Dyer, 1975; Schweinhart, Weikart, & Larner, 1986a; Stallings, 1974).

SOCIALIZATION EFFECTS OF CHILD-CARE IDEOLOGIES

Ideologies involve concepts about human life and behavior. It has been well documented, as discussed in past chapters, that cultural or ethnic ideology influences socialization practices. People from different cultural and economic backgrounds hold different views of what constitutes appropriate child care (Honig, 1995). Yet much of the existing literature on child-care practices has been toward a monocultural model of optimum care (Greenfield & Suzuki, 1998; Bromer, 1999; Miller, 1989).

Miller (1989) examined the nature of early socialization taking place in quality day care centers serving infants and toddlers from families of different social classes. She found differences in language and social interaction according to the socioeconomic status of the center. She also discovered that parents tend to seek out and employ caregivers outside the family whose child-care ideologies generally match theirs.

The centers in Miller's study included Center A (Alphabet Academy), which served a working-class, relatively low-income clientele; Center B (Balloons and Bunnies Learning Center), which served a middle-class clientele with modest incomes; Center C (Color-Coordinated Country Day School), a highly educated professional clientele with affluent means; and Center E (Le Exclusive Enfants School), an executive, elite clientele with affluent means. Miller focused on the verbal interaction and role expectations between adults and children because language, according to Bernstein (1979), mediates and is mediated by one's perception of reality as well as one's social role. Thus the language of caregivers who spend much of the day talking and responding to children has an impact on the development of values, roles, and culture-specific behaviors.

Caregivers in the centers gave evidence of differing perceptions of the needs of babies (Miller, 1989). In centers A and E, crying was not necessarily perceived to indicate a need, so it wasn't responded to as such. For example, in Center A a baby who cried for days was said to have just wanted her mama. A bottle or pacifier was not given to soothe the baby because it was not allowed. The attitude was that the children "holler for a few days and then they forget about them [their mothers]."

In centers B and C, crying was almost always perceived to indicate a need. In Center B, whenever several babies started to cry, they were said to be either hungry or tired, although not much was done except telling the babies to stop. In Center C, when a baby cried, the adults were responsible for finding a solution, and if nothing they came up with worked, the parents were called.

In Center E, crying was perceived as a simple annoyance typical of babies and sometimes was indulged and sometimes was ignored.

According to Miller, the caregiver's response to babies crying represents the world as they perceive it. If the world appears to be warm, gentle, and compliant, that is the way they interact with the children—meeting their needs, comforting, and giving verbal encouragement ("You'll be fine; I'm here now"). If, on the other hand, caregivers perceive the world to be cold, hard, and unbending, they respond to children with epithets ("You scaredy-cat," "You naughty boy"), pointing out their failures and denying indulgences as a way of habituating and, thereby, protecting them from future hurts and disappointments and avoiding false expectations.

A child socialized to existence in a setting of poverty and inequality may have low expectations and low self-esteem but highly effective coping skills. The child socialized to exist in a protected, middle-class environment might be confident, verbal, and creative, but unprepared for life's daily hazards, especially when the real world proves colder and harder than expected.

That humans replicate for their children their own perceptions of social reality based on their experiences in the larger society was demonstrated by the different expectations communicated to children by caregivers in Miller's study (1989). For example, although both the low-socioeconomic and the high-socioeconomic day care reported that they would have toddlers "clean up" spilled milk, the low-socioeconomic caregiver said she would "make" them clean it up and the high-socioeconomic caregiver said she would "invite" them to do it.

In Center C, the center with the affluent, highly educated professional/managerial parents (doctors, lawyers, professors), there was a high level of give and take among caregivers and children. Children negotiated with caregivers for autonomy when caregivers made demands. Caregivers regarded a child's resistance to obey as an indication that perhaps their expectations were unwarranted or the child's primary needs were not being met. Thus the caregiver adjusted her expectations and demands to gain the child's cooperation. Children were treated with respect. Since achievement of responsible independence was a goal for children in Center C, the rights and interests of individual children were the focal point of curriculum decisions. These children were being socialized to fit into the world of their privileged parents, who were primarily employed in self-directed, creative, and highly respected occupations.

In Center E, the center serving primarily executive, elite parents, the degree of measurable performance by children in academic tasks was the focal point of curriculum decisions. Children were positively reinforced for absorbing as much memorized information as they could reasonably handle via abstract symbols for quantities, letters, and geometric shapes. Adults controlled most of the use of time, space, and objects.

Children who resisted authority demands were at first ignored, then firmly redirected if they persisted. Compliance, receptivity, and attentiveness were valued by caregivers, but so was high-quality performance. These caregivers were socializing the children to fit into their parents' world, in which compliance, loyalty to the company, and ability to perform on cue help one rise through the hierarchy of power and money.

In Center B, the middle-socioeconomic status center, children were expected to depend on caregivers, compete with peers for attention, and take circumstances in stride. The children's resistance to caregivers' demands was tolerated.

Safety, avoidance of conflict, adherence to set routines, and maintenance of the status quo seemed to be the criteria for curriculum decisions. The attitude was that development and learning would take their normal courses in a safe, nurturing environment. Thus these caregivers were socializing the children to fit into their parents' world, where they were middle-level supervisors in factories, small businessowners, and participants in other occupations in which one may be less able to control the circumstances surrounding one's work due to being at the mercy of one's superiors or economic trends.

One's occupational success in such circumstances may depend on avoidance of conflict and adherence to set procedures.

In Center A, the center with a semiskilled and unskilled, working-class family clientele, children were treated as underlings with few rights. Teachers were to be obeyed without question even though resistance was expected. Resistance was arbitrarily punished. Conformity and group cohesion along with rote memorization were the bases for curriculum decisions. The children were not overprotected or directly controlled during rowdy physical playtimes. Children had become adept in dealing with the physical environment. These children had learned to cope with environmental dangers, long periods of boredom, and lack of material resources. They learned to tolerate discomfort, care for the physical needs of one another, suppress impulses, and passively resist authority. They also became used to punishment while also becoming impervious to it. Academic work was passive and drudging. These children were being socialized to live in their parents' world, which generally consisted of doing menial and repetitive work while being at the mercy of forces outside their grasp.

The significance of Miller's description of socialization in child-care facilities for children under age 3 is its attempt to analyze different cultural ideologies that may be typical of various socioeconomic statuses and may unwittingly contribute to structures of social inequity in the larger society. Also, when nonparental child care complements family ideology and behavior, it is more likely to be beneficial for the child; when it differs, it is more likely to be harmful (Lamb, 1998). Thus, to provide optimal socialization experiences for children, a more detailed analysis of the consequences of caregiving ideologies and styles must occur.

COLLABORATIVE CAREGIVING

To provide a beneficial caregiving environment for children, it is critical for professionals who care for infants and children to collaborate with families regarding socialization goals (Bromer, 1999; Greenfield & Suzuki, 1998). At different ends of a continuum are cultural frameworks for socialization, *individualism* and *collectivism* (*see* box). The primary goal in an *individualistic* society is *independence*—children are encouraged to be autonomous and self-fulfilled; social responsibilities are motivated by personal choice. The primary goal in a *collective* society is *interdependence*—children are encouraged to be subordinate and responsible in relating to others; achievements are motivated in terms of service to the group, usually the family (Greenfield & Suzuki, 1998). In a diverse society, such as the United States, both parents and caregivers represent different degrees of individualism and collectivism. These can be observed in such attitudes as sleeping arrangements (Should the baby sleep alone or with its parents?), carrying (Should the baby be carried in a baby carrier close to his or her mother's body, or put in an infant seat to be physically separate, but in view of his or her mother?), feeding (Should the baby be fed whenever he or she cries, or should a certain schedule be adhered to?) (Bhavnagri, 1997).

Diversity in socialization goals can also be observed in communication styles with infants. An American mother is likely to label objects verbally so the child will learn the names of things in the environment ("That's a car. It's red. Look! It has four wheels."). A Japanese mother is likely to focus more on the sharing of an object than on labeling it ("Here's the car. I give it to you; you give it to me. Thank you!") (Greenfield & Suzuki, 1998).

Perhaps parents and nonparental caregivers should set aside "transition time" when the child enters a child-care setting. During this time parent and caregiver observe each other interact with the child and discuss socialization goals, methods, and outcomes. Observation and discussion should take place at regular intervals. Evidence for this recommendation comes from a study of child-care facilities in three Canadian cities of major immigrant influx (Bernhard, Lefebvre, Kilbride, Chud, & Lange, 1998). The investigators found that parents and teachers were unaware of their basic differences in socialization goals, particularly respect for authority, social skills, and learning. Also, there were substantial differences over what constitutes appropriate parenting at home. Thus there needs to be more linkages between home and child care in order to provide developmentally appropriate practices for diverse groups of children (Bredekamp & Copple, 1997).

Collaborative caregiving also refers to the support child caregivers can provide to parents because of their knowledge of child development and developmentally appropriate practices. Support includes the following:

- listening to parents
- empathizing
- translating emotional responses into concrete ones that can be acted upon
- modeling methods of guidance and discipline
- providing opportunities for support groups and parent education.
- enabling the family to link with services in the community

Some Cultural Frameworks for Socialization in Caregiving Settings

Independence-Oriented	*Interdependence-Oriented*
Individual achievement is valued.	Group cohesiveness is valued.

Values

Independence-Oriented	*Interdependence-Oriented*
• competition is encouraged	• mutual help is encouraged
• toys promoting individual enjoyment or mastery are provided	• toys promoting turn-taking or collaboration are provided
• self-help skills are reinforced	• helping others is reinforced

Independence-Oriented	*Interdependence-Oriented*
Object-focused activities are emphasized.	People-focused activities are emphasized.

Activities

Independence-Oriented	*Interdependence-Oriented*
• Children are stimulated and learn from playing with toys and things.	• Children are stimulated and learn from observing and interacting with people.
• Babies are put on mats or in playpens to play with things.	• Babies are held by adults most of the time.

Communication of feelings is openly expressive.	Communication of feelings is restricted.
Communication	

• Children are encouraged to talk about feelings of happiness, sadness, fear, or anger. • Children are permitted to question rules and authority figures.	• Children are expected to subordinate their feelings to the harmony of the group. • Children are not permitted to question rules or authority figures.

Source: Adapted from Bromer, J. (1999). Cultural variations in childcare: Values and action. *Young Children, 54*(6), pp. 74–75.

CAREGIVERS AND CHILD PROTECTION

American ideology (a macrosystem) regarding children is that they should be protected from harm and maltreatment. If the family doesn't do this, then the government must. Child protective laws, such as the Child Abuse Prevention and Treatment Act (CAPTA) of 1974, have been passed. CAPTA defines maltreatment and lists professionals who must report suspected cases to their local child protective agency. Child caregivers and educators are among the mandated reporters. Sometimes caregivers notice that a child's appearance, behavior, or way of interacting differs from that of the other children. Caregivers with child development training and experience are able to recognize deviations from what is considered normal development. Although states vary in their specific definitions of maltreatment and their procedures as to when and how to report it, the box titled "Indications of Possible Maltreatment" provides useful general information. Intervention programs are discussed in Chapter 10.

Maltreated children do not usually "tell." They may be distrustful of all adults. They are even unlikely to express hatred toward abusing parents. There is little understanding of the parents' behavior. Often children believe the abuse occurred because they did something wrong. Thus they may be confused and even frightened by another adult's concern. They may also worry about their parents' retaliation if they tell (O'Brien, 1984). With this understanding, child caregivers and educators can be involved in

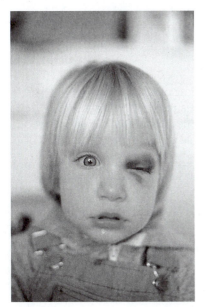

Physical abuse, exemplified by the bruise on this child's eye, must be reported to child protective services.

identification, support, providing a stable environment, and modeling ways to express feelings appropriately and resolve conflicts.

Indications of Possible Maltreatment

<u>**Physical Abuse:**</u>
Physical indicators
Bruises

- Unexplained bruises and welts on the face, lips, mouth, torso, back, buttocks, or thighs, which often reflect the shape of the object used to inflict the injury, for example, electric cords, belts, buckles, and sticks. ("Normal" bruises or welts do not usually cause lacerations, deep discoloration, or other trauma to the extent injuries from abuse do.)
- Bruises that regularly appear after absences, weekends, or vacations.

Burns

- Burns in unusual places, especially on the soles of the feet, palms of the hands, the back, and the buttocks. (These are often caused by cigars or cigarettes.)
- Burns resembling sock-like or glove-like markings on the hands or feet or "doughnut" burns on the buttocks or genital area. (These burns are caused by forced immersion in scalding liquids.)
- Appliance or tool burns that leave a pattern mark of the object (iron, electric burner, fireplace tool, etc.)
- Rope burns on the arms, legs, neck, or torso. (These appear when children are tied to beds or other structures.)

Fractures and other injuries

- Unexplained fractures (particularly to the nose or facial structure) in various stages of healing. Fractures that are a result of child abuse frequently cannot be explained by one episode of trauma. They often have not healed properly and have some additional patterns of stress in terms of growth that are evident upon examination.
- Multiple fractures appearing in different parts of the body (ribs, vertebral compression or spinal fractures)
- Injuries that are in various stages of healing, are clustered, or form regular patterns over the same injured area
- Unexplained swelling of the abdomen, localized tenderness, and constant vomiting

(continued)

- Human bite marks, especially when they are recurrent and/or appear to be adult size

Behavioral indicators

- Unexplained behavior patterns, such as fear of adult contact, apprehension when other children cry, fear of parents, or fear of going home
- Chronic tardiness, poor attendance, increased withdrawal, preoccupation, or simply the need to talk to someone
- Inability to establish good peer relations and, often, aggressive acting-out behavior
- Restlessness or inability to sit down

Physical Neglect:
Physical indicators

- Constant hunger
- Poor hygiene
- Inappropriate dress for weather conditions
- Unattended physical or medical needs
- Lack of supervision in especially dangerous situations or activities over long periods of time

Behavioral indicators

- Alcohol or drug abuse
- Begging for or stealing food; making statements that indicate there is no guardian or parent at home
- Extended stays at school (early arrival or late departure)
- Constant fatigue, listlessness, or falling asleep in class

Sexual Abuse and Exploitation:
Physical indicators

- Difficulty in walking or sitting
- Torn, stained, or bloody underclothing
- Complaints of pain or itching in the genital area
- Bruises or bleeding in external genital, vaginal, or anal area
- Venereal disease in the genital area, mouth, or eyes

(continued)

Behavioral indicators

- Unwillingness to change clothes for gym class or to participate in physical education class
- Bizarre, sophisticated, or unusual sexual behavior or knowledge in younger children, including withdrawal, fantasy, or infantile behavior
- Verbal reports by the child of sexual relations with a caretaker or parent
- Fear of certain people or places
- Withdrawal
- Clinging to parent more than usual
- Behaving as a younger child
- Acting-out the abuse with dolls or peers
- Excessive masturbation

Even though sexual abuse is often deceptively nonviolent, it is disabling and emotionally harmful. It involves the employment, use, or coercion of any child to engage in sexually explicit conduct. It includes indecent exposure, obscene phone calls, pornographic pictures (viewing or taking), fondling, oral or genital stimulation, and sexual intercourse. It may occur over a long period of time, beginning gradually, or it may occur as rape.

Emotional Abuse:

Just as physical injuries can scar and incapacitate a child, emotional cruelty can similarly cripple and disable a child emotionally, behaviorally, and intellectually. Obviously, individual incidents of emotional abuse are difficult to identify and/or recognize and are, therefore, not mandated reporting situations. However, the interests of the child should be primary, and if it is suspected that the child is suffering from emotional abuse, it should be reported. Furthermore, if there is an indication that emotional abuse is being inflicted willfully and causing unjustifiable mental suffering, reporting is required. Regardless of whether or not the situation is one requiring mandatory reporting, cases should be diverted to some sort of treatment as soon as possible.

Behavioral indicators

- Withdrawn, depressed, apathetic behavior
- Antisocial or "acting out" behavior
- Displaying other signs of emotional turmoil (repetitive, rhythmic movements, inordinate attention to details, no verbal or physical communication to others)
- Unwittingly makes comments about own behavior: "Daddy always tells me I'm bad"

(continued)

Emotional Deprivation:

Like emotional abuse, emotional deprivation can leave serious scars on a child. It, too, is difficult to recognize or identify, and is only a mandated reporting situation if willfully intended and if serious mental suffering results. However, the same precautions apply: in the best interests of the child, suspected emotional deprivation should be reported and/or referred for some type of intervention treatment.

Physical indicators

- Speech disorders
- Lag in physical development, frailty, refusal to eat
- Failure to thrive

Behavioral indicators

- Thumb or lip sucking (habit disorders)
- Constantly "seeking out" or "pestering" other adults for attention and affection
- Attempted suicide
- Antisocial or destructive behavior
- Sleep disorders, inhibition of play, neurotic traits
- Behavior extremes (such as compliant/demanding, passive/aggressive)
- Hysteria, phobias, or compulsive traits

Parent Attitudes:

Some noticeable indicators in parental behavior that may indicate abuse are as follows:

- Blaming or belittling child
- Overly defensive or abusive reaction when approached about problems concerning the child
- Apathetic or unresponsive attitude
- Showing little concern about the child—as evidenced by lack of interest in what child is doing in school and lack of participation on parent's or child's part in school activities
- Finding nothing good or attractive in the child

Sources: Child Abuse Prevention Handbook. *Crime Prevention Center (1988). Sacramento, CA: California Department of Justice; National Clearinghouse on Child Abuse and Neglect (1996).*

Epilogue

*C*hild care is a significant socialization setting. Family involvement is essential to the caregiver in socializing the child; it is thus a collaborative effort. Mary Poppins modeled appropriate practices with the Banks children as did Anne Sullivan with Helen Keller. Both Mary and Anne were available to the parents as consultants. ■

SUMMARY

Child, or day, care refers to care given to children by persons other than parents during the day or part of the day. It can be at the child's home, at another home, or in a center.

Quality care involves (1) a caregiver who provides warm, loving care and guidance for the child and works with the family to ensure that the child develops in the best way possible; (2) a setting that keeps the child safe, secure, and healthy; and (3) activities that help the child develop emotionally, socially, mentally, and physically. Quality care is also judged by whether the program is developmentally appropriate. Objective measures of quality include size of the overall group, caregiver–child ratios, and caregiver training in child development. Voluntary accreditation systems exist nationally to establish higher-quality standards than are required by law for both child care centers and family day care homes.

Child care and educational practices have been affected by macrosystems—historical events, political values, technological change, and sociocultural change.

Child care began in this country at the beginning of the nineteenth century as a social service for poor immigrants. It was mainly custodial. Some middle-class families viewed child care as potentially enriching. By the 1960s, child-care programs began to flourish because of the increase in mothers of young children entering the labor force and the recognition of the importance of the early childhood years for later development. Along with the increase in child-care programs came a concern about their quality.

The correlates and consequences of child care on the child that have been examined are emotional, social, and intellectual. Basically, day care children in quality programs do not differ from home-care children in their attachments to their mothers. Day care children differ somewhat from home-care children in their relationships with peers. Day care children have been found to be more self-sufficient, outgoing, and aggressive with others than are home-care children. Generally, day care children's intellectual performance has been shown to be higher than that of children from similar family backgrounds who did not attend a quality child-care program. This is especially true of lower-socioeconomic status children.

A federally funded program for disadvantaged children, Head Start, provides intervention to enable such children to enter school ready to learn. The rationale for government intervention comes from research on the importance of early experience on intellectual development, as well as political attitudes regarding prevention of poverty. Even though there are many kinds of intervention programs, most investigators seem to agree that in order to enable the child to become a competent member of society, the child's family must be involved. Also, the earlier and longer the intervention, the better the results. The problem, however, with assessing the socialization outcomes of intervention programs is that so many variables pertaining to the child, the family, and the day care program must be taken into account.

Child care impacts the community, too. Child care fosters future contributors to society. Economically, it is less costly to fund child-care programs with tax dollars than it is to fund other services such as special education, welfare, or programs for juvenile delinquents. Child care provides work for adults in the community, thereby contributing economically.

The future challenge will be providing more choices in quality child care, due to the increased need. Some ways that center-based child-care options can be increased is for businesses to provide services for their employees, such as leaves, flextime, financial assistance for child care, resources and referrals, in-kind contribution to child-care facilities in the community, and/or on-site child care. Another way is for elementary schools to extend their services to include children younger than 5 years as well as extend the hours normally in session, although there is the fear that this will introduce academics into child care.

Different types of child care (in-home care, family day care, center-based care) have different effects on socialization due to the varying opportunities for interacting with adults, other children, and materials. Having several adults with whom to interact as well as children in a safe, orderly, stimulating environment is related to intellectual and social competence.

Some curriculum models found in preschool programs are cognitively oriented, Montessori, direct instruction, and developmental interaction. Curriculum influences socialization in that the specific skills a program emphasizes are likely to be the ones exhibited by the child. Teacher-directed curricula such as direct instruction, generally produce children who score higher on achievement tests. Learner-directed curricula, such as Montessori and developmental interaction (as well as the cognitively oriented curriculum, generally), tend to foster autonomy, problem-solving skills, and cooperation.

Caregivers influence socialization by their cultural ideologies. These ideologies affect caregivers' language and social interaction with children. Thus caregivers from child-care centers of varying socioeconomic statuses were found to have different expectations of children, which, in turn, affected the socialization practices and outcomes in the centers.

To provide a beneficial caregiving environment for children, it is critical for professionals who care for infants and children to collaborate with families regarding socialization goals; one end of the spectrum being individualism and the other collectivism. Collaborative caregiving refers to the support provided to parents based on knowledge and experience.

American ideology regarding children is that they should be protected. Caregivers and educators are mandated reporters by law for child maltreatment, which includes physical abuse, neglect, sexual abuse and exploitation, emotional abuse and deprivation.

ACTIVITY

Purpose: To assess the socialization that occurs in the child-care facilities in your community.

1. Look in the phone book and choose two child-care facilities in your community to visit. Note whether they are half- or full-day facilities and whether they serve infants/toddlers, preschoolers, and/or school-agers.

2. Describe each facility—physical setting, teacher–child ratio, ages of children, hours, fees, equipment (outdoor and indoor), toys, and creative materials.

3. Observe the interaction between the adults and the children. Describe.

4. Observe the interaction between the children. Describe.

5. What kind of curriculum is implemented?

6. Is there parent involvement and/or education in the program? Describe.

7. Are there support services (health, nutrition, counseling, referrals) for families of the enrolled children? Describe.

RESOURCES

Educational Resources Information Center's Clearinghouse on Elementary and Early Childhood Education (ERIC/EECE)
http://ericeece.org/

International Nanny Association
http://www.nanny.org

National Association for the Education of Young Children
http://www.naeyc.org/naeyc/

National Association for Family Child Care
http://www.nafcc.org/

National Child Care Information Center
http://nccic.org/abtnccic.html

National Clearinghouse on Child Abuse and Neglect
http://www.calib.com/nccanch

National Institute on Out-of-School Time
http://www.wellesley.edu/wcw/crw/sac

RELATED READINGS

Baker, A. C., & Manfred-Petitt, L. A. (1998). *Circle of love: Relationships between parents, providers, and children in family child care.* St Paul, MN: Redleaf Press.

Bender, J., Flatter, C. H., & Sorrentino, J. (1998). *Half a childhood: Quality programs for out-of-school hours.* Nashville, TN: School Age Notes.

Besharov, D. J. (1990). *Recognizing child abuse.* New York: Free Press.

Clarke-Stewart, K. A. (1993). *Daycare* (rev. ed.). Cambridge, MA: Harvard University Press.

Cochran, M., & Larner, M. (1990). *Extending families.* Cambridge, MA: Cambridge University Press.

Dombro, A. L., & Bryan, P. (1991). *Sharing the caring: How to find the right child care and make it work for you and your child.* New York: Simon & Schuster.

Elkind, D. (1987). *Miseducation: Preschoolers at risk.* New York: Knopf.

Forward, S., & Buck, C. (1988). *Betrayal of innocence.* (rev. ed.). New York: Penguin.

Garbarino, J., Guttman, E., & Seely, J. W. (1986). *The psychologically battered child: Strategies for identification, assessment and intervention.* San Francisco: Jossey-Bass.

Gormley, W. T. (1995). *Everybody's children: Child care as a public problem.* Washington, DC: The Brookings Institution.

Helfer, R., & Kempe, C. H. (1987). *The battered child* (4th ed.). Chicago: University of Chicago Press.

Hohmann, M., & Weikart, D. P. (1995). *Educating young children: Active learning practices for preschool educators and child care programs.* Ypsilanti, MI: High/Scope Press.

Kontos, S. (1992). *Family day care: Out of the shadows and into the limelight.* Washington, DC: National Association for the Education of Young Children.

Larner, M., Halpern, R., & Harkavy, O. (Eds.). (1992). *Fair start for children: Lessons learned from seven demonstration projects.* New Haven, CT: Yale University Press.

Wrigley, J. (1995). *Other people's children.* New York: Basic Books.

Zigler, E. F., & Lang, M. E. (1991). *Child care choices: Balancing the needs of children, family, and society.* New York: The Free Press.

"The direction in which education starts a man will determine his future life."

— **Plato**

ECOLOGY OF THE SCHOOL

Prologue

LEARNING: INSTINCT OR INSTRUCTION? PROCESS OR PRODUCT?

Emile, *a classic novel by Jean Jacques Rousseau (1762), tells of a child's education from infancy to adulthood. Emile's education was to take place on a country estate under the guidance of a tutor who would nurture his natural abilities. Emile was not to be exposed to societal influences that might corrupt him, such as books and other people's words.*

Emile would first learn about the world through his senses. According to Rousseau, the senses are the first teachers and, therefore, are more efficient and desirable than formal learning in a school-room with a teacher and a curriculum. By observing his environment, Emile would acquire knowledge of nature, geography, and science.

Emile was indeed a child of nature in that he was allowed to follow his instinctive curiosity, express himself as he desired, and not be required to conform to society's morals or the usual ways of teaching subjects. Rousseau believed formal education was based on symbols (e.g., words, numbers, maps). A child could learn the names of countries and cities, but not know how to navigate his way to town without getting lost. Emile would learn by doing—his eyes would be his compass, adding informaton to his repertoire as he became capable of understanding, and as the information became necessary. By the time Emile was 13-years-old he would have enough practical experience to be ready for formal schooling. He would also be able to deal with the "corrupt" influences of government, economics, business, and the arts because, at this age, he would be capable of evaluating information based on real experiences.

The "deschooling" philosophy described in Emile *is ongoing today. Many children like Emile are being educated at home, as it is legal for parents to take charge of their child's education from kindergarten to college (Kantrowitz & Wingert, 1998). A primary reason for home schooling is to protect children from the "corrupt" influences of school—drugs, alcohol, sex, violence. A secondary reason is to maintain their curious nature to learn. Home schooling enables children's learning to be more individualistic and spontaneous according to their interests. For example, if a child is fascinated with dinosaurs, a trip to the museum is easier to arrange than it would be in a school setting where approval and planning for a class fieldtrip must take place. Do children learn best when they pursue their interests and the teacher guides them? Or when the teacher constructs a curriculum and motivates them with rewards (praise, points, grades, and so on)?* ∎

- *What and how should children learn?*
- *Is learning a process or a product?*
- *Should content or curiosity drive the curriculum?*
- *Should schools teach society's accumulated knowledge (a "core" curriculum), or stress skills to learn how to learn (fostering individualism and creativity)?*

Figure 6.1   An Ecological Model of Human Development

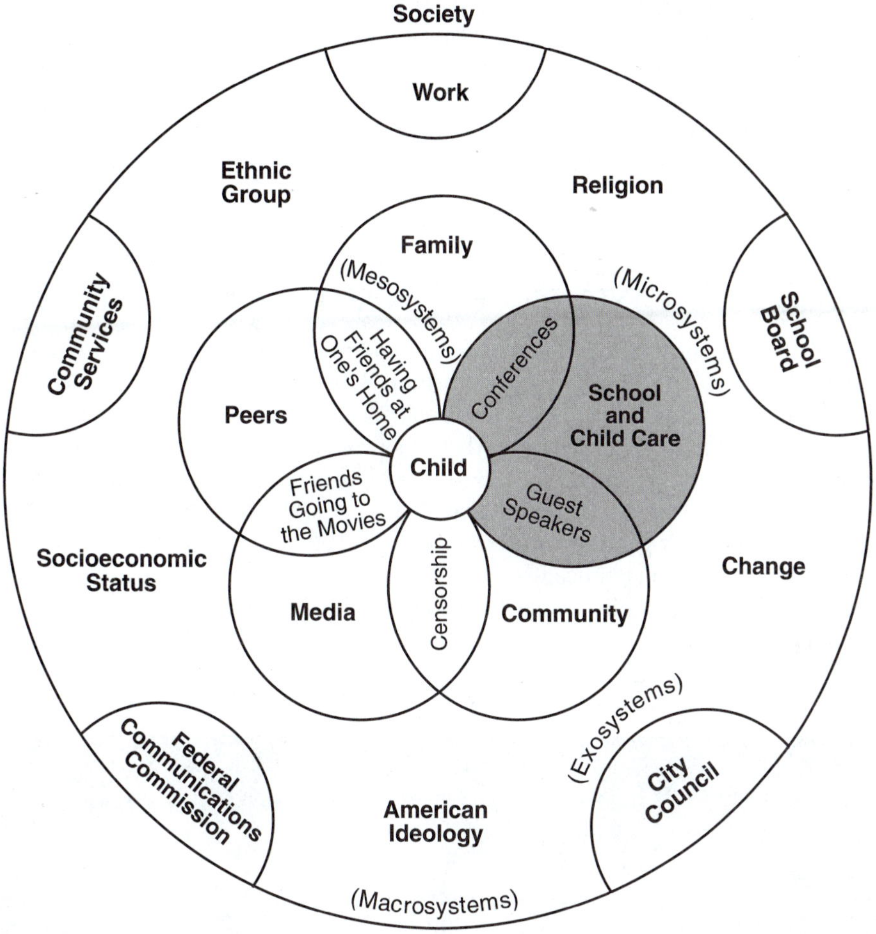

The school is a significant influence on the child's development.

THE SCHOOL'S FUNCTION AS A SOCIALIZING AGENT

This chapter examines the school as a microsystem in which children develop, as well as the linkages, or mesosystems, between school and family, school and peer group, school and media, and school and community.

The school's function as a socializing agent is that it provides the intellectual and social experiences from which children develop the skills, knowledge, interest, and attitudes that characterize them as individuals and that shape their abilities to perform adult roles. Schools exert influence on children by their educational policies leading to achievement, by their formal organization of the introduction of students to authority, and by the social relationships that evolve in the classroom. Some of these influences are intentional, such as instruction in a specific subject; and some are unintentional—for example, competitive grading, possibly leading to low motivation.

The primary function of education, from *society's* perspective, is the transmission of the cultural heritage: the accumulated knowledge, values, beliefs, and customs of the society. To transmit culture and maintain it, society must be provided with trained people who can assume specialized roles, as well as develop new knowledge and technology. The function of education from the *individual's* perspective is to acquire the necessary skills and knowledge to become self-sufficient as well as able to participate effectively in society.

MACROSYSTEM INFLUENCE: SOCIETY'S EXPECTATIONS

The school's current function in society is more universal, formal, and prescriptive, as is illustrated by the goals for schooling set forth in Table 6.1. These goals emerged from a detailed study of schooling led by John Goodlad (1984) in a sample of communities across the United States representing urban, suburban, and rural areas, as well as different socioeconomic statuses. Elementary, junior high, and high schools were included in the observations. Questionnaires were given to teachers, parents, students, and administrators regarding their goals for education.

In sum, school is a significant socializing agent because it transmits the culture; it transmits skills; it transmits values and beliefs; and it prepares individuals for citizenship and work roles.

These students are learning a craft.

Table 6.1   Goals for Schooling in the U.S.

A. ACADEMIC GOALS
  1. Mastery of basic skills (reading, writing, arithmetic) and fundamental processes (communicating ideas, using information resources)
  2. Intellectual development (accumulate general knowledge; think rationally, independently, and critically; solve problems; be curious)

B. VOCATIONAL GOALS
  3. Career education–vocational education (select a suitable occupation based on interest and abilities, develop appropriate work attitudes and habits, become economically independent and productive)

C. SOCIAL, CIVIC, AND CULTURAL GOALS
  4. Interpersonal understandings (various values, relationships, cultures)
  5. Citizenship participation (understand history and representational government, make informed choices, contribute to the welfare of others and the environment)
  6. Enculturation (awareness of values, behavioral norms, traditions, achievements of one's culture and other cultures)
  7. Moral and ethical character (evaluate choices, conduct, develop integrity)

D. PERSONAL GOALS
  8. Emotional and physical well-being (develop self-awareness, coping skills, time-management skills, healthy habits, physical fitness)
  9. Creativity and aesthetic expression (develop originality in problem-solving, be tolerant of new ideas, appreciate various forms of creativity)
  10. Self-realization (evaluate abilities and limitations, set goals, accept responsibility for decisions made)

Sources: J. I. Goodlad, (1984). *A Place Called School.* New York: McGrawHill, pp. 51–56; J. A. Johnson, V. L. Dupuis, D. Musial, G. E. Hall, & D. M. Gollnick (1999). Introduction to the Foundations of American Education, 11th ed. Needham Heights, MA: Allyn and Bacon.

PHILOSOPHIES OF TEACHING AND LEARNING

There are many types of schooling or educational programs, each having many variations. For the sake of simplicity, the programs discussed here are categorized according to their emphasis on who takes responsibility for the learning that takes place—the teacher or the learner (*see* Table 6.2). In reality, however, most programs emphasize both teacher and student responsibility for learning, but to different degrees. Since different programs provide different learning environments, experiences, and interactions, the school's program influences a child's development and socialization in a particular way.

Teacher-directed educational environments (sometimes referred to as "traditional") usually subscribe to the philosophy that the functions of the school are to impart basic

Table 6.2   Teacher- and Learner-Directed Settings

TEACHER-DIRECTED (TRADITIONAL)	LEARNER-DIRECTED (MODERN)
Structure	
Day is organized by teacher and divided into time segments according to subject	Program is prepared by teacher based on student abilities and interest; time spent on activities depends on interest; activities not divided into specific subjects
Management	
There are many rules for appropriate behavior (being moral, having manners, following directions, paying attention, being quiet, sitting still, being neat)	Teacher encourages children to discuss standards of conduct and take responsibility for their behavior
Curricula	
Predetermined by teacher and/or textbook	Subjects determined by student ability and interest
Emphasis on reading, writing, arithmetic, science, social science	Activities and problem-solving experiences based on student interest
Knowledge considered an end in itself; what is studied is preparation for life	Knowledge considered a means to an end, the process of living; subject matter grows out of experience
Motivation	
Extrinsic (grades)—success mainly a function of how well the required tasks are mastered according to teacher's standards	Intrinsic (child's interests)—success is mainly a function of self-evaluation (based on accomplishment of a self-chosen goal)
Advancement determined by subjects and tests passed/time spent in system	Advancement according to activites chosen and skills developed
Competitive	Cooperative
Method	
Teacher teaches generally the same thing at the same time to all students or a group of students	Learning is individualized and students are responsible for their own learning
Teaching style is dominative	Teaching of process
Teaching of content	Teaching style is integrative
Direct encouragement of children's participation	Indirect encouragement of children's participation

Source: Adapted from George H. Morrison (1980). *Early childhood education today* (2nd ed.). (Columbus, OH: Merrill), pp. 146–149; 152–153. Reprinted by permission of the publisher.

This classroom is organized to provide many learner-directed activities.

factual knowledge (reading, writing, arithmetic) and preserve the American cultural heritage (Toch, 1996). Those who support this philosophy believe that education should include homework, tests, memorization, and strict discipline. They view the school as a place where hard work and obedience are expected. The teacher structures the curriculum. Subjects chosen are based on the teacher's, school's, or community's goals.

Roots of teacher-directed learning can be traced back to Plato's *Republic*. Plato's thesis stated that the mind is what it learns, so the content of curricula is vital for an educated society.

Learner-directed educational environments (sometimes referred to as "progressive" or "modern") usually subscribe to the philosophy that the function of the school is to develop the whole child. Curriculum emerges from the child's interests and abilities, and knowledge is constructed as the child is capable of processing it (Toch, 1996). This process is called "constructivism."

Roots of learner-directed learning can be traced back to Rousseau's *Emile* (1762). Rousseau concentrated on the development of the *child* rather than *subjects* to be taught. His thesis stated that *how* learning occurs is more important than *what* is taught.

John Dewey (1859–1952), influenced by Rousseau, was the first progressive educator. He believed that education should place emphasis on the children and their interests, rather than on subject matter. Dewey also believed that education was a process of living, not a *preparation* for living. Those who subscribe to this philosophy believe learning occurs spontaneously and is best when children can interact with materials and people in their environment. Learning materials may be grouped in various centers, which children explore. Children are given opportunities for inquiry and discovery. They become involved in their own learning by making choices about what they will learn. Subject matter is integrated into student activities.

To determine the extent to which a philosophy shapes teaching practices, Putnam (1983) observed the classroom interactions in six inner-city kindergartens—three of which followed a traditional or *teacher-directed* approach to reading readiness and three of which followed an interactive or more *learner-directed* view of reading.

Teachers in traditional kindergartens assume that prior to trying to read, children should develop a set of foundational skills—visual and auditory discrimination, letter-naming, beginning word sounds, and so on—that would allow them to be successful when they learn to read in first grade. For example:

> Mrs. Hall's kindergartners have just listened to a song about *Mr. D.,* who loves *d*oughnuts, *d*ogs, *d*eer, and other things that begin with *d*. Mrs. Hall then asks the children to name other things that begin with the *d* sound. "Raise your hand; don't call out, speak in a sentence," she says. One child says, "I sit at a *d*esk." "Very good, 'desk' begins with *d,*" replies Mrs. Hall. After several responses the children are given worksheets on which they are to circle pictures of items beginning with a *d*.

Thus, in the traditional, or *teacher-directed* approach to reading readiness, the children are supposed to sit quietly, follow directions, listen attentively, and talk only when called upon to answer a question. Discussion with fellow classmates is frowned upon (Putnam, 1986).

In contrast, teachers in the interactive or *learner-directed* kindergartens create a reading environment by these approaches:

- Giving children plentiful opportunities to listen to literature and nonfiction being read aloud
- Providing opportunities for children to act out and discuss the readings
- Allowing children to express their understanding of the readings through art
- Enabling the children to experiment with writing and reading their own "books"

There is some instruction in letter sounds, but most of the focus is on interpreting whole messages. The children are encouraged to collaborate with one another in talking, asking questions, and comprehending material. The children spend time each day "reading" a book (looking at pictures, reciting the story, and trying to decode the words) or "writing" a story (drawing, inventing spelling, and talking about ideas). The teacher moves around listening to pretend readings, asking the writers to "read" their stories, helping with invented spelling, answering questions, and praising efforts. Thus, in this *learner-directed* approach to reading readiness, the children have a greater degree of control, choice, and responsibility (Putnam, 1986).

SOCIALIZATION OUTCOMES OF DIFFERENT SCHOOL SETTINGS

What does research say about the effects of *teacher-* and *learner-directed* programs on socialization?

Table 6.3   Classroom Management: Goal Structures and Socialization

GOAL STRUCTURES	TYPE OF INSTRUCTIONAL ACTIVITY	IMPORTANCE OF GOAL FOR SOCIALIZATION	STUDENT EXPECTATIONS	EXPECTED SOURCE OF SUPPORT
Cooperative	Problem-solving; divergent thinking or creative tasks; assignments can be more ambiguous with students doing the clarifying, decision making, and inquiring	Goal is perceived as important for each student, and students expect group to achieve the goal	Each student expects positive interaction with other students; to share ideas and materials; support for risk-taking; to make contributions to the group effort; dividing the task among group members; to capitalize on diversity among group members	Other students
Individualized	Specific skill or knowledge acquisition; assignment is clear and behavior specified to avoid confusion and need for extra help	Goal is perceived as important for each student, and each student expects eventually to achieve this goal	Each student expects to be left alone by other students; to take a major part of the responsibility for completing the task; to take a major part in evaluating his or her progress toward task completion and the quality of his effort	Teacher
Competitive	Skill practice; knowledge recall and review; assignment is clear with rules for competing specified	Goal is *not* perceived to be of large importance to the students, and they can accept either winning or losing	Each student expects to have an equal chance of winning; to enjoy the activity (win or lose); to monitor the progress of his/her competitor to compare ability, skills, or knowledge with peers	Teacher

Source: Adapted from David W. Johnson and Roger T. Johnson (1999). *Learning together and alone: Cooperative, competitive, and individualized learning* (5th ed.), pp. 6–8. Reprinted by permission of Allyn and Bacon, Needham Heights, MA.

In a review of approximately 200 research studies on elementary school programs, Horowitz (1979) noted the different socializing effects of *modern* and *traditional* settings. In general, he found children in *modern* settings have a more positive attitude about school and their teachers than do children in *traditional* settings. They are more likely to find friends of both genders. They also are involved in cooperative work more often and show more autonomy, or self-reliant behavior. He did not find any significant differences in the academic achievement of children in *modern* and *traditional* settings. However, later studies (Good & Brophy, 1986) indicate that students in *traditional, teacher-directed* classrooms perform better academically than students in *modern learner-directed* programs.

Modern and *traditional* environments provide different opportunities for cooperative work. In *traditional* environments teachers generally teach to the whole class and children work individually; sharing information is seen as cheating. In *modern* classrooms there is considerable small-group effort and an emphasis on developing a cooperative work ethic (Atkinson & Green, 1990; Minuchin & Shapiro, 1983).

We can conclude, then, that different patterns of competence emerge as a result of the different experiences children have in various programs (Toch, 1996). More specifically, instructional settings involving how students relate to each other and how they relate to the teacher to accomplish educational goals also affect socialization outcomes.

Instructional settings can be organized into "goal structures" (Johnson & Johnson, 1999). There are three types of goal structures: **cooperative**—students work together to accomplish shared goals; **competitive**—students work against each other to achieve goals that only a few students can attain; and **individualized**—one student's achievement of a goal is unrelated to other students' achievement of a goal (*see* Table 6.3).

Each type of goal structure, according to Johnson and Johnson, promotes a different pattern of interaction among students. A *cooperative goal structure* promotes positive interpersonal relationships such as sharing, helping, trust, and acceptance. A *competitive goal structure* promotes comparisons and mistrust. An *individualized goal structure* promotes student–teacher interaction and responsibility for oneself. Table 6.3 describes the conditions under which each goal structure is most effective in promoting the desired learning.

An interesting application of the cooperative type of goal structure was described by Aronson and Patenoe (1996). The goal of the activity was to get students in a newly integrated classroom to interact positively with one another. The students were divided into small groups and given tasks in which they had to cooperate with each other in order to succeed. Each student was given a piece of information that the rest of the group needed in order to finish the task. All the members had to share their pieces of information with the others. Aronson called this "the jigsaw-puzzle method." The results were higher achievement, a decrease in social insults, higher self-esteem, and improved attitudes toward school. Several successful adaptations of cooperative goal structures have been developed to include children with disabilities and those who are ethnically diverse and to prepare students for an increasingly collaborative workforce (Slavin, 1991).

Thus, the way teachers manage the classroom environment, including arranging the room, planning the activities, observing behavior, and organizing groups, affects the socialization taking place in that classroom.

THE SCHOOL, CHANGE, CHALLENGE, AND CHOICE

In a changing society the challenge continually facing educators is how to transmit the society's diverse cultural heritage, as well as prepare individuals for the future. What aspects of past knowledge must be taught for survival in the present, and what coping skills must be taught for survival in the future? With new knowledge being discovered every day, choices have to be made. For example, most jobs being created today require workers who can (1) read, write, and compute at high levels; (2) analyze and interpret data, draw conclusions, and make decisions; and (3) function as part of a team (Haycook, 1991).

From its inception, the public school system was intended to be a vehicle for social change. Schools, however, do not execute their functions in a vacuum. They are affected by macrosystems such as history, politics, economics, religious values, cultural values, and technology, and are linked to other microsystems such as the family. They must teach children from diverse backgrounds with diverse skills. Therefore, in order to equalize opportunities, schools must implement a variety of programs in addition to basic reading, writing, and arithmetic (Levine & Levine, 1996).

> Policy mandates like desegregation and mainstreaming dramatically changed the social environment of the school. These forces have expanded and complicated the mandate of the public school well beyond the traditional academic "three Rs," identifying multiple and sometimes conflicting goals. The school has become a potential intervention site for almost every social problem affecting children (Linney & Seidman, 1989, p. 336).

Schools are supposed to have preventative programs such as sex education to help students avoid unplanned pregnancies, as well as the spread of AIDS and other sexually transmitted diseases; health classes that discuss the danger of substance abuse; and conflict resolution to prevent violence. Schools are also supposed to keep up with technology, such as requiring computer literacy.

Elementary schools traditionally taught academic skills and good citizenship. Gradually, development of critical thinking skills, individuality and self-concept, and interpersonal relationship skills crept into the curricula. The reasons for the gradual changes were many. The classic writings of John Dewey (*Democracy and Education*), Jean Piaget (*To Understand Is to Invent*), B. F. Skinner (*The Technology of Teaching*), Carl Rogers (*Freedom to Learn*), to name a few, influenced educational practices. More recently the work of Lev Vygotsky (*Mind in Society*) has been adapted for the classroom.

The political climate from the late 1950s to early 1970s, evidenced by the passage of certain legislation providing federal money for new programs, was also supportive of change. For example, the Economic Opportunity Act of 1964 provided federal money for preschool programs for disadvantaged children, the Elementary and Secondary Acts of 1965 (Title I) provided federal aid to education, and the Education for All Handicapped Children Act of 1975 (revised in 1990 to become the Individuals with Disabilities Education Act) mandated a free and appropriate education for all children with disabilities. Thus, federal aid to education allowed schools to benefit more children by individualizing programs to meet individual needs. It also enabled schools to experiment with new programs in order to be more successful in meeting those needs. To illustrate, bilingual education was mandated in school districts with high population rates of children whose native language was not English. Children in such programs were taught the specified

Scientific knowledge is one of the National Educational Goals.

curriculum in their native languages while they learned English as a second language. The philosophy behind bilingual education is that it prevents non- or limited-English-speaking children from being academically disadvantaged due to not understanding the language of the teacher. During the 1980s, however, federal aid to education was reduced; public education was felt to be the responsibility of the states. This appeared to some as a lack of "national purpose" in education.

A report, titled "A Nation at Risk: The Imperative for Educational Reform," by the National Commission on Excellence in Education (NCEE) appointed by the government in 1983, helped create a public demand for change in the public schools. The report charged that U.S. citizens "have lost sight of the basic of schooling" and that "the educational foundations of our society are presently being eroded by a rising tide of mediocrity that threatens our very future as a nation and a people" (NCEE, 1983). The report advocated a number of directions for reform, including the following: (1) There must be a greater consensus by Americans on the goals of schooling. (2) There must be renewed emphasis on "the basics" (reading, communicating, and computing) in learning. (3) Standards of excellence must be established. (4) More capable people must be motivated to train and stay in the teaching profession. (5) The U.S. economic position in the world community necessitates higher levels of education for *all* students (Chafel, 1997).

As the twenty-first century approached, debates regarding the function of school had not changed very much. To address the charges made by the report, government, business, and educational leaders developed six national education goals, announced in 1990 and reconfirmed in 1999 via the Educational Excellence for All Children Act proposed by President Bill Clinton. They state that by the year 2000,

1. All children in America will start school ready to learn.
2. The high school graduation rate will increase to at least 90%.
3. American students will leave grades four, eight, and twelve having demonstrated competency in challenging subject matter including English, mathematics, science, history, and geography; and every school in America will ensure that all students learn to use their minds well, so they may be prepared for responsible citizenship, further learning, and productive employment in our modern economy.
4. American students will be first in the world in science and mathematics achievement.
5. Every adult American will be literate and will possess the knowledge and skills necessary to compete in a global economy and exercise the rights and responsibilities of citizenship.
6. Every school in America will be free of drugs and violence and will offer a disciplined environment conducive to learning.

Although all of these goals are not likely to be reached by the year 2000, they remain targets worth striving for. The philosophy is that schools and students will rise to the expectations and standards set for them.

Reaching the goals requires significant improvements in a wide range of services for children, including health care, child care, parent education, and family support. It also requires many changes in schools, teacher education, and testing. Finally, it requires the involvement of businesses, communities, politicians, colleges, and universities, as well as you.

In order for any education strategy to be implemented and school socialization to be effective, children must come to school ready to learn. To assess what exactly was involved in "school readiness," the Carnegie Foundation for Advancement in Teaching took on the task of examining the influences of birth, family, child-care arrangements, workplace, and community supports (Boyer, 1991). The results of this study will be discussed later.

To address the transition from school to work, especially for the high school graduates who don't go to college or those who drop out, some states have established funding for apprenticeship programs in areas such as health, machine tooling, and entrepreneurship.

To address the ambitious challenge of meeting the goals, the known effects of various types of schools, programs, and teaching styles on children's development will be examined.

IMPACT OF TECHNOLOGY: COMPUTERS

Schooling for the future includes being prepared for the world of work. Learning to use computers is essential to successful functioning in any society. This is a good example of the impact of a macrosystem (change) on an exosystem. Your bank statement is computerized, thereby requiring fewer people to provide you with information in less time. Your doctor may use a computer to assist with a diagnosis. Along with television and telephones, computers have revolutionized communication. Computers enable users who have access to the Internet to get information from anywhere in the world. In response to technological change, most schools (high, middle, elementary, and even preschools) have purchased computers to serve as educational tools.

The computer is an interactive tool that enhances learning in a variety of subjects. It can present and store information, motivate and reward learners, diagnose and prescribe, provide drill and practice, and individualize instruction (Levine & Levine, 1996; Oppenheimer, 1997). It can support a wide range of learning styles because it enables children to construct their own knowledge (Haugland & Wright, 1997; Papert, 1993). Effectiveness of the computer as a tool for learning depends on how it is used by teachers and students, as well as the software selected.

Computers are not really new to education. In the past, computers were used mainly for programmed instruction, which involved reading information and answering questions. Depending on one's responses, one branches into different program areas or goes back for more information and practice. The learning that occurs is determined by reacting to the program rather than discovery by the learner, although sometimes children discover different ways to get the same result by experimenting with different commands. Today, educational software includes interactive games, Web sites on the Internet to visit, discussion groups via e-mail.

How does computer education affect children? Does the computer foster independence at the expense of developing social skills? Does the computer enhance certain skills at the expense of creativity? Computers deal with facts. They do not convey or receive emotions. If computers become a primary medium of communication, especially in school, what happens to the socializing impact of the teacher through attachment and modeling? What happens to other mechanisms of socialization such as reasoning and group pressure?

According to Jane Healy (1991, 1998), the computer provides visual and sometimes auditory stimulation. However, optimal learning occurs, especially for preschoolers, when several senses are involved. The young child needs to manipulate things, as well as see them, in order to construct an understanding of the world.

Computers can be used as an adjunct to regular classroom activities, rather than a replacement. For example, computers can facilitate children's creative writing by using word processing to help simplify physical aspects of writing, as well as manipulate writing structure (Daiute, 1983). When students don't get stuck on handwriting, spelling, and grammar, they are freer to express thoughts. However, some children exhibit *parallel* thinking (like hypertext) rather than *sequential* thinking (Oppenheimer, 1997). They don't connect their thoughts in a logical way; they just list things without understanding the relationship (Healy, 1991, 1998).

Creating software programs can encourage problem-solving skills and logic. For example, Seymour Papert (1999) developed a system using a computer language called LOGO, in which children learn mathematics by *being* mathematicians. LOGO is programmable, as opposed to direct-manipulation software. By controlling the movements of the "Turtle," the children (as young as age 3) are learning about numbers, shapes, velocities, and rates of change, as well as problem-solving. Various LOGO programs are used today in school for biology, physics, and driver's education, to name a few (Papert, 1993). Designing computer programs requires the child to think hypothetically. ("If I choose this command, then this will happen.") Programmable software, such as LOGO, enables the user to construct knowledge.

Computers can be used for collaboration and research. Students can network with each other in the classroom on projects. With a telephone hook-up, they can access information from libraries, universities, government databases, and any "online" service subscribed to by their school. With computer-interactive multimedia capabilities, such as graphics, sound, and compact disks, students can "visit" museums, planetariums, and other countries, or go back in history. New software is being developed for learning via computer simulation. For example, the standard biology laboratory experiment of dissecting a dead frog can now be simulated. Some driver education programs start students on computers.

In sum, computers contribute to schooling for the future in that they can individualize instruction to accommodate different learning styles; they can be used for routine tasks, thereby freeing teachers to provide more creative ones; they can help develop self-directed learners, logical or hypothetical thinkers, and problem-solvers; and they can provide access to infinite information. Parents and teachers must enable children to develop critical thinking skills to evaluate appropriate software, as well as the plethora of information on the Internet. In doing research on the Internet, students must learn to distinguish facts from opinions and reliable resources from unreliable ones.

Finally, computer technology has been utilized to link home and school or hospital and school for ill children, school to school for specialized instruction, and business to school for "virtual field trips." Such utilization is known as "distance education."

IMPACT OF VIOLENCE

The National Academy of Sciences defines **violence** as "behaviors by individuals that intentionally threaten, attempt, or inflict harm on others" (Elders, 1994). Parents, teachers, students, and communities are very concerned about the rise in school violence in recent years. The shootings of 12 students and a teacher in 1999 at Columbine High School in Colorado alerted society to the negative outcomes of being rejected by peers, of being victims of bullying, and most importantly, of being disengaged from family, school, and community.

To have an optimal environment for learning, schools must be safe. Violence transcends all socioeconomic levels of schools and communities. Its roots are as much a part of a family's dysfunctional way of solving problems, as a community's racism, sexism, and high unemployment. If children grow up in families that practice spousal or child abuse or neglect they will be more likely to exhibit aggressive behavior in school. They may also model the violent behavior they see in neighborhoods (Verdugo, Kuther, Seidel, Wallace, Sosa, & Faber, 1996). Many believe that the pervasiveness of violence in the media and its portrayal as the normal means of conflict resolution gives children the message that violence is acceptable and is an effective way to solve problems (Elders, 1994).

The availability of guns and knives enables anger to be vented physically. Children have turned to gangs and weapons for the protection they believe they have not received from parents, teachers, and/or community members (Children's Defense Fund, 1998).

Children who grow up in violent communities are at risk for emotional and psychological problems because growing up in a constant state of fear makes it difficult for one to establish trust, autonomy, and social competence (Wallach, 1993).

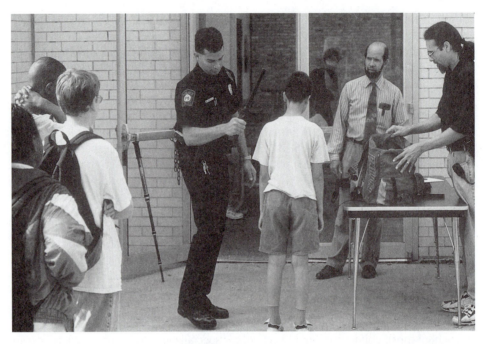

School violence has become a national concern, and schools have taken steps to protect their students.

Growing up in an impoverished neighborhood, one that lacks recreational and employment opportunities, as well as many successful adult role models, leads to alienation of children. Children do not develop feelings of safety and nurturance; instead, they often develop feelings of hopelessness (National Research Council, 1993), leading to "learned helplessness," a motive to be discussed in more detail in Chapter 11. In addition, poverty appears to inhibit the capacity of families to parent and hence to achieve social control over adolescents (Sampson & Laub, 1994). Although violence does occur in suburban and rural communities, it is more prevalent in urban communities (Verdugo et al., 1996).

What is being done? Some schools have hired security guards, installed metal detectors, and/or given teachers cellular phones, but these are merely small deterrents to a problem the roots of which lie in a "socially toxic environment." To cut those roots, all of a child's ecological systems have to participate.

How can micro-, meso-, exo-, and macrosystems work to combat violence?

The *macrosystem,* or government, can implement laws, such as stricter policies on gun control and the portrayal of violence in the media (both of which are objectionable to a significant number of people). It can increase law enforcement in communities. It can provide funding for preventive programs in schools and families. Violence prevention in schools may involve having more counselors available to students, training teachers to intervene with children who are social isolates, bullies, or victims. Violence prevention in families may involve parent education and/or counseling.

The *exosystem,* such as business, can provide jobs, financial assistance to rebuild impoverished communities, and role models for youth. Businesses can support schools by giving time and money, providing opportunities for field trips, guest speakers, and fund after-school activities.

The *mesosystem,* exemplified by the link between schools and families, can empower families to share the responsibility for creating a safe school environment (Stomfay-Stitz, 1994). This means accompanying children to and from school and being involved in school activities. The mesosystem, exemplified by the link between communities and families, can provide services to support families (examples will be discussed in Chapter 10), thereby proactively contributing to the prevention of violence.

The *microsystem,* referring here to the school itself, can implement a curricular priority at all grade levels of anger management (learning cues to when angry feelings get out of control and how to deal with them appropriately) and conflict resolution (learning positive strategies to resolve differences). Consistent behavior standards and consequences, as well as academic expectations, must be established. Classes for parents in parenting methods, as well as violence prevention, should be available. Teacher inservice training should include methods for dealing with disruptive or uncooperative behavior before it escalates. Teachers need to be more responsive to bullies, victims, and social outcasts at all school levels. Teacher training should also include working with diverse groups and knowledge of how to connect with appropriate community resources (medical, psychological, and economic). Children should learn to respect differences and be empathetic to others (Verdugo et al., 1996).

Preventing Violence

Some Strategies to Resolve Conflicts Before they Escalate into Violent Behavior

Emotional Regulation

- Enable children to verbalize angry feelings and presumed cause (young children may need some suggested words).
- Redirect anger to appropriate physical activity (pounding play-doh, running).

Empathy

- Role play to get the other person's perspective.

Problem-Solving

- Discuss various solutions to conflict that are agreeable to all involved parties.

Mediation

- Involve an adult or trained peer—listen to all perspectives and give assistance in working out a compromise.

THE SCHOOL'S LINKAGES TO OTHER ECOSYSTEMS

Since American children spend approximately 180 days per year for approximately 12 years in school (and more, if children attend preschool), the schools they attend and the teachers they encounter play significant roles in their socialization.

The school, by exposing children to different experiences, direct and vicarious, opens new avenues to them with which they would not otherwise have come into contact. A direct experience may be having a part in a play, for example. A vicarious experience may be seeing a movie about another country.

The school, in designating programs and curricula, selects which experiences a child will have. In other words, the school determines which aspects of culture are to be transmitted. Often the government influences program development and curriculum content (influence of an exosystem). For example, after the Soviet Union launched the first satellite into space in 1957, the U.S. government passed the National Defense Education Act of 1958, which provided federal funds for science, math, and foreign-language programs, thereby enabling children to be socialized to compete globally.

The school is the formal system in which children learn. However, children learn informally in their families, peer groups, communities, and via the media. To optimize the socializing influence of the school, supportive linkages or mesosystems, must be developed with these other contexts.

In *theory,* public education in the United States enables any child, according to his or her abilities, to acquire the skills necessary to fulfill virtually any role in the society. In *reality,* however, today's students are so diverse that educational opportunities are not equal. For example, factors such as family income, family structure, and parents' education have been correlated with grade repetition, special services, and dropping out of school (Young & Smith, 1997). Also, because schools have different resources, different philosophies of education, and different teachers, children's learning abilities are affected accordingly.

School–Family Linkages

The effectiveness of the school as a socializing agency depends to a major degree on the kinds of families its children come from (Coleman, 1966; Jencks, 1972; Levine & Levine, 1996). Generally, the school has been less effective in educating children from low-socioeconomic-status families. Such children, in addition to being poor, are often from minority groups. The reasons generally attributed for the school's lessened effectiveness are the fewer resources available for education in poor communities, the expectations of the teachers (most teachers are middle class), and the lack of certain preschool experiences expected of children their age by public schools. For example, sitting still at the table when working or eating is generally expected of school-age children, but some children do not have a table at home large enough to accommodate all the family members at one time, so there are no formal sit-down meals; instead, family members eat "on the run." Consequently, these children will have trouble in school until they learn to conform to sitting still. In addition, schools in lower-class neighborhoods tend to be *teacher-directed,* emphasizing conformity and order in the classroom, whereas schools in middle-class neighborhoods tend more toward *self-directed learning.* Students who don't learn self-motivation are likely to experience difficulty as they progress in school (Levine & Levine, 1996).

Since it has been demonstrated that the effectiveness of school as a socializing agent depends on the degree of consistency, or supportive linkages between children's home environments and their educational environment, (Levine & Levine, 1996; Minuchin & Shapiro, 1983), this may explain why schools generally are less effective in educating children from lower socioeconomic levels.

As was discussed in the Chapter 5, beginning in the 1960s, the federal government attempted to remedy some of the inequalities in educational opportunities by providing intervention programs for children from lower socioeconomic levels. The rationale behind intervention programs was to provide learning experiences and skills disadvantaged children lacked due to their environments. Most intervention programs require that schools and families work together. Family involvement will be discussed in Chapter 7.

The school's influence in the socialization process differs according to the value placed on the school by the family (Gordon, 1971; Schaefer, 1991). In other words, if a family believes the school is very important in imparting cultural heritage (accumulated knowledge, values, and so forth) to their children, the family will support the school. The family will tell children that school is important, that school will help them achieve in life, that the teacher knows best. Parents will see that children do their homework and will respond to teachers' requests for behavioral change. Studies have shown that parental involvement is related to the child's school performance, and the degree of involvement is related to the level of education attained by the parents (Levine & Levine, 1996).

If, on the other hand, the family does *not* believe the school is a very significant socializing agent, parents will not take much interest in the child's work brought home; they may ignore the teacher's requests for help to change the child's behavior, and may even relate negative experiences they had at school to the child.

Schools in poor communities have extra challenges in educating children due to fewer economic resources and lack of supportive attitudes toward the school.

School–Child Linkages

Certain psychological characteristics of a child, such as *learning style,* may determine which type of learning environment is optimal to that child's development (Levine & Levine, 1996; Reynolds & Gerstein, 1992).

Learning style is defined as

> . . . that consistent pattern of behavior and performance by which an individual approaches educational experiences. It is the composite of characteristic cognitive, affective, and physiological behaviors that serve as relatively stable indicators of how a learner perceives, interacts with, and responds to the learning environment. It is formed in the deep structure of neural organization and personality that molds and is molded by human development and the cultural experiences of home, school, and society (Bennett, 1995, p. 164).

Learning style, then, is an aspect of socialization.

Learning styles can be observed in children by various criteria. For example, does the child learn best by watching? by listening? by moving his or her body? Does the child achieve more alone or in a group? Is the child better at breaking down a whole task into components (analysis) or relating the components to each other to form a new whole (synthesis)? Is the child motivated by pleasing the teacher, by concrete rewards? by internalized interest? Does the child need much or little structure to carry out a task?

Recently, attention has been given to psychologist Howard Gardner's theory of multiple intelligences. Gardner (1983, 1999) delineates a variety of intelligences: linguistic, logical–mathematical, spatial, musical, bodily–kinesthetic, interpersonal, intrapersonal, existential and naturalist. Historically, the schools have primarily focused on linguistic and logical–mathematical. Gardner's theory has significant implications for meeting the individualized needs of various children. For example, different ethnic groups (as will be discussed later) tend to value and develop different areas of intelligence by the way they solve problems. Thus, by assessing children's learning styles in addition to developing individual learning profiles for them describing their strengths and weaknesses according to Gardner's categories of intelligences, teachers can empower all children to succeed.

School–Peer Group Linkages

Children's attitudes about learning can be influenced by the peer group to which they belong. The peer group can thus help or hinder the school's role in socialization. The following are some examples:

> Brian is not too sure of his status with his peers in class. The high school he attends has a strong tradition of academic excellence and has many intramural scholastic competitions. Brian's peers expect best efforts, which are rewarded by social recognition. Those who lag are put down. Brian works very hard academically to meet the standards of his peer group.
>
> Todd, on the other hand, has a group of friends who believe it is not "cool" to carry books, give evidence of having done homework, or work hard academically. Todd, in choosing a group of friends whose value it is to "keep cool," probably is not working up to his full potential academically.

Business and media link with schools by advertising products and sponsoring activities.

That peers influence the educational process was demonstrated by Coleman (1961) in a classic study on adolescent values. He found that in most high schools, boys value athletic ability and girls value popularity. This is still true today as evidenced by the labeling of peer groups in junior high school and high school (Kinney, 1993)—"brains" or "nerds," "jocks," "populars," or "normals," or "unpopulars." Thus students who are dependent on their peers for approval are less likely to endorse school and family values of academic success.

Research has established that under certain circumstances, such as attaining a superordinate goal (a group grade), the use of peers in a cooperative learning setting (students share responsibility for solving academic tasks and preparing reports) increases student achievement more than a teacher-directed setting. In addition, working together in a cooperative learning setting improves student self-esteem, social relations (particularly in the area of ethnic relations), and acceptance of students with disabilities who have been mainstreamed or included (Johnson & Johnson, 1999; Slavin, 1991).

SCHOOL–MEDIA LINKAGES

Television characters creep into preschool and elementary school classrooms in the form of superheroes (Superman, Batman, X-men, Power Rangers). While preschool children have always played "pretend," this generation's crop of superheroes are violent (Levin, 1998). When young children take on the persona of their favorite superhero, they behave in ways unlike their ordinary selves. (Bobby knows hitting hurts, but when he becomes Superman, hitting is OK because he is "wiping out the bad guys.")

Many schools deal with superhero play and toys by banning them. However, the school can turn such play into an opportunity to teach appropriate nonviolent conflict resolution (Boyd, 1997). For example, children can be enabled to verbalize the problem, discuss alternative solutions, and/or role play various scenarios. A battle between two superheroes for space or a toy might be redirected to something like a collaborative search for miniature creatures from outer space. Children's cognitive and communication skills are limited, so they need adult guidance to learn appropriate social skills.

Not only do TV characters find their way into the classroom, so does advertising and commercialism. For many years, children have become mini-entrepreneurs, selling magazines, wrapping paper, and candy to their relatives and neighbors as part of school fundraisers. However, now the school has become a mecca for corporations to advertise to children because, in return, the corporation donates much-needed equipment. Corporations view the classroom as a new market for customers. For example, a company may donate athletic equipment in return for putting their logo on the school's team uniforms. A more controversial example is Channel One, a company that supplies schools with satellite dishes, cable connections, TV monitors, and VCR equipment in exchange for broadcasting its programs—including ads—to students for a certain amount of time each day (Aidman, 1995). In addition to the commercialism, a significant problem is that neither the Channel One required programming nor the commercials are subject to curriculum review by teachers, parents, or administrators. A number of educational organizations, such as the National Education Association and the National Parents and Teachers Association, are working on alternatives.

School–Community Linkages

Communities allocate resources for schools. They may use tax money to fund school construction or services. They may pass laws requiring builders to include a school in a new housing development. They set school boundaries (districts), thereby influencing the economic and/or ethnic composition of schools.

Communities, due to their size and budget, influence the size of schools. Generally, large schools are found in large communities, small schools in small communities. Communities with ample budgets can afford to have more schools per student capita, hence smaller schools and classes. Studies have been done relating the size of a school to socialization. Specifically, researchers (Barker & Gump, 1964; Linney & Seidman, 1989) have found that students in *small* schools engage in a greater variety of activities than students in *large* schools. Students in *small* schools hold more leadership positions than those in *large* schools. While there may be more choices of activities in large schools, students have to compete for acceptance to teams and extracurricular activities, like the newspaper. Consequently, many students don't "try out." Thus the size of the school influences the kind of socializing experiences students have in that participation in extracurricular activities helps develop leadership skills, responsibility, cognitive and social competence, and personality development.

The size of the classes within a school also influences socialization. Classes are considered "large" if they have over 25 students, "small" if they have less than 20 students, and "regular" if they are in between. In *large* classes, as the size of the group increases, participation in discussion by each child decreases; interaction with the teacher also decreases (Barker & Gump, 1964; Linney & Seidman, 1989). In *small* classes, more learning activities take place and the greater interaction among students enables them to understand one another, which results in an increase in cooperative behavior. Teachers have more time to monitor students' "on-task" behavior and can provide quicker and more thorough feedback to students. Also, potential disciplinary problems can be identified and resolved more quickly (Pate-Bain et al., 1992).

That the size of the learning environment affects socialization was demonstrated in a large-scale experiment (Finn & Achilles, 1990) in which kindergarten students and teachers were assigned randomly to small and large classes within each participating school. Students remained in these classes for two years. At the end of each grade, they were given standardized tests in reading and mathematics. The results showed that students in reduced-size classes in both subject areas outperformed students in the regular-size classes. The study showed that minority students in particular benefited from the smaller class environment. As a result of the studies on class size, the federal government has mandated a maximum number of students per teacher depending on the grade.

The businesses in a community can support schools by donating resources and time ("Adopt-a-School"). A business can donate equipment, offer expert guest speakers, provide fieldtrips, and/or offer apprenticeship training to students. Such supportive linkages enable children to understand the connection between school learning and the world of work, as well as discovering new role models to emulate (Swick, 1997).

Communities may also have certain traditions that are reflected in its schools. For example, San Juan Capistrano, California celebrates the return of the swallows every spring. There is a parade in which the local schools participate—students decorate floats, bands play, drill teams perform.

THE TEACHER'S ROLE AS A SOCIALIZING AGENT

The most powerful socializing influence of the school lies in those who translate program goals into action—the teachers (Brophy, 1992). Teachers provide the environment for children's learning. They understand children's needs, interests, and abilities and can feel empathy for children's fears of failure. The teacher has the ability to encourage children to explore, to satisfy their natural curiosity, and to love learning—to love it so much that it becomes part of their lives forever. The teacher also plays a major role in helping children learn to deal with positions of authority, to cooperate with others, to cope with problems, and to achieve competence.

The teacher is responsible for selecting materials relevant to the learner, for managing the group dynamics in the classroom, and for interacting individually with each child. When teachers interact with their students, they communicate attitudes about learning and behavior, as well as feelings about individuals. Below are some of the things effective teachers do (Levine & Levine, 1996):

- Provide time and opportunity to learn; pace instruction accordingly.
- Communicate high expectations for student success.
- Involve all students in learning activities by engaging them in discussion and providing motivating work.
- Adapt levels of instruction to learning needs and abilities of students.
- Ensure success for students as they progress through curriculum.

This teacher is a powerful influence on learning through his ability to stimulate the children's interest and engage their involvement.

Thus the teacher–student relationship forms a different social experience for each child, and, therefore, leads to different developmental outcomes.

Teachers as Leaders

A classic study done by Lewin, Lippitt, and White (1939) compared the effects of three leadership styles (authoritarian, democratic, or authoritative and **laissez-faire,** or permissive) on three groups of 10-year-old boys. The boys were assigned randomly to one of three after-school recreational groups engaged in craft activities. The groups were led by three adults who behaved in different ways. In the *authoritarian* situation, the leader determined the group's policy, gave step-by-step directions, dictated each boy's particular task, assigned children to work with one another, was subjective in his praise of the children's work, and stayed aloof from group participation. In the *democratic* situation, the leader allowed the boys to participate in setting group policy, gave the boys a general idea of the steps involved in the project, suggested alternative procedures, allowed them to work with whomever they wished, evaluated them in a fair and objective manner, and tried to be a member of the group. In the *laissez-faire* situation, the leader gave the group complete freedom to do as they wished, supplied material or information only when asked, and refrained almost completely from commenting on the boys' work.

The style of leadership was shown to have a definite effect on the interactions within each group. The boys in the authoritarian situation showed significantly more aggression toward one another and were far more discontented than the boys in the democratic condition. They also produced more work than the other two groups. The boys in the democratic group showed less hostility, more enjoyment, and continued to work, even when the leader left the room, which was not true of the other two groups. Finally, the laissez-faire group accomplished relatively little; the boys were frequently bored and spent much time "fooling around."

Do teachers' leadership styles influence the learning environment in the classroom? In several studies, Good and Brophy (1986) report that a teacher who is clearly the leader and authority and who directs the class toward specific goals (direct instruction) promotes achievement. In this learning environment, little emphasis is placed on discussion, student ideas, discovery learning, or other types of indirect instruction. Jonathon Kozol in *Savage Inequalities* (1991) disagrees. He describes the plight of poor inner-city children trying to learn from teachers who can't relate to their students' experiences in overcrowded schools with dilapidated equipment. Herbert Kohl, in his classic book *36 Children* (1967), describes the remarkable progress in language and thinking abilities made by the children in his class when he brought books, art, and play materials to class and allowed the children to explore them freely and make discoveries. Kohl acted as a facilitator, a helper in the acquisition of knowledge, and in so doing, allowed the children to participate in their own learning. Kohl (1984) believes children learn best from teachers who are role models, who love learning.

Still another way of viewing the teacher's role as a leader is that of a mentor who guides participation (Rogoff, 1990). For example, when a teacher shows a child how to be more successful at doing number problems by putting the numbers in boxes on the graph paper, the teacher is not only guiding the child's participation, but is also providing support for success from one level to the next. Thus teachers facilitate children's capacities to reach their full potential. Lev Vygotsky (1978) called the space between what a learner can do independently and what he or she can do while participating with more capable others the **zone of proximal development (ZPD).** The effective teacher is one who is sensitive to the students' zone of development and provides appropriate independent, as well as collaborative, activities to enhance learning.

An Example of the Zone of Proximal Development

My mother wanted to learn how to use the word-processing program on my computer. I demonstrated a few commands and let her practice, telling her to call me if she got stuck. When she felt she had mastered the basics, I showed her how to do more complicated things. With my assistance, my mother was able to learn more quickly than she would have on her own.

TEACHERS AS MANAGERS

Teachers' ability to manage a classroom affects their effectiveness as socializing agents. For example, Kounin's (1970) classic research on classroom management showed that the key to successful management was in preventive measures rather than consequential measures. Thus the differences between successful and unsuccessful classroom managers lay in the planning and preparation of instruction, so that inattention and boredom were prevented.

Kounin found that student inattentiveness and misbehavior were often linked to problems of discontinuity in a lesson, which in turn were linked to inadequate preparation by the teacher. For example, a teacher who is giving instructions on how to do a book report and stops to find some appropriate books in the closet is likely to have lost the students' attention by the time the books are located. On the other hand, if a teacher has the exemplary books displayed on a table while the book report instructions are being given, it is likely that inattentiveness will be prevented.

Did you ever have teachers who had "eyes in the back of their heads"? Such teachers seem to know what their students are doing without looking and therefore are quick to react to potential problems. Kounin refers to this type of teacher behavior as "with itness." Teachers who are "with it" respond immediately to incidents rather than waiting, quash minor problems before they turn into major ones, do not overreact to incidents, and focus accurately on the individuals involved in the incident rather than blaming someone wrongly. When students realize that the teacher knows what is going on, they are less likely to become involved in unproductive behavior.

Another characteristic of successful classroom managers is the ability to "overlap"—that is, to deal with more than one activity at the same time (Good & Brophy, 1997). For example, while working with a group of students in one corner of the room, a teacher provides an appropriate motivating statement to a child who is wandering about, not involved in an activity. Also, transitions from one activity to the next are smooth, not disruptive. "When you complete the chapter, you may work on the computer"; rather than "All books away; it is time for your test now."

In sum, then, teachers who succeed in producing substantial achievement gains in their students prevent most potential problems from occurring and are able to move activities along or give presentations without confusion or loss of focus. They also provide activities that are at the appropriate developmental level for their students and are interesting enough to hold their attention; they monitor the entire class continuously and can do two or more things simultaneously without breaking up the flow of learning (Brophy & Good, 1986; Good & Brophy, 1997).

TEACHERS' CHARACTERISTICS

Teachers who try to work closely with each child and who understand group dynamics are more likely to provide a successful and rewarding learning environment. For example, studies (Agne, 1992; Brophy & Good, 1986) have found that successful, or effective, teachers are those who are warm, enthusiastic, generous with praise, and have high status. Also, successful teachers communicate well and are responsive to students. Conversely, unsuccessful, or ineffective teachers are aloof, critical, and negative. They tend to communicate in ways that are difficult for students to understand and are unresponsive to students' needs. Teachers who are warm and friendly in their relationships with children are likely to encourage favorable rather than aggressive behavior and constructive, conscientious attitudes toward schoolwork.

When teachers communicate with children, learning is influenced; when teachers ask questions, verbalization from the child is elicited. For example, teachers' verbal styles have been found to have an impact on the development of language skills in preschool children (Schickendanz, 1990). Teachers who use expansive verbal descriptions and who encourage the children to converse with each other effect an increase in their students' verbal skills. It was also found that teachers who use reinforcement (verbal praise, smile, touch) are able to foster the learning of certain tasks. Preschool children who were observed in the presence of a friendly, approving adult behaved in a more exploratory, inquisitive manner than when a critical, aloof adult was present (Moore & Bulbulian, 1976).

The relationship of teachers' characteristics to their degree of success and their impact on socialization can be explained by the classic research of Bandura and Walters (1963) on modeling. They point out that "models who are rewarding, prestigeful or competent, who possess high status, and who have control over rewarding resources are more readily imitated than are models who lack these qualities" (p. 107).

Students who model their teachers pick up subtle behaviors and attitudes about learning. It would follow, then, that the most important influence on students' achievement is the competent teacher. More specifically, a competent teacher is one who is committed to work, is an effective classroom manager, is a positive role model with whom students can identify, is enthusiastic and warm, continues efforts for self-improvement in teaching, possesses skill in human relationships, and is able to adapt his or her skills to a specific context (Good & Brophy, 1997; Linney & Seidman, 1989).

TEACHERS' EXPECTATIONS

Do teachers' expectations affect the achievement and behavior of students? Rosenthal and Jacobson (1968) in their book *Pygmalion in the Classroom* described a classic experiment in which they had all the teachers in an elementary school give a test to their students that was designed to identify intellectual "bloomers" (those who would show an academic spurt during the year). Actually, the test was a nonverbal IQ test and, unknown to the teachers, did not predict future intellectual spurts. After the test, however, the researchers provided the teachers with a list of bloomers. The bloomer list was not based on the test; instead, it was a random list of names from the teachers' rolls. Eight months later, all the children were retested with the same IQ test. The designated bloomers did, in fact, demonstrate significant intellectual growth. The children in the first and second grades showed the most growth. This study raised the question—are teachers trapped by their self-fulfilling prophecies?

Rosenthal and Jacobson's study generated a lot of controversy because of methodological weaknesses and the inability of others to replicate the original results. Brophy and Good (1986) pointed out that attempting to induce teacher expectations by providing phony information generally has not shown results. However, studies observing actual teacher behavior in the classroom have shown the effects of expectancy.

Brophy and Good explain the reality of teacher expectations as follows: teachers usually receive data about students at the beginning of the school year (test scores, past grades, family and health information, comments by previous teachers), which influence their expectations of students for achievement and behavior. Because of these expectations, the teacher tends to treat students differently. Students then react to the teacher differently. The students' behavior and achievement reinforce the teacher's expectations. Gradually, the students' self-concepts, motivation, and levels of aspiration reflect these expectations. If continued throughout the year, the students' performances will match or fulfill what the teacher expected or prophesized in the beginning of the year.

In addition to students' past records of achievement and behavior, teachers' expectations can also be influenced by certain student characteristics, such as socioeconomic class, ethnicity, gender, personality, physical attractiveness, speech characteristics, and handwriting (Brophy & Good, 1986; Good & Brophy, 1997; Proctor, 1984).

An Example of How the Self-fulfilling Prophecy Operates

Mrs. Levins gets a child named Roy in her third-grade class who has moved several times and has below-normal achievement scores for his age recorded in his cumulative folder. As Mrs. Levins reviews the rest of the folders belonging to the children in her class, she finds she has three children (Sarah, Andrew, and Cary) who have consistently scored well above normal on achievement tests and whose folders also contain notes from previous teachers about what a joy each one was to teach. Upon observing Mrs. Levins midyear, we find that she waits less time for Roy to answer her questions than she does for Sarah, Andrew, or Cary. We also find that she is more critical of Roy than she is of the others and demands less of him in terms of work.

Of course, not all teachers translate their expectations into the type of behavior described in the example. Some teachers do not form expectations that continue throughout the year; rather, they change their expectations on the basis of the students' performances. Teacher expectations about students do not by themselves have a direct impact on student behavior; it is only when the expectations are communicated to the students and when selective reinforcement results in shaping their behavior that teacher expectations have an impact.

Therefore, it is only when teachers become aware of possible biases in their behavior, caused by their expectations, that they can then try to interact objectively with each child.

TEACHER–SCHOOL RESPONSES TO GENDER

Why do girls perform better academically than boys in elementary school, but falter in high school? For example, girls do not do as well as boys in science and math by the time they reach adolescence (American Association of University Women [AAUW], 1991; Maccoby & Jacklin, 1974). That teachers treat boys and girls differently in school has been well documented (Minuchin & Shapiro, 1983; Tittle, 1986). Studies consistently show that boys have more interventions with teachers than do girls (Streitmatter, 1994). For example, it has been found (Serbin, O'Leary, Kent, & Tonick, 1973) that teachers are more responsive to the disruptive behavior of boys than girls and more likely to reprimand boys. When children request attention, teachers generally respond to boys with instructions and to girls with nurture. In addition, girls receive more attention when they are close to the teacher, whereas boys are given attention from a distance.

It has also been found that the feedback received by boys and girls on the intellectual quality of their work differs. Boys receive considerable criticism for failing to obey the rules, whereas girls receive criticism related to their performance. Boys attribute their failure to do well to lack of effort; girls attribute their failure to do well to lack of ability

These ethnically diverse children are involved in a cooperative learning task compatible with their learning styles.

(Dweck, Davidson, Nelson, & Enna, 1978). Do some girls, then, give up trying to be successful when they reach high school, due to the responses their elementary teachers have given them? There is evidence that girls generally take fewer advanced math classes than do boys in high school and college (AAUW, 1991; Sadker & Sadker, 1985, 1994).

According to a report by the American Association of University Women (AAUW, 1991), schools are shortchanging girls. Specifically, the contributions and experiences of girls and women are still marginalized in textbooks. Sexuality and the realities of sexual activity (pregnancy, disease, rape) are rarely discussed in schools. There has been little change in gender-segregated enrollment patterns in vocational education (girls primarily are enrolled in office and business-training programs, whereas boys are in programs leading to higher paying trade jobs). Teachers must be trained to foster assertive and affiliative skills in both girls and boys. School curricula and textbooks should be monitored for gender stereotypes and provide positive role models for both girls and boys. Gender-role socialization will be discussed in more detail in Chapter 12.

TEACHER–SCHOOL RESPONSES TO ETHNIC DIVERSITY

The macrosystem ideology that the school is responsible for socializing the ethnically diverse is wedded to American immigration policy; those who live and work here must learn good citizenship. They must accept democratic values as well as adhere to the laws and principles of the Constitution.

Macrosystem philosophies influencing how diverse ethnic groups should be socialized, especially by the school, are *assimilation* (microcultures take on the macroculture), *melting pot* (all cultures blend into one), and *cultural pluralism* (micro- and macroculture coexist).

Assimilation involves the process whereby one group gives up its characteristics and takes on those of another group. The school has traditionally served the socialization needs of the majority culture. For a long time it was felt that in order for diverse ethnic groups to be assimilated into society, they had to adapt to the majority culture's ways. Examples of assimilation are English immersion programs in schools, printing voting pamphlets in English, and celebrating American holidays. An important influence in this attitude was Elwood P. Cubberley (1919), a historian of U.S. education and an educational leader. Cubberley advocated an intensive effort to Americanize the children of immigrants. He felt that it was the obligation of the public schools in areas of great immigrant concentrations to assimilate the children of the newcomers into the superior "American race." His view was generally accepted by school administrators and teachers.

Later, the idea of America as a *melting pot* became a popular approach to socializing immigrants and ethnic minorities. The melting-pot concept was first expressed by Hector Saint-John de Crevecoeur, who wrote in 1756, "Here in America individuals of all nations are melted into a new race of men" (cited in Krug, 1976). Advocates of the melting-pot theory deplored the hatreds and feuds that the immigrants brought with them from Europe and perpetuated in the United States, but they acknowledged that there was much good in their respective ethnic groups. They believed that the new emerging U.S. culture must be built not on the destruction of the ethnic values and mores of the various immigrant groups, but on their fusion with existing U.S. civilization, which itself was never purely Anglo Saxon but a product of the interaction of Anglo Saxon elements with the French, Spanish, Dutch, Native Americans, and African Americans.

The melting-pot concept presupposes respect for the ethnic heritage of the immigrants because it accepts their intrinsic values and their potential contribution to the cultural melting process that was—and is—taking place in the United States of America. This process envisions the emergence of a new American people. The melting-pot theorists rejected the idea of Anglo Saxon superiority expressed by Cubberley and others. In the melting pot, all ethnic groups are equal, all to be reshaped into a new entity.

An example of the melting-pot philosophy is *Esperanto,* a language invented in 1887 for international use. It is based on word roots common to the main European languages. Currently, there is an Esperanto League of Cyberspace. Another example is intermarriage between people of different races or religions.

Today, the approach to the socialization of ethnically diverse groups has become associated with *cultural pluralism,* principally developed by Horace M. Kallen (1956), which accepts the existence of a mainstream "American" culture, or macroculture. Kallen has maintained that the dominant culture will benefit from coexistence and constant interaction with the cultures of other ethnic groups—in other words, "unity in diversity." The various ethnic groups, or microcultures, should accept and cherish the common elements of U.S. cultural, political, and social mores as represented by the public schools, but they should by their own efforts support supplemental education for their young to preserve their ethnic awareness and values:

> [This philosophy] embraces the ideals of mutual appreciation and understanding of various cultures in society; cooperation of diverse groups; coexistence of different languages, religious beliefs and life styles; and autonomy for each group to work out its own social purposes and future without interfering with the rights of other groups (Ornstein & Levine, 1982, p. 245).

An example of the socialization philosophy of cultural pluralism is the concept of bilingual/multicultural education, which will be discussed later.

Background for School and Teacher Response

In general, children from ethnically diverse or minority families are much more likely to be poor, and therefore at risk for negative developmental outcomes than are other children (Reed & Sautter, 1990). "Minority" refers to an *ascribed,* or given social status, not necessarily a *statistical,* or actual one. Sometimes the label "minority" can be a "self-fulfilling" prophecy (Garcia, 1998). For example, workers from some ethnic minority families find it hard to get work when the economy slows down, and they are usually paid less for the work they do than are Anglos (Levine & Levine, 1996). In addition, the educational level of certain ethnic groups, in general, is lower than that of Anglos (Cohen, Pettigrew, & Riley, 1972; Coleman, 1966; Levine & Levine, 1996).

Since education has become a more and more important requisite for success via employability, children from some ethnic minority families are generally disadvantaged in their quest for the "American dream," equal opportunity to achieve one's inborn potential. In other words, their capacity for achievement is handicapped because of their ascribed social status as minorities in U.S. society. A long history of prejudicial attitudes has been difficult to change. Attitudes will be discussed in Chapter 11.

Until recently, the philosophy in the United States of socializing ethnic minorities was assimilation. Those who did not learn the language or "American" ways failed to become effective members of the larger society because they could not achieve in school—which meant that their knowledge of the world about them remained limited, as did the opportunities available to them as adults. Thus their statuses remained low.

Various societal responses have attempted to address the unique socialization needs of ethnically diverse groups to enable resiliency and success. Laws have been passed, such as the Civil Rights Act of 1964, which prohibit discrimination on the basis of race, gender, or national origin in public accommodations, federally assisted programs, and by employers. Financial assistance has been allocated to schools and to community programs providing services to ethnic minorities, such as bilingual educational programs. And parents have been required to become involved with the school in the socialization of their children.

Historically, it has been very difficult to break the cycle of inequality of opportunity. Because ethnic minority parents were denied equal political rights, they were not involved in community affairs. They were neither elected to school boards or city councils, neither were they appointed to committees or commissions. Ethnic minority representation on higher education faculties was rare. Thus, until recently, ethnically diverse groups had no place in decision-making bodies, such as government or education, or in advisory capacities. Not only could they not be advocates for themselves, they could not provide leadership role models for their young.

To try to break the cycle of inequality, and as part of President Lyndon Johnson's War on Poverty, the U.S. Office of Education commissioned a study on the equality of educational opportunity. This concern over educational opportunities illustrated society's view in the 1960s regarding its obligation to meet the special socialization needs of ethnic minorities—that diverse groups should have educational opportunities in accordance with their talents and abilities.

James Coleman (1966), a sociologist at Johns Hopkins University, was given prime responsibility for surveying nearly a million pupils in 6,000 different schools across the nation to determine whether students were succeeding in accordance with their ability and, if not, why they were not. This famous survey, known as the Coleman Report, found that non-Anglos and Anglos usually attended different schools. Non-Anglos did less well than Anglos in verbal and nonverbal skills, reading comprehension, arithmetic skills, and general information. The difference became greater as they progressed through school. Coleman found that the school's social composition had the most influence on individual achievement. In other words, children were influenced by their classmates' social class backgrounds and aspirations. African Americans from low-socioeconomic statuses attending school with Anglos from low-socioeconomic statuses did not achieve as well as African Americans from low-socioeconomic statuses attending school with Anglos from middle-class socioeconomic statuses.

Some interpreted the report as concluding that integration of schools and communities would eventually resolve the problem of unequal achievement. They reasoned that if poor African American children interacted with middle-class Anglo children, their achievement would improve. Others, who felt integration was either unattainable or would take too long, advocated compensatory education. They reasoned that poor African American children's achievement would improve if they were given more educational and related services, such as tutoring, reading specialists, preschool, parental participation, and so on. As was discussed in Chapter 5, various types of compensatory educational programs appeared in the 1960s, with varying results.

Since the Coleman Report found that there was a strong association between children's achievement levels and their attitudes, which came from family background, regarding their personal sense of control over their own destinies, it was felt that parental participation in school and parental control over educational decision making might make a critical difference in children's achievement. Even though research (Lazar, 1977; Schorr, 1997; Schorr, & Schorr, 1988) has shown that early intervention programs that include parents (participation and education) have resulted in improved test scores of participants; it has also been shown that these improvements peter out in elementary school unless intervention is continued (Bronfenbrenner, 1977; Levine & Levine, 1996).

Ethnically diverse students who perform poorly in school do so for a number of possible reasons (Bennett, 1999; Ornstein & Levine, 1989):

1. *Inappropriate curricula and instruction.* The lessons teachers plan and the kinds of materials teachers have been trained to use are often inappropriate for some ethnically diverse children. Often the children are unfamiliar with the terminology and concepts, and many are unfamiliar with the language.

2. *Differences between parental and school norms.* Since the parents of ethnically diverse children are likely to be unfamiliar with school norms and learning experiences, they are unlikely to reinforce such behaviors as creative thinking, reasoning, and self-direction.

3. *Lack of previous success in school.* Failure to achieve in the early grades leads to low self-esteem and a lack of feeling of control over what happens in school. Consequently, the motivation to try harder is diminished, and learned helplessness results.

4. *Teaching difficulties.* Teachers of ethnically diverse children often become frustrated because of lack of success in the classroom. The students who do not succeed in school can exhibit behavioral problems. This provides an additional burden for the teacher, especially since most teachers are not adequately trained in dealing with behavioral problems.

5. *Teacher perceptions and standards.* Because of published data and because of what they may have experienced, teachers of ethnically diverse children are likely to have low expectations. These perceptions often result in a self-fulfilling prophecy, in that standards are lowered and students' low performance levels are reinforced. In other words, teachers who believe their students cannot learn are less likely to motivate them beyond their current performance level; therefore, the students do not succeed. Teachers who believe that their students can learn are more likely to design appropriate learning experiences that stimulate them to succeed.

6. *Segregation.* Children from ethnically diverse groups are more likely to attend school with their ethnic minority peers; or if they attend an integrated school, they are more likely to be placed in special classes than are Anglo children. Consequently, they are reinforced by peers who have similar backgrounds as well as similar educational needs. These peer groups similarly lag in school performance levels. Thus there is no motivation to succeed among the peer group because high performance by an individual would make that individual different from his or her friends, and the price to pay for nonconformity— ostracism—is too great for many children to handle.

7. *Differences in teacher/student backgrounds.* Teachers with middle-class backgrounds may experience particular difficulties in understanding and motivating their lower-class students. Problems of this type are more likely to occur in the case of Anglo teachers working with disadvantaged minority students.

Schools reflect the communities from which they draw their students, as well as those from which they draw their teachers (Garcia, 1998). Sometimes there is a wide range of socioeconomic statuses represented in classrooms. While ethnic minority groups are represented in greater numbers than Anglos in the lower-socioeconomic classes, the disparity between oppression and privilege affects all.

Classism is the differential treatment of groups of people because of their class background and the reinforcement of those differences through values and practices of societal institutions, such as schools. Socioeconomic class, as was discussed in Chapter 3, is based on income, educational attainment, occupation, and power. Where a family falls on the continuum from poor to rich affects the manner in which its members live, how they think and act, and the way in which others react to them (Gollnick & Chinn, 1998).

We are all socializing children in "a world of contradictions." On the one hand, children learn that everyone is "created equal" and that each individual has the right to "pursue happiness" (the *Declaration of Independence*); and that we as a nation are united to provide for the "common good" (the *Constitution*). On the other hand, in the community, children observe that certain groups of people are exploited while others compete for resources and power. "Despite its egalitarian principles, the United States has been moving away from, not toward, more equitable distribution of wealth, especially during the last two decades" (Ramsey, 1998, p. 45).

Dealing with life's inevitable inconveniences is dependent on class. For example, if your car breaks down, do you bring it to a service station for repairs, rent a car, and go about your business? Or do you ask a relative or friend to help you fix it while you depend on others and public transportation to take you where you need to go? When you get sick, do you go to a doctor knowing that whatever the treatment, it will be covered by your insurance? Or do you go to bed and try to heal yourself? Likewise, in the classroom children who have access to books, computers, and trips can navigate more successfully through school projects than those who have few resources at home.

Consequences of classism in school are subtle, but significant. One consequence is that a large number of students from lower-socioeconomic statuses are assigned to low ability groups in their early years, setting them on a track that is difficult to alter (Levine & Levine, 1996). Another consequence is segregation of peer groups along socioeconomic lines, especially in middle or junior high school (Davidson & Schniedewind, 1992). What possessions students have, what neighborhoods they live in, what clothing they wear, the language and vocabulary they use can all interfere with positive social interaction, thereby reinforcing inequality in society.

Bilingual/Multicultural Education

An increasing number of ethnically diverse children with limited English proficiency (LEP) are attending U.S. schools and are at risk for failure. Research shows that disproportionately high numbers of ethnic minority students do not finish school, and disproportionately high numbers of those who do remain in school are achieving far below their potential (Bennett, 1999). Through legislation, the federal government has tried to equalize opportunities for diverse groups. The basis for a variety of legislative acts and court decisions is Title VI of the Civil Rights Act of 1964 which states that "No person is the United States shall, on the grounds of race, color, or national origin, be excluded from participation in, be denied the benefits of, or be subjected to discrimination under any program or activity receiving federal financial assistance."

In 1974, Congress passed the Equal Educational Opportunity Act requiring schools to take "appropriate action" to overcome the language barriers of students who cannot communicate in English. The Supreme Court decision of 1974 in *Lau* v. *Nichols* held that schools receiving federal funds could not discriminate against children of limited or no English-speaking ability by denying them language training. It ruled that the civil rights of the students involved in the suit had been violated because the school had not provided an equal educational opportunity for them. The court gave school districts a choice of providing instruction in the child's native tongue while learning English (bilingual education), English as a second language (ESL) training, or other specialized services. The purpose of bilingual education is to help students achieve both communicative and academic competence (Garcia, 1998).

Many schools have added a multicultural component to bilingual education. A major goal is to prepare culturally literate citizens who can function effectively in their own microculture, other microcultures, and the macroculture (Banks, 1994). We live in a world that is becoming increasingly interdependent on other cultures about which most of us are culturally illiterate. Thus it is both desirable and necessary that we understand diversity as well as impart this understanding to our children. Multicultural education should meet the needs of all children so that they can progress to their fullest potential in this ever-changing world.

Do bilingual–multicultural programs meet the unique socialization needs of ethnically diverse children? There are still some issues that need to be resolved before this question can be answered (Levine & Levine, 1996). At one end of the continuum are those who believe the language and culture of diverse ethnic groups must be preserved to develop and maintain positive individual and group identity in an equitable society. At the other end of the continuum are those who believe that ethnic minority children will be better prepared to compete in society if they are immersed as soon as possible in English-language instruction. In between, there are a variety of approaches to enable the LEP student to make the transition from native language to English.

The research on the effects of bilingual–multicultural education is inconclusive (Levine & Levine, 1996) Many factors in addition to language proficiency contribute to a child's success in school—individual learning ability, socioeconomic status, family involvement, effective teaching, to name a few.

The potential of the school for meeting the special socialization needs of ethnically diverse children can be increased by providing opportunities for parents and children to make educational decisions that reflect their needs. One way is through the encouragement of family involvement in school, to be discussed in Chapter 7. Another way is to include ethnically diverse individuals in decision making and/or governing bodies, such as school boards, city councils, planning commissions, advisory boards, and committees.

The teacher's role in enabling successful educational outcomes for ethnically diverse children is to understand how their socialization experiences may differ from the majority and to modify teaching methods accordingly (Chapter 7 outlines some suggestions).

Students from different ethnic groups have notably different experiences in school. For example, Chinese, Japanese, and some Southeast Asian children have succeeded in American schools, whereas some other Asian, Pacific, and Native American children are less successful (Tharp, 1989). Because teachers are generally from the majority culture and they invoke the ways of the majority culture, educational underachievement by minority groups is usually blamed on incompatibilities between the child's culture and that of the school (Levine & Levine, 1996).

Research indicates that individual learning styles vary; children's learning styles may be related to their ethnic socialization, and teachers should respond accordingly (Banks, 1994). However, teachers often communicate in the style of their own culture. For example, the time a teacher waits for a child to respond to a question and the time the teacher waits before talking again was compared between an Anglo and a Navajo teacher of the same group of third-grade Navajo students (White & Tharp, 1988). The Navajo teacher waited considerably longer than the Anglo teacher after the children responded before talking again. What was perceived by the Anglo teacher as a completed response was often intended by the child as a pause, which the Anglo teacher had interrupted. On the other hand, while Navajo students preferred long wait times between responses, Native Hawaiian students preferred "negative" wait times; that is, the listener speaks without waiting for the speaker to finish (White & Tharp, 1988). This is often interpreted by teachers from other ethnic groups as rude interruption, but in Hawaiian society it demonstrates involvement and relationship (Tharp, 1989).

Another variation related to ethnic socialization is behavior. For example, American children are taught to look directly at an adult when being spoken to; many African American, Mexican American, and Asian American children are taught to lower their eyes. This behavior may be interpreted as disrespect. Teachers must develop an awareness of how ethnic background affects actions (McIntyre, 1992). The next chapter will explore in more detail the socialization of ethnically diverse children and how to involve families in the school.

TEACHER–SCHOOL RESPONSES TO RELIGIOUS DIVERSITY

As was discussed in Chapter 3, religion is a significant socializing mechanism in the transmission of values and behavior. Traditions, rituals, and religious institutions reinforce those values taught in families.

Although the political ideology in the United States advocates separation of church and state (including public school), the two often intersect (Gollnick & Chinn, 1998). For example, the words, "One nation, under God, . . ." are in the Pledge of Allegiance, and the statement, "In God we trust" is on U.S. currency. The degree that religious ideologies intersect with public school curricula and policies is significant in the socialization of all children who attend public school. Issues that have been controversial are school prayer, the teaching of evolution, sex education, censorship of certain books, and the celebration of certain holidays.

Teachers need to be sensitive to the values of the families in the community in the context of a diverse society, while at the same time implementing the educational goals of the school district.

TEACHER–SCHOOL RESPONSES TO CHILDREN WITH DISABILITIES

Due to changes in the law that reflect public attitude—that education is a *right,* not a privilege—the school has become a designated agent for identifying children with disabilities and including them in educational activities that are available to all children. Therefore, the attitudes, history, and laws regarding individuals with disabilities are discussed here.

A **disability** refers to the reduction of function or the absence of a particular body part or organ. An **impairment** refers to diseased or defective tissue.

Children with disabilities are those who have been evaluated as being mentally retarded, hard of hearing, deaf, speech impaired, visually impaired, seriously emotionally disturbed, autistic, orthopedically impaired, other health impaired, deaf–blind, multidisabled, traumatically brain injured, or as having specific learning disabilities and who, because of those impairments, need special education and related services.

The terms *disability* and/or *impairment* are used today instead of *handicap* in order to dispel negative stereotypes. The dictionary, for example, defines *handicap* as something that hampers a person: a disadvantage, a hindrance. People in wheelchairs are disabled. They are handicapped only when they try to enter a building with steps. A person may be handicapped in one situation but not in another. For example, Ray Charles is handicapped in *reading* music because he is blind. He certainly is not handicapped, however, in *playing* music. Thus, for children with disabilities, the main aim of socialization should be to minimize the effects of their disabilities and to maximize the effects of their abilities.

There are some common assumptions about individuals with disabilities that affect interaction with them. Assuming that individuals with disabilities are helpless can lead to solicitude or overprotectiveness. The assumption that individuals with disabilities are incapable can lead to ostracism or neglect.

Assumptions and practices that promote the deferential and unequal treatment of people because they are different physically, mentally, or behaviorally is called **handicapism.** The word *handicap* is thought to be derived from the practice of beggars who held "cap in hand" to solicit charity, thereby reflecting a dependent position (Biklen & Bogdan, 1977). The media have contributed to certain attitudes associated with disabilities. For example, children's stories tell of evil trolls, hunchbacks, or witches (who are old and deformed in some way), thus promoting an attitude of fear. While handicapism has a long history, the media are trying to include people with disabilities in TV shows and advertisements. Teachers need to be sensitive to handicapism and view children as individuals with abilities and disabilities, if applicable.

Background for School and Teacher Response

Historically, we can delineate four stages of attitudes toward people with disabilities that have affected their socialization (Hallahan & Kauffman, 1998; Kirk, Gallagher, & Anastasiow, 1997). (1) During the pre-Christian era, people with disabilities tended to be banished, neglected, and/or mistreated. (2) During the spread of Christianity, they were protected and pitied. (3) In the eighteenth and nineteenth centuries institutions were established to provide separate education. (4) In the latter part of the twentieth century, there was a movement toward accepting people with disabilities and integrating them into the mainstream of society to the fullest extent possible ("full inclusion"). Currently, laws enable individuals with disabilities to receive a free and equal education and to compete for jobs without discrimination.

In the early years of U.S. history there was no concept of classification according to the type of disability. The concept of individual differences, as we know it today, was not understood or appreciated. In those early years there were no public provisions for people with disabilities. Such individuals were "stored away" in charitable houses or remained at home without educational opportunities.

In the early 1800s, residential schools were established in some states for people with disabilities. Those institutions offered training in a protective environment, often spanning the life of the individual. As the population of the United States increased and as large numbers of people congregated in the growing cities, the population of children with disabilities in any one place also increased. Parents and educators sought ways of keeping the children with disabilities in their home communities because residential schools were far away, making it difficult for parents to visit their children. Therefore, in the latter part of the nineteenth century, special classes were introduced in the public schools.

The most significant influence on the history of special education has been the advocacy of the parents of children with disabilities. They raised money for treatment centers and research. They stimulated governmental organizations for new legislation that would provide funds for research, professional training, treatment, transportation, financial assistance, community health, and many other related needs.

As the special-class movement grew, so did the research on the effectiveness of special-class placement. Some research indicated that special-class placement provided a more supportive and sheltered social environment for exceptional children, but other researchers found that special-class placement did little to increase the learning and achievement of children (Dunlop, 1977).

In 1968, Lloyd Dunn wrote a classic article in the field of special education that drew serious widespread attention to the issue of special-class placement. The article questioned the appropriateness of special classes for many children labeled "educable mentally retarded." Dunn estimated that 60% to 80% of the pupils enrolled in classes for the mildly retarded were from low-socioeconomic-status backgrounds, "including Afro-Americans, American Indians, Mexicans, and Puerto Rican Americans, those from nonstandard English-speaking, broken, disorganized and inadequate homes, and children from other non middle-class environments" (p. 5). In 1973, Jane Mercer found that among children labeled as retarded by the public schools, there were 2 times as many African Americans and 4.5 times as many Mexican Americans as might be expected from their proportion in the general population. Conversely, only half as many Anglo children were labeled as retarded. Were the public schools using the special classes as a dumping ground for children who were not successful in the regular classroom, regardless of the reason?

Studies done during the late 1960s and early 1970s (Avery, 1971; Beez, 1968) indicated that teacher expectations were lower for labeled children than for others. Lowered expectations tend to reduce the chances of reaching optimal developmental capacity. A strong impetus for inclusion of students with disabilities into regular classes came from parents who claimed their children were not developing their full potential in special classes because not much was expected of them—they were receiving a "watered-down" curriculum.

The prevailing attitude up until the mid-1970s was that the school's role was to educate the majority. Thus any students who might interfere with that role should be isolated if possible, or else not served. Those who were served were put in special classes to be trained by experts. Those who were not served by the public schools generally received no education at all, unless their families could afford a private tutor.

In 1975, Congress passed PL 94-142, the Education for All Handicapped Children Act, which required that children with disabilities be educated in a regular public classroom wherever possible. It applied to children age 3 to 21. In 1986, an amendment was passed, PL 99-457, to serve children from birth to age 3 in order to minimize the risks of developmental delays due to lack of appropriate services early on. In 1990, the name of the Education for All Handicapped Children Act was changed to the Individuals with Disabilities Education Act (PL 101-476). In 1991, the Americans with Disabilities Act (PL 101-336) was passed to ensure nondiscriminatory treatment of people with disabilities in areas of their lives such as employment, use of public facilities, transportation, and telecommunications.

Individuals with Disabilities Education Act

In 1990, the Individuals with Disabilities Education Act (IDEA) was passed. It provides federal money to states and local agencies to educate children with disabilities age 3 to 21. Because of the possible effects of early categorization, IDEA allows states to use the category "developmental delay" for preschool children with special needs. Each state has specific criteria and evaluation procedures for determining children's eligibility for early intervention and special services, including what constitutes developmental delay (Wolery & Wilbers, 1994).

Many children are diagnosed early by physicians as having specific conditions, such as cerebral palsy or spina bifida. However, many other children, due to environmental variables such as abuse, exposure to toxins or disease, or poverty, are at risk for developmental delays or disabilities (Wolery & Wilbers, 1994). Such children are often not identified as such prior to their contact with social workers or teachers. Thus early childhood professionals are significant identifiers of children with special needs. This identification can occur through informal observations of children, screening with developmental scales, and vision and hearing screening (Meisels & Provence, 1989; Meisels & Wasik, 1990).

IDEA requires *nondiscriminatory evaluations* appropriate to a child's cultural and linguistic background of whether a child has a disability and, if so, the nature of the disability. A reevaluation must occur every three years. Parental approval is required.

The main purpose of the act is to guarantee that all children with disabilities have available to them a free and appropriate public education. The principal method of guaranteeing the fulfillment of that purpose is via the *Individualized Education Program* (IEP). Any child receiving special education services must have an IEP written at the beginning of each year and reviewed at least once a year. The IEP is basically a form of communication between the school and the family. It is developed by the group of people responsible for the child's education—the parents, the teacher, and other involved school personnel. The exact format varies, depending on the particular school districts; however, all IEPs must include the following:

1. A statement of the child's present levels of educational performance.
2. A statement of annual goals, including short-term objectives.
3. A statement of the specific special education and related services to be provided to the child, and of the extent of the child's participation in regular education environments, including initiation dates and anticipated duration of services.

A child with disabilities can be integrated into the classroom with the support of special equipment and assistance from the teacher.

4. Required transition services from school to work or continued education (usually by age 14 to 16).

5. Objective criteria, evaluation procedures, and schedules for determining whether instructional objectives are being met.

The Individuals with Disabilities Education Act also requires that students with disabilities be placed in the *least restrictive environment* (LRE). This means that such students should be included in school programs with nondisabled students to the maximum extent appropriate. Supplementary services such as attendants, tutors, interpreters, transportation, speech pathology and audiology, psychological services, physical and occupational therapy, recreation, and medical and counseling services enable inclusion. Supplementary aids such as wheelchairs, crutches, standing tables, hearing aids, embossed globes, braille dictionaries, and books with enlarged print, also enable inclusion. Inclusion can be for the entire day or appropriate portions of the day.

Figure 6.2 Meeting the Special Socialization Needs of Children with Disabilities

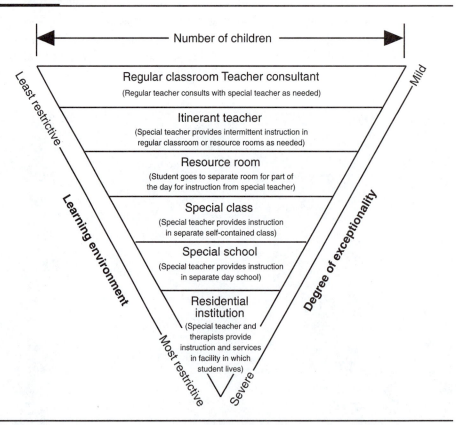

Source: Adapted from "Special Education as Developmental Capital" by E. Deno, 1979. *Exceptional Children, 37,* pp. 229–237. Copyright 1970 by the Council for Exceptional Children. Reprinted with permission.

Inclusion

Inclusion is the educational philosophy of being part of the whole, that children are entitled to fully participate in their school and community. Is such a concept appropriate for all children with disabilities? Some believe in full inclusion (Lipsky & Gartner, 1989; Stainback, Stainback, East, & Sapon-Shevin, 1994), advocating appropriate support services as needed by all children.

Others believe in partial inclusion, providing a continuum of services as well as integration in regular classrooms and regular activities whenever possible. They acknowledge the need for special, supplementary services or even separate schooling, if necessary (Keogh, 1988; Smith & Bassett, 1991). The rationale for the availability of comprehensive special services is that students with disabilities may need more intensive, individualized instruction, and it helps ensure that students without disabilities in the regular classroom get appropriate education (Kaufman, 1989). Figure 6.2 diagrams how varying degrees of inclusion and separation might be implemented.

The debate regarding optimal socialization environments for those with disabilities goes on. Many schools all over the country serving children ages 3 to 21 are experimenting with various educational reforms, especially using peers as socialization agents in an integrated or mainstreamed classroom (Fulton, 1994).

Summary of Effective Schools and Schooling

- *Schooling goals*—school provides clear standards of achievement and excellence.
- *School–family linkages*—family provides resources according to socioeconomic status and positive attitudes to support schools by being involved and ensuring children come to school ready to learn.
- *School–child linkages*—psychological characteristics of child temperament, motivation, learning style influence ability to learn.
- *School–peer group linkages*—cooperative activities increase learning.
- *School–media linkages*—schools use TV, videos, and computers appropriately, critical thinking skills taught.
- *School–community linkages*—community provides resources and positive attitudes to support schools; size of school and class influences adult–child interactions.
- *School programming*—traditional (or teacher-directed) and modern (or learner-directed) programs have different socialization effects.
- *Teacher's characteristics*—successful teachers are democratic leaders and good classroom managers; are warm, enthusiastic, generous with praise; have high status and positive expectations; respond sensitively to gender, ethnicity, disability.
- *Safety*—school provides protection for children and is proactive in violence prevention.

Epilogue

The school's basic function in society is to develop future contributing citizens. Philosophies on teaching and learning vary as to the best way to accomplish this. Rousseau's philosophy was learner-directed (let the child's natural curiosity determine what is learned); formal traditional schooling is teacher-directed (the teacher determines what is learned by the child); home schooling can be either or both.

Teachers implement the learning process and products in a variety of ways. They are partners with students in learning. They provide instruction, set standards, reinforce, extinguish, and/or punish. Teachers are facilitators of knowledge. They are role models, give feedback, and utilize reasoning. Teachers are mentors or experts and students are apprentices. They structure, collaborate, transfer knowledge.

For the school to be an effective socializer, parents must be involved in their child's education.

SUMMARY

The school is an agent of socialization in that it is a setting for intellectual and social experiences from which children develop the skills, knowledge, interest, and attitudes that characterize them as individuals and that shape their abilities to perform adult roles.

Schools exert influence on children by their educational policies leading to achievement, by their formal organization of introducing students to authority, and by the social relationships that evolve in the classroom.

The primary function of education from society's perspective is the transmission of the cultural heritage—the accumulated knowledge, values, beliefs, and customs of the society. To transmit culture and maintain it, society must be provided with trained people who can assume specialized roles, as well as develop new knowledge and technology.

The function of education from the individual's perspective is to acquire the necessary skills and knowledge to become self-sufficient and able to participate effectively in society.

Society's expectations of schools are expressed in academic, vocational, social, civic, cultural, and personal goals.

Philosophies of teaching and learning range from teacher-directed programs to learner-directed ones.

Teacher-directed (traditional) educational environments usually subscribe to the philosophy that the functions of the school are to impart basic factual knowledge and preserve the cultural heritage. Traditional education includes homework, tests, memorization, and strict discipline. Learner-directed (modern) educational environments subscribe to the philosophy that the function of the school is to develop the whole child. Curriculum emerges from the child's interests and abilities.

Socialization outcomes differ according to the setting. Children in traditional settings perform better on academic tasks and are "on-task" more often than children in modern settings. Children in modern settings have a more positive attitude toward school, are involved in more cooperative work, and show more autonomy than children in traditional settings.

In a changing society, the challenge continually facing educators is how to transmit the cultural heritage, as well as prepare individuals for the future. Educators have approached this dilemma differently. Some believe only academic skills, cultural heritage, and good citizenship should be taught. Others believe critical thinking skills, self-concept, and interpersonal-relationship skills should be included in the curriculum.

To address criticisms of the school's ability to socialize effectively and to produce well-educated graduates, the government proposed "Goals 2000."

Schooling for the future involves being prepared for the world of work; knowing how to use computers and software as tools is essential to successful functioning in our society. Effectiveness of the computer as a learning tool depends on how it is used by teachers and students, as well as the software selected.

To have an effective environment for learning, schools must be safe. Violence is rooted in families and communities. Children model parents' behavior and see violence in the media and in the community as a way to solve conflicts, have access to guns and knives, and turn to gangs for protection. Children who are rejected by their peers, are at risk for violent behavior, as are children who are disengaged from caring adults.

The school's function as a socialization agent is affected by the larger macrosystem context—history, politics, economics, religious values, cultural values, and technology. It is also affected by mesosystem linkages to the microsystems of family, peer group, media, and community.

The most powerful socializing influence of the school lies in those who translate program goals into action—the teachers. The teacher plays a major leadership role in helping children learn to deal with positions of authority, to cooperate with others, to cope with problems, and to achieve competence. Types of leaders are classified as authoritarian, democratic, and laissez faire (permissive).

The teacher is responsible for selecting materials relevant to the learner, for managing the group dynamics in the classroom, and for interacting individually with each child. Goal structures (cooperative, individualized, competitive) have different socialization effects.

Effective teachers are warm, enthusiastic, generous with praise, and have high status. These characteristics lead to their becoming role models for children. Other characteristics of successful teachers are the ability to communicate well and responsiveness to students.

Teachers' expectations of children often influence their interactions with them and, consequently, the children's performance. Teachers need to be aware of the effects of the self-fulfilling prophecy. Teachers also need to be aware of their responses to gender—generally teachers give more attention to boys for their work and girls for appropriate behavior—as well as to children from diverse ethnic groups, different social classes, religions and to children with disabilities.

The school's response to ethnic diversity is that it has traditionally served the needs of the majority culture. For a long time the attitude toward the socialization of ethnic minorities was assimilation—teaching them to adapt to the ways of the majority culture. Later, the idea of a cultural blending (the melting pot) became popular. Today, the socialization approach has become associated with the theory of cultural pluralism, that the mainstream of the majority culture should coexist and interact with the various cultural minorities for the benefit of all. Bilingual/multicultural education is an example.

The school's response to religious diversity must be sensitive regarding which religious values intersect with educational goals.

The school's response to children with disabilities is to provide special education and related services as required.

The history of socialization of individuals with disabilities spans banishment and neglect to pity and protection, to segregation and education. Currently, the trend is toward integration or inclusion into the mainstream of society.

The Individuals with Disabilities Education Act guarantees that all children with disabilities will have available to them a free and appropriate education. The act requires nondiscriminatory evaluations to determine whether or not a child is disabled. The act also requires that an Individualized Education Program (IEP) be written for each child, which is developed by the school personnel in conjunction with the parents. Students with disabilities must be placed in the least restrictive environment (LRE), and supplementary aids and services must be provided as necessary. What constitutes "the least restrictive environment" is controversial along with the concept of full inclusion versus partial inclusion.

ACTIVITY

Purpose: To understand the school's influence on socialization.

1. Choose two elementary school classrooms (same grade) to observe. One should be primarily teacher-directed, or traditional; one should be primarily learner-directed, or modern. (You may have to go to two different schools.)

2. Describe the physical arrangement of each classroom environment.

3. Describe the activity going on during the time of your observation in each classroom. How are simultaneous activities (computer work and reading group, for example) handled? What about transitions from one activity to another?

4. Describe the social interaction (for example, warm/hostile, flexible/inflexible, caring/uncaring) between the teacher and children in each classroom. Note teachers' responses to gender and ethnic diversity (and disability, if included).

5. Can you draw any conclusions regarding the socialization of the children in each classroom?

RESOURCES

Association for Childhood Education International
http://www.udel.edu/batemau/acei

Center for the Prevention of School Violence
http://www.ncsu.edu/cpsv/

Educational Resources Information
Center (ERIC)
http://ericeece@uiuc.edu

U.S. Department of Education
http://www.ed.gov

National Education Association
http://nea.org

RELATED READINGS

Dewey, J. (1944). *Democracy and education.* New York: Free Press.

Egan, K. (1997). *The educated mind: How cognitive tools shape our understanding.* Chicago: University of Chicago Press.

Farnham-Diggory, S. (1990). *Schooling.* Cambridge, MA: Harvard University Press.

Gardner, H. (1999). *Intelligence reframed: Multiple intelligences for the 21st century.* New York: Basic Books.

Ginott, H. (1972). *Teacher and child.* New York: Avon Books.

Goodlad, J. I. (1984). *A place called school: Prospects for the future.* New York: McGraw-Hill.

Gordon, T. (1974). *T.E.T.: Teacher effectiveness training.* New York: Wyden.

Hallahan, D., & Kauffman, J. (1997). *Exceptional learners: Introduction to special education* (7th ed.). Boston: Allyn and Bacon.

Healy, J. (1991). *Endangered minds: Why children don't think and what we can do about it.* New York: Touchstone.

Heck, S. F., & Williams, C. R. (1984). *The complex roles of the teacher: An ecological perspective.* New York: Teachers College Press.

Holt, J. (1970). *How children learn.* New York: Dell.

Kidder, T. (1989). *Among schoolchildren.* New York: Avon.

Kozol, J. (1991). *Savage inequalities: Children in America's schools.* New York: Crown.

Papert, S. (1999). *The children's machine: Rethinking school in the age of the computer* (2nd ed.). New York: Basic Books.

Steinberg, L. (1996). *Beyond the classroom: Why school reform has failed and what parents can do.* New York: Touchstone.

"Every American ought to have the right to be treated as he would wish to be treated, as one would wish his children would be treated."

— **John F. Kennedy**

Chapter 7

RISK AND RESILIENCE: IMPACTS OF CHILD/FAMILY/SCHOOL/COMMUNITY LINKAGES

Prologue

FROM OPPRESSION TO OPPORTUNITY

Victor Hugo's classic novel, Les Misérables *(1862), about how oppressive life was for the indigent, tells of Jean Valjean, a man sentenced to prison for stealing bread for his sister's starving family. Because he tries to escape numerous times, his sentence is lengthened to 19 years. When he finally is set free, he becomes a beggar and is befriended by a priest. An embittered man battling for survival, Jean reacts the priest's kindness by stealing his silver. However, when Jean is caught by the police, the priest tells them the silver was a gift. This charitable act changes Jean's entire life.*

During the years that follow, the ex-convict prospers, and even becomes mayor of a town. He attempts to atone for his past by helping the poor.

All the while, he is pursued by the detective, Javert, who maintains society's prevailing view that a condemned person cannot reform. Javert is so zealous that he arrests a man who resembles Jean. Jean, who no longer has self-serving motives, steps forward to prevent an innocent man from going to prison.

A modern tale with a similar theme of transforming oppression into opportunity is the life of "The Golden Boy," Oscar De La Hoya. Oscar grew up in a poor neighborhood in East Los Angeles. As a child he was often frightened by the other kids who were bigger than he. He would run home crying when bullied. His father realized Oscar had a problem because not fighting back when attacked was hardly a Mexican custom. His father, a boxer, obliged Oscar to go to a boxing gym for training when he was 5-years-old. Oscar's father remained a strong influence throughout Oscar's childhood. He was an authoritarian parent, insisting on strict standards of behavior and consequences for disobedience.

Even though young Oscar did not want to become a boxer, the incentive for continuing his training was the trophies he won and the attention he received. Every time he won a fight, his uncles would give him money—a quarter, 50 cents, a dollar.

Not only did Oscar grow up to be a boxing champion, he also has become a champion for less fortunate children in his community, setting an admirable example for others. He is the primary founder of a nonprofit organization dedicated to sponsoring Olympic hopefuls and to providing educational scholarships. According to the brochure, his youth center provides "a safe, sound, and positive training environment emphasizing self-esteem and success through dedicated hard work, good citizenship, achieving passing school grades, and abstinence from drugs and alcohol." Oscar is proud of his Latino heritage; he initiates all his press conferences in Spanish.

Jean Valjean from the past and Oscar De La Hoya from the present are examples of resiliency despite growing up in "at-risk" environments. ■

- *What made Jean Valjean and Oscar De La Hoya resistant to a life of crime?*
- *Do you agree that, once condemned, always condemned?*
- *How can adversity breed responsibility?*

This chapter examines linkages between the child and the microsystems of family and school, and community as well as to the macrosystem of society, to better understand how "risk" can be turned into "resilience." *Risk* refers to endangerment. Children at risk are vulnerable to negative developmental outcomes, such as dropping out of school, substance abuse, violence, teenage pregnancy, unemployment, and suicide. What are some risk factors affecting infants and children? They can be classified as *genetic* (such as mental retardation), *prenatal* (such as drug exposure), *perinatal* (such as health care), and *environmental* (such as poverty) (Rickel & Becker, 1997).

    Resilience refers to the ability to recover from, or adjust easily to, misfortune or change. Studies of psychological resiliency have revealed factors that enable children to

Figure 7.1   An Ecological Model of Human Development

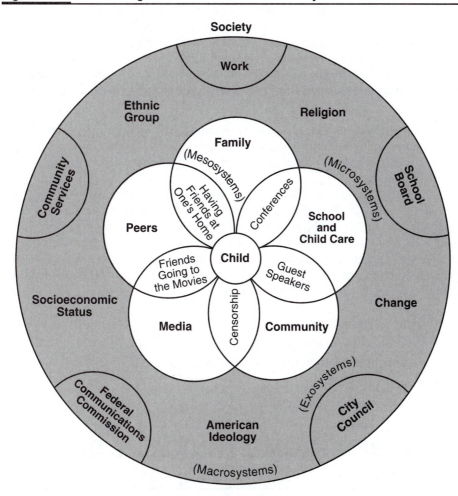

All children are affected by how exosystems and macrosystems provide support for their diverse socialization needs.

thrive despite difficult or traumatic environments (Garbarino, 1995b; Rikel & Becker, 1997). For example, psychologist Emmy Werner began studying infants at risk in Hawaii over 40 years ago (Werner, 1993). The children came from families who were chronically poor, alcoholic, and abusive. Expecting negative developmental outcomes for the children, she was surprised to find that approximately one-third of those she followed grew into emotionally healthy, competent adults. They had close friends, supportive marriages, attained a high level of education, and mastered vocational skills.

What enabled these children to become resilient to a traumatic childhood? The resilient children had a sense of autonomy and personal responsibility; they related to others positively; perhaps most significantly, they had established a bond with an adult caregiver or mentor. Apparently, the "substitute" parent and positive relationships and experiences act as buffers against negative developmental outcomes.

> . . . these buffers make a more profound impact on the life course of children who grow up under adverse conditions than do specific risk factors or stressful life events. They appear to transcend ethnic, social class, geographical, and historical boundaries. Most of all, they offer us a more optimistic outlook than the perspective that can be gleaned from the literature on the negative consequences of perinatal trauma, caregiving deficits, and chronic poverty. They provide us with a corrective lens — an awareness of self-righting tendencies that move children toward normal adult development under all but the most persistent adverse circumstances (Werner & Smith, 1992).

The implications of such research are profound. The findings mean that parents, schools, community services, and others can help children develop into healthy, contributing adults by working together to build a socially nourishing environment (Garbarino, 1995b).

Groups who have traditionally been oppressed—children of diverse ethnicity, children who have disabilities, and children from families with identified risk factors (for example, poverty, substance abuse, domestic abuse, maltreatment)—will be examined to understand how the school can provide optimal socialization experiences and resiliency for children. Most important, that the school must work with families, as well as children, has been documented by much research (Connors & Epstein, 1995). Specifically, when families get involved in school, their children:

- get better grades and test scores;
- graduate from high school at higher rates;
- are more likely to go on to higher education;
- behave more positively; and
- are more achievement-oriented.

CHILDREN FROM ETHNICALLY DIVERSE FAMILIES

The Great Seal of the United States used on many official documents and coins contains the motto "E pluribus unum" (one out of many). This statement symbolizes that national strength and unity comes from diversity of individuals.

The United States is composed of many diverse ethnic groups. According to the U.S. Bureau of the Census (1998), 11% of the population identified themselves as Hispanic in origin, 4% as Asian–Pacific Islanders, 13% as African Americans, and 1% as Native Americans. About 73% of Americans classify themselves as non-Hispanic White, and approximately 9.3% of the population reported being foreign-born.

Americans speak many languages. More than 32 million speak a language other than English at home; 17 million speak Spanish; 2 million speak French; and more than 1 million speak German, Chinese, or Italian (U.S. Bureau of the Census, 1998). If the population growth to the year 2050, based on life expectancies, fertility rates, and immigration, is projected, it can be concluded that the gap between majority and minority ethnic groups is narrowing. This fact, plus the movement toward a global economy (discussed in Chapter 1), points to the importance of understanding ethnic diversity.

> As the preschool teacher was helping the children settle down on their mats for naptime, she noticed red marks on Jenny Truong's neck and forehead. She asked Jenny how she got them and Jenny replied that her father put them there. The teacher, suspecting child abuse, reported it to the police.

People from various Asian countries believe that internal winds cause illness. However, by bringing the wind to the surface, the illness can leave and that person will be

Some children are socialized to lower their eyes to indicate shame.

healed. The way this is done is by "scratching the wind away," or "coining." A coin dipped in oil or menthol is vigorously rubbed against the head, neck, chest, back, or wherever the symptoms are exhibited. The skin is rubbed until it turns red (Dresser, 1996).

> One day a fifth-grade teacher noticed that Juanita, normally a tidy youngster, had a brown smear of dirt on one arm. That day and the next, the teacher said nothing. However, when Juanita came to class with the mark on her arm the third day, the teacher told her to go wash her dirty arm. When Juanita said it was not dirty, the teacher told her not to argue and to do as she was told. Juanita complied.
>
> Several days later, Juanita was taken out of school by her parents to attend the funeral of her sister. Two weeks had passed and Juanita had still not returned to school, so the principal went to her home to find out why. Juanita's mother told the principal that when someone is ill, each family member places a spot of oil and soil somewhere on the body. "We are one with nature. When someone is ill, that person is out of balance with nature. We use the oil and soil of our Mother, the earth, to show her we wish our sick one to be back in balance with nature." When Juanita's teacher made her wash her arm, our oneness with nature was broken. That is why her sister died. The teacher caused her death; Juanita can never return to her class" (Garcia, 1998).

Respect for cultural and ethnic differences requires teachers to be sensitive to a variety of customs. Asking appropriate questions and listening carefully can help avoid misunderstandings.

The National Association for the Education of Young Children (NAEYC, 1996a, p. 5) has taken the following position:

> For optimal developmental and learning of all children, educators must *accept* the legitimacy of children's home language, *respect* (hold in high regard) and *value* (esteem, appreciate) the home culture and promote and encourage the active involvement and support of all families, including extended and nontraditional family units.

Teacher sensitivity can be used to enable children to be tolerant and respectful of differences. When a kindergarten boy from India was called "garbage head" by his classmates because his hair smelled of coconut oil, the teacher planned a series of activities in which she and the children compared coconut oil to a variety of shampoos, conditioners, mousses, and gels. After much discussion about all the different things people put on their hair, the children came to realize that everyone's hair has a particular smell and coconut was simply one of a vast array (Ramsey, 1998).

Understanding diversity in microcultures or minorities involves examining the macroculture or majority. Historically, political and social institutions in the United States developed from a Western European tradition. The English language and American legal system were derived from English common law. The American political system of democratic elections comes from France and England (Gollnick & Chinn, 1998). Thus, American formal institutions, such as government, schools, business, health and welfare agencies, show White, Anglo Saxon, Protestant influences, often referred to as the Protestant Ethic.

Despite the fact that the macroculture is composed of people who are not White, Anglo Saxon, or Protestant, there are certain basic values that are shared to some degree by all members of the macroculture. Generally, the American macroculture is characterized by the following (Arensberg & Niehoff, 1975; Stewart & Bennett, 1991; Williams, 1960b):

- Emphasis on active mastery rather than passive acceptance—individuals are responsible for what happens to them.
- Valuation of the work ethic—industriousness, ambition, competitiveness, individualism, independence. Status is based on occupation, education, and financial worth.
- Stress on assertiveness and achievement—achievement is valued above inheritance.
- Valuation of fairness—equal opportunities in social, political, and economic institutions.
- More interest in the external world of things and events rather than the internal world of meaning and feeling—achievement and success are measured by the quality of material goods purchased.
- Emphasis on change, flow, movement—new and modern are better than old and traditional; emphasis is on future rather than past or present.
- Belief in rationalism, rather than traditionalism—not accepting things just because they have been done before; there has to be a logical reason for doing something.
- Emphasis on peer relationships rather than superordinate–subordinate; advocates equality, or horizontal relationships, rather than hierarchy, or vertical relationships.
- Focus on individual personality (individualism, independence) rather than group identity and responsibility (collectivism, interdependence)—idealizes an adaptive and outgoing personality rather than a conventional, introverted one.
- Relationships to others (impersonal or objective); communication is direct or confrontational.
- Personal life and community affairs are based on principles of right and wrong rather than on shame, dishonor, or ridicule.

How are these values exemplified in young children's behavior? "Most children in the United States learn that nature is something you conquer and exploit. In the sandbox they often 'build roads' or 'dig to the other side of the world'" (Ramsey, 1998, p. 61). Children are also encouraged to be actively engaged in activity rather than be "bored" as verified by the quantity of toys parents bring on long car rides.

The degree to which individual U.S. citizens subscribe to the general value of the macroculture depends, in part, on the microculture, or ethnic group to which the individual belongs. The degree may also depend on how much an individual must interact with the formal societal institutions for support (Gollnick & Chinn, 1998). For example, if one receives a government loan to further his or her education, one has to prove attendance at a college or university and comply with regulations for repayment.

Until recently, most of the research on child development has been carried out in the context of the dominant macroculture. Consequently, the development of Anglo-American, middle-class children has come to be considered the norm for all children regardless of the ethnic, cultural, or economic context they inhabit. Thus, to get a broad perspective of child development and to foster understanding of diverse ethnic children, the socialization backgrounds and consequent learning styles of African

Americans, Hispanic Americans, Native Americans, and Asian Americans will be examined, recognizing that there are many other diverse, but less populous groups. The concept of learning style offers a value-neutral approach to understanding individual differences among ethnically diverse students. Learning styles are discussed as extremes, but are really the ends of a continuum, with variations in between (Bennett, 1998). The following discussion comprises *generalizations* from research. These generalizations are common, but do not necessarily apply to all children of a *particular* ethnic group (the groups are classified to resemble those of the U.S Bureau of the Census).

SOCIALIZATION OF AFRICAN AMERICAN CHILDREN

African Americans identify themselves as a single ethnic group because they share a common history, language, and culture. African Americans generally exhibit the following tendencies related to learning style (Bennett, 1998; Hilliard, 1992):

- Viewing things in their entirety and not in isolated parts. (Euro-Americans tend to believe that anything can be divided into pieces and those pieces add up to the whole.)
- Approximating space, number, and time instead of being exact. (Euro-Americans tend to value preciseness.)
- Appearing to focus on people and their activities rather than on objects.
- Preferring inferential reasoning to deductive or inductive reasoning.
- Proficiency in nonverbal communication. (Euro-Americans tend to be "word-dependent" for communication.)

These characteristics, known as a *relational cognitive style,* are significant because school, which is part of the macroculture, usually requires an analytical, rather than relational, approach to learning. An *analytical cognitive style* involves breaking down the whole into parts and studying each part, whereas a *relational* one involves how the parts connect or fit together to form a whole. Children who function with a different way of thinking, or cognitive style, and who have not developed analytical skills to process information will be poor achievers early in school and will do worse as they move to higher grade levels (Hale-Benson, 1986).

A *relational cognitive style* is associated with learning by observation, modeling, and apprenticeship rather than learning through verbal instruction, the teaching method most commonly used in American schools. To illustrate, Joan tells how she learned to prepare salmon as a child. After watching her mother, she was allowed to gradually take on portions of the task and to ask questions only if they were important. Once she told her mother that she didn't understand how to do "the backbone part." So her mother took an entire fish and repeated the deboning because, according to her, it is not possible to understand "the backbone part" except in the context of the whole fish.

Researchers (Hilliard, 1992; Ramirez & Castaneda, 1974; Tharp, 1989) suggest that children develop learning or cognitive styles based on the socialization they receive in their families and peer groups—although there are still many unanswered questions about cognitive styles. Children who live in families that are structured so that the members have defined roles, have specific times set aside for doing certain activities such as eating and sleeping, and who have experiences with formal styles of group organization (relating to a leader, following goals, receiving feedback) have been observed to have an *analytical cognitive style*. On the other hand, children who live in families that are less structured in that the roles are shared, individuals eat when hungry, and sleep when tired, are more likely to exhibit a *relational cognitive style*.

Other socialization outcomes, according to some studies (Bennett, 1998; Hale-Benson, 1986), are that many African American children tend to be more oriented toward feelings and personal interaction and are more proficient at nonverbal communication than are Anglo children. For example, Anglo children who are oriented toward objects have numerous opportunities to manipulate objects and discover properties and relationships. These experiences with objects are preparatory toward school, which is also object-oriented, using books, computers, learning centers, and so on. Many African American children, on the other hand, get a lot of experience interacting with people (Hale-Benson, 1986). Communication in these interactions may differ from that of Anglo children; talking may jump from topic to topic rather than following a linear sequence from the beginning of the story to the end (Ramsey, 1998).

The high degree of person orientation found in many African American children may account for their seeming indifference to books and other school materials and may explain why teachers report that many African American children have trouble working independently. Thus traditional education settings might consider a more flexible and personal approach to children who have such a person orientation (Bennett, 1998).

Creating a Supportive Learning Environment for African American Children

1. Provide an environment in which children can work together cooperatively on projects.
2. Provide activities that permit experimentation and improvisation.
3. Classroom books and materials should have African American role models. African American folktales and proverbs should be part of the curriculum.
4. When the child communicates, focus on his or her correct understanding rather than on inaccurate pronunciation.
5. Relate learning activities to real and immediate needs as well as provide opportunities for involvement. For example, learning about nutrition can be accompanied by a cooking activity; learning math concepts can be done by setting up a pretend store with fake money; reading can be related to street signs and finding one's way to school, home, or a park (Hilliard, 1992).

SOCIALIZATION OF HISPANIC AMERICAN CHILDREN

Hispanic Americans represent a diverse historical, genetic, and cultural group. The three largest Hispanic groups are Mexican Americans, Puerto Ricans, and Cubans. Others included in this group by the U.S. Bureau of the Census have origins from Spanish-speaking countries of the Caribbean, Central or South America, and Spain. Each group, while sharing a common Spanish culture, differs in experience. The Mexican American

These children are enjoying learning by working cooperatively on an activity that permits experimentation and improvisation.

experience primarily is from the southwestern United States and Mexico, the Puerto Rican experience is generally northeastern and urban, and the Cuban experience is largely from the southeastern United States (Melendez, Cole-Melendez, & Molina, 1989). According to Ramirez and Castaneda (1974), the Spanish and Indian heritage of Mexican Americans may range from zero to 100%. The Spaniards who came to Mexico varied in cultural origin. They included individuals of Iberian, Greek, Latin, Visigoth, Moroccan, Phoenician, Carthaginian, and other backgrounds. Some of those with a Spanish heritage prefer to be called *Latinos*. However, most government documents use the Hispanic reference. (If in doubt, ask the person how he or she wishes to be called.) In spite of this diversity, there is a commonality in basic values and consequent learning styles among most Hispanic Americans that is imparted to children. These values can be classified as follows (Bennett, 1998): identification with family, community, and ethnic group; personalization of interpersonal relationships; status and role definition in family and community; and a field-dependent cognitive style.

Identification with Family, Community, and Ethnic Group

Hispanic Americans traditionally have a strong sense of loyalty to their family, community, and ethnic group. Their orientation is collective and interdependent. The group (family, community, or other Hispanic Americans) takes precedence over the individual. Children are encouraged very early on to achieve for their families. This contrasts with the macroculture's definition of achievement, which entails accomplishment for the benefit of the individual (Garcia, 1992).

Even though the school may be recognized as important, when a family member needs help, one drops everything to assist, regardless of obligation outside the family whether at work or school (Dresser, 1996). Thus a child may be absent if a relative is ill, or if a younger sibling needs care while the mother goes to the doctor.

Identification with community includes the church, generally Catholic. Catholicism emphasizes respect for convention and significant adults such as parents and teachers. Disrespect is considered sinful.

Identification with ethnic group is exhibited by Hispanic Americans as pride in their heritage, culture, and language.

Teachers need to involve parents in their child's education to extend the socialized value of interdependence. Teachers also need to provide cooperative activities to extend the socialized value of collectivism. Teachers should not "Anglocize" children's names (call "Roberto," "Robert").

Personalization of Interpersonal Relationships

An emphasis on interpersonal relationships and a commitment to help others is part of the Hispanic American value system. Also, interpersonal relationships are personal and humanistic in that there is great sensitivity to the needs and feelings of others. This sensitivity relates to both verbal and nonverbal communication. It permits the individual to read and understand another person's feelings without forcing that person to be embarrassed by pleading for help. This probably explains why Hispanic American children, especially males, seldom ask for help with their schoolwork, even though they may be doing poorly. It also explains why Hispanic American children who have been sexually abused have even more difficulty than do Anglo children in telling their parents or other adults. Hispanic American children are accustomed to expressing needs in an indirect, nonverbal way that is often unfamiliar to many teachers, whereas in their own communities such indirect expressions always meet with a response.

Relationships between teachers and learners in traditional Hispanic American communities are very close and personalized. Thus the relationship between teacher and child is the most important aspect of the teaching process. The objectivity and impartiality of many teachers are often interpreted as rejection. Therefore, teachers should be close to the child and use direct social rewards, such as "You did that very well."

Status and Role Definition in Family and Community

Hispanic American children are expected to respect the status and feelings of others and to demonstrate acceptable social behavior by assuming the responsibilities of their assigned roles. Parents place as much emphasis on social roles and behavior as they do on academic education. They are often confused when school personnel do not seem to understand that a child's duties at home, such as having to stay home to care for younger family members, are just as important as the child's education at school. Parents may also be concerned when teachers do not emphasize classroom control or do not demand respect from their students. The ideal teacher in the Hispanic American community is nurturant, firm, and shows concern for the well-being of the child. The teaching technique used most often in the Hispanic American community is modeling—do it the way the teacher does it.

Gender roles are clearly defined in Hispanic American traditional communities. Men are considered to have more status in business and politics; women have more status in religion, child rearing, and health care. Teachers should be cautious about forcing Hispanic American children from traditional families to do tasks or take on roles that contradict their gender roles.

Field-Dependent Cognitive Style

Research suggests that Hispanic Americans tend to prefer holistic, concrete, social approaches to learning (Bennett, 1998; Ramirez & Castaneda, 1974). This style of learning is referred to as *field-dependent* and usually implies the person works well in groups and perceives things in terms of the whole context. A *field-independent* learning style, on the other hand, describes an analytic and logical approach to tasks and usually implies that the person relates well to impersonal, abstract information, independent of the context.

The reason Hispanic American children tend to be more *field-dependent* than Anglo American children is that they tend to be socialized to be open, warm, committed to mutual dependence, cooperative, sensitive to the feelings of others, and respectful of adults and social convention (Escobedo & Huggans, 1983; Greenfield & Suzuki, 1998; Ramirez & Castaneda, 1974).

Creating a Supportive Learning Environment for Hispanic American Children

1. Indicate acceptance verbally ("That dress is such a pretty color." "I like the way you helped Roberto fold his paper.") or nonverbally (smiling, patting, hugging).

2. Personalize the classroom and curriculum whenever possible. Ask questions such as "What did your family do in the storm?" or "How did you celebrate your birthday?" Display children's stories and creative work.

3. Involve the students' families whenever possible—verbal and written communications, invitations to the classroom to observe or share a skill.

4. Recognize and affirm the language and the culture of the students—holiday celebrations, language instruction, culture and history lessons. Have appropriate books and posters in the classroom.

5. Employ group activities involving cooperative learning. Individuals often get to know each other best when working together in a group toward goals (Vasquez, 1990).

SOCIALIZATION OF NATIVE AMERICAN CHILDREN

There are over 500 native groups in the United States. The U.S. Bureau of the Census groups together American Indians, Eskimos, and Aleuts. Native Americans are diverse in language, tribal customs, religious beliefs, and ways of earning a living. However, they share many values and have a unified world view.

During their many centuries in North America, the Indians developed tribal societies and traditional ways of life. Education in the tribal society, which taught the values of cooperation and collective organization, prepared children for a meaningful, competent life (Robbins, 1974; Weinberg, 1977).

Children were socialized via an extensive kin network. Religion played an extremely important role. For example, if children misbehaved, they were told that the evil spirits would punish them. Tradition and rituals also had a large part in the socialization process. For example, praising learning accomplishments in public ceremonies was a tribal strategy to stimulate learning. Socialization was also accomplished by imitating adults in the realm of play.

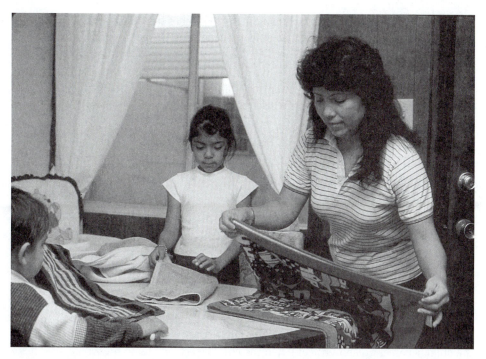

These children are learning by observing and modeling their mother and by working cooperatively on a task.

Names given to children signified personal identity. The name could change as the child showed significant achievements. For example, if a boy successfully hunted a deer, "deer hunter" would be added to his name.

Oral literature was the means by which tribal history and culture were passed on. The elder members of the tribe told stories of the past. Sometimes this would be part of the rites of passage, preparation for the formal ceremony when a child would become an adult.

The following are some general cultural characteristics of traditional Native Americans (Bennett, 1998; Soldier, 1985):

- Orientation toward the extended family. The child is considered an important member of the family group; the family provides a psychological support system throughout the individual's life. Cousins are considered as close as brothers. Emphasis is placed on cooperation, helping those in need, and respect for elders. Family and tribal matters may take precedence over school attendance.

- Fostering of sharing and group ownership. This means that to a Native American child who has not been socialized to understand individual ownership ("These are *your* crayons"), *your* may mean belonging to the group. Thus, if Lee cannot find his pencil, he borrows Steve's without asking because whatever belongs to the group the Native American child regards as his or hers, too.

- Teaching children not to "show up" (demonstrate individual superiority over inferiority) their peers. Thus they may not exhibit competitive behaviors in classroom settings such as responding to "Who has the best work?" However, when performance is socially defined as benefiting the peer society, Native American children compete well ("Which group has read the most books?")

- Learning by observation and being patient. At home, many Native American children are not rewarded for curiosity and for asking questions; parents may even use legends and fables to discourage curiosity.

- Teaching children to drop their heads as a sign of respect and compliance rather than look directly at the adult, as is expected in the macroculture.

- Status in Native American cultures is based more on who you are (family name) than what you have.

- Time orientation is generally more present-oriented than future-oriented. Time is viewed as a continuum, with no beginning and no end. Ceremonies, for example, begin when the participants are ready, rather then punctually at the scheduled time.

Studies on the learning styles of Native American children have established the importance of visualization in learning (Bennett, 1998). These children generally learn through careful observation, noticing, for example, the behavior and expressions of adults, the changing weather conditions, the terrain, and so on. After observing an adult do a task, the child takes over small portions of the task under the guidance of the adult; the child becomes an apprentice. When the child feels ready to do the whole task, he or she practices it in private. Thus failures are not seen and don't cause embarrassment, but success is demonstrated for the adult with pride (Vasquez, 1990).

This Native American child is learning the task of weaving by intently watching her grandmother and occasionally assisting her, exemplifying apprenticeship.

Creating a Supportive Learning Environment for Native American Children

1. It is a tradition not to ask a person's name directly; learn it from a friend.

2. Inquire before bringing any animals into the classroom. Some animals are not to be touched or looked upon for various reasons. Some individuals believe in reincarnation, and all forms of life are to be treated with respect.

3. Death is not a subject to be discussed in the classroom.

4. Do not plant seeds in the classroom for a science project; most Native Americans believe that the earth provides enough room for growing things.

5. When preparing food in the classroom, find out the way to prepare and serve to which the Indian children are accustomed.

6. During certain seasons certain games are not to be played. Find out the taboos before introducing games and activities.

7. Family ties are very strong, and children call their cousins "brothers" and "sisters." Respect this custom.

8. Invite community members to the classroom to share skills.

9. Use small groups, where children can help each other. Avoid individual competition.

10. Stress short-term, present-oriented goals. Present required tasks as a whole before breaking them into parts. Let children practice tasks on their own until they feel ready to show them to the teacher (Bennett, 1998; Soldier, 1985).

In general, Native American children also prefer holistic over analytic learning. In community storytelling, for example, Navajo children are not asked to recite details of a story or to dissect it; instead, they are expected to listen quietly to the long telling of stories (Tharp, 1989). Thus teachers of Native American children who frequently interrupt narrative events with questions produce sharp cultural discongruity (Phillips, 1983).

Children who are taught to quietly respect adults and not be too quick to show mastery at a task, may be viewed as withdrawn compared to their outspoken, attention-seeking American peers. They may also be judged as unmotivated (Ramsey, 1998).

SOCIALIZATION OF ASIAN AMERICAN CHILDREN

Asian Americans include individuals of Chinese, Filipino, Japanese, Asian Indian, Korean, Vietnamese, Hawaiian, Samoan, Guamanian, and Asian Pacific Island ancestry. While there are many differences among these ethnic groups, there are also some similarities in traditions. These are as follows (California Department of Education, 1986, 1987, 1989, 1992, 1994; Saracho & Spodek, 1983):

- Emphasis on tradition, conformity, respect for authority, and submergence of individuality. This is exhibited in respect for age, avoidance of calling attention to oneself, avoidance of confrontation, and concerns with etiquette or good form.

- Emphasis on loyalty to the family, control of behavior through guilt and shame, formality in interpersonal relationships, and restraint in displaying affection and emotion. This is exhibited in the way others are addressed and in the way offending or embarrassing others is avoided. Also, there is a reluctance to talk about personal things and unpleasant topics.

- Respect for education, expectation for a formal student–teacher relationship, achievement-consciousness.

- Motivation for shared or collective achievement, rather than individual. This is exhibited by achieving for the honor of the family.

Compared to the research on learning styles of other American ethnic groups, there is a scarcity of information on Asian American learners. Children who come from a country where many do not get a formal education (for example, the Hmong) have different ways of approaching cognitive tasks required in school than those children coming from countries where formal education is necessary for success (Bennett, 1998; Thuy, 1983). Japanese Americans, for example, have the highest literacy rate of any ethnic group in the United States, tend to do well financially, and have been assimilated into the macroculture (Bennett, 1998). Similarities between the Buddhist–Confucian ethic of hard work and that of the Protestant Ethic may be part of the explanation.

This parent supervises his child's homework, emphasizing the importance of effort and hard work.

According to studies (Stevenson & Lee, 1990; Stevenson, Siglor, Lee, Kitamura, Kimura, & Kato, 1986), Japanese students consistently are top performers on achievement tests in both math and science. One possible influence is the time spent on homework. Japanese children are expected to practice all their lessons at home, and the mother is present to supervise and help. Another possible influence is the emphasis Japanese parents place on effort and hard work.

Japanese and American families provide different socialization experiences to prepare children for work in the classroom (Hess, 1986). For example, Japanese mothers interact with their children in a way such as to promote internalization of adult norms and standards, whereas American mothers rely more on external authority and direction. Japanese mothers demonstrate how to perform a task correctly, expecting the child to eventually master it internally; guidance is gentle and supportive. American mothers rely more on verbal instructions, external rewards, and punishment.

While some Asian children do very well on tests on homework assignments, they may not participate in class discussions, not sharing ideas, and may be reluctant to work with other students on group projects. This is because such children have been socialized to view the teacher as the complete source of knowledge. The student's job is to listen, take notes, memorize, follow directions, and recite. Students' ideas are not requested nor are they valued. Such students are taught not to ask questions, argue, or challenge the teacher (Dresser, 1996).

Creating a Supportive Learning Environment for Asian American Children

1. Appeal to family honor to praise a child ("Your parents will be very proud" instead of "You did the best job").

2. Have a wide variety of instructional techniques to accommodate differing learning styles. For example, allow extra time for reflective thinkers to respond to questions. (This, of course, applies to all children.)

3. Introduce group problem-solving to encourage flexibility and fluency in thinking. Children might also be asked to examine interesting pictures or objects to stimulate creative writing. Acceptance of all ideas and reward for productivity versus accuracy can also enhance creative thinking.

4. Be aware of cultural superstitions. For example, the number four in Japanese, called *shi,* also means death. Chinese prefer even numbers to odd numbers. Filipinos avoid having their picture taken in a group of three because they believe that to do so would result in one of the trio dying or being involved in a serious accident.

5. Be aware of cultural symbolism. For example, the color white signifies death to the Chinese, whereas it signifies purity and cleanliness to Koreans. Black is an expression of mourning to most Asians. Having one's name written in red is offensive and may be interpreted as a sign of death (California State Department of Education, 1986, 1987, 1989, 1992, 1994; Dresser, 1996; Saracho & Spodek, 1983).

CHILDREN WITH DISABILITIES

Children with disabilities are at risk for negative developmental outcomes unless they receive support. As was discussed in Chapter 6, laws have enabled individuals with disabilities to be included in the mainstream of society. Access to equal educational opportunities has become very significant in the socialization of children with disabilities to enable them to become optimally functioning adults and resilient to risk of negative developmental outcomes.

Not only have laws been passed to give individuals with disabilities certain equal access rights, but educators have modified the teaching environment to include the following (Hallahan & Kauffman, 1998):

1. *Individualized instruction,* whereby the child's abilities rather than prescribed academic content provide the basis for teaching techniques.
2. *Adaptation of the curriculum to various learning styles,* whereby visual, auditory, and tactile learners are motivated to succeed.
3. *Collaboration with various professionals,* whereby services such as medical, physical therapy, speech therapy, and counseling are provided.
4. *Peer tutoring,* whereby children with greater abilities help those who are in need.

Some examples of how the educational environment and teaching strategies can be modified to include children with disabilities can be found in the appendix.

A child with disabilities enjoys an outing in the park with her brother and dog.

SOCIETY, EDUCATION, AND CHILDREN WITH DISABILITIES

The Individuals with Disabilities Education Act (IDEA), discussed in Chapter 6, requires that children with disabilities be placed in the "least restrictive environment." This means inclusion with nondisabled peers wherever possible.

In order to determine and maintain optimal placement, IDEA requires that an individualized education program (IEP) be written annually and reviewed by the (1) child, (2) parent, (3) teacher, (4) professional who has most recently evaluated the child, and (5) principal or school district special resource person. The IEP must specify educational goals, methods for achieving those goals, and the special educational/resource services to be provided to meet the child's needs.

Since the IEP is a vehicle that enables children with disabilities to interact with peers who do not have disabilities, teachers must provide appropriate interactive activities. An example of an appropriate interactive activity is cooperative learning. *Cooperative learning* as an educational goal structure was discussed in Chapter 6. It involves a set of strategies that organizes students into small groups of five or six and gives them a task to solve cooperatively. Students are enabled to learn problem-solving techniques and how to constructively work with others. The child with disabilities can be part of the group, making a contribution according to ability (Kirk, Gallagher, & Anastasiow, 1997). Cooperative learning structures also provide opportunities for reinforcement and tutoring.

Reinforcement increases the chance of a behavior being repeated. Thus children without disabilities can reinforce certain behaviors in children with disabilities (for example, sharing), and children with disabilities can do likewise (for example, helping).

While helping children to learn, *tutoring, or direct instruction,* also provides an opportunity for close social interaction. The learner gets instruction, and the tutor gains sensitivity to others, communication skills, and an opportunity to nurture. While the learner gains individual attention and an opportunity for cognitive growth, the tutor gains self-confidence and esteem.

SCHOOL LINKAGES: IDENTIFICATION AND ASSESSMENT

In 1986, Congress passed PL 99-457, which addressed the needs of infants, toddlers, and preschoolers with disabilities. It also recognized that families play a large role in the socialization of children with disabilities. Consequently, PL 99-457 provides that, whenever appropriate, the preschooler's IEP will include instruction for parents; it then becomes an Individualized Family Service Plan (IFSP). A variety of programs are available to meet the needs of preschool children with disabilities. These can be home-based or center-based and can be full- or part-time.

An Early Intervention Program was authorized by PL 99-457 to establish a state grant program for infants and toddlers with disabilities from birth to age 2 who are at risk for special needs. In this context, *at risk* refers to children who are not currently identified as impaired or disabled, but who are considered to have a greater than usual chance of developing a disability due to conditions surrounding their birth or home environment (Heward & Orlansky, 1988, p. 4). At-risk conditions include the following:

- *Established risk*—identified by an early medical diagnosis (cerebral palsy, spina bifida, Down's syndrome) or a later one through manifestation of developmental delays or deviations (language delay, physical or mental retardation, delay in psychosocial development or self-help skills).

- *Biological risk*—children with a history of prenatal, perinatal, or postnatal events that increase the probability of later developmental problems (premature birth, genetic predispositions, serious illness).

- *Environmental risk*—children whose early life experiences (maternal and family care, health care, nutrition, opportunities for expression of adaptive behaviors, and patterns of physical and social stimulation) are so limiting that they impart a high probability for delayed development.

PL 99-457 is supported by evidence that shows providing early educational and therapeutic programs for children with disabilities and their families reduces the number of children who will need intensive or long-term help (Lerner, Mardell-Czudnowski, & Goldberg, 1987). Therefore, it is crucial to diagnose and assess a child who has special socialization needs as soon as possible.

For children with certain kinds of disabling conditions, identification can occur at birth—for example, Down's syndrome and various physical deformities. Behaviors not usually exhibited by normal infants can be identified shortly after birth—for example, extreme lethargy, continual crying, convulsions, and paralysis. There are, however, many disabling conditions that are not readily apparent and may not be suspected until later—for example, learning disabilities.

Since more and more children are attending various types of preschool programs, teachers and others who work on a daily basis in such programs are in a unique position to assess young children. By observing and recording specific child behaviors that occur excessively, or that occur instead of appropriate behavior, the teacher can identify children who may have potential disabilities.

Teachers and parents can observe behavior through a variety of techniques: anecdotal records, checklists and rating scales, time samples, and measurements of behavior. *Anecdotal records* report a child's adaptive behavior in various situations. *Checklists and rating scales* are used to compare a child's development against the norms or averages. *Time samples* record everything a child does for a certain period of time each day (for example, from nine to ten o'clock for five consecutive days). *Measurements of behavior* record the frequency of a behavior, the duration of the behavior, the antecedents of the behavior, and the consequences of the behavior.

The teacher observation form (an assessment of general development for preschool children—*see* Appendix) provides a model that may be used to indicate the necessity for referral to other professionals—a pediatrician for health problems; an otologist for auditory problems; an ophthalmologist for visual problems; a neurologist for neurological problems; an orthopedist for bone, joint, or muscle problems; a psychologist or psychiatrist for emotional problems; and so on.

There are many other assessment devices available, in addition to the teacher observation example provided in the appendix. Some general ones are designed for a particular population and some assess specific areas of development. For example, a *medical assessment* consists of a medical history and a physical examination. The medical history in-

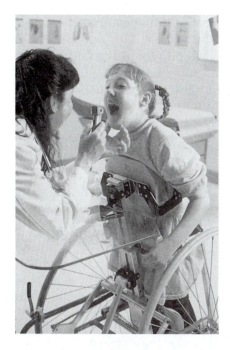

Appropriate assessment is important in order to get supportive services as early as possible.

cludes specific information about the prenatal as well as the postnatal development of the child. Unusual aspects of the family's history are noted. Complications during pregnancy and birth, illnesses in the early years, and developmental milestones (such as the age the child walked or talked) are also included in the assessment. The physical examination assesses developmental normalities and abnormalities.

A *psychological assessment* includes a psychological evaluation and a measurement of intelligence. The evaluation assesses perceptual, motor, language, social, and emotional development. The intelligence test used depends on the child's age. For an infant, the tests usually measure sensorimotor development; however, the accuracy of predicted intelligence from such tests is debatable. After age 2, intellectual development can be assessed more accurately.

Assessment, of course, is meaningless unless adequate follow-up and services are provided for children who need them. Services may involve corrective or supportive medical services and/or special educational programs. Corrective or supportive medical services may involve prosthetic devices and/or medication, plus physical and/or psychological therapy. Special educational programs can involve services at home (a professional works with the parent and child; the parent carries on the program between visits by the professional); services in a center (the child attends a center for several hours a day for education and therapy); or supportive services enabling the child to be mainstreamed (transportation, tutoring, interpreting, and so forth).

Services may also involve social work or counseling. For example, certain prescribed medical treatment that is to be carried out at home may necessitate training the parent (dialysis, diet therapy, physical therapy, for example). Social or counseling services may include advocacy for the child—informing the family of the services to which the child is legally entitled. Thus the professional serves as an educator, a supporter, and a resource.

Assessment must be an ongoing process; hence, the IEP or IFSP, previously discussed, is used. When children are continually assessed, their performance can then indicate the need to modify the special program.

Any program designed to meet the special needs of children with disabilities must involve the family, for several reasons (Gargiulo & Graves, 1991; Heward, 1996):

- Since parents of a child with disabilities will often be responsible for implementing the educational program at home, they need additional training.

- Parents can contribute much valuable information to the program staff regarding the behavior and performance of their child.

- In order for professionals to work with parents for the optimal development of the child, the particular dynamics of the family with a child with disabilities must be understood—the feelings (hopes, disappointments, frustrations, joys) and interactions.

Recognizing that parents are family members with myriad responsibilities and individual needs and preferences has a profound influence on parent–professional relationships in special education settings. The same concept of individuation embraced by the field of special education as pertinent to children and youth also applies to parents and other family members.

COMMUNITY LINKAGES: INCLUSION

The community, via legislation, has facilitated integration of individuals with disabilities into society. Not only do those with disabilities have a right to receive an appropriate ed-

---

Strategies for Professionals to Involve Families

1. Recognize and show that parents are significant contributors to their child's development. Call on parents for advice, help, support, and critical evaluations.

2. Present a realistic picture of what the child's program is designed to accomplish.

3. Keep an ongoing communication with parents. Provide written information regarding due process procedures, parent organizations, and other relevant matters as well as oral and written information about the child's progress.

4. Show parents you care about their child. Call, write notes, spend time listening to parents' concerns.

5. Keep parents informed as to how they can help their child at home. Enable parents to enjoy their children.

6. Use parents' ideas, materials, and activities to work with the child.

7. Know community services and resources so you can refer parents when necessary.

8. Be yourself. Don't appear to know all the answers when you don't; don't be afraid to ask for advice or refer parents to others.

9. Recognize that diverse family structures and parenting styles will influence parent participation.

10. Help parents grow in confidence and in self-esteem (Gargiulo & Graves, 1991; Heward, 1996).

ucation; they also have the right to equal employment opportunities and the right to enjoy the services provided by the community. The macrosystem behind such legislation is rooted in the principles of equal opportunity, independence, and economic self-sufficiency (Hardman, Drew, & Egan, 1999).

The Vocational Rehabilitation Act of 1973 (PL 93-112) amended in 1992 serves as a "bill of rights" for individuals with disabilities in order to guarantee equal opportunity. It requires that federal agencies and all organizations holding contracts or receiving funds from the U.S. government have affirmative action programs to hire and promote qualified persons with disabilities. It enforces an earlier law requiring that all buildings constructed with federal funds or buildings owned or leased by federal agencies have ramps, elevators, handrails, wide aisles, or other barrier-free access for persons who are disabled. It also prohibits discrimination against qualified persons with disabilities—students, employees, and receivers of health and other services—in all public and private institutions receiving federal assistance. For example, employers can ask about a person's ability to perform a job, but cannot inquire if she or he has a disability. In 1990, the Americans with Disabilities Act (ADA) was passed. It bars discrimination in employment, transportation, public accommodations, and telecommunications. This law guarantees access to all aspects of life—not just those that are federally funded—for people with disabilities. The law specifies that "reasonable accommodations" be made according to the disability a person has. For example, telephone companies must provide services so that individuals with hearing or voice impairments can use ordinary telephones, all new construction and renovations of facilities must be accessible to those with disabilities, employers must restructure jobs and modify equipment as reasonably required.

Since the community has opened up opportunities for the livelihood and employment of individuals with disabilities, schools and support professionals must be involved in enabling those persons to make the transition from home to community. This means inclusion in leisure and social functions as well. The community has to make not only physical accommodations, such as designated parking spaces and ramps, but also open leadership and/or advisory positions on boards; provide sensitivity training to businesses; and be more welcoming to individuals with disabilities in the neighborhood. For example, in one community, the Performing Arts Center installed special headphones in every seat for anyone who might be (or might become) hearing impaired.

CHILDREN AT RISK FOR NEGATIVE DEVELOPMENTAL OUTCOMES

A growing number of children do not necessarily meet the definition of disabled, but they are at risk for psychological, social, or academic problems (Hardman, Drew, & Egan, 1999). They come from families that may have poor marital relations, practice domestic abuse, lack social support networks, experience unemployment, exhibit depression, and/or engage in substance abuse (Rogosch, Cicchetti, Shields, Toth, 1995).

Various types and observable signs of maltreatment were explained in Chapter 4; here the masked effects that interfere with development are discussed. Some of these less obvious developmental consequences for the child that may result from the quality of parenting in a dysfunctional family include difficulty in regulating emotions, insecure attachments, difficulty achieving autonomy, aggressiveness with peers, noncompliance with adults, and difficulty in readiness to learn (Rogosch, Cicchetti, Shields, & Toth, 1995). It is important for teachers and caregivers to understand the interactive dynamics in at-risk families in order to provide support to enable them to be involved in their children's learning.

CHILDREN PRENATALLY EXPOSED TO DRUGS

Substance abuse has been consistently linked with poor parenting and poor family functioning; addicted parents' primary relationship is with drugs, not with their children (Thompson, 1998). One group of children from at-risk families are those prenatally exposed to drugs or alcohol. Commonly abused drugs include crack cocaine, heroin, marijuana, tranquilizers, and stimulants. Substance-exposed infants exhibit low birth weights, sleeping and eating disorders, and increased irritability (Hardman, Drew, & Egan, 1999). Not only are there physical and health problems but psychological and behavioral ones as well. For example:

> Five-year-old Jeffrey's foster parents are at their wits' end. Jeffrey has just hit the neighbor's cat with a golf club. Fortunately, the cat was quick to move, so only its tail got the brunt of the blow. Jeffrey is in perpetual motion most of his waking hours. He even has a hard time sitting still while eating or in front of the TV. Suddenly, he may burst into tears, or laughter, or trance-like states that can last an hour or more (Green, 1990).

Jeffrey is a victim of his mother's addiction to crack cocaine, which she smoked during her pregnancy. Why the concern with such children?

About 15% of women of child-bearing age are substance abusers. A conservative estimate of the incidence of prenatal exposure to illicit drugs in the United States is 11% of live births (Hardman, Drew, & Egan, 1999).

Implementing interventions for mothers and their babies who have been exposed to drugs is challenging and expensive. Many drug-exposed babies are placed in foster care, which is costly, too. There is also the cost of special education and services, which can be two or three times the amount spent on a child in a regular program at a public school (about $5,000 per year).

Due to his mother's addiction to drugs, Jeffrey was removed from her care shortly after birth and placed in foster care. Jeffrey's antisocial behavior is likely to be related to the effects the drugs had on Jeffrey's developing brain in utero; cocaine causes blood vessels to constrict, thereby reducing the vital flow of oxygen and other nutrients to the brain as well as to other organs. Because fetal cells multiply rapidly in the first few months of development, the fetus is deprived of an optimal blood supply for normal growth.

Prenatal cocaine exposure affects brain chemistry as well. The drug alters the action of neurotransmitters, the messengers that travel between nerve cells and help control a person's mood and responsiveness. Such changes may explain the unusual behavior, including impulsiveness and moodiness, seen in some prenatally cocaine-exposed children as they mature (Toufexis, 1991).

Caring for prenatally cocaine-exposed babies is frustrating because they respond differently to natural adult overtures such as cooing, tickling, and bouncing. While normal babies gurgle and laugh, babies prenatally exposed to drugs stiffen or scream. The mothers feel rejected and end up avoiding trying to make further contact, unless they are given the opportunity to learn how not to overstimulate the infant (Toufexis, 1991; Tyler, 1992).

As these children reach preschool- and school-age, they don't relate to other children or adults appropriately. They tend to ignore rules, have temper outbursts, be aggressive, and be unable to concentrate (Green, 1990; Hardman, Drew, & Egan, 1999). Thus they have special socialization needs, and their caregivers need to learn techniques to optimize their development.

CHILDREN WHOSE PARENTS ABUSE ALCOHOL

Another group of children from at-risk families are those whose parents abuse alcohol. According to the American Academy of Child and Adolescent Psychiatry (AACAP, 1999), one in five adult Americans lived with an alcoholic while growing up. **Alcoholism** is a chronic, progressive, and potentially fatal disease. It is characterized by excessive tolerance for alcohol and physical dependency or pathologic organ changes, or both—all the direct or indirect consequences of the alcohol ingested.

Alcohol is so common in our society that we seldom think of it as a drug. Yet beer, wine, and liquor are all central-nervous system depressants. They are similar to barbiturates and other sedative drugs in slowing down bodily functions such as heart rate and respiration.

Alcohol consumption during pregnancy can produce abnormalities in the developing fetus. Alcohol interferes with the delivery of nutrients to the fetus, impairs the supply of fetal oxygen, and interferes with protein synthesis.

A specific cluster of abnormalities appearing in babies exposed prenatally to alcohol abuse (heavy drinking) was described and named "Fetal Alcohol Syndrome" (FAS) by

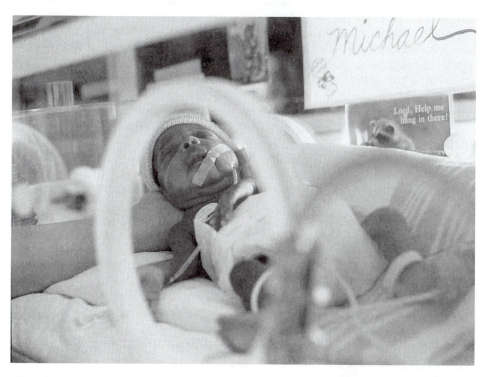

This baby was prenatally exposed to his mother's substance abuse resulting in physical and mental birth defects.

Jones and his colleagues (1973). Among the distinguishing features of this syndrome are prenatal and postnatal growth retardation; facial abnormalities, including small head circumference; widely spaced eyes; short eyelid openings; a small, upturned nose; and a thin upper lip. Most FAS children are mentally retarded. FAS is the leading known preventable cause of mental retardation. Now warnings of possible birth defects are required on alcoholic beverages and in establishments that serve alcohol.

Behavior problems appear in infancy and persist into childhood; the most common are irritability, hyperactivity, poor concentration, and poor social skills. Sometimes affected children display other physical problems such as defects of the eyes, ears, heart, urinary tract, or immune system (Aaronson & MacNee, 1989).

Children whose parents abuse alcohol are frequently victims of incest, child neglect, and other forms of violence and exploitation (Leershen & Namuth, 1988; Mayes, 1995).

Children whose parents abuse alcohol are prone to a range of psychological difficulties, including learning disabilities, anxiety, attempted and completed suicides, eating disorders, and compulsive achieving. The problems of most of such children remain invisible because their coping behavior tends to be approval-seeking and socially acceptable. They do their work, do not rock the boat, and do not reveal their secret. Many are high achievers and eager to please. Yet their adaptation to the chaos and inconsistency of an alcohol-abusing family often results in developing an inability to trust, an extreme need to control, excessive sense of responsibility, and denial of feelings, all of which result in low self-esteem, depression, isolation, guilt, and difficulty maintaining satisfying relationships. These and other problems often persist throughout adulthood (Leershen & Namuth, 1988; Tubman, 1993).

Janet Geringer Woititz (1990), in her classic book, *Adult Children of Alcoholics,* and Claudia Black (1991) in her classic book, *It Will Never Happen to Me,* discuss some common traits exhibited by adult children of alcoholics, such as guessing what is normal behavior, having difficulty following a project from beginning to end, lying instead of telling the truth, having difficulty having fun, constantly seeking approval, feeling they are different from other people, and tending to lock themselves into a course of action without giving consideration to consequences. As adults the wounded child within impairs emotional expressions (feelings are repressed) and relationships (trust) are difficult.

The child is often embarrassed by his or her parents. The ashamed child does not invite friends home and is afraid to ask anyone for help. The child also feels anger toward the alcoholic parent for drinking and may be angry with the nonalcoholic parent for lack of support and protection. The child may even feel guilty perceiving himself or herself as the cause of the parent's drinking (AACAP, 1999).

Although the child tries to keep the parent's alcoholism a secret, teachers, friends, relatives, or other caring adults may sense something is wrong. The following behaviors may signal a problem (AACAP, 1999):

- Failure in school; truancy
- Lack of friends; withdrawal from classmates
- Delinquent behavior, such as stealing or violence
- Frequent physical complaints, such as headaches or stomachaches
- Abuse of drugs or alcohol
- Aggression toward other children

- Risk-taking behaviors
- Depression or suicidal thoughts or behavior

Whether or not their parents are receiving treatment for alcoholism, these children can benefit from programs such as Al-Anon and Alateen. Therapists can help these children to understand they are not responsible for the drinking problems of their parents. Therapists can also help the family, particularly when the alcoholic has stopped drinking, develop healthier ways of relating to one another. For example, a problem emerging during recovery stems from the familial responsibilities undertaken by children during active parental alcoholism. When parents are drinking, children may run the household and care for younger siblings. The recovering alcoholic generally tries to reassume these responsibilities. Children are then asked to become children again instead of "little adults" or "parents." Because they are unaccustomed to behaving like children, the transition back to more traditional familial roles may cause conflict between parents and children (AACAP, 1999).

Thus the consequences of living in an alcoholic family are particularly difficult for young children and adolescents because alcoholism affects the process of socialization of values, morals, attitudes, behavior, gender roles, self-control, and self-concept. The effects of alcoholism depend on the child's age, gender, relationship to the drinking and nondrinking parents, relationship to other family members, or other social networks.

CHILDREN EXPOSED TO DOMESTIC VIOLENCE

Children exposed to domestic violence are at risk for negative developmental outcomes. *Domestic violence* may be defined as "the systematic abuse by one person in an intimate relationship in order to control and dominate the partner" (Kearny, 1999, p. 290). Abusive behavior can be physical, emotional, mental, and/or sexual. Domestic violence can be found in all socioeconomic classes and cultures (Greenfield, 1998). Most is experienced by women, although some men experience it, too (Kearny, 1999). The government plays a significant role in preventing negative outcomes from domestic violence. It has passed laws making violence against women a crime and provided funding for shelters, counseling, and hot lines (National Coalition Against Domestic Violence, 1999).

Children who are exposed to domestic violence often experience the following feelings (Kearny, 1999, p. 291):

- *Anger*—They are angry at the abuser for the violence, at the victim, or themselves for not being able to stop the violence.
- *Fear/terror*—They are afraid that the mother or father will be seriously injured or killed, that they or their siblings will be hurt, that others will find out and then the parents will be "in trouble," or that they will be removed from the family.
- *Powerlessness*—Because they are unable to prevent the fights from happening, or to stop them when the violence occurs, they feel out of control.
- *Loneliness*—They feel unable or afraid to reach out to others, feeling "different," or isolated.

- *Confusion*—They are confused about why it happens, choosing sides, what they should do, what is "right" and "wrong." They are also confused about how the abuser can sometimes be caring, and at other times, violent.
- *Shame*—They are ashamed about what is happening in their home.
- *Guilt*—They feel guilty because they may have caused the violence, or they should have been able to stop it, but couldn't
- *Distrust*—They don't trust adults because experience tells them that adults are unpredictable, that they break promises, and/or that they don't mean well.

Breaking the silence surrounding domestic violence and providing appropriate intervention can help exposed children become resilient.

Strategies for Teachers of Children Exposed to Domestic Violence

- **Identification.** Be alert to changes in emotional, social, and/or learning behaviors. Ask the child, "What is wrong?" (Does the child not want to go home? Is the child unusually attached to his or her teacher? Is the child withdrawn? Is the child aggressive or a bully?)
- **Support.** Be available to listen to the child and acknowledge his or her feelings without being judgmental. Help the child to develop ways to release his or her feelings appropriately.
- **Modeling.** Exhibit nonviolent cooperative ways of solving problems.

TOWARD RESILIENCY

The concept of *resiliency* was introduced at the beginning of this chapter. Children who were found to be resilient against negative developmental outcomes were those who had established a bond with an adult caregiver or mentor. To enable resiliency, then, families must develop linkages with schools and communities to avail children of many possible supportive adults and potential mentors.

What are the ways families can become involved in school? There are three major ways: (1) decision making—determining school programs and policies; (2) participation—working in the classroom as paid and volunteering instructional assistants; and (3) partnership—providing home guidance to their children to support learning and extend school goals. For example, Yale University psychiatrist Dr. James Comer (1988) found by involving parents of minority children in these three aspects, parent distrust of the school was overcome. Students were viewed as having unmet needs rather than as having behavioral problems. The children were served by a mental health team as well as by resource teachers. There was a Crisis Room, where counselors provided positive alternatives to antisocial behavior. There was a Discovery Room, where teachers motivated learning based on children's interests and curiosity. The program thus joined social and intellectual skills. Parents' help was enlisted, and the school became a source of self-esteem and community pride.

Figure 7.2   Child–Family–School Linkages

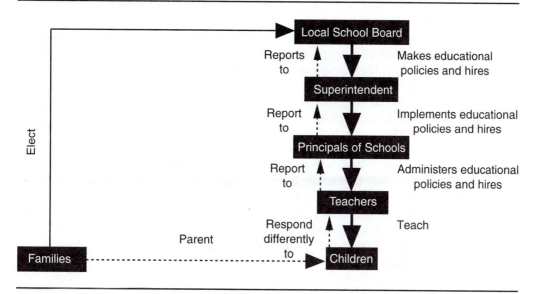

Families also become involved in school and education when they vote. They elect people to serve on the local school board to make decisions about educational goals, school facilities, budget allocations, personnel, student standards of achievement and conduct, and evaluation methods. Obviously, this interaction is indirect, but nonetheless influential (*see* Figure 7.2). Direct interaction occurs when families go to the school their children attend and talk to the administrators and teachers.

THE IMPORTANCE OF FAMILY INVOLVEMENT IN SCHOOLS

Whereas socialization of the child begins in the family, the school extends the process by formal education. The outcome of this joint effort depends considerably on the relationship between family and school. Many research studies from preschool to elementary school to high school (Cochran & Henderson, 1986; Epstein & Dauber, 1991; Henderson & Berla, 1994; Lazar & Darlington, 1982; Nettles, 1990) have provided evidence showing that when schools work together with families to support learning, children tend to succeed in school and afterward. These studies point to family involvement in learning as a more accurate predictor of school achievement than is socioeconomic status. Specifically, when families (1) create a home environment that encourages learning, (2) express high (but not unrealistic) expectations for their children's achievement and future careers, and (3) become involved in their children's education at school and in the community, children from low-socioeconomic-status and ethnically diverse families fare comparably to middle-class children.

For example, schools that have turned around truancy rates dramatically let the students know they care. In some cases, schools use a system in which every student is assigned one teacher to be sure that the student gets to school. The teacher makes wake-up calls and occasionally drops by the child's home on Saturdays to keep up school interest.

If there is any sign of reluctance about going to school, the teacher will explore why and, if necessary, refer the student to appropriate social services. Successful schools, then, really work on human connectedness (Henderson, 1990; Steinberg, 1996).

On the other hand, the effectiveness of the school or family can be eroded by conflict, confusion, lack of consensus in goals, or mismatch in motivation or cognitive skills (Hess & Holloway, 1984; Levine & Levine, 1996). For example, a mismatch in the way language is used in a community and in school can result in learning problems for the child (Heath, 1983; Levine & Levine, 1996). A child who communicates in Black English dialect will have difficulty in a classroom where standard English is the norm.

Why is family involvement in schools so important to the school's ability to socialize? When families are involved, children benefit by having more positive attitudes toward learning, better attendance, fewer placements in special education, better grades, and being more likely to graduate high school and go to work or continue their education. When families are involved, they gain confidence in the school, the teacher, and themselves. Often they are motivated to continue their education. The school benefits by having community support, higher teacher morale, and better student achievement.

Thus the school needs to interact with the family so that socialization goals for the child are complementary rather than contradictory. For example, in several studies of students in the early grades of school (Overt & Donald, 1998; Tizard, Schofield, & Hewison, 1982), those children (of all reading levels) who were asked to read to their parents gained in reading skills (a school goal), whereas the control group of children did not.

The key to forming complementary goals for the child is communication. The school and the family need to talk to each other about their attitudes regarding education and parenting. What are the parents' expectations for the child's achievement and behavior at school? What are the school's expectations for the child's activities at home?

THE SCHOOL'S ROLE IN ENCOURAGING FAMILY INVOLVEMENT

Studies report that parents of young children with some college background and in the middle- to upper-socioeconomic statuses have the most involvement in school (Berger, 1995; Epstein, 1995). As children progress from elementary school to upper grades, parental contact with school diminishes. Inner-city parents, single parents, dual-earner parents, and parents of secondary schoolchildren express the desire to be more involved as well as the frustration with the school and teachers for not being more accessible.

To collaborate with parents and empower them, Indianapolis schools implemented weekly tutoring sessions, assignment monitoring, and workshops that enable parents to learn how to help their underachieving students. The program demonstrated that the school cared about the parents and the success of their children (Hyde, 1992).

However, not all parents are interested in becoming involved in their child's school. Why? Perhaps some disliked school as children, and their attitude prevents them from wanting to communicate with their child's teacher. Some may feel that parents are called to the school only when there is a problem. Perhaps some are so involved with working that they are too tired to make the effort. Or perhaps some parents do not speak English fluently enough to feel comfortable talking to the teacher.

What can the teacher do to break through these barriers? Probably the most effective way to break a barrier to communication is to allay the fears that built up that

Table 7.1   Developing Parent–Teacher Partnerships

A collaborative relationship depends on:

- Trust ("I know you will inform me if John is having problems with his homework.")
- Mutual respect ("I admire your patience.")
- Open communication ("I don't understand the requirements.")
- Honesty ("I had hoped for more challenging work for Susan.")
- Active listening ("I understand you to mean . . .")
- Openness ("Conferences make me nervous, too.")
- Flexibility ("If you can't come tomorrow, the next day will be fine.")
- Caring ("I hope you are feeling better.")
- Understanding ("I'm sure you must be disappointed with that grade.")
- Shared responsibility ("Let's work together drilling Matt on his multiplication tables.")
- Full disclosure of information ("Here are all of Mary's standardized test scores since first grade.")

Source: Martin and Waltman–Greenwood (1995).

barrier. If parents will not come to school because they are afraid to hear bad things about their child, make it a habit to send positive notes home and call parents to let them know their child is doing well. If parents are very involved in their work, perhaps they could share their work with the class—visit the class, arrange a trip for the children to visit their workplace, or share information with their child so the child can share it with the class. If the parents' English is limited, invite them to visit the class to see their child's work—let them know that you would like to meet them because you care about their child. Their language facility is unimportant. Provide a translator, if possible.

Basically, parents need confidence, support, and praise. Parenting is work—hard work. In the business world, hard work is recognized by praise from supervisors, salary raises, or commissions, but in the home, the hard work of child rearing often goes unrecognized by the child. A teacher who is able to communicate to parents the positive results of their jobs as parents is, in effect, building their self-esteem and breaking down their doubts about their competence as parents. A teacher who can communicate respect for parents has taken the first step toward motivating the parents to become involved. The sustenance of that involvement then depends on the teacher's genuine and constant interest.

FAMILY–SCHOOL LINKAGES AND CHILDREN'S READINESS TO LEARN

To illustrate the significance of child, family, and school linkages, this chapter concludes by discussing the nation's primary educational goal: that all children will come to school "ready to learn." The challenge of reaching this goal for macrosystems, microsystems, and mesosystems employ the following strategies (Boyer, 1991, pp. 136–143):

1. *A healthy start.* Good health and good schooling are inextricably interlocked, and every child, to be ready to learn, must have a healthy birth, be well nourished, and be well protected in the early years of life.

2. *Empowered parents.* The home is the first classroom. Parents are the first and most essential teachers; all children, as a readiness requirement, should live in a secure environment where empowered parents encourage language development.
   a. Parents must speak frequently to children and listen.
   b. Parents must read to children.
   c. Parents must build a bridge between home and school.

3. *Quality preschool.* Since many young children are cared for outside the home, high-quality programs are required that not only provide good care but also address all dimensions of school readiness.

4. *A responsible workplace.* If each child in America is to come to school ready to learn, we must have workplace policies that are family friendly, ones that offer child-care services and give parents time to be with their young children.
   a. Provide available leave time.
   b. Have flexible scheduling.
   c. Enable job sharing.
   d. Link with community child-care services.

5. *Television as teacher.* Next to parents, television is the child's most influential teacher. School readiness requires television programming that is both educational and enriching.
   a. Commercial companies selling children's products should help underwrite quality programs.
   b. Establish a Ready-to-Learn cable channel.

6. *Neighborhoods for learning.* Since all children need spaces and places for growth and exploration, safe and friendly neighborhoods are needed, ones that contribute richly to a child's readiness to learn.
   a. Have well-designed indoor and outdoor parks.
   b. Provide readiness programs in libraries, museums, zoos.
   c. Establish ready-to-learn centers in malls where college students can volunteer their services.

7. *Connections across the generations.* Connections across the generations will give children a sense of security and continuity, contributing to their school readiness in the fullest sense.
   a. Build bridges between child care and senior citizen centers.
   b. Build bridges between child care and community grandteacher programs.

In conclusion, children who are ready to succeed in school are healthy, immunized against disease, well nourished, and well rested. Their early experiences have given them a start in learning to cooperate, exercise self-control, articulate their thoughts and feelings, and follow rules. They are trusting and have a feeling of self-worth. They explore their environment actively and approach tasks with enthusiasm (U.S. Department of Education, 1991b).

Communities provide many learning experiences for children and their families, as exemplified by this museum.

What Families Can Do to Enable Children to be Ready to Learn

- Express your love
  Spend time with your child
  Talk and listen
  Help child to be independent (let child do things he/she is capable of)
- Use everyday opportunities to teach about the world
  Talk about scenery, weather, news
  Figure things out together—how much time has passed, how to divide the
  pie, how to repair the toilet
  Enable child to follow directions
  Plan together (activities, goals)
- Encourage questions
  How does this work?
  Why did this happen?
- Give approval for trying new things
  Reward accomplishments
  Make it understood that mistakes happen—what can we learn?
  Stimulate creativity
- Instill a love of books
  Model reading
  Read to your child
  Answer questions

Visit the library

Tell stories and have child tell them, too

- Get involved in school

  Talk about school positively

  Visit school

  Encourage attendance

  Support homework

- Limit TV viewing

  Select appropriate programs

  Encourage reading and imaginary and physical activities

  Discuss programs with child

- Encourage writing

  Have child write and/or draw thank-you notes, messages, stories

- Develop math concepts

  Cook together

  Play games

  Give allowance money to save and spend

- Develop science concepts

  Encourage collections

  Observe plants and animals

  Visit museums

- Develop social studies concepts

  Discuss current events

  Observe national holidays

  Demonstrate good citizenship by being well informed, discussing decision
    making, voting

- Get involved in the community (Hatcher & Beck, 1997)

  Visit workplaces (post office, fire department, factory, office)

  Visit historical sites

  Participate in community service

- Be a model of lifelong learning (Rich, 1992)

  confidence ("I can do it")

  motivation ("I want to do it")

  effort ("I'm willing to try hard")

  responsibility ("I follow through on commitments")

  initiative ("I am a self-starter")

  perseverance ("I finish what I start")

  caring ("I show concern for others")

  teamwork ("I work cooperatively with others")

  common sense ("I use good judgment")

  problem-solving ("I use my knowledge and experience effectively")

What Schools Can Do to Enable Children to be Ready to Learn

Many schools have interpreted the concept of "readiness" to mean children's ability to succeed at school-related tasks and have used entrance testing to make this evaluation (Lewit & Baker, 1995). For example, **standardized tests,** those in which an individual is compared to a norm on specifically selected items, have been developed to assess kindergarten readiness. The National Association for the Education of Young Children (1988) asserts that such tests are inappropriate for young children because each child comes from a unique set of family experiences. What one family makes available for its children, another does not. Some children travel extensively; others seldom go outside their immediate community. Some children speak a language other than English. Some have had preschool experiences; others remained at home. Also, there are maturational differences that influence children's ability to perform well on standardized tests—for example, the ability to listen and follow instructions, control a pencil, and sit still for a certain period of time.

If the concept of readiness were shared by the school, the school could do more to individualize school curricula and group children by developmental readiness instead of by age only (Lewit & Baker, 1995). Thus, children who were of the legal age to attend school but were not as "ready" as their peers to learn due to diverse family backgrounds, such as those discussed in this chapter, could be provided with developmentally appropriate activities. In addition, **authentic assessments,** those which evaluate real performance showing mastery of a task (for example, a portfolio of a child's writing or art), could be used rather than solely relying on standardized paper-and-pencil tests.

In conclusion, the *school* should be ready for children to learn when they come to school, just as *children* should be ready to learn when they come to school.

Epilogue

*T*o enable children to be resilient to risk, linkages must be developed between children, families, schools, and communities. To succeed, children must have caring and mentoring relationships with adults. Jean Valjean's life was turned around by a caring priest. Oscar De La Hoya had consistent family support. Both Jean Valjean and Oscar De La Hoya became role models for others. ■

SUMMARY

Linkages between the child, family, school, and community are necessary to optimize socialization, especially for children at risk for negative developmental outcomes, such as children from diverse ethnic groups, those who have disabilities, those exposed to domestic violence, and those from families with other identified risk factors. The purpose of these linkages is to enable resiliency. Resiliency in children is more likely to occur when they receive understanding and support from adults.

Ethnic diversity needs to be understood because the United States is composed of many diverse ethnic groups, Americans speak many languages, and the world is moving toward a global economy.

The U.S. macroculture—usually defined as white, Anglo Saxon, Protestant—generally shares certain values. The degree to which individual U.S. citizens subscribe to the general values depends, in part, on the microculture or ethnic group of which the individual is a member. The degree may also depend on how much an individual must interact with the formal institutions in U.S. society (school, government, health and welfare agencies) for support.

Learning, or cognitive, styles are aspects of socialization that have implications for education. Generally, Anglo Americans prefer analysis, deductive reasoning, accuracy, individual and competitive work, and verbal communication. This is an analytical and field-independent cognitive style.

Generally, African Americans view things in their entirety, use approximations, focus on people, prefer simultaneous involvement in activities, and are proficient in nonverbal communication. This is a relational, field-dependent cognitive style.

Generally, Hispanic Americans subscribe to the following values: identification with family, community, and ethnic group; personalization of interpersonal relationships; and status and role definition in family and community. Their learning style tends to be relational and field-dependent.

Generally, Native Americans are oriented toward the extended family. Sharing and group ownership are fostered. They are socialized in their families by observation. They are more present-oriented than future-oriented. Their learning style tends to be visualization and modeling. Children gradually take over tasks via apprenticeship. They prefer holistic concepts rather than analytic ones.

Generally, Asian Americans are socialized to place emphasis on tradition, conformity, and respect for authority, and to submerge individuality. There is respect for education, age, and etiquette. Their learning style tends to be relatively nonverbal. Emphasis is placed on hard work and effort. Adult standards are expected to be internalized early.

Children from certain ethnic minority families are at risk for negative developmental outcomes not only because they are more likely to be poor, but also because they are more likely to achieve less educationally than others. The exception is Asian American children, who, by and large, are surpassing their peers in academic achievement. To equalize educational and employment opportunities, various mechanisms have evolved—legislation, financial assistance to education, and the requirement of family involvement in education.

To enable children with disabilities to be resilient to risk, society and schools have provided support. Laws requiring individuals with disabilities to be included in the mainstream of society have been passed. Educational methods have been modified to include children with specific disabilities to optimize their socialization.

The Individuals with Disabilities Act (IDEA) requires that an individualized education program (IEP) be written annually specifying educational goals, methods, and resources/services required to meet the child's needs. Also, PL 99-457 provides for a variety of programs for infants, toddlers, and preschoolers with disabilities and includes instruction for parents in the socialization of their child via an Individualized Family Service Plan.

The community, via legislation, has aided integration of individuals with disabilities. The Vocational Rehabilitation Act of 1973 and, more recently, the Americans with Disabilities Act of 1990 guarantee certain rights to individuals with disabilities, such as affirmative action and access. Thus schools and support professionals must be involved in transition from home to community.

At-risk families include those that, due to poor marital relations, domestic abuse, lack of a social support network, unemployment, depression, and/or substance abuse might become dysfunctional and maltreat a child.

One group of children from at-risk families are those prenatally exposed to drugs or alcohol. The costs to care for and educate these children are great.

Another group of children at risk are those whose parents abuse alcohol. Children of alcoholics are frequently victims of maltreatment including neglect, abuse, and incest.

They are likely to experience a range of psychological difficulties as well as birth defects and be at risk to become alcoholics themselves. Shame, secretism, withdrawal, aggression, learning problems, and risk-taking behaviors are common.

To enable resilience in all children, especially those at risk, bonds must be fostered with adult caregivers. This is best accomplished via linkages between the child, family, and school. Children exposed to domestic violence are at risk for negative developmental outcomes. To enable such children to become resilient, teachers can identify them, give support, and model appropriate behavior.

Family involvement is the most important influence on children's success in school, because the family is the primary socializer of children. Thus, in order for the educational goals of the school to be effective with children, parental support must be obtained. Some of the benefits of parental involvement in school are positive attitudes toward learning, higher academic achievement, and higher aspirations on the part of the children. Some of the benefits for the parents who are involved are higher self-esteem and more interaction with their children.

Family involvement can occur in decision making, participation, and/or partnership. Parents need encouragement and support from teachers. Teachers need good communication skills.

The significance of child/family/school linkages is demonstrated in the nation's number-one education goal, that all children will come to school "ready to learn." "Readiness" encompasses health, nutrition, and social/emotional factors. Families can enable children to be ready by nurturance, communication, encouraging learning, and getting involved in school. Schools can enable "readiness" by individualizing the curriculum, by providing activities that are developmentally appropriate, and by using authentic assessments rather than relying on standardized tests.

ACTIVITY

Purpose: To understand child/family/school interaction in your community.

1. Locate an elementary school in your community that involves families.

2. Interview the principal or other school administrator.
   a. How does the school motivate families to become involved (letters, phone calls, visits, open houses, conferences, and so on)?
   b. What activities do families participate in (decision making, volunteering, partnering with teachers, and so on)?
   c. Does the school link with the community (fieldtrips, guest speakers, financial and/or equipment donations from businesses, provide school facility for community functions, and so on)?
   d. How does the school provide for children from various ethnic groups and for children with disabilities?
   e. What does the school do to identify children at risk for learning problems?

3. Evaluate your findings, making recommendations where appropriate.

RESOURCES

America Goes Back to School
http://www.ed.gov/family/agbts

Bureau of Indian Affairs
http://www.boi.gov/bureau-indian-affairs.html

Coalition for Asian American Children & Families
http://www.cacf.org/

Hispanic Culture
http://www.literacynet.org/

Institute for Disabilities Research and Training, Inc.
http://www.idrt.com/

Mental Health Net—Facts for Families
http://www.cmhc.com/factsfam.htm

National Black Child Development Institute
http://www.nbcdi.org/

National Coalition Against Domestic Violence
http://www.ncadv.org

National Institute on Alcohol Abuse and Alcoholism
http://www.niaa.nih.gov/

National Institute on Drug Abuse
http://www.nida.nih.gov/

National March of Dimes/Birth Defects
http://modimes.org

National PTA/Children First
http://www.pta/

Office of Bilingual Education and Minority Languages Affairs
http://www.Ed.Gov/offices/OBEMLA/

Phi Delta Kappa International Connecting Educators
http://www.pdkintl.org/

RELATED READINGS

Bennett, C. E. (1998). *Comprehensive multicultural education: Theory and practice* (4th ed.). Boston: Allyn and Bacon.

Berger, E. H. (1995). *Parents as partners in education: Families and schools working together* (4th ed.). Englewood Cliffs, NJ: Prentice-Hall.

Black, C. (1991). *It will never happen to me* (rev. ed.). New York: Ballantine Books.

Booth, A., & Dunn, J. (1996). *Family–school links: How do they affect educational outcomes?* Mahwah, NJ: Lawrence Erlbaum.

Byrnes, D. A., & Kigler, G. (Eds.). (1996). *Common bonds: Anti-bias teaching in a diverse society.* Wheaton, MD: Association for Childhood Education International.

Derman-Sparks, L. (1989). *Anti-bias curriculum: Tools for empowering young children.* Washington, DC: National Association for Education of Young Children.

Epstein, J. L. (1996). *School and family partnerships.* New York: Basic Books (Westview Press).

Farnham-Diggory, S. (1992). *The learning-disabled child.* Cambridge, MA: Harvard University Press.

Featherstone, H. (1980). *A difference in the family.* New York: Basic Books.

Garbarino, J., Eckenrode, J., & Barry F. D. (1997). *Understanding abusive families: An ecological approach to theory and practice.* San Francisco: Jossey-Bass.

Geffner, R. A., & Jouriles, E. N. (1998). *Children exposed to marital violence: Theory, research, and applied issues.* Washington, DC: American Psychological Association.

Locke, D. C. (1998). *Increasing multicultural understanding: A comprehensive model* (2nd ed.). Thousand Oaks, CA: Sage.

McCracken, J. B. (1993). *Valuing diversity: The primary years.* Washington, DC: National Association for the Education of Young Children.

Quackenbush, S., Villareal, S., & McKinney, L. E. (1992). *Handle with care: Helping children prenatally exposed to drugs and alcohol.* Santa Cruz, CA: ETR Associates Network Publications.

Ramsey, P. G. (1998). *Teaching and learning in a diverse world: Multicultural education for young children* (2nd ed.). New York: Teachers College Press.

Rich, D. (1992). *Megaskills* (rev. ed.). Boston: Houghton Mifflin.

Rothenberg, P. S. (1998). *Race, class, and gender in the United States: An integrated study* (4th ed.). New York: St. Martin's Press.

Stewart, E. C., & Bennet, M. J. (1991). *American cultural patterns: A cross-cultural perspective* (rev. ed.). Yarmouth, ME: Intercultural Press.

Strauss, M. A., Gelles, R. J., & Steinmetz, S. (1980). *Behind closed doors.* Garden City, NY: Anchor.

Werner, E. E., & Smith, R. S. (1992). *Overcoming the odds: High-risk children from birth to adulthood.* Ithaca, NY: Cornell University Press.

Wolery, M., & Wilbers, J. S. (Eds.). (1994). *Including children with special needs in early childhood programs.* Washington, DC: National Association for the Education of Young Children.

York, S. (1991). *Roots and wings: Affirming culture in early childhood programs.* St. Paul, MN: Toys n Things Press.

"Without friends no one would choose to live, though he had all other goods."

— Aristotle

Chapter 8

ECOLOGY OF THE PEER GROUP

Prologue

PEER, PRESTIGE, PERSUASION, AND POWER

Mark Twain's famous story, Tom Sawyer *(1876), takes place in a Mississippi River town before the Civil War. It tells of Tom's adventures and maneuverings to outwit his conventional but caring Aunt Polly, as well as his escapades with his friends, especially Huckleberry Finn.*

One beautiful summer Saturday morning, Aunt Polly gives Tom the chore of whitewashing the fence. As Tom surveys the massive area he has to paint, he begins to dip his brush in the bucket while musing how cruel is his fate. Why should he have to work while his friends have the day to play? He knew if the other boys saw him, they would tease and harass him. He remembers the trinkets in his pocket—maybe he could offer them as a bribe in exchange for a few hours of work. Suddenly, he has an inspiration!

He picks up the brush with new vigor just as Ben, the boy whose ridicule he most dreads, comes skipping and whistling down the street pretending to be a steamboat. Tom ignores him.

Ben laughs, "Ha, ha. You gotta work. I'm goin' swimmin'."

Tom replies, " Oh, it's you, Ben. I hadn't noticed. You call this work?"

"Whitewashing's work if I ever saw."

"Well maybe it is, and maybe it ain't; but it sure suits Tom Sawyer. A boy doesn't get to whitewash every day, you know."

Tom takes great care and pretended pride in his work so effectively that Ben says, "Hey, let me try that."

"No, I reckon, that would not do . . . see, Aunt Polly is awful particular about this fence. It's got to be done very careful; I reckon there ain't one boy in a thousand, that can do it the way it's got to be done."

"Oh, come on, let me just try . . . I'd let you, if you was me, Tom."

"Ben, I'd like to, honest; but Jim wanted to do it and Aunt Polly wouldn't let him. Sid wanted to, and she wouldn't let him neither. So, see how I'm fixed? If you were to tackle this fence and anything were to happen . . ."

"Oh, shucks, I'll be careful; I'll even let you have my apple."

"Well, OK, here."

Tom gives up the brush with reluctance on his face, but eagerness in his heart.

A similar scene occurs as various friends pass by. By the time Ben is fagged out, Tom has already traded the next chance to Billy for a kite, then to Johnny for a dead rat on a string, and so on, hour after hour.

Tom spent a nice idle time the whole day with lots of company and many new acquisitions. And the fence got three coats of whitewash.

Tom's outlook on the world changed. He had discovered how to manipulate his friends by making them covet something that seemed difficult to attain.

In a contemporary study of seventh- and tenth-graders in the suburbs of Boston, Harvard Professor Richard Weissbourd (1996) tells of the case of 14-year-old Stephen Brewer.

Stephen was instrumental in forming a gang called the Sunvalley Estates Bad Boys (SEBB). The gang began by playing pranks on elderly people watching cable TV. They would hide in the bushes near the senior's home and aim a remote control channel selector to randomly change channels. More recently, however, some of the members have been involved in vandalism, intimidating younger children, and abusing drugs.

Stephen complains there is nothing to do. There is no public transportation to the Estates, so if you are too young to drive or don't have access to a car, you are marooned. Some children are involved in team sports, but depend on parents for transportation. The older children who have transportation can work at local restaurants.

What makes being trapped harder for Stephen is that he hates being home. His parents divorced several years ago and he lives with his mother and older brother, Kevin, who has a learning disability. Much of his mother's time is spent advocating for Kevin.

Stephen likes hanging with the Bad Boys because it gives him status and popularity at school. His role in the gang is that of bodyguard, so the other kids depend on him for protection. However, because he has been in so many fights and his grades have plummeted, he is in danger of being retained for a year at school. Stephen is afraid to reform because others will step in and claim his status with his friends.

While Tom Sawyer and Stephen Brewer have leadership roles in their respective peer groups, Tom's is productive whereas Stephen's is destructive. Why?

According to Weissbourd, children's peer groups tend to become destructive when children lack positive sources of recognition, especially meaningful opportunities that extend into adulthood. Tom lived with a supportive adult who was committed to making him "turn out right." The chores he was required to do were meaningful, even though he didn't like them. Stephen, on the other hand, felt abandoned; first by his father due to the divorce, and then by his mother because of her involvement with his brother, and finally by his school that seemed to always be punishing him. ■

- *What is the appeal of the peer group?*
- *What makes one a leader, able to manipulate peers?*
- *Why does social pressure influence people to conform to others?*
- *What influences positive goals versus negative goals for the peer group?*

THE PEER GROUP AS A SOCIALIZING AGENT

Peers are equals; they are usually of the same gender and age and have similar social statuses and interests. Experiences with peers enable children to acquire a wide range of skills, attitudes, and roles that influence their adaptation throughout life (Rubin, Bukowski, & Parker, 1998). Peer groups are significant socializers, contributing beyond the influence of family and school because (1) they satisfy certain belonging needs;

(2) they are often preferred to other socializing agents; and (3) they influence not only social development, but cognitive and psychological development as well.

As more mothers are being employed, more and more children are being cared for in group settings. Children are experiencing social interaction with peers today earlier and for longer periods of time than they were a generation ago. Also, school-age children and adolescents who are not supervised by adults after school are more likely to turn to their peers for support. We examine various influences here.

THE SIGNIFICANCE OF PEERS TO DEVELOPMENT

Peer groups satisfy certain basic human needs to develop optimally. These are the need to belong to a group and interact socially as well as the need to develop a sense of self (a

Figure 8.1   An Ecological Model of Human Development

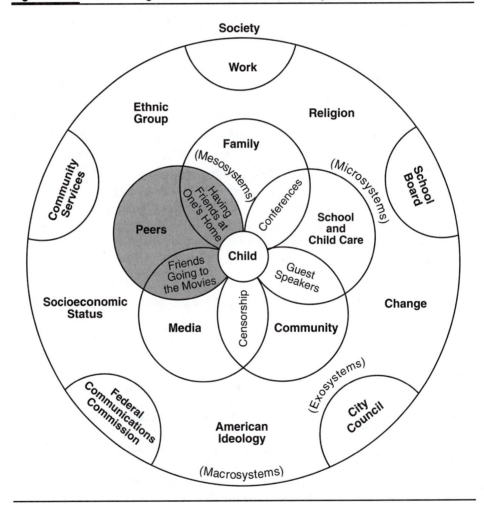

Peers are a significant influence on the child's development.

personal identity). Belonging to a peer group enables one to have social interactions with others and have experiences independent of parents or other adults. By socially interacting with others, we derive an opinion of ourselves. We referred to this concept of self in Chapter 2 as "the looking glass self" (Cooley, 1964) and "the generalized other" (Mead, 1934). We think of ourselves as having pretty hair, cute freckles, or a large nose because others tell us so. We think of ourselves as clever, as fast runners, or as good at drawing by comparing our skills to those of others.

Sense of Belonging and Social Interaction

Child peer relationships are influenced by individual temperamental characteristics that may set the stage for certain types of parent–child relationships and social behaviors (Rubin, Bukowski, & Parker, 1998). For example, parents who provide opportunities for their children to have contact with peers may coach their children to interact positively and may intervene when negative behavior occurs (Pettit & Mize, 1993). Parent–child relationships from infancy to middle childhood will be examined to better understand how they influence peer relationships.

Infancy/Toddlerhood (Birth to Age 1.5 or 2).   The sense of belonging develops first within the family. A baby gets the feeling he or she "belongs" to his or her mother when the mother holds, soothes, and meets the baby's needs. Babies whose mothers or caregivers are sensitive and responsive to their needs—for example, feeding them when they are hungry and comforting them when they are frightened—are *securely attached* (Ainsworth, 1979; Rubin, Bukowski, & Parker, 1998). The importance of attachment in socialization was discussed in Chapter 2. Attachment theory suggests that the child who enjoys a secure attachment relationship with his or her caregiver is likely to possess a model to imitate for responsiveness to others (Sroufe & Fleeson, 1986; Rubin, Bukowski, & Parker, 1998). In addition, it is believed that a secure attachment provides a secure base for exploratory behavior (Ainsworth, 1978). In other words, infants and toddlers who are secure in their relationship with their caregivers feel confident in leaving them to explore their environment (including objects and people) because they know their caregiver will be available to touch base with should the need arise. On the other hand, babies who are *insecurely attached,* those who have experienced parental rejection or inconsistency or care, tend to avoid peer relationships (Troy & Sroufe, 1987).

Babies who form *secure attachments* during their first year are described at age 3.5 as socially involved with their peers. Children who are *securely attached* tend to approach others with positive expectations more readily than do children who are *insecurely attached* (Ainsworth, 1979; Jacobson & Wille, 1986; Rubin, Bukowski, & Parker, 1998). They are often leaders proactively engaged in activities (Park & Waters, 1989). In contrast, a child who has experienced *insecure attachments* in which his or her needs were met insensitively or inconsistently may have negative expectations toward peers, acting as if peers will be rejecting (Howes, Matheson, & Hamilton, 1994). Such children may exhibit withdrawal or aggressive behavior (Rubin, Bukowski, & Parker, 1998).

After toddlerhood, a gradual shift occurs in the relative importance of adults and peers in children's lives. Children who attend preschool increasingly look to their peers for attention and decreasingly seek proximity to the caregivers (Hartup, 1983). This was demonstrated by Corsaro (1981) in a field study done in a preschool with children ranging in age from 2 years, 11 months to 4 years, 10 months. Field notes and videotapes showed that the children rarely engaged in solitary play and that when they found themselves alone, they consistently tried to gain entry into ongoing peer activities: "Can I play? I'll be your friend." Also, children who were involved in peer activities often protected the interaction by resisting children who attempted to gain access: "You can't play; you're not our friend." Thus, the more important peers become to the child, the more expansive are his or her social experiences.

Early Childhood (Age 2 to 5 or 6). Preschool children's social interactions are affected not only by how secure they feel in their attachment to their mothers but also by the willingness of adults to provide opportunities for social interaction (Ladd & LeSieur, 1995). For instance, where the family resides determines the number of same-aged children living nearby. The willingness of parents to invite other children to their home or to take their child to another's home, and whether or not a child attends a preschool program, affect the amount of social interaction that can take place.

Parenting style has been found to influence children's competence interacting with peers. *Authoritative* (democratic) parenting has been associated with children's social–behavioral competence and confidence (Baumrind, 1973). *Authoritarian* (adult-directed), *permissive* (child-directed), and *indifferent–uninvolved* parenting styles, in contrast, have been linked to low competence in social interaction (Ladd & LeSieur, 1995). It is likely that children model parental interactions with their friends.

Middle Childhood (Age 6 to 12 or 13). By school age, opportunities for social interaction increase. Children spend most of the day with other children—in class, on the school bus, and in the neighborhood. Children no longer need adults to structure their social interactions. In the middle years, children become more and more dependent upon the recognition and approval of their peers, rather than that of adults. Their sense of belonging extends and expands. Interestingly, however, it was found that children whose parents took an active role in arranging and organizing their peer relations (inviting specific children to the home, encouraging the child to participate in a school or community group, and discussing the child's friends and interactions) tended to develop closer, more harmonious ties with peers (Ladd & LeSieur, 1995).

Sense of Self and Personal Identity

The social influences contributing to the self-concept at various stages of development will be examined.

Infancy–Toddlerhood. Infants as young as 6 months look at, vocalize to, smile at, and touch other infants, thereby distinguishing themselves from others (Hay, 1985). As babies develop, relations with peers change, becoming more reciprocal. For example, at about a year, their smiles, vocalizations, and playful activities are often imitated or reacted to (Howes & Matheson, 1992). During the second year, toddlers use words to communicate and can coordinate their behavior with that of a playmate (Rubin, Bukowski, & Parker, 1998).

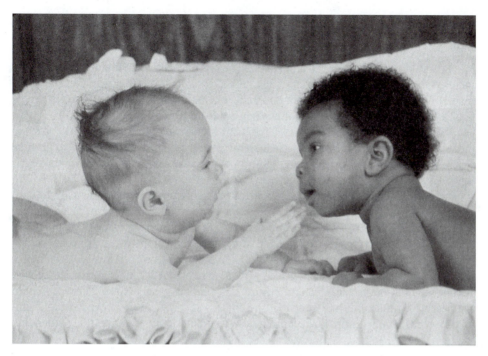

These babies are already interested in each other as distinct human beings.

Early Childhood. When children begin to play in groups, generally after age 2 or 3, they have a chance to play a variety of roles that were not available to them in the family context. Now they have to grapple with and work through issues of power, compliance, cooperation, and conflict (Kemple, 1991). Such issues contribute to the development of a sense of self and personal identity in that they give children the opportunity to be assertive regarding ownership and to negotiate regarding desires: "That's my puzzle; you can't play with it." "If you let me ride the bike, I'll let you hold my doll."

Middle Childhood. For the middle-years child (age 6 to 12 or 13), the peer group is attractive because it provides opportunities for greater independence than does the family, thereby enhancing the sense of self. Did you ever build a fort or a tree house when you were a child? The underlying idea, of course, was for the group to have a place of its own, where it could be independent of adult supervision and where unwanted children could be excluded.

In the peer group, children can say what they feel without being told, "You should not say things like that." Or they can make suggestions without being told, "You're too young to do that." Or they can do things without being told, "It will never work" (as an adult might say).

Middle-years children, especially toward preadolescence (age 11 to 13), long to find others like themselves; to know that others share their doubts, their fears, their wishes, and their perceptions. The peer group is an important source of self-confirmation in that children learn, by comparing their thoughts and feelings with those of others, that they are not really different or "weird." Thus belonging to a group clarifies personal identity and enhances self-esteem. The concern about acceptance in the peer group is often exhibited by gossip. Teasley and Parker (1995) found that much gossip among middle-years children is negative, involving defamation of third parties. Children like to discuss who are their friends and who are their enemies.

Peers also provide empathy and support for one another when children's desires for independent actions are in conflict with adults' demands: "My father won't let me touch his CD player! He's so mean!" "Can you believe Mrs. Millard made me clean the whole floor after school just because I shot one spit-wad? It's not fair!"

The peer group, in addition to clarifying and supporting one's identity, also provides models for what one can become. Peers show what is worth doing and how to do it. It was probably your friends who taught you how to dance and to like popular music, as well as influencing what style clothes you wore.

Achieving personal identity is a slow and difficult process during which children turn to their peers instead of their parents for certain kinds of support. However, entrance into the peer group creates some difficulties of its own (Grusec & Lytton, 1988). First, there is the change from protected to unprotected competition. At home, squabbles between children can be settled by adults; in the peer group one has to learn to protect oneself, whether it be getting to the swing first or not letting someone tease you. Second, the responses expected and rewarded at home and school are different than in the peer group. At home and at school the child is encouraged to be obedient and submissive. In the peer group, however, self-assertion and domination are the virtues that are rewarded.

Adolescence.   Adolescence (about age 13–18) is a time in our society when peer group activities escalate, one reason being that adolescents are not fully included in the adult world of responsibility and recognition for contributions. Therefore, they turn to peers. Adolescents often experience differences in the values of the family and those of the peer group. For example, academic achievement is an important value in some families whereas among some groups of adolescents, athletic performance seems to be more important (Steinberg, 1996). Normally, which values are adolescents more likely to adopt: their family's or their friends'? According to Hans Sebald (1989, 1992), adolescents turn to their parents in regard to scholastic or occupational goals—in general, *future-oriented decisions.* They turn to their friends in regard to clothing, social activities, dating, or recreation—in general, *present-oriented decisions.* On *moral issues,* parental values dominate; on *appearance,* such as grooming, peer values dominate (Niles, 1981).

Parenting styles (described in Chapter 4) have been found to be associated with adult versus peer influence. Parents, as was discussed, do influence with whom their children interact. The following findings link child–parent relationships to child–peer relationships.

- *Authoritative* parents, who are warm, accepting, neither too controlling nor too lax, and consistent in their child rearing management, generally have children who are attached and internalize their values. These children have little need to rebel or to desperately seek acceptance from peers (Fuligni & Eccles, 1993). They usually associate with friends who share their values, so they are not faced with negative peer influences (Fletcher, Darling, Steinberg, & Dornsbuch 1995).

- *Authoritarian* parents, who are very strict, cold, and do not adjust to their adolescent's need for greater autonomy, typically have children who alienate themselves from parental values and are attracted to the peer group to gain understanding and acceptance (Fuligni & Eccles, 1993). These adolescents are at risk for negative peer influences.

- *Permissive* parents, who indulge their children by not providing standards, rules, or behavioral consequences and/or who ignore their children's activities, typically risk having adolescents who are attracted to antisocial peer groups (Dishion, Patterson, Stoolmiller, & Skinner, 1991).

Do these generalizations relating parenting styles to peer group attraction apply to diverse ethnic groups? This is a question still being researched. It is known that some ethnic groups place more emphasis on interdependence and social support networks than do Anglos, who tend to emphasize independence and individuality (Greenfield & Suzuki, 1998). Social support networks include extended family members as well as friends. This was documented in a field observation study by Hutchison (1987) that took place in public parks in Chicago and included 18,000 groups engaged in various leisure activities. In general, Anglos engaged in more individualized activities, Hispanics engaged in the most family–peer combined activities, and Blacks engaged in the most peer-oriented activities.

Thus the significance of peer group attraction may differ according to ethnic origin. Peer groups may provide connection to the community and positive social support regardless of parenting style; or because of the peer group's attractiveness, the peer group may become a negative influence on values and behavior.

To conclude, in achieving a personal identity, a major task for the child is to be able to balance group identification with personal autonomy while forging a personal role within the group. To participate in the activities of the group requires developing the skills for its games, as well as mastering the rules and agreements that govern its activities. In reaching a balance between group identification and personal autonomy, children must weigh loyalty to group norms against personal norms and parental norms. They must develop their roles in the group structure (leading or following, for example) and must cope with feelings of being accepted, popular, unpopular, or rejected (Grusec & Lytton, 1988; Minuchin, 1977; Rubin, Bukowski, & Parker, 1998). Thus the peer group contributes to a sense of self.

How Peers Influence Development

Humans who do not have normal peer relations are affected in their later emotional development. The long-term effects of prior peer relations during childhood have been studied (Asher & Coie, 1990; Hartup, 1983; Rubin, Bukowski, & Parker, 1998) and have indicated that poor peer relations in childhood are linked to the later development of neurotic and psychotic behavior and to a greater tendency to drop out of school. Psychologists actually find that sociometric measures (measures of patterns of attraction and rejection among members of a group, discussed later in the chapter), taken in the elementary grades predict adjustment in later life better than other educational or personality tests: "The child's peer group seems to be a sensitive barometer of current and future adjustment problems" (Asher, 1982; Hymel, Bowker, & Woody, 1993; Parker & Asher, 1987). Why is this so? One's ability to deal with the social world requires communicative skills, a repertoire for coordinating one's actions with those of others, reciprocity, cooperation, and competition. These competencies develop via interactions and experiences in the peer group. In addition, peer groups have certain norms for behavior, sometimes positive (cooperation, for example) and sometimes negative (exclusion of some children or rebelliousness, for example). Children learn to compete for status in the peer group by compliance with group norms (*"followership"*) and creation of group norms (*leadership*) at appropriate times.

The social interactions with peers contribute to the child's cognitive understanding of his or her culture. Collaboration with peers through language and play enables the child to construct thoughts (Berk & Winsler, 1995).

SOCIAL BEHAVIOR

Social development involves behavior that is influenced by the understanding of others' feelings and intentions, the ability to respond appropriately, and the knowledge of consequences of one's actions. Being part of a social group involves conforming to group norms. The degree of social conformity that an individual exhibits depends on age, situation, stage of cognitive development, and psychological factors.

Studies (Berndt, 1979; Brown, Clasen, & Eicher, 1986; Foster-Clark & Blyth, 1991) show that children become most susceptible to the influence of peers in middle childhood and become less conforming in adolescence.

Even when it is known to be wrong, middle-years children still go along with the majority opinion of the group (Berenda, 1950). In a classic study, 90 children age 7 to 13 were asked to compare the lengths of lines on 12 pairs of cards. They had already taken this same test in school. This time, however, the children participating in the experiment were tested in a room with the eight brightest children in their class. Answers were given aloud. These eight children had been instructed beforehand to give 7 wrong answers out of 12. The results pointed to the power of group influence. Whereas almost all the subjects had given correct answers to the seven critical questions in the original test taken in school, only 43% of the 7- to 10-year-olds, and only 54% of the 10- to 13-year-olds gave correct answers on the second test in the group setting. The rest changed their former answers to match the group's, which were intentionally incorrect.

Such conformity is even more apparent in ambiguous situations where children are unsure about what they should do or are supposed to do (Cohen, Bornstein, & Sherman, 1973; Hartup, 1983; Steinberg, 1996). For example, Thomas Berndt (1979; Berndt & Ludd, 1989) gave a questionnaire to students ranging from third to twelfth grade, asking how they would respond to various hypothetical situations (*prosocial, neutral, antisocial*). A question exemplifying a *prosocial* situation asked the students whether they would help a classmate with a report if asked by their peers, instead of doing what they wanted to do, which was helping another classmate operate the film projector. A question exemplifying a *neutral* situation asked the students whether they would go to a movie if asked by their peers, even if they were not particularly interested in that movie. A question exemplifying an *antisocial* situation asked the students whether they would steal some candy if a peer wanted help in doing it.

One of Berndt's (1979) findings was that conformity to antisocial behavior and neutral situations peaked in the ninth grade and then dropped off to previous levels. Another finding was that conformity to prosocial behavior peaked in the sixth grade and then

Figure 8.2   Conformity Peaks

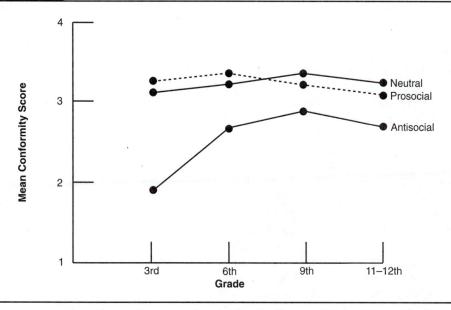

Prosocial conformity peaks at sixth grade, whereas antisocial conformity peaks at ninth grade.

Source: T. J. Berndt (1979). Developmental changes in conformity to peers and parents. *Developmental Psychology, 15,* 608–616. Copyright © 1979 by the American Psychological Association. Reprinted by permission.

dropped. In general, the sixth- to ninth-graders exhibited the most conforming behavior. The results are plotted in Figure 8.2.

Berndt also found that whether or not people conformed to the group depended upon the particular situation—how "good" or "bad" they felt about it. Students were more likely to conform to situations they did not feel very "bad" about. Thus personal standards do affect one's likelihood of conforming to the peer group.

According to Harris (1995), children not only learn the importance of conforming to be accepted by the peer group, they also learn the dynamics of power, manipulation, and popularity. They learn how to compete for status within the group by combining "leadership" and "followership" skills (Adler & Adler, 1998). Thus conformity exhibited at a given time may depend on whether the child is leading or following.

SOCIAL COGNITION

On the basis of these studies, it can be seen that the peer group becomes an increasingly powerful socializing agent during the period of development between early childhood (age 2 to 5) and preadolescence (about age 11 to 13). Why are children age 11 to 13 more susceptible to peer group influences than children of other ages?

Even though children interact with one another increasingly from infancy on, the ability to cope with complex social messages increases with age. For example, children under age 7 do not have the cognitive ability even to be aware of peer pressure to conform or the consequences for deviance. They have difficulty taking another's point of view and cannot therefore project what the peer group thinks of them. Much documentation has been accumulating regarding the connection between social development and cognitive development. This connection is referred to as **social cognition;** the conceptions and reasoning about people, the self, relations between people, social groups, roles, and rules, and the relation of such conceptions to social behavior (Shantz, 1983).

Young children between ages 7 and 11 are in the stage of cognitive development that Jean Piaget (1952) termed the "stage of concrete operations." The concrete operational stage is characterized by the ability to apply logical, systematic principles to help interpret specific experiences but also by the inability to distinguish between assumptions, or hypotheses, and facts, or reality.

According to David Elkind (1981a), concrete-operational children make assumptions about situations and people that they are convinced are real and true ("assumptive realities"), no matter how illogical they are. For example, U.S. children of this age who have seen a globe at school might try to dig a hole in the ground to get to China, because China is on the other side of the globe (I used to do this at the beach). No amount of adult logic in terms of distances can dissuade them. In regard to people, concrete-operational children assume they are clever. David Elkind calls this "**cognitive conceit,**" the exhibition of too much faith in one's reasoning ability. The concept of cognitive conceit is illustrated in some favorite stories of children of this age—for example, *Peter Pan* (a child who outwits Captain Hook, an adult) or *Alice in Wonderland* (a young girl who makes the queen look like a fool).

Because children under age 11 often think they know it all, they sometimes feel they do not have to pay attention to the opinions of others, be they adults or other children. "I don't have to" (a common remark at this age), then, is not really defiance but a statement about concrete-operational children's beliefs about their abilities (1952).

About age 11, children become capable of logical thought. Piaget called this the "stage of formal operations." It is characterized by the ability to think logically about abstract ideas and hypotheses as well as concrete facts; one can now construct all the possibilities of a proposition—the ones related to fact and the ones contrary to fact. Preadolescent children, then, can conceptualize their own thoughts and discover the arbitrariness of their assumptions. They also discover rules for testing assumptions against facts ("reality testing"). This leads to diminished confidence in their ability, especially their cleverness. Preadolescent children are aware of the reactions of others and the need to conform to their expectations. This new awareness exhibits itself in the **imaginary audience**—the belief that others are as concerned with one's behavior and appearance as one is oneself. Thus preadolescent children believe they are the focus of attention. Because of this, they strive extra hard to be like their peers so that they will not stand out.

As preadolescent children approach adolescence (about age 13 to 15), the imaginary audience comes to be regarded as an assumption to be tested against reality. As a consequence of this testing, adolescents gradually come to recognize the difference between their own preoccupations and the interests and concerns of others. Therefore, conformity decreases because adolescents realize they are expected to conform to some situations, but can be independent in others. Adolescents have also developed greater social skills and a greater reliance on their own judgment.

One reason preadolescent children are more conforming than other age groups is that their level of cognitive development is capable of logical thought; that is, they can project how others react and evaluate their assumptions. However, they have not yet had the experience of testing their assumptions on reality, for example:

When my daughter began junior high school, she refused to take the backpack I had bought her for her books. She said, "All the kids will laugh at me; only kids in elementary school use backpacks." I asked her what the junior high kids used to carry their books. Exhibiting preadolescent assumptions, she did not know exactly (she had not been there yet), but she thought they used satchels. For the first week of school, she carried her books loosely in her arms. When the second week of school came, she grudgingly put her books in the backpack, saying she was tired of dropping books and that her arms ached. One day after school had been in session for about a month, I picked up my daughter at school. I noticed that a lot of kids had backpacks. I said nothing, but I thought to myself, "She assumed all the other kids would have satchels and she didn't want to be different. She had to make sure that enough other kids had backpacks before she would take hers to school." Can you remember being reluctant to do something before you saw others do it? What were your concerns?

Psychosocial Development

Another reason preadolescent children are more conforming than other age groups is that they are entering Erikson's (1963) fifth psychosocial stage of development—*Identity versus Identity (Role) Confusion* (Who am I, and what is my role in life?). Erikson's stages were discussed in Chapter 2. In the process of finding an identity, preadolescent children repeat the crises of the earlier stages—*Basic Trust versus Basic Mistrust* (Do I generally trust people, or distrust them?); *Autonomy versus Shame and Doubt* (Am I confident I can be independent, or am I doubtful about my ability to be independent?); *Initiative versus Guilt* (Do I feel good about starting new things or meeting new people, or do I feel guilty?); and *Industry versus Inferiority* (Do I feel competent about my abilities, or inferior?).

> The growing and developing youths, faced with this psychological revolution within them, and with tangible adult tasks ahead of them, are now primarily concerned with what they appear to be in the eyes of others as compared with what they feel they are (Erikson, 1963, p. 261).

They are trying out roles and using the reactions of others to judge how well the roles fit their self-concept. Thus, in the process of wondering "Who am I?" children beginning this psychosocial stage of development tend to "temporarily overidentify to the point of apparent complete loss of identity, with heroes of cliques and crowds" (Erikson, 1963, p. 262).

Erikson explains the clannishness and cruelty of excluding those who are different from the group as a defense against a sense of identity confusion. Preadolescent children who are on the brink of entering the identity-versus-role-confusion stage look to the peer group for their identity. The group's symbols and rituals (ways of dressing, ways of behaving, attitudes, opinions), as well as its approval and support, help define what is good and what is bad, thereby contributing to the development of ego identity. Identifying with a group and excluding those who are not like the members of the group helps children identify who they are by affirming who they are not. As preadolescence gives way to adolescence, young people begin to derive an identity from the accumulation of their experiences, their abilities, and their goals. They begin to look within themselves rather than to others for who they are. The peer group, then, serves to mediate between the individual and society playing a powerful role in shaping the individual's identity (Adler & Adler, 1998).

Peer Group Socializing Mechanisms

The socializing mechanisms that peers employ to influence one another's behavior are reinforcement or approval and acceptance, modeling or imitation, punishment or rejection and exclusion, and apprenticeship (novice learns from expert).

Reinforcement.   One important way in which children influence each other is through reinforcement, or giving attention. Approving another's behavior (smiling, laughing, patting, hugging, verbalizing praise) increases the likelihood of that behavior recurring. The behavior could be sharing, or it could be aggression against another (Martin & Pear, 1996). Reinforcement also involves acceptance into the group. Criteria for acceptance will be discussed later.

That reinforcement increases behavior rather than the degree of friendship was demonstrated in a study in which young children age 4 and 5 performed better at simple tasks when a child they disliked praised their performance than when a child they liked did so (Hartup, 1964, 1983).

Sometimes reinforcement is unintentional but it is still effective. To illustrate, a study (Patterson, Littman, & Bricker, 1976) showed that some preschool children reacted to physical aggression (bullying) by becoming passive, assuming a defensive posture, crying, telling the teacher, retrieving their property, or retaliating with aggression. When the aggression was responded to with reinforcers such as passiveness, defensiveness, or crying, the aggression tended to be repeated on the same victim. When the aggression was responded to with proactive behavior such as telling the teacher, retrieving property, or counteraggression, the aggressor or bully tended to behave differently toward the former victim. Unintentional passivity to aggression, then, generally reinforces it toward the victim; action serves to redirect the aggression away from the victim.

To determine whether certain social stimuli functioned as reinforcers, Furman and Masters (1980) observed and recorded rates of laughter and praise (positive reinforcers); crying, physical attack, and disapproval (negative reinforcers); and other expressions (neutral reinforcers) in preschool children. They found that behaviors classified as positive reinforcements were twice as likely to be followed by similar affective behaviors, whereas punitive acts were more than five times as likely to be succeeded by negative behaviors. Parents and teachers need to be alert to patterns of peer reinforcement so that peers can be used effectively to help change negative or disruptive behavior. Some studies follow that illustrate how this can be done.

Modeling.   Children also influence each other through modeling, or imitation. Modeling is related to conformity, previously discussed. Observing a child behave in a certain manner can affect another's consequent behavior in three different ways (Bandura, 1977, 1989):

1. The observing child may learn how to do something new that previously could not be done (such as drawing a picture of a dog) or that would probably not have been thought of (such as riding a bike with "no hands").

2. The child may learn the consequences of behavior by observing someone else. For example, pinching another results in being punished by the teacher, or getting to the swings first results in getting the longest turn.

3. A model may suggest how a child can behave in a new situation. For example, when the children lined up at the edge of the pool for their first dive, Maureen was first. She said, "I can do it. I've watched my brother hundreds of times." As the instructor was showing her how to hold her arms and keep her head down, the others watched nervously. In a second, she hit the water, and in another few seconds she popped up smiling. The others relaxed.

In a classic study by Bandura, Ross, and Ross (1965), children who were shown a film in which a model struck a doll, sat on it, and screamed at it later copied the model's aggressive behavior when given a similar doll to play with. Other researchers (Hartup,

This child is intent on modeling her friend.

1983; Hartup & Coates, 1967) studied a group of 4- and 5-year-old children who were asked to watch one of their classmates work out problems. The classmate, the model, received some trinkets for doing the task. This model put aside some of the trinkets for a mythical child. The children who watched were then asked to do the problems, and the model left the room. They were also given trinkets and were also given the opportunity to save some trinkets for "the other child." Another group of 4- and 5-year-olds, who did not watch a model do the problems and exhibit altruistic behavior, were asked to do the same problems, were given trinkets, and were given the opportunity to save some for "the other child." The children who observed altruistic behavior gave more trinkets than those who did not.

Modeling does influence behavior; the extent sometimes depends on the situation. Active behavior is more likely to be imitated than passive behavior. The extent of the influence also depends on the observer's perception of the model. A model who is similar to the observer and has desirable or admirable traits is more likely to be imitated than one who is not very similar to the observer or who has traits not particularly desirable to the observer. The observer's ability to produce the observed behavior also influences modeling (Bandura, 1977, 1989).

Studying children in preschool classes has shown that a great deal of imitation, some positive and some negative, of both verbal and motor acts occurs in day-by-day interactions (Abramovitch & Grusec, 1978). Imitation seems to decrease from preschool to age 10, perhaps because deferred, rather than immediate, imitation and other subtle forms of observational learning become more favored as children get older. Dominant children in a group are imitated more often by the others, but they imitate the others as well (Grusec & Lytton, 1988).

Modeling, as a socializing method compared to reinforcement, has broader effects. A large number of children can be influenced by one carefully selected model, whereas direct reinforcement requires one-to-one interaction between the teacher and the learner. Modeling can provide a means of inducing behavior that otherwise might not occur. It may give the child an idea for doing something never done before, or it may remind the child of something done before and induce the child to repeat it (Bandura, 1989). Using reinforcement as a behavior modification technique requires waiting for the behavior to appear and then reinforcing it (Martin & Pear, 1996).

Punishment. Still another way in which children influence each other is through punishment—teasing, physical aggression, or rejection by the group. Criteria for rejection will be discussed later. An extreme of such punishment is being a victim of bullying. Victims are usually withdrawn, passive, shy, insecure, and have difficulty asserting themselves in a group. Bullies are usually dominant, aggressive, impulsive, angry, and have a low frustration tolerance. Bullying and victimization require adult intervention strategies to be discussed later (Crick, Casas, & Ku, 1999; Olweus, 1993).

Sometimes children are rejected or punished by peers because of physical characteristics (being overweight, for example) or behavioral characteristics (bragging, dominating, or criticizing, for example) (Adler & Adler, 1998; Coie, Dodge, & Kupersmidt, 1990; Parkhurst & Asher, 1992). The consequence of being punished by exclusion and teasing by the peer group are described in the box "Peers, Power, Pecking Order, and Punishment."

Peers, Power, Pecking Order, and Punishment

Peer groups in schools are manifested in the formation of cliques—friends who view themselves as mutually connected. Cliques are a significant contributor to children's and adolescents' quests for identity.

In elementary school, cliques are hierarchical friendship groups based on popularity and prestige. By the time children reach high school, the clique social hierarchy is stratified. Typically, one finds "jocks," "preppies," or "populars"; "brains," or "nerds"; and "unpopulars" (Eder, 1995). High school social life was popularized in the media by the TV show *Beverly Hills, 90210*. By interacting within and between friendship groups children learn what kind of social competence they possess. The high status clique is the "populars"; below them are the "wannabes" (the group that hangs around hoping for inclusion); next are smaller, independent groups; and at the bottom of the social hierarchy are the "social isolates" (those who only occasionally find playmates) (Adler & Adler, 1998).

Cliques are dominated by leaders. They are exclusive in nature, so that not all individuals who desire membership are accepted. The critical way that cliques maintain exclusivity is through careful membership screening. Acceptance or rejection of potential new members is linked to the power of the leaders. Leaders derive their power through popularity and use it to make decisions and influence social stratification (pecking order) within the group (Adler & Adler, 1998).

In their observations of preadolescents in school, Adler and Adler (1998, p. 76) found that the popular clique "set the tone for, and in many ways influenced, the behavior of the entire grade." Maintaining membership took a concerted effort of conforming to desires of the leaders. The exclusivity of membership was a reward for those who were "in" and a punishment for those who were "out." The "wannabes" tried to be "cool" by imitating the "populars"—their clothing, hairstyles, buying the same music, and using the same vocabulary (Eder, 1995). Their conforming behavior is reinforced because, occasionally, they are invited to participate in clique activities even though they are not fully accepted into the group.

Those who are "out," the "social isolates" (the "loners," "drifters," "dweebs," "nerds"), are excluded because they are different in some way—appearance, behavior, and/or language. Those who are "in" or the "wannabes" treat them poorly by teasing and laughing at them. It is as though everyone in the pecking order offsets his or her own insecurities by humiliating the individuals who are lower in status (Thorne, 1993). The exclusion of the "social isolates" from nearly all cliques' social activities coupled with the extreme degradation they suffer takes a heavy toll on their feelings of self-worth.

The significance of these findings from peer group studies was manifested in 1999 at Columbine High School in Littleton, Colorado, where two social isolates, Harris and Klebold, shot and killed 12 students and a teacher, as well as themselves. Interviews with students and community members pointed to the injustice and harassment done to Harris and Klebold by the "jocks," combined with their disengagement from caring adults (Wilson & Mishra, 1999). That such rage was acted out when cliques and cruelty have been around for years in children's groups, poses a disturbing question. In 1961, James Coleman studied 11 high schools of varied socioeconomic statuses and found similar peer group stratification, similar values (athletes having the highest prestige; brains and unpopulars, the lowest), and similar behavior. The adolescents in his study seemed to accept things as "normal" for high school life; so why did the Columbine tragedy occur?

Apprenticeship.   Throughout this chapter, references have been made to the influences of peers, such as in having introduced you to rock music, having taught you to dance, or having "educated" you about sex. The concept intended by such references was of someone with more expertise helping someone with less, as in an apprenticeship. The concept of apprenticeship as a method of socialization was discussed in Chapter 2. Traditionally, the word *apprenticeship* has been used in the world of work—a novice becomes an apprentice under a master until he or she learns a trade well enough to succeed alone.

Lev Vygotsky (1978) postulated that a more knowledgeable person, such as a teacher or an expert peer, initially guides the learner's, or novice's, activity. Gradually, the two begin to share the problem-solving functions, with the novice taking the initiative and the expert peer correcting and guiding when the novice falters. Finally, the expert peer cedes control and acts as a supportive audience.

An illustration of Vygotsky's hypothesis might be your learning how to ride a two-wheeler bike from a friend who had mastered the skill. Your friend shows you how to get on the bike, how to balance, how to pedal, and how to stop. You get on the bike while your friend supports it. Your friend holds on while you pedal. After many falls, you can finally balance and pedal at the same time, so your friend lets go (but runs after you yelling instructions on how to stop).

Vygotsky believed that engaging in such apprenticeship activities advances the novice's level of development. Vygotsky suggested that a novice's boundaries lie between (1) his or her actual development, or what he or she can do independently; and (2) his or her potential development, or what he or she can do while participating with more capable others.

For example, my husband has a talent for drawing. I persuaded him to take an art class to develop his ability further. The students in the class submitted their drawings every week for peer review and would get suggestions for improvement while the instructor served as a moderator. At the end of the course, my husband's drawings were significantly more elaborate and sophisticated than when he began the class. Peer review is a technique also used in other classes, such as writing or speech.

Vygotsky, as was discussed in Chapter 2, calls the space between the learner's two boundaries the *zone of proximal development (ZPD)*. Schools are implementing the concept of ZPD in cooperative goal structures (discussed in Chapter 6) peer collaboration, conflict resolution, peer tutoring, and peer counseling. Peer groups provide apprenticeships for learning many things; these, as was said, can be positive or negative.

FUNCTIONS OF THE PEER GROUP

The peer group provides the setting and the means for children to achieve some of the developmental tasks of early and middle childhood (Duvall & Miller, 1985; Havighurst, 1972; Zarbatany, Hartmann, & Rankin, 1990), especially social competence: getting along with others, developing morals and values, learning appropriate social and cultural roles, and achieving personal independence (Rubin, Bukowski, & Parker, 1998). Developmental tasks were discussed in Chapter 2.

GETTING ALONG WITH OTHERS

Playing with children of the same age is a vehicle for socializing the capacity to "get along" by learning to give and take. Getting along involves recognition of the rights of others. The peer group provides children with opportunities for understanding the limitations that group life places upon the individual: "At my house I can play with my Legos all I want, but at preschool I have to share." "When I'm with my friends, I can't always have my way. We talk about what we're going to do on Sunday, trying to please everyone. If Barbara, Joan, and Carol want to go shopping and I don't, the group tells me if I come with them, they'll stop by my favorite ice-cream place on the way home. Even though I don't get my way, I get the feeling I'm wanted and that the group is trying to please me. I agree to go shopping."

The ability to get along is developmentally progressive in that it involves both seeing things from another's perspective and verbal communication (Grusec & Lytton, 1988). It depends then on increasing cognitive abilities as well as social experiences. Some studies (Clarke-Stewart, 1992; Lamb, 1998) have shown that young children who are in child-care centers are more socially competent than those who are cared for at home but are also more aggressive. It is likely that these children learn early how to "stick up" for themselves and compete for toys.

DEVELOPING MORALS AND VALUES

The development of **morals** (distinguishing right from wrong) and **values** (determining what is worthwhile) occurs in a social setting. By interacting with others, the child comes to know what is and what is not acceptable behavior. Children usually learn morals and values from parents and other adults via instruction, reasoning, modeling, reinforcement, and punishment. Children usually learn morals and values from peers by real experiences (learning by doing).

Most studies of the development of morals and values involve school-age children and adolescents who are capable of articulating judgments about hypothetical dilemmas, as will be discussed in Chapter 11. However, research by Judy Dunn (1988) on the beginnings of social understanding, which is the cornerstone of moral development, has shown that from 18 months on, children understand how to hurt, comfort, or exacerbate another's pain. They also understand the consequences of their hurtful actions toward others in their own environment, as well as being able to anticipate the response of adults to their own and to others' misdeeds. Preschoolers enter the peer group setting with a rudimentary understanding of social rules influenced by their family context. As children develop, peer group experiences expand this understanding (Rubin, Bukowski, & Parker, 1998).

Understanding rules is part of moral development in that both involve formulation of rules, rule-following, cooperation, limit-setting, division of roles, and territoriality: "Consciousness of rules cannot be isolated from the moral life of the child as a whole" (Piaget, 1965, p. 50). Rules are related to morals in that both have to do with established guides for conduct. In the peer group, common rules based on common experience begin to develop. These rules may be devised to meet a specific situation; they may be copied from adults' rules or those of older children. Between age 3 and 7, children sometimes observe the rules of the group and sometimes not. Even when playing together, children of this age play "each one on his own" (Piaget, 1965, p. 27)—everyone has his or her own views of the way the game is played—without any real regard for the codification of the rules.

Between age 7 and 8, children "begin to concern themselves with the question of mutual control and of unification of the rules" (Piaget, 1965, p. 27), even though their understanding of the rules may be rather vague. Between age 11 and 12, children fix the rules in their groups; everyone in the group understands and observes them. For example, in the game of Four Square, whoever misses the ball is out. Everyone knows that rule. However, some groups will make rules regarding how the ball is returned, like "no babies." A "baby" is a ball bounced so lightly that it barely comes off the ground and, therefore, is almost impossible to get. Thus, if a child wants to belong to the group, the rules must be respected and obeyed. If "babies" are not allowed, one cannot use them if one wants to continue to play with the group. Learning the conditions attached to belonging to the group, then, is the way children are socialized as to the requirements for participation. It is also a way in which children develop morality.

Piaget (1965) contrasts two types of morality. One type, *heteronomous morality* or **morality of constraint,** consists of behavior based on respect for persons in authority. It is imposed by a prestigeful and powerful source, usually the parent or another adult. This type of morality fosters the ideal that to obey the will of the authority is good; to obey one's own will is bad. Such morality is fostered in the family and in school. The other type, *autonomous*

In game-playing, children's moral development is influenced through practicing such activities as rule-following, cooperation, and limit-setting.

morality or **morality of cooperation,** consists of behavior based on mutual understanding between equals. It involves the acceptance of rules because they are necessary for continuance of group life. If one wants to participate in the group, one freely accepts the rules, and these rules are imposed upon oneself by oneself. This type of morality emerges from the mutual respect of the children in the group. Thus peer group participation—participation among equals—helps foster *morality of cooperation,* whereas *morality of constraint* is more likely to be fostered in authoritarian, adult-dominated situations, such as in the family or school.

In our society, we must obey certain rules because they were imposed by an authority, whether or not we agree (draft registration, for example). We also impose certain rules upon ourselves for the benefit of group life (compromise with a neighbor regarding the property line, for example). To participate effectively in society, then, children need both types of morality training. To exemplify, studies (Devereaux, 1970; Ladd & LeSieur, 1995) have shown that children who came from homes with moderate to high levels of discipline and control and who had a great deal of peer group experience were autonomous and had strong moral character. On the other hand, children who came from homes characterized by high permissiveness or high punitiveness and who had a great deal of peer group experience were "peer conformists" or "chameleons." Studies on parenting styles, discussed in Chapter 4, also showed that authoritative parents were more likely to have children who exhibited independence and social competence (Baumrind, 1973; Ladd & LeSieur, 1995).

It would seem, then, that the peer group helps children in the *process* of developing morals, whereas the level of moral development is greatly influenced by parenting styles. Recent research (Bogenschneider, Wu, Raffaeli, & Tsay, 1998) documents the importance of contingent linkages between parents and peers in moral behavior.

LEARNING APPROPRIATE SOCIOCULTURAL ROLES

While the family imparts sociocultural roles, such as *independence* and *interdependence,* the peer group gives the child opportunities to try out roles learned at home (Greenfield & Suzuki, 1998). The child gains an understanding of the individual's responsibility in a group situation. For example: Does one exercise *autonomy* and respect peers' right to free choice ("I want to play Scrabble, what game do you want to play?"); or does one exercise *empathy,* anticipating the desires of peers ("I know you like to play Chess, so let's play.")? Does one communicate in a *direct, assertive* manner ("I want to try your new bike.") or in an *indirect, passive* manner ("That's a nice new bike you got.")? Does one *compete* with peers for *individual* recognition or *cooperate* with peers for *group* recognition? Does one *confront* conflict or *avoid* it?

An example of how appropriate sociocultural roles are learned can be seen when children who have never had to share things at home or who have never had to take turns learn to do so in the peer group or else be excluded. From the peer group, children receive feedback about their behavior and skills. Your peers will not hesitate to tell you when you are acting dumb. Children not only learn the sociocultural roles of cooperation and appropriate behavior from each other, they also learn how to compete. They evaluate their skills in terms of whether they can do better than, as well as, or worse than others in the group. They also learn methods of conflict resolution. An example of cultural conflicts is when children have been socialized by their families to emphasize

By everyone doing the same activity under the teacher's direction these children learn regimentation and social control.

cooperation in the group or on a team with children who have been socialized to emphasize competition. "Two immigrant Latina players talk about wanting the team to work as a unit. They complain that the Euro American girls just want themselves to look good sometimes even at the expense of the team's performance" (Greenfield & Sukuki, 1998, p. 1091).

The box, "Development of Sociocultural Roles through the Peer Group" illustrates how societal values influence what is considered appropriate for young children's sociocultural roles. Gender role is another example of a societal sociocultural role that the peer group helps teach children. Children learn from their peers what is culturally acceptable and admirable for both boys and girls (Best, 1983; Pitcher & Schultz, 1983; Thorne, 1993). For example, Jerry, age 4, wanted to join a group of girls who were playing with their dolls. Jerry had a doll at home that he bathed and dressed while his mother or father bathed his baby sister. When Jerry approached the girls, they said, "Boys don't play with dolls!" Peer pressure for *appropriate* gender-type play has been observed to begin as early as age 2 (Fagot, 1985; Maccoby, 1990).

Peer groups generally segregate boys and girls beginning in preschool (Maccoby, 1990). In the preschool years, girls become interested in small group games in small spaces, games that allow them to practice and refine social rules and roles (for example, playing in the house corner). Boys engage in larger group games that are more physically active and wide-ranging. These games tend to have a more extensive set of explicit rules that involve reaching a defined goal. The games tend to be competitive (for example, the "good guys against the bad guys," in the form of Batman or Darth Vader, with the goal being "to save the world"). Thus segregated peer group play leads to different outcomes for boys and girls in achievement motivations, personal relationships, and self-concepts (Dweck, 1981). Gender roles will be discussed in more detail in Chapter 12.

Sex Education and Sexual Activity

The peer group is often the imparter of sex education. Children and adolescents share their knowledge with each other—knowledge they may have gained from their families, from the media, from school, or from friends. With their limited cognitive ability, they often have an incomplete understanding of sexual behavior, which, combined with their friends' incomplete understanding, distorts the total picture of sex.

Observations of elementary school-age children in the United States demonstrate

Development of Sociocultural Roles Through the Peer Group

The peer group can provide a mechanism whereby the socialization goals of the macrosystem are implemented. How three countries shape their children were studied by observing and comparing 4-year-olds in Chinese, Japanese, and American preschools. It was found that these countries viewed preschools as agents that preserve certain traditional cultural values even in times of social change (Tobin, Wu, & Davidson, 1989).

In China, a collective society valuing interdependence, social change has caused the government to mandate only one child be born to a nuclear family. Therefore, preschools are expected to provide experiences with peers that will counter the undivided attention that the only child gets from parents and grandparents.

In Japan, a society that values fitting in and working cooperatively with others, Japanese parents believe that preschools enable their children to learn this traditional value by functioning in a large group. Social change in Japan has resulted in shrinking birthrates and movement of young people away from their extended families. When families were large and many relatives lived close by, Japanese children could learn social skills in their families and identify with members of a group; now the preschool has become the vehicle.

In the United States, a society valuing independence and individuality, social change has evidenced itself in family mobility, employment of mothers, and the growth of single-parent families. Parents have turned to preschools to provide stability, enrichment, and guidance for children.

Based on interviews with teachers, administrators, parents, and child development specialists, preschools in all three cultures stressed the importance of learning to cooperate and be a member of a group. In addition, Chinese preschools especially valued learning citizenship, discipline, and perseverance. Japanese preschools especially valued learning sympathy, empathy, and concern for others. American preschools especially valued learning self-reliance and self-confidence.

Chinese children are taught citizenship via regimentation and orderly conduct. The role of the preschool is to instill values of self-control, discipline, cooperation, and responsibility. Children do the same activities at the same time under the direction of the teacher, whether it be calisthenics, singing, or building with blocks. The children copy what the teacher does; no talking is permitted. The children line up to go to the bathroom at a specified time. Children are taught to regulate bodily functions to synchronize with the group. Sociocultural roles of interdependence, order, and conformity are thereby reinforced.

Whereas Chinese preschools maintain order by direct adult control, Japanese preschools seek to maintain order by relying on the peer group to deal with disputes and misbehavior. The children arrive at school and play with their friends until the "clean-up" song. They are led by the teacher in group exercises. Once seated at their tables, the children begin a workbook project. The teacher makes no attempt to stop the talking, laughing, or even playful fighting that occurs. After their work, there is free play and then lunch. A little girl tells the teacher about a particularly raucous boy, but the teacher just encourages her to go deal with the problem herself. Eventually, the fighting ceases, and the children listen to a song before settling down to rest. Thus the Japanese child's preschool experience involves learning to enjoy ties to peers, to transfer the warmth of the parent–child relations to other relationships, and to learn to balance informality with formality, emotion with control, and family with society. Sociocultural roles of interdependence and harmony are thereby reinforced.

American children generally experience much freedom of choice and expression at preschool. The preschool is expected to make young children more independent and self-reliant. Its function is to promote individuality, autonomy, problem-solving, cognitive development, and friendship in children. Whereas Chinese preschools instill discipline primarily by regimentation, modeling appropriate behavior, criticism, and praise, and Japanese preschools instill it by fostering a sense of concern for the group, American preschools instill discipline by fostering a sense of individual rights.

The American children observed began their day with free play until all the children arrived. The teacher then gathered everyone together for "show and tell," thereby encouraging individual expression. After a flannel-board story and a song, the children were told they could choose to go to any of the several learning centers set up for that day. The learning centers consisted of an art project, the housekeeping corner, blocks, books, manipulative toys, a cooking center, and water play. The children moved about freely. The teachers assisted the children in the learning activities. A disruptive child was told by the teacher that his actions may have caused another child to get hurt and was told to sit in the "time-out" chair to think about what he had done. Sociocultural roles of independence and individual rights are thereby reinforced.

Thus, the peer group in preschool settings serves as a vehicle by which children learn certain cultural values. In China, children learn to conform to the group by the teacher structuring the activities accordingly, criticizing those who don't conform, and praising those who do. In Japan, children learn to get along in the peer group by the teacher's encouragement and noninterference. In the United States, children learn to respect other children's rights by the teacher interceding in conflicts, explaining why they are hurtful or unsafe and providing a consequence (Tobin, Wu, & Davidson, 1989).

that girls and boys are very aware of the opposite gender (Best, 1983; Thorne, 1993). Children continually talk about who "loves" whom and who is "cute." As preparation for later heterosexual relations, children play chase-and-kiss games. Usually, the girls try to catch the boys and kiss them, pronouncing they have "cooties." The others who watch will engage in laughing and teasing.

In the United States, the onset of sexual activity is influenced by peers, gender, and ethnic orientation (Brooks-Gunn & Furstenberg, 1989). One's peers establish the norm for initiating sex. Assumptions (rather than actual knowledge) about what one's peers are doing has been found to be associated with sexual behavior (actual behavior is difficult to research due to disclosure reluctance). In teens age 15 to 19, studies have found early dating to be associated with early intercourse (Brooks-Gunn & Furstenberg, 1989). Historically, boys have been much more likely to engage in sexual intercourse earlier than girls. This may have been due to peer pressure "to become a man" as well as not having to bear the consequences of becoming pregnant. However, the gap between the onset of sexual activity by gender has narrowed (Miller, Christopherson, & King, 1993). This may be due to media influence portraying females as sexual seductresses and easier access to contraception. Parental influences on sexual behavior are believed to outweigh peers and the media if there is a feeling of connectedness and support as well as open communication (Brooks-Gunn & Furstenberg, 1989; Small & Luster, 1994).

Onset of sexual behavior in teens differs according to ethnic orientation, with Blacks reporting the earliest, followed by Hispanics, then Anglos (Brooks-Gunn & Furstenberg, 1989; Katchadourian 1990). However, ethnicity may not be solely influential (Adams, Gullotta, & Markstrom-Adams, 1994). As socioeconomic status decreases, sexual activity has been found to increase. Teens from single-parent families report a higher incidence of sexual activity. Adolescents who attend church, do well in school, and are on academic rather than vocational tracks report lower activity. Thus, other factors usually linked with ethnic orientation, in addition to possibly greater peer affiliation, could explain the ethnic differences found in the onset of sexual behavior.

In the United States, adolescents receive information on sex and sexuality from parents, school, media, and peers (Katchadourian, 1990; Thornburg, 1981). Topics such as love, contraception, ejaculation, homosexuality, intercourse, masturbation, petting, and prostitution are discussed with peers. Schools provide information on topics such as abstinence, sexually transmitted diseases, menstruation, semen production, and pregnancy. Parents transmit their attitudes about sex, love, and marriage. The media presents the excitement of sex without the consequences. Thus knowledge about sexual *behavior* apparently comes from peers and the media, whereas the *mechanics of reproduction* apparently comes from parents and schools.

Regarding the danger of sexually transmitted diseases and the consequences of teen pregnancy, adults need to be "tuned-in" to the role that peers and other socializing agents play in sex education. They need to talk to children before puberty about love, marriage, sex, and reproduction and continue to communicate throughout adolescence, being "askable," available, and willing to answer questions.

ACHIEVING PERSONAL INDEPENDENCE AND IDENTITY

As was discussed earlier, peer groups enable children to become increasingly independent of adults. "Individuals juggle different and often conflicting images of self between the childish self shown to their families and the maturing self shown to their peers" (Adler & Adler, 1998, p. 198). In addition, as children get older, peers become increasingly important as social support (Belle, 1989). **Social support** refers to the resources (tangible, intellectual, social, emotional) provided by others in times of need. Tangible support includes sharing toys, clothes, and money. Intellectual support includes giving information or advice. Social support involves companionship. Emotional support involves listening and empathy.

Children develop their identities through meaningful interactions and accomplishments in the peer group. Children begin to view the peer group as a reference group beginning about age 7 or 8 and increasing through adolescence (Levine & Levine, 1996).

Peers provide validation for the self: "Do you like my hair?" "C'mon, let's play ball." "I have a secret to tell you."

Peers provide encouragement to try out new things: "I'll join Girl Scouts if you will too." "Do you want to go camping with me 'n' my dad?"

Peers provide opportunities for comparison: "I beat Sam in the race." "Sally made the team, but I didn't."

Peers enable self-disclosure. Children are more likely to disclose their innermost feelings to trusted friends than to adults (Parker & Gottman, 1989): "I'm in love with Brad; I let him French kiss me."

PEER GROUP ACTIVITIES: PLAY

A general view of peer group activities in a developmental context is presented first to understand the psychological, social, and cognitive capabilities of children. A specific discussion of the stages and types of play engaged in by children follows.

INFANT/TODDLER PEER ACTIVITIES (BIRTH TO 2 YEARS)

Peer groups emerge early in the child's life, the time varying according to the family situation, including attachment and play patterns, the availability of age-mates, and the temperament and social competence of the child (Parke, 1990). Research suggests that peer sociability is influenced by the relationship with the caregiver. When caregiving is sensitive and responsive, babies learn how to send and interpret emotional cues, which carry over to peer relationships (Vandell & Mueller, 1995).

Observations of babies in institutions have shown that even at 2 months babies are oriented toward the movements of a baby in an adjoining crib (Bridges, 1933). Between 6 and 8 months, babies look at each other and sometimes touch each other; between 9 and 13 months, they sometimes fight, mainly over toys (Hay, 1985; Vincze, 1971). It has also been found that during the second year toddlers interact positively with peers, once conflicts over toys have been resolved (Hughes, 1998; Rubenstein & Howes, 1976). They imitate each other (Asendorpf & Baudoniere, 1993) and show responsiveness (Howes, 1988).

Children become increasingly able to "empathize" with others—first on an emotional level, then on a behavioral level. For example, it has been found that by the end of the first year, babies often cry when they observe another baby crying; by the middle of the second year, they pat or hug the crying baby; by the end of the second year, they offer specific kinds of help, like a toy or a Band-Aid (Saani, Mumme, & Campos, 1998). Then they also begin to "empathize" cognitively. For example, the studies of Zahn-Waxler and Radke-Yarrow (1982, 1990) and Zahn-Waxler and colleagues (1992) showed that during the second year, children's responses to distress of others become increasingly differentiated and their ability to comfort increasingly effective. They were more likely to empathize with family and friends than they were with strangers. They were also more likely to verbalize their empathy and respond sensitively: "Please don't cry; I'll let you play with my doll."

EARLY CHILDHOOD PEER ACTIVITIES (2 TO 5 YEARS)

From age 2 to age 5, the frequency of peer interaction increases and becomes more complex (Rubin, Bukowski, & Parker, 1998). Sometime about age 3 or 4, children begin to enjoy playing in groups—at first, usually on an informal and transitory basis (Howes, 1988). Young children, however, are limited in their friends. Playmates come from the immediate neighborhood—or from school, if parents are willing to chauffeur or have friends over.

Successful social relationships depend on the ability of one person to take the point of view of another, the ability to empathize, and the ability to communicate. Generally, children under age 3 not only cannot take another's point of view or empathize, they also lack the skills for effective two-way communication. Even though some children under age 3 do exhibit some prosocial behaviors, such as empathy, they also exhibit some antisocial behaviors, such as selfishness and aggressiveness. According to Dunn (1988), social understanding just begins to be exhibited by 18 months in the family setting. Then one must have experiences with peers to implement one's understanding of social situations effectively.

Developmental advances in cognition and language enable preschoolers to engage in more and more complex social interactions. They participate in more cooperative ventures, but they also exhibit more aggression. They direct more speech to their peers, as well (Rubin, Bukowski, & Parker, 1998).

MIDDLE CHILDHOOD/PREADOLESCENT PEER ACTIVITIES (6 TO 12 YEARS)

The middle years represent a change in the proportion of social interaction involving peers; approximately 10% of the social interaction for 2-year-olds involves peers, whereas for 6- to 12-year olds it is more than 30%. The remainder is spent with siblings, parents, and other adults (Rubin, Bukowski, & Parker, 1998). The settings of peer interaction also change during the middle years from supervised (home and preschool) to more unsupervised (neighborhood).

As children reach school age, they spend some of their time hanging around informally, talking, teasing, "roughhousing," and bike riding, but they often move spontaneously into group games. Such games involve the development of skill, understanding, and acceptance of rules, and the ability to cooperate as well as compete.

As children's physical and mental capacities and interests mature, the quality of their games changes; they tend to reflect the culture and they are apt to be more

A place secluded from adults allows children to experiment with different roles, behaviors, and interactions.

gender-specific (Best, 1983; Hughes, 1998; Sutton-Smith, 1972). For girls, there are jump rope, hopscotch, jacks, dolls, and playing house or school. Boys play baseball, football, cars, trains, cops and robbers, or spacemen. According to Sutton-Smith (1972), games involving verbal and rhythmic content, such as guessing games, have traditionally been played predominantly by girls, whereas physically active games and organized sports have been played mostly by boys. Chasing and teasing games have been played by both genders.

Game patterns change with cognitive development (Hughes, 1998). Children become more and more capable of handling complex rules and strategies. According to Sutton-Smith (1972), children age 6 to 9 enjoy simple games with dramatic content (cops and robbers). Older children like games requiring strategy, such as checkers or chess, as well as organized team sports.

Games also change with children's psychological development. For example, their self-concepts change. Sutton-Smith (1972) points out that in younger children's games, such as Simon Says or Giant Steps, the person who is "It," operating from a home base, is safe and has power to control the moves of the others. The structure of these games provides a nonthreatening opportunity for children to venture into a leadership role. From about age 10 on, the games enjoyed involve a central figure who is vulnerable to attack by others who seek the leadership role (King of the Castle). Older children also enjoy competitive games, where one wins and one is defeated, because these types of games offer the experience of competence.

Children's games reflect the culture in which they live. For example, according to Parker (1984), competitive games, such as soccer, basketball, or football, offer practice in territorial invasion. Card games offer practice in bluffing and calculating odds. All games involve memory, manipulation, and strategizing. Games of culture offer opportunities for children to practice skills they will need in adult life (Hughes, 1998).

Today, children generally spend less time in spontaneously organized play (*stickball, hide and seek, marbles, jacks*) than they did a generation ago because children can buy many prepared board games with printed instructions and rules, as well as computer and video games. The sandlot neighborhood versions of baseball and football have given way, for many children, to organized sports supervised by adults, such as Little League or soccer; sports that come with rule books and procedures. One reason is safety; parents fear letting their children play unsupervised because of traffic, crime, and kidnapping issues. Another reason is to provide structured time spent after school, especially when both parents are employed. Adult–peer group linkages are discussed later in more detail. While children gain many physical, cognitive, and social skills from adult-organized play, they are not getting too many opportunities to experience making and revising their own rules and enforcing them with their peers.

THE SIGNIFICANCE OF PLAY

Perhaps the most revealing context for peer relationships is play. **"Play** is behavior that is enjoyed for its own sake" (Evans & McCandless, 1978, p. 110). Play, according to Jean Piaget (1962), is the way the child learns about his or her environment because its interactive nature allows for construction of knowledge. Vygotsky (1978) and Berk & Winsler (1995) believed play to be an imaginary situation governed by social rules. Play contributes to development in that it enables the child to separate thought from actions and objects. It also enables the child to move from impulsive activity to planned goals and self-regulation (instead of taking a desired toy, the child asks permission to play with it). Anna Freud (1968) viewed play as an acceptable way to express emotions and impulses. Groos (1901) described play as a way for children to practice skills necessary for adult life. These various functions of play enable therapists and educators to learn what the child feels and understands by observing his or her play activities.

Mildred Parten (1932) examined the developmental changes in children's social play over years ago. On the basis of observations of children at "free play" at nursery school, she described the following categories of play, based on social interactions, which are still applicable today:

1. *Solitary*—the child plays alone and independently. The child seems to concentrate on the activity rather than on other children who may be nearby. Solitary play is typical of infant/toddlers.

2. *Onlooker*—the child watches other children playing. Conversations with the others may be initiated. Though there is no actual engagement in the play being observed, the child is definitely involved as a spectator. Two-year-olds engage in a considerable amount of onlooker play.

3. *Parallel*—the child plays alone, but with toys like those that other children are using, or plays in a manner that mimics the behavior of playing children. Parallel play is common among 2- and 3-year-olds, but diminishes as the child gets older.

These children are engaged in parallel play; they enjoy playing next to each other while engaged in a similar activity, but true interaction doesn't take place.

4. *Associative*—social interaction and communication are involved in associative play, but with little or no organization. Children engage in play activities similar to those of other children; however, they appear to be more interested in being associated with each other than in the tasks at hand. Associative play is common among 3- and particularly among 4-year-olds.

5. *Cooperative*—social interaction in a group characterizes cooperative play. The activity is organized, and the group has a purpose—for example, a group building a fort together, a group playing "store," or a game of baseball. Cooperative play is the prototype for the games of middle childhood. Cooperative play begins to be exhibited by 4- to 5-year-olds.

Contemporary research shows that these play forms emerge in the order suggested by Parten, but earlier forms may coexist with later forms, rather than being replaced by them (Howes & Matheson, 1992). However, the complexity of the form does change with age (Rubin & Coplan, 1992). Children will combine *type* of play with what Parten classified as *stage* of play. For example, when children pretend, they may do it solitarily or cooperatively (Hughes, 1998).

Brian Sutton-Smith (1971) categorized play by type of activity—*imitative, exploratory, testing,* and *model-building:*

1. *Imitative Play*—during the first year of life, the baby imitates the parent. During the second year of life, the child can put together parts of acts already imitated or observed in new combinations. In the third year, children imitate whole roles,

such as mother or father. Most of this early imitative play consists of imitation of the important and powerful people in children's lives. Between 4 and 6, imitative social play tends to be governed by one player acting as a central person and the others acting in satellite roles, by players taking turns and alternating the roles, or by all the players doing much the same thing at the same time.

2. *Exploratory Play*—in the first year, the child explores—touches, tastes, and manipulates. In the second year, the child also empties, fills, inserts, puts in and out, pulls, stacks, and rolls. In the third year, the child arranges, heaps, combines, transfers, sorts, and spreads. Novel manipulations are a delight to the child and can be manipulations of objects or of words.

3. *Testing Play*—in many types of play, what children are actually doing is testing themselves. During the second year, children test their motor skills. They pull wagons, lift objects, climb, run, and jump. As children get older, they test themselves in games. They compete with others to measure their skills, both physical and intellectual. They also test their emotions, such as fear and anger.

4. *Model-Building Play*—about age 4, model-building play becomes explicit, when blocks are organized into buildings, trucks into highway traffic, dishes into tea parties. Children begin to put elements of their experiences together in unique ways.

As can be seen, children's play becomes more complex and interactive with age. The increasing social nature of play requires a combination of physical–motor skills, inter-personal skills, and cognitive skills. Through play, children discover their capacities. They explore and test their physical and mental abilities against their own standards and in comparison to others. Children often issue a challenge just to see if they can make their bodies and minds do what they want them to: "I bet I can climb to the top of that tree"; "I can figure out that puzzle in five minutes!"

Young children often engage in rough-and-tumble play. This type of play involves fighting, wrestling, and/or chasing. It is viewed more as "mock" aggression rather than "real" aggression (Hughes, 1999). Children in many cultures exhibit it, as do young animals. Thus it may have evolutionary survival roots to develop protective skills in the young.

A very common type of *pretend play* among young children is "superhero/heroine play" (Kostelnik, Whiren, & Stein, 1986). Superheroes and heroines emerged in radio, comics, movies, and television. Some examples are Buck Rogers (1920s), Superman and Batman (1930s), Wonder Woman (1940s), Captain Video (1950s), Captain Kirk (1960s), Luke Skywalker and Princess Leia (1970s), He-Man (1980s), Ninja Turtles and Power Rangers (1990s), and Tarzan and Zena (2000). What super characters have in common is that they possess powers children wish they themselves had: they are good, strong, can fly, swim under water, change the shape of their bodies, and overcome all obstacles they may encounter. In other words, they are in control—no one tells them what to do, they know what is right, and they have respect and approval from others. Unfortunately, in this kind of play some children exploit being in control by intimidating others and, therefore, cause hostile and hurt feelings.

Superhero/heroine play allows children to experience power and prestige unavailable to them in their daily lives. It also provides them with concrete models whose behavior is easy to emulate, unlike real-life models, whose behavior is often too ambiguous or complex for children to figure out. Finally, it gives children a chance to experience concretely abstract values such as honor, justice, courage, honesty, and mercy. While some preschools ban superhero/heroine play because it usually involves aggression, others use it to enable children to be creative rather than imitative ("How would Darth Vader fix that broken chair?" (Levin, 1998).

PEER GROUP INTERACTION: FRIENDSHIP

What children generally *do* in peer groups as they develop has been discussed. Now the relationships children form when interacting with peers, as well as why some children are successful in making friends while others are not, will be examined.

DEVELOPMENT

Like the activities children engage in as they develop, their social relationships and friendships also become more complex and interactive with age. To illustrate, two studies will be described.

Toddlerhood to Early Childhood

Carolee Howes (1988) studied the social interaction and friendship formations of young children in a child-care setting. While young children's social competence is limited by their cognitive development, apparently early experience with peers enhances interaction skills. She found that 13- to 24-month-old toddlers differentiated friends among available playmates at their child-care center. These friendships were marked by emotional responsiveness (happiness in seeing each other or comforting in times of stress). Children age 25 to 36 months were able to distinguish between the emotional and play components of friendship by approaching different peers when in need of comfort and when wanting to run or wrestle.

Selman and Selman (1979) interviewed more than 250 individuals between the ages

Friendship Stages	Approximate Ages
Momentary playmateship	<4 years
One-way assistance	4–9 years
Two-way, fair-weather cooperation	6–12 years
Intimate, mutually shared relationships	9–15 years
Autonomous interdependent friendships	>12 years

3 and 45 to get a developmental perspective on friendship patterns. They delineated five stages, described as follows.

Early Childhood

Most children under age 4 and some older ones are in the first stage—*momentary play-mateship*. They are unable to consider the viewpoint of another person and can think only about what they want from the friendship. Friends are defined by how close they live ("He's my friend; he lives next door") or by their material possessions ("She's my friend; she has a doll house and a swing set").

Early to Middle Childhood

The second stage is *one-way assistance*. About age 4 until about age 9, children are more capable of telling the difference between their own perspectives and those of others. However, friendship is based on whether or not someone does what the child wants that person to do ("He's not my friend anymore; he didn't want to play cars"). Youniss and Volpe (1978), in a study of the friendships of children between age 6 and 14, found that the 6- and 7-year-olds thought of friendship in terms of playing together and sharing material goods ("She plays dress-up with me"; "She always shares her candy with me").

Middle Childhood

In the third stage—*two-way, fair-weather cooperation*—children age 6 to 12 acknowledge that friendship involves give and take. However, they see friendship as mutually serving individual interests rather than mutually cooperating toward a common interest. ("We are friends. We do things for each other"). Youniss and Volpe found that 9- and 10-year-olds regard friends as those who share with one another ("Someone who plays with you when you don't have anyone else to play with"). At this age, children emphasize similarities between friends, as well as equalities and reciprocities ("We all like to collect baseball cards. We trade them and give doubles to our friends who are missing those. No one brags."). Children of this age are beginning to recognize that friendship is based on getting along—sharing interests, ideas, and feelings.

Middle Childhood to Adolescence

The fourth stage is one of *intimate, mutually shared relationships*. Children between age 9 and 15 can now view a friendship as an entity in itself. It is an ongoing, committed relationship that incorporates more than just doing things for each other; it tends to be treasured for its own sake and may involve possessiveness and jealousy ("She is my best friend. How can she go to the movies with Susan?"). Youniss and Volpe report that the 12- and 13-year-olds in their study carried the earlier principles of equality and reciprocity further ("If someone picks on me, my friend helps me. My friend does not leave me to go off with some other kids.").

Adolescence to Adulthood

Finally, there is the stage of *autonomous interdependent friendships*. About age 12, children are capable of respecting their friends' needs for both dependency and autonomy

("We like to do most things together and we talk about our problems, but sometimes Jason just likes to be by himself. I don't mind.").

Are there gender differences in friendships? Generally, girls refer to best friends as someone you can have an intimate conversation with and who is "faithful" more than do boys; boys refer more to the companionship nature of best friends and the sharing of activities (Lever, 1976; Maccoby, 1990).

Is there a link between the ability to have friends and emotional adjustment in adulthood? Reviews of the literature on peer relationships verify a link between problematic childhood peer interactions and adjustment difficulties in adolescence and adulthood (Kupersmidt, Coie, & Dodge, 1990). In the next section, we look at some reasons for peer acceptance and rejection, as well as how to help children be more successful in making friends. Generally, having friends and being accepted by the peer group are related in that children who are well-liked by peers have many opportunities to make friends. However, it is not always so that children who are rejected by the peer group do not have friends. Children who are rejected by the group, but have at least one friend, have fewer problems later in life than those who are rejected and also have no friends (Howes, 1988; Rubin, Bukowski, & Parker, 1998).

Sociometry

Techniques called **sociometry** have been developed to measure patterns of acceptance, neglect, and rejection among members of a group. Sociometry originally was used in school classrooms but is now widely used in other settings, such as recreational, work, or prison. Contemporary researchers typically use sociometry to identify the extent to which children prefer to be with certain peers (Parkhurst & Asher, 1992).

A sociometric rating is easy to conduct; it involves asking children questions anonymously about each other and tabulating the results. For example: Who is your best friend? With whom would you prefer and not prefer to work on a project? With whom would you share a secret? For preschoolers, it can be implemented by showing each child photographs of classmates and asking which ones with whom he or she likes and dislikes to play. Child with the most "liked" votes are popular; the ones with the most "disliked" are neglected or rejected.

Sociometric results can help adults facilitate the inclusion of neglected or rejected children into the group. By careful observations, adults can assess where the neglected or rejected child needs intervention (Kemple, 1991)—*social* (Does the child cooperate? share? boast?); *emotional* (Does the child interpret other's emotions correctly? empathize?); *language* (Does the child make relevant responses to peers' communications? communicate desires clearly?); and *physical* (Does the child resort to aggression to resolve conflicts?) Adults can choose appropriate intervention strategies or sociotherapy.

ACCEPTANCE/NEGLECT/REJECTION BY PEERS

The significance of being accept, neglected, or rejected by peers came to the attention of the media in 1999 when two rejected adolescents shot 12 students and a teacher at the school they attended in Colorado. Apparently the athletes who repeatedly teased them were the targets for retaliation. Which children are readily accepted by the group? According to several studies (Asher, Gottman, & Oden, 1977; Dodge, 1983; Hartup, 1983; Rubin, Bukowski, & Parker, 1998), a child's acceptance by peers and successful interactions with them depend on willingness to cooperate and interact positively with other children. Children who are popular with their peers tend to be healthy and vigorous, capable of initiative, and well poised. They are also adaptable and conforming, as well as dependable, affectionate, and considerate.

Being yourself, being happy, showing enthusiasm and concern for others, and showing self-confidence but not conceit are among the characteristics that lead to popularity (Hartup, 1983; Rubin, Bukowski, & Parker, 1998). Certain physical and intellectual factors can also affect a child's popularity. Studies have shown that, on average, children who are physically attractive are more popular than those who are not (Adams & Crane, 1980; Adler & Adler, 1998; Ritts, Patterson, & Tubbs, 1992). A study of 6- to 10-year-old boys (Hartup, 1983) revealed that the boys with muscular physiques were more popular than boys who were skinny or plump, perhaps this correlates with consistent findings that athletic ability is related to popularity (Adler & Alder, 1998; Coleman, 1961). Children who are more intelligent have been found to be more popular than those who are less intelligent (Berndt, 1983; Rubin, Bukowski, & Parker, 1998). Other studies have shown that the ability to use language and communicate ideas effectively helped in peer acceptance (Gottman, Gonso, & Rasmussen, 1975; Kemple, 1991). In general, popular children approach others in a friendly manner, respond appropriately to communications interpreting emotional states correctly and are generous with praise and approval.

Prosocial behavior is the most consistent correlate of peer group acceptance (Wentzel & Erdley, 1993). Socialization of pro- and antisocial behavior will be discussed more thoroughly in Chapter 12 (*see* Table 8.1 for a summary of characteristics of children accepted, neglected, and rejected by peers).

Family interaction patterns play a role in children's successful integration into the group (Hartup, 1989, 1996). In the family, children learn to express and interpret various emotions such as pleasure, displeasure, attachment, and distancing. Children also learn to respond to such emotional expressions as well as regulate their behavior according to family requirements. Thus social competence, which leads to peer acceptance, begins in the family.

Which children are neglected or rejected by the group? The rise and fall of children's likes and dislikes causes almost every school-age child to feel neglected or rejected at some point by other children. The child not asked to play, not chosen to be on the team, not invited to the party, or excluded from the club feels that a crucial part of his or her world has been shattered. Why a child is neglected or rejected can be due to the child's shyness or lack of social skills. Children who do not know how to initiate a friendship, who are withdrawn, who misinterpret others' emotional states, who have difficulty communicating, who are bossy, who are disruptive in class, and/or who rarely praise their peers are not readily accepted by the group. Also, children who are poor losers, who cheat or whine, and who are aggressive are not welcome in most children's groups. Antisocial behavior is the most consistent correlate of peer rejection (Coie & Cillessen, 1993; Coie, Dodge, & Kupersmidt, 1990).

Sometimes children are rejected for reasons they cannot change or even understand. For example, *Blubber* by Judy Blume (1974) is about an overweight girl who is the brunt of her fifth-grade classmates' teasing and scapegoating: "She won't need a coat

Table 8.1 Summary of Characteristics of Children Accepted/Neglected/ Rejected by Peers

ACCEPTED	NEGLECTED/REJECTED
Cooperative	Shy
Positive in interactions	Withdrawn
Capable of initiating interaction	Dishonest
Adaptable and conforming	Unsporting attitude when losing
Understanding emotional expressions	Incapable of initiating interaction
Shows concern for others	Socially unskilled
Able to communicate effectively	Unable to interpret others' emotional states
Happy	Unable to communicate easily
Dependable	Whiny
Affectionate	Disruptive
Considerate	Miserly with praise
Well-poised	Bossiness
Generous with praise	Aggressive
Intelligent	"Different" physically, behaviorally, academically
Friendly	Negative social reputation
Self-confident (not conceited)	
Physically attractive	
Athletic ability	
Prosocial behavior	
Positive social reputation	

this winter; she's got her blubber to keep her warm." Sometimes children are teased and ostracized from the group because of they are different physically (weight, height, skin color); behaviorally (accent, speech impediment, style of dress, religious preference); academically (learning disabled, gifted); or even their names (Hartup, 1983; Langlois, 1986; Sandstrom & Coie, 1999). The following story appeared in the *Los Angeles Times* (1982):

A 9-year-old boy named Alfonse wrote a letter to Senator Alfonse D'Amato (R-N.Y.), asking him how he got his name. The boy couldn't ask his father why he was named Alfonse, because his father had died. He wrote that he hated his name because the kids at school joked about it. D'Amato wrote back that the name Alfonse means "prepared for battle," and when you're young, "you'd better be." D'Amato also wrote that when he asked his father why he was named Alfonse, his father replied, "Son, your Uncle Alfonse was a very wealthy man, and that's how we got the down payment on the house." The senator recommended that young Alfonse tell his friends to call him Al.

Family problems can have damaging effects on children's peer relations (Baker, Barthelemy, & Kurdek, 1993; Burton, 1985). For example, children whose parents are getting a divorce may act out feelings of anger and fear at school, eliciting rejection from peers in the process. Children who have an alcoholic parent may feel reluctant to bring friends home, as well as avoid making close friends due to embarrassment. Likewise, abused children or children of homosexual parents or parents with a disability or health impairment may isolate themselves from others to avoid telling a family secret.

While many studies suggest that children's behaviors and characteristics contribute to how well liked they are by peers, according to Kemple (1991) it is important to consider the role that peers play in maintaining a child's level of social acceptance. Once a child has established a reputation as someone who is nice and fun to play with, acceptance is easy; whereas for a child who has a reputation of being unpleasant, acceptance is difficult.

In sum, factors linked to acceptance (initiating and maintaining a relationship) enable group belonging; whereas factors linked to neglect and rejection (unsociable, disruptiveness, aggressive) make it difficult to belong to a group. Dodge (1996) proposes these factors are influenced by how children cognitively process social information.

PEER SOCIOTHERAPY

Selman and Selman's (1979) developmental stages of friendship have been used in **peer sociotherapy,** an intervention to enable children who have trouble making and keeping friends learn to relate to others. By assessing their levels of social relationships with others, a therapist or teacher can sometimes help children to move on to the next developmental level.

Children who have difficulty making friends can be helped by giving them a chance to play with younger children. Some researchers (Bullock, 1992; Howes, 1988) have found that socially withdrawn preschoolers become more sociable after they have had a chance to play, one on one, with children one to two years younger than themselves during play sessions. The researchers conclude that being with younger children gives socially withdrawn children a chance to be assertive in initiating and directing activity. Once they experience success with younger children, they are better able to interact with children their own age.

Children who have difficulty reading other children's social cues may benefit by watching others who interact successfully. This can be done in real situations with an adult coach, watched on video tape, or performed by puppets (Bullock, 1992).

Also, having a friend in a new situation, such as school, or in a stressful situation, such as divorce, helps the child cope and better adjust to what is going on (Ladd, 1990). This is another reason why it is important to enable children to make friends.

In order to help children who are not readily accepted by their peers get along better, Oden and Asher (1977) identified four categories of social skills, based on the research on popularity: *participation* (playing with others, paying attention); *communication* (talking and listening); *cooperation* (taking turns, sharing); and *validation–support* (offering encouragement or help).

Improving Children's Social Skills

The following are some guidelines that teachers and parents can use for improving children's social skills (Asher, 1982; Bullock, 1992). Monitoring children's interactions enable them to:

Model
- Observe how others interact positively
- Imitate behaviors and communications that were successful in promoting friendship

Participate
- Get involved with others
- Get started on an activity, a project, or a game
- Pay attention to the activity
- Try to do your best
- Help someone who is younger

Cooperate
- Take turns
- Share the game, materials, or props
- Make suggestions if there's a problem
- Work out a mutually agreeable alternative, if there is disagreement about the rules

Communicate
- Talk with others
- Say things about the activity or about yourself
- Ask a question about the activity
- Ask a question about the other person
- Listen when the other person talks
- Look at the other person to see how he or she is doing

Validate and Support
- Give some attention to the other person
- Say something nice when the other person does well
- Smile
- Have fun
- Offer help or suggestions when needed

A group of unpopular school-age children were coached on these specific skills. The coaching sessions involved demonstration (instruction and role modeling), discussion (explanation and feedback), and shaping by reinforcing desired behavior (behavior modification). A year later, the group of unpopular children who were coached showed more sociability and acceptance by peers than the control group of unpopular children who were not coached. Coaching strategies have also been employed successfully with preschool as well as school-age children (Mize & Ladd, 1990).

Another study (Sandstrom & Coie, 1999) found that elementary school children who were initially rejected could have their statuses with peers improved by participating in extracurricular activities as well as having their parents monitor their social interactions (arranging for play with cooperative peers, intervening in conflicts).

How Can Teachers Help Rejected Children Gain Acceptance?

For children to effectively implement newly learned social skills in the classroom, the teacher must be able to offer on-the-spot guidance in various situations (Kemple, 1991). For example, in conflict situations the adult serves as a mediator, encouraging each child to voice his or her perspective and generate potential solutions leading to compromise (Bullock, 1992; Stein & Kostelnick, 1984).

Also, teachers can provide on-the-spot guidance to help with communication patterns, such as "Joey, I don't think Jackson understands why you don't want to play fire engines; can you tell him why? Maybe you can say what you can both do together."

A child who has difficulty interpreting others' emotional states can be guided with suggestions such as "Look at Sarah's face; do you think she likes it when you push her?"

This teacher is providing on-the-spot guidance to facilitate a compromise.

Sometimes a child's behavior may have to be interpreted to the group in order to facilitate acceptance. For example, a child who makes fun of a group playing a game may be doing so in order to be included: "I think Trey is trying to figure out how he can be an ambulance driver; if you don't need another one, maybe he can be the emergency room doctor."

Finally, the teacher's attempts to help a disliked child find a niche in the peer group may sometimes be more successful if the child's family is involved (Sandstrom & Coie, 1999). Teachers can discuss skills being taught and request parents' support with siblings and neighborhood peers (Kemple, 1991).

NEGATIVE PEER INFLUENCES: BULLIES, GANGS

Dan Olweus (1993) has extensively studied bullies and their victims at school. He defines *bullying* or victimization as being "exposed, repeatedly and over time, to negative actions on the part of one or more other students." Negative actions, or harassment, include threats, taunts, teasing, being called names, making faces or dirty gestures, a well as hitting, kicking, pinching, and physically restraining another.

Bullies tend to have the following characteristics:

- Domination needs—need to feel powerful, superior
- Impulsive, low frustration tolerance, easily angered
- Usually physically stronger than peers
- Difficulty adhering to rules
- Generally oppositional, defiant, aggressive
- Show little empathy
- A relatively positive self-concept
- Engage in antisocial behavior

Victims tend to have the following characteristics:

- Usually physically weaker than peers
- Poor physical coordination
- Exhibit fear of being hurt or hurting themselves
- Cautious, sensitive, quiet, passive, submissive, shy
- Anxious, insecure, unhappy
- A relatively negative self-concept
- Difficulty asserting themselves
- Often relate better to adults than peers

What can be done?

- Awareness, supervision, and involvement by adults
- Interventions with bullies by parents, teachers, and peers that do not reinforce harassment

- Class rules with consequences, training in alternative behaviors, role playing, cooperative learning
- Interventions with victims to alter their negative self-concept, training to be assertive and respond in nonreinforcing ways to threats (ignoring, humor)

Why do peer groups sometimes engage in negative behavior? Peers (or, more specifically, "hanging around with the wrong crowd") are often blamed for delinquency and substance abuse, but in reality the single most consistent characteristic of delinquents is lack of support and socialization by their families (Jackson & McBride, 1985; Rutter, Giller, & Hagell, 1998). Antagonistic relationships between parents are often found to exist in families with antisocial children (Patterson, Reid, & Dishion, 1992; Rutter, 1971). When children do not have their needs met in their families, they often turn to their peers. Adolescents become delinquent because they are socialized into it, particularly by peers (Dishion, McCord, & Poulin, 1999; Goldstein, 1991; Zober, 1981). How this occurs is illustrated in William Golding's *Lord of the Flies,* published in 1954.

A group of English schoolboys ranging in age from 6 to 12 crash-lands on a deserted island. The adults are killed, and the youngsters, despairing of rescue, set out to build their own society. At first, the older boys try to draw on their memory of English society, but they do not remember enough, and there are no elders they can turn to for guidance. They establish their own system of socialization, first by investing authority in a leader chosen on the basis of appearance and perceived power (he possesses a conch shell), and then by setting up rituals to provide order amid the chaos. However, disagreements and conflict soon give way to savagery, and Piggy, the continual reminder of adult standards of behavior, is brutally killed before the rescuers arrive. The children, not remembering how to resolve differences, resort to competition for status and power and aggression to get them.

Social change, microsystems (family, school, community) under stress, and consequent lack of support for children tend to be associated with an increase in delinquency rates (National Research Council, 1993). Many young people lack positive adult role models. The gap between the consumerism perpetuated by the media and reality may entice young people to turn to delinquency. Personality factors may contribute to the reasons some adolescents become delinquents. It is known that those who become delinquent are more likely to be defiant, ambivalent to authority, resentful, hostile, impulsive, and lacking in self-control (Goldstein, 1991; Thompson & Dodder, 1986). Those who get poor grades in school, have been reported for classroom misconduct, and have trouble getting along with other children and teachers have been shown to possess a greater tendency to become delinquents (Ladd & LeSieur, 1995; Lindre, Miller, & Porter, 1997). Therefore, the peer group may be the setting in which preexisting antisocial behavior due to family factors, social change, personality characteristics, or being out of synch with the school is reinforced (Goldstein, 1991; Rubin, Bukowski, & Parker, 1998).

"A **gang** is a group of people who form an allegiance for a common purpose and engage in unlawful or criminal activity" (Jackson & McBride, 1985, p. 20). Gangs are of concern not only because of their antisocial activities, but also because of their increase (Goldstein, 1991). Gangs usually consist of males, although there are female gangs. Gang members identify themselves via names, clothes, tattoos, slang, sign language, and graffiti. The problem of gangs is spreading throughout our society like a plague. They are present in neighborhoods and schools, impacting businesses, recreation, and education (Landre, Miller, & Porter, 1997). Daily news stories depict the tragedy of gang violence. Gangs steal, hurt, and kill. Innocent bystanders are often victims.

What is the appeal of gangs? Gangs give members companionship, guidance, excitement, and identity (Goldstein, 1991). When a member needs something, the others come to the rescue and provide protection (Landre, Miller, & Porter, 1997). Gang members have experienced failure and alienation in their lives. They tend to live in depressed or deprived environments, which their families may be helpless to change. Because they feel they can't accomplish anything individually, gang members band together in order to exercise influence over their lives (Jackson & McBride, 1985).

The homes of gang-oriented children are characterized by either high permissiveness or high punitiveness (Devereaux, 1970). The parents of such peer-oriented children also show less concern and affection, and by such passive neglect, rather than active maltreatment, push their children to look to their peers for support (Condry & Simon, 1974; Ladd & LeSieur, 1995).

Youngsters living with both natural parents were found to be less susceptible to pressure from peers to engage in deviant behavior than youngsters living in single-parent homes or with stepfamilies. Thus the integrity of the home is an important protector against pressure toward deviant behavior (Steinberg, 1987).

Gang members have significantly lower levels of self-esteem compared to their nongang peers. They also could name fewer adult role models than did their nongang peers (Wang, 1994).

Some sociological forces in the formation of gangs are racism, socioeconomics, family structure, and belief system (Jackson & McBride, 1985):

1. *Racism*—gangs are usually made up of one race, thereby being a source of identity and support.

2. *Socioeconomics*—gang members usually come from poor families in densely populated areas where there is competition for resources, although recently there are increasing numbers of gangs from middle-class neighborhoods.

3. *Family structure*—gang members usually come from families with minimal adult supervision; a mother-headed family; a two-adult family in which the father, stepfather, or boyfriend is a negative role model; or a family that has a gang lineage.

4. *Belief system*—gang members believe they are victims and blame society for their problems. They also feel that since society hasn't helped them, they are justified in protecting themselves outside of society's rules.

POSITIVE PEER INFLUENCES: PEER COLLABORATION, TUTORING, COUNSELING

The peer group is not always a liability; it can also be a resource. Collaboration, tutoring, and counseling are methods encouraged by adults to enable peers to be supportive of one another.

Peers that *collaborate* learn to solve problems through consensus. Peers that *tutor* learn how to analyze and synthesize information for others. Peers that *counsel* learn how to care, help, and give support to others.

Peer *collaboration* with different outcomes are discussed by Piaget and Vygotsky. According to Piaget (1965), when children interact they discover others have opinions and perspectives different from theirs. As a result, they reorganize their cognitive structures (accommodate) to fit discrepant information. Thus Piaget believed cognitive development was more likely to occur from *conflict* with same-age peers than from interaction with older children and adults (Berk & Winsler, 1995). Vygotsky (1978), on the other hand, believed cognitive development resulted from *collaboration* with peers. Peer conflict could only contribute to heightened understanding if the disagreement was compromised or resolved. Vygotsky emphasized the importance of mixed-age groups that provide each child opportunities to interact with more knowledgeable companions and give each child a chance to serve as a resource for others. More expert peers can serve as mentors, models, or tutors, whereas novice peers can be apprentices. Adults must guide collaborative activities, teaching social and problem-solving skills, intervening when necessary (Berk & Winsler, 1995).

Peer *tutoring* is exemplified by inclusion programs wherein a child with a disability is assisted by a classmate academically and/or socially (Vaughn, Bos, & Schumm, 1997). Peer tutoring provides a *zone of proximal development* (ZPD), as discussed earlier, in which what one is capable of learning independently is potentially increased by participating with more capable others.

An example of peer *counseling* is "positive peer culture" or PPC (Vorrath & Brendtro, 1985). PPC involves a group of peers with an adult leader. It is designed to "turn around" negative youth subculture and mobilize the power of the peer group to foster positive behavior. A person is not asked whether he or she wants to *receive* help, but whether he or she is willing to *give* help. As the person becomes of value to others, he or she increases feelings of self-worth (Vorrath & Brendtro, 1985). PPC believes that delinquent youth, who are often rebellious and strong-willed, have much to contribute when redirected. Those who have encountered many difficulties in their lives are often in the best position to help others. PPC provides its students with what they did not get from other socializing agents: care and learning to be responsible for oneself as well as others.

A group home for troubled girls had severe drug-abuse problems. The result of the many attempts to suppress this activity was a cold war between staff and youth. Suspicion, searches, and restriction became commonplace. That was a year ago.

Now staff members no longer police students for drugs, and the climate of intrigue is gone. As a new girl enters, her peers confiscate any drugs she may have and tell her, "We don't have to use dope around here." Drug problems are dealt with openly in a helpful, matter-of-fact way. Group members state with strong conviction that when a person has good feelings about herself, she no longer needs to get high on drugs.

ADULT/PEER GROUP LINKAGES

Adults play a significant role in "setting the stage" for peer group experiences. Earlier, the adult role was discussed in terms of secure attachment and arranging for friends to get together in the home. According to Steinberg (1996), the neighborhood in which a child lives influences whether the peer group has *positive* or *negative* effects. Neighborhoods that include parents who are *involved* in schools, who participate in organized activities for children (sports, arts, scouts), and who *monitor* their children, tend to have children who provide *positive* peer influences for one another. On the other hand, neighborhoods that include parents who are *disengaged* from school and community activities tend to have children who provide *negative* peer influences for one another. Thus parents can influence whether a child's peer group experiences are positive or negative by knowing who their child's friends are, and by being involved in their child's activities.

Peer groups linked to and structured by adults include teams, clubs, Scouts, and church groups. They differ, due to their organization, from the peer groups (neighborhood or school groups of friends) that have been discussed so far, which are formed and maintained by the children themselves. Whereas child-structured groups are casual and informal, adult-structured groups are purposeful and formal.

Adult-structured and child-structured groups differ in their socializing influences on children. When adults organize groups, there are rules, guidelines, or suggestions about appropriate or expected behavior in an activity. Adults supply the structure by verbal instructions, praise, criticism, feedback about the activity or the child's performance, or modeling ways to perform the activity. The structuring of a setting influences the behavior that goes on within it. For example, formal groups organized by adults encourage children to play according to established rules, to be compliant, and to seek guidance as well as recognition from adults; however, groups organized by the children themselves encourage children to be active and assertive with peers, to take initiative, and to behave independently (Huston, Carpenter, Atwater, & Johnson, 1986). Studies of preschool children have found that girls prefer more adult-structured groups (Carpenter, Huston, & Holt, 1986; Powlishta, Gerbin, & Moller, 1993). A similar pattern of gender differences was shown to exist for school-age children (Carpenter, 1983; Huston, 1983; Maccoby, 1990).

Groups structured by adults are also characterized by the different values that are imparted to children. Clubs may be formed at church, at school, or in the community. The church club may serve the purpose of fellowship—getting to know children of similar religious backgrounds. At school the club may provide extracurricular activities for interested children—for example, computer club, chorus, or drama club. In the community the club may be for recreation (the Y) or for character building (Scouts). For example, the ideology of the Boy and Girl Scouts of America is to foster patriotism, reverence, leadership, and emotional development. Children are encouraged to develop self-reliance by accomplishing certain tasks to earn badges—for example, water safety or cooking.

SPORTS

Sports are "organized interactions of children in competitive and/or cooperative team or individual enjoyable physical activities" (Humphrey, 1993, p. 3). In the United States, sports are not only a major form of recreation, but are also considered a means of achieving physical health. Sports are also regarded as a way for children to learn leadership skills, loyalty, and other desirable traits, and as valuable training in competitiveness and give-and-take relationships. Organized sports is also a vehicle for promoting the development of talent.

Sports are a pervasive part of American culture. Sports lingo, "competition, teamwork, winning the game" is widely used in the corporate world (Murphy, 1999).

The American attitude toward sports is revealed by the statistics: over 20 million U.S. children, age 6 and older, play on organized sports teams—over 2.5 million play Little League baseball, more than 1 million play organized football, and the other 17 million are involved in such sports as hockey, soccer, swimming, track, and gymnastics (Poinsett, 1997).

Do all children benefit from the experience? According to many, no (Murphy, 1999). Some children do learn a lot about themselves and their capabilities, about their potential for improvement (however modest), about the value of teamwork, about the fun of sports, and about the lifelong importance of physical fitness (Poinsett, 1997). Some children, unfortunately, are humiliated by their experience in organized sports. Perhaps they are being pushed to succeed by their parents; not being able to live up to their parent's expectations, they become discouraged and end up hating the sport or themselves. I remember watching many Little League games while my son was involved. It was not uncommon to hear a father yell to his son from the stands, "You dummy, how could you miss that ball? Wake up!"

When I was 11 years old, I was on a softball team. I desperately wanted to be the pitcher, but I wasn't chosen. My throwing was accurate, but it wasn't fast enough. The coach put me in centerfield because I was also a good fielder. I was so crushed that I almost quit. What I didn't understand then was that the team already had a good pitcher, but the shortstop made a lot of errors and the right- and leftfielders were daydreamers. The coach's logic was to put me in centerfield because I could catch and throw, and because I could also run fast, I could get the balls missed by the others. It took me quite a few games to understand that teamwork makes everyone play better because teamwork coordinates all the individual abilities. No matter how good one person on the team is, if the others are not playing well, the team can't win. I wanted to be the pitcher because I wanted to be the star. I learned that stars don't succeed without the support of the cast.

In some cases the coach of a team may place more emphasis on winning than on playing. Winning can mean several things. It can mean self-improvement and a sense of accomplishment when a player's performance improves, or it can mean beating the other team. When winning is narrowed down to beating the other team, undue pressures are put on children (Galton, 1980; Humphrey, 1993). If children are ridiculed, belittled, or threatened when they fumble, or if the coach gives attention only to the better players, then some children are not benefiting from participating on that team. On the other hand, if the coach gives extra support to those lacking in confidence, they will benefit in more ways than just improving their athletic skills. Thus sports training can be of benefit in developing an attitude of positive thinking and setting goals that go beyond what one thinks one can presently do. A significant factor is that coaches consider the developmental needs of children and foster an environment based on respect for effort rather than just for winning (Murphy, 1999). For example:

> At a gymnastics competition I saw a girl fall off the bar. She was not hurt, but her confidence was shaken. Her coach told her the mistake and made her do the routine again correctly even though it would not count for points. The girl took a deep breath, focused, and completed her flip on the bar. Everyone applauded. The girl learned not to give up if perfection is not achieved on the first attempt and that effort can be as appreciated by the audience as much as the performance.

In this soccer game it appears as though some girls are getting more enjoyment than others.

Adult Leadership Styles

Groups led by adults can differ markedly according to the kind of leadership provided. Leadership style influences socialization, as illustrated by a classic series of studies (Lewin, Lippitt, & White, 1939; Lippitt & White, 1943) that distinguished three kinds of adult leadership and measured their effects on groups of 10-year-old boys. The boys were organized into clubs and worked on such activities as soap carving, mask making, or mural painting. The three kinds of leadership were categorized as follows.

1. *Authoritarian*—policies, activities, techniques, and delegation of tasks were dictated by the leader. Praise and criticism of the group members' work was subjective. ("You are good at that.") The leader did not actively participate in the group's activities.

2. *Democratic (Authoritative)*—policies and activities were determined by group discussion. Techniques and delegation of tasks were presented by the leader in terms of alternatives from which the group members could choose. Praise and criticism were objective. ("Your soap carving has a lot of detailed work; it must have taken you a lot of time to do that.") The leader participated in the activities.

3. *Laissez-faire (Permissive)*—policies, activities, techniques, and delegation of tasks were left up to the group members. The leader supplied materials for the projects and was available for information, if requested. Comments about the group members' work were very infrequent. The leader did not participate in the group's activities.

Since each adult in the studies rotated the three leadership styles, differences in the group's behavior were determined to be a function of the style of leadership, rather than the leader's personality. Children in the groups with authoritarian leaders became either submissive or aggressive. The boys were discontented with the activities and worked less constructively when the leader left the room. They tended to be competitive with one another. Children in the groups with democratic leaders had high morale. The boys were involved in their group goals and were cooperative. They sustained their level of activity even when the leader left the room. Children in the groups with laissez-faire leaders were disorganized and frustrated. The boys made efforts to mobilize themselves as a group, but were unable to sustain their efforts.

In all three situations, the behavior of the adult set the tone for group effort (*see* Table 8.2). Within each situation, children got different messages about how to make decisions and work with others toward a goal.

Adult-Mediated Interaction

How adults mediate, or structure, the social interaction within a peer group—specifically, whether it is competitive or cooperative—influences children's behavior. To illustrate, psychologist Mustaf Sherif (1956) and his colleagues (Sherif, Harvey, White, Hood, & Sherif, 1961) conducted a series of naturalistic classic experiments in which middle-class, white, Protestant boys, 11 years old, were recruited and sent to a camp

Table 8.2	Socialization Effects of Leadership Styles
ADULT	**CHILDREN**
Authoritarian	aggressive submissive discontented competitive
Democratic	high morale cooperative self-supporting, cohesive
Laissez-faire	disorganized frustrated nonsupporting, fragmented

during the summer. He demonstrated that within a few weeks two sharply contrasting patterns of behavior in this sample of normal boys could be brought about by adult mediation. The sample was divided into two separate groups of boys (the Rattlers and the Eagles) who did not know each other. The counselor/observers were able to transform each group into a hostile, destructive, antisocial gang by various strategies, such as competitive sports where winning was all-important, and letting each group know the other group was "the enemy." Then the counselor/observers were able, within a few days, to change each group into cooperative, constructive workers and friends who were concerned about the other members of the community. Various problems at the camp were set up to foster cooperative spirit. For example, a water line was deliberately broken so that both groups of boys would have to work together to fix it. Another time, the camp truck broke down on the way to town for food. The boys had to help get the engine started.

Several findings emerged from Sherif's (1956) and his colleagues' (Sherif et al., 1961) naturalistic experiments regarding peer group behavior:

1. Groups tend to *stratify,* with some individuals assuming more dominant roles and others more submissive ones.
2. Groups develop *norms.* **Norms** are standards that serve to guide and regulate individuals' actions as members of a group.
3. Frustration and competition contribute to hostility between groups.
4. Competition *between* groups fosters cohesiveness *within* groups.
5. Intergroup hostility can often be reduced by setting up a *superordinate,* or common, goal that requires the mutual efforts of both groups. When overriding goals that are real and important for all concerned need to be achieved, then hostility between groups diminishes.

The significance of these studies of peer group dynamics is that it suggests strategies for enabling children to work together.

The findings on cooperation and competition were implemented by a team of researchers at Johns Hopkins University (Johnson & Johnson, 1999; Slavin, Devries, & Hutten, 1975). A Team Games Tournament (TGT) was developed to see if cooperation in a competitive setting would increase academic achievement. In TGT, four or five children of varying academic ability, gender, and race are put on a team. Teams are equated on average ability level. Individuals compete with individuals who are members of other teams. Each person's game score is added to those of the others on the team to form a team score. Team members cooperate by studying as a group and helping each other prepare for the tournament. TGT has had positive effects on mathematics achievement in the junior high school; language arts achievement in elementary school, and, in general, on attitudes about subject matter and classroom procedures. Increases have occurred in class solidarity, helping friendships among girls and boys as well as among children of differing ethnic backgrounds. A sample sociometric test, a measure of acceptance or rejection by the group, revealed that children who succeeded as team members were liked more than when they succeeded as individuals.

Epilogue

*P*eers are significant socializers. Acceptance by the group influences self-concept, behavior, and values. Rejection by the group can have damaging developmental consequences, as exemplified by the tragic shootings in 1999 at Columbine High School by two social outcasts.

Desire to be part of the group and have status within it is why children conform. Children compete within the group for power and leadership roles; leaders make the rules and manipulate the others, as exemplified by Tom Sawyer and Stephen Brewer. Whether the peer group engages in positive or negative behavior generally depends on influences of other socializing agents, such as family, school, and community. Tom had a strong family influence (his aunt kept constant "tabs" on him) and he found many things to do in his community, as well as friends with whom to do them. Stephen, on the other hand, did not have the involved attention of his parents, who were divorced. He felt abandoned by his father and ignored by his mother, who had to attend to his learning-disabled brother. He had negative experiences in school and found "nothing to do" in his community, so he had to look for things to keep him occupied and give him status in the eyes of friends to make him feel worthwhile. Thus, Tom's peer experiences were positive in that they contributed to his social skills; Stephen's peer experiences were negative in that they resulted in vandalism. ■

SUMMARY

Peers are a group of equals, usually of the same age, gender, and socioeconomic status, who share the same interests. Beyond the family and school, peers influence acquisition of skills, attitudes, and roles.

Having a group of friends meets certain needs of belonging and social interaction as well as promoting a sense of self and personal identity.

The need to belong is first established in the family via attachment. Infants and toddlers who are securely attached are more likely to interact socially with others. Opportunities for social interaction are influenced by parents.

The peer group influences the sense of self in that it provides opportunities for comparisons to others. It also influences personal identity in that it provides opportunities for independence from adults and allows children to "learn by doing." Children work through issues of power, compliance, cooperation, and conflict.

As children enter the middle years of childhood (age 6 to 12 or 13), the peer group becomes increasingly important. Experiments show that children become more susceptible to the influence of peers in middle childhood (especially around preadolescence, age 11 to 13) and become less conforming in adolescence. The reasons for this have to do with the child's cognitive level (transition from Piaget's stage of concrete operations to formal operations) and stage of personality development (entrance into Erikson's psychosocial stage of identity versus identity confusion). Also, the child's social cognitive abilities are becoming more complex.

The relative importance of adult and peer influence depends on parenting style, particular values, and ethnicity. Children of authoritative parents are less likely to be influenced by peers than are children of authoritarian or permissive parents. Parents, in general, are more likely to influence future decisions and values; peers, present ones. Ethnic groups valuing interdependence are more group-oriented than ethnic groups valuing independence.

The socializing mechanisms that peers employ to influence one another's behavior are reinforcement (approval and acceptance), modeling, punishment (rejection and exclusion), and apprenticeship (novice learns from expert).

The peer group functions to enable children to accomplish certain developmental tasks: getting along with others, developing morals and values, learning appropriate sociocultural roles, and achieving personal independence and identity. Peers are a significant source of sex education and an important influence on sexual activity.

When children get together in informal groups, they play. Play has cognitive, social, psychological, and adaptive functions for adult life.

Parten identified categories of play based on social interactions: solitary, onlooker, parallel, associative, and cooperative. Sutton-Smith identified four types of play based on activities: imitative, exploratory, testing, and model-building.

As children develop, their play, as well as their social relationships, becomes more complicated. Selman and Selman delineated five stages of friendship: momentary playmateship; one-way assistance; two-way, fair-weather cooperation; intimate, mutually shared relationships; and autonomous, interdependent friendships.

Sociometry is a set of techniques to measure acceptance, neglect, and rejection among members of a group. Children who are readily accepted by the peer group tend to be healthy, vigorous, initiating, well-poised, adaptable, conforming, dependable, affectionate, considerate, happy, enthusiastic, concerned for others, and self-confident. Family interaction patterns play a role in children's successful integration into the group.

Children who are neglected or rejected by the peer group tend to have difficulty initiating a friendship, have difficulty communicating, rarely praise their peers, and are shy, poor losers, cheaters, whiners, or aggressive. Sometimes children are rejected because they are different physically, behaviorally, style of dress, academically, or their names. Family problems can have damaging effects on children's peer relations.

Selman and Selman have applied their developmental stages of friendship in peer sociotherapy. Children who have trouble making and keeping friends can sometimes be helped to move on to the next developmental level.

Ways to help children improve their social skills and be more acceptable to their peers are modeling, participation, communication, cooperation, and validation/support. Children who were coached in these categories were more sociable and acceptable to their peers than those who were not coached.

Peer groups can have negative effects on children. Bullies who victimize children can cause psychological, as well as physical harm. Delinquency usually occurs in the peer groups whose members lack family support. Gangs are allegiances that engage in unlawful activities.

The influence of peers can be positive, too. Peer groups can be used to solve problems, educate, and help others with appropriate adult guidance. Examples are peer collaboration, tutoring, and counseling.

Groups structured by adults differ from those structured by children in that adults provide values, rules, and suggestions. Examples of adult-structured peer groups are clubs, teams, and recreation groups. Team sports are discussed in terms of their value for learning competitiveness and cooperation, and gaining self-esteem.

Groups led by adults can differ markedly according to the kind of leadership provided by the adult. Children in groups with authoritarian leaders tend to become either submissive or aggressive. Children in groups with democratic (authoritative) leaders tend to cooperate and have high morale. Children in groups with laissez-faire (permissive) leaders tend to be disorganized and frustrated.

How adults mediate, or structure, the social interaction within a peer group (competitive or cooperative) influences children's behavior. For example, frustration and competition contribute to hostility between groups, competition between groups fosters cohesiveness within each group, and intergroup hostility can often be reduced by setting a superordinate, or common, goal that requires the mutual efforts of both groups.

ACTIVITY

Purpose: To understand peer influences at different ages on attitudes, values, and behavior.

1. Choose at least six children (two preschoolers age 4 to 5; two elementary school children age 7 to 9; and two middle school children age 11 to 13). Separately ask each one the following questions, marking parents (P) or peers (pr) in the appropriate column in the chart below.

2. Write a summary of about a page on which choices were most influenced by parents and which were most influenced by peers. Explain. Did you notice an age difference regarding peer influence? Explain. Did you notice a personality difference, such as being shy or outgoing, in those children who chose peers over parents—or vice versa? Explain.

Child's name and age	Preschool		Elementary school		Middle school	
1. Who do you tell about what happened at school (your mom or dad or your friends?						
2. Who do you ask about which TV show you should watch?						
3. Who has helped you decide what you want to be when you grow up?						
4. Who most often helps you decide who your friends should be?						
5. Who do you talk to most about games or sports you would like to play?						
6. If someone hurts your feelings, whom do you talk to about it?						
7. Who suggests books to you to read (or toys to play with)?						
8. Who do you ask about what you should wear?						
9. If something exciting happened to you, whom would you tell first?						
10. Who tells you about snack foods to try?						

RESOURCES

American Youth Soccer Organization
http://www.soccer.org/

Boy Scouts of America
http://www.bsa.scouting.org/

Big Brothers/Big Sisters of America
http://www.bbbsa.org/

Boys and Girls Clubs of America
http://www.bgca.org/

Girl Scouts USA
http://www.gsusa.org/

Little League
http://www.littleleague.org/

RELATED READINGS

Asher, S. R., & Gottman, J. M. (Eds.). (1981). *The development of children's friendships.* Cambridge: Cambridge University Press.

Bukowski, M. W., Newcomb, A. F., & Hartup, W. W. (Eds.). (1996). *The company they keep: Friendship during childhood and adolescence.* New York: Cambridge University Press.

Dunn, J. (1988). *The beginnings of social understanding.* Cambridge, MA: Harvard University Press.

Elkind, D. (1981). *Children and adolescents: Interpretive essays on Jean Piaget.* New York: Oxford University Press.

Garvey, C. (1990). *Play.* Cambridge, MA: Harvard University Press.

Goldstein, A. P. (1991). *Delinquent gangs: A psychological perspective.* Champaign, IL: Research Press.

Harris, J. R. (1998). *The nurture assumption.* New York: Free Press.

Herron, R. E., & Sutton-Smith, B. (1971). *Child's play.* New York: Wiley.

Landre, R., Miller, M., & Porter, D. (1997). *Gangs: A handbook for community awareness.* New York: Facts on File Inc.

Olweus, D. (1993). *Bullying at school: What we know and what we can do about it.* Cambridge, MA: Blackwell.

"The medium is the message."

— *Marshall McLuhan*

ECOLOGY OF THE MASS MEDIA

Prologue

MESSAGES, METAPHORS, AND MIMES

*L*ong before people recorded events as history, the media used to share group traditions and values was oral stories that were passed from one generation to another. People developed the media of folktales and myths to attempt to explain natural phenomena and to make sense out of human nature. If a lesson or useful message was added to the story, it was called a fable.

A famous storyteller in ancient Asia Minor was Aesop. He served King Croesus as an entertainer, mime, and diplomat. Aesop's fables used animal characters with human qualities as metaphors to deliver his messages; that way the tales would not offend those for whom the lesson was intended. His fables traveled by word-of-mouth from one country to another and from old to young.

A very popular tale was "The Boy who Cried Wolf." It's about a boy who is employed to tend sheep but who is often bored with the task. One day he decided to create a little excitement by running into the village crying, "Wolf! Wolf!" When the villagers came to the rescue with clubs and pitchforks, they see nothing but the grazing sheep. This is such fun for the boy that a few days later he cried "Wolf!" again; once more the villagers came to help him and left empty-handed.

Several days passed when a wolf actually wanders out of the forest. The boy cried, "Wolf! Wolf! This time, however, the villagers ignored him, believing it to be just another one of the boy's tricks. Meanwhile, the wolf had a hearty meal of sheep.

The moral of the story is, one who lies will not be believed even when one speaks the truth.

Today's messages are not only spread orally, but via print and pictures as well. A modern fable is Roald Dahl's (1964) book, Charlie and the Chocolate Factory. The moral message in this elaborate tale of five children, similar to that of "The Boy Who Cried Wolf," is it pays to be honest and good.

Willy Wonka offers a tour of his chocolate factory and a lifetime supply of Wonka Bars to the lucky five children who find a golden ticket in their chocolate bars. The winners are Augustus Gloop, a greedy boy; Veruca Salt, a spoiled girl; Violet Beauregarde, a girl who constantly chews gum; Mike Teavee, a boy who does nothing but watch television; and Charlie Bucket (the hero), a kind and caring boy (he cares for his ailing relatives).

On the appointed day, the children accompanied by their parents show up at the Chocolate Factory for a tour. As they visit each room, one by one all the children, except Charlie, get into trouble because of their bad habits. For every mischievous deed, the factory workers—the Oompa Loompas—sing a metaphor and mime the appropriate lesson to be learned.

For example, Mike Teavee, the TV buff, is most fascinated by Willy Wonka's television chocolate room. Willy invented a machine to send chocolate to people's homes much the same way TV sends images. The children are told not to disturb anything in the room, but while Willy is demonstrating the machine, Mike disobeys and steps in front of the camera. He is instantly zapped and reduced to tiny particles that disappear into the air, later to reappear on the TV screen as a miniature Mike Teavee.

The Oompa Loompas sing the following message (Dahl, 1964, pp. 145–147):

The most important thing we've learned,
So far as children are concerned,
Is never, Never, NEVER let
Them near your television set—
Or better still, just don't install
The idiot thing at all.
In almost every house we've been,
We've watched them gaping at the screen.
They loll and slop and lounge about,
And stare until their eyes pop out. . . .

But did you ever stop to think,
To wonder just exactly what
This does to your beloved tot?
IT ROTS THE SENSES IN THE HEAD!
IT KILLS IMAGINATION DEAD!
IT CLOGS AND CLUTTERS UP THE MIND!
IT MAKES A CHILD SO DULL AND BLIND
HE CAN NO LONGER UNDERSTAND
A FANTASY, A FAIRYLAND!
HIS BRAIN BECOMES AS SOFT AS CHEESE!
HIS POWERS OF THINKING RUST AND FREEZE!
HE CANNOT THINK—HE ONLY SEES! . . .

What used the darling ones to do?
How used they keep themselves contented
Before this monster was invented?
Have you forgotten? Don't you know?
We'll say it loud and slow:
THEY . . . USED . . . TO . . . READ! They'd READ, READ, AND READ.

At the end of the factory tour, the only child left who did not get into trouble was Charlie. Willy Wonka bequeaths the Chocolate Factory to Charlie because he had proved himself to be trustworthy. The other children go home with their lifetime supplies of chocolate bars, the promised reward for having found the lucky tickets in their candy.

While both stories are similar in that they are fables intended to influence the moral behavior of those who hear or read them, they differ in how children's misbehavior is treated. The boy who cries "Wolf" is ignored by the villagers and loses his sheep to the wolf (learning by doing); all the children who misbehave in Willy Wonka's factory while they still get their supply of chocolate as promised, they don't get the factory (learning via punishment). ■

- *Does the form of the media (an oral fable, a printed story, a television show) make a difference in the message's impact on the audience?*
- *Do media shape culture, reflect it, or transform it?*
- *Do media stimulate critical thinking or inhibit it?*
- *Is media access to information a cultural equalizer or cultural divider of the information-rich and one information-poor?*

THE ROLE OF MASS MEDIA IN THE UNITED STATES

Media, the plural of *medium,* refers to a type of communication. A medium is an intervening means through which a force acts, or an effect is produced. This chapter discusses **mass media,** the form of communication in which large audiences quickly receive a given message via an impersonal medium between the sender and the receiver—for example, radio, television, movies, books, popular music, newspapers, magazines, and computers. The significance of the mass media (a microsystem) as a socializer is examined. Specifically, television, movies, books, magazines, popular music, computers, and video games are explored. How many children fantasize or build their dreams around what they have seen on television or read in books? How many young people have unrealistic expectations about the world of work, family life, and relationships? For example, many TV programs and movies that appeal to teenagers portray the teenager as wise and the adult as dumb. Such a portrayal gives adolescents the unrealistic expectation that they can assume an adult identity without much effort (Elkind, 1984). Some classic examples are Peter Pan and Pippi Longstocking; some contemporary ones are Bart Simpson and Madeline.

Whereas the media is a microsystem, its influence is often dependent on family variables, such as what (videotapes, books, CDs) is purchased, what alternative leisure activities (games, sports, museums, trips) are pursued, and/or how much adult supervision accompanies media exposure (Dorr & Rabin, 1995). To better understand how the various media influence children's socialization, their ecology is analyzed: "It is not what the media does to people but what people do with the media" (Lull, 1980, p. 198).

Marshall McLuhan's (1964) famous aphorism, "The medium is the message," means that media are extensions of the human being outside itself and "the 'message' of any medium as the change of scale or pace or pattern that it introduces into human affairs" (p. 8). Thus the mass media are *shapers of culture* in that their intervention affects us in some way. Culture includes the knowledge, beliefs, customs, skills, and patterns of behavior of a group of human beings. The mass media are also *spreaders of culture* in that they extend our capacity as human beings to process information and, in so doing, transform us in some way.

These interveners can *change* experience, *enhance* experience, or *interfere with* experience. Mass media can, for example, change the neutral experience of going to sleep into a frightening one for a child, by presenting monsters coming out from under a bed. Television can enhance the experience of a parade by providing close-up shots, supplying comments, and increasing the pace of the action. Television can also interfere with the experience of imagining what a storybook character looks like by choosing an actor with

Figure 9.1   An Ecological Model of Human Development

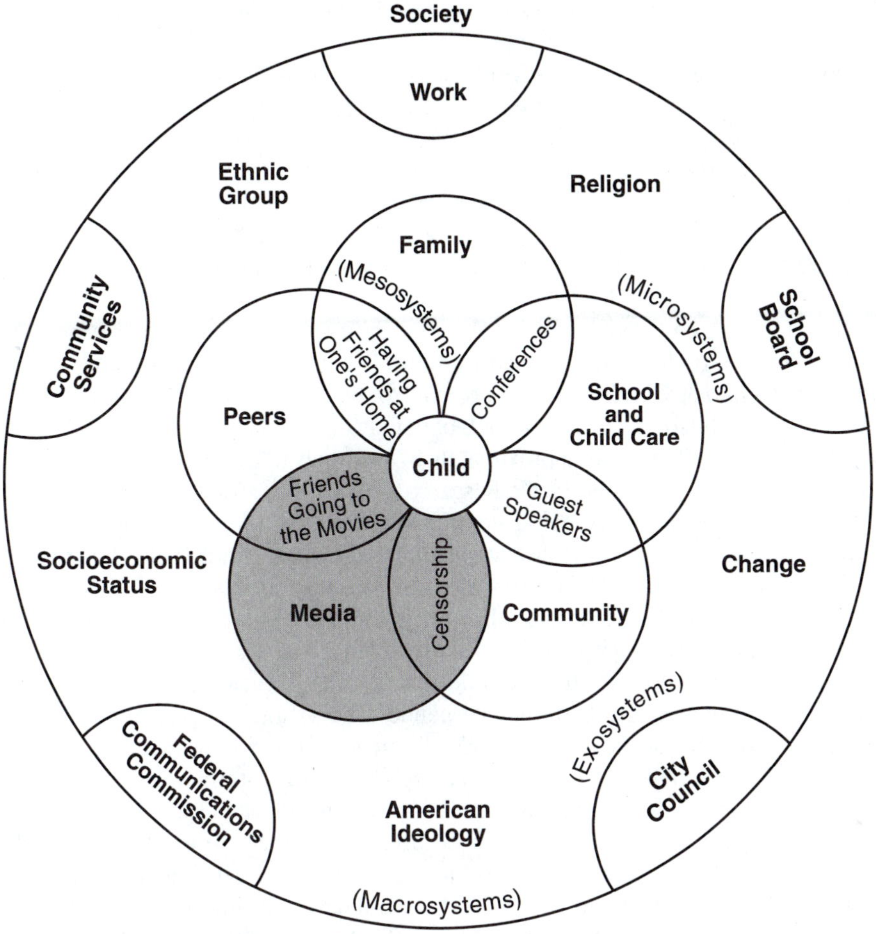

The media contribute to the socialization of the child.

certain characteristics to play the role. Movies can employ computer graphics and simulations to alter reality.

Extending our human capacity to process information changes the way we perceive the world. We can, via television, "see and hear things happening at the other end of the world" (Esslin, 1982). Satellite communications have transformed the world into a "global village" by compressing time and distance. According to McLuhan (1989), we now live in a global village that has become a global theater. Because of the electronic media revolution, we perceive ourselves differently than people did 50 years ago. Whereas learning about the world through reading is solitary, single-sensory, and gradual learning about the world through television, movies, and videos is massive, multisensory, and immediate. For example, how many of you followed the car chase of O. J. Simpson, or "attended" the funeral of Princess Diana? Learning about the world through computers equipped with the multimedia of graphics and sound is creative in that the user can make infinite combinations and projections with the available information. It is difficult to tell what is real and what is computer-simulated in some of today's movies.

More than 35 years ago, television was described in *TV Guide* as follows:

> What I think must be said is that television is not just a great force in modern life, but that it virtually is modern life. What, one might ask, doesn't it do? It gives us — be we rich, poor, snowbound, bedridden, or slow-witted — the time, the weather, the small news, sport news, now in spoken headlines, now in pictured narrative, now at the very scene of the crime or the coronation itself. It plays, sings, whistles and dances for us, takes us to movies and theaters, concerts and operas, prize fights and ball games, ski jumps and tennis tournaments. . . . It teaches you French, rope dancing, bird calls and first aid; provides debates and seminars and symposiums, quizzes and contests and it tells you jokes, gags, wheezes, wisecracks, jokes and jokes (Krononberger, 1966, p. 15).

Not much has changed except for TV's availability, choices, and pervasiveness. Most children growing up today have access to multiple channels, videotapes, and computer discs. This technology enables viewers to control what they will watch and when they will watch it. To illustrate the impact of technology on television viewing habits, the average U.S. household receives approximately 57 channels (3 times the number available in 1985), according to Nielsen Media Research. In addition, 85% to 90% of U.S. households have VCRs, which were not as common in the early 1980s, and most homes are wired for cable or have a satellite dish, compared to 20% in the mid-1980s (Lowry, 1999).

Most research on the role of mass media in socialization has been concerned with pictorial media, especially television, but print and sound media also have an impact. Television and movies have been criticized for violence and sex, but as will be seen later in this chapter, some books and music do the same. While books enhance language and cognitive development, some stereotype gender and ethnic groups. Some think the medium of music influences children. We all know from personal experience that setting words to music makes them easier to remember. Many commercials take advantage of this concept (Rosenfeld, 1985). We also know that music can alter our mood—make us relaxed or get us excited. Music has been used as therapy—for example, in breaking through the psychological isolation of autistic children (Rosenfeld, 1985). That computers can connect to the Internet, are interactive, and have multimedia capabilities makes them a potentially influential socializing agent (Postman, 1992). Since 1994, computers have expanded from 25% to 47% of U.S. homes and the percentage of people online has increased sixfold from 6% to 35% (Lowry, 1999).

BROADCASTING IN THE UNITED STATES

In order to understand the impact of the media on children, the broadcast system under which radio and television operates (Leibert & Sprafkin, 1988; Levin, 1998) is described. The mass communication system in the United States is generally characterized by private ownership and dedicated to corporate profits (this does not of course apply to public TV).

The broadcast media are subject to control by the Federal Communications Commission (FCC). That is, the federal government controls the frequencies, transmitting power, and transmitting times of radio and TV. During the 1930s, Congress established the principle that the airwaves belong to the people. Therefore, the government, through an agency, could legally issue licenses and control transmitters in the interest of the people. In addition to federal regulations, there are also state and local laws pertaining to broadcasting. Cable channels, because they do not use the public airwaves, are not under the same obligation to serve the public interest as broadcast television.

The FCC can award a license to broadcast when such an action is "in the public interest, convenience, or necessity." However, there are no clear standards for what constitutes "serving the public interest." When frequencies are available, they are auctioned to the highest bidder. The FCC is thus supposed to encourage competition. It is also prohibited from censoring program content. However, broadcasters must refrain from using obscene material and, until recently, had to regulate the amount of time allocated to commercials.

There are no comparable FCC rules for cable (pay) television or videocassettes. In 1984, the FCC lifted some of its restrictions under the general movement of the Reagan administration to deregulate and to reduce government intervention. The FCC held that marketplace competition could best serve children's interests. Two trends resulted from this shift in policy: educational content declined, and advertising increased. These developments led Congress to enact legislation known as the Children's Television Act of 1990. This law imposed a limit of 10.5 minutes of TV commercials each hour for children's programming on weekdays and 12 minutes an hour on weekends.

In 1997, most of the television industry implemented a rating system intended to give parents advance information (see box—Parental Guidelines) about the content of programs. Specifically, the guidelines address the degree of violence, foul language, and sexually suggestive content allowed. Television manufacturers are now installing V-chips—computer chips that can be programmed to block undesirable programs—in all new sets. They are also available as add-ons for existing TVs. These V-chips will enable families to set their own viewing standards.

Radio and TV make their profits from advertising. The broadcaster sells the advertiser time. Advertisers choose the vehicle—the program—that will expose the demographic audience best suited for their commercials. Within this system, control over content really rests with the audience. If the audience is not interested in the content of a program, the program is dropped. Thus the tastes and interests of viewers and listeners serve as indirect but powerful controls.

The main emphasis of mass communication in the United States is on entertainment (Huston, Zillman, & Bryant, 1994). Generally, the major media aim their content at the broadest spectrum of viewers in order to win the attention of the largest number of consumers to the products advertised on their programs. A major result is that the broadcast media must then continually produce a "mass culture" geared to popular or majority tastes. However, with new available technologies, such as cable, video, and computers audiences have become more fractionated, so advertisers have to target their products to special interests. Audiences become more fractionated as family income increases (Dorr & Rabin, 1995; Lowry, Jensen, & Braxton, 1999). This is because there are more TV sets as well as more choices of available technologies in higher socioeconomic statuses.

Therefore, as long as the broadcast media in the United States are designed to attract audiences to sell products, they will convey messages that are likely to influence attitudes and behavior (Huston, Zillman, & Bryant, 1994).

Parental Guidelines (TV and Movies)

Television

There are two categories of ratings, one for children's programs and one for programs not specifically designed for children. The ratings are as follows:

The following categories apply to programs designed solely for children:

 All Children. *This program is designed to be appropriate for all children.* Whether animated or live action, the themes and elements in this program are specifically designed for a very young audience, including children ages 2–6. This program is not expected to frighten young children.

Directed to Older Children. *This program is designed for children age 7 and above.* It may be more appropriate for children who have acquired the developmental skills needed to distinguish between make-believe and reality. Themes and elements in this program may include mild fantasy or comedic violence, or may frighten children under the age of 7. Therefore, parents may wish to consider the suitability of this program for their very young children. Programs containing fantasy violence that may be more intense or more combative than other programs in this category are designed as TV-Y7-FV.

The following categories apply to programs designed for the entire audience:

General Audience. *Most parents would find this program suitable for all ages.* Although this rating does not signify a program designed specifically for children, most parents may let younger children watch this program unattended. It contains little or no violence, no strong language, and little or no sexual dialogue or situations.

Parental Guidance Suggested. *This program contains material that parents may find unsuitable for younger children.* Many parents may want to watch it with their younger children. The theme itself may call for parental guidance and/or the program contains one or more of the following: moderate violence (V), some sexual situations (S), infrequent coarse language (L), or some suggestive dialogue (D).

Parents Strongly Cautioned. *This program contains some material that many parents would find unsuitable for children under age 14 years of age.* Parents are strongly urged to exercise greater care in monitoring this program and are cautioned against letting children under the age of 14 watch unattended. This program contains one or more of the following: intense violence (V), intense sexual situations (S), strong coarse language (L), or intensely suggestive dialogue (D).

Mature Audience Only. *This program is specifically designed to be viewed by adults and therefore may be unsuitable for children under 17.* This program contains one or more of the following: graphic violence (V), explicit sexual activity (S), or crude, indecent language (L).

When a program is broadcast, the appropriate icon should appear in the upper left corner of the picture frame for the first 15 seconds. If the program is longer than one hour, the icon should be repeated at the beginning of the second hour. Guidelines are also displayed in TV listings in a number of newspapers and magazines.

Movies

G	**GENERAL AUDIENCES**	All ages admitted.
PG	**PARENTAL GUIDANCE SUGGESTED**	Some material may not be suitable for children.
PG-13	**PARENTS STRONGLY CAUTIONED**	Some material may be inappropriate for children under 13.
R	**RESTRICTED**	Under 17 requires accompanying parent or adult guardian.
NC-17	**NO ONE 17 AND UNDER ADMITTED**	

PICTORIAL MEDIA: TELEVISION AND MOVIES

Television and movies have evoked many concerns, especially about their content, their socializing effects on children, and how the public should respond. Movies include videos as well as those seen in theaters.

Television has certain properties that distinguish it from other media (Singer, Singer, & Zuckerman, 1990):

- Attention demand
- Brevity of sequences
- Rapid succession of presented material
- Visual orientation

Children are a special audience in regard to the medium of television (Dorr, 1986; Levin, 1998). Because of cognitive immaturity, they are generally assumed to be more vulnerable than adults to the amount of time spent watching TV and to believing that the images they see are real; that violence is the way to solve problems; that one should buy what is advertised; that the values, stereotypes, and behavior portrayed on TV constitute the way one should be: "Television is a particularly appealing medium to young children in part because many of its images and modes of representation are readily understood; it does not require the child to learn a complicated system of decoding as reading does, for example" (Huston, Zillman, & Bryant, 1994, p. 5). As a result, television has major socializing potential.

CONCERNS ABOUT TELEVISION AND MOVIES

Advances in television broadcasting have created changes in the sleep habits, meal arrangements, use of leisure time, and conversation patterns of millions of U.S. families (Huston, Zillman, & Bryant, 1994; Leibert & Sprafkin, 1988). Mass communications have also created changes in our culture. New products advertised via television, magazines, newspapers, and the Internet can be adopted in a very short time. The rapid spread of other cultural forms, such as fashion fads, hairstyles, and types of music or sports, can be stimulated by the media. All of these changes have understandably given rise to some concern.

> It has never been much of a secret . . . that movies influence manners, attitudes, and behavior. In the fifties, they told us how to dress for a rumble or a board meeting, how far to go on the first date, what to think about Martians or, closer to home, Jews, blacks, and homosexuals. They taught girls whether they should have husbands or careers, boys whether to pursue work or pleasure. They told us what was right and what was wrong, what was good and what was bad; they defined our problems and suggested solutions (Biskind, 1983, p. 2).

Statistics on TV Viewing*

- Preschoolers (age 2 to 5) view about 15 hours of TV per week. Preschoolers spend most time viewing weekdays from 10 A.M. to 4:30 P.M. and evenings from 8 P.M. to 11 P.M.

- School-age children (age 6 to 11) watch about 23 hours of TV per week. Most of their viewing time is in the evening.

- Saturday morning "Kid Vid" viewing accounts for only about 14% of the total time children spend watching TV.

- Two-thirds of children age 8 and older have a TV set in their bedroom as do one-third of children ages 2 to 7.

Sources: Nielson, 1998; Kaiser Family Foundation, 1999.

Time Spent Watching TV and Movies Is Time Away from Other Activities

The statistics on TV viewing habits indicate that, on average, children spend nearly 3 to 5 hours a day in front of the television set and often do it with little parental monitoring (Huston & Wright, 1998; Kaiser Family Foundation, 1999). Young children from economically and educationally disadvantaged backgrounds spend even more time watching TV than do children from more affluent, better-educated families (Dorr, 1982; Huston & Wright, 1998).

Obviously, if children are spending that much time in front of the television set or VCR, activities that they might otherwise be engaged in, such as reading, hobbies, games, sports, and family or peer interaction, are being neglected. As Urie Bronfenbrenner (1970c) wrote:

> Like the sorcerer of old, the television set casts its magic spell, freezing speech and action, turning the living into silent statues so long as the enchantment lasts. The primary danger of the television screen lies not so much in the behavior it produces — although there is danger there — as in the behavior it prevents: the talks, the games, the family festivities and arguments through which much of the child's learning takes place and through which his character is formed. Turning on the television set can turn off the process that transforms children into people.

Family Life and Rituals. Rituals are shared customs or ceremonies that give life meaning (Bria, 1998). Marie Winn (1977), in *The Plug In Drug,* discusses what has happened to family life and rituals with the advent of television. She defines family rituals as "those regular, dependable recurrent happenings that gave members of a family a feeling of belonging to a home . . . those experiences that act as the adhesive of family unity" (p. 124).

> For example, when I was a small child, my grandmother had weekly family dinners, at which we children got to tell all the adults about our achievements and then gloried in their praise. We also got to listen to adult gossip. When we got bored by the conversation, we'd explore my grandmother's house. She had drawers full of old clothes, pictures, and letters—she never threw away anything. Or we'd play cards, and if we lost, we could always hustle a game with one of the adults, who would see to it that we'd win. That was before my grandmother bought a TV.

Although television may have replaced extended family conversations around the dinner table, card games, or singing songs, it has become an integral part of family life in that viewing is an activity that usually occurs with other family members, especially for young children. Parents and siblings provide a model of how to use television, and children are exposed to what their parents and siblings view simply because they are in the same household (Huston & Wright, 1998). A generation ago, when only about 50% of homes had more than one TV set, families assembled to watch shows together. Now, with the majority of households having multiple televisions, opportunities for shared experiences decrease (Lowry, 1999).

Family Interactions.   Time spent watching TV affects family interactions—development of relationships, communication, and resolutions of problems. Interpersonal relationships take work. To get along with someone, you must be able to communicate your feelings and wishes as well as receive that person's feelings and wishes. When these feelings and wishes are *compatible,* the two individuals are said to "get along"; when they are *incompatible,* the two must compromise in order to get along. The compromise may involve taking turns or modifying one's desires. Although parents and children are often in close proximity when watching TV, sometimes touching and hugging, they tend to talk less to one another when viewing TV than in other activities (Wright, St. Peters, & Huston, 1990).

The values of working at interpersonal relationships in children's development are numerous. The children get language training. They must use words to express feelings and wishes. They must receive a message and process it and respond to it. By having to listen to another's message, the child is also moving away from egocentrism (the inability to see things from another's point of view). Finally, the child is involved in problem-solving, if a compromise has to be reached. These values or attributes of working at an interpersonal relationship are interfered with by the high incidence of television viewing. If, however, parents discuss the show with their children, they can provide some interactive experiences.

Telling the Difference Between Reality and Fantasy

According to Piaget (1962), young children think very differently from adults. They believe that everything that moves is alive, that the sun follows them when they go for a walk, and that dreams come in through the window at night when they sleep. Preschool children believe that the cartoon characters and actual people they see on television are all equally "real" and are inside the television set. This is because they have difficulty conceptualizing the distinction between a pictorial representation and an actual one. They also have difficulty understanding pretense (Flavell, Miller, & Miller, 1993). Preschool children believe that they can turn off a program and that the same program will be on when they turn on the set again (as if one were putting a marker inside a book). For the preschool child, reality (*actual* objects) and fantasy (*images* of objects) are likely to be interchangeable. Flavell (1986) demonstrated the difficulty that preschoolers have distinguishing appearance from reality. For example, 3-year-olds assert that a rock-shaped sponge really is a rock as well as looking like one. However, children over age 5 can make the distinction.

Preschool children usually cannot distinguish the commercial from the program. This may be because they can only deal with one "script" at a time (Flavell, Miller, & Miller, 1993). They also accept the message literally and uncritically. Because of their stage of cognitive development, preschool children are unable to understand that advertisements are intended to sell products rather than entertain them. The gullibility of preschool children can be dangerous. A number of children each month are brought to hospital emergency rooms with broken bones from leaping from tops of buildings or smashing objects with bare hands—a sad way to find out you are not Superman. One 4-year-old spent two days in intensive hospital care after swallowing 40 children's vitamins—the TV commercial said vitamins would make him "big and strong real fast" (Leibert, Neil, & Davidson, 1973). It is not until about age 7 that children realize ads are intended to be persuasive messages. And although ability to evaluate advertising claims increases with age, even adolescents exhibit gullibility (Dorr & Rabin, 1995).

Because young children confuse reality and fantasy, many of their ideas about the world beyond their families and neighborhood come from television programs and movies (Cantor, 1998; Greenfield, 1984). The more limited the life experiences or economic circumstances of children, the more likely they are to believe what they see on television. Although some people believe that fantasy on television can lead to imaginative and creative expression, it also permits children (especially troubled ones) to retreat from real-life situations and can encourage them to seek immediate gratification of their impulses or instant solutions to problems (Comstock & Paik, 1991).

"Television substitutes its own image of reality (usually made to the specifications of adult media executives) for the image of reality the child is beginning to form as he develops his capacity for symbolic activity" (Gatz, 1975, pp. 415–418). In effect, TV is saying, "This is the world the way it is." Because children have not experienced much of the real world, they accept what TV portrays as the truth and neglect to test it against reality.

As children get older (between age 5 and 7) and have more experience with different types of TV programming, as well as reality, they can later recognize form and content cues denoting fact and fiction on TV (Wright, Huston, Reitz, & Piemymat, 1994). By about age 7 or 8, children come to distinguish between things that are real and those that are make-believe on television. At first, they judge according to format (cartoons are make-believe and live-action shows are real). Then they come to realize that certain things portrayed on TV—whether animated or live—are physically impossible (people can't fly like Superman). They come to evaluate reality on TV based on whether things in the story match what exists in the real world (a police story is real because police are present in the community). By about age 10, children begin to understand that some programs are script-acted for the purpose of telling a story, while others show real events that actually happened, such as news and documentaries (Cantor, 1998).

Imagination. Jean Piaget (1962) believed the thinking process involves a balance between the demands the outside world makes on us (objectivity) and the demands we make on the outside world (subjectivity). When this balance is shifted in the direction of the data presented by the world, we *imitate*. When it is shifted in the direction of our interpretation, we *imagine*. "Imaginative play," writes Piaget (1962), "is a symbolic transposition which subjects things to the child's activity without rules or limitations" (p. 87). When a child plays, the world bends itself to the child's wishes. For example:

5-year-old Tammy went to her room after lunch, having come home from kindergarten. She didn't nap anymore, but her mother felt she needed some quiet time alone before going outside to play with her friends. Tammy got out her model horses and "galloped" them around her bed on the floor. The horses spoke to each other—they were arguing over space to graze. Tammy then got out her blocks and attempted to build a barn for one of the horses. She succeeded in building the sides but could not get the roof to stay on without tumbling on the horse. The play then abruptly changed to a rodeo, and the blocks used to build a barn became an obstacle course. The horses, no longer arguing, took turns jumping and turning corners, complete with sound effects. Forty-five minutes had passed, and Tammy emerged from her room cheerful and ready to play with her friends.

These children are engaged in imaginative play.

Television makes imagination subservient to imitation. Further, TV's images become reality for the child, who is then unable to later break through that mindset when the real world is experienced. For example, studies by Singer and Singer (1990) found that children, age 3 to 8, whose play themes reflected specific television references to cartoons, superheroes, and action-detective shows were more likely to be aggressive. The children's imagination was measured by an inkblot test. It was found that those with the least imagination, who also watched television with large amounts of violence, were most likely to imitate the aggression in school. They also found that the imaginative children were less likely to engage in impulsive acts or gross aggression.

Although television does not ordinarily stimulate imaginative play and creativity, children do find ideas for make-believe play in everything around them, including television. In a review of the research, Van der Voort and Valkenburg (1994) found that television's influence on imaginative play depended on the type of program. Benign, nonviolent programs did not directly affect imaginative play, whereas programs with high levels of violence reduced imaginative play. However, certain educational programs were exceptions in that they did enhance imaginative activities.

While imaginative play and creativity may be reduced by heavy viewing, if an adult watches TV with a child, the adult can stimulate the child's imagination by asking questions about the show, interpreting words and actions on the show, and suggesting various alternative solutions to what is happening.

Effects of the Prevalence of Violence in Television and Movies

"Television and movies, by their very nature, have the ability to introduce children to frightening images, events, and ideas, many of which they would not encounter in their entire lives without the mass media" (Cantor, 1998, p. 3). An example is **violence,** defined as the "overt expression of physical force against others or self, or compelling action against one's will and pain of being hurt or killed or actually hurting or killing (Gerbner, Gloss, Jackson-Beck, Jeffries-Fox, & Signorielli, 1978). Violence on TV is measured in terms of *prevalence, rate,* and *role.* Prevalence is the extent to which violence occurs in the program; rate is the frequency of violent episodes; and role is the number of characterizations of violence or victimization. Violence on television is a concern because, over the years, there has been an increase in violence on children's Saturday morning programs as well as on prime time television (8 to 11 P.M.) (Condry, 1989; Mediascope, 1996). The National Television Violence Study (NTVS) (Mediascope, 1996) has demonstrated that not all violence portrayed on TV has similar effects on children. Characterization in which the perpetrator is attractive is more likely to influence the viewer's identification and modeling. When violence is justified, goes unpunished, or shows no harm or pain to the victim, it is also more likely to influence viewer behavior.

According to the Center for Media and Public Affairs (CMPA 1999), scenes of serious violence (physical force) hammer TV viewers and moviegoers every 4 minutes (CMPA 1999). A majority of the 10 most violent television movies carried a PG-13 rating and a majority of the 10 most violent television shows were rated TV-PG. The concern is not only the prevalence of violence, but that it is portrayed as necessary and relatively harmless.

While it may be difficult to prove that excessive viewing of televised violence can or does provoke violent crime in any *one* individual, it is clear that if children watch a great deal of televised violence, they will be more prone to behave aggressively than those children who do not watch TV violence (Geen, 1994). The NTVS (1996) demonstrated that the context in which most violence is presented on TV poses certain risks for viewers: (1) learning to behave violently, (2) becoming more desensitized to violence, and (3) becoming more fearful of being attacked. Characteristics of the child such as age, real experiences, temperament, and cognitive developmental level, influence the impact of viewing violence. Explanations from psychological research for these findings follow.

Observational Learning.   Observational learning is based on Albert Bandura's (1974, 1989) social cognitive theory; we learn by observing and imitating behavior. This theory states that role models, especially attractive ones, act as stimuli to produce similar behavior in the observer of the role model. The behavior is learned by being imitated, rewarded, or reinforced in a variety of ways. Responses produced often enough and over a long enough period of time maintain the behavior. Bandura outlines four steps necessary for this process: (1) attention to the stimulus, (2) retention of the observed behavior and consequences, (3) ability to reproduce the behavior, and (4) motivation to perform the observationally learned behavior.

Are children likely to learn and remember new forms of aggressive behavior by watching them on TV? If children learn and remember, will they practice the behavior? Yes, research shows that children do learn and remember novel forms of aggression seen on TV or in films. They are more likely to remember the behavior learned by observation if they have tried it at least once. Whether or not children will practice the behavior depends on the similarity of the observed setting and their real setting; that is, if they imitate an observed aggression and it "works" (is reinforced) in solving a problem or attaining a goal, it is likely to be repeated. For example, a young child who sees Superman punching a criminal to retrieve a bag of money and prevent innocent bystanders from getting shot might be likely to try the observed aggressive behavior to take a toy away from another child, not having comprehended the concept of the Superman scene—that aggression is justifiable for protection. If the child's aggressive behavior results in getting the toy, the child is likely to repeat the behavior. Thus, children may learn aggressive behavior from TV, but whether or not they perform it depends on factors within the child such as anger, as well as the situation (Condry, 1989; Huston & Wright, 1998; Leibert & Sprafkin, 1988).

Attitude Change.   Watching television influences people's attitudes. The more television children watch, the more accepting they are of aggressive behavior. It has been shown that persons who often watch television tend to be more suspicious and distrustful of others, and they also believe there is more violence in the world than do those who do not watch much television (Comstock & Paik, 1991; Pearl, 1982).

Attitudes in psychological theory are attributions, rules, and explanations that people gradually learn from observations of behavior. Therefore, it can be assumed that if someone watches a great deal of television, attitudes will be built upon the basis of what is seen, and the attitudes will, in turn, have an effect on behavior.

Apparently, young children are more willing to accept aggressive behavior of other children after viewing violent scenes (Paik & Comstock, 1994; Thomas & Drabman, 1975). However, studies have shown that children's attitudes are changed if adults discuss the program (Huston & Wright, 1998). In an experimental study (Huesmann, Eron, Klein, Brice, & Fisher, 1983), one group of children who regularly watched violent programs were shown excerpts from violent shows. They then took part in discussion sessions about the unreality of television violence as well as alternative strategies to solve conflicts, and wrote essays. Another group, who also watched many violent programs, were shown nonviolent excerpts followed by a neutral discussion of content. The group who took part in the sessions on unreality and alternative strategies were significantly less aggressive than the control group.

Arousal.   Arousal theories examine physiological changes in the body and subsequent emotions that occur when viewing violent episodes. One response might be *desensitization.*

Does viewing violence on TV decrease one's sensitivity to it in real life? Research shows that as a result of the repetition of violence in the media, classical desensitization takes place. **Desensitization,** the gradual reduction in response to a stimulus due to repeated exposure, is practiced in behavior therapy. It is used to get over a fear. For example, the more exposure to riding in an airplane, the less the fear of flying. There was a story several years ago in the newspaper depicting this very kind of desensitization. A masked burglar gagged and tied a woman to a chair while he robbed her home of valuables. He had told her 5-year-old son to watch television and not to call the police until the show was over. Four hours later, the son phoned. Apparently, the boy's emotional sensitivity to the real event had been so reduced as to not react immediately. Also, the boy may have been so accustomed to seeing similar events on TV that he was not cognizant of the seriousness of the real event.

A study of school-age boys who regularly looked at violent programs showed less of a physiological response when they looked at new violent programs (Pearl, 1982), compared to boys who were not used to viewing much violence (Condry, 1989). If viewing violence desensitizes one to aggression, then the material will have to be more and more graphic in order to keep the audience attentive. Some TV critics believe this is exactly what has occurred.

Another response might be *increased aggression* due to the increase in general arousal, which occurs because viewing televised violence releases socialized constraints on one's behavior. Thus, televised aggression can have a disinhibiting effect, making subsequent aggression, after viewing violence, more likely, especially in certain situations (Condry, 1989).

TV Advertising Messages

Every hour of television is carefully planned to contain enough minutes for "commercial messages." By selling commercial messages to advertisers, TV stations are able to defray the costs of their programs. Commercials are cost effective. Even though seconds cost thousands of dollars, mailings to individuals would cost much more. The federal agency responsible for regulating TV commercials is the Federal Trade Commission (FTC). The Better Business Bureau, to which most advertisers belong, has a self-regulatory Children's Advertising Review Unit.

Annually, on average, children between ages 2 and 11 are exposed to between 20,000 and 40,000 television commercials. The number of product commercials has increased steadily (Condry, Bence, & Scheibe, 1988; Kerkman, Kunkel, Huston, Wright, & Pinon, 1990). On a typical Saturday morning, the average young viewer may see over 100 child-directed commercials. Including advertising directed specifically at them, children are exposed to toy, cereal, sugared snacks, and beverage commercials.

Why advertise to children? Children have decades of buying power ahead of them and, unlike adults, they have no preconceived product preferences. They are open to suggestion and are impulsive (Stabiner, 1993). Advertisers report that children start asking for brand names as early as 2 years old. One successful way to gain a child consumer is to give the child a sense of power or importance. For example, Kool-Aid was marketed as a product "just for kids." Also, it contained coupons that children could save and trade in for toys (Stabiner, 1993).

Gorn and Goldberg (1982) directly tested the effects of exposure to commercials for sugared snacks on children's actual food selections. The study was conducted in a summer camp setting with children who were between age 4 and 8. During each of 14 consecutive days, the children viewed a different half-hour, Saturday morning cartoon. Four experimental groups were devised according to the nature of the commercials: (1) sweetened snack foods, such as candy, Cracker Jacks, and Kool-Aid; (2) fruit, such as orange juice or grapes; (3) public service announcements that emphasized the value of eating a balanced, nutritional diet; and (4) no commercials. The commercials took up 4.5 minutes during a half-hour show. Snack choices were made available each day immediately after the television viewing. The snack choices consisted of orange juice, Kool-Aid, two fruits, and two candy bars. The children exposed to the sweetened snack food commercials selected Kool-Aid and candy more often than did the other groups. The children exposed to the fruit commercials selected the most orange juice and more fruit than the sweetened snack group.

As the National Institute of Mental Health report confirms, "television seems to be doing a rather poor job of helping its audience to attain better health or better understanding of health practices." The report cites evidence showing a disproportionate number of commercials for sweet and snack foods, compared to nutritious foods (Pearl, 1982). Much research since the report documents that children who watch a lot of TV are fatter than children who watch less (Dorr & Rabin, 1995; Huston & Wright, 1998). This is partially due to lack of physical activity and partially due to the tendency to snack when watching TV.

Gullibility. Young children take things literally, rather than figuratively, which makes them more vulnerable to advertising messages (Stabiner, 1993). Although most children by age 3 distinguish program content from commercials, children below age 8 seldom understand that the purpose of the ad is to sell something. Research suggests that repeated exposure to ads turns children into mini-salespersons who make demands on their parents for what they see advertised on TV (Kunkel & Roberts, 1991). Their parents, in turn, complain that advertising causes conflict in the parent–child relationship ("I want" versus "You can't have").

Whereas children below age 8 do not understand the persuasive intent of advertising and are, therefore, particularly vulnerable to its appeals, children over age 8, who are more aware of the purposes of advertising, are still apt to be persuaded by appeals that are subtly deceptive or misleading (Huston, Watkins, & Kunkel, 1989). For example, they don't understand product disclosures or disclaimers, comparative claims, the real meaning of endorsements by famous characters, or the use of premiums, promotions, and sweepstakes (Council of Better Business Bureaus, 2000).

To illustrate the fact that young children do not critically evaluate the commercials they see, one study (Atkin & Gibson, 1978) showed that children often take advertisements literally. Two cartoon characters, Fred Flintstone and Barney Rubble, said a cereal was "chocolatey enough to make you smile." When asked why they wanted the cereal, two-thirds of the children said because of the chocolate taste, three-fifths said because it would make them smile, and over half said because Fred and Barney like it. Another study (Atkin & Gibson, 1978) reported that children who saw a cereal advertisement with a circus strongman lifting a heavy weight believed that eating the cereal would make them strong.

Despite increased awareness of the purpose of advertising, even older children find commercials convincing. In a study of 8- to 14-year-old boys, celebrity endorsement of a racing toy made the product more attractive; including live racetrack footage led to exaggerated estimates of the toy's features as well as decreased awareness that the ad was staged (Ross, Campbell, Wright, Huston, Rice, & Turk, 1984).

An increasing development in children's program production is the making of programs that feature characters corresponding to toys (Levin, 1998), "toy tie-in" marketing. In essence, these are program-length

Marketing products to children has become common.

commercials and constitute unfair soliciting of children, according to Action for Children's Television (Condry, 1989; Huston & Wright, 1998; Leibert & Sprafkin, 1988). Product-related programming is of concern for reasons other than its commercial intent. Its content is "formulaic" and stereotyped (Huston & Wright, 1998). Children's play with program-featured toys was found to be more imitative and less imaginative than play with other toys (Greenfield, Yut, Chung, & Land, 1990). Another new development causing concern is interactive TV programming. Children buy the required toy, such as a gun, aim it at the screen, and exchange fire with on-screen enemies (Tuchscherer, 1988). Recently, interactive toys ("Teletubbies") have been developed for children as young as 1 year.

Adolescents are affected by TV commercials, too. According to the Centers for Disease Control (1994), by glamorizing smoking, cigarette advertising increases the likelihood that teenagers will experiment with cigarettes. The same holds true for alcohol (U.S. Department of Health and Human Services, 1992).

If children are influenced by TV ads for toys and foods, what about all the medication commercials? Although ads for medicine are not intentionally directed at children, children are nevertheless exposed to them. Do the ads give children the perception that drugs give quick relief for pain or stress? Does exposure to such advertising increase the likelihood that children will turn to drugs when they have problems? These questions are being researched. What is known so far is that children in stressful families (divorce, alcoholism, abuse, and/or economic problems) watch more television, reportedly to escape their problems (Dorr & Rabin, 1995). According to Neil Postman (1982, pp. 43-45), New York University Professor of Communication Arts and Sciences,

> A commercial teaches a child three interesting things. The first is that all problems are resolvable. The second is that all problems are resolvable fast. And the third is that all problems are resolvable fast through the agency of some technology. It may be a drug. It may be a detergent. It may be an airplane or some piece of machinery, like an automobile or computer.

The essential message of a commercial, then, is that people have problems—lack of confidence, lack of friends, lack of money, lack of health, and so on, and these problems are solvable through the product advertised.

According to James McNeal (1987), author of *Children As Consumers,* advertisers are attuned to children's developmental stages and their needs for peer approval, status, and independence. The basic advertising message being communicated, then, is "things make the person."

Commercialism not only invades the home, it is present in the school as well. Chapter 6 discussed some advertising strategies (Channel One, fundraisers, sponsorships of clubs and sports). Are the promotional messages and commercial influences undermining the integrity of children's education (Aidman, 1995)? Studies demonstrate that students in schools with Channel One show a greater consumer orientation and intent to purchase products than students not exposed to Channel One (Huston & Wright, 1998).

Perpetuation of Values (Behavior, Sexuality, Stereotypes)

Values refer to qualities or beliefs that are viewed as desirable or important. They influence attitudes, motives, and behavior.

As has been discussed, children not only watch "Kid Vid" but spend much of their viewing time watching "adult" programs (action/dramas, situation comedies, news). The problem with this is that an adult knows about certain aspects of life—its tragedies, its contradictions, its unfairness, its mysteries, its joys—whereas a child does not have the intellectual capabilities or the life experiences to comprehend these aspects. What television does, then, is communicate the same information to everyone simultaneously, regardless of age, level of education, or experience. And, in the quest for new material to hold its audience, television has been increasingly exposing its audiences to life experiences previously considered forbidden: explicit sexuality, adultery, family violence, incest, corruption, extreme violence, pornography, and horror. Consequently, "with TV's relentless revelation of all adult secrets, it is not inconceivable that in the near future we shall return to the thirteenth- and fourteenth-century situation in which no words were unfit for a youthful ear" (Postman, 1982). If so, what values are being perpetuated?

Behavior.   According to Dr. Isidore Ziferstein, a fellow of the American Psychiatric Association, television has presented to children a set of "anti-values" regarding behavior (Larrick, 1975). For example:

- *Anti-interpersonal relations values:* A woman kills her husband in order to get his insurance.
- *Anticooperation values:* Life is presented on television as consisting of conflicts, strife, and war.
- *Antidemocratic values:* Television heroes succeed by operating outside the law.

Thus the viewer does not get much information on cooperation, peace, and obeying the laws. A television show often contains more excitement, adventure, power, and violence than the average person experiences in a lifetime. By comparison, everyday life seems boring (Huston & Wright, 1998).

Not all shows present negative values; some exhibit socially desirable behaviors that benefit others. Studies have shown that children who watch altruistic behavior (generosity, helping, and cooperation) on television become more altruistic themselves (Comstock & Paik, 1991). For example, children who watched a prosocial episode of *Lassie,* in which Lassie's master risked his life by hanging over the edge of a mineshaft to rescue Lassie's puppy, exhibited more prosocial behavior than did children who watched a neutral episode of *Lassie* (Sprafkin, Leibert, & Poulos, 1975). While many children's TV shows today are designed to illustrate prosocial behavior, there are few *lasting* effects unless an adult watches the show with the child and discusses the positive behavior as well as encourages the child to model it. Unfortunately, research shows that not many adults do so (Dorr & Rabin, 1995).

According to Fred Rogers, host and producer of *Mister Rogers' Neighborhood:*

So much of what we see on television is so terrifically limited. Just think of the problem solving on television that people are exposed to and how in so many instances, it is so uncreative. If somebody gets angry with somebody else, he just annihilates that other person. Children look to adults to discover how they solve problems. . . . It would be helpful for kids to see that there is a wide variety of ways to deal in a constructive fashion with what the world hands out (Boyer, 1983, p. 1).

Sexuality.   Presentation of behaviors, lifestyles, and attitudes that are felt to be harmful to children has led some parents to organize into groups to protest against what they consider to be invasions of family and religious values. For example, TV is bolder about sexual activity than it was several years ago. The shows of the 1970s that caused a furor only talked about sex, whereas the shows of the late 1980s and 1990s present sex acts visually. Men and women are now seen in bed together. Moreover, these presumably copulating couples are typically not married to each other. Finally, sex acts previously considered taboo, such as sexual abuse, incest, rape, and prostitution, are now openly discussed and depicted on TV (Greenberg, 1994; Leibert & Sprafkin, 1988).

A significant portion of adolescents' sex education comes from prime-time TV programming. Watching shows depicting premarital, extramarital, or nonmarital sex affects the moral values of young teens in that they report such sexual behavior to be acceptable. However, family discussions of values can intervene (Bryant & Rockwell, 1994).

Young people today are exposed to an incessant flow of sexual images. Television and movies have increasingly included nudity, profanity, and sexually explicit activities. Sex appeal and sexual activity are glamorized. Unfortunately, much less attention is paid by the media to the potential consequences of casual sexual behavior. It wasn't until 1995 that TV and radio carried ads for condoms (Jaffee, 1998).

Stereotypes.   **Stereotypes** are oversimplified representations of members of a group. Stereotypes generally conform to a pattern of dress or behavior that is easily recognized and understood. Generally, stereotypes are less real, more perfect, or imperfect,

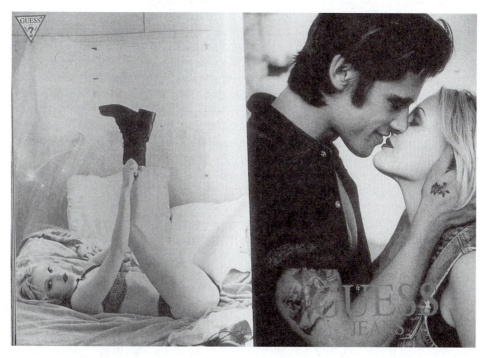

Advertising sells more than products; it sells a message. These ads exemplify equating sexual desirability with purchasing the product.

more predictable than their real-life counterparts. Some stereotyping on television may be unavoidable, due to the format; 30- or 60-minute programs do not allow for full character development. Many minority groups—women, older people, African Americans, Italians, Hispanic Americans, Asian Americans, Native Americans, and Middle Eastern Americans—claim that television and movies either ignore them or distort them. In a study (Scheibe, 1989) of 2,135 commercials containing more than 6,000 characters, it was shown that men outnumbered women. However, females made up the majority of characters in commercials for cleaners, hygiene/beauty products, apparel, and toys; whereas males appeared in ads for alcohol, cars, leisure/travel, and financial services. TV commercials overrepresented young adults by 3:1. Most of the characters on TV commercials were Anglo (94%); nearly all the rest were African American. Other ethnic groups were underrepresented relative to their true demographic distribution in the population. Finally, TV commercials overrepresented white-collar, managerial, and professional occupations while underrepresenting blue-collar occupations.

In situation comedies or action dramas, ethnic minorities are most often associated with violence, servile occupations, or comic roles. Studies show that both African American and Anglo children accept television's stereotypes of ethnic minorities and their lifestyles as realistic. On the other hand, the portrayal of ethnic minorities on children's programs has become more and more favorable. Research shows that prosocial programs reflecting ethnic variety tend to have a beneficial effect on children's perception of, and interactions with, minority groups (Comstock & Paik, 1991).

Gender stereotypes have decreased on TV but are still prevalent in behavior, relationship, and occupational roles (Comstock & Paik, 1991; Huston & Wright, 1998). Males outnumber females on children's TV, and males dominate in action roles. They exert authority, display bravado, or demonstrate competence or expertise. Females dominate in nurturing roles and dependent behavior. A metaanalysis of show correlations between television viewing and gender-role stereotyping (Signorella, Bigler, Liben, 1993). Although children who have stereotyped beliefs are likely to be attracted to stereotyped shows, it was demonstrated in a classic study that the television show *Freestyle,* with boys in nurturing roles and girls as mechanics, changed the perceptions of its sixth-to-ninth-grade viewers (Johnston & Ettema, 1982). When school viewing was accompanied by class discussion changes in stereotypes and attitudes endured in a nine-month follow-up (Huston & Wright, 1998).

Both the young and the old are represented differently from reality on TV (Condry, 1989). The typical female on television is young (under age 35), whereas men are generally older. Elderly women are portrayed on TV as victims of crime 30 times more often than is so in real life. Older men are portrayed as successful and powerful. The effect of these stereotypes is that children assume that the real world mirrors that of TV unless they have actual experiences to alter this perception (Dorr & Rabin, 1995).

How do children perceive ethnicity and class as represented by the media? In a study of 1,200 children representing African American, Asian, Latino, and Anglo ethnic groups (Children Now, 1998), it was found that children believe it is very important to see their own ethnic group on television. Anglo children reported seeing people of their group most frequently, followed by African American children. Asian and Latino children see people of their groups much less frequently. All groups recognized media's use of stereotypes, frequently attributing positive traits and roles to Anglo characters, and negative traits and roles to minorities.

The Effect of TV Watching on Children's Reading and Communication Skills

In addition to watching TV, reading and communicating are ways children learn about the world. There is concern that time spent in front of the TV has been responsible for the general decline in reading levels and test scores on standardized tests, such as the Scholastic Aptitude Test (Healy, 1998; National Commission on Excellence in Education [NCEE], 1983). This is because TV viewing takes time away from other pursuits, such as reading, hobbies, attending concerts, and visiting museums—pursuits that enhance intellectual development as measured by college entrance exams.

According to research reviews (Neuman, 1991; Winn, 1977), there is no doubt that children read fewer books when television is available to them. This is probably because it is human nature to opt for the activity requiring less effort (entertainment) rather than the activity requiring more effort (reading). However, family values regarding what constitutes "useful" leisure activities can be very influential on what children choose to do (Neuman, 1991).

Television has the potential to motivate reading. For example, an award-winning show, *Reading Rainbow,* broadcast on public television, has proven to encourage reading. Once a book is spotlighted on the show, libraries and bookstores report an increase in demand (Trelease, 1995).

Information Processing.   Many educators report that children who watch a lot of television show a low tolerance for the frustration involved in learning. Watching television accustoms the child to being entertained. Programs such as *Sesame Street* and cartoons, all designed for children, "tend to give students unrealistic expectations of teachers. Kids are so used to being entertained by personalities on TV that they expect teachers to do the same" (Fiske, 1980, p. 55). Further, students accustomed to being entertained by "show biz" techniques become bored with schoolwork that requires complex thought or sustained concentration. Children may have attention and listening problems (Healy, 1999). Once again, adult involvement in viewing and discussion can be influential by stimulating children to think about what they have seen (Dorr & Rabin, 1995).

Reading is an active process in that it involves the creating of images in the reader's mind through symbols: the printed words. Television viewing, on the other hand, does not involve decoding and transformation of symbols; the whole sensory message and experience are there all at once. Information processing involves selecting content to attend to based on interest, past experiences, and cognitive development (Huston & Wright, 1998).

Until recently, there was little research on how the brain absorbs information from TV. TV primarily stimulates the right half of the brain, the part that specializes in emotional responses, rather than the left half, which specializes in analytical thinking. By connecting viewers to instruments that measure brain waves, one researcher found periods of right-brain activity outnumbering left-brain activity by a $2:1$ ratio (Mann, 1982). Because reading demands complex mental manipulations, a reader is required to concentrate far more than a television viewer. In reading, the reader has control over the pace. If the material is not understood, the reader can reread, slow down, or go to other sources for elucidation before continuing. Similarly, if the material is familiar, or easily understood, the reader can skip over it, speed up, or skim it. Also, if the material evokes an emotional reaction, readers can stop and experience their feelings, then return to the printed material without having lost anything.

Television's pace cannot be controlled by the viewer—another reason it impacts the viewer's ability to concentrate (Healy, 1999). The TV program continually moves forward; what is misunderstood by the viewer remains so, and what evokes delight cannot be slowed down. The increased use of VCRs may overcome this limitation in that videos can be slowed down and repeated. Television is essentially a visual medium. Pictures shown move very rapidly (the average length of a slot on network TV is about three seconds). Although words are spoken, it is the picture that contains the most important meaning. Because viewing the rapid succession of pictures doesn't allow time for the viewer's own reflections, some researchers have speculated that television viewing leads to an impulsive rather than reflective style of thought and to a lack of persistence in intellectual tasks. Evidence comes from studies where television viewing was restricted and children were tested on intellectual impulsiveness and reflectivity, as well as on ability to wait (Greenfield, 1984; Healy, 1999).

Television has made significant contributions to children's realms of experience, their vocabulary, and their ability to communicate. The challenge for educators and parents, then, in regard to improving academic skills, is to capitalize on the useful aspects of children's viewing experiences.

SOCIALIZING INFLUENCES OF TELEVISION AND MOVIES

In a comprehensive review of all evidence on the effects of television on children, Comstock and colleagues conclude that television should be considered a major socializer of children (Comstock & Paik, 1991; Comstock & Scharrer, 1991). However, it is difficult to pinpoint the exact effects of television on behavior because of other mediating or intervening influences, such as the viewer's cognitive developmental level, needs, attitudes, motives, habits, interests, values, morals, beliefs, and experiences (Huston & Wright, 1998) (*see* Figure 9.2). For example, teens who need to feel part of the group are more influenced by ads touting the "in" clothes, perfume, or CD than are adults whose need for belonging has been met. For another example, some of my college students who watch certain talk shows said they could not relate to some of the topics because what was being discussed was against their moral beliefs. These mediating influences determine what viewers will selectively attend to in their environments.

Thus, media effects are bidirectional. "Children are not just recipients of media messages; they choose the content to which they are exposed, and they interpret the content within their own frames of reference. They receive media messages in contexts of family, peers, and social institutions, all of which may modify or determine how children integrate messages into their existing store of information and beliefs" (Huston & Wright, 1998, p. 1027).

Selective Attention

The senses (sight, hearing, touch, taste, and smell) are equipped to respond to stimuli in the environment. However, it is impossible to pay attention to everything going on about us; thus we select, or consciously attend to only some of the available stimuli.

Figure 9.2   Mediating Influences that Affect the Impact Media Messages Have on Behavior

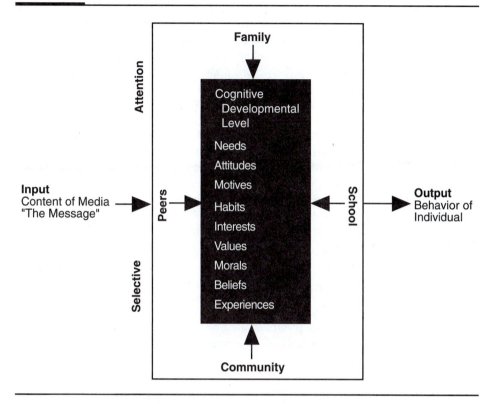

Research has been done on infants and children in order to understand what parts of their environment they attend to. Selective attention is crucial to learning because children's perceptions and concepts of the world depend on which aspects of it get their attention. The following are examples of classic research findings that illustrate the role of selective attention in learning.

Babies respond to movement. A 5-day-old who is sucking on a pacifier will stop sucking if a light moves across its visual field (Haith, 1966). Babies also respond to novelty. One-day-old babies will look longer at a patterned surface than at a plain one (Fantz, 1965). Children between age 2 and 3 years tend to pay more attention to the color of the object than to the form, whereas children between age 4 and 6 tend to prefer form to color (Stevenson, 1972). As children grow, their attention tends to focus on what they judge to be the important aspects of a situation. Eight-year-olds are more capable than 4- to 6-year-olds of deliberately ignoring irrelevant information when confronted with a problem (Bjorklund, 1994; Osler & Kofsky, 1965).

Although children become increasingly better at selective attention as they get older due to attentional strategies they have developed, it is not until about age 7 that they can purposely ignore "attention-grabbers" (Bjorklund, 1994), such as colors or songs used in advertisements.

As children approach adulthood, they selectively attend to those messages that are related to their individual interests, are consistent with their attitudes, are congruent with their beliefs, and are supportive of their values. For example, children will spend more time watching families on television that are similar to theirs in regard to ethnicity or single- or step-parenthood (Dorr & Rabin, 1995; Huston & Wright, 1998).

John Condry (1989) summarized what specific aspects of television children attend to in his book, *The Psychology of Television.* Starting in infancy, the amount of time children spend looking at a TV set while it is on increases steadily with age. The largest increase comes between the age 2 and 3. Preschool children show elevated attention to women, puppets, animation, strange voices, lively music, auditory changes, and rhyming, repetition, and alliteration. Children of this age pay less attention to men, animals, inactivity, and still pictures. Commercials capitalize on these findings.

Older children pay attention to more complexities as they gain in cognitive development. They are now able to understand story plots and characters. They are attracted to action, adventure, and family situation comedies. School-agers need to attend to visual techniques more so than do adolescents to understand the story line (Comstock & Paik, 1991). In general, media cues that attract attention are "outstandingness," novelty, contrast, and how closely the cue is related to the viewer's frame of reference.

Adults as Mediating Influences

Since we do selectively attend to our environment from infancy onward, we likewise selectively attend to the messages communicated by television. Television programmers may be able to manipulate the level of "outstandingness," novelty, or contrast, or to

By viewing TV with their children, these parents can mediate the messages broadcast.

attract the audience's attention by controlling the input, but it is up to the viewer to choose whether that message belongs in his or her frame of reference by being aware of the mediating influences (cognitive developmental level, needs, attitudes, motives, habits, interests, values, morals, beliefs, and experiences).

Parents, especially, can mediate the amount and level of attention given to TV by their children by being the primary socializers in their children's frames of reference. Their children will be more likely to attend to messages on TV that conform to their family's interests, attitudes, beliefs, and values. Parents, teachers, and older siblings are probably most important in determining television programming effects on children (Comstock & Paik, 1991; Pearl, 1982). Early evidence of this importance was found in a first-year evaluation of *Sesame Street*. It was shown that those children who watched the show with their mothers and talked to them about the show learned more than did other children (Ball & Bogatz, 1970). This finding was supported by later research on the vocabulary development of preschoolers (Rice, Huston, Truglio, & Wright, 1990).

These are several ways in which parents can mediate television viewing: (1) by controlling the number of hours of television exposure, (2) by checking ratings and evaluating what kinds of programs may be viewed, (3) by viewing television with their children and discussing the programs, and (4) by arranging family activities other than television viewing.

Several studies (Corder-Bolz, 1980; Dorr & Rabin, 1995; Huston & Wright, 1998) support the value of significant others' involvement in children's television viewing. For example, one study (Wilson & Weiss, 1993) showed that co-viewing a show with older siblings increased preschoolers' enjoyment of and decreased their arousal to a scary program. Another study (Haefner & Wartella, 1987) showed that co-viewing changed 6- and 7-year olds' evaluations of certain characters in two programs.

Why is significant other or adult mediation important? For one reason, children do not "see" television in the same way adults do; according to Marieli Rowe, executive director of the American Council for Better Broadcasts, "The impact television has on a viewer depends to a great extent on what the viewer brings to TV" (Condry, 1989; Skalka, 1983). Adult viewers can analyze and evaluate content. They can tune out irrelevancies, absorb complicated plots, and understand underlying messages. For the most part, children cannot.

For another reason, as was said previously, young children cannot distinguish fantasy and reality; their understanding is based on appearances. They do not know what is fact and what is opinion. They neither have had the experiences nor do they possess the knowledge to enable them to comprehend the basis of many events that occur in the world. Yet they are exposed to the whole world through the television screen before they have even developed an understanding of their own immediate world. We do not expect children to read a book before they can recognize letters. Adults, then, must develop strategies to mediate children's television viewing according to their values and their children's cognitive developmental level.

COMMUNITY–MEDIA LINKAGES

It is generally agreed that TV is here to stay. Even though some alternatives to broadcast (free) TV are available, it is the programs broadcast over the airwaves "in the public interest" that have stimulated community concern:

Children and families live in a media environment that is not of their own making. They can select from what is available, but they do not have many opportunities to change the menu. Decisions about production and distribution of most mass media are made by private corporations. In this country, because of the First Amendment to the Constitution, those decisions are protected from government interference except in unusual circumstances (Huston, Zillman, & Bryant, 1994, p. 9).

The community's response, therefore, has been to develop alternatives to commercial television, such as the Public Broadcasting Service (PBS), cable and satellite TV, video recorders to tape particular shows and to view selected movies, and to form public interest groups.

The Public Broadcasting Service (PBS)

One response to what were felt to be the deficiencies of commercial television was the establishment of the Public Broadcasting Service (PBS), through the Public Broadcasting Act, which became law in 1967. PBS is an alliance of local community and educational stations financially supported by the Corporation for Public Broadcasting and by annual membership fees of licensees as well as by selling time to advertisers. Supplemental funds come from grants from the National Endowment for the Humanities, from universities, and from big corporations, with the aim of providing more specialized, diversified, and high-quality programs to reach specific age, social, and cultural groups.

Some examples of children's programs broadcast on PBS are *Sesame Street*—designed for preschoolers (programs are creative and educational); *Wishbone*—designed for school-agers (adaptations of excellent children's literature to promote reading), and *Scientific American Frontiers*—designed for young adolescents (about stimulating scientific discoveries).

The main problem that public television faces is financial; specialization is costly. If the public wants the quality PBS provides, it will have to financially support its local community PBS station.

Cable and Satellite Television

Families that pay for cable television or have purchased satellite dishes can view certain channels that show movies, sports, and educational programs. One such channel, available only through cable TV, is Nickelodeon—a television channel for children. Every day there are shows for children age 2 to 15. For example, there are songs for young children, adventures for middle-years children, and talk shows for teenagers.

Cable TV also provides music television (MTV) in which rock stars "act out" rock music. Occasionally, the portrayals are surrealistic, have sexual imagery, and/or violence (Greenberg, 1994). Many religious groups as well as parent groups have, unsuccessfully, tried to ban such violence and suggestive music because the lyrics were said to provide a bad influence on children (Cocks, 1985; Dougherty, 1985). Particularly active has been the Parents Music Resource Center (PMRC). This group charged in a congressional hearing that rock music influences sexual morality, violence, drug use, and Satanism

(Gore, 1987). Recently, however, MTV and the American Psychological Association (APA) joined forces to enlighten viewers to the dangers of violence on TV. The research on popular music will be discussed later in this chapter.

Videocassette Recorders

The business community has provided expanded uses of television. In many homes, television sets are currently used as display terminals for videotapes or discs and video games. Over three-quarters of the TV households in the United States own videocassette recorders. Families that have home videocassette recorders can play a more active role in selecting and managing their leisure time. A home video recorder enables you to rent tapes of selected movies or instructional tapes to show at home. It also enables you to record shows you don't want to miss.

Schools use videocassette recorders, too. Teachers can record television shows and play them back in their classrooms. The advantage of such a medium is that the tape can be stopped at any point for a discussion. Sometimes videos are used to illustrate literature. Viewing Zeffirelli's *Romeo and Juliet* aided my son's understanding of Shakespeare's play.

The proliferation of videos makes movies produced for the big screen accessible and affordable. Unless adults mediate the selection, young people can be similarly exposed to violence, sexuality, and "antivalues" as was discussed in regard to TV.

Public Interest Groups

Another response to what were felt to be the deficiencies of commercial television was the formation of public interest groups. These groups were formed to pressure the broadcasters for change, to lobby the government for regulations, and/or to educate the public to monitor its own viewing habits and those of its children. They have been influential in developing the rating system for television and movies.

An example of such groups is Action for Children's Television (ACT), which was founded in 1968 by a concerned parent (Peggy Charren) who mobilized 30 friends for the purposes of reducing violence on children's TV, reducing the number of commercials on children's shows, and preventing program hosts or celebrities from advertising on their shows. It is now a national organization that positively encourages networks to provide more and better-quality programming for children by giving annual awards to broadcasters that have made significant contributions to children's television and by providing parents, teachers, and others with educational material.

Another example of a public interest group is the National Citizens' Committee for Broadcasting (NCCB), which distributes information outlining public TV rights and methods for legislation. The NCCB annual "violence index" was instituted to increase public awareness of advertisers that sponsor shows with a high incidence of violence.

Finally, the National Parents and Teachers Association (PTA) has become involved in educating parents and teachers on how they can help children develop critical viewing skills (see the box titled "Strategies for Television Viewing").

Video games actively engage children in media technology.

School–Media Linkages

PBS stations carry a variety of programs specifically developed for the classroom, referred to as educational television (ET). Many teachers nationwide use ET as part of their curriculum, and millions of school-age children receive a portion of their regular instruction through television. Supporters of television in the classroom suggest that ET provides memorability, concreteness, and emotional involvement, and also stimulates reading, encourages class discussion, and promotes student interactions (Greenfield, 1984). As was discussed, educational television has been criticized because many programs are financed by corporations that advertise their products on the show. It is felt that the classroom should not be a marketplace.

Schools have tried various tactics to control children's viewing habits. Some schools ask parents to keep children away from the tube entirely. Some recommend setting limits of a certain number of hours per day or specifying only certain shows. Other schools have taken steps to educate parents on the effects of TV on academic performance, rather than making across-the-board rules. Parents are encouraged, then, to develop their own family policies. Still other schools give parents ideas of alternative activities to TV viewing.

Some schools work with parents on developing critical viewing skills in children. The television networks have cooperated with the schools in this regard by producing detailed study guides for teachers to use as learning aids. The scripts of some shows are available to schools to stimulate interest in reading. An example of such a show broadcast by CBS was *Skeezer,* based on the book by Elizabeth Yates.

Obviously, the success of the school efforts to ban, limit, provide alternatives, or develop critical viewing skills for television depends on the cooperation of the family.

FAMILY–MEDIA LINKAGES

There can be no doubt that television as a medium of communication and information is of extreme potential value. Shows such as *The American Experience, Nova,* and *National Geographic* enrich viewers by exposing them to history, culture, geography, science, and travel—perspectives of life that they may never have experienced. Shows such as *Barney, Sesame Street,* and *Mister Rogers' Neighborhood* can provide children with models of cooperation, altruism, self-control, and empathy. Research shows that exposure to television programs that provide models of prosocial behavior enhances children's prosocial tendencies (Friedrich & Stein, 1973; Leibert & Sprafkin, 1988). Parental co-viewing of the prosocial program and discussion are even more enhancing (Dorr & Rabin, 1995; Huston & Wright, 1998).

As was discussed, parents must exercise their primary responsibility in regulating and monitoring their children's viewing habits. In a democratic society, it is ultimately the viewer who bears responsibility for the effects of television; families must accept that responsibility by not viewing what is offensive and/or by supporting public interest groups.

Unfortunately, studies (Dorr & Rabin, 1995; Huston & Wright, 1998) indicate that parental involvement in children's viewing is infrequent. Some children are allowed to watch what and when they want. Other children are restricted to how early and how late they may watch. Still others have restrictions on their total viewing time per day. And some children are restricted to viewing certain approved shows. While many shows are viewed with other family members, especially siblings, two intensive, longitudinal studies of young children and their families concluded that parents did not use the time to mediate the shows (St. Peters, Marguerite, Huston, Wright, and Eakins, Desmond, Singer, & Singer, 1990).

Parental involvement is difficult for many families, because the parents may both work. In some families, the child comes home after school to an empty house and turns on the television for companionship. In other families, the television unintentionally becomes an "electronic babysitter" while the parent is busy with chores, caring for other children, or engaged in some activity. In these families, then, the message children get from television is not mediated by significant adults in their lives. Thus television becomes a powerful socializing agent for these children. Parents who rely on television to occupy children while they are busy might consider using selected videotapes and/or purchasing a channel blocker. However, all parents should teach their children how to watch TV selectively and critically.

Strategies for Television Viewing and Developing Critical Viewing Skills in Children*

1. *Know what your children watch and when.*

   A log of how much time they spend in front of the tube will often speak for itself about whether TV is playing too large a role in their lives.

   Be alert to the content of the program as well as the commercials. Notice ways in which viewing affects your children's behavior. Do they become transfixed after watching for a while? Or does viewing make them tense and lead to fighting? What effects does it have on family communication when you all watch together?

How are ethnic groups, gender roles, and age groups presented? How are conflicts resolved?

2. *Know the ratings and choose what to watch.*

Don't leave watching to chance—you wouldn't put a refrigerator in your children's room and allow them to eat what they wanted on the chance they would eventually meet their nutritional requirements. Learn to turn off the set when your choice is over.

3. *Set limits.*

Talking over a set of guidelines with family members, agreeing upon them, and sticking to them is effective in establishing a new routine for viewing TV. For example, your family may choose to ban TV during dinner, to allow viewing only after other responsibilities (homework, chores) have been done, or to allow each family member to have a choice of selecting a program each week.

Help children choose activities to do when the TV is off (read a book, draw a picture, play a game).

4. *Whenever possible, view with children.*

When watching with young children, point out what is real and what is fantasy.

When values presented on TV conflict with your family values, say so! When values agree, say so too!

- Discuss the differences between fantasy and reality.
- Discuss conflict situations and how problems could be solved without violence.
- Discuss situations involving cooperation, and note behaviors your child might imitate.
- Point out characters who represent a variety of ethnic groups.
- Point out men/women who represent a variety of occupations.
- Discuss food advertisements in terms of what is healthy and nutritious.
- Discuss toy advertisements in terms of play potential, safety, and age appropriateness.

5. *Use the time in front of the TV to benefit the child.*

Television can be a rich source of vocabulary development. Explain new words to children.

Television can expand a child's horizons. Talk about other places in the world, other cultures, new experiences.

Television programs can stimulate reading of related material if the child is encouraged.

Television can stimulate discussion on sensitive topics by older children—such as drugs, rape, and teenage pregnancy—and thus may provide the opportunity for parents to discuss such topics.

Source: *Action for Children's Television*

PRINT MEDIA: BOOKS AND MAGAZINES

Compared to pictorial media, such as television, print media are more difficult to investigate experimentally because they are often long, have complex structures, and provoke more individual imagery than does television. Thus it is difficult to separate the socializing effects of the *content* of the book or magazine from the socializing effects of the *interpretation* of the reader.

Unlike the pictorial media, where the visual image is provided, the print media describe in words the images of the writer. These words must then be translated into visual images by the reader. Obviously, reading is much more personal than is television viewing because the visual image one is able to conjure up from printed words depends on one's personal vocabulary, one's reading ability, and one's real-life experiences.

Also, it is difficult to compare the effects of books and TV on socialization because, until children gain a fair amount of reading skill, an adult usually reads books to them. Therefore, the adult is present to explain, answer questions, and adjust the tempo of the book to the child's level of understanding and interest. In addition, adults choose most of the books young children read. Parents and relatives buy them. Teachers assign certain books, and librarians choose which books will fill the library shelves. Thus, adults play a large role in determining the influence books will have on children, whereas this has not been the case in television viewing.

The role that print media are known to play in socialization is that of passing on culture to the next generation. The print media teach history, values, morals, ideals, and attitudes. Former Secretary of Education William Bennett felt so strongly that American children should be exposed to the basic human values of self-discipline, compassion, responsibility, friendship, work, courage, perseverance, honesty, loyalty, and faith that he edited *The Book of Virtues: A Treasury of Great Moral Stories* (Bennett, 1993). He believes that stories are the way children learn what virtues look like, what they are in practice, how to recognize them, and how they work.

THE POWER OF PRINT COMPARED TO OTHER MEDIA: LITERACY

Literacy, being able to communicate via reading and writing, is the core of an educated person. According to Postman (1986, p. 2) "the written word endures, the spoken word disappears." That print media make a powerful contribution to literacy may seem obvious, but why?

Different media elicit different thinking skills (Healy, 1990). Meringoff (1980) and colleagues (Char & Meringoff, 1981) compared the abilities of young children to comprehend and reproduce narratives presented in different media (stories in print versus stories on television and radio). They found that even when the same soundtracks were used, television focused children's attention on *actions of characters,* while radio or book format directed attention to the *quality of the language.* Children were more likely to consider television as an experience apart from themselves when answering questions about the program, whereas they were more likely to include their own personal

These boys can discuss their interpretation of the book they are reading together, thereby enhancing its socialization effects.

experiences when answering questions about stories in books. Thus print and pictorial media require different ways to process information.

The print media has more potential to socialize because of the greater involvement of adults. Adults motivate children to notice print by pointing out signs and labels. They read books to children. They encourage children to recognize letters and to write:

> The development of literacy is a social process, embedded in social relationships, particularly in children's relationships with parents, siblings, grandparents, friends, caretakers, and teachers. These people serve as models, provide materials, establish expectations, and offer help, instruction, and encouragement (McLane & McNamee, 1990, p. 7).

When adults become involved in children's experiences with print, children are exposed to values, attitudes, behaviors, and skills related to written languages. Children learn how to derive meaning from print (McLane & McNamee, 1990). The ability to glean meaning, then, opens up the world of history, culture, science, and so on to the child. This conclusion is based on Vygotsky's (1978) writings that children's learning is increased with the help of an expert, a phenomenon referred to earlier in the book as "the zone of proximal development."

Television, too, has the potential of actively involving viewers and contributing to literacy (Huston & Wright, 1998; Neuman, 1991). It provides concrete behavior that can be imitated. Adults can enhance the meaning for children from TV shows via co-viewing and discussion. ("Can you think of a better way to solve that problem besides hitting?"

"How do you think the show should have ended?" "The kind of food they are advertising is unhealthy.")

HOW BOOKS AND MAGAZINES SOCIALIZE CHILDREN

Throughout time, history and culture have been passed on, first orally, then via writing (hieroglyphics, letters, diaries), then via print. Therefore, the print media has become a significant socializer.

Books are written language. Language, as was discussed in Chapter 2, enables socialization to take place. Language makes ideas and communication of these ideas possible; language also makes it possible to replace action with thoughts. Language enables humans to internalize attitudes of others. Language is the means of passing on the cultural heritage from one generation to the next.

Magazines are written language, too; but they are infused with pictures and advertisements, sometimes in greater proportion than their articles. This means a socializing effect is consumerism. Magazines usually cater to special interests, such as fashion, sports, computers, science, pets, and therefore contribute to the knowledge base of their readers.

Jim Trelease (1995), in *The Read-Aloud Handbook,* cites evidence stressing the importance of reading for building knowledge. Reading aloud improves children's *listening comprehension,* a skill that must occur before *reading comprehension.* It is the activity of reading aloud to children that enables them to become successful readers. Reading aloud is so important because it is personal and, therefore, enhances attachment. In Chapter 2, it was said that socialization begins with personal attachment. Reading aloud provides a model for children to imitate:

> Children who are not spoken to by live and responsive adults will not learn to speak properly. Children who are not answered will stop asking questions. They will become incurious. And children who are not told stories and who are not read to will have few reasons for wanting to learn to read (Haley, 1989, p. 19).

Ellen Spitz (1999), in *Inside Picture Books,* analyzes books that adults have read to children for generations like *Goodnight Moon* (Brown, 1947) and *Where the Wild Things Are* (Sendak, 1963). She discusses how well-known picture books transmit psychological wisdom, convey moral lessons, and shape tastes. Hidden in these familiar stories are the anxieties of childhood, such as fear of separation and loss, or threat of aggression. Reading to children builds a special bond between the reader and listener.

Influences on Development

The way children use their brains causes physical changes in their neural wiring. Children who are stimulated and are actively engaged in experiences have more neural connections than children who have fewer experiences (Begley, 1997). These neural connections allow for different functions, so the child with more connections not only can master more skills, but is also more adaptable in learning them. One can get to a destination more successfully if one knows alternative routes to use in case of road work or traffic. Some brain functions influenced by books are language, readings, cognitive, and psychological development.

Language and Reading Development.   Books enhance language development. The relationship of children's language to the amount of reading done by them and the amount of reading aloud to them was examined. It was found that children who are read to often and read a lot on their own are more advanced in their language development than children who are rarely read to and do not read very much on their own (Chomsky, 1972; McLane & McNamee, 1990).

Part of the explanation for the effect of reading on language development, compared to talking and/or other media, is that literary language is more structured and more complex. The language in children's books, then, is more complex and richer in syntactic patterns than the language used in children's television programs (Healy, 1990; Postman, 1992). Television engages the child in a passive way with language, whereas reading books and telling stories engage the child in an active way. Active use of language has more impact on language development than does passive listening (Barclay, Benelli, & Curtis, 1995).

Books also enhance reading development. Research indicates that children who are read to learn to read earlier and more easily than children who are not read to. It has been shown that children who learned to read early had been read to and had had someone to answer their questions (Barclay, Benelli, & Curtis, 1995; Schickendanz, 1986; Teale, 1984).

Cognitive Development.   Books nourish cognitive development. Not only do they provide information and concepts, they also provide vicarious experiences and stimulate the imagination of the child. For example, *The Very Hungry Caterpillar* (for preschoolers) by Eric Carle (1986) helps teach a child the days of the week, how to count to five, and how a caterpillar becomes a butterfly, all in bright pictures.

Books can be used to help children gain an understanding of themselves and others across time and space (Norton, 1999). For example, *Snowflake Bentley* (for school-agers) by Jacqueline Martin (1998), is a 1999 **Caldecott Medal** winner (an award given yearly for the most distinguished American picture book for children). The book takes children back to the days when farmers worked with ox and sled and had to use lanterns to see at night. Wilson Bentley, the protagonist, loved snow more than anything and wanted to capture the beauty of snowflakes with his camera.

By reading aloud to children, adults can enhance children's language development as well as the desire to read on their own.

Psychosocial Development. Books provide models for children—models of behavior, models of gender roles, and models of occupational roles. For example, *Mothers Can Do Anything* (for preschoolers) by Joe Lasker (1972) demonstrates the variety of jobs mothers can hold, including scientist, linesman, artist, and lion tamer.

Books can also be used to impart a desired value system. For example, Jerry Spinelli's (1997) *Wringer* (for school-agers) is the 1999 Honor Book winner of the **Newbery Medal,** an award presented yearly for the most distinguished contribution to American literature for children. The book is about a 10-year-old boy, Palmer LaRue, who does not want to be a "wringer" on his birthday. Becoming a "wringer" is an annual rite of passage in a town in Pennsylvania where young boys get to wring the necks of pigeons wounded in the town's pigeon shoot fundraiser. When his three bullying friends suspect he is sheltering a stray pigeon, Palmer decides to take a stand against conformity and peer pressure.

Literature can be of value in helping children cope with and master problems of importance in their lives (Bettelheim, 1976; Cashdan, 1999). For example, some fairy tales and folk stories deal with aggressive and negative traits of human beings and indicate ways of coping with them. Folk and fairy tales lie at the roots of every culture and, despite geographical differences, have many similarities in theme (Baker, 1981; Norton, 1999): tribal history, local history, myth, legend, trickster, and entertainment. Folk and fairy tales are appealing to children because they explain things in terms to which children can relate.

Books offer children the opportunity to explore and understand their own feelings and the feelings of others. For example, in *The Hundred Dresses* (for school-agers), a classic by Eleanor Estes (1944), a group of schoolchildren realize too late that their cruelty has destroyed the happiness of a poor girl, Wanda Petronski, and her family, who immigrated to the United States from Poland. Wanda attempts to win a place in the group by telling of the hundred dresses she owns. However, she wears the same faded dress to school every day and is teased by the other girls because of it and because she has a funny name. The ostracism that the Petronski family experiences compels them to move away. Soon afterward, Wanda's hundred dresses—that is, her drawings of 100 dresses—are presented in an art contest. The girls finally understand Wanda's feelings, but it is too late to undo that cruelty. This book helps children understand what values are truly important and also that mistakes cannot always be rectified.

Literature, then, can help children understand the realities of life. It can provide them with models of behavior that are useful in dealing with problems; it can also help children understand the consequences of certain behaviors.

CONCERNS ABOUT BOOKS AND MAGAZINES

Books can elicit some of the concerns that were described earlier in this chapter regarding television, such as fantasy being confused with reality, violence, the perpetuation of certain values and stereotypes, and even commercialism (toy tie-ins). The degree to which books should reflect the reality of the times leads to controversy regarding how the characters solve problems and how they are portrayed (Norton, 1999).

Fantasy and Reality

Some books have young characters who overcome obstacles, apparently caused by adults, through real problem-solving or through fantasy. The lack of strong adult role models in such books has been a cause for controversy (Norton, 1999). For example, Maurice Sendak's *Where the Wild Things Are* (1963) illustrates Max's imagination when, because of his misbehavior, his mother sends him to his room without supper. This book was banned in some schools because its illustrations were regarded as "frightening" to young children and because of its message. Others highly recommend the book because readers can identify with Max and his strong feelings expressed through fantasy.

The Goosebumps books, a series of monster mysteries for the under-12 set, by R. L. Stine, were introduced to school-agers through school book clubs. There are five basic plots written in a clipped style thick with thumps and gasps. They are advertised on TV and have games and toys for children to act out the plots, thereby blurring the boundaries of fantasy and reality (Gelline, 1996). Critics say they don't promote literacy but they do promote commercialism.

A popular series for the over-12 set is *Harry Potter* by J. K. Rowlings. Apparently these best sellers are stimulating children's imaginations due to their blend of fantasy, magic, mystery, and reality.

Some classic juvenile series books have been criticized for being formulaic such as *Nancy Drew* and *The Hardy Boys* books by Edward Stratemyer. The themes are danger, mystery, and excitement. Stratemyer's formula consisted of capturing the reader's interest on the first page, providing a dramatic highpoint in the middle of every chapter, and ending each chapter with a "cliff-hanging event." Romances, westerns, and mysteries usually contain a great deal of action; the characters are ideal types, and the ending is happy. Such books purvey an unrealistic view of life, based on the following questionable assumptions (Carlsen, 1980, pp. 52–53):

1. Children and adolescents are more perceptive than adults; if they could switch places with adults, they could do a better job at everything adults generally do.
2. Dramatic changes, such as in personality or personal appearance, can occur in a short period of time.
3. Premonitions turn out to be accurate.
4. There is a solution for every problem, and it is usually a simple one.
5. One's physical appearance indicates one's character.
6. People are either good or bad. Good always wins over bad, and bad people are punished.
7. It is OK for the good people to use deceptive or illegal techniques because they have the right goals—"The end justifies the means."
8. Heroes and heroines are the culture's male and female stereotypes (handsome, brave males and pretty, dainty females). They also tend to have anglicized names (Nancy Drew).
9. Villains are different from the cultural ideal stereotypes. They may be fat, hairy, or dark. They also tend to have foreign-sounding names (Fu Manchu).
10. The wealthy tend to be corrupt, whereas the lower and middle classes tend to be good.

Books, as has been said, are agents of socialization. Psychologist Bruno Bettelheim (1976) wrote, "The acquisition of skills . . . becomes devalued when what one has learned to read adds nothing of importance to one's life." Books should help a child examine values, sort them out, and make decisions. Reading stereotyped and formula fiction is unlikely to achieve such ends. Research shows that children's attitudes and achievements are affected by certain biases in books (Norton, 1999). As a response, Bennett (1993) compiled his book of moral stories and poems to influence children's values.

Violence

Children were exposed to violence in stories and fairy tales long before there was television, and it has been shown that children imitate aggression from storybooks, just as they do from television (Neuman, 1991). Bettelheim (1976) and Cashdan (1999) believe fairy tales help children cope with their strong emotions on an unconscious level:

> It seems particularly appropriate to a child that exactly what the evildoer wishes to inflict on the hero should be the bad person's fate—as the witch in "Hansel and Gretel" who wants to cook children in the oven is pushed into it and burned to death . . ." (Bettelheim, 1976, p. 144).

In *The Witch Must Die,* Cashdan (1999) explores how fairy tales help children project their own inner struggles with good and evil onto battles enacted by characters in the stories. Thus, the violence we, as adults, see in literature for young children, especially in fairy tales, is really a catharsis, a mechanism for release of strong feelings. According to Charlotte Huck (1996), however, a well-written book enables the reader to empathize with the human suffering of people's inhumane acts, whereas television or films are more apt to concentrate on the act itself.

A well-written book can provide a perspective on people's pain and suffering because the author has time to develop the characters, which is not true of television. In a book, the reader gets to know the motives and pressures of each individual and can understand and empathize with the characters (Norton, 1999).

Stereotyping

Stereotypes continue to appear in children's books, textbooks, and magazines as they do on TV. Males, Anglos, and middle-class families tend to be overrepresented. Men and boys are more likely to be active and presented in adventuresome or exciting roles; females are more likely to be passive or dependent and presented in inconspicuous or immobile roles. Fairy tales, especially those made into Disney movies are good examples ("Cinderella," "Snow White and the Seven Dwarfs," and "Beauty and the Beast"). Minority groups are underrepresented and, when they are shown, they are usually portrayed as conventional and middle class (Dougherty & Engle, 1987; Gollnick & Chinn, 1998; Sadker, Sadker, & Klein, 1991).

Recently, however, more and more changes have begun to be exhibited in children's literature. Specifically, award-winning books have begun to show improvement in the equitable portrayal of gender and cultural diversity (Dellman-Jenkins, Florjancic, & Swadener, 1993; MacLeod, 1994). A study by Dougherty & Engle (1987) assessed the gender-role distribution of characters in a sample of Caldecott Medal books from 1981 to 1985. They compared their assessment to a similar study done 14 years earlier by

Weitzman (1972) of Caldecott Medal books from 1967 to 1971. The early study found that males in the titles of picture books outnumbered females 8:1. The later study found males still outnumbering females, but in a ratio of 12:1. While the early study found males to be portrayed as active and females as passive, the later study found instances of females being portrayed as active and independent; in these instances, the females occupied central roles in the story. Similar findings occurred in an analysis of sexism in Newbery Medal award books from 1977 to 1984 (Kinman & Henderson, 1985).

Similar changes generally have occurred in elementary school textbook gender-role stereotyping. Since 1972, when Scott, Foresman and Company was the first publisher to issue guidelines for improving the image of women in textbooks, all major publishers have issued recommendations for reducing inequities in instructional materials (Levine & Levine, 1996). However, Myra and David Sadker (1994), in their research on sexism in schools, found twice as many boys and men as girls and women pictured in language arts textbooks; and in a 631-page history text, only 7 pages were related to women.

Reality is still misrepresented in children's books (Britton & Limpkin, 1983; Gollnick & Chinn, 1998). For example, in an attempt to correct an imbalance of ethnic minority males, who in reality make up about 6% of the labor force, these figures are overrepresented in that they are depicted in 17% of the working roles in basal readers. Individuals with disabilities, on the other hand, are underrepresented. Whereas about 10% of the population are disabled, only 2% are shown in basal reader series. People over age 55, who make up over 20% of the population, are not only underrepresented, but are often shown walking in parks, rocking in chairs, and being cranky. Finally, less than 1% of the families portrayed in basal readers have single parents, even though about half of the children reading these books are likely to spend part of their childhood with only one parent.

A problem in solely depending on a textbook for classroom instruction is that sometimes the validity of its content is not questioned. Gollnick and Chinn (1998) recommend critically examining the following in textbooks:

1. *Invisibility*—the underrepresentation of certain groups.
2. *Stereotyping*—the attribution of rigid roles to certain groups.
3. *Selectivity and imbalance*—the interpretation of issues and situations from only one perspective.
4. *Unreality*—the exclusion of sensitive and controversial topics.
5. *Fragmentation and isolation*—separating issues, information, and contributions of certain groups from main instructional materials rather than integration.
6. *Linguistic bias*—the omission of feminine and ethnic group references, pronouns, and names.

Concern about the effects of school textbooks on gender-role stereotyping, attitudes about ethnic minorities and people with disabilities, and acquisition of values has caused some state boards of education to adopt guidelines for purchase.

Ten Quick Ways to Analyze Children's Books for Ethnic and Gender Stereotypes*

1. Check the illustrations—look for stereotypes, tokenism (presentation as a symbol with no real significance), and who is doing what.
2. Check the story line—what is the standard for success? How are problems presented, conceived, and resolved in the story? What is the role of women?
3. Look at the lifestyles.
4. Weigh the relationships between people.
5. Note the heroes.
6. Consider the effects on a child's self-image.
7. Consider the author's or illustrator's background.
8. Check out the author's perspective—is the perspective patriarchal or feminist? Is it Eurocentric, or do minority ethnic perspectives also receive attention?
9. Watch for loaded words (those that ridicule or have insulting overtones).
10. Look at the copyright date—books on minority themes began appearing in the mid-1960s, but they were usually written by white authors. Not until the 1970s did children's books begin to reflect the realities of a multi-ethnic society, as well as exhibit more gender equity.

Council on Interracial Books for Children

Magazines for teenagers have been around for decades; for example, *Seventeen,* a magazine for teenage girls was first published in 1944 and still dominates sales (Palladino, 1996). It has articles on fashion, cosmetics, celebrities, and relationships. Teenage boys prefer to read magazines about sports, cars, or computers (Jaffe, 1998).

A study (Evans, Rutberg, Sather, & Turner, 1991) was done sampling 10 issues each of three widely circulated female-oriented magazines *(Seventeen, Sassy,* and *YM)* to identify messages directed at teenage girls and how they related to female identity. It was concluded that the road to happiness for girls is to attract males by physical beautification (presumably by purchasing the products advertised in the magazine). Many articles implied that female self-esteem should be related to body image, physical attractiveness, and satisfaction with one's weight. Relatively few articles discussed personal enhancement through professional development or leadership. Few articles promoted intellectual pursuits, sports, or the social issues most women face.

BOOKS, SOCIALIZATION, AND DEVELOPMENTAL LEVELS OF CHILDREN

The developmental level, or cognitive stage, of a child influences the socializing effect of books on that child. How children selectively attend to their environment, perceive information, process it in their brains, remember it, and use it are influential factors.

Several authors (Huck, 1996; Norton, 1999) believe that children's favorite stories correspond to their stages of cognitive development, described by Piaget as follows:

Preoperational Stage (About Age 2 to 7)

Children about age 2 to 7 who are in the preoperational stage, are neither able to deal with more than one aspect at a time, nor are they able to deal with complex relationships or abstractions. Thus folktales, for example, which repeat each event from the beginning—such as "The Gingerbread Boy"—are very appealing to preoperational children, especially 2 to 4-year-olds. Such folktales are cumulative; that is, they bring all previous events into the present to build a visible scene for the reader. Examples of classic books that appeal to older preoperational children are *Blueberries for Sal* by Robert McCloskey (1948) and *Harry the Dirty Dog* by Gene Zion (1956).

As preoperational children begin to understand seriation (arranging things in a sequence), they become interested in stories that have characters of increasing size, such as "The Three Bears"—or stories that denote growth, such as the classic, *Peter's Chair* by Ezra Jack Keats (1967). Books can extend and reinforce children's developing concepts—the sequence of time, for example.

Concrete Operational Stage (About Age 7 to 11 or 15)

As children move from the preoperational to the concrete operational level of thought (about age 7 to 11 or 15), their ability to understand literature expands. At this level, thought is more flexible and reversible, so they can understand stories within such classic stories as Leo Lionni's (1968) *The Biggest House in the World.* They can also understand flashbacks and shifts in time periods, and so project themselves into the past and future. Finally, concrete operational children can more easily identify with other points of view and are able to understand a wide variety of books. Informational books can expand their interests and experiences. Biographies can provide them with models with whom to identify.

Formal Operational Stage (About Age 11 or 15)

The intellectual developmental stage of formal operations (about age 11 or 15) is characterized by abstract, logical thought. Children in this stage can reason from hypotheses to conclusions. They can hold several plots or subplots in their minds simultaneously and see interrelations among them. They can also interpret abstract symbols and different meanings in literature. They can analyze and evaluate what they read. They are able to understand the values presented in books and can examine various issues presented from different viewpoints. For example, in Marjorie Rawlings' (1938) classic *The Yearling,* Jody's parents reluctantly consent to his adopting an orphan fawn because he is so lonely. The two become great friends, but when the fawn destroys the family's meager crops, Jody realizes he must sacrifice the fawn. In giving up what he loves, he leaves behind his own yearling days. Books can provide role models, morals, and attitudes for children to explore. Books play an important role in socialization at this time because formal operational children are beginning to develop a sense of self, including a gender-role identity, a moral code, and a set of values.

So far, media designed by adults for children has been examined. Now sound media, some of which are created by youth for youth, will be explored.

SOUND MEDIA: POPULAR MUSIC

What sets today's popular music apart from television and books is that it is an expression of the youth culture and also that it effectively alienates many adults (Elkind, 1994; Jaffe, 1998). "Pop" music usually refers to rock, even though other types of music may go in and out of vogue.

According to a review of the research on popular music (Christenson & Roberts, 1990), children's interest in rock music accelerates at about the third and fourth grades, and by the time of early adolescence, teens listen to music (radio, CDs, tapes, music videos) from 2 to 5 hours each day. Girls listen more than boys. African Americans and Hispanics watch music videos more than Anglos.

Music taste preferences become more specific as children get older. Boys generally prefer the louder forms of rock, but girls generally prefer softer, more romantic forms. Ethnicity and socioeconomic status also play a role in music choice. African Americans report a preference for soul, rap, and rhythm and blues; Hispanics lean toward salsa; Anglos say they like all types of rock. The medium of vocal music is a socializing influence in that it engages one's attention and emotions with the sound while espousing certain values with the lyrics (American Academy of Child & Adolescent Psychiatry [AACAP], 1997; Jaffe, 1998). However, motivation, experience, knowledge, and self-concept are factors in the interpretation of the lyrics. For example, some studies (Prinsky & Rosenbaum, 1987; Thompson, 1993) have discovered that preadolescents and adolescents often don't understand or attend to the underlying themes in the lyrics. Other studies (Larson, 1995) report music listening as as fantasy experience to explore possible selves (images of power and conquest, rescue by an idealized lover). This effect is magnified by music videos with their visual, as well as audio components (Strouse, Buerkel-Rothfuss, & Long, 1995) and reduced by the presence of family members who disapprove (Thompson & Larson, 1995).

Throughout time and across cultures, people have always created and listened to music. It was a form of communication, emotional expression, art, celebration, tradition, and enjoyment. The media of records, radio, television, and videos provided the ways and means for popular music.

Teenagers in the 1950s were attracted to a form of popular music, known as "rock 'n' roll." The term was coined by Alan Freed (1922–1956) on his radio show in 1951. Teens liked the dance beats and rhythms, the wailing instruments, and the emotional vocal tones of the singers (Gay, 1998). The music and dance often celebrated sexuality and other freedoms beyond what most adults considered to be acceptable boundaries (Gay, 1998). The general themes of the lyrics were alienation, romantic longing for an ideal partner, and frustrated sexuality (Jaffe, 1998). As teenagers demanded more rock music be played on the radio and purchased more records, the genre spread to other media (TV, movies, audiotapes, and later, videotapes and compact discs). By the 1960s, rock music was featured in movies about gangs and juvenile delinquents, reinforcing an association between teenage music and alienation (Jaffe, 1998).

With its origins in the music of slaves and other downtrodden groups, rock music has always spoken to values and points of view outside the mainstream, values frequently divergent from or in opposition to adult culture. . . . Rock music offers an antidote to and an escape from the unrelenting socialization pressures that emanate daily from family and school. Popular music does not tell its listeners to delay gratification and prepare for adulthood. Rather, it tells young people that the concerns they have today are of importance, that they merit expression in music, and that one ought to value one's youth and not worry so much about the future (Larson, Kubey, & Colletti, 1989, pp. 584, 596–597).

Does listening to music about sensual gratification or reckless behavior influence teenagers' behavior, or are troubled teens attracted to such music because it reflects their state of confusion? Consistent with the hypothesis that solitary music listening allows adolescents to explore their possible selves, one study (Took & Weiss, 1994) concluded that heavy metal and rap music empower male teenagers and provide them with an identity "complete with clothes and hairstyle." Such music also offers a peer group with only similar music taste as a requirement for entry.

Arnett (1991) suggests that adolescents' fascination with the despairing lyrics of heavy metal music is a *symptom* of alienation, not its *cause*. For some teens, drug use and careless behavior provide an escape from a chaotic family environment. Acting on the lyric suggestions reflects an absence of parental supervision. For most fans, heavy metal music serves not as a source of anger and frustration, but as a release.

Popular music provides many adolescents with a means of identifying with a particular group or performer (Larson, 1995), especially when real positive role models are lacking in the young person's life. Going to concerts, collecting rock stars' music, wearing certain clothing, adopting certain hairstyles, getting tatooed or body pierced can all

Teens at this rock concert are enjoying each other's company as well as the music.

be part of an adolescent's search for identity—it's a style to "try on," a group of which to be a part. Performers are powerful image-makers; their affect on children depends on the role of other significant socializing agents, such as family and friends.

The question that remains is whether the songs *reflect* the values of a particular generation or whether they *influence* that generation's values. Concern centers on the issue of contagion. **Contagion** is the phenomenon in which an individual exposed to a suggestion will act on it. For example, there is a real concern about metallic rock that portrays sex and violence (AACAP, 1997). Groups of adults have formed in opposition to "rockporn"; a number of wives of government officials have formed the Parents' Music Resource Center (PMRC). They, as well as some PTAs and others, have pressured the Recording Industry of America and the National Association of Broadcasters not to record or air controversial songs or videos and to establish a rating system similar to the one used for movies. Some recording companies have already given in to identifying record albums and cassettes that possess certain explicit lyrics, and some radio stations do not air controversial music (Rice, 1996).

Such a rating system, however, may attract the young people that the adults are trying to protect to the very material that they are being warned against. It has to be kept in mind, though, that a medium's influence as a socializing agent, whether it be television, books, or music, depends on its ability to capture the attention, emotions, and motivations of its audience.

A highly controversial provider because of its ability to captivate young audiences is MTV, or Music Television, which was first introduced in 1983. MTV is a 24-hour rock music, cable television channel that promotes new songs by accompanying them with visual dramatization. These videos have been criticized for their violence, sexism, substance abuse, and sexual content (American Academy of Pediatrics, 1996) as well as stereotyping ethnic groups (Rich, Woods, Goodman, Emans, & DuRant, 1998). "Shake Your Bon Bon," by Ricky Martin (1999), exemplifies sexism and sexual content in that it shows a bunch of guys on the street looking up at a girl dancing in front of a window in her underwear.

A concern about the marriage of music to television is that about 43% of all adolescents in the United States view MTV at least once a week (Thompson, 1993). Mental images once formed by rhythm, beat, and perceived lyrics are now created by special effects on video. That these images are often sexual and/or violent leaves us with this question: Do they influence teen behavior, or are they an outlet for fantasy and aggressive feelings? Another concern is the commercialism. Music videos show images that sell the product (Gay, 1998); therefore, what messages are really being promoted must be questioned.

INTERACTIVE MEDIA: COMPUTERS AND VIDEO GAMES

COMPUTERS

Nearly 69% of children have a computer at home and 45% have Internet access. They spend an average of 1/2 hour per day using the computer for fun, compared to about 3 hours per day watching TV (Kaiser Family Foundation, 1999).

The role of computers in education was examined earlier, and it was concluded that computers are tools to assist instruction in that they present information, enable students to practice skills, enable creativity (an essay, for example) because time doesn't have to be spent on mechanics (spelling, for example), and allow for assessment. The interactive capabilities of computers with CD-ROMS and modems allow for practically unlimited access to information.

Computers are also an excellent medium for learning by doing (Papert, 1993). For example, certain programs enable children to create figures, plan, and solve problems. However, parents and educators must be selective in choosing educational software that will enhance, not detract, from cognitive development. According to Healy (1998), many programs allow the child to select tasks to be done and level of difficulty; adults need to mediate such selections. Also, "hands-on" learning should precede computer use and virtual reality should not replace genuine experience, Healy warns.

What about the socializing effects of computers outside the educational domain? What are the influences on a child's development of playing computer games? How do children cope with access to all kinds of information on the Internet without having developed critical thinking skills? What about access to information negating family values, such as pornography? How can children discern commercial interests from educational ones? The Internet has become the family encyclopedia, library, newspaper, entertainment center, mailbox, chat room, and marketplace.

Neil Postman (1992), communications professor, is worried that as society uses new technology, it becomes shaped by it. New technologies alter how we learn, what we think about, and what we think with. Postman exemplifies how the printing press changed what was meant by "information," then how television changed how "news" was defined, and now how the computer is changing the concept of "truth." He advises that every culture negotiate with technology.

To negotiate with the interactive capacity of the computer, how children use it needs to be explored. One fear is that children who have home computers will be social isolates and choose solitary activities over interactive ones. So far, this has not been widely proven. One study (Sleek, 1998) of people who regularly log on to the Internet, over a 2-year time span, found that as use of the Internet increased, the number of social activities engaged in and social support experience decreased. On the other hand, children often *use* a computer to attract playmates as if it were a desirable toy. They also use it, as in the classroom, to do collaborative activities (Crook, 1992; Haugland & Wright, 1997; Weinstein, 1991).

Another fear regarding the available interactive technology is that, due to economics, some groups of children will not have access. While children from lower socioeconomic families may have computers available to them at school or the public library, they are unlikely to have them at home (Lepper & Gurtner, 1989). Therefore, they may lag behind the very skills needed to succeed in our increasingly computer-dependent society. Are we creating a gap between the information-rich and information-poor?

Finally, the nature of an interactive medium creates the fear of children accessing information that negates their family's values. Any information accessible by a computer and a modem is open to the child who knows how to use the system. The Internet is a web of connections to people and data. Through a modem and various computer software, one can connect to banks, businesses, government, stores, libraries, universities, people with certain interests, and so on. How does such access affect children? Most likely, it will depend, like the influence of all the other media that has been discussed, on the involvement of parents. Parents will have to enable children to develop critical thinking skills to evaluate the information and services accessible on the Internet. Parents can now, with certain software, block out parts of the Internet (pornography, for example) to which they don't want their children exposed. The problem with such "filter" software is that it blocks access to Web sites via certain banned words, so it may block "breasts" links to pornography as well as "breasts" links to cancer. Recently, the Federal Trade Commission (FTC) set privacy rules to protect children from data gathering online marketers, requiring parental permission prior to obtaining information.

As Postman (1992) eloquently elaborates in his book *Technopoly: The Surrender of Culture to Technology,* we must take charge of the technology that is running our lives and place it within the larger context of human goals and social values. The American Library Association suggests the following rules for Internet safety for children:

- Never give your name, address, phone number, or school name to anyone you meet online.
- Never go into a new online area that will cost extra without parental permission.
- Never give out a credit card number online.
- Always tell parents or a trusted adult if something online is scary or confusing.
- Never arrange to meet anyone in person met online.

Computers open a world of information to children.

COMPUTERIZED VIDEO GAMES

Playing video games on the television screen is an alternative to watching television. These games can be educational in that certain skills such as math, spelling, and reading can be reinforced. Some video games require the player to use certain strategies: "Video games are the first medium to combine visual dynamism with an active participatory role for the child" (Greenfield, 1984, p. 101).

Video games represent the fusion of media technology: television and computer. The major forces in the current entertainment video game market are *Nintendo* and *Pokémon,* although many other interactive systems are available, some in videotape format and others in compact disk format. The main concern of these popular interactive games is the prevalence of aggression and gender-role stereotyping as well as their rule-bound logic designed by the programmers (Dietz, 1998; Provenzo, 1991). Pokémon is an example of a multimedia phenomenon (Solomon, 1999). It ranked first in popularity among TV shows for children age 2 to 11. It is also a video game, a card game, and a toy. The most popular categories of video games are fantasy violence, sports, general entertainment, human violence, and educational games (Cesarone, 1994).

Studies show that males play video games more than females (Cesarone, 1994). TV producers and video game manufacturers may produce violent games for this audience. The demand for such aggressive games may arise from a need to have strong role models, rather than from male hormones.

Studies show an increase in the aggressive feelings of children after having played a hostile game. Whether these games are helpful in letting off steam or in encouraging hostile behavior remains uncertain (Cooper & Mackie, 1986; Griffiths, 1991), but they do contribute to children's acceptance of violence as a way to solve problems (Levin, 1998).

Epilogue

*M*edia transmit cultural values whether they are via oral tradition, pictures, print, sound, or computer. For example, both the boy who cried "wolf," and Charlie Bucket learned it pays to be truthful. Media users must cultivate critical thinking skills to evaluate how media messages compare to personal and family values. Adults must be involved in children's media use, just as adults were involved in socializing the boy who cried "wolf" and Charlie Bucket. The villagers taught the boy a lesson by ignoring his third wolf cry. Willy Wonka taught Charlie a lesson by bequeathing him the chocolate factory for being kind and caring. ∎

SUMMARY

Mass media are exemplified in this chapter by broadcast television, books, movies (including videos), magazines, popular music, computers, and video games.

Media are intervening things through which forces act or effects are produced. They are shapers, spreaders, and transformers of culture.

Whatever is broadcast on the airwaves in the United States must be in the public interest. The responsibility of determining what constitutes public interest rests with the broadcasters. Some government regulations exist regarding children's television, which are monitored by the Federal Communication Commission, the agency that grants licenses to broadcasters. Recently, a rating system has been developed for TV viewers.

Television in the United States is mostly perceived as a form of entertainment. Television's multisensory experience forces its audience to employ selective attention. Selective attention depends on one's frame of reference—one's needs, attitudes, motives, habits, interests, values, morals, beliefs, and experiences. The mediating or intervening effects of selective attention make research on the specific effects of television on children confusing. Parental or older sibling involvement has been shown to have a mediating effect.

The following concerns regarding pictorial media are: time spent watching TV and movies, changes in family life rituals, distinguishing reality from fantasy and interactions, affect on imagination, the prevalence of violence, the effect of advertising, the perpetuation of certain values (sexuality, stereotyping), and TV's effect on reading and communication skills.

Television, because of its prevalence, does have influence. It influences behavior, attitudes, values, and expectations, especially for children. In that respect it is a significant socializing agent.

In this democratic society, where freedom of speech prevails in the media, the choice and challenge rest with parents and teachers to mediate children's frames of reference and to impart attitudes, habits, values, and morals so that children will selectively attend to those messages that are already within their frames of reference.

The community's linkage to media (broadcast television) has been to develop alternatives, such as the public broadcasting system, cable and satellite television, video recorders, and computerized video games. Another response has been the formation of public interest groups to pressure broadcasters to change programming, lobby the government for regulations, and educate the public regarding the importance of monitoring its television-viewing habits, especially those of its children.

The school's linkage to media is to teach critical viewing skills as well as to provide educational programs in the classroom. Some suggestions for the family to mediate television and develop critical viewing skills are to know the ratings; know what your children watch and when; choose what to watch; set limits; view with your children whenever possible; and use the time in front of the TV to benefit the child.

Print media (books and magazines) are more difficult to investigate experimentally than are pictorial media (television and movies). Unlike the pictorial media, where the visual image is provided, the print media describe in words the images of the writer. These words must then be translated into visual images by the reader. The visual image one is able to conjure up from printed words depends on one's vocabulary, one's reading ability, and one's real-life experiences. The print and pictorial media require different ways to process information.

It is difficult to compare the socializing effects of print and pictorial media because adults are more likely to mediate books than television. Until children gain a fair amount of reading skill, adults usually choose their books and read to them.

Reading is important for building knowledge. Reading aloud to children enables them to become successful readers. Reading aloud enhances personal attachment, which is a basic ingredient of socialization. It also improves listening skills, which are necessary for reading comprehension. And it provides a model for children to imitate.

Print plays a role in socialization in that it passes on culture to the next generation. It teaches history, values, morals, ideals, and attitudes.

Books also socialize children by influencing language and reading development, cognitive development, and psychosocial development. One of the criteria influencing the effect of books on a child's socialization is the developmental level, or cognitive stage, of the child.

Some concerns regarding the influence of print media on children revolve around certain themes and values perpetuated in comic books, juvenile series books, romances, westerns, mysteries, and magazines. Other concerns involve unrealistic life views, violence, consumerism, and stereotyping.

Sound media (popular music) is a socializing influence in that it engages one's attention and emotions with the sound while espousing certain values with the lyrics. Whether or not children's values and behavior are influenced by the lyrics is questionable because other mediating factors, such as relationships and self-concept are involved. Popular music provides many adolescents with a means of identifying with a particular group or performer. Such identification may affect dress, behavior, friends, and self-concept.

The interactive media—computers and video games—have provoked many questions regarding their socializing effects. While their use in the classroom to assist instruction generally expands the nature of learning, the effects of their use at home is under debate. The current fears are diminished social interaction, playing computer games, access to information on the Internet without necessary critical skills, and access to information negating family values.

Video games represent the fusion of media technology: TV and computer. Games can be educational and/or for entertainment. Some concerns are portrayal of violence, stereotyping, and rule-bound logic.

ACTIVITY

Purpose: To increase your awareness of television's impact.

1. Monitor a child's (or your own) television viewing behavior for a week, using the chart on page 415 as a model.

2. Note the total viewing hours for the week.

3. Keep track of the time spent in other leisure activities for a week.

4. Analyze your findings to determine what types of shows are viewed and the potential impact of their content and commercial messages on viewers.

Date, Day, Time	Name and Type* of Show	Description of Action (Conflicts/ Cooperation)	Description of Role Portrayal (Ethnic, Gender, or Occupation)	Number and Kind† of Advertisements

*Type—comedy, sports, news, drama, cartoon, musical, mystery, and so on.
†Kind—food, toy, beverage, medicine, public service, and so on.

RESOURCES

American Library Association
http://www.ssdesign.com/

American Advertising Federation
http://aaf.org

Federal Communications Commission
(FCC)
http://www.fcc.gov/

KIDSNET
http://www.kidsnet.org/

Media Literacy Online Project
http://interact.uoregon.edu/MediaLit/

Motion Picture Association of America
(MPAA)
http://www.mpaa.org/

Public Broadcasting Service (PBS)
http://www.pbs.org/

RELATED READINGS

Adler, R. P. (1980). *The effects of advertising on children.* Lexington, MA: Lexington.

Cantor, J. (1998). *"Mommy, I'm scared": How TV and movies frighten children and what we can do to protect them.* San Diego: Harcourt Brace.

Carlsen, G. R. (1980). *Books and the teenage reader.* New York: Harper & Row.

Cashdan, S. (1999). *The witch must die: How fairy tales shape our lives.* New York: Basic Books.

Cassell, J., & Jenkins, H. (Eds.). (1999). *From Barbie to Mortal Kombat: Gender and computer games.* Cambridge, MA: MIT Press.

Comstock, G. & Scharrer, E. (1999). *Television: What's on, who's watching, and what it means.* San Diego, CA: Academic Press.

Condry, J. (1989). *The psychology of television.* Hillsdale, NJ: Lawrence Erlbaum.

Greenfield, P. M. (1984). *Mind and media: The effects of television, video games and computers.* Cambridge, MA: Harvard University Press.

Haugland, S. W., & Wright, J. L. (1997). *Young children and technology: A world of discovery.* Needham Heights, MA: Allyn and Bacon.

Healy, J. (1999). *Failure to connect: How computers affect our children's minds— for better and worse.* New York: Touchstone Books.

Jowett, G., & Linton, J. M. (1989). *Movies as mass communications* (2nd ed.). Newbury Park, CA: Sage.

Levin, D. E. (1998). *Remote Control childhood? Combating the hazards of media culture.* Washington, D.C.: National Association for Education of Young Children.

Levine, M. (1996). *Viewing violence: How media violence affects your child's and adolescent's development.* New York: Doubleday.

Lull, J. (Ed.). (1987). *Popular music and communication.* Newbury Park, CA: Sage.

Norton, D. E. (1999). *Through the eyes of a child: An introduction to children's literature* (5th ed.). Upper Saddle River, NJ: Prentice-Hall.

Packard, V. (1980). *The hidden persuaders.* New York: Pocket Books.

Postman, N. (1985). *Amusing ourselves to death: Public discourse in the age of show business.* New York: Penguin.

Postman, N. (1992). *Technopoly: The surrender of culture to technology.* New York: Vintage Books.

Provenzo, E. F., Jr. (1991). *Video kids: Making sense of Nintendo.* Cambridge, MA: Harvard University Press.

Spitz, E. H. (1999). *Inside picture books.* New Haven: Yale University Press.

Trelease, J. (1995). *The read-aloud handbook* (4th ed.). New York: Penguin.

"No man is wise enough by himself."

— *Titus Maccius Plautus*

Chapter 10

ECOLOGY OF THE COMMUNITY

Prologue

THE CONCEPT OF COMMUNITY—UTOPIAN OR UTILITARIAN?

John Donne (1572–1631) wrote, "No man is an island entire of itself; every man is a piece of the continent; a part of the main . . ."

A community is a group of people having something in common. A community is created because no individual is self-sufficing; everyone has many needs, so one turns to others to help satisfy those requirements to survive. When interdependence between people becomes the norm, rules or common policies for group behavior are usually established formally or by custom. Formal rules require leaders to execute them. When a community establishes formal rules and leaders, it becomes a republic. Plato (427–347 B.C.) described the ideal community, a utopia, in The Republic. In such a utopia, everyone fulfills his or her function and works for the good of all. Upbringing and education prepare individuals for their particular functions in the community and for citizenship.

In Plato's ideal republic, rational leaders with ethical knowledge rule because they understand what is good in human life: What is beneficial for the community is beneficial for the individual. For example, the community agrees to common social rules concerning safety, theft, truth-telling, and promise-keeping because these provide individual protection. Plato's vision was criticized in his day as well as today. Can such a utopia exist in reality in that its leaders are rational and ethical? Can it be utilitarian or practical in that there is agreement among citizens on what is beneficial for all?

George Orwell (1946) expressed his anti-utopian views in his satirical novel, Animal Farm. Having been treated poorly, the animals on Manor Farm oust their drunken human master and take over the management of the farm. At first, all the animals have a collective spirit. Everyone willingly works overtime, productivity soars, and everyone has plenty to eat. The rules for the new animal community are painted on the barn:

The Seven Commandments

1. *Whatever goes upon two legs is an enemy.*

2. *Whatever goes upon four legs, or has wings, is a friend.*

3. *No animal shall wear clothes.*

4. *No animal shall sleep in a bed.*

5. *No animal shall drink alcohol.*

6. *No animal shall kill any other animal.*

7. *All animals are equal (Orwell, 1946, p. 33).*

Within the first season, the pigs appoint themselves to be the leaders because of their assumed intelligence (or could it be they were "pig-headed"?). "We pigs are brain workers. The whole management and organization of the farm depend on us. Day and night, we are watching over your welfare. It *is for your sake that we drink that milk and eat those apples" (p. 42). By now the pigs have succumbed to the temptations of privileges and power. They begin to edit the rules to benefit themselves while rationalizing their violence and greed: "Some animals are more equal than others." They sell the old dog, Boxer, to the glue factory for money to buy booze. Once again the rest of the animals are left hungry and exhausted, no better off than they were when humans ran the farm.*

While Plato envisioned benevolent, idealistic leaders (a utopian community), Orwell envisioned manipulative, practical leaders (a utilitarian community). Plato focused on the benevolent, empathetic side of human nature, whereas Orwell took into account the malevolent, selfish side.

Since the establishment of the United States as a republic, government leaders, via legislative policies, shaped communities and the services they provided. Throughout history some leaders were motivated by altruistic concerns, others by egotistical ones. Federal and state governments, due to political ideology, pressure from lobby groups, and fluctuations in funding, influenced the number and types of programs government leaders made available to support families and children. Then there was the conflict between the separate urgings of distinct, diverse individuals and the imperative of one people, one voice—should leaders do what is best for certain persons, or should they do what is best for all? How is the motto of the United States, which is printed on all currency, E. pluribus unum, meaning one out of many, be interpreted? ■

- *How can we approach the concept of an ideal community while oscillating between individualism and collectivism, independence and interdependence, and equality and competition?*
- *Does the individual shape the community or does the community shape the individual?*
- *How can we know what is best for all, who is qualified to decide, and what policies will best help those in need?*

COMMUNITY—STRUCTURE AND FUNCTION

A **community** includes a group of people living in the same geographic area (neighborhood, town, or city) under common laws; it is also a group of people having fellowship, a friendly association, a mutual sharing, and common interests. **Community ecology** comprises the psychological and practical relationships between those people and their social, as well as physical, environments. The crucial component of a community is the relationship of people to one another and the sense of belonging and of obligation to the group.

The community is a microsystem in which much socialization and development take place. The need for community was expressed very well in an article titled "Yearning for Community" (Freedman, 1986) that appeared in my college alumni magazine. The author laments, "I suddenly find myself, at 30, in my sixth new town since college graduation, my third graduate program, living on the edge of unfamiliar suburbs in Seattle." The author's nostalgia from reading the alumni news each month stems not from missing the college she knew, but from missing the community of which she was a part of for 4 years.

She goes on to say, "I was raised in suburban New York, in a family half Jewish, half (Greek Orthodox) Catholic. I went neither to Hebrew nor Sunday school, and my family belonged to no church or temple." When she tried to get tickets for a Yom Kippur service at a local temple, she was told there were no more seats; and even if there were, she would have been charged $90 to sit with total strangers.

She mourns for her roommates: "Now they're scattered, these writers, lawyers, psychologists, teachers, Jews, gentiles, to San Francisco, Baltimore, Greenwich, Bethesda, Manhattan—as my own siblings are scattered to Philadelphia and Boston. Only my parents remain in the same place. Suddenly I envy them, even their country club set." The author of "Yearning for Community" bemoans her lack of geographic ties, religious ties, friendship ties, and family ties; and she is not alone. Community ties have eroded almost everywhere for the following reasons (Schorr, 1997): (1) Fear of violence deters people from gathering informally in public spaces; (2) advances in transportation and communication have enabled people to move far from family and friends in order to work; (3) technological advances make it less necessary to leave home for entertainment; and (4) the larger scale of most institutions and businesses makes it harder to connect with others.

The need for community is both psychological and practical, or economical. Psychologically, humans need companionship and the emotional security that comes from belonging to a social group whose members share the same ideas and patterns of behavior. Practically, humans need to cooperate with fellow beings in order to share in the necessities of life—food, shelter, and security. The concept of community can be small and nearby, as when one refers to one's neighborhood. Or it can be large and far-reaching, as when one refers to one's country or to society in general.

A community is structured to have five functions (Warren, 1983):

1. *Production, distribution, consumption*—the community provides its members with the means to make a living. This may be agriculture, industry, or services.

2. *Socialization*—the community has means by which it instills its norms and values in its members. This may be tradition, modeling, and/or formal education.

3. *Social control*—the community has the means to enforce adherence to community values. This may be group pressure to conform and/or formal laws.

4. *Social participation*—the community fulfills the need for companionship. This may occur in a neighborhood, church, business, and so on.

5. *Mutual support*—the community enables its members to cooperate to accomplish tasks too large or too urgent to be handled by a single person. Supporting a community hospital with tax dollars and donations is an example of people cooperating to accomplish the task of health care.

Communities, small or large, perform these functions in many different ways. The ways in which an individual community performs these functions influence the socialization of children growing up there.

Figure 10.1   An Ecological Model of Human Development

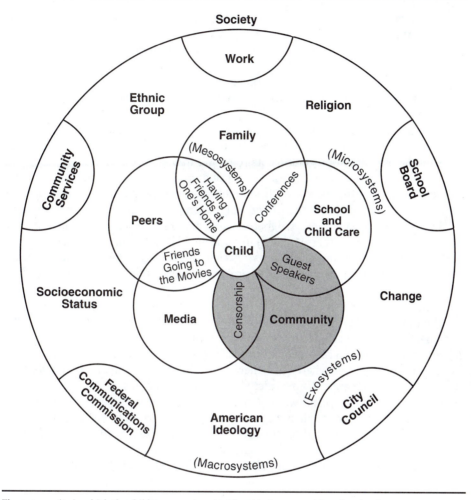

The community in which the child grows up is a significant influence on his or her development.

THE COMMUNITY'S INFLUENCE ON SOCIALIZATION

The neighborhood or neighborhoods (nearby geographic areas) in which we grew up conjure up rich imagery of what constitutes a community (common ties among people). We may picture a small town with a minimall consisting of several stores, the gas station, and the movie theater; the outlying streets with a church or two, the school, and homes separated by bushes or fences. We may picture apartment houses grouped closely together on the street, with the bus stop on the corner and the park and school several blocks away. We may picture acres of farmland and the town, miles away, with a large mall that we visited only once a week. We may picture a large housing tract with lawns, cars, bicycles, and no sidewalks.

Part of the imagery of the neighborhood in which we grew up involves the people who lived there. How did they earn a living? We may picture farmers, shopkeepers, laborers working in factories or mines, or people rushing to and from work dressed in business suits.

How did the people in our community instill in us their norms and values? We may visualize the schools we attended or the clubs we belonged to. We may remember some community traditions like the Fourth of July picnic when everyone brought food to share, or the annual school music festival when every class had certain songs to sing, or we may remember the razzing from the boys on the street when we wore our new shoes.

How did our community enforce its rules? We may picture everyone watching over everyone else and knowing that if we did something wrong, Mrs. Nader would be sure to tell Mother. We may picture the police officer on the corner or the sheriff's car patrolling the streets. We may picture the neighborhood bully beating up someone for being a "rat fink."

How did the people in our neighborhood community socialize with one another? We may visualize our mothers gathered in someone's kitchen or on the street in front of someone's house—a group of men entering a bar after work—a group of adults dancing in the church social hall. Or we may remember our homes filled with company on various occasions.

How did the people in our neighborhood community help one another? We may recall the flurry of activity after the Masons' house burned down. Everyone contributed clothing, food, or household items. We may think of the Garcias' house after their 2-year-old was killed by a car—people crowded inside, talking quietly and crying. We may picture the hospital room where our father spent several weeks—filled with plants, flowers, and cards from friends. We may picture the waiting room of a medical clinic and the cries of sick children, or people waiting in line to fill out forms at a government office.

The community is a socializing agent because it is where children learn the role expectations for adults as well as for themselves. It is in the community that children get to observe, model, and become apprentices to adults; it is in the community that children get to "try themselves out." Socialization requires active involvement:

> For the things we have to learn before we can do them, we learn by doing them. We become just by doing just acts, temperate by doing temperate acts, brave by doing brave acts . . . states of character are formed by doing the corresponding acts (Aristotle, *Methaphysics* [Book 1, ch. 1]).

PHYSICAL FACTORS

Research has shown that certain characteristics of the physical environment of the community influence behavior (Bell, Greene, Fisher, & Baum, 1996). These are *population density and characteristics, noise, arrangement and types of houses, and play settings*.

Population Density and Characteristics

Population density refers to the number of people occupying a certain area of space. High population density can have positive effects on social relationships in that people have many opportunities to mingle, provided there are spaces (places to sit or play) to do so (Etzioni, 1993).

High population density can also have negative effects, such as excessive social contact, reduced behavioral freedom, scarcity of resources, personal space violations, and inability to maintain desired privacy (Bell, Greene, Fisher, and Baum, 1996).

People who report excessive, unwanted social interactions and insufficient privacy, have been observed to socially withdraw. The consequence of social withdrawal is a breakdown in socially supportive relationships (Evans, Palsane, Lepore, & Martin, 1989).

Studies (Rodin, 1976; Rodin, Soloman, & Metcalf, 1978) have demonstrated the relationship between residential density and susceptibility to **learned helplessness**. Learned helplessness, discussed in a later chapter, describes the condition of people who have developed a sense of apathy due to their perception that they have no control over events. This occurs when they feel that their actions no longer influence outcomes. (Did you ever get low grades no matter how hard you studied in a class and, consequently, didn't put forth your best effort on the final because you figured "What's the point"?)

Rodin (1976) found that children who lived in high-density areas were less likely than those in low-density areas to try to control the amount of rewards they would get if they performed certain tasks. She also found that when initially given a frustrating task that was not related to getting rewards, the children who lived in high-density areas did worse on a later task that was related to getting rewards than those who lived in low-density areas.

Density does therefore appear to influence learned helplessness. The density of environment tends to affect people's perception of control over that environment—the higher the density, the less control one feels one has. For example, fire, floods, earthquakes, hurricanes, and tornadoes are much more damaging in high-density environments than in low. In addition, they serve as reminders of how vulnerable one is to natural forces one cannot control, no matter how technologically advanced society becomes. When people continually experience loss of control, which apparently occurs more often in high-density areas, they are likely to lose the motivation to act; they become helpless.

Additionally, communities characterized by high density have been found to be associated with violence and higher crime rates than communities with low density (Limber & Nation, 1998). For example, Sampson (1983) found the rates of victimization were three times greater in high-density versus low-density neighborhoods, even after holding other demographic variables constant. Also found was a relationship between multifamily housing units and crime rates. Thus continual exposure to violence and crime most likely contributes to feelings of helplessness.

The rate of population turnover in a neighborhood influences the interactions with newcomers, as well as the degree of community involvement (Bell et al., 1996; Garbarino, 1992). The degree of transience in a neighborhood affects both those who remain and those who move. When people do not plan to remain in a neighborhood more than a few years, they tend not to get involved in community activities. Those who do remain in the neighborhood make fewer efforts to establish close personal ties with newcomers whom they expect to depart.

Neighborhoods differ in the extent to which they include people from differing ages, and varying income levels, religious, ethnic, or educational backgrounds (Garbarino, 1992). *Homogeneous* neighborhoods include people of similar backgrounds; *heterogeneous* neighborhoods include people of differing backgrounds.

Children who grow up in homogeneous neighborhoods—for example, like many suburban neighborhoods—have few opportunities to interact with children or adults who differ in their backgrounds and values. Children whose neighborhoods are accessible to a larger town only by car have little opportunity to even observe the work world of adults. Children who grow up in heterogeneous neighborhoods—for example, like some urban neighborhoods—are more likely to have opportunities to interact with children of differing backgrounds at school or on the playground. Because stores and businesses are more accessible, children have more opportunities to interact with adults in their work roles.

Noise

Noise is "unwanted sound" (Bell et al., 1996). High levels can lead to hearing loss, increases in arousal levels, and stress. It can interfere with attention.

Cohen, Glass, and Singer (1973) studied children living in a large, high-rise apartment complex situated over a noisy highway in New York City. They found that the exposure to noise on the lower floors of the complex was more severe than on the upper floors. The researchers controlled for other factors such as social class and air pollution. They found that the children on the noisier lower floors had poorer hearing discrimination than the children on the upper floors. Moreover, the hearing problems of children on the lower floors may have influenced their poorer reading performance in school.

A study conducted by the California Department of Health Services linked freeway noise to poorer school test scores (Savage, 1983). The study compared third- and sixth-graders in nine sets of two comparable schools, one set located near a freeway and one farther away. The children in the noisy schools generally did less well academically in reading and mathematics than their counterparts in quieter schools. One sixth-grader said, "We can't hear the teacher, and she gets mad because we don't hear what she says." Another child said, "You can't concentrate when the trucks are passing." Noise interferes with verbal communication and may affect productivity (Bell et al., 1996).

In another study (Evans, Hygge, & Bullinger, 1993), third- and fourth-grade children who lived near the Munich International Airport and were chronically exposed to airport noise, found that they had higher stress levels (measured by blood pressure, heart rate, and blood levels of

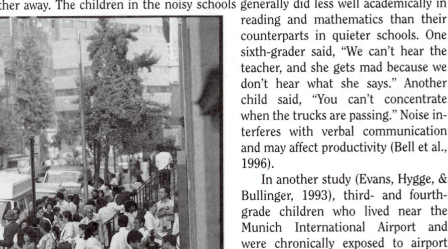

Much interaction with a variety of people is possible in this highly populated neighborhood; however, some people may experience a feeling of being crowded.

stress hormones) when performing cognitive tasks than children who lived in quieter neighborhoods.

In conclusion, whether noise hurts or helps performance depends on the type of noise, the complexity of the task, and individual factors such as personality and adaptation level (Bell et al., 1996).

Arrangement and Types of Houses

The way houses and streets are arranged affects the interactions between people living in a neighborhood (Bell et al., 1996; Garbarino, 1992). When houses face the street or a courtyard, people have a common place of contact. Children living in such a setting usually play on the court or sidewalk or in the street, provided there is not much traffic. This direct access to the outside maximizes the potential for parental supervision (Taishido Study Group, 1984/1985). In other words, children can be watched from inside simply by looking out. On the other hand, houses that have no common area, such as apartments, minimize the potential for parental supervision. When children in such houses leave to play, their actions cannot be supervised unless the children are accompanied by a parent or other adult.

Play Settings

Play settings influence socialization by the types of activities that occur in them and by whether or not adults are present to supervise. Some neighborhoods provide playgrounds for children, and the type of equipment available appears to affect their use (Rivkin, 1995). A study (Hayward, Rothenberg, & Beasley, 1974) comparing different playground settings (*traditional, modern, adventure*) found that the availability of the play materials clearly influenced the play activity. The *traditional* playground setting had swings, a slide, a teeter-totter, and a sandbox. The *modern* playground had various sculptures upon which children could climb, crawl, and slide. The *adventure* playground had old lumber, tires, crates, bricks, and rocks.

Children were interviewed and observed in each of the settings. Preschool children often accompanied by adults used the *traditional* and *modern* playground more often; school-age children and teenagers used the *adventure* playground more often. The children in the *traditional* and *modern* playgrounds were involved with using the equipment, whereas children in the *adventure* playground were involved in expressing ideas and fantasies.

ECONOMIC FACTORS

Economic factors in a community play a central role in shaping the daily lives of families who live and work there. Local economic systems vary depending on the jobs, goods, and services provided by the business sector of the community. When a local plant closes, the employees are forced to find work elsewhere, often at lower wages. Often they have to bridge the income gap by working more hours. Thus, wage earners have fewer hours to spend with their families.

Community economics have affected the costs of housing, transportation, education, and health care, all of which have risen steadily since the 1970s and today consume substantially more of a typical family's income than they did 30 years ago. In recent decades, the average working family's tax burden has also risen.

To accommodate family lifestyle to economic changes in the community, more than two-thirds of mothers with young children are working in the labor force (U.S. Bureau of the Census, 1998). When mothers work, adjustments have to be made in the workplace and in communities. As will be discussed later, the main adjustments involve businesses becoming more responsive to families and, as was discussed in Chapter 5, communities providing quality child care.

Children's economic well-being is directly related to that of their families. When families have an adequate income, they are better able to meet their children's material, intellectual, and emotional needs and help them become healthy, productive adults. Yet today, children, especially those in single-parent families, are the poorest Americans (Children's Defense Fund [CDF], 1998; McLoyd, 1998). Failure to address the economic needs of families, especially the threat of poverty, leads to social consequences affecting individuals, families, and the whole community. Examples of such ills are more crime and delinquency, more substance abuse, more school failure, more child abuse and neglect, more teenage childbearing, more unhealthy children, and lower productivity by tomorrow's labor force. These problems impose enormous costs on the community, including expenditures for treatment of illnesses and chronic health conditions, special education, foster care, prisons, and welfare (CDF, 1998; National Commission on Children [NCC], 1991). Social problems and their costs will be discussed in more detail later.

Community economics, specifically unemployment, is related to how children in families are socialized. There is evidence that economic hardship threatens the psychological well-being of parents and undermines their capacity for supportive child rearing. When parents have difficulty coping financially and share their problems with their chil-

Some neighborhood designs foster people interaction.

dren, children experience increased psychological distress (McLoyd, 1998; McLoyd & Wilson, 1990).

Many inner-city neighborhoods are plagued by the highest level of joblessness since the Depression (Wilson, 1995). Unemployment, as experienced in different neighborhood settings, has different connotations and hence effects on children. A jobless family that lives in an area of relatively low employment and poverty differs from a jobless family that lives in a predominately poor neighborhood. Neighborhoods plagued with high levels of joblessness tend to have high levels of crime, gang violence, and drug trafficking. The decline of legitimate employment opportunities tends to build up incentives to sell drugs (Fagan, 1993). For example, children see the drug dealers with cars, fancy clothes, and money; things they don't see at home. They also have trouble connecting the role of education to post-school employment because most of the adults in their community don't work in spite of having gone to school (Wilson, 1995).

Surprisingly, the effect of unemployment on children has not always been found to be negative. A classic longitudinal study by Glen Elder (1974), discussed in Chapter 1, demonstrated that adolescents whose fathers lost their jobs had to assume certain responsibilities in the family to keep it functioning. This contribution to family welfare enabled the adolescents to adjust successfully to adult life. They did well in school, were satisfied with their marriages, and had successful careers. However, such positive outcomes were not true of children under age 14 whose fathers lost their jobs. They were resentful, lost respect for their fathers, and did not generally adjust well to adult life. They were vulnerable to impaired development because at the time economic crisis hit their families, they were most dependent and in need of a role model.

The different findings in present studies and those of the Depression may be due to the type of supportive relationships the child or adolescent had with relatives and non-relatives during the time of economic hardship (Coleman, 1990). These social supports include common values of neighborhood residents to maintain effective social control (supervise children's activities, monitor children's behavior, and motivate children to be productive).

SOCIAL AND PERSONAL FACTORS

In addition to the physical and economic factors in a community, there are certain other characteristics, less tangible and more individualistic, that influence socialization. These are the *neighborhood setting* and the *patterns of community interaction*. **Neighborhood** refers to people and places nearby, whereas **community** refers to people and places having something in common.

The Neighborhood Setting

The neighborhood is the geographic setting in which children generally spend their unstructured time (Garbarino, 1992). The neighborhood is where children explore, interact with other children, observe adults engaged in work or other activities, and have various experiences themselves.

Neighborhood settings differ not only in the physical environments (streets, parks, facilities) available for children, but also in the social environments (who is available to interact with whom). Since children are minimally mobile, they play close to home and interact with those who live close by. Medrich and his colleagues (Medrich, Roizen, Rukin, & Buckley, 1981) studied how children in different neighborhoods spent their time after school. Five neighborhoods (their names were changed for publication) exemplify how different settings affect children's daily experiences and hence their socialization. Were any of these similar to neighborhoods you grew up in?

These examples illustrate how the neighborhood setting affects children's mobility, exposure to adults, friendship patterns, and types of play (Berg & Medrich, 1980; Medrich, Roizen, Rubin, & Buckley, 1981).

Mountainside

Mountainside has no sidewalks, and its streets are hilly. The houses are set back from the road, and you get a feeling of isolation. The shops, library, school, park, and recreation center are clustered in "the village" at the base of the hill, several miles from most of the houses. Children spend most of their free time close to home because it's not easy to get around in this neighborhood—the hills are too steep for bicycles. They play baseball and soccer in diamonds they have painted on the streets. They build tree houses and rope swings and share them with other neighborhood children. The children interact with few adults other than their parents, and that doesn't seem to bother them. They have to rely on their parents to drive them to lessons or recreational facilities.

Rosewood

Rosewood is a neighborhood with sidewalks and connecting streets on which the children ride their bicycles and play softball. There are few boundaries between the houses. The neighborhood is centered on the school. Anyone can get there within a seven-minute walk, and many children use the playground as a meeting place. Rosewood is heterogeneous in character and dense with children. The majority of children are Anglo, but a large proportion are African American. Friends are chosen on the basis of similarities in age and race.

Bancroft

Bancroft is a neighborhood with no sidewalks or street lamps. The roads are narrow and patched with asphalt. Most houses cannot be seen from the street. Yards are separated by fences. In Bancroft both parents are apt to work, and children are frequently left on their own when not at school; children are expected to stay close to home after school so parents know where they are. Children's time is often spent in the company of brothers and sisters. Children rarely leave their block except to go to school, run an errand, or keep an appointment. This may be because the school and park both front on streets heavy with traffic.

Glenn

Glenn begins where the trucking companies and shipping warehouses along a freeway exit end. The houses look like fortresses. There are a lot of apartments. Neighbors sit on bannisters, and children hang around the streets. Although buses and large trucks run through continually, there are no stop signs. Shops and churches are located mostly in one area; all have gated locks because vandalism rates are high. There is a park with a recreation center that many people frequent. Glenn is a neighborhood with strong ethnic ties—most families are African American, a lot are Hispanic, and few are Anglo. Friendships seem to be formed along ethnic lines, and tightly knit adolescent gangs are common.

Eastside

Eastside is a neighborhood with stark streets and debris collecting at the curbs. Yards are fenced, and most lack trees. Despite its physical appearance, the neighborhood is vibrant with street life. Many Eastside families migrated from the South and talk with one another about relatives back there or recent visits. The children congregate on the street. Many go to the community center, where they are eligible for free lunch. Friendships are formed easily according to whoever is nearby. Not only are peers considered to be friends to children, but so are neighbors and shopkeepers. Children have a lot of comfortable relations with different adults. The schoolyard can be reached in five minutes, and children often gather there to play. Age doesn't seem to matter regarding playmates, but skills count. It is not uncommon to find a broad age range of children getting together to play ball.

Patterns of Community Interaction

Community interaction is an important factor in development because, according to Bronfenbrenner (1979, 1989), the developmental potential of a setting, in this case the community, is enhanced as a function of the number of its supportive links with other settings the child might be in, such as the family or school. This section examines patterns of community interaction.

Patterns of interaction vary considerably with the size of a community. In a small town, one person may interact directly with almost every other person in a given week or month. In contrast, a resident of a large city might conceivably roam the streets without ever seeing a familiar face.

The social density, or the degree to which an environment contains a diversity of roles and experiences for children to learn from and for parents to draw upon, affects families and children. A dense setting contains a variety of businesspeople as well as a variety of ages and ethnic groups. Such a setting provides many opportunities for children to learn what community relations are all about. Such a setting also affords families a choice of social networks upon which they can rely for support (Garbarino, 1992; Hareven, 1989).

Interaction in a small town involves close contact with relatives, friends, and acquaintances. Because of this, people in a small community tend to be involved in each other's lives—their marriages, their children, their illnesses, and their employment are subjects of discussion, concern, and gossip. Interaction in a large city, on the other hand, involves less personal contact, but more impersonal interactions. For example, interactions with coworkers, bankers, clerks, and bus drivers may occur daily, but only in the context of the specific roles they perform. For personal interactions, residents of large cities must rely on immediate family members and voluntary associations (church, PTA, lodge, club).

The norms of a small town are more homogeneous than those of a large city, and are also more widely understood and accepted (Garbarino, 1992). Because of this consensus, socialization of children tends to proceed more smoothly in a small town than in a large city. In a small town, shared convictions about what is right or wrong, proper or improper, tend to be passed on from generation to generation and become institutionalized. In other words, the unwritten local customs become the common law. The community, then, becomes the medium through which the basic values, norms, and customs of society are interpreted and reinforced through repeated interaction of community members.

As an example of an institutionalized *value* mediated by the community, "Honor thy father and mother" may mean that community members ask children if their parents know where they are before inviting them into their homes. An example of a *norm* mediated by the community might be the appropriate ways of dressing—it may not be appropriate to wear shorts certain places in town. An example of a *custom* mediated by the community might be how people greet one another—"Hello, how are you?" or "Hi, y'all." "What's happening?" or shaking hands or bowing.

Unlike a small town, a large city brings together people from a wide variety of ethnic, religious, regional, educational, and occupational groups, all of whom are products of their own socialization. The majority of the population may have similar values, but their norms and ways have not been institutionalized. Therefore, large cities must rely more on formal rules and regulations for influencing behavior than on informal methods. For example, in a small town it is highly unlikely that you would play your stereo loudly at 11 P.M. Your behavior is regulated by courtesy to your neighbor. In a large city, however, where neighbors often do not know each other, behavior might have to be regulated by rules restricting noise to certain hours.

Mechanisms of social control differ in small towns and large cities. In a small town, residents know they are under constant surveillance and that any misconduct will become a matter of community concern. Social control is due to fear

These neighbors are interested and involved in each other's lives.

of social rejection and gossip. In large cities, the police and courts are more often relied upon to provide social control by using formal sanctions.

Industrialization and urban growth have been accompanied by increasingly impersonal forms of interaction, according to Ferdinand Tonnies (1957/1987). His book *Gemeinschaft und Gesellschaft*, considered to be a classic, defines two basic types of social relationships. *Gemeinschaft* relationships are mutually dependent and caring. People relate to each other because they are kin, because they live in a particular locality, or because they are likeminded and wish to pursue a common goal. *Gemeinschaft* relationships are close, informal, interpersonal, and intimate. There is mutual trust and concern, as well as willing cooperation. *Gesellschaft* relationships, on the other hand, are independent and contractual. People relate to each other because it is a practical way of achieving an objective, like paying for services rendered. *Gesellschaft* relationships are associative and formal. They are characterized by individualism and mutual distrust. Typically, interactions are for a particular purpose. Children who primarily experience *gemeinschaft* relationships have very different socialization experiences than children who primarily experience *gesellschaft* relationships.

The decline of contemporary morality has been blamed on too much "gesellschaft" or "individualism" in communities and not enough "gemeinschaft" or "communalism" (Etzioni, 1993; Hayes & Lipset, 1993/1994). Those who favor communalism do so because they feel the norms of responsibility common to *gemeinschaft* communities should be emphasized to "counterbalance" the selfishness of individualism. Those who favor individualism do so because it is embedded in the American culture and because they feel that Americans should use the tools with which their individualistic culture provides them (efficiency, specificity, or practicality, for example) to fix the social problems, such as crime or substance abuse, common to *gesellschaft* communities. What kind of social relationships did you primarily have in the community or culture in which you grew up, and how did they influence you?

Basic Social Relationships

Gemeinschaft	*Gesellschaft*
mutually dependent	independent
caring	contractual
informal	formal
intimate	associative
trusting	mistrusting
kin	employers/managers
friends	employees
neighbors	business associates
special-interest groups	achievement objectives
collectively oriented	individually oriented

CHILD–COMMUNITY LINKAGES

The community is a setting that provides much potential for learning. Libraries, museums, zoos, farms, businesses, people's experiences, and collectibles (family heirlooms, antiques, photographs, and so on) are all rich sources for involving children (Hatcher & Beck, 1997).

To illustrate the community's potential for learning, an experiment was initiated in Philadelphia to try a "school without walls" (Brenner & Von Moschzisker, 1971). Students in grades nine to twelve were chosen by lottery from eight school districts; neither economic nor academic background was a factor. There was no school building; each of the eight areas had a headquarters with office space for staff and lockers for students. All teaching took place within the community. Art was studied at the art museum; biology was studied at the zoo; vocational education took place at various business locations. A higher than average percentage of students who attended went on to college.

Many school districts have *alternative schools* that follow this model. The philosophy of alternative education is that "the child, like the adult, learns the art and technique of citizenship, not through admonitions or through lectures on civics, but from involvement in real issues" (Hatcher & Beck, 1997; Ward, 1978, p. 184). Some high schools and colleges have combined work–study programs, in which students can apply theoretical knowledge learned in school to practical experience at work. Existing schools can find many ways of using the community as an educational resource—inviting guest speakers to class, going on fieldtrips, and working on a community project (planting trees, participating in a parade, raising money for the needy, and so on).

Today, many high schools around the country require students to perform community service in order to graduate. This was a result of the passage of the National and Community Service Act of 1990, which gave grants to schools to develop and implement student-involvement projects (Levine & Levine, 1996). Projects can include environment conservation, hospitals, child-care facilities, law enforcement, and social service agencies, to name a few.

Part of the National School Goals 2000, reform strategies discussed in Chapter 6, is the commitment of communities to learning. The business community can facilitate child socialization by fostering school and related educational work or recreational projects in several ways. Members of the business community can provide specific schools with materials, financial aid, human resources, and professional support. (Some communities refer to such a project as "Adopt-a-School.") They can serve on school advisory councils or on school boards. They can offer schools the use of business settings for job placement or offer field sites for work experience programs. (Harcourt College Publishers does these things.)

A specific example of a cooperative business–school venture to facilitate child socialization is operated by the Boston Private Industry Council Partnerships. John Hancock, an insurance company, collaborates with various schools in Boston to motivate disadvantaged minority children toward academic and career achievement. Classes of eleventh and twelfth graders are transported twice a week to the company, where they learn business skills to give them a head start for permanent positions at John Hancock or another company. In addition, employees at the company volunteer at the schools, and the company sponsors workshops for parents on "partnering" as well as for students to find summer jobs.

In conclusion, child–community linkages are established when citizens (parents, educators, businesspeople, religious groups, service providers, legislators) become involved in working toward mutually beneficial goals that focus on the positive growth and development of children (Pagano, 1997). It is only through a concerted effort by parents, educators, business leaders, and community leaders that we can produce a future generation of contributing and effective people (Schorr, 1997). Specific business practices supporting families were discussed in Chapter 3.

COMMUNITY SERVICES

Lisbeth Schorr (1997), in her book *Common Purpose,* quotes anthropologist Margaret Mead: "Never doubt that a small group of thoughtful, committed citizens can change the world; indeed, it is the only thing that ever has." Schorr gives examples of community services (family, educational, and welfare) throughout the country that have succeeded by injecting flexibility and creativity into bureaucratic policies that govern their existence.

Why are community services necessary? One reason is the increasing population. As more people compete for available resources, more people need supportive services to survive—job assistance, housing assistance, financial support, food subsidies, and medical care. As people live longer, the number of years that they are likely to depend on Social Security payments for support in their retirement years, as well as on Medicare for their health insurance, increases. As advancements in science occur, more people's lives are prolonged. These people may have diseases or disabilities that prevent them from working; they, too, will need financial assistance as well as other services to survive.

A second reason is the changing nature of the family. More births to teenagers, more divorces, more single-parent families, and more employed mothers mean an increasing need for such services as financial assistance, social services, and child care. The mobility of families has caused separations from relatives. Thus families turn to the community for support when relatives are unavailable.

A third reason lies in the increasing urbanization of communities. The centralization of industries in certain areas and the consequent migration—from rural to urban areas—of people seeking employment has increased the number of people living in a smaller amount of space. Therefore, people living in cities must turn to the community for various kinds of services—recreational, for example. Because of the high density of people living in a small area, the community is expected to provide open-space areas for recreation. Rural areas, because they are less populated, have fewer public services than urban areas.

PUBLIC AND PRIVATE AGENCIES

Agencies providing services can be public or private. Public agencies are financed by taxation. They are administered within the legal framework of the local, state, or federal government. *Private* agencies are financed by donations and/or fees. Some funds may come from Community Chest or United Way. They are established by individuals or philanthropic, religious, fraternal, or humanitarian groups; their management is the responsibility of a board of directors.

Public Agencies

Historically, U.S. charitable organizations voluntarily assumed the responsibility of maintaining the social welfare of the community. The Depression of the 1930s convinced the government of the need to step in to help its citizens (Zaslow et al., 1998), hence the gradual increase in public welfare agencies over the past 60 years (Garbarino, 1992; McLoyd, 1998). Because public welfare agencies are government institutions, they depend on legislation to appropriate funds for their administration and services. Legislation to appropriate tax monies for an agency is generally related to the approval and support of the citizens. (Citizen support, or advocacy, will be discussed later in this chapter.) Most public agencies operate at the local (county, city, town) level. Their structures differ according to state and local laws.

Private Agencies

Private or voluntary social agencies have traditionally been organized to meet a community's particular problems of caring for orphans and neglected children, unwed mothers, individuals with disabilities, the aged, and the indigent. They have also been organized to meet problems of alcohol abuse, drug abuse, and certain specific diseases. When a private agency is set up, it must comply with local and state laws. Donations are solicited, a board of directors is chosen to represent various parts of the community, a constitution is drawn up, and committees are appointed to oversee the various functions of the agency—for example, a finance committee, a buildings and maintenance committee, a public relations committee, and so on. Since the agency depends on citizen donations, continuous communication with the public regarding its activities is necessary.

The actual services the agency provides are under the control of a director, appointed by the board, who oversees a professional staff. In contrast to public agencies, which according to law have to accept every client who meets the legal requirements for eligibility, voluntary agencies are not under obligation to serve every applicant (Maidman, 1984). Generally, private agencies are more focused in the services they provide and can therefore be effective only with certain persons. For example, a public agency dealing with adoptions must legally serve all races and religions, but a private adoption agency can focus on only one religion. The public agencies, then, may serve more people, but the private agencies can provide more in-depth services to fewer people.

Most local communities have a policy regarding the establishment of private agencies. Before a new agency can be supported, there must be an investigation into what resources already exist in the community and what needed facilities or services the community is lacking. Partnership usually develops between public and private agencies so that each supplements and supports the other.

Examples of private social agencies are the Child Welfare League of America, the Alliance for Children and Families, Catholic Charities USA, the Association of Jewish Families and Children's Agencies, the Aid Association for Lutherans, the American Red

Cross, and the March of Dimes Birth Defects Foundation. There are also many private nonprofit organizations that serve local communities.

PREVENTIVE, SUPPORTIVE, AND REHABILITATIVE SERVICES

Community services can be categorized as *preventive, supportive,* or *rehabilitative.*

Preventive services attempt to lessen the stresses and strains of life resulting from social and technological changes and to avert problems—for example, parks and recreation programs set up in rapidly developing urban areas. These parks and recreational services are meant to be used by children in their free time to keep them from engaging in delinquent behavior.

Supportive services deal with educational programs, counseling services, health services, policies related to demographic changes, employment training, and community development projects. These services maintain the health, education, and welfare of the community.

Rehabilitative services enable people to participate in the community effectively.

Preventive Services: Parks, Recreation, and Education

The purpose of **preventive services** is to provide for people's needs for space, socializing, physical activity, and mental stimulation. Children need room to play and explore. Families need places to go to relax and enjoy each other's company. Everyone needs space to exercise and be physically fit. Many community members enjoy taking classes to learn new skills or to broaden their perspectives on life (culturally, historically, technologically, linguistically, and so on).

Open spaces have been set aside for enjoyment as far back in history as early Greek and Roman civilization. As Western European cities grew, parks or plazas were established. The first parkland in America to be designated for the public was purchased in 1660. As the colonies grew, so did the number of parks. One of the best-known parks, which was established in about 1853, is Central Park in New York City. The 843 acres of land were reserved for the purpose of recreation and relief from urban conditions. Other large cities followed New York's example (Rivkin, 1995).

In the 1890s and early 1900s the public began to pressure the government to assume responsibility for community recreation. This pressure was probably due to the growth of large cities and resultant lack of play space for children. The government responded by setting up agencies and organizations to provide recreation for children. By 1900, some 14 cities had made provisions for supervised play and, in 1906, the Playground and Recreation Association of America (now called the National Recreation Association) was set up. Its purpose was to promote community recreational facilities and programs.

Some of the services that community parks and recreation programs supply are providing and maintaining natural or designed environments, promoting physical fitness, and offering classes to enable people to develop interests and skills for use of their leisure time or to enhance their employability.

The environments provided and maintained by parks and recreation departments may include parks with play equipment, marked trails in which flora are labeled or historical events recorded on signs, museums with varying exhibits, zoos, botanical gardens, planetariums, and aquariums.

Some of the programs promoting physical fitness and interest and skill development include organized team sports and classes in tennis, fishing, sailing, photography, and arts and crafts. Opportunities for camping and other trips may be provided. Special events, such as hobby shows, pet shows, or camping demonstrations, may be sponsored by parks and recreational programs. Some communities have classes in computers, languages, parenting, art, and astronomy, to name a few.

There are many federal agencies as well as state and local agencies responsible for administering recreational programs. Some examples of federal agencies performing this service are the National Park Service and the Cooperative Extension Service. The National Park Service, created in 1916 under the U.S. Department of the Interior, is the federal agency responsible for managing the 29 national parks. This service attempts to keep national park resources as natural as possible. For example, dead trees are allowed to stand or fall in order to provide homes and food for wildlife. Historical sites are sometimes reconstructed to provide visitors with a feeling of "what it was like then."

The Cooperative Extension Service, under the Department of Agriculture, was originally designed to improve the rural economy by providing educational services and information to farmers. It works through the state agricultural colleges and county agricultural agents to provide direct community services. An example of one of the services is the establishment and maintenance of 4-H clubs. Many children participate. They learn farm and home skills, science, and camping, and participate in various recreational activities. The mission of 4-H (head, heart, hands, and health) is to enable young people to become self-directing, productive, and contributing members of society through learn-by-doing experiences.

Many state agencies responsible for park and recreational services have functions similar to their federal counterparts. However, some functions vary greatly from state to state—such as the actual services provided to local communities, the laws regarding protection and conservation of wildlife and natural resources, and the maintenance of lands and waters for public use.

Some of the private and voluntary groups providing recreational services to children in the community are the Boy Scouts of America, Girl Scouts of America, Boys' and Girls' Clubs of America, American Red Cross, Young Men's Christian Association (YMCA), and

Young Women's Christian Association (YWCA). These agencies promote certain values, emphasize learning by doing, and are concerned with personal development; their leaders come from the community and serve as role models. For example, the Boy Scouts of America promotes the ability of young people to do things for

A park in the middle of the city for all to enjoy.

themselves and others. Leaders train the boys in self-reliance, courage, and good citizenship. In addition, patriotism is emphasized. For another example, the Boys' and Girls' Clubs of America, which includes boys and girls, age 6 to 18, who are at risk for behavioral, social, or academic problems, provide programs and services to significantly enhance children's lives and enable youth to develop skills to become employable. The clubs also build knowledge to engage in positive behaviors and safe health practices, as well as to become responsible citizens.

Supportive Services: Family and Child

The purpose of family services is to preserve a healthy family life by aiding the family members to achieve harmonious relationships. Whereas friends and neighbors function as an informal support system (*Gemeinschaft*) to families, family services function as a formal support system (*Gesellschaft*). In helping families, family services consider the influence on the family of ethnicity, religion, and pattern of organization (Feldman & Scherz, 1987; Schorr, Both, & Copple, 1991).

Referrals. Problems that threaten the stability of family life include discord between husband and wife, discord between parent and child, illness, accidents, economic problems, desertion, delinquency, teen pregnancy, and alcohol or drug abuse. Family service agencies provide referrals to specific agencies dealing with these specific problems. They also give counseling, which may include advice on budgeting and home management, vocational opportunities, and family relationships.

Economic Assistance. Both public and private social agencies offer family services. Generally, public agencies offer services based on the family's economic need (families must meet legal eligibility requirements to qualify for assistance)—for example, in arranging financial assistance, finding a job, and locating affordable and suitable housing. Assistance may also include the distribution of food and medicine as well as child-care services. Private family service agencies are concerned primarily with personal problems and emotional maladjustment problems of members of the family rather than problems due to economics. Private agencies do, however, provide financial help in emergencies (especially when the family is waiting to see if it qualifies for public assistance or when the family has recently immigrated to the United States and does not qualify for public assistance). Family agencies may deal with personal problems involving an economic commitment such as placement of children in special schools or camps, or placement of adults in mental institutions or homes for the aged.

Counseling. Family services include marriage counseling, prenatal and family planning, family life education, homemaker services, and senior citizen services. Counseling services help marriage partners meet their marital responsibilities and resolve marital conflicts. They may also help in emotional maladjustment problems such as lack of communication between parents and teenagers, in premarital counseling, or in problems involved in adjusting to divorce. Prenatal care and family planning services promote the mental and physical health of children (and mothers) from the prenatal stage onward. Family planning includes birth control education. Child guidance services include family therapy and parenting training.

Table 10.1   Empowering Families to Help Themselves

FAMILY SUPPORT AND PRESERVATION	TRADITIONAL SERVICES
• Build on family strengths	• Emphasize family deficits
• Focus on families	• Focus on individuals
• Respond flexibly to family needs	• Program and funding source dictate services
• Reach out to families	
• Treat families as partners in goal-setting	• Have strict eligibility requirements
• Offer services in home or homelike setting	• Workers set goals and solutions
	• Services are office-based
• Respond quickly to needs	• Often have waiting lists

Source: Children's Defense Fund (1994). *The state of America's children yearbook, 1994.* Washington, DC. Author.

Family Preservation.   The Family Preservation and Support Services Program was officially enacted by the federal government in 1993. States receive money to develop family preservation and support services, thereby changing the way services have traditionally been delivered to families (*see* Table 10.1).

The purpose of family preservation services is (1) to keep the family safe, (2) to avoid unnecessary placement of children in substitute care and the consequent high human and financial cost, and (3) to improve family functioning so that the behavior that led to the crisis will be less likely to reoccur (Cole & Duva, 1990). Family preservation services offer a mix of counseling, education, referrals, concrete assistance, and advocacy. An example is family life education, which includes education in home economics and management, parenting, and family relationships. Homemaker services send a "homemaker" to the home when the mother is temporarily unable to care for the family. The service enables the family to stay together and carry on in crises such as hospitalization, chronic illness, and impairment due to a disabling condition.

Keeping families together involves protecting children's safety in the home and strengthening families' abilities to deal with their problems. Family preservation programs may include intensive family-based crisis-intervention services. For example, when a child is at risk for abuse, rather than remove the child from the family, a trained professional goes to the home to give practical assistance on immediate problems and parenting training, and helps to link the family with other support services in the community.

Senior Citizens.   Senior citizen services may include economic assistance, in-home care, day care, institutionalization, recreation, Meals on Wheels (a program that delivers meals to the homes of the housebound), friendly visiting, and arranging for other community services to "adopt a grandparent" (for example, a child-care center might welcome the experience and extra help a senior citizen could provide for the children).

Child Health and Welfare.   The term *child welfare* encompasses care for indigent, neglected, abused, deserted, sick, disabled, maladjusted, or delinquent children. The purpose of child welfare agencies is to protect the physical, intellectual, and emotional well-being of children (Zaslow, Tout, Smith, & Moore, 1998). Child welfare services entail providing (1) economic and personal aid to children living in their own homes, (2) foster care for children who have no home or cannot remain with their own families, and (3) institutional care when children cannot be placed in a foster home or cannot remain with their own families (Nazario, 1988).

Traditionally, children whose families could not care for them, due to death, illness, or poverty, were placed in institutions. Private agencies and charitable organizations took the major responsibility for child welfare. Today, however, children are enabled to remain with their families; they are removed only as an emergency measure—for example, in cases of abuse. The need for financial aid to mothers in order to preserve the family was first emphasized at the White House Conference on the Care of Dependent Children in 1910. The first national welfare legislation was passed as part of the Social Security Act of 1935 (Zaslow et al., 1998). Public funds are available under the Aid to Families with Dependent Children (AFDC) Program. The government administered public agencies via taxation to enable families to provide a minimum of shelter, food, clothing, and medical care for their children. In 1998, the Family Support Act was passed. It implemented the Job Opportunities and Basic Skills Training (JOBS) Program that provided education and job training, as well as child care, for mothers with young children to enable them to make the transition from government assistance to independence. Today, the Personal Responsibility and Work Opportunity Reconciliation Act of 1996 sets time limits for the transition.

The states carry out maternal and child health programs with the financial support of the federal government. These programs include family planning services, prenatal clinics, well-baby clinics for regular medical examinations of young children, hearing and vision screening, home delivery, nursing, dental services, and mental health services.

The state governments also administer programs that provide services for children with disabilities, partially financed by matching funds from the federal government. Services include locating children with disabilities (physicians, nurses, and teachers do the referrals); providing medical, surgical, and corrective services for them; providing facilities for diagnosis, hospitalization, and rehabilitative care; and providing aids and prosthetic appliances, physiotherapy, and medical social services.

Protective.   There is a need for services that provide protection for children against abuse and neglect. Protective services are usually invoked upon a report from a teacher, doctor, or neighbor. An investigation of the family takes place and, depending on the circumstances, the child may be removed from the home and temporarily placed in foster or institutional care until the parents can prove they can care for the child appropriately. Often the parents must receive counseling and take classes in child development and parenting.

Children's services also include the care and protection of children born out of wedlock. Typical services for unmarried mothers include financial assistance, prenatal care, hospitalization, and counseling. Educational programs (child development, parenting, health and nutrition, vocational, and academic education) are often included.

Child Care.   Child-care centers serve preschool children of employed mothers. Most care is for children age 2 to 5, but more and more centers are serving infants and toddlers. Some centers include health and educational services as part of their programs. Extended day care programs serve school-age children whose parents are employed. Children come to the center before and after school, as necessitated by their parents' work schedules. Extended day care programs are sometimes located in elementary schools and sometimes in community centers. When necessary, the extended day care program provides transportation between school and center.

Foster Care. Foster care services are provided for neglected or abused children who need protection, as well as for children whose parents are temporarily unable to care for them. Foster homes are carefully selected by the community social service agency. Children placed in these homes are closely supervised by the agency, which provides money for room and board, clothing, medical and dental care, and often an allowance for the children. Counseling services are provided for the foster parents.

Adoption. In contrast to foster care, adoption is a social and legal process by which a child becomes a permanent member of the adopting family, with legal rights, including that of inheritance. The social process of adoption seeks to provide children of incapacitated or deceased natural parents with a healthy home environment. The legal process seeks to ensure that separation from natural parents is resorted to only when absolutely necessary and only on the basis of consent, if the parents are alive. Social agencies arranging for adoption conduct investigations to match the child and the adoptive family. Character, motivation, age, finances, and sometimes ethnic and religious background are examined.

Rehabilitative Services: Correction, Mental Health, Special Needs

The purpose of rehabilitative agencies is to enable individuals to effectively participate in the community.

Correction. Correctional services are provided for children, youths, and adults who have difficulties abiding by the legal rules of community life. What constitutes deviant behavior varies among different social groups. Some children may be encouraged by their friends and neighbors to behave delinquently—for example, stealing may be a prerequisite to being accepted by the neighborhood gang. Another child in another neighborhood who behaves similarly may be brought to a social agency, such as a child guidance clinic. Still another child may be arrested and cited before the juvenile court.

Since human behavior is influenced in part by the customs of the society in which we live, some deviant behavior may stem from conflicting values within and between ethnic groups in society (Garbarino, 1992). For example, different ethnic groups may have different attitudes toward fighting. Societal mores, as expressed by the U.S. legal system, punish aggressive acts, especially if the aggression harms someone or someone's property. A particular ethnic group may feel that aggression is the only acceptable way to avenge an insult. For example, in Hispanic culture, *macho* behavior, or male dominance, which includes physical power, evolved due to the need to defend the honor of females, many of whom were victims of invading Spaniards (Vigil, 1980).

Children under age 18 who are deemed neglected or delinquent are under the jurisdiction of the juvenile court. The juvenile court is not a criminal court; it does not file charges against the child. Therefore, there is no jury to determine guilt or innocence. Rather, the court attempts to understand the causes for the particular maladjustment and determines which steps must be taken for rehabilitation.

In order to understand the causes for the maladjusted or deviant behavior, the child and his or her family background are examined. Also, the physical, socioeconomic, and cultural conditions under which the child is living are explored.

Juvenile court judges may place children under the supervision of their parents in their home, with the stipulation that the family receive counseling. Or children may be removed from their homes and placed in foster care or institutions. Judges may even require children (or their parents) to pay for damages caused by the delinquent behavior.

Mental Health. Children are usually referred to local child guidance clinics by teachers, medical personnel, or the court. Behavioral problems indicating the need for referral include truancy, running away, lying, stealing, vandalism, setting fires, and extreme aggressiveness. Other behaviors may include excessive shyness, apathy, daydreaming, withdrawal, excessive fearfulness, enuresis, eating disorders, and nightmares. Child guidance clinics provide medical and psychological examinations for the child. The parents and often the siblings come for treatment, as well as the child. There is coordination with the school.

Special Needs. Services for recent immigrants to the United States encompass education (English language, American history, government, and culture), financial assistance,

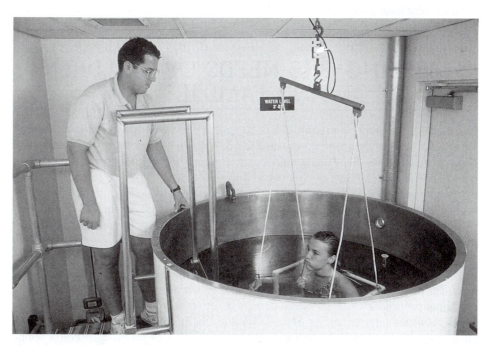

Agencies provide therapeutic services for those with special needs to enable optimal development.

Table 10.2 Types of Community Services: A Summary

PREVENTIVE AGENCIES	SUPPORTIVE AGENCIES	REHABILITATIVE AGENCIES
parks	family and child services	correction
recreation	referrals	mental health
education	economic assistance	special needs
	counseling	
	family preservation	
	senior citizens	
	child health and welfare	
	protective care	
	child care	
	foster care	
	adoption	

housing assistance, and vocational counseling, as well as referrals to other agencies providing specific services.

Services for people with disabilities emphasize rehabilitation. Self-help and productive work are the goals of rehabilitation. These services encompass evaluation, special education, financial assistance, counseling, vocational training, recreation, and referrals for treatment (*see* Table 10.2).

MEETING THE NEEDS OF CHILDREN AND FAMILIES

Even though different communities can provide a variety of services, some of which were described earlier, many do not provide enough to adequately meet the needs of children and families. Sensitizing individuals, especially individuals on decision-making bodies, to the unmet needs of children and to society's obligation to respond to those needs is known as *child advocacy*. In general, **advocacy** refers to the process of supporting a person, group, or cause. *Society* can mean public agencies, such as the government or the school; private agencies, such as religious groups or businesses; or concerned members of the community.

To publicize the need for advocacy for children, in 1977 the Carnegie Council on Children, under the leadership of Kenneth Keniston, published the report *All Our Children: The American Family under Pressure*. This report describes how the effects of U.S. social policy (or lack of it) have been detrimental to family life. The Children's Defense Fund publishes reports on *The State of America's Children* annually. The purpose of such reports is to educate the nation by drawing attention to the need for better public policies regarding children and families citing, for example, the high infant mortality rate in the United States compared to other nations. The Children's Defense Fund (discussed later) points to the lack in our country of a social policy that guarantees adequate health care to mothers and children.

The Children's Defense Fund also emphasizes that we are the only industrial democracy that lacks a system of income supports for families with children. It calls attention to the high number of children living below the official poverty line, the bare-bones level that the federal government estimates is necessary to meet a family's minimal subsistence needs.

The National Commission on Children ([NCC] 1991), also described later, points to the school system in the United States, which is supposed to equalize opportunities for all children, as manifesting a tremendous gap between rich and poor, ethnic minority and Anglo, by the time children reach the twelfth grade.

If the life chances for children are to be improved, then parents and anyone who cares about children must become involved in public policy; they must become advocates for children. As can be seen in Table 10.3, our children's needs are still not being met publicly or privately. According to many concerned with the welfare of children and youth, the United States has made a minimal investment in caring for its future citizens (CDF, 1998; Child Welfare League of America, 1987; NCC, 1991).

Twenty years after the Carnegie Council's report, the National Commission on Children was created by Congress and the president "to serve as a forum on behalf of children of the Nation." The commission, comprised of parents, grandparents, teachers, health and child development experts, business leaders, professionals, elected officials,

Table 10.3   Moments in America for Children

Every 9 seconds	a child drops out of school.
Every 10 seconds	a child is reported abused or neglected.
Every 15 seconds	a child is arrested.
Every 25 seconds	a child is born to an unmarried mother.
Every 32 seconds	a child sees his or her parents divorce.
Every 36 seconds	a child is born into poverty.
Every 36 seconds	a child is born to a mother who did not graduate from high school.
Every minute	a child is born to a teen mother.
Every 2 minutes	a child is born a low birthweight.
Every 3 minutes	a child is born to a mother who received late or no prenatal care.
Every 3 minutes	a child is arrested for drug abuse.
Every 4 minutes	a child is arrested for an alcohol-related offense.
Every 5 minutes	a child is arrested for a violent crime.
Every 18 minutes	an infant dies.
Every 23 minutes	a child is wounded by gunfire.
Every 100 minutes	a child is killed by gunfire.
Every 4 hours	a child commits suicide.

Source: Children's Defense Fund (1998). *The state of America's children yearbook, 1998.* Washington, DC: Author, p. xvii.

and so on, became official in 1989. Their mandated task was to assess the status of children and families in the United States and to propose new directions for policy and program development in order to improve the opportunities for every young person, regardless of circumstances, to become a healthy, secure, educated, economically self-sufficient, and productive adult. The Commission's final report, *Beyond Rhetoric: A New American Agenda for Children and Families* (NCC, 1991), made recommendations in nine major areas: (1) ensuring income security, (2) improving health, (3) increasing educational achievement, (4) preparing adolescents for adulthood, (5) strengthening and supporting families, (6) protecting vulnerable children and their families, (7) making policies and programs work, (8) creating a moral climate for children, and (9) providing costs and financing.

How Can the Community Help to Optimize Children's Development?

1. *Establish a local commission for children and families.* This commission should find out what is being done in the community and what needs to be done for children and families. More specifically, it should examine the adequacy of existing programs, such as maternal and child health services, social services, day care facilities, and recreational opportunities.

   The commission should include representatives of the major institutions dealing with children and families, as well as business, industry, and labor representatives. Older children, who can speak from their own experience, should also be included.

2. *Establish a neighborhood family center.* A place that provides a focal point for leisure, learning, sharing, and problem-solving should be established in a school, church, or community building. To eliminate the fragmentation of human services, the center should be the place where community members receive information on family health, social services, child care, legal aid, and welfare. The center should emphasize cross-age rather than age-segregated activities.

3. *Foster community projects.* Projects involving cleaning up the environment; caring for the aged, sick, or lonely; and planning parades, fairs, and picnics are excellent ways for community members of all ages to learn to work together and appreciate each other's talents and skills. These projects should provide an opportunity for young people to act as collaborators rather than subordinates.

4. *Combat alcohol, drugs, and violence.* Provide successful community role models for children. Work with families and schools to give children skills to solve problems without having to resort to substance abuse or violence. Work with families and schools on strong sanctions against substance abuse and violence.

5. *Foster youth participation in local policy bodies.* Every community organization affecting children and youth should include teenagers and older children as voting members. These would include such organizations

as school boards, recreation commissions, health boards, and welfare commissions.

6. *Plan communities to consider the children who will be growing up in them.* When planning and designing new communities, some of the factors that should be considered are the location of shops and businesses where children can have contact with adults at work, recreational and day care facilities readily accessible to parents as well as children, provision for a family neighborhood center and family-oriented facilities and services, availability of public transportation, and "places to walk, sit, and talk in common company" (Bronfenbrenner, 1980; Garbarino, 1995b; U.S. Department of Education, 1994).

Specific issues addressed were a yearly refundable tax credit for children; a government guaranteed, minimum child support payment, as well as tough enforcement; continuation of the job training program, as well as child care and health insurance to assist low-income families make the transition from welfare to working; and communities taking responsibility for health care and education programs. Recommendations included development of a universal system of health insurance, expansion of Head Start to all income-eligible children, and improvement of the quality of education and accountability. The commission also felt that public support for family services should be continued; that businesses should have family-oriented policies; that the quality, availability, and affordability of child-care services should be improved; that community-based family support programs should be developed and expanded; and that there should be an increase in salaries and training opportunities in early childhood and welfare fields. Finally, the commission asserted that there be more diligence in the public and private sectors in terms of giving children and adolescents clear, consistent messages about personal conduct and responsibility to others, and that the allocation of financial resources be shared by the private and public sectors.

ECONOMIC ASSISTANCE

In 1996, 20.5% of all children in the United States were living in families with incomes below the poverty line ($16,000 for a family of four). In comparing ethnic groups, the poverty rate for African Americans was 39.9%, for Hispanic Americans it was 40.3%, for Asian Americans it was 19.5%, and for Anglo Americans it was 16.3% (U.S. Bureau of the Census, 1998). Some facts about poor children (CDF, 1998) are interesting:

- 3 in 5 are Anglo
- 1 in 3 live in a suburban neighborhood
- 1 in 3 live in a family with married parents
- 2 in 3 live in a working family

Many families are poor even though one or both parents are employed. Many poor families are large and represent various ethnic minority groups, although the largest recent increase in poor families has been among Anglos under age 30 (U.S. Bureau of the

Census, 1998). Both family structures and the labor market affect the duration of childhood poverty (Corcoran & Chaudry, 1998). A common feature of poor families is that the head of the household is less educated than heads of nonpoor households. A large proportion of poor families are headed by single women. Families headed by single mothers are more likely to be poor due to the cost of child care and the lower average wage paid to women than men (CDF, 1998).

The Need for Economic Assistance

Rafael Gomez works as a gardener for a landscape company. He earns $350 per week. He and his wife have five children, ranging in age from 6 months to 12 years. Mrs. Gomez stays home to care for the family. The rent for a three-bedroom apartment in a dilapidated building is $425 per month. The Gomez children wear hand-me-down clothes from each other and from relatives. The family does not own a car, or have medical insurance.

Joan Thomas is age 20; has three children, age 1 month, 2, and 4. She gets government assistance for welfare, food, and medical services. Her husband recently deserted her. Since she first became pregnant while in high school, she never completed her education. Because her education is lacking, so are her job opportunities. She would like to work, but knows that the job would be low paying because of her lack of skills and she worries about the cost of child care and her ability to juggle all the responsibilities.

A number of federal programs attempt to alleviate some of the conditions of poverty.

- *Temporary Assistance for Needy Families (TANF)*—a federal and state matching program that provides temporary financial support for families with children. Eligibility, work requirements, and time limits for benefits are set up by individual states. (This welfare reform program replaced Aid to Families with Dependent Children [AFDC].)

- *Unemployment Compensation*—covering all workers in the labor force. It is financed by employers' contributions, intended to maintain about 50% of a worker's income for a temporary period of involuntary unemployment. The program is administered by federal and state governments.

- *Social Security Survivor or Disability Benefits*—administered by the federal government; payments come from the Social Security Trust Fund, through taxes on employer and employee. Benefits of those who have Social Security benefits, but who die or become disabled, are paid to their survivors or dependents.

- *Supplemental Security Income (SSI)*—providing a guaranteed minimum income for the aged and disabled.

- *Veterans' Benefits*—paid by the federal government to survivors or dependents of veterans who die or are disabled in the service.

- *Child Nutrition Services*—federally funded programs administered by the states. These are intended to improve the nutritional standards of low-income families. Included are the Food Stamp Program in which participants buy food stamps, according to a formula based on income and family size, for a cost less than the value of the food to be bought and then use the stamps for food, the National School Lunch Program, the Special Supplemental Food Program for Women, Infants, and Children (WIC), and the National School Breakfast Program.

- *Other Services*—a variety of social services are funded through state grants in Title IV and Title XX of the Social Security Act. Large proportions of these funds provide day care for children of employed mothers and other child welfare services. Title I of the Elementary and Secondary Education Act and Head Start provides educational and related services to low-income children. Child health programs and Medicaid also provide services to poor families.

Why have the federal programs not alleviated poverty? According to the Children's Defense Fund (1998), five major factors have been pushing more and more children and families into poverty. These factors exemplify how exosystems and macrosystems affect children:

1. The persistently high rate of unemployment among parents
2. The inability of parents to earn high enough wages to escape poverty
3. The growth in the number of female-headed households due to divorce and out-of-wedlock births
4. Inadequate education and job training
5. The reduction of budgets in governmental programs

Unemployment and low-wage employment has outcomes other than poverty: loss of self-worth, increased family tensions, alcoholism, and abuse. When the economic support system of a family breaks down, often so does its ability to provide emotional support (Huston, McLoyd, & Coll, 1994).

Economists Ross and Sawhill (1975) as well as others (Huston, McLoyd, & Coll, 1994; Wilson, 1995) reported that family disintegration increased in families whose head was unemployed for a long period of time, compared to similar families not experiencing long-term unemployment. For example, at a congressional hearing, the former president of the United Automobile Workers testified that as unemployment increased, so did the number of people seeking assistance because of alcoholism and child abuse (Marcossen & Fleming, 1978).

Which public policies are designed to overcome the effects of economic problems, especially unemployment? In addition to unemployment compensation, the federal government creates certain jobs and provides certain tax exemptions. To create jobs, local units of government (cities, towns, counties) can submit applications for federal money to pay for local public construction—for example, road and street improvements or building additions. The local community thus both relieves unemployment and gets some funds for public works. The federal government also creates certain jobs by giving money to local units of government to hire unemployed individuals. Thus needed public services are provided (clerks, park attendants), and jobs are created for those in need.

Tax exemptions are provided for those receiving unemployment compensation; they are granted to businesses hiring certain individuals, such as the disabled or those in government work-training programs; and they are granted for child care required by the mother's employment.

There are still problems in the welfare system of public support for the poor, such as the income level at which the government considers a family poor enough to receive assistance, the funding levels for welfare-to-work programs, implementation of job training, and employment prospects, child care, housing, and adequate health care, coverage (Behrman, 1997a, b).

Homeless Families

Related to poverty is the ability of a family to provide shelter. Homeless families with children are the fastest growing segment of homeless Americans. Families with children make up more than one-third of the nation's homeless population (CDF, 1998).

The threat of homelessness is even graver than the statistics suggest because millions of families are just one crisis away from losing their homes. A crisis could be an unexpected expense, illness, disability, or loss of a job. Other families are at risk for homelessness because they spend most of their income on housing and have no financial cushion if their rent goes up or their income falls even slightly (CDF, 1998).

Homelessness is the result of many simultaneous trends: shrinking incomes for many young families, rising housing costs, a decreasing supply of low-cost housing, decline in government housing assistance, and deinstitutionalization of the mentally disabled (CDF, 1998). A significant number of homeless youths are runaways who have left or been kicked out of their homes (Levine & Levine, 1996). An alarming trend is the number of homeless who were formerly children in foster care (Balk, 1995). Nearly all state child protective services stop foster care payments when children reach age 18; few young people have the skills at this age to be self-supporting.

Other problems associated with the homeless population are poverty, poor health, inadequate education, poor employment prospects, and social isolation (CDF, 1998). Homeless children suffer psychological, as well as behavioral and educational, consequences (McCormick & Holden, 1992).

The incidence of homeless families has increased greatly.

The following illustrates a church's response to a local homeless family.

Thomas Green, age 6, took his stuffed dog and lay down on the mattress with his sister, Eva, age 3, who was already asleep. The mattress was a piece of foam rubber donated to the church that was to be Thomas's home for the next few months (the town had no public shelter for the homeless). Thomas's mother, Vicki, had been living in motel rooms with the children and whomever was her current boyfriend until he left or was arrested. Vicki took odd jobs in between boyfriends to support herself and the children, but being a high school dropout, her skills were limited and so, consequently, were her work opportunities.

In the morning, Vicki took Thomas to the nearby school to enroll him in kindergarten. He had to repeat it because he moved so many times the previous year that his school attendance didn't enable him to be ready for first grade. Eva was invited to go to the church preschool while Vicki spent the day looking for work.

Local governments frequently have been unable or unwilling to deal effectively with the problems of homeless familes and children, and the federal government also has provided only limited assistance (CDF, 1998). The federal government gives funds to states for temporary shelters and money to schools to assure homeless children access to free public education.

Teachers need to be sensitive to the characteristics observed in homeless children, such as depression, anxiety, severe separation problems, poor quality relationships, shyness, aggressiveness, sleep disorders, temper tantrums, and short attention spans (McCormick & Holden, 1992). Many homeless parents have substance abuse problems, are victims of domestic violence, and have fragmented social support networks (McCormick & Holden, 1992).

HEALTH CARE

As a nation, we spend enormous amounts of money on health care. For insured persons, we have an excellent health care system that includes crises and serious illnesses, but we have inadequate preventative and public health care (CDF, 1998). There are serious inequities in health standards for low income and ethnic minority families, too few medical resources in rural and inner-city communities, too little prenatal care for many women, and not enough regular immunizations against disease (CDF, 1998; NCC, 1991). To address these inadequacies, the Children's Health Insurance Program (CHIP) was enacted in 1997. Federal funds are granted to states to design and implement programs.

The Need for Health Care

Thu Truong, 7 years old, developed a high fever and a cough one Saturday night. His mother gave him aspirin and some cough syrup, but by Sunday the fever was still high and the cough was worse. Mrs. Truong decided to take him to the emergency room, because she has no regular doctor (she relies on health clinics for medical care). It took her an hour and a half by bus to reach the hospital. Because Thu was not "critical" (bleeding profusely, not able to breathe, for instance), he had to wait an hour before a doctor was available to examine him.

Lara Michaels had her third baby several weeks prematurely. The baby remained in intensive care for 2 months. Al Michaels' insurance policy did not cover newborn health care, so the Michaels face an enormous hospital bill that will keep them in debt for years.

The most important factors influencing child health occur before birth. A baby is likely to grow into a healthy child when the mother had good nutrition during childhood and during pregnancy, received prenatal care early in pregnancy, is between age 20 and 35, is in good health, has not been pregnant recently, and does not abuse drugs or alcohol. A baby is more likely to have a low birthweight (under 5.5 lb.) and/or birth defects, or die, when its mother was poorly nourished, has no prenatal care, is under age 18, is in poor health (has a sexually transmitted disease, for example), has just been pregnant, smokes, or abuses drugs or alcohol. The infant mortality rate in the United States remains high compared to other industrialized nations (CDF, 1998). Thus females need to be educated *before* they get pregnant about their future child's health.

Early and continuous health care for children after birth saves lives and helps minimize long-term health problems. High-quality preventive, primary, and remedial pediatric health care can ensure that problems that can develop during infancy, such as respiratory, neurologic, or orthopedic impairments, are detected and treated. Health professionals working with low-income schoolchildren have found that they are twice as likely as middle- and upper-income children to be suffering from one or more untreated medical conditions. Such untreated problems as vision, hearing, and dental as well as anemia and mental health and developmental conditions can impair a child's ability to benefit from school, thus affecting that child's later life (CDF, 1998; NCC, 1991).

In addition, a population of children born exposed to drugs or alcohol is especially vulnerable to serious physical and mental disabilities, as well as behavior problems and learning impairments. Acquired immune deficiency syndrome (AIDS), threatens a growing number of children each year, primarily through transmission from their mothers before or at birth. The risk of human immunodeficiency virus (HIV), which can develop into AIDS, is also growing among adolescents who are intravenous drug users or sexually active (NCC, 1991).

Human-made environmental hazards increasingly threaten the health of all children. For example, absorption or inhalation of lead causes damage to the central nervous system, mental retardation, and blood and urinary-tract infection. Thus technological advances must continually be monitored regarding their environmental impact on health and safety.

Some government health programs for children follow.

- *Medicaid*—a program that provides matching money to the states to pay for medical services for the indigent and medically needy. Children who are eligible for Medicaid receive early and periodic screening, which involves diagnoses and treatment.
- *Maternal and child health services*—services that provide money from the federal government to states for projects to reduce infant mortality and improve the health of low-income mothers and children. Also supplied to states is money for projects that provide comprehensive health care to low-income children up to age 21; money for projects that provide dental care for low-income children, and also money for outreach, diagnosis, and medical and related services for low-income and medically indigent children who are physically disabled. There are also neighborhood health centers, migrant health centers, and Native American health services.
- *Centers for Disease Control*—federal funds provided to the states for purchase of vaccines.
- *Child nutrition programs*—include school lunch programs, school breakfast programs, and special food programs for low-income children and children with disabilities in day care or other nonresidential settings. Also included is the Women, Infants and Children Program (WIC), which provides nutritious food to low-income pregnant and lactating women, and children under age 4 who are at nutritional risk.

Support for Families

Traditionally, many U.S. family services have been provided by private voluntary organizations on a charitable basis. In recent years, more and more public agencies have begun to play a part in services to families. Unfortunately, the combination of public and private social services is often fragmented and uncoordinated, but there are successful collaborative examples across the country (Schorr, 1997).

Government programs providing some support to families include the following.

- *Child welfare services*—fund state efforts to preserve families by strengthening abilities to address their problems and avoid unnecessary foster care, and to reunite with their parents children who have been placed in foster care.
- *Social services block grant (Title XX)*—provides various preventive, counseling, and other support services for low-income children and families as well as for vulnerable, abused, and neglected children and their families.
- *Child and adolescent service system program*—helps ensure that youths with serious emotional problems receive needed mental health services by improving coordination among the numerous agencies responsible for them.

The Need for Family Support Services

Jill Sanger, age 15, lives in a suburban town. Her father is an engineer for an aerospace company and often works late. Her mother is not employed but is involved in school and community activities, as well as caring for her 10-year-old twin brothers and 6-year-old sister. Jill has been reported truant from school on several occasions. She refuses to communicate with her parents and has become involved with drugs. Her parents want to get help.

Helen Black, recently divorced, has two young children. Her ex-husband is lax in sending child support payments. Helen wants to become a computer programmer and feels confident she can get a job. Someday, she would like to buy a computer and work at home. Meanwhile, however, she must go to school, and needs child care.

Jack (age 13) and Sally (age 12) Baker have been cared for and supported by their mother since their father deserted them when Sally was a year old. When Jack was 6 and Sally was 5, however, their mother became very ill. She had to be hospitalized for 3 months and then recuperated for 6 months. Having no relatives, the children were placed in foster care. When their mother could again care for them, they were returned to her. A year later, however, their mother had a relapse and the children were placed in another foster home. This time they were separated because a home was not available that would take both of them.

Two changes in family structure have accelerated tremendously in the past few years—the increase in the number of women employed, especially mothers of young children under age 6, and the growth in the number of children living in families headed by one parent, primarily the mother. Among the family supports that can respond to the needs of poor mothers, employed mothers, and single mothers, as well as to the needs of the children, is a system of quality child-care services, in home or center settings.

As was discussed in Chapter 5, families seeking child care for their children can choose (where available) child-care centers, family day care homes, or home care by a relative, neighbor, or paid person. Even though some centers and some day care homes are licensed, this is no guarantee of quality, since enforcement of licensing standards may be minimal. Some children have to care for themselves (*see* box, "Latchkey Children: Self-care").

Government programs assisting families experiencing such changes include the following.

- *Income tax deductions*—deduction of child-care expenses by employed mothers.
- *Subsidized day care (such as Head Start and Title XX)*—federal and state matching funds for a wide variety of social services, including day care.

Although some children flounder when having to be responsible for themselves, others (especially children over age 10) flourish. They enjoy the independence and have learned what to do if various situations arise, such as a stranger coming to the door, the electricity going out, not feeling well, and so on (Belle, 1999). Apparently, developmental

Latchkey Children: Self-care

Mothers who are employed and have school-age children often do not or cannot make provision for after-school care. The children are referred to as "latchkey children"—children who have to let themselves into their homes with a key. Unsupervised by adults, latchkey children are vulnerable to delinquency, vandalism, injury, rape, and drug use (Collins, Harris, & Susman, 1995).

There are other problems, as well, for latchkey children. Studies comparing latchkey children ranging in age from 5 to 12 with their supervised counterparts, it was found that children who are left alone to care for themselves and/or siblings often feel afraid regardless of their age, capabilities, or parents' assurances (Behrman, 1999; Belle, 1999; Long & Long, 1982). Perhaps their fearfulness stems from warnings and cautions about people coming to the door, about cooking, and about various household problems that might occur.

Latchkey children are usually restricted to their homes until their parents return. They are generally prohibited from having friends over. Sometimes older latchkey children are given the responsibility for caring for younger siblings.

It took a tragedy to bring national attention to the problems surrounding latchkey children. A little boy, 5 years old, left alone in his house while his mother worked was accidentally shot and killed by a police officer who mistook the background noise of the television and the shadow on the wall of the toy gun as threats to his life. He didn't see the little boy until it was too late.

outcomes from self-care depend on characteristics of the child, family circumstances (Is someone available by phone?), and neighborhood features (Is it safe?) (Vandell & Su, 1999)—see box "Is Your Child Ready for Self-Care?.

SPECIAL CHILD-CARE SERVICES

Some children have special needs—they are disabled, maltreated, or abandoned by their families; they are orphans, or runaways from desperate situations.

Abused and neglected children have recently received more national attention, due in part to the establishment in 1974 of a National Center on Child Abuse and Neglect. Abused, neglected, or abandoned children, as well as orphans and sometimes runaways, are often placed in foster homes. Foster care is funded by federal, state, and local sources. Foster care provides temporary care when children cannot be cared for in their own homes for any of the following reasons: death or illness of a parent, divorce or desertion, inadequate financial support, abuse or neglect, and behavioral problems with which the parent cannot cope. The problems with foster care placement are several. For example, relatively few foster parents have training in dealing with maltreated children; some children placed in foster care drift from one home to another, never returning to their own homes. Some children may even be abused by their foster parents.

In spite of the fact that many children placed in foster care are eligible for adoption, it seldom happens. Present legislation results in the loss of federal support for foster children if they are adopted by the family with which they reside. Support is not only financial—it includes medical, dental, and clothing allowances. Many private insurance companies will not cover preexisting medical conditions that some of these children have. However, there is a government Adoption Assistance Program that provides financial grants to families adopting "hard to place" children. These children include those with health problems (physical or emotional) or disabling conditions and those having an ethnic minority background.

In many states, terminating parental custody is very difficult; therefore, the child cannot be legally adopted. Often, this is damaging to the child's emotional health because the child does not know to whom he or she really belongs (Nazario, 1988).

In addition to foster care funding and adoption assistance, some other governmental programs for children with special needs include the following (*see also* Table 10.4).

- *The Child Abuse Prevention and Treatment Act*—authorizes grants to states to assist them in developing and strengthening programs designed to prevent child abuse and neglect while providing treatment for its victims.

Table 10.4   Summary of Various Federal Assistance Programs for Children and Families

POVERTY	CHILD HEALTH	SUPPORT FOR FAMILIES	SPECIAL CHILD-CARE NEEDS
Temporary Assistance for Needy Families	Medicaid	Child Welfare Services	Foster care
Unemployment Compensation	Maternal and Child Health Services	Social Services Block Grant (Title XX)	Adoption Assistance Program
Social Security Survivor or disability benefits	Children's Health Insurance Programs	Child and Adolescent Service System Program	Child abuse prevention and treatment
Supplemental Security Income	Centers for Disease Control	Income tax deduction for child-care expenses	Family violence prevention and services
Veteran's Benefits	Child Nutrition Programs	Subsidized child care (e.g., Head Start)	Head Start
Child Nutrition Services	Head Start		
Other services—child care educational, health			
Homeless assistance			

- *The Family Violence Prevention and Services Program*—supports local programs that provide immediate shelter and related services to family violence victims and their children.

The Need for Special Child-Care Services

Julie was born prematurely and required special care when her mother brought her home from the hospital one month after she was born. After a week at home, Julie had lost a significant amount of weight and was listless. She was diagnosed as suffering from "failure to thrive" due to neglect and was placed in foster care. Her mother, just 18 years old, had a history of drug abuse. She had trouble keeping track of medical appointments, filling prescriptions, and meeting Julie's needs. In one year, Julie was shifted three times from her mother's care to foster care. Julie's current foster mother wants to adopt her, but the biological mother will not sign the papers.

Kenny, age 13, is the oldest of four children. Both his parents are alcoholics. Kenny has been involved in some stealing incidents in the neighborhood, but he was never reported to the police because the shopkeepers felt sorry for him. Kenny stole when his father spent his paycheck on booze and there was no food in the house. Recently, however, Kenny has been hanging around with some older kids who deal in drugs. Kenny sees this as an easy way to make money and get out of the house. The first time he tries to make a sale, though, he gets caught.

Mike was born without hip sockets. In order for him to walk normally and use his legs, he needs several surgeries. In addition to the surgeries, he will need special equipment such as a walker to keep mobile until he heals. He will also need daily physical therapy to strengthen his muscles. Unfortunately, Mike's father deserted the family after Mike's birth; he couldn't deal with having a disabled son. Mike's mother has to work to support Mike and his two older sisters. She has no medical insurance, neither does she have the time or energy to give Mike the special care he needs.

Is Your Child Ready for Self-Care?

Yes or No?

1. Do you consider your child old enough to assume self-care responsibilities?
2. Do you believe your child is mature enough to care for himself or herself?
3. Has your child indicated that he or she would be willing to try self-care?
4. Is your child able to solve problems?
5. Is your child able to communicate with adults?
6. Is your child able to complete daily tasks?

7. Is your child generally unafraid to be alone?

8. Is your child unafraid to enter your house alone?

9. Can your child unlock and lock the doors to your home unassisted?

10. Is there an adult living or working nearby whom your child knows and can rely on in case of an emergency?

11. Do you have adequate household security?

12. Do you consider your neighborhood safe?

If you answered "no" to any of the above questions, it is highly recommended that you delay or abandon plans to leave your child in self-care until positive responses can be given for all of the questions (Long & Long, 1983).

LINKING COMMUNITY SERVICES TO FAMILIES AND SCHOOLS

To be effective in supporting children's development, child-care services should be comprehensive in that they link with health, nutrition, social services, and education for children and their parents (CDF, 1998). Such collaboration strengthens the immediate environment of vulnerable children making them more resilient to stress (Hurd, Lerner, & Barton, 1999).

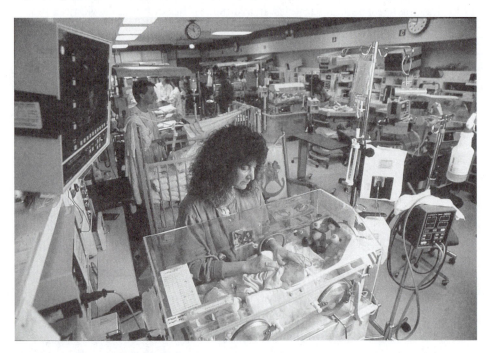

The increase in premature live births has caused an increase in the need for special child-care services, such as intensive hospital nursing care.

Examples of comprehensive service linkages between children, families, and schools are the Head Start Preschool Program (discussed in Chapter 5) and the Brookline Early Education Program (BEEP) for prekindergarten children in the public schools. Head Start addresses the physical, emotional, cognitive, and family support needs of the child. BEEP focuses on family involvement and empowerment in children's education.

Examples of service linkages between children, families, and communities are child-care resource and referral agencies, providing information to parents regarding child-care arrangements, health and social services, parent education, family friendly businesses and university programs, providing model schools, teacher training, and collaboration with schools in the community (Hurd, Lerner, & Barton, 1999).

ADVOCACY

Advocacy is the process of supporting a person, a group, or a cause. How to be an advocate for children and families, as well as examples of child advocacy groups are discussed here.

HOW TO BE AN ADVOCATE

In addition to the unmet needs of children examined earlier, there are still many others, such as child maltreatment, a more humane system of juvenile justice, and transition programs for young people leaving protective community services to become independent functioning adults. If these things bother you and you want to do something about them, you need to know how to become an advocate (NAEYC, 1996b; Phillips, 1981):

1. *Make a personal commitment*—speak out, write, and be heard regarding a certain problem or need.

2. *Keep informed*—do research and get facts. For example, if the problem in your neighborhood is lack of after-school care for children, find out how many families could benefit from such a service, what facilities would be available, what licensing requirements exist, what the cost would be, and so on. Find out what is currently being done to alleviate the problems or meet the need (publicly and privately). For example, do any public schools in your areas remain open after regular hours?

3. *Know the process*—determine what must be done. Set priorities, and have a plan of action for how to use the information most effectively.

4. *Express your views*—write letters, send e-mail, make telephone calls, talk in person to those in decision-making roles.

5. *Get support*—seek allies both outside the system and inside the system (people or organizations that have the power to make changes).

6. *Be visible*—be physically present at hearings, meetings in the community, in legislators' offices.

7. *Show appreciation*—when those in power respond positively to your request by taking action or speaking publicly, send a "thank-you" message immediately.

8. *Monitor implementation*—legislation often outlines intent and directions, as it is a result of compromise; continue to watch the specifics in order to correct misinterpretations or problems; analyze budgets.

9. *Build rapport and trust*—be a reliable source of information to those in power so you will be trusted; volunteer to help your elected official; influence legislation.

10. *Educate your legislators*—meet new decisionmakers, keep them informed by sending them articles, invite them to speak at meetings and visit targeted progams; influence appointments to advisory boards.

Advocacy in Action

The people in my town wanted a new library. The one room, with floor-to-ceiling shelves, was woefully inadequate for a population of almost 25,000. A group of citizens got together and presented their desires to the city council. A committee of citizens and council members was formed to gather facts. (How many people wanted a new library? What were the populations of other towns that had library buildings? How many books would be required? How far did schoolchildren have to go to find a library that met their educational needs adequately?)

Once the need for a new library had been established, a plan of action was set: the city would apply for funds from the county and match those funds, a building site would be located, architects would be invited to submit plans for the library, and a contest would be held so the citizens could choose the plans that best suited them. Support had to be gotten from decisionmakers at the county level of government so they would agree to fund the proposal. It took many letters and presentations at meetings to convince the county to support the project financially. In the interim, there was much discussion regarding where the library would be built and what design to choose. In the end, there were many compromises, but the library got built to the satisfaction of most. And those who advocated for children got almost half the library devoted to books for children and young people.

CHILD ADVOCACY GROUPS

An advocacy group can form to solve and monitor a particular problem, or it can be an ongoing support group for children's problems in general, or it can be a lobby to government. The oldest federal agency for children, the Children's Bureau, is located within the U.S. Department of Health and Human Services' Administration for Children and Families. It is responsible for assisting states in the delivery of child welfare services including child protective services, family preservation and support, foster care, adoption, and independent living.

An example of an ongoing children's advocacy group, mentioned earlier, is the Children's Defense Fund (CDF), developed in 1973 to provide a strong and effective voice for all the children in America who cannot vote, lobby, or speak for themselves. Particular attention is paid to the needs of poor and minority children and those with disabilities (CDF, 1998).

CDF's goal is to educate the nation about the needs of children and encourage preventive investment in children before they become ill, drop out of school, suffer family breakdown, or get into trouble. CDF monitors the development and implementation of federal and state policies (CDF, 1998).

Being an effective advocate requires knowledge of both the facts and the law. Careful research into various situations must occur before advocacy efforts at reforms can take place. Advocacy involves not only research and pressure for legislative reform but also follow up on implementation of the reform. CDF staff includes specialists in health, education, child welfare, mental health, child development, adolescent pregnancy prevention, family income, and youth employment.

The work of another ongoing children's advocacy group, the Child Welfare League of America (CWLA), is grounded in the knowledge and understanding of the needs of children and their families. The league takes the position that advocacy is an important aspect of the total responsibility of contemporary child welfare agencies. According to the league's philosophy, a contemporary social agency cannot merely be a provider of services; it must also be concerned with the general welfare policies of the community. It must take into account the external forces and conditions that affect people's ability to function. Child welfare agencies are expected to help change unfavorable community conditions that affect children and their families adversely (Goffin & Lombardi, 1988). In this respect, CWLA employs an ecological approach to human development.

Agencies that belong to the CWLA must be committed to securing the fullest measure of services and rights to which children are entitled, halting processes and procedures that are adverse to children's interests, promoting humane and rational response by government and others to the needs of children and families, discovering gaps in services and proposing ways to fill them, and focusing public attention on the nature and extent of problems and on possible solutions (Whittaker, 1983).

There are many children's advocacy groups on a local level as well as on the national level. In some cases, local groups join together to form a national coalition in order to influence national public policy. A familiar example of this is the National Congress of Parents and Teachers (PTA), which is devoted to improving relations between home and school on behalf of children.

CHILD MALTREATMENT AND WHAT YOU CAN DO ABOUT IT

Inappropriate parenting practices resulting in child abuse or neglect were discussed in Chapter 4, and the role of the caregiver in protecting children who might be maltreated was discussed in Chapter 5. Here, advocacy for children is exemplified in the law (macrosystem influence) and in the community services provided to help families in need of emotional support and parenting skills, as well as children who have been mal-treated (mesosystem influence of linkages between the community and families).

1. *Know your state's child abuse/neglect law* (O'Brien, 1984). Every state requires that suspected child abuse be reported, but every state defines abuse differently and has different reporting procedures. You can get a copy of your state's law from a department of social services; a law enforcement agency; a state, district, city, or county attorney's office; or a regional office of child development.

2. *Who must report?* Injury, sexual molestation, death, abuse, or physical neglect that is suspected of having been inflicted upon any child under age 18 by other than accidental means *must* be reported by the following persons:

- physician
- surgeon
- teacher
- child caregiver
- dental hygienist
- ophthalmologist
- pharmacist
- commercial film and photographic print processor
- dentist
- chiropractor
- osteopath
- podiatrist
- nurse
- hospital intern or resident
- foster parent
- group home personnel
- marriage, family, child counselor
- school personnel
- social worker
- county medical examiner
- psychologist
- law enforcement officer
- audiologist
- clinical laboratory technician
- speech pathologist
- others having responsibility for child care

3. *Know how to report abuse and neglect according to the law.* The box in Chapter 5 titled "Indications of Possible Maltreatment" describes physical and behavioral indicators of possible abuse. If you consistently notice several of the indicators over a period of time, you have a valid reason to report your observations.

Every state requires that a report of suspected child abuse be made "immediately" or "promptly." This means that as soon as you suspect abuse, you must inform the appropriate agency. The person taking the call is trained to determine whether it is an emergency situation and an immediate response is required or whether it can wait a few days. The response depends on the age of the child, the severity of the abuse, and how accessible the child is to the perpetrator. In a typical protective service investigation of alleged maltreatment, the professional must decide not "Has this child been matreated?" but rather "Is this maltreatment extreme enough to justify community intervention?"

Once an investigation is made by a social worker and a police officer, it is determined whether or not to remove the child into protective custody. If the child is removed, he or she is placed in an institution until the court decides on final placement. The court hearing must take place within a specified time (usually 72 hours) after the child has been taken into protective custody. The child and the accused abusers are assigned different lawyers. The court can require a family preservation program, such as counseling or parent education, along with supervision by a social worker. The court can rule that the child be placed in an institution or in foster care for a specified time while the accused become rehabilitated. Then another hearing takes place to determine whether the family is ready for reunification.

You do have legal protection when you report. This means that people who report abuse in good faith are granted immunity from civil and criminal court action, such as lawsuits, even if the report, when investigated, turns out to be erroneous. There are cases where some individuals have been wrongly accused of child abuse or neglect. Families who are wrongly accused can go through much turmoil. So be very sure (observe and take notes to document what you see) before you report the suspected abuse. A national organization for victims of child abuse laws, called VOCAL, exists to address their concerns.

Treatment or Intervention Programs for Child Maltreatment

Beyond the challenge of identifying and assessing maltreatment, agencies and practitioners confront the challenge of providing effective treatment or intervention programs. In order to protect the child, *legal intervention* is the first requirement (Goodman, Emery, & Haugaard, 1998).

Once suspected abuse or neglect is reported to the appropriate authorities, a social worker and/or a police officer is sent to the home or school to investigate. If it is determined that the child is endangered, the child is placed in protective custody—which usually means the child is taken away from the parents or guardians and is brought to a state, county, or city institution until the case is heard in court (usually within 72 hours). Some communities assign a child advocate to the child, usually a trained volunteer with an interest in helping children. The child advocate supports the child through interviews with police and lawyers as well as going to court with the child, if necessary.

If, on the other hand, it is legally determined that the child is not in immediate danger but there may be some risk of future abuse or neglect, the social services agency, as directed by the court, may provide a variety of support services to the family. Such services may also be required if and when the child is returned home after being in protective custody.

The following are various types of *therapeutic intervention* or *treatment* used with abusive families, depending on the particular case (Goodman, Emery, & Haugaard, 1998; Wolfe, 1994). The individual child, the family, and the community context (what is available and/or ethnically amenable) must be considered in deciding the most effective treatment (Garbarino, Guttman, & Seely, 1986).

- *Family preservation.* The child remains at home under the supervision of the protective agency. The child protective worker visits the home on a scheduled basis. The worker can teach child development and child management to the parents.

- *Homemaker services.* A person employed by the appropriate community agency helps the family with home management and child care.
- *Parent education.* The parents take a formal course given in their community.
- *Child care.* The child is cared for during the day at a center or in a family day care home.
- *Family therapy.* A therapist addresses the whole family's interaction patterns.
- *Kinship care.* The child is temporarily (or permanently) placed in the care of grandparents or other close relatives.
- *Foster care.* The child is temporarily placed in another home until his or her family can provide adequate care.
- *Parent groups.* The parents are required to join a support group, such as Parents Anonymous (a voluntary organization of child abusers), and/or become involved in their child's school.
- *Institutionalization.* The child is temporarily placed in an institution for abused/neglected children until his or her family can provide adequate care.
- *Residential family care.* The whole family moves into a supervised environment.
- *Adoption.* When returning the child to his or her home is unwise or impossible, the child is put up for adoption. This avoids interminable foster care.

Support. The goals of treating the abusive family are to give help to the parents with their problems, give help to the children with their problems, and improve the relationship between parents and children in order to prevent further abuse (Cole & Duva, 1990).

Before any changes can be made in the abusive adults' behavior, it must be realized that they may have unmet needs and frequently must be "parented" themselves before they can become adequate parents to their children. This support can come from therapy, a parent aide, or a group such as Parents Anonymous. Also, the parents have to want to make changes in their behavior. They have to understand their own self-destructive patterns and the consequences of them.

Parents Anonymous, founded in 1970, now has chapters all over the country. Parents can join on their own or can be ordered to join by the court. When parents join Parents Anonymous, they are told how to handle anger or frustration—for example, going into a room alone and then screaming, kicking, or pounding. The point is to get the aggression out on objects so that no one gets hurt. Members share their difficulties and try to work them out at meetings, with the help of other members. They try to develop solutions to their problems and to learn to feel better about themselves. The members maintain a network of telephone numbers so that they can call one another for support when they feel a crisis coming on.

Parents are children's primary role models, the most important people in their lives. Much of what children learn about dealing with stress and conflict is patterned on their parents' behavior (Iverson & Segal, 1990). Thus, Children's Village, a treatment facility for abused children and their families, and other programs like it reflect the current attitude among social service professionals that treatment for abuse should include reeducating the parents and strengthening the family wherever possible, while making sure that the victimized child is protected.

Some of the changes that abusive parents need to make in their behavior include the following.

- The parents have to learn to deal appropriately with emotions and stress. They need to increase their repertoire of coping mechanisms in dealing with frustration. They need to become less isolated and learn to turn to others when in need of help or support. They should be able to develop an improved self-esteem and be increasingly able to enjoy life.

- The parents need to develop more realistic expectations of themselves and of others. They also must work on breaking potentially self-destructive patterns of interpersonal relationships. For example, a mother must learn not to continually become involved with passive–aggressive men. A passive–aggressive person tends to resist the demands of others in an indirect way—procrastination, inefficiency, forgetfulness, complaining.

- The parents must learn what is age- and developmentally appropriate behavior for children. They must also learn to tolerate and understand children's negative behavior. They must view the child as an individual, rather than a personal need-satisfying object. To do this, they must learn empathy and respect for the child's individuality. Finally, the parents must learn to express affection toward the child, both verbally and physically.

Prevention.   Social agencies have begun to develop various programs to help troubled families. With the passage of the Child Abuse Prevention Act in 1974, government funds have been available for research on effective preventive programs. Some programs are based on parent effectiveness training, which concentrates on developing good communication between parents and their children. These programs theorize that abuse often occurs because parents do not understand or know how to react to their children's expressions of need and affection. Other programs teach behavior modification techniques. The aim of these programs is to give alternatives to physical punishment when disciplining children. Parents are trained to notice their children behaving appropriately and to reward them accordingly. In some communities, hotlines provide counseling advice, available any time of the day.

Still other programs concentrate on preventing abuse, even before birth. For example, Johns Hopkins University has such a preventive program for high-risk mothers. These women are sought out while pregnant. They are counseled and may choose abortion. Those who choose to have their children are given classes in parenting, health, and nutrition. They are also assisted in planning their future education and career as well as in learning how to use the community services available to them.

Effective Community Services

- The earlier intervention is undertaken in a child's life, the better the outcome.
- Comprehensive approaches are more effective than limited interventions.
- Services must be easily accessible to individuals, and aggressive outreach may, in some cases, be required.

- Staff involvement in, and knowledge of, the situation are critical.
- Stable, caring adults, including mentors, are important role models.
- Parental involvement is crucial to success with children.
- Involvement in the school system is a key element of successful intervention.
- Highly structured programs are the most successful.

Source: *Rickel & Becker, 1997, pp. 7–8.*

Epilogue

A community can be both utopian (idealistic) and utilitarian (practical)—utopian in the sense that it values families and children; utilitarian in the sense that it requires widespread citizen involvement to support families and children, balancing individualism and collectivism (E. pluribus unum). *If children are to grow up to be contributing members of adult society, they will need positive role models, mentors, and leaders.*

SUMMARY

The community comprises a group of people living in the same district under common laws who have a sense of fellowship among themselves. Community ecology comprises the relationship between those people and their environment.

The community is structured to have five functions: production/distribution/consumption, socialization, social control, social participation, and mutual support. These functions are performed in many different ways by different communities, and the ways these functions are performed affect the socialization of the children growing up in them.

The community influences socialization through the role models it provides for adults, such as earning a living, socializing with one another, and helping one another. The community influences socialization by the way the people in it instill their norms and values in children. And the community also influences socialization by the way it enforces its rules. Finally, the community is where children can "try themselves out" and by so doing learn the consequences of their behavior.

Some physical factors in the community that have an impact on socialization are population density and characteristics, noise, arrangement and types of houses, and play settings.

Economic factors in a community play a central role in shaping the daily lives of families who live and work there. Economics affects unemployment rates, whether mothers seek employment, ability of young adults to afford homes of their own, and cost of living.

Certain social and personal factors, such as the neighborhood setting and the patterns of community interaction, influence socialization. The neighborhood setting affects children's mobility, exposure to adults, friendship patterns, and types of play.

Community interaction is important to the development of the child because of its supportive links to the family or school. Community relationships can be classified as informal, mutually dependent and caring (*Gemeinschaft*), or formal, independent, and contractual (*Gesellschaft*).

Children can be involved in the community in order to learn. Libraries, museums, zoos, farms, businesses, and people's experiences are all rich sources for involvement.

The community can be better used by children if the school can treat the community as an educational resource. The community can also be better used by children if the community itself—the business community, for example—opens itself to children.

Suggestions for community practices include establishing a local commission for children and families, establishing a neighborhood family center, fostering community projects, fostering youth participation in local policy bodies, and planning communities so as to consider the children who will be growing up in them.

Community services are necessary because of the increasing population, the changing nature of the family, and increasing urbanization.

Community agencies can be public or private. Some community services are preventive, such as parks, recreation, and education agencies; some are supportive, such as family and child services; and some are rehabilitative, such as correction, mental health, and special needs agencies.

Community services have attempted to meet the needs of children and families, but many needs are still unmet, such as economic, health, support, and special child care needs.

Child advocacy is the process of sensitizing individuals and groups to the unmet needs of children and to society's obligation to provide a positive response to those needs.

To be an advocate, one must make a personal commitment, keep informed, know the process, express one's views, get support, be visible, show appreciation, build rapport and trust, and educate one's legislators.

Child maltreatment, an example of child advocacy, must be reported to police or social agencies. Professionals and persons responsible for child care are required by each state to report suspected cases of child abuse or neglect immediately. In turn, they are granted immunity from being sued if the investigation proves false.

Various treatments for the abusive parents include therapy, training in child development and child management, parent education, support groups, and supervision by a child protective agency. Various programs for the child include hospitalization when necessary, residential care, child care, foster care, adoption, and therapy. Choice, as well as effectiveness, of such intervention programs depends on the individual child, the family, and the community context.

The main goal in treating the abusive family is to improve the relationship between the parents and children in order to prevent further maltreatment.

ACTIVITY

Purpose: To learn about the services in your community.

The following are 10 hypothetical case studies involving families and children in a community. Please read each of these case studies and select one family (or make up your own hypothetical one* that you would like to help by completing the following:

1. Provide the family with a list of three agencies that may be helpful to them in their particular situation. Your list should include the following information about each agency (share with your class): (a) name of agency, (b) address, (c) telephone, (d) hours, (e) services provided, (f) eligibility, (g) fees, and (h) area served.

2. Choose one of the three agencies on the list, call to make an appointment to visit the agency, and interview one person employed there (for example, director, counselor, teacher, therapist, or case worker). In this section of your report, be sure to include the following information:

   a. What steps the agency would take to help this hypothetical family (person). Explain the services provided by this agency.
   b. For the person interviewed at the agency, describe requirements for the job, educational background, previous experience, job satisfactions/dissatisfactions, and so on.
   c. For the agency itself, give the number of employees, physical layout, number of people served, and so forth.

Case Study 1   Wilson Family

Mr. Matt Wilson is 67 years old, and his wife has recently died. His daughter and her family live in another state, and they have persuaded Matt to sell his home and move close to them. After he has found an apartment and gotten somewhat settled, Matt's family notices that he is having a difficult time adjusting. He seems continually depressed and sometimes confused. He does not leave his apartment often (although he has a car and drives), he spends his days watching television, and doesn't seem to seek out other people. He is also not eating properly, and his family is afraid that his physical, as well as mental, health will begin to decline rapidly.

Is there help available for Matt in your community? What would you recommend to Matt's family in order to help him?

*Ideas—At-risk infants (premature, drug- or alcohol-exposed), relative with a terminal disease, transition programs for 18-year-olds no longer eligible for special or protective services, disaster (tornado, fire, hurricane, earthquake) assistance, and so on.

Case Study 2   Johnson Family

You are a first-grade teacher at an elementary school. You are especially worried about one of the students in your class, Michael Johnson. He always seems to arrive at school extra early (usually about 30 minutes). He is never dressed appropriately for the weather, and his general appearance is sloppy. His schoolwork is on grade level. However, at times his behavior is aggressive and hostile (especially toward classmates). On several occasions you have noticed bruises on Michael, and when you've asked him about these, he was really evasive. During your first parent/teacher conference, you share your concerns with Mrs. Johnson. She breaks down and tells you that her husband, Michael's stepfather, is very hard on him. He is sarcastic, always belittling Michael, and at times gets physically violent with him. Mrs. Johnson asks you for help. What is your role as a teacher? What assistance is available to Michael and to his family in your community?

Case Study 3   Peterson Family

Mary Peterson is a single parent living in your community. She has three children, Pam (16), Brian (14), and Lynn (12). Mary works full time, and the three children all attend school. Mary's oldest daughter, Pam, has always been a good student and has had a nice group of friends. Pam has rarely had any problems that could not be worked out easily. Recently, however, Pam has been very withdrawn and moody. She spends a lot of time in her room, and Mary suspects that she is crying a lot. When confronted, Pam gets emotional and shouts at Mary, "Mind your own business and leave me alone!" Mary questions her other children about Pam's behavior. Finally, Lynn tells her Mom that Pam thinks she is pregnant. Where would you suggest that Pam and Mary Peterson go for help in this situation? What kind of assistance is available to them in your community? Who can help Pam explore her options and make a decision about this pregnancy?

Case Study 4   Meyers Family

Paula and Larry Meyers live in your community with their two children, Kelly (4) and Lisa (18 months). Lisa is not showing the normal development Kelly did at this age, and Paula is very concerned. Lisa is not yet standing or walking. She does not respond to the family with love and affection and often seems to be in her own little world. Their pediatrician has suggested that the Meyers take Lisa to a neurologist for some testing. After extensive tests, it is determined that Lisa has cerebral palsy. Paula and Larry want to provide Lisa with every possible opportunity for a normal life. What services are available to Lisa and her family in your community? Where would you recommend the Meyers go to get assistance?

Case Study 5   Simmons Family

Martin Simmons lives in your community with his wife Sue and their 14-year-old son, Steve. Martin has worked for a large engineering firm in the area for the past 12 years. Recently, due to cutbacks, Martin lost his job. He has been unemployed for the past 8 months, and his family is really feeling the pressure of his job loss. Martin had been actively looking for a job for the first month of his unemployment. Lately, however, he has begun drinking more and more and looking for work less and less. Since he began drinking, his relationship with his wife and especially with his son Steve, has suffered a tremendous strain. Sue is convinced that Martin is becoming addicted to alcohol and feels he is settling deeper and deeper into a depressed state. Steve is angry with his dad, and they are continually fighting with one another. Sue has asked you to help her find assistance for herself and for her family. What agencies would you suggest the Simmons family contact for assistance?

Case Study 6   Hernandez Family

During lunch break on the junior high school playground, you notice a group of boys in a small circle intently examining something. As you approach the group, Roberto hastily shoves something in his pocket. In the haste, a joint drops on the ground. You pick it up and escort the group to the principal's office. You learn that Roberto had gotten the marijuana from his older brother, who is in a gang, and had brought it to show his friends. Mr. and Mrs. Hernandez are called, and a conference is scheduled. After explaining the situation to the parents, where do you refer this family for help?

Case Study 7   Lambert Family

Mrs. Lambert waits to speak to you after picking up her daughter at the day care center. She tells you her husband has been laid off and that his unemployment checks will stop next week. She can't pay the tuition at the center, and she has no other place to leave her daughter while she works. She must work to pay the rent and buy food. She hopes her husband will find work soon (he spends all day looking), since there are unpaid bills piling up. The family no longer has medical insurance since the father lost his job. They have several doctor bills to pay for a severe ear infection their daughter had last month. The family car's tire treads are so worn that driving is unsafe, yet the car is the family's only means of transportation to work, the day care center, and the store. Mrs. Lambert is terrified of having her family become homeless. Where would you refer Mrs. Lambert for help?

Case Study 8   Sullivan Family

You are a prekindergarten teacher at a local preschool. Brian is a student who turned 5 in November. Brian's behavior in class is causing problems for you and for the other students. He has difficulty sitting still, attending long enough to a story, completing any activities, and keeping his hands to himself. Brian is easily frustrated and is prone to temper tantrums and outbursts of aggression. Mrs. Sullivan, a single parent, has experienced the same problems with Brian at home. What could be the cause of Brian's behavior, and where would you refer this family for help?

Case Study 9   Nguyen Family

A child enters your public school preschool class the first day and speaks no English. You wait for his mother to pick him up so you can get some information about the child. The mother's English is very limited. You resort to communicating in simple words combined with gestures. You even draw pictures in order to communicate. You learn that the family has recently arrived from Vietnam and is staying with relatives who were sponsored to come to the United States the previous year. The father works in a local electronics factory, and the mother is expecting another child in 3 months. The mother is most anxious that her son, as well as herself and her husband, learn English and the "American way" as quickly as possible. Where do you refer this family for help with American culture?

Case Study 10   Horvath Family

For the past 2 years, Mr. Horvath has brought and picked up two of his children, aged 4.5 and 5.5, to the children's center. You have never met the mother. One day a woman comes to the center claiming she is the Horvath children's mother. She asks to have them released to her. You refuse because her name is not on their information form. She produces a court document stating she has legal custody of the children and demands they be released to her. You assign someone to watch the children while you call the police and the father (immediate attention is required by the legal authorities). The father admits the mother was granted legal custody, but she was continually drunk, so he took them. He has had them for 2 years, and she has never even visited them once. What do you advise him to do?

RESOURCES

Boys' and Girls' Clubs of America
http://www.bgca.org

Centers for Disease Control and
Prevention
http://www.cdc.gov/

Children's Defense Fund
http://www.childrensdefense.org/

Child Welfare League
http://www.cwla.org/

Department of Health and Human
Services
http://www.os.dhhs.gov/

Families USA
http://www.familiesusa.org/

Office of Juvenile Justice and
Delinquency Prevention
http://www.najrs.org/

Social Security Administration
http://www.ssa.gov/

RELATED READINGS

Belle, D. (1999). *The after-school lives of children: Alone and with others while parents work.* Mahwah, NJ: Lawrence Erlbaum.

Editors of Time/Life Books (1976). *The community.* New York: Time/Life Books.

Etzioni, A. (1993). *The spirit of the community: The reinvention of American society.* New York: Touchstone.

Garbarino, J. (1995). *Building a socially nourishing environment with children.* San Francisco: Jossey-Bass.

Garbarino, J., Dubrow, N., Kostelny, K., & Pardo, C. (1992). *Children in danger: Coping with the consequences of community violence.* San Francisco: Jossey-Bass.

Goffin, S. G., & Lombardi, J. (1988). *Speaking out: Early childhood advocacy.* Washington, DC: National Association for Education of Young Children.

Nazario, T. A. (1988). *In defense of children: Understanding the rights, needs, and interests of the child.* New York: Charles Scribners.

Rickel, A. U., & Becker, E. (1997). *Keeping children from harm's way: How national policy affects psychological development.* Washington, DC: American Psychological Association.

Rivkin, M. S. (1995). *The great outdoors: Restoring children's rights to play outside.* Washington, DC: National Association for Education of Young Children.

Schorr, L. B., & Schorr, D. (1997). *Common purpose: Strengthening families and neighborhoods to rebuild America.* New York: Anchor Books.

Shirk, M., Bennett, N. G., & Aber, J. L. (1999). *Lives on the line: American families and the struggle to make ends meet.* Boulder, CO: Westview Press.

Warren, R. L., & Lyon, L. (1983). *New perspectives on the American community.* Homewood, IL: Dorsey Press.

Whittaker, J. K., & Garbarino, J. (1983). *Social support networks: Informal helping in the human services.* New York: Aldine.

"Are you good men and true?"

— *William Shakespeare*

IMPLICIT SOCIALIZATION OUTCOMES

Prologue

VIRTUE VERSUS VICE

Concepts of good and bad and right and wrong are the foundation of society because they encompass how people should treat one another. Such moral concepts have been immortalized and realized through religion, laws, history, and literature.

Moral messages are often found in stories read to children. For example, the classic fairy tale, *The Goose Girl*, by the Brothers Grimm is about deception and lying. A servant woman usurps her mistresses' identity in order to marry a prince in a distant land.

The queen had a daughter who was promised in marriage to a prince who lived far away. When it came time for the wedding, the queen provided the princess with her dowry and a servant woman, a maid-in-waiting, who was pledged to look after the princess and deliver her safely to the bridegroom.

The servant lies to the queen when she promises to care for the girl and takes advantage of the princess's naiveté and inexperience depriving the princess of her royal clothes, jewelry, and furnishings; things that would identify her as the bride-to-be.

Upon arrival at the prince's palace, the servant again lies, telling the king that she is the princess and the girl accompanying her is just someone she picked up along the way who was looking for work. The king bids the girl (princess) to help look after the geese.

Eventually, the king, suspecting deceit, asks the imposter to propose a punishment for someone who is a fraud. Believing her secret safe, she advises that an imposter should be put naked into a cask studded inside with sharp nails and dragged by two horses along the street until dead. The king then tells her that she has pronounced her own fate.

Deception and lies are, unfortunately, common practice in today's society. For example, businesses cut corners, use "bait-and-switch" tactics, or deceive customers to increase their profits. Pretense is also prevalent on new technology such as the Internet, where ethical rules are not yet firmly established. Television, movie, and rock stars; sports heroes; and political leaders behave as though possessions, money, power, and prestige are ends that justify lying; ends that are more important than self-respect, honor, and high regard by loved ones.

Modern "heroes" who have been caught include President Richard Nixon who, in the Watergate scandal, spied, stole, and lied to maintain his power; Jimmy Swaggart, television evangelist, who was caught with a prostitute; scientists who "adjust" data to get grants to fund their research; college basketball players who "fix" games by missing shots in order to get money; movie stars who abuse substances and engage in violent behavior; and President Bill Clinton who committed adultery and lied about it to maintain his power and avoid censorship.

While what happens to the woman in *The Goose Girl* represents a concrete punitive consequence, a "built-in check" for moral behavior or for wrongdoers, today's famous wrongdoers have alternatives if they get caught—the publicity makes them marketable for talk shows, book deals, and movies.

The danger from such alternatives is for all children who, due to cognitive immaturity and lack of experience, are especially vulnerable to the influence of deceitful role models, particularly when they see wrongful behavior being rewarded.

What happened to society's "built-in check" for moral behavior? According to Sissela Bok (1989), author of Lying: Moral Choice in Public and Private Life, *certain societal values compete with personal morals:*

The very stress on individualism, on competition, on achieving material success which so marks our society, also generates intense pressures to cut corners. To win an election, to increase one's income, to outsell competitors — such motives impel many to participate in forms of duplicity they might otherwise resist. The more widespread they judge these practices to be, the stronger will be the pressures to join, even compete, in deviousness (p. 244).

Thus, the social incentives for deceit (to achieve success) in our society today have become more powerful than the controls (to be dishonored).

- *Why do people vary in their motives for good behavior (fear of getting caught, or "do unto others as you would have others do unto you," or self-respect)?*
- *How does the pressure for success (achievement, power, wealth) blur the line between right and wrong?*
- *How can the incentive structure in society for moral behavior be changed (for example, enable honesty, rather than deceit, to be more worthwhile; or at least disable some of the gains from deception)?*

The outcomes of socialization that will be examined in this chapter and the next are *implicit* (ones that are not immediately apparent or are indirect)—values, morals, attitudes, and motives—and *explicit* (ones that are relatively apparent or are direct)—behavior, gender roles, and self-esteem. These outcomes are the result of child, family, school, peer, and community interaction, referred to in Chapter 1 as mesosystems. Also influencing the development of these outcomes are exosystems, such as parents' work or school board policies, and factors in a person's macrosystem, such as religion, ethnicity, or even change (such as in the time one grows up as compared to when one's parents grew up).

VALUES

Values are qualities or beliefs that are viewed as desirable or important. Values are outcomes of socialization. Some of our values reflect the values of our parents, our teachers, our religion, our culture, or our friends. Some reflect what we have read, or seen on TV or film, as well as what we have directly experienced. The following example illustrates different generational values and different moral reasoning.

The boxed example that follows demonstrates that Tammy placed more value on what her friends thought than what her parents thought. Her parents, on the other hand, placed more value on obeying the law and following the community policy in regard to minors drinking alcohol than on Tammy saving face with her friends.

Tammy wanted to have a party for her graduation from high school. The neighborhood where she lived with her family had a recreation room, which was rented out for a nominal fee to various groups for meetings, club functions, and parties. Tammy's parents, Tom and Cheryl, agreed to let Tammy have the party provided the rules for rental were followed. One rule was that parties for minors had to be chaperoned, another was that there could be no more than fifty people, another was that the room had to be cleaned after the party, and the last was that no alcohol could be served to minors. Tammy agreed to all but the last: "How can you have a graduation party without beer? C'mon, get real . . . no one will come!" "Sorry," said Tom, "you want a party, you have to abide by the rules." "OK, OK, but we better have great food," Tammy grumbled.

One week before the party, Cheryl got a phone call from a parent of a girl she did not know. The parent wanted to confirm that there was in fact a party, and that beer would be served, and that the cost of a formal invitation to enter was $5. Cheryl could hardly contain her shock and anger. Apparently, a flier had been distributed at school "advertising" the party. Cheryl thanked the parent and said there would be no such party.

Cheryl told Tom what happened and together they confronted Tammy. Tammy said it was one of her friends who had distributed the flier (Tammy would not tell who). Tom said he was extremely disappointed that she hadn't stopped her friend, as they had agreed to the rules for the party—especially no alcohol—in advance; as a result, there would be no party. Tom explained that advertising the party, especially one in which beer would be served, was setting up her parents for trouble—uninvited kids having to be denied entrance to the party and leaving angry neighbors calling the police—and he and Cheryl being responsible for any alcohol-related accidents. Tammy listened and said she understood her father's position but that he and Cheryl were out of touch with reality—all graduation parties have booze—that they didn't understand her position—she couldn't have a party and not do what was expected. "Well, then, I guess the party is off," said Tom, "because we had expectations, too."

The next evening several of Tammy's friends came over to beg Tom and Cheryl to reconsider. They claimed drinking was going to occur on graduation night whether or not Tammy had the party. Tammy's having the party would at least keep the kids from driving around drunk, and the best way to prevent alcohol-related accidents was to let Tammy have the party, take everyone's car keys, and have all the kids spend the night.

Cheryl said, "That's an interesting argument but, first, I feel morally wrong serving kids alcohol; second, the recreation room belongs to the community, and the rules cannot be broken; and third, it is illegal for kids under twenty-one to drink in this state."

Tom shook his head and said to Cheryl, "The values of this generation are so different from those of ours. Why does booze have to be the essential ingredient for having a good time?"

Figure 11.1 An Ecological Model of Human Development

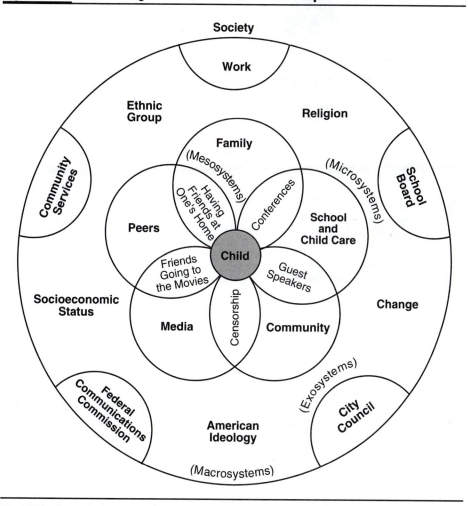

The child's values, morals, attitudes, and motives are outcomes of his or her socialization

In American culture, as portrayed by the media, there is much value placed on drinking alcohol as a means of having fun, whereas in certain religious and ethnic groups, drinking alcohol is considered sinful. Thus some people might experience conflict in social situations.

As soon as children can understand language, they have access to their parents' and their culture's values (Damon, 1988). As children develop cognitively and can interpret the meaning of their social interactions and real experiences, they begin to construct their own values, which will change and be redefined as they get older.

VALUES, DECISIONS, AND CONSEQUENCES

How does one come to know what is personally important? A technique known as **values clarification** which is the process of coming to know what is personally worthwhile or

Many adolescents in this culture equate alcohol with having a good time.

desirable in life, at any particular time can be used. It can help individuals understand their own personal moral codes, their attitudes and motives, their prosocial or antisocial behavior, their gender roles, and themselves. For example, in teaching about the founding of America, a *fact* level might explore dates and events; a *concept* level might discuss emigration and freedom of religion; a *values* level might address questions, such as: What is so important to you that if it were taken away, you would leave your country? If you left what would you take with you? A values clarification exercise can be found in the chapter activity.

Values clarification involves making decisions—choosing among alternatives. Sometimes the process is difficult because values may conflict. For example, Tom and Cheryl had to choose between their values of respect for the law and family harmony; Tammy had to weigh her value of preserving friendship against that of respecting the law. At other times the process of values clarification is easy because certain basic *human* values are enshrined in the laws of most civilized societies. The Ten Commandments are an example of basic human values, some of which ("Thou shalt not kill") are also found in laws. There are also certain values that are basic to a particular society. An example of a basic *societal* value is the Bill of Rights, which lists the rights and freedoms ("freedom of speech," for instance) assumed to be essential to people in our society.

Human values and societal values are part of our cultural heritage. Many of the decisions we make are based on such learned values. Still other values are *personal* in that they develop through experiences and relationships. Differences in social and personal interactions make for a wide divergence in human values. For example, some people value money over leisure time. They would rather spend most of their time working in order to earn money to afford a large house or an expensive car. Others would rather schedule their work so that they have some time for leisure—time to enjoy their families, their homes, or their environments—even if, by so doing, they earn less money.

Divergence in values is manifested in parenting styles, as was discussed in Chapter 4. Some parents believe the most effective way to raise a child is to be *authoritarian;* others believe an *authoritative* style is best; still others believe a *permissive* style is optimal. Value outcomes in adolescents has been found to be related to delinquency, substance abuse, and sexual activity (Goff & Goddard, 1999). Teens valuing fun/enjoyment and security were strongly identified with delinquency and substance abuse, whereas those valuing self-respect, a sense of accomplishment, and a warm relationship with others exhibited a low frequency of delinquent behavior and substance abuse. Sexual activity was found to be related to wanting a warm relationship with others.

Divergence in values is also manifested in governmental policies. For example, during the 1960s many social programs emerged as part of the War on Poverty; in the 1980s many social programs were cut back or eliminated as a way to achieve the goal of a balanced budget. The 1990s bore the goal of building a nation of learners. Health care seems to be a priority for 2000.

Values of specific groups have an impact on governmental decisions and consequent policies, as was mentioned in the discussion on advocacy in Chapter 10. A pertinent example of how group values influence public policy is the Human Capital Initiative, launched by professional associations in the behavioral sciences (National Science Foundation, 1994). This initiative provides government funding to support human capital research that contributes to a theoretical understanding of the processes that shape the intellectual, physical, and psychological capacities for productive citizenship. The National Science Foundation seeks to support research in six priority areas recommended by the representatives of the behavioral sciences:

1. Building strong neighborhoods
2. Educating for the future
3. Employing a productive workforce
4. Fostering successful families
5. Overcoming poverty and deprivation
6. Reducing disadvantages in a diverse society

Since the 1970s, many people have begun to question the role of the federal government in services to children and families (Schorr, 1997; Children's Defense Fund, 1998). Some believed that many of the country's expensive public health and public welfare programs, such as child abuse and neglect programs, residential and outpatient psychotherapy, and rehabilitation following avoidable accidents, might be greatly reduced if parents were more effective in nurturing and socializing their children. Whereas most people value the importance of the family to children, few supported the 1980 White House Conference on Families proposal to implement universal parent education in the schools (Caldwell, 1986). Thus, although people may share a value, they might not agree as to how to implement it.

This chapter and the next will explore some of the components of values (morals, attitudes, motives, behavior, gender roles, and self-esteem) and discuss how they have become outcomes of socialization.

MORALS

Morals encompass the individual's evaluation of what is right and wrong. They involve acceptance of rules and govern one's behavior toward others. Breach of morals provokes judgmental and emotional responses (Damon, 1988; Turiel, 1998).

Morality involves *feeling,* which includes empathy and guilt (Hoffman, 1988). Morality also involves *reasoning,* which includes the ability to understand rules, distinguish right from wrong, and take another person's perspective (Kohlberg, 1976; Piaget,

1965; Selman, 1980). Finally, morality involves *behaving,* which includes prosocial and antisocial acts (Eisenberg, 1986), as well as self-control of impulses.

Children acquire self-control over impulses from family and culture via reinforcement for obedience and sanctions for wrong doing. They construct moral reasons from social interactions (experience in collaboration and conflict) according to their cognitive and emotional development (Turiel, 1998).

The development of morals has been of concern since the beginning of civilization. In prescientific periods, philosophers and theologians debated the moral status of the newborn infant—was the infant inherently good, bad, or neutral? The outcome of these debates had important implications for child rearing. Those who believe a child is morally good tend to be more relaxed and more permissive in their parenting styles. Those who believe a child is morally bad tend to be stricter and more authoritarian in their parenting styles in order to socialize the child to be "good." Those who believe the child is morally neutral tend to place more emphasis on the interaction between parent and child because they believe morals develop from experiences of being good and bad, and observing right and wrong.

People differ not only in their beliefs about the inherent nature of children but also in their beliefs about what is and what is not acceptable behavior. In other words, people's moral codes differ. Sometimes one's moral code is guided by external rules, such as parental approval, convention, or the law; other times one's code is guided by internal rules, such as self-approval or self-condemnation. Moral variability does not stem solely from the influence of diverse groups such as family and culture, it reflects the flexible thinking of individuals interpreting aspects of their social worlds (Turiel, 1998).

DEVELOPING A MORAL CODE

Morality develops out of the necessity for people to get along with one another. It involves obeying society's rules for daily living, such as not stealing, not assaulting, not maligning another's character, and so on. It also involves one's conscience, or personal rules, for interacting with others, such as being kind, cooperative, and helpful.

As children develop, their morality changes. Infants and toddlers do not distinguish right from wrong. Thus when they conform to parental demands it is usually because they are attached and fear loss of love. Preschoolers and school-agers consider right and wrong to be opposite ends of a spectrum, with nothing in between. They are not capable of factoring "on purpose" or "by mistake" into the judgment of wrongdoing. Adolescents begin to view right and wrong as a matter of degree. They take into account intention in judging an act.

Not only does children's development influence their moral codes, but so do intelligence, motivation, the need for approval, self-control, and the particular situation (Bandura, 1991).

Most psychologists (Damon, 1988; Kohlberg, 1976; Piaget, 1965; Turiel, 1998) believe that one's moral code develops through social interaction in a societal context. According to Robert Simon, author of *Bad Men Do What Good Men Dream* (1996, p. 316), "a measure of psychological health is the presence of values and standards that throughout life provide the mentally healthy person with a moral rudder. The conscience of a healthy person is firm but fair and adaptive, not harsh and punitive."

Piaget's Theory of Moral Development

Piaget (1965) defined morality as "the understanding of and adherence to rules through one's own volition." Piaget analyzed morality from the perspective of how an individual's social experiences result in the formation of judgements about social relationships, rules, laws, and authority (Turiel, 1998). He approached the question of how one develops a moral code by observing and participating in children's games (games of marbles). He reasoned that games contain complex systems of rules that must be followed in order to play the game. These rules are handed down from one generation to another and are preserved solely by the respect that is felt for them by individuals. Since morality consists of a system of rules and the essence of all morality can be found in the respect an individual acquires for these rules, one can understand children's developing morality by studying their adherence to game rules.

Piaget worked with a group of Swiss schoolboys, ranging in age from 4 to 13. He asked them questions about the rules of the game: What are the rules? Where did they come from? Could they be changed? Piaget found that for the youngest children (age 4 and 5), the rules were poorly understood and were not binding. For the middle group of children (age 6 to 9), rules were regarded as having been made by an authority ("morality of constraint") and were therefore sacred and unchangeable. Following rules is quite rigid; any bending of the rules results in "That isn't fair!" For the oldest group (age 10 to 13), rules were regarded as law emanating from mutual consent ("morality of cooperation"); rules must be respected if you want to be loyal to the group, but rules can be changed if the majority of the group agrees.

Generally, children's moral reasoning shifts from the belief that one is subject to another's law or external control (**heteronomous morality**) to the belief that one is subject to one's own law or internal control (**autonomous morality**). As children develop, they begin to understand that things are not totally right or totally wrong. They can also gradually see things from other perspectives and, therefore, can consider the intentionality of an act when deciding whether the act is right or wrong.

That younger children reason about the wrongness of an act in terms of the amount of damage done rather than whether the act was done purposefully or accidentally was examined by Piaget. Reading pairs of stories like the following, to children of varying ages, he asked which character in the stories was naughtier:

A little boy who is called John is in his room. He is called to dinner. He goes into the dining room. But behind the door there was a chair, and on the chair there was a tray with fifteen cups on it. John couldn't have known that there was all this behind the door. He goes in, the door knocks against the tray, bang go the fifteen cups, and they all get broken!

Once there was a little boy whose name was Henry. One day, waiting for a time when his mother was out, he tried to get some jam out of the cupboard. He climbed up on a chair and stretched out his arm. But the jam was too high up and he couldn't reach it and have any. But while he was trying to get it, he knocked over a cup. The cup fell down and broke.

Piaget found that for the younger children interviewed, the goodness or badness of the actors in the story was related solely to the extent of the consequences. They judged John to be naughtier than Henry because John had broken more cups. Older children, however, recognized the role of intention behind the acts. They judged Henry to be naughtier than John because Henry had been purposefully sneaking something whereas John had had an accident.

Contemporary researchers have corroborated Piaget's findings (Jose, 1990; Smetana, 1981; Suls, Gutken, & Kalle, 1979). For example, in a study of 136 children from kindergarten, first, third, and fifth grades, the investigators found that only the fifth-grade children were able to take intentions into account.

Kohlberg's Theory of Moral Development

Lawrence Kohlberg (1976), influenced by Piaget's work, developed a theory of moral development after twenty years of interviewing children, adolescents, and adults in different cultures (*see* Table 11.1). He proposed that there was no consistent relationship between parental conditions of child rearing and various measures of conscience or internalized values because morality cannot be imposed, it has to be constructed as a consequence of social experiences (Turiel, 1998). Kohlberg presented his subjects with stories involving moral dilemmas and questioned them about the stories. Probably the best known is the following.

> A woman in Europe was near death from cancer. One drug might save her, a form of radium that a druggist in the same town had recently discovered. The druggist was charging $2,000, ten times what the drug cost him to make. The sick woman's husband, Heinz, went to everyone he knew to borrow money, but could get together only about half of what it cost. He told the druggist that his wife was dying and asked him to sell it cheaper or let him pay later. But the druggist said "no." The husband was desperate and broke into the man's store to steal the drug for his wife. Should the husband have done that? Why (Kohlberg, 1969, p. 379)?

Clearly, there is no "right" answer to this story (or for the others Kohlberg used). On the one hand, there are the husband's feelings; on the other, there are the legal rights of the druggist.

Based on the *reasoning* behind the responses to the stories (*see* Table 11.2), Kohlberg concluded there are six distinct stages, or perspectives, of moral development, which are associated with changes in the individual's intellectual development; each perspective is broader taking into account more variables or aspects of a moral problem (Higgins, 1995). The stages begin at about age 6 and continue to adulthood. It is important to note that children and adults sometimes operate at several different stages simultaneously. Kohlberg's findings are listed below (cited in Lickona, 1977):

1. The stages of moral reasoning are the same for all persons, regardless of culture.

2. Individuals progress from one stage to the next.

3. Changing from stage to stage is gradual. The change results from many social experiences.

4. Some individuals move more rapidly than others through the sequence of stages. Some advance further than others—for example, only 25% of U.S. adults were found to reason at stage five (principled morality).

Table 11.1 Stages of Moral Development

LEVEL AND STAGE	WHAT IS RIGHT	REASONS FOR DOING RIGHT	SOCIAL PERSPECTIVE OF STAGE
Level I. <u>**Preconventional**</u> **Stage 1:** Heteronomous morality	To avoid breaking rules backed by punishment, obedience for its own sake, and avoiding physical damage to persons and property.	Avoidance of punishment, and the superior power of authorities.	*Egocentric point of view.* Doesn't consider the interests of others or recognize that they differ from the actor's; doesn't relate two points of view. Actions are considered physically rather than in terms of psychological interests of others. Confusion of authority's perspective with one's own.
Stage 2: Individualism, instrumental purpose, and exchange	Following rules only when it is to someone's immediate interest; acting to meet one's own interests and needs and letting others do the same. Right is also what's fair, what's an equal exchange, a deal, an agreement.	To serve one's own needs or interests in a world where you have to recognize that other people have their interests, too.	*Concrete individualistic perspective.* Aware that everybody has his or her own interest to pursue and that these interests conflict, so that right is relative (in the concrete individualistic sense).
<u>**Level II. Conventional**</u> **Stage 3:** Mutual interpersonal expectations, relationships, and interpersonal conformity	Living up to what is expected by people close to you or what people generally expect of your role as son, brother, friend, etc. "Being good" is important and means having good motives, showing concern about others. It also means keeping mutual relationships, such as trust, loyalty, respect, and gratitude.	The need to be a good person in your own eyes and those of others. Your caring for others. Belief in the Golden Rule. Desire to maintain rules and authority, which support stereotypical good behavior.	*Perspective of the individual in relationships with other individuals.* Aware of shared feelings, agreements, and expectations, which take primacy over individual interests. Relates points of view through the concrete Golden Rule, putting oneself in the other person's shoes. Does not yet consider generalized system perspective.
Stage 4: Social system and conscience	Fulfilling the actual duties to which you have agreed. Laws are to be upheld except in extreme cases where they conflict with other fixed social duties. Right is also contributing to society, the group, or institution.	To keep the institution going as a whole, to avoid the breakdown in the system "if everyone did it," or the imperative of conscience to meet one's defined obligations (easily confused with stage 3 belief in rules and authority).	*Differentiates societal point of view from interpersonal agreement or motives.* Takes the point of view of the system that defines roles and rules. Considers individual relations in terms of place in the system.

(continued)

Table 11.1 *continued*

LEVEL AND STAGE	WHAT IS RIGHT	REASONS FOR DOING RIGHT	SOCIAL PERSPECTIVE OF STAGE
Level III. **Postconventional, or Principled** **Stage 5:** Social contract or utility and individual rights	Being aware that people hold a variety of values and opinions, that most values and rules are relative to your group. These relative rules should usually be upheld, however, in the interest of impartiality and because they are the social contract. Some nonrelative values and rights like *life* and *liberty,* however, must be upheld in any society and regardless of majority opinion.	A sense of obligation to law because of one's social contract to make and abide by laws for the welfare of all and for the protection of all people's rights. A feeling of contractual commitment, freely entered upon, to family, friendship, trust, and work obligations. Concern that laws and duties be based on rational calculation of overall utility, "the greatest good for the greatest number."	*Perspective independent of formal rules.* Perspective of a rational individual aware of values and rights (such as fairness) prior to social attachments and legal contracts. Integrates perspectives by formal mechanisms of agreement, legal contract, objective impartiality, and due process. Considers moral and legal points of view; recognizes that these sometimes conflict and finds it difficult to integrate them.
Stage 6: Universal ethical principles	Following self-chosen ethical principles. Particular laws or social agreements are usually valid because they rest upon such principles. When laws violate these principles, one acts in accordance with the principle. Principles are universal principles of justice: the equality of human rights and respect for the dignity of human beings as individual persons.	The belief as a rational person in the validity of universal moral principles, and a sense of personal commitment to them.	*Perspective of a moral point of view from which social arrangements derive.* Perspective is that of any rational individual recognizing the nature of morality or the fact that persons are ends in themselves and must be treated as such.

Source: "Moral Stages and Moralization," by Lawrence Kohlberg, from *Moral Development and Behavior,* edited by T. Lickona, copyright © 1976 by Holt, Rinehart and Winston, Inc., reprinted by permission of the publisher.

5. Although the particular stage of moral reasoning is not the only factor affecting people's moral conduct, the way they reason does influence how they actually behave in a moral situation.

6. Experiences that provide opportunities for role taking (assuming the viewpoints of others, putting oneself in another's place) foster progress through the stages. For example, children who participate in many peer relationships tend to be at more advanced moral stages than are children whose peer interaction is low. Within the family, children whose parents encourage them to express their views and participate in family decisions reason at higher moral stages than children whose parents do not encourage these behaviors.

In summary, at the **preconventional level,** the individual seems to be motivated by the personal consequences of the behavior—*How will I be affected?* Preconventional moral reasoning focuses on individual results. At the **conventional level,** the individual

Table 11.2 Types of Moral Judgments Made in Heinz's Dilemma

	Pro	Stage 1	Con
I. Preconventional Level [What will happen to me?]	If you let your wife die, you will get in trouble. You'll be blamed for not spending the money to save her, and there'll be an investigation of you and the druggist for your wife's death.	Action is motivated by avoidance of punishment, and "conscience" is irrational fear of punishment.	You shouldn't steal the drug: you'll be caught and sent to jail. If you do get away, your conscience will bother you, thinking how the police will catch up with you at any minute.
	Pro	**Stage 2**	**Con**
	If you do happen to get caught, you could give the drug back, and wouldn't get much of a sentence. It wouldn't bother you much to serve a short jail term, if you have your wife when you get out.	Action motivated by desire for reward or benefit. Possible guilt reactions are ignored and punishment viewed in a pragmatic manner. (Differentiates own fear, pleasure, or pain from punishment—consequences.)	You may not get much of a jail term if you steal the drug, but your wife will probably die before you get out, so it won't do you much good. If your wife dies, you shouldn't blame yourself; it isn't your fault she has cancer.
	Pro	**Stage 3**	**Con**
II. Conventional Level [What will others think of me?]	No one will think you're bad if you steal the drug, but your family will think you're an inhuman husband if you don't. If you let your wife die, you'll never be able to look anybody in the face again.	Action motivated by anticipation of disapproval of others, actual or imagined–hypothetical (e.g., guilt). (Differentiation of disapproval from punishment, fear, and pain.)	It isn't just the druggist who will think you're a criminal; everyone else will, too. After you steal it, you'll feel bad thinking how you've brought dishonor on your family and yourself; you won't be able to face anyone again.
	Pro	**Stage 4**	**Con**
	If you have any sense of honor, you won't let your wife die because you're afraid to do the only thing that will save her. You'll always feel guilty that you caused her death if you don't do your duty to her.	Action motivated by anticipation of dishonor; that is, institutionalized blame for failure of duty, and by guilt over concrete harm done to others. (Differentiates formal dishonor from informal disapproval. Differentiates guilt for bad consequences from disapproval.)	You're desperate, and you may not know you're doing wrong when you steal the drug. But you'll know you did wrong after you're punished and sent to jail. You'll always feel guilty for your dishonesty and lawbreaking.

(continued)

can look beyond personal consequences and consider others' perspectives—*What will they think of me?* Conventional moral reasoning focuses on upholding the rules of society. At the **postconventional level,** the individual considers and weighs the values behind various consequences from various points of view—*How would I respect myself if I . . . ?* Postconventional moral reasoning considers principles that may be more important than upholding society's rules or laws.

Table 11.2 *continued*

	Pro	Stage 5	Con
III. Postconventional Level [What will I think of myself?]	You'd lose other people's respect, not gain it, if you don't steal. If you let your wife die, it would be out of fear, not out of reasoning. So you'd just lose self-respect and probably the respect of others, too.	Concern about maintaining respect of equals and of the community (assuming their respect is based on reason rather than emotions). Concern about own self-respect; that is, to avoid judging self as irrational, inconsistent, nonpurposive.	You lose your standing and respect in the community and violate the law. You'd lose respect for yourself if you're carried away by emotion and forget the long-range point of view.

	Pro	Stage 6	Con
	If you don't steal the drug and let your wife die, you'd always condemn yourself for it afterward. You wouldn't be blamed and you would have lived up to the outside rule of the law, but you wouldn't have lived up to your own standards of conscience.	Concern about self-condemnation for violating one's own principles. (Differentiates between community respect and self-respect. Differentiates between self-respect for general achieving rationality and self-respect for maintaining moral principles.)	If you stole the drug, you wouldn't be blamed by other people, but you'd condemn yourself because you wouldn't have lived up to your own conscience and standards of honesty.

Source: Nicholas J. Anastasiow. *Educational Psychology: A Contemporary View,* p. 131. Copyright © 1973 by Random House, Inc. Reprinted by permission of the publisher.

For example, a current law in the United States is that all 18-year-old men must register with the Selective Service System. The rationale behind this rule is that if our country needed men for defense, these men could be called. A postconventional-level individual, who is generally a law-abiding citizen, may choose not to register because it violates his moral code, which says that only volunteers should be called for service; no one should be forced to fight.

Kohlberg (1976, 1986) believes that most children under age 9 are at the preconventional level of moral development (stages 1 and 2). Some preadolescents also score at this level. Most adolescents, and adults, reason at the conventional level (stages 3 and 4) when faced with moral dilemmas. A small percentage of older adolescents may reach the postconventional level (stages 5 and 6). Adults who are at the postconventional level are only a minority. Recently, stage 6 was removed from the Kohlberg moral judgment scoring manual, but it is still considered to be theoretically important (Santrock, 1996).

Kohlberg's stage theory has been criticized by some investigators even though his work has had significant influence on subsequent research (Turiel, 1998). For example, it has been shown that people who *score* at different stages in the hypothetical moral dilemmas presented *behave* identically in reality (Haan, Smith, & Block, 1968). Conversely, people who *exhibit* different moral behavior often *score* at the same stage of moral reasoning (Fodor, 1971). Thus one's moral code consists of both moral reasoning (how one believes one should behave in a certain situation), and moral behavior (how one actually does behave in a certain situation). For some individuals, there is a difference between the two (Hartshorne & May, 1928; Kurtines & Gewirtz, 1991; Kurtines &

Greif, 1974). When people think about real-life moral problems, they tend to rank at a lower stage than on hypothetical stage (Turiel, 1998).

Some of the criticisms of Kohlberg's theory focus on his methodology. For example, the extensive use of language in the stories may make it difficult for those who are not well-educated to reason at the higher level (Simpson, 1974). For another example, the differences in the responses of females compared to the responses of the original male sample sheds some doubt on the applicability of Kohlberg's delineated stages of moral reasoning to all human development (Gilligan, 1977), although this is not conclusive (Turiel, 1998; Walker, 1991).

Carol Gilligan (1982, 1985) argues that Kohlberg's theory views morality only from a perspective of justice. The **justice moral perspective** (individualistic) emphasizes the right of the individual. When rights of individuals conflict, equitable rules of justice must prevail. Cultures with an individualistic orientation exhibit just such a moral perspective. According to Gilligan, a perspective of morality that is not given significance by Kohlberg is that of *care.* The **care moral perspective** (collectivistic) sees people in terms of their connectedness with others. In other words, the welfare of others is intrinsically connected to one's own welfare. People share in each other's fortunes and misfortunes and must accept responsibility for one another's care. Various cultures around the world that have a collective orientation socialize children to have such a care moral perspective. For example, children and adolescents growing up in India give priority to interpersonal relationships in moral conflict situations, whereas most American children and adolescents give priority to individual rights (Miller & Bersoff, 1993).

In the United States, boys and girls are generally socialized differently in regard to moral perspectives. Boys are generally socialized to acquire a morality of justice in that individualism and separateness are emphasized, whereas girls are generally socialized to acquire a morality of care in that attachment and connectedness are emphasized (Damon, 1988). Cultural differences can exaggerate gender differences in children's moral orientations. Anthropologists have reported that contrasts between boys' and girls' values are far sharper in traditional cultures than in Western technological societies. For example, girls in agrarian parts of Africa tend to be more nurturant and cooperative than boys in those cultures (Edwards & Whiting, 1980).

In order to illustrate the influence of gender socialization (gender roles will be discussed in Chapter 12) on morality, Gilligan related examples of boys' and girls' reasoning regarding the Heinz dilemma, such as the following (Gilligan, 1982, pp. 26–28):

Jake: For one thing, human life is worth more than money, and if the druggist only makes $1,000 he is still going to live; but if Heinz doesn't steal the drug, his wife is going to die. *(Why is life worth more than money?)* Because the druggist can get $1,000 later from rich people with cancer, but Heinz can't get his wife again.

Amy: Well, I don't think so. I think there might be other ways besides stealing it, like if he could borrow the money or get a loan or something, but he really shouldn't steal the drug—but his wife shouldn't die either. *(Why shouldn't he steal the drug?)* If he stole the drug, he might save his wife then, but if he did, he might have to go to jail, and then his wife might get sicker again, and he couldn't get more of the drug, and it might not be good. So, they should really just talk it out and find some other way to make the money.

In these examples, Jake's sense that people sometimes must act on their own, even in opposition to others if they are to do the right thing, is contrasted with Amy's assumption that people can work out their problems by "talking it out."

Because Amy sees the social world as a network of relationships, she believes that the solution to the problem lies in making Heinz's wife's condition known to all concerned, especially the druggist. Surely, then, the people will work something out that will be responsive to the wife's needs. Jake, on the other hand, assumes no such consensus among those involved in the dilemma. So Jake believes Heinz may need to take the law into his own hands if he is to protect his rights. Jake concludes that Heinz's wife is a legitimate part of Heinz's rights by logically calculating the unique value of the wife's life as compared to the money the druggist can get for the drug from others (Damon, 1988).

Despite the criticisms, Kohlberg's model of moral development has stood the test of time. Most psychologists agree that morality, no matter which perspective you take, is developmental; that is, children universally progress through stages of understanding, and even though the timing of the progression and the highest stage reached are individual, the sequence of the stages is the same. "Debates now center on the roles of emotions and judgments, on the individual and the collectivity, on the contributions of constructions of moral understandings and culturally based meanings, and on how to distinguish between universally applicable and locally based moralties" (Turiel, 1998, p. 868).

INFLUENCES ON MORAL DEVELOPMENT

Situational Contexts

The situation or context an individual is in often influences actual moral behavior. Situational factors include the nature of the relationship between the individual and those involved in the problem, whether others are watching, previous experience in similar situations, and the value society places on various responses (Turiel, 1998). For example, killing in self-defense is condoned, whereas killing for revenge is sanctioned.

The relation between moral reasoning and moral behavior is not always clear. People may believe in honesty and feel that individuals who cheat on tests should be punished, yet those same people may cheat on their income tax returns. One classic study (Krebs, 1967) found that in a sample of sixth-graders, the behavior of resisting temptation was related to children's stage of moral development, as delineated by Kohlberg. However, another study of a group of 7- to 11-year-olds found no relation between moral reasoning (based on intentionality and justice) and the individual child's behavior when resisting temptation in a laboratory situation (Grinder, 1964).

Elliot Turiel (1983, 1998) explains that the inconsistencies exhibited in individuals' moral reasoning are influenced by whether they judge the situation to be a "moral" or a "conventional" situation. According to Turiel, a *moral situation* involves other people's rights or welfare being affected (you cannot hit other children), whereas a *conventional situation* involves rules promoting appropriate behavior in a social group (you must not interrupt when someone else is talking).

Judith Smetana (1981, 1985, 1989) finds that even 2.5- to 3-year-olds distinguish between moral and conventional rules. Young children view moral transgressions, such as hitting, stealing, and refusing to share, as more serious and deserving of punishment than not saying "please" or forgetting to put away a toy. Thus young children seem to have a greater understanding of rules in different situations than Piaget originally assumed.

Temperament, Self-Control, and Self-Esteem

Moral development may be affected by an individual's temperament (the innate characteristics that determine an individual's sensitivity to various experiences and responsiveness to patterns of social interaction), level of self-control (the ability to regulate one's impulses, behavior, and/or emotions), and self-esteem (one's regard, value, or favorable opinion of one's self).

Kochanska's (1993, 1995) studies on children's temperament (inhibited or shy, impulsive or aggressive) and conscience development conclude that children's temperaments can affect parenting methods. For example, maternal reasoning, polite requests, suggestions, and distractions predicted internalized conscience development in inhibited 2- and 3-year-olds, but not in impulsive children. Impulsive children were found to comply with directives when they had a secure attachment; power assertion resulted in anger and defiance. The method, then, to internalize morals for such children is to maintain the affection of the parent.

Additionally, moral development may be related to one's self-control. Some studies (Mischel, 1974; Mischel, Shoda, & Peake, 1988) show that preschool children who exhibit self-control in that they are able to defer immediate gratification are more successful than their more impulsive age-mates to resist the temptation to cheat at experimental games. Also, these self-controlled preschoolers are rated by adults as more self-competent and socially responsible ten years later in adolescence.

Finally, moral development may also be influenced by one's self-esteem; specifically, the extent to which an individual needs approval from others (Hogan & Emler, 1995). For example, a longitudinal study (Dobkin, Tremblay, Masse, & Vitaro, 1995) showed that the need to receive approval from others was related negatively to the level of moral behavior. Specifically, the greater the dependency on others for esteem, the more likely to abuse substances and engage in antisocial acts. On the other hand, results also showed that the need for approval from oneself and feeling competent was positively related to the level of moral behavior and consequent avoidance of drugs.

Age, Intelligence, and Social Factors

Kohlberg and his colleagues (Colby, Kohlberg, Gibbs, & Lieberman, 1983) reported data from a 20-year longitudinal study of moral judgment in boys age 10, 13, and 16 when first assessed. The data supported the theory that moral reasoning is significantly linked with age, IQ, education, and socioeconomic status. It also showed that stage 4 did not emerge in a majority of individuals until early adulthood (the twenties). In addition, the data indicated no distinction between individuals at the stages 5 and 6, using available assessment techniques.

Several researchers (Walker & Taylor, 1991; Youniss, 1981) believe that one's moral code develops through social interaction—through discussion, debate, and emergence of consensus. This may explain why those growing up in democratic societies, whose existence depends on consensus among the majority, score at the higher levels (Bronfenbrenner & Garbarino, 1976; Miller, 1995; Simpson, 1974).

Jerome Kagan (1984) believes the morality of most persons to be directed more by emotions than by reasoning. Avoidance of unpleasant feelings and achievement of pleasant feelings are the major motivations for morality. Unpleasant feelings include fear of punishment, social disapproval, and failure, as well as guilt and uncertainty. Pleasant feelings include affection, pride, sense of belonging, and contribution.

Family

The family is a social system and, therefore, has rules of conduct in order that its members get along. Many of these rules are similar to those of society at large—for example, prohibitions against lying, stealing, aggression, and disorderly conduct. In both family and society, misbehavior is discouraged through sanctions such as disapproval and punishment; good behavior is encouraged through approval. The goal is for the child to develop a conscience. *Conscience* is a word that traditionally refers to the "cognitive and affective processes which constitute an internalized moral governor over an individual's conduct" (Aronfreed, 1968).

Although Kohlberg rejected the role of parents in a child's construction of morality, Damon (1988) believes that since parents first introduce the child to the laws and logic of a social system, they are a crucial ingredient in the child's moral development. The child-rearing methods that parents implement have an impact on the moral development of children. Several investigations found that parents who discuss various issues with their children, such as the Heinz story, and the values behind such issues, tend to promote more advanced moral thought (Walker & Taylor, 1991).

Other researchers (Eisenberg & Murphy, 1995; Hoffman, 1970, 1983; Hoffman & Saltzstein, 1967) have found that children of parents who are punitive tend to have *externally focused consciences* (a description that generally corresponds to Kohlberg's stages 1–3). Children who have externally focused consciences are "good" in order to receive praise, avoid punishment, or please others. Children of parents who are warm and affectionate tend to have *internally focused consciences* (generally corresponding to Kohlberg's stages 4–6). Children who have *internally focused consciences* are "good" in order to fulfill their duty or conform to their own standards. *Internally focused consciences* can be conventional (tradition-oriented) and rigid, or humanistic (person-oriented) and flexible. A humanistic conscience develops when parents are not only affectionate but also use induction as a socializing technique—they explain the reasons for their demands and discuss the impact of the child's actions on others.

Hoffman and Saltzstein (1967), in a classic study, identified three kinds of parental discipline techniques that are related to conscience development: *power assertion, love withdrawal,* and *induction.* In one study, these researchers asked seventh-graders (matched for intelligence and social class) which method of discipline their parents ordinarily used. They also asked the parents which method of discipline they had used when their child was 5 years old. The children were rated for conscience development along several dimensions: severity of guilt, as expressed in story completions; acceptance of responsibility for wrongdoing, as judged by teachers; tendency to confess misdeeds, as reported by mothers; judgment of right and wrong independent of rewards and punishment; and consideration for other children, as judged by classmates.

Results showed that discipline by *power assertion* was associated with low ratings on conscience development; discipline by *induction* was associated with high conscience ratings; and discipline by *love withdrawal* was not significantly associated with conscience development.

More recent studies have also demonstrated the relationship between parental socialization methods and moral development. For example, one study (Kochanska,

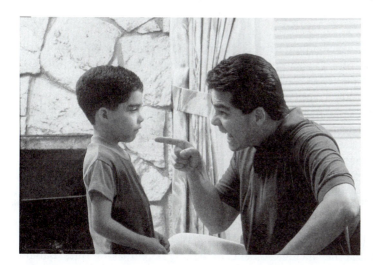

This parent's harsh and punitive child-rearing methods will likely influence this child to have an externally oriented conscience in that the child behaves out of fear of punishment.

1991) found that mothers who deemphasized power strategies when trying to get their toddlers to comply to their rules had children who, when studied six years later, had a more internally focused conscience. Another study (Kuczynski, Kochanska, Radke-Yarrow, & Girnius-Brown, 1987) found that mothers who used strategies of direct control were associated with children who used strategies of direct defiance, whereas mothers who used negotiations had children more likely to use negotiations. Thus children seem to model parental socialization methods.

It must, however, be kept in mind that moral reasoning is a complicated process involving perception, emotions, desires, and judgment. Even though children's earliest social interactions occur in the family influencing moral development, these biologically influenced factors are significant (Turiel, 1998).

Peers

Reciprocity is a fundamental ingredient of all human interchange—"Do unto others as you would have them do unto you." Reciprocity is learned by doing through social interaction—I say something, you answer; I smile, you smile back; I grab your toy, you hit me; I share my cookies with you, you play with me.

Kohlberg (1976, 1985) and others (Damon, 1988; Saltzstein, 1976) believe that social interaction, especially the opportunity to take the role of another person and the opportunity to generate rules democratically, can enhance moral development. Children who have more opportunities for participation in the family, peer groups, and social settings may develop faster in moral thought and behavior than children who lack these supports. It was found that children who grew up on an Israeli kibbutz—with its intense peer-group interaction, opportunities for shared decision making, and cooperative work responsibilities—typically reached stage 4 or 5 in adolescence. In contrast, children who were reared in situations where there was limited social exchange were often still at stage 1 or 2, even in late adolescence (Lickona, 1977; Santrock, 1996). Direct training in role taking may even induce people to advance in Kohlberg's developmental stages (Saltzstein, 1975; Santrock, 1996).

Social conflicts between peers are a source of moral development (Killen & Nucci, 1995). Conflicts can stimulate children to take different points of view in order to restore balance in social situations, to consider the rights of others, and to coordinate others' needs with those of self.

School

Schools influence moral development through their programs and their staff (Kohlberg, 1985; Silberman, 1970). Since, according to Piaget, moral development begins with the understanding and acceptance of rules, it will be useful to examine the relationship of the approach with classroom rules and moral development.

All programs have rules. The purpose of rules in a classroom is to ensure an optimal learning environment. If learning is to take place, students cannot interfere with one another or with the teacher. Students must respect and cooperate with one another when differences arise, they must learn how to compromise.

As has been discussed, traditional programs tend to emphasize rigid adherence to rules regarding behavior, interpersonal relationships, and manners. Teachers who implement traditional programs tend to be *authoritarian* in that they make the rules and dole out the rewards and consequences. Modern programs also have rules, but they tend to be more flexible in their approach. Teachers who implement modern programs tend to be *authoritative* in that they include students in the process of making rules. Damon (1988, 1999) believes that for teachers to enhance children's moral development, children need guidance with reasoning, positive role models, and involvement in group discussions for decision making, social interaction, and perspective-taking. For example, one four-year study (Higgins, 1995) demonstrated that students in a modern, or democratic, high school were more advanced in moral reasoning than students in a traditional, or autocratic, high school. A discussion of what *authoritative* teachers specifically do to enhance moral development follows.

Reasoning   Whether the rules emanate from external sources or internal sources, how the teacher communicates the rules, keeping in mind children's cognitive development, can have an impact on children's moral development. Consider the teacher who says, "You can't go out to recess until all your materials are put away," versus the teacher who says, "Here, let's put your materials away so that no one will step on them and get hurt." The first teacher is merely parroting a rule, whereas the second teacher is giving the child the reasoning behind the rule. The first teacher may get compliance, but will not be fostering moral development; the second teacher will.

Modeling   Teachers create the atmosphere for modeling responses. Research has shown that modeling has a positive effect on moral development (Bandura, 1991). There is no comparable substitute for a teacher who models compassion, honesty, altruism, and justice. The teacher who encourages children to share, yet when asked for a certain book by another teacher says, "No, I'm sorry; we are going to use it later," and then does not, is not being an effective model. On the other hand, the teacher who says, "Let's see this film now (recess time), so Mr. Johnson's class will still have time to see it today, and I'll take you out to recess after the film," is being an effective model for cooperative behavior.

Group Discussions.   Certain activities incorporated into classroom programs have been found to foster moral development. For example, research (Higgins, 1995; Kohlberg, 1985; Lickona, 1991) has indicated that group discussions on moral issues can raise a person's level of moral reasoning. Group discussions can deal with various problems in the classroom, such as how certain transgressions (fighting, taking other people's things, tattling) should be handled. Or they can involve planning a group project. Such group projects tend to reduce egocentrism and foster cooperation because an opportunity is provided for everyone to listen to everyone else, and everyone can make a contribution. Many teachers use the team approach for group projects. For example, suppose a group of children on a team has to present an animal project to the class. One child records the information from books, another illustrates it, another writes a poem about it, and another organizes and narrates the information to the class. The children choose their jobs. They help each other, so the project represents their best team effort.

Still another group discussion technique that enhances moral development is the presentation of moral dilemmas to the class. The following is an example for middle-years children:

> Joe's father promised he could go to camp if he earned the $50 to pay for it, but he changed his mind and instead asked Joe to give him the money he had earned. Joe lied and said he had only earned $10 (which he gave to his father). He then went to camp using the other $40 he had made. Before he went, he told his younger brother, Alex, about lying to his father. Should Alex tell their father? Why or why not (Good & Brophy, 1986, p. 121)?

The significance for moral development is not in the answers but in the reasoning behind them. Dilemmas should be related to the student's level of cognitive development and interest. Discussions revolving around such dilemmas help students clarify their values, make choices, and understand the consequences of their choices. Hearing what others say also broadens their perspective and their alternatives.

As was said earlier, perspective taking—giving children roles to play and discussing them—has been found to enhance moral development (Gibbs, 1995; Staub, 1971). Through role playing, children learn to view events from a variety of points of view. They learn what it feels like to be helpless, what it feels like to be helped, and what it feels like to be the helper. For example, how would you feel if you lost your dog? How would you feel if it were returned to you? How would you feel if you returned a lost dog to someone else?

Kohlberg suggests that teachers ask students questions about moral issues and listen to their explanations, in order to gain insight into their level of moral thought. He has found that discussions that are one stage above an individual's present level of moral reasoning are most effective in this regard. Finally, Kohlberg urges teachers to deal with situations posing broad problems and issues, rather than focus too much on discussions involving specific classroom rules and routines because these specifics cannot be generalized (Kohlberg, 1980, 1985; Lickona, 1977, 1991).

The box titled "Suggestions for Promoting Moral Growth in the Classroom" lists some other suggestions for fostering moral development.

Suggestions for Promoting Moral Growth in the Classroom

1. Build a sense of community in the classroom where the students learn together in an atmosphere of respect and security.
2. Provide opportunities for the children to have a voice in establishing the rules of the classroom and the consequences for not following them.

3. Give reasons for consequences, stressing where possible the effect of the child's action on the group.

4. Discuss differences between rules for the good order of the school and rules affecting justice and human relations.

5. Provide opportunities for collaborative peer group work.

6. In stories and discussions of everyday experiences, help the children to consider the feelings of other persons, real or fictional.

7. Role play experiences from daily life events that lead to disappointments, tensions, fights, and joys in order to provide opportunities for the students to see the event from perspectives other than their own.

8. Discuss concepts of fairness and unfairness.

9. Using stories, literature, history, current events and/or films, stimulate discussions that will provoke higher-stage reasoning.

10. Be a role model and point out other role models as they occur in classroom activities.

Sources: R. Duska and M. Whelan (1975). *Moral development: A guide to Piaget and Kohlberg.* New York: Paulist Press; A. Higgins (1995). *Educating for justice and community: Lawrence Kohlberg's vision of moral education.* In W. M. Kurtines and J. L. Gewirtz (Eds.). *Moral development: An introduction.* Boston: Allyn & Bacon.

Mass Media

As has been discussed, television is a significant socializing agent. Does it affect moral behavior? Some believe that TV and other popular media have helped create a large number of people who think it's perfectly OK to grab what they want and to do what they want, and the only bad thing is getting caught.

In a study of television and the moral judgment of young children, kindergartners who were heavy TV viewers (based on a television diary kept by their mothers) were found to exhibit less advanced moral reasoning when interviewed than those children who watched little TV (Rosenkoetter, Huston, & Wright, 1990).

Television may contribute to disruption of moral behavior. Specific programs have been followed by antisocial acts (Levin, 1998)—for example, various school shootings following news coverage of the Columbine High School massacre in Littleton, Colorado; or the 5-year-old boy who set fire to his home killing his 2-year-old sister, following a similar episode on *Beavis and Butt-head;* or the13-year-old boy and his friend who were acting out the Russian roulette scene from the movie *The Deer Hunter* with a real gun (the boy died instantly).

The National Television Violence Study concluded that not only does violence pervade TV, it also involves repeated acts of aggression against a victim that go unpunished (Mediascope, 1996). Huesmann (1986) proposed that such repetition results in a cumulative learning process, having specific effects on short- and long-term behavior. One effect is that children learn new ways of aggressing by watching aggressive models. A second result is that socialized restraints over aggressive impulses are weakened because many violent acts are performed by heroes and are rationalized in the story context as "good triumphing over evil." The message portrayed, then, is that aggression is an appropriate tool for those who believe they are in the right (Coie & Dodge, 1998). A third effect of viewing violence is desensitization—emotional responsiveness is reduced. A fourth result is that the observer's sense of reality is altered. Frequent viewers compared to infrequent ones, believe that real-world violence is more common, that the world is less safe, that group stereotypes are more valid, and that their chances of being victimized are greater (Coie & Dodge, 1998).

Since young children attend primarily to the consequences of acts and not intentions, they are unlikely to understand moral messages of programs, even when these are explicit. When children identify with televised models, they copy the observed behavior and accept the models' attitudes. It has been demonstrated that children's aggressiveness increases after being exposed to an aggressive model and children's altruism increases after being exposed to an altruistic model (Levine & Sprafkin, 1988). Thus the particular moral behavior children are exposed to on television is likely to influence their moral behavior. For example, what are the effects on children of observing rule-breaking on television? The research literature reveals that observational learning can play a potent role in shaping responses to situations in which breaking an established rule will bring immediate gratifications or benefits to the transgressor. It has been demonstrated that children exposed to a model who breaks an established rule will break rules more often in the absence of an adult than will those who have not been exposed to such an example. On the other hand, it has also been established that children who have been exposed to a model who adheres to established rules are more likely to adhere to

When aggressive models are successful, they are likely to be imitated.

rules, even when they are highly tempted and when their transgression will not be detected (Bandura, 1991; Leibert & Poulos, 1976).

Community

Some psychologists (Damon, 1988; Miller & Bersoff, 1993; Turiel, 1998) believe that moral development is influenced by the cultural ideology in one's community. For example, as discussed in other chapters, cultural ideology can be oriented toward individualism or collectivism. Individualistic cultures emphasize rights and justice, whereas collectivistic cultures emphasize duties and obligations. These different ideologies influence values and morals in that community members judge behavior accordingly. Individualistic cultures value personal goals; collectivistic cultures value shared goals. Moral concepts in individualistic communities are interpreted in terms of independence, autonomy, self-reliance, and individual rights. Moral concepts in collectivistic communities are interpreted in terms of interdependence, conformity, duty, obedience toward authority, tradition, and social harmony. In moral dilemmas, individualistic communities judge whose rights have been violated, whereas collectivistic communities judge what obligations were not fulfilled (Turiel, 1998).

The interaction of the socializing agents in a culture and the individual's intellectual level of development and motivation determines the level of moral development. Bronfenbrenner and Garbarino (1976) describe three developmental levels of morality that are similar for individuals in all cultures.

- Level one: *Amoral.* The individual's motivation at this level is basically to seek pleasure and avoid pain. The only moral judgment involved is self-interest. This level of morality is quite normal for very young children, but when it persists into adolescence or adulthood, it is considered to be deviant behavior for the individual and hazardous for the society in which he or she lives (corresponding to Kohlberg's stages 1 and 2).
- Level two: *System of social agents.* The individual's motivation at this level comes from allegiance to others, either to certain individuals or to groups. The individual behaves in such a way as to gain approval (corresponding to Kohlberg's stages 3 and 4).
- Level three: *Values and ideas.* The individual's motivation at this level is personal principles, one's own system of beliefs. The individual does not depend on other socializing agents for direction (corresponding to Kohlberg's stages 5 and 6).

According to Bronfenbrenner and Garbarino, individuals who attain level three have had experiences in which abstract thinking, speculation, and decision making were supported. In order for these experiences to take place, one needs to have some competitive allegiances that create enough tension within the individual to stimulate thought about loyalties and critical behavior. In other words, when people are exposed to a variety of settings and social agents representing different expectations and moral sanctions, conflict is produced. This conflict causes people to look within themselves for moral convictions with which they are comfortable. On the other hand, individuals who are exposed to a single setting are exposed to only one set of rules. Since they do not experience conflict, they need not look within themselves for resolution.

Support for Bronfenbrenner's (1970b) theory comes from his findings of differential moral judgments between Russian boarding school students and Russian day school students. The boarding school students who were exposed to a single socializing agent (school), made moral judgments that were more authority-oriented than those made by the day school students who were exposed to multiple socializing agents (school, parents, peers). The children were asked to respond to various moral dilemmas, such as the following.

You and your friends accidentally find a sheet of paper the teacher lost. On this sheet are the questions and answers for a quiz that you are going to have tomorrow. Some of the kids suggest that you do not say anything to the teacher about it, so that all of you can get better marks. What would you really do? Suppose your friends decided to go ahead and keep the paper. Would you go along with them or refuse? (*Absolutely certain, fairly certain, I guess so.*)

Other moral dilemmas included going to a movie recommended by friends but disapproved of by parents, neglecting homework to be with friends, and accidentally breaking a window and running away.

This moral dilemma test was used by Bronfenbrenner and Garbarino (1976) on groups of 12-year-old boys and girls in thirteen different societies, to find out if being exposed to **pluralism** (of the existence of more than one belief system), was related to the development of level three moral judgment. The thirteen participating countries were ranked on pluralism. Children growing up in the 1970s in countries that ranked high on pluralism, such as the United States and West Germany, were less authority-oriented and had more plural ideas about moral dilemmas than children growing up in the countries that ranked low on pluralism, such as Poland and Hungary. Thus cultures that allow individual freedom and in which diversity is common produce children who are likely to have had experiences that stimulate abstract thinking, speculation, and decision making. These experiences occur because of the existence of differing socializing agents competing for the individual's allegiance. The individual has to make some personal choices. The process of choosing (values clarification) leads to the development of moral judgment characteristic of level three.

Bronfenbrenner and Garbarino explain that experiences involving exposure to differing socializing agents do not occur in many cultures, and that is why cross-cultural comparisons of levels of moral development show differences among same-aged individuals. Pluralistic societies, those having many socializing agents with differing values, are more likely to produce individuals with level three moral judgment, whereas monolithic societies, those whose socializing agents have a singular value system, are less likely to do so. Pluralism per se, is no guarantee that individuals will be motivated to attain level three moral judgment. There must be integration or a common goal between the individual and the various socializing agents for the conflict over allegiance to occur. For example, a common goal of socializing agents in the United States is achievement. Parents urge children to work hard and do their best, teachers motivate achievement with grades, and friends cheer the kid who hits a home run for the team.

Occasionally, however, these socializing agents compete for one's loyalty as, for instance, when team practice conflicts with plans to study for a test. Which socializing agent gets one's loyalty then? When there is no common goal, conflict does not occur. For example, when Joan comes home from school, her mother asks her to empty the trash. Joan had already promised her friend she would go over to her house after school to work on a school project. There is no competition between socializing agents for Joan's loyalty because she can easily accomplish both activities.

Other research supports the theory that the more socializing agents one is exposed to that have a common goal, yet sometimes compete for allegiance, the more likely one is to have level three moral judgment. For example, studies of high school students have found that their stage of moral reasoning was positively related to the quantity and quality of their social participation (school clubs, friendship groups, leadership role), whether judged by teachers, peers, or themselves (Turiel, 1998). For another example, 14- and 17-year old Finnish adolescents who experienced Western individualistic educational practices, compared to adolescents of the same age who grew up in Estonia during the period of Soviet socialism with collectivistic educational practices, exhibited more internal moral reasoning (Keltikangas-Järvinen, Terav, & Pakaslahti, 1999).

In conclusion, moral development is socially constructed (Davidson & Youniss, 1995). It represents an individual's scheme of personal and societal values that include a coordination of emotions, thoughts, and actions (Turiel, 1998). If one acts exclusively on personal values, one may too often overlook the rights and privileges of others in the social environment. To illustrate, in the example discussed at the beginning of the chapter, Tammy overlooked her parents' liability if they break the law and allow her to have a party with alcohol because she is more concerned with her peers. On the other hand, if one acts on societal values or social convention, contract, or laws, one may fail to see how they can unjustly affect a given individual. For example, Tammy's parents did not fully understand her position in feeling she had to fulfill the expectations of her peers because they were more concerned with their responsibilities.

Thus, mature moral development—which is influenced by one's capacity to anticipate the future, to predict consequences, and to put oneself in another's place, along with one's level of self-esteem—is the ability to make rational decisions that balance one's own personal value system with the value system of society.

ATTITUDES

The Pratt Family: Their Attitudes about Football

Bill Pratt loves football. He's anxious about Saturday's game because it is the play-off for the league championship. Since Bill made the team last year as a high school sophomore, he has been more conscious about his diet and sleep habits. He has also neglected his schoolwork a bit. Bill's younger sister, Julie, hates football. She thinks it's a dumb, boring game, where everybody piles up on everybody else. Bill's dad used to be the star quarterback for his high school team. He is devoted to the game. It was he who encouraged Bill to try out for the team, and it was he who used to toss a football to Bill when Bill was only about 3 years old. Bill's mother's attitude toward football is one of fear. She is proud of her son's accomplishments, but would rather he participate in a different sport. She worries about the possibilities of injury. She is also concerned about Bill's drop in grades.

An **attitude** is a tendency to respond positively (favorably) or negatively (unfavorably) to certain persons, objects, or situations. Bill's dad had a positive attitude about football, whereas Bill's sister had a negative one.

Prejudice is an attitude. The word means "prejudgment." It generally refers to the application of a previously formed judgment to some person, object, or situation. It can be favorable or unfavorable. Usually, prejudice comes from categorizing or stereotyping. Bill accused his mother of being prejudiced against football when she objected to his joining the team.

A **stereotype** is an oversimplified, fixed attitude or set of beliefs that is held about members of a group. Stereotypical attitudes usually do not allow for individual exceptions. Bill's sister stereotypes football players as "dumb jocks." When she heard her mother prodding Bill about his grades, she teased Bill: "See? You're turning dumb just like the other goons."

Attitudes are composed of beliefs, feelings, and behavior tendencies. Most psychologists agree that attitudes determine what we attend to in our environment, how we perceive the information about the object of our attention, and how we respond to that object. Thus attitudes guide behavior. For example, if one has the attitude that intelligence is genetic, then one will not support educational programs for children with learning problems in school.

DEVELOPMENT OF ATTITUDES

The development of attitudes is influenced by age and cognitive development. For example, according to Goodman (1964) and Derman-Sparks (1989), ethnic attitudes develop in the following sequence.

- Phase I—awareness of ethnic differences, beginning at about age 2.5 to 3.
- Phase II—orientation toward specific ethnic-related words and concepts, beginning at about age 4.
- Phase III—true attitudes toward various ethnic groups, beginning at about age 7.

This developmental sequence is probably due to the reaction of others to children's appearance—remarks about skin color, hair, and facial features alert one to the fact that people look different. Cognitive development also enters into the explanation. As children develop cognitively, they are more able to categorize (assimilate and accommodate) differences. Experience with differences promotes more awareness.

Other research has supported Goodman's delineation of ethnic attitudes. Reviewing many studies of Anglo children's attitudes toward other groups, Aboud (1988) analyzed that 4- to 7-year-old Anglo children were already aware that "white" is the ethnic identity favored by the society. They referred to other groups as "bad" or with negative characteristics. ("He's lazy because he's colored.") Many African American children felt ambivalent about being African American and were envious of Anglo children. Hispanic children followed a similar pattern. After age 7, however, children of all ethnic groups were less prejudiced toward other groups and had more positive attitudes toward their

The friendship between these children is more important than societal attitudes about race.

own group. Aboud explained young children's prejudicial attitudes as due to cognitive immaturity rather than malice.

As children learn of the existence of ethnic categories, they also become aware of the evaluations attached to them. These evaluations come from the family, the peers, the school (including teachers and textbooks), and the media. Exemplifying how color attitudes can be transmitted subtly, a 1993 Caldecott Honor Book (recognition given for pictures), *Seven Blind Mice,* by Ed Young (1992), is about seven blind mice, each a different and brilliant color, whose task is to identify an object. The white mouse solves the riddle and correctly identifies the object as an elephant. Many have criticized the book, complaining that the white mouse is portrayed as the "savior," thereby perpetuating prejudicial attitudes of "white supremacy" (Jacobs & Tunnell, 1996).

Whether children pick up subtle messages from the media depends on their real-life experiences and interactions, especially with parents. Studies of young children show that those with the most prejudicial attitudes have parents who are authoritarian, who use strict disciplinary techniques, and who are inflexible in their attitudes toward right and wrong (Aboud, 1988; Boswell & Williams, 1975; Katz, 1975). Thus rigid parental attitudes influence similar ones in their children.

Prejudicial attitudes are not only found in regard to ethnic differences but in regard to disabilities as well. In a longitudinal study of children's attitudes toward those with mental *illness,* Weiss (1994) found that by the time children entered kindergarten, they already had stigmatized attitudes, which remained stable after being examined eight years later. However, perception of those with mental *disabilities* had changed from being stigmatized to being more acceptable. Perhaps the inclusion of children with mental disabilities in schools and their inclusion in the media and community have influenced the attitude change.

Steps in the Development of Prejudice

Awareness

Being alert to, seeing, noticing, and understanding differences among people even though they may never have been described or talked about. Children model behavior they observe in adults they look up to.

Identification

Naming, labeling, and classifying people based on physical characteristics that children notice. Verbal identification relieves the stress that comes from being aware of or confused by something that you can't describe or no one else is talking about. Identification is the child's attempt to break the adult silence and make sense of the world. Children mimic what they see, hear, and read about.

Attitude

Thoughts and feelings that become an inclination or opinion toward another person and their way of living in the world. Children may displace their feelings on others who are less powerful.

Preference

Valuing, favoring, and giving priority to one physical attribute, person, or lifestyle over another, usually based on similarities and differences. Children understand the world from the perspective of their own experience.

Prejudice

Preconceived hostile attitude, opinion, feeling, or action against a person, ethnic group, or their lifestyle without knowing them. Children generalize their personal experiences to the world.

Source: S. York (1991). *Roots & Wings: Affirming Culture in Early Childhood Programs*. St. Paul, MN: Toys 'n' Things Press, pp. 169–170.

INFLUENCES OF SIGNIFICANT SOCIALIZING AGENTS ON THE DEVELOPMENT OF ATTITUDES

Here the influences of family, peers, media, community, and school on children's attitudes toward those who are similar and those who are different are examined.

Family

Parents have a large impact on children's attitudes and values. Many studies have shown that the attitudes of children tend to resemble those of their parents. For example, 76% of a national sample of high school seniors favored the political party favored by both of their parents (McGuire, 1985). Ethnic prejudice also follows this general pattern. The ethnic prejudices of Anglo elementary school children tend to resemble those of their parents, as do the ethnic prejudices of African American elementary school children (Aboud, 1988).

Modeling   An explanation of the resemblance of children's and parents' ethnic attitudes is that children develop attitudes through role modeling. Children identify with models who are powerful and admirable. Through the process of identification they begin to assume on attitudes of the people they would like to emulate (parents, relatives, friends, fictional heroes or heroines, television and movie characters, rock stars).

Instruction   We often think of the ethnic majority as being prejudiced against ethnic minorities. However, prejudice is present in ethnic minorities, too. The following description illustrates how a Jewish boy's parents tried to socialize him to be prejudiced against Christians because they had been persecuted by prejudiced Christians.

> My first impressions of Christianity came in the home, of course. My parents brought with them the burden of the Middle Ages from the blood-soaked continent of Europe. They had come from the villages of Eastern Europe where Christians were feared with legitimate reason.
>
> When occasionally a Jewish drunk was seen in our neighborhood, our parents would say, "He's behaving like a Gentile."
>
> For in truth, our parents had often witnessed the Polish, Romanian, Hungarian, and Russian peasants gather around a barrel of whiskey on Saturday night, drink themselves into oblivion, "and beat their wives." Once in a while the rumor would spread through the tenements that a fellow had struck his wife, and on all sides we heard the inevitable, "Just like a Gentile."
>
> Oddly enough, too, our parents had us convinced that the Gentiles were noisy, boisterous, and loud—unlike the Jews. It is indeed strange how often stereotypes are exactly reversed.
>
> If we raised our voices, we were told, "Jewish boys don't shout." And this admonition covered every activity in and out of the home: "Jewish boys don't fight." "Jewish boys don't get dirty." "Jewish boys study hard."
>
> It wasn't until I was in school and was subjected to the influence of Gentile teachers and met Gentile social workers and classmates that I began to question these generalizations. Then I began to read and I found myself finally dismissing all prejudice from my mind (Golden, 1962, p. 210).

The example illustrates one way children learn attitudes—by instruction. Young children accept as true the statements of their parents and others they admire because, with their limited experience, they are not apt to have heard anything different.

According to Ramsey (1998), children assimilate ethnically related attitudes, preferences, and social expectations at an early age. They understand the world in terms of absolutes and believe overgeneralizations. Therefore, because of their cognitive level of development, they are receptive to global stereotypical and prejudicial comments of adults.

Reinforcement and Punishment.   The socializing techniques of reinforcement and punishment are also involved in the way children learn attitudes. For example, it has been demonstrated that attitudes toward ethnic groups can be influenced simply by associating them with positive words (reinforcement), like *happy* or *successful,* or negative words (punishment), like *ugly* or *failure* (Aboud, 1988; Lohr & Staats, 1973). For another example, negative attitudes about individuals with disabilities, such as they are vocationally limited or socially inept, are reinforced when such individuals are excluded from the mainstream of society (Gollnick & Chinn, 1998).

Peers

According to recent research (Eccles, Wigfield & Schiefele, 1998), peers are influential regarding attitudes and behavior in that children compare the acceptability of their beliefs with those of their friends. Children and adolescents whose peers are academically motivated are more likely to do well in school.

Coleman's (1966) classic study showed how prejudicial attitudes were molded among high school students. For example, one study (Margolis, 1971) found that the main factor affecting African Americans' association with Anglos was how they thought their African American friends would react.

Peers are also very influential in the development of gender-role attitudes, as was discussed in Chapter 8, as well as influencing who is accepted or rejected from the group based on similarities and/or differences. Because preadolescent children have a great need to identify with the peer group, someone who is ethnically different or who has a disability is often excluded (Gollnick & Chinn, 1998). Other attitudes influenced by peers involve dress, dating, personal problems, and sex (Sebald, 1986, 1989).

Because peer opinion is important to children, peers can be used to influence attitudes regarding achievement. Cooperative learning settings enable peers to help each other learn by sharing resources and modeling academic skills. Also, inclusion of diverse children in such cooperative learning groups reduces stereotypical and prejudicial attitudes (Eccles, Wigfield, & Schiefele, 1998).

Mass Media: Television and Movies

Children and adolescents frequently cite television as a source of information that influences their attitudes about people and things (Comstock & Paik, 1991; Jensen, 1999). "You see so much violence that it's meaningless. If I saw someone really get killed, it wouldn't be a big deal. I guess I'm turning into a hard rock," said an 11-year-old. "When I see a beautiful girl using shampoo or a cosmetic on TV, I buy them because I'll look like her. I have a ton of cosmetics," said a 13-year-old. Several studies have reported that middle and high school students rate the mass media as their most important source of information and opinions, even more important than their parents, teachers, and friends (Comstock & Paik, 1991). Television, as was discussed in Chapter 9, is a source of social stereotypes. For example, while the occupational roles of African Americans have become more varied from the subservient roles shown in the past, other minority groups are often cast as villains or victims (Leibert & Sprafkin, 1988). To illustrate, Arab Americans have experienced negative stereotyping in movies. They are often portrayed as villains, criminals, or terrorists, as well as enacting taboo acts of American society (Bennett, 1999).

Although television and movies have generally had the reputation of perpetuating negative attitudes, they also have the potential for bringing people to new levels of empathetic understanding. Various documentaries and biographies of ethnically diverse historical and sports figures aired on TV, such as *The Jackie Robinson Story,* give viewers insight. Movies such as *Schindler's List* and *Life is Beautiful* bring awareness to the plight of Jews during World War II.

However, merely being exposed to ethnic minorities is not effective in changing attitudes over a long period of time; children have to be taught nonstereotypical attitudes directly (Bigler & Liben, 1990). Similarly, while there are more programs on TV today

Participation of individuals with disabilities in athletic events has helped communicate positive attitudes regarding their abilities.

portraying women in traditionally male-dominated activities, to really influence children's gender-role attitudes, adults have to engage in discussion and provide nonstereotypical activities (Dorr & Rabin, 1995).

Mass Media: Books

That books are influential in attitude formation is evidenced by the controversy stirred up by some, resulting in their removal from library shelves (Norton, 1999). For example, in the 1960s, Garth Williams's *The Rabbit's Wedding* (1982) was criticized because the illustrations showed the marriage of a black rabbit and a white rabbit. In the 1970's, Maurice Sendak's (1970) *In the Night Kitchen* was taken off some library shelves because the child in the story was nude. In the 1980s, Helen Bannerman's *The Story of Little Black Sambo,* which was first published in 1899 and had enjoyed much popularity over the years, was attacked for being offensive to African Americans due to the story line and crudely drawn figures of characters with stereotypical features.

The major controversies in children's books include how attitudes regarding stereotypes (gender, ethnicity, disabilities), sexuality, violence, profanity, and family problems are portrayed (Feldstein, 1989).

That books can be used to influence attitudes is evident in *McGuffey's Reader,* popular in U.S. schools in the early part of the twentieth century. The reader contained stories with moral messages. William Bennett (1993), former U.S. Secretary of Education, published *The Book of Virtues* for a similar purpose. Spitz (1999) claims that even when they are not intended to do so, "picture books provide children with some of their earliest takes on morality, taste, and basic cultural knowledge, including messages about gender, race, and class. They supply a stock of images for childen's mental museums" (p. 14). A classic book defying gender stereotypes is *The Story of Ferdinand* by Munro Leaf (1936). Ferdinand is a bull who would rather smell the flowers than fight; the attitude portrayed is that it is OK to be yourself rather than conform to cultural role prescriptions.

Community

The community influences attitudes by its customs and traditions. For example, in certain countries only men are allowed into the teahouses to socialize; women stay home. Prior to the civil rights movement, there were signs labeling the bathrooms in southern communities ("White," "Colored"). In many communities today one finds signs that say "adults only." These examples all illustrate attitudes of discrimination by gender, ethnicity, and/or age. Such attitudes are acquired by children because they represent the status quo in their environment.

Is the community population diverse? Does it represent many ethnic groups? Or, is it homogeneous? Do the people who live there have similar backgrounds? How do different people in the community interact? As has been discussed, research shows that positive interactions with people different from oneself tend to foster positive attitudes toward them.

A community's attitudes are reflected most obviously in the ways it chooses to spend its tax money. This in turn affects the services it provides. Is money spent on educational programs, recreation, preventive services, support services, and compensatory services? By examining a community's budget, one can determine rather quickly, for example, the degree to which children and families are valued. Children are very likely to incorporate their community's attitudes into their own attitudes.

The attitudes of the community toward providing support for its families are likely to affect the level of stress and social pathology experienced by some families (Etzioni, 1993; Schorr, 1997). These families, then, may come to feel a loss in their ability to control what happens to them (Seligman, 1975). On the other hand, several studies have reported that social support received by children is one important resource that protects them against the negative effects of life stressors (Sandler, Miller, Short, and Wolchik, 1989).

Specific social pathologies involving families that have been related to the community's attitude of support (or lack of) are infant death and disease, teenage pregnancy, juvenile delinquency, and child abuse and neglect (Garbarino, 1992). Communities that provide prenatal and perinatal support to young, high-risk mothers have lower infant mortality rates (Children's Defense Fund, 1998; Schorr, 1997). One reason for this is that attitudes toward mothering and child health change for the positive. Community attitudes toward providing support and guidance to pregnant teenagers are influential in the teenagers' attitudes toward birth control, education, and occupational goals (Furstenberg, 1976). Community attitudes regarding law enforcement, recreation, youth employment, and curfews can affect the level of juvenile delinquency (Garbarino, 1992). Finally, the attitudes of the community members toward helping one another can affect the level of child abuse and neglect in community families by influencing parenting attitudes. Mothers in communities of high support reported that their children were significantly easier to care for than did the mothers in communities of low support (Garbarino & Sherman, 1980).

School

Schools influence attitude formation. A review of various studies (Sadker, Sadker, & Klein, 1991) illustrated how gender-role stereotyping is perpetuated in schools. Schools that separate male and female activities and encourage boys to play in the "block corner" or take science classes and girls to go to the "housekeeping" area or take English classes, for example, are teaching children which activities are "gender appropriate." Teachers who project their gender-typed expectations on boys and girls reinforce traditional gender-role behavior. In other words, if a teacher *expects* boys to be more active and aggressive than girls, the teacher will tend to allow this behavior. Likewise, a teacher who *expects* girls to be passive and docile will likely encourage girls to conform to this pattern.

Although teachers are generally committed to the idea of ethnic and/or gender equality, biased attitudes in the form of certain classroom practices still emerge, such as the "self-fulfilling prophecy," in which teacher *expectations* of performance influence *actual* performances (Good & Brophy, 1986). However, classroom organization can be very effective in influencing attitudes toward others. For example, researchers (Johnson & Johnson, 1999; Johnson, Johnson, & Maruyama, 1983) tried to identify conditions in schools that led to positive attitudes regarding ethnically diverse students as well as students with disabilities. They found when members of both heterogeneous and homogeneous groups cooperated instead of competed to achieve a common goal, greater positive attitudes occurred among the group members. These positive attitudes included more realistic views of self and group members, greater expectations of success, and increased expectations of favorable future interactions with group members (regardless of how different were the individuals).

CHANGING ATTITUDES ABOUT ETHNIC DIVERSITY

According to Aboud (1988), attitudes about ethnic diversity, especially prejudice, take different forms in children according to age. Prejudice in children under age 7 is due to cognitive immaturity, rather than malice. Prejudice is often exhibited because of children's frustrations with authority; they turn on other groups perceived to have less power or status.

Katz and Zalk (1978) examined the following different techniques to counter the ethnically biased attitudes of Anglo second- and fifth-graders (as determined by a test). All four methods were found to be effective on a short-term basis, and two were effective for a long time.

1. *Increased positive ethnic contact.* Children worked in interethnic teams at an interesting puzzle and were all praised for their work.
2. *Vicarious interethnic contact.* Children heard an interesting story about a sympathetic and resourceful African American child.
3. *Reinforcement of the color black.* Children were given a marble (which could be traded in for a prize) every time they chose a picture of a black animal.
4. *Perceptual differentiation.* Children were shown slides of an African American woman whose appearance varied, depending on whether or not she was wearing

glasses, one of two different hairdos, and smiling or frowning. Each different-appearing face had a name, and the children were tested to see how well they remembered the names.

After two weeks, the children's levels of prejudice were measured again. All the groups who had been exposed to any of the four techniques showed less prejudice than did children in the control groups. Four to six months after the experiment, a second posttest showed that the children who had learned to perceive differences in the African American faces and those who had heard the stories about African American children had more positive attitudes than those in the other two groups. Younger children showed more gains than older children.

Apparently, prejudicial attitudes can be changed by enabling children to have positive experiences (both real and vicarious) with ethnic minorities. When an adult mediates the experience by pointing out individual differences, it is especially effective. Thus children learn to view people as individuals rather than as representatives of a certain group with certain fixed characteristics.

An experiment was carried out to help children feel what it is like to experience prejudice, to be discriminated against (Weiner & Wright, 1973). Anglo third-grade children were divided into two groups randomly: the Orange people and the Green people. On one day, the Orange children were "superior"; they were praised by the teacher and given preferential treatment in the day's activities. On this day, the Green children were discriminated against; they were criticized and denied privileges. On the second day, the positions were reversed: the Green children were favored, and the Orange children were discriminated against. On the third day, and again two weeks later, the children's ethnic beliefs were measured. Compared to children who had not had this experience, the experimental class expressed fewer prejudicial beliefs about African Americans and were significantly more likely to want to have a picnic with African American children. Thus prejudiced attitudes can be changed by role taking—experiencing the feelings that discrimination brings.

A similar experiment was carried out in an Iowa third grade by teacher Jane Elliott using blue and brown eyes as criteria for superiority and inferiority. It was documented in the film *Eye of the Storm* (1971) and repeated with adult parole officers, documented in *A Class Divided* (1992). The children interviewed as adults, as well as the parole officers reported a major change in their attitudes toward diversity as a result of the experiment.

MOTIVES

A *motive* is something that causes a person to act. The theory that people are motivated to act by the urge to be competent, or achieve, is attributed to Robert White (1959). According to him, people of all ages strive to develop skills that will help them understand and control their environment, whether or not they receive external reinforcement. People act to pursue different goals, but why do some persist and some give up? Explanations can be categorized as (1) within-person changes from cognitive or emotional maturation, and (2) socially mediated developmental changes resulting from contexts children experience as they grow, such as family, school, or peer group (Eccles, Wigfield, & Schiefele, 1998).

Creating an Antibias Environment

The classroom should include the following:

1. Images in abundance of *all* the children, families, and staff in your program. Photos and other pictures reflecting the varying backgrounds of the children and staff should be displayed attractively.

2. If the classroom population is racially/ethnically homogeneous, images of children and adults from the major racial/ethnic groups in your community and in U.S. society.

3. Images that reflect accurately people's current daily lives in the United States working and with their families during recreational activities.

4. A numerical balance among different groups. Be sure that people of color are not represented as "tokens"—only one or two.

5. A fair balance of images of women and men, shown doing "jobs in the home" and "jobs outside the home." Show women and men doing blue-collar work (e.g., factory worker, repair person) and pink-collar work (e.g., beautician, salesperson), as well as white-collar work (e.g., teacher, doctor).

6. Images of elderly people from varying backgrounds performing different activities.

7. Images of differently abled people from varying backgrounds shown doing work and with their families in recreational activities. Be careful not to use images that depict differently abled people as dependent and passive.

8. Images of diversity in family styles: single mothers or fathers, extended families, gay or lesbian families (families with two mothers or fathers), families in which one parent and a grandmother are the parents, interracial and multiethnic families, adopted families, differently abled families (the atypical person may be either a child or a parent).

9. Images of important individuals—past and present. These should reflect racial/ethnic, gender, and abledness diversity, and should include people who participated in important struggles for social justice.

10. Artwork—prints, sculpture, and textiles by artists from varying backgrounds that reflect the aesthetic environment and the culture of the families represented in your classroom and of groups in your community and in the United States.

Source: L. Derman-Sparks, and the Antibias Task Force (1989). *Antibias curriculum: Tools for empowering young children.* Washington, DC: National Association for the Education of Young Children, pp. 11–12.

Before exploring influences on motives, some related terms are defined. **Achievement motivation,** the motivation to be competent, expresses itself in behavior aimed at approaching challenging tasks with the confidence of mastery. This motivation has been linked to one's *locus of control*. **Locus of control** refers to how one *attributes* his or he

Figure 11.2   Relationship between Attribution and Actual Performance

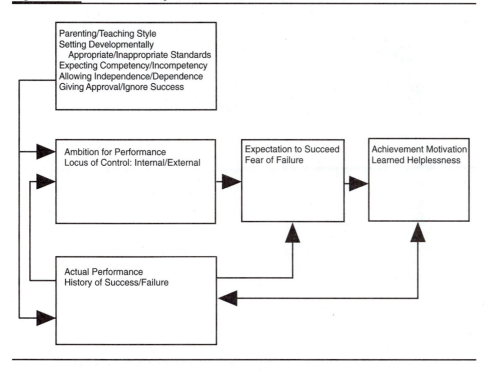

performance, or where a person places personal responsibility for successes or failure—inside or outside oneself. (Am I responsible for my grade, or is the teacher?) When one feels he or she has *no* control over events and, therefore, no responsibility, one is no longer motivated to achieve; one has *learned helplessness*. **Learned helplessness** is a phenomenon exhibited by people who no longer perform effectively in a number of situations (they have learned to be helpless as opposed to competent). How achievement motivation is related to *locus of control* and to *learned helplessness* will be discussed. The relationship of **attributions** explanations for performance to actual performances is outlined in Figure 11.2.

ACHIEVEMENT MOTIVATION

People differ in their motivations to achieve. To assess the differences in strengths of people's achievement motives, in a classic study David McClelland and his colleagues (1953) developed a projection technique, using selected picture cards from the Thematic Apperception Test (TAT). The technique assumes that when asked to write stories about the pictures, people will project their feelings about themselves onto the characters in the pictures shown to them.

The pictures show such scenes as two men ("inventors") in a shop working on a machine, a young boy and a violin, or a boy sitting at a desk with an open book in front of

This girl's achievement is influenced by her personal responsibility to perform and her confidence of success.

him. Subjects are asked to answer the following questions about the pictures:

1. What is happening? Who are the persons?
2. What were the circumstances leading up to the situation in the pictures?
3. What are the characters thinking? What do they want?
4. What will happen? What will be done?

The assessment of the stories involves noting references to achievement goals (concern over reaching a standard of excellence). Subjects who refer to achievement goals are often rated high in achievement motivation; subjects who rarely, or never, refer to achievement goals are rated low.

Achievement *motivation* is often correlated with *actual* achievement behavior (Camara, 1986). The motivation to achieve, however, may evidence itself only in behavior that the child values. For example, a child may be highly motivated to achieve, and this may be exhibited in athletics, but not in schoolwork. Thus different situations have different achievement-attaining values for children (Eccles, Wigfield, & Schiefele, 1998; Harter & Connell, 1984).

Development of Achievement Motivation

How does the motivation to achieve develop? The origins of individual differences in achievement motivation (also called "need achievement") have most often been linked to parenting practices. In a classic study (Rosen & D'Andrade, 1959), two groups of 10-year-old boys having similar socioeconomic backgrounds and IQ scores but different levels of achievement need were observed in their homes with their parents watching them do a task. The task was rather difficult. It involved building a tower out of irregularly shaped blocks while blindfolded and restricted to the use of one hand. The parents were told to watch the boy do the task. The parents could say or do anything they pleased, but they could not touch the blocks. They were also told the height of the tower the "average boy" would erect and were asked to predict (confidentially to the researchers) how well their son would do. The parents of the *high need-achievement* boys predicted a better level of performance than did the parents of the *low need-achievement* boys. This probably indicates the parents' usual behavior of setting higher standards of excellence for the child to strive for.

While the boys were doing the task, the parents of sons with *high achievement needs* were more encouraging and more likely to reward accomplishment with warm praise. Fathers of the *high need-achievement* boys were warm and friendly while their sons were working, but did not interfere with their sons' decisions regarding how to complete the task, other than giving a hint or two. (They allowed for independence.) The fathers of *low need-achievement* boys, on the other hand, were more domineering, in that they gave specific directions on how to complete the task and were more likely to show irritation when things went awry.

Apparently, the parents of the *high need-achievement* boys set high standards of excellence for them, but not so high as to discourage the boys. They also allowed the boys to solve problems independently and communicated approval. In contrast, the parents of the *low need-achievement* boys set standards that were either too high or not high enough; they were less likely to permit independence in solving the problem. In short, parenting styles are related to the development of need achievement in that they set standards of excellence, expect competence, allow independence, and communicate approval after success. These characteristics are components of the *authoritative* parenting style. Many more recent studies correlate *authoritative* parenting with achievement in children and adolescents (Baumrind, 1973; Eccles, Wigfield, & Schiefele, 1998; Lamborn, Mounts, Steinberg, & Dornbusch, 1991; Steinberg, Elmen, & Mounts, 1989).

When some investigators (Hermans, Terlaak, & Maes, 1972) questioned teachers, they learned that children with high achievement motivation were viewed as being more interested in striving toward goals, showing a higher degree of personal responsibility for their work, and being more persistent in following through on tasks they had begun. Research has demonstrated that achievement motivation is a relatively stable characteristic of personality. Longitudinal studies have demonstrated a consistent relationship between the level of achievement motivation in preschool, elementary school, and high school (Deci & Ryan, 1985; Eccles, Wigfield, & Schiefele, 1998; Feld, 1967; Kagan & Moss, 1959).

Achievement Motivation and Parenting Practices/Expectations

A study of the antecedents of achievement motivation was done by McClelland and Pilon (1983). They related mothers' reports of child-rearing practices when their children were 5 years old to the children's achievement motivation scores when the children were in their thirties. The mothers had been interviewed in 1951 in a study of child-rearing practices. Twenty-five years later, the children were interviewed to assess their achievement motivation.

McClelland and Pilon consistently found a relationship between child-rearing practices emphasizing scheduled feeding and conscientious toilet training (putting the child on the potty at regular times and watching for clues that the child needs to urinate or defecate) and achievement motivation for males and females from low- and middle-class backgrounds. It is likely that the scheduled feeding and conscientious toilet training were examples of standards of excellence set by the parents. Parental expectations play a significant role in children's motivation to achieve (Ginsberg & Bronstein, 1993; Parsons, Adler, & Kaczala, 1982; Phillips, 1987a).

McClelland and Pilon also found that child-rearing practices emphasizing early independence (by age 5) were *not* significantly related to adult achievement motivation. Perhaps parental expectations for independence by age 5 freed the parents of their role in continually communicating standards to the child. Or perhaps expecting the child to be independent by age 5 was too high a standard. There are indications that when the achievement standard is set at an unrealistic level, the effect is opposite to what was intended. Thus children who are expected to do well on tasks with which they are too young to cope exhibit a lower level of achievement motivation. These children, instead of learning to achieve, learn to give up. The desire to achieve, then, is created by optimally challenging the child—providing a task that can be done with effort (not too easy) so that the accomplishment is meaningful (Burhans & Dweck, 1995; McClelland, 1961). Such tasks are referred to today as *developmentally appropriate*.

In sum, the child-rearing environment of children who show high achievement motivation includes developmentally appropriate timing of achievement demands (early, but not too early, and continuing encouragement), high confidence in child's abilities, a supportive affective family environment (orientation toward exploration and investigation as well as positive feedback), and highly motivated role models (Eccles, Wigfield, & Schiefele, 1998). These research findings provide the rationale for parent involvement in school. Parents who take an active interest in their children's school performance are more likely to have children who achieve in school than parents who are not interested in their children's school performance.

Achievement Motivation, Child Expectations, and Attributions

Individuals' actual achievement behavior depends not only on their motivation to achieve but also on whether or not they *expect* to achieve and whether or not they fear failure. People are more likely to work hard when they perceive a reasonable chance to succeed than when they perceive a goal to be out of reach. Children's expectations of success can be measured by asking them to predict a certain grade, indicate how sure they are that they can solve a particular problem, and select the hardest task they think they can do from a collection of tasks varying in difficulty (Phillips, 1987a).

Children with high expectations for success on a task usually persist at it longer and perform better than children with low expectations (Eccles, 1983; Eccles, Wigfield, & Schiefele, 1998). Research (Carr, Borkowski, & Maxwell, 1991) has found that children with high IQs and high expectations of success in school did, in fact, get the highest grades; whereas children with high IQs and low expectations received lower grades than children with low IQs and high expectations.

One's expectation of success is related to (1) one's history of success or failure, (2) one's perception of how difficult the task is, and (3) the attributions for one's performance. Generally, one who has been successful most of the time in the past expects to succeed in the present and future; one who has failed most of the time in the past expects to fail in the present and future.

In some situations, however, people who usually succeed, fail; conversely, people who usually fail, succeed. A second possible factor, then, operating in an individual's expectation of success can be how difficult one originally perceived the task to be. Failure on a task perceived to be very easy results in a different self-evaluation than failure on a task perceived to be very difficult.

A third possible factor operating in an individual's expectation of success is to what the individual's performance is attributed (Weiner, 1992). People can attribute performance to themselves (their ability or their effort), to others (the teacher's opinion of one or the teacher's ability to teach), to the situation (the test too difficult or the room too noisy), or to luck. Where one places responsibility for success (or failure) is referred to as one's *locus of control,* discussed next.

LOCUS OF CONTROL

Locus of control relates to one's attribution of performance, or sense of personal responsibility. Individuals who have strong beliefs that they are in control of their world, that they can cause things to happen if they choose, and that they can command their own rewards have an **internal locus of control** (one is responsible for one's own fate). These people attribute their success (or failure) to themselves. Individuals who perceive that others or outside forces have more control over them than they do over themselves have an **external locus of control** (others or events are responsible for one's fate). These people attribute their success (or failure) to things outside themselves.

Regarding control beliefs, Skinner (1995) stressed the importance of perceived relationships between a person's actions and his or her success or failure. Achievement is related to whether the person thinking he or she controls the outcome. As children get older their understanding of causality and explanations for outcomes becomes more differentiated. Specifically, 7- and 8-year-olds consider factors of luck, effort, ability, more powerful than others; whereas 11- and 12-year-olds consider unknown factors, external factors (luck more powerful than others), and internal factors (ability and effort) in attributing locus of control.

How is locus of control measured? Julian Rotter (1966, 1971) developed a locus of control scale that is used to study the internal–external dimensions of personal responsibility. The Internal–External Scale is constructed so that each item can be scored as internal or external. Some sample items are given in the box titled "Measuring Locus of Control." Subjects are to indicate, in each pair of statements, the more appropriate of the two.

Locus of control is an aspect of personality that interests educators because children with an internal locus of control generally do better academically (Nowicki & Segal, 1974; Swick, 1986). Research shows that these children are generally more competent and effective than those with an external locus of control. For example, in an experiment that required subjects to work on a verbal ability test, children with internal loci of control budgeted the time allotted them in a way that related to the difficulty of each item, whereas children with external locuses of control did not (Gozali, Cleary, Walster, & Gozali, 1973). And in a review of more than 100 studies, Findley and Cooper (1983) found that internals earn higher grades and outperform externals on standardized achievement tests.

The explanation behind the relationship between locus of control and academic achievement is that internals view outcomes as within their control. So if they succeed, they can figure out what they did correctly and do it again. If they fail, they believe they can change the outcome in the future by exerting more effort to correct their mistakes (for example, study harder or differently). They develop a *mastery-oriented attribution.* Externals, on the other hand, view outcomes as outside their control. So if they succeed, they attribute it to good luck, and if they fail, they attribute it to bad luck or lack of ability. Since they don't attribute the outcomes of their performance to their own efforts or strategies, they give up quickly. They develop a *helpless-oriented attribution* (Dweck & Leggett, 1988).

Measuring Locus of Control

I more strongly believe that:

1. a. Promotions are earned through hard work and persistence.
   b. Making a lot of money is largely a matter of getting the "right breaks."
2. a. There is usually a direct connection between how hard I study and the grades I get.
   b. Many times, the grades teachers give seem haphazard to me.
3. a. The number of divorces in our society indicates that more and more people are not trying to make their marriages work.
   b. Marriage is largely a gamble; it's no one's fault if it doesn't work.
4. a. When I am right, I can usually convince others that I am.
   b. It is silly to think that one can really change another person's basic attitudes.
5. a. In our society, earning power is dependent upon ability.
   b. Getting promoted is really a matter of being a little luckier than the next person.
6. a. If one knows how to deal with people, they are really quite easily led.
   b. I have little influence over the way other people behave.
7. a. People can change the course of world affairs if they make themselves heard.
   b. It is only wishful thinking to believe that one can really influence what happens in society at large.
8. a. I am the master of my fate.
   b. A great deal that happens to me is probably a matter of chance.
9. a. Getting along with people is a skill that must be practiced.
   b. It is impossible to figure out how to please some people.

Source: J. B. Rotter (1971). "Who Rules You? External Control and Internal Control," *Psychology Today*, 5, 37–42. Reprinted from *Psychology Today*. Copyright 1971 by the American Psychological Association.

A review of the literature on locus of control (Eccles, Wigfield, & Schiefele, 1998; Young & Shorr, 1986) confirmed that internal locus of control was significantly related to age (older children are more internal), gender (elementary school-age girls are more internal than boys), socioeconomic status (middle- and upper-class children exhibit greater internality than do lower-class children), and achievement. These findings are probably related to the diverse socialization experiences of these groups.

Development of Locus of Control

How does locus of control develop? Piaget's observations of infants led him to conclude that it is not until about age of 5 or 6 months that children show awareness that their own actions can bring about an effect. However, behavior does not become intentional or goal directed until between about 8 and 12 months. A favorite game of infants this age is "drop and fetch." The infant drops a toy from the highchair or playpen, and the parent fetches. Therefore, it is about age 1, according to Piaget, that children begin to distinguish between events caused by their own actions and those that are not (Flavell, Miller, & Miller, 1993). Once children begin to understand that they have an impact on their environment, they begin to experiment with various autonomous behaviors—"No, me do it" is commonly heard in the second year.

Children gradually develop a sense of control when things that happen to them are contingent upon their actions. As has been discussed in relation to Erik Erikson's (1963) theory of personality development, parental responsiveness to children's needs leads to attachment and a sense of trust (first year). When children are allowed to be autonomous, they gain a feeling of control; if not given opportunities to be autonomous, they feel self-doubt (age 2–3). If children are allowed to initiate activities, they will feel a sense of control over their environment, rather than guilt over wanting to control it (age 4–5). When children enter school, their experiences there will affect their feelings of industry or inferiority (age 6–12). These are crucial years for development of self-esteem in that a sense of control and self-determination is related to the perception of self-competence (Beane, 1991).

Thus locus of control develops through one's actions on the environment and one's interactions with others. The outcomes of these actions and interactions influence whether people attribute what happens to them to internal or external causes. The reason

This child is given the opportunity to correct a mistake, thereby gaining a feeling of autonomy. Such opportunities enable children to gain a sense of control and lead to self-confidence.

children growing up in lower-class families tend to demonstrate a less internal locus of control than do those from middle-class backgrounds (Bain, Holliman, & McCallum, 1989; Stephens & Delys, 1973) may be due to different parenting styles or to the different environments experienced by lower- and middle-class children. Lower-class children have fewer opportunities to develop a sense of being in control or determining life outcomes. For example, financially, they have fewer choices. The box titled "How Parents and Teachers Can Help Children Develop an Internal Locus of Control" provides some methods for enabling children to associate their actions with outcomes.

How Parents and Teachers Can Help Children Develp an Internal Locus of Control

1. *Be responsive to children from the moment they are born.* Be affectionate, comforting, attentive. They need to know someone will respond to their actions, or else they will feel they have no control over their own actions.

2. *Let children accept consequences for their actions.* If they spill milk, give them something with which to clean it up.

3. *Avoid performing tasks children can do for themselves.* Encourage effort, allow children to make mistakes, and don't expect adult performance.

4. *Give children developmentally appropriate responsibilities.* For example: age 3, put toys away; age 5, make bed; age 7, set and/or clear table.

5. *Give feedback.* Let children know when they have performed well and, if need be, how they can improve.

6. *Be an example of a person who makes things happen.* Don't wait for things to happen and then react.

7. *Encourage children's special interests.* Provide opportunities for children to initiate things themselves by questions and stimulating activities.

8. *Set standards and limits for behavior.* Explain the reasons for the rules ("You need to be home by 6 o'clock so we can all have dinner together").

9. *Show respect for children and for their accomplishments.* ("What an interesting painting; can you tell me about it?" rather than, "What is that? It doesn't look like a kitty.")

10. *Allow children to make appropriate decisions that affect them.* ("You can have six children at your birthday party; whom would you like to invite?" "Do you want to play soccer this year?")

LEARNED HELPLESSNESS

Martin Seligman has presented evidence in his books, *Helplessness* (1975) and *Learned Optimism* 1990), that people become passive and lose motivation when placed in situations where outcomes are unaffected by their behavior. These people believe they are pawns of external circumstances; as a result, they learn to be helpless.

When does helplessness first appear? Research on infants shows that infants exposed to mobiles that spin independently of their actions do not learn to control new

This child is feeling helpless because his assignment is too difficult, so he gives up and daydreams.

mobiles presented to them that can be activated by turning their heads. In contrast, infants exposed to stationary mobiles, and to mobiles that spin contingent upon their actions (head or arm moving), evidence no difficulty in learning to control the new mobiles. These differences in performance are still present after six weeks without any exposure to a mobile (Fincham & Cain, 1986). Thus certain experiences involving the ability to control outcomes can affect even infants.

Gunnar (1980) demonstrated that the ability to control the onset of a potentially frightening toy reduces fear and increases positive approach responses in 12-months-old infants. Similar findings regarding control have been demonstrated in studies of infant attachment. When a baby cries and the mother responds to his or her needs, the baby experiences a "sense of control" even though he or she is not cognitively aware of it at first. Apparently, this sense of control, or trust that mother will meet baby's needs, enables the baby to develop a secure attachment to the mother (Ainsworth, 1982; Frankel & Bates, 1990).

As children get older and the number of their experiences with objects and people increases, their *perceptions* of being able to control outcomes and their ability to understand cause and effect influence when and if they manifest learned helplessness as opposed to motivation to achieve (Eccles, Wigfield, & Schiefele, 1998; Fincham & Cain, 1986). Figure 11.2, illustrated earlier in this chapter, summarizes the factors involved in attributions for performance and their relationship to actual performance.

By age 4, some children give up on even developmentally or age-appropriate tasks, such as building a tall tower out of blocks (Cain & Dweck, 1995). These nonpersistent children believe they can't do the task and report feeling badly after failures. Persistent children, on the other hand, believe they can succeed on challenging tasks if given more time and if they try harder. Nonpersistent children describe their parents as critical or punitive ("Daddy's going to get mad"). Persistent children describe their parents as supportive and encouraging ("Try it again, you'll do better next time").

Many economically-deprived persons and some ethnic minorities have learned that they exert little control over their lives. Due to experiences they have had, they feel that the external educational, economic, social, and political systems control them. For example, poverty makes higher education a luxury, but without it, people lack the skills and assurance to change their condition. Perhaps the lack of motivation attributed to the lower class is really due to their lack of control over personal outcomes (National Commission on Children, 1991).

In a series of studies on learned helplessness (Dweck, 1975; Dweck & Bush, 1976; Dweck & Gillard, 1975; Dweck & Reppucci, 1973; Elliot & Dweck, 1991), Dweck (1991) found that when children believe their failures are due to uncontrollable factors in themselves such as lack of ability (for example, "I failed the math test because I'm dumb in math"), their subsequent task performance deteriorates after failure. If, however, children believe their failure was due to lack of effort, they try harder on subsequent tasks and often show improved performance.

How Parents and Teachers Can Help Children Who Have Learned Helplessness

1. *Know the individual abilities (strengths and weaknesses) of the child, and set realistic goals for tasks*—not too easy or too hard, challenging enough to make the child work, yet guaranteed to enable the child to succeed.

2. *Provide opportunities to learn by doing*—experiencing consequences of one's actions leads to a sense of autonomy.

3. *Give feedback as soon as possible for the task performed*—evaluation leads to insight into successes and failures. ("Maybe if you'd wash your brush after using each color, you wouldn't always end up with black.")

4. *Give encouragement for trying and for persistence*—"You worked really hard on cutting a straight line; I bet with just a little bit of practice you'll be able to do it."

5. *Let children know it is OK to make mistakes*—that is how we learn. Ask children how they can correct their mistake next time.

6. *Provide structured opportunities for decision making*—"Do you want to wear the red or the blue sweater?" rather than "Do you want to wear a sweater?" "Do you want to brush your teeth first or put on your pajamas before bed?" "You may do your math homework or spelling now."

7. *Explain to children that actions have consequences*—desirable behavior leads to positive consequences, but undesirable behavior leads to negative consequences (finishing your work gets a star; not cleaning up when told to do so means you must clean up later when everyone else goes outside to

play). Implementing positive and negative consequences enables children to learn to take responsibility for their actions.

8. *Teach children they have the power to make changes, and point to things they control*—"Remember when you couldn't pump yourself on the swing? Now look how high you can go!"

9. *Avoid high levels of competition*—stress cooperation or activities in which every child can make a valued contribution.

10. *Model achievement motivation*—show pride in accomplishments.

In several studies, Dweck found that girls are more likely than boys to demonstrate learned helplessness that comes from attributing lack of ability to themselves. Boys more often tend to believe that when they do not do well, it is because they have not worked hard enough. Since the boys and girls scored similarly on achievement tests, it can be inferred that ability was similar but that locus of control was different. Dweck and her colleagues looked to the teachers to see if there was differential feedback to boys and girls relating to failure. They found that when boys submitted poor work, they were generally reprimanded for sloppiness, not paying attention, or lack of effort. Girls who submitted poor work were generally told, "You didn't do it right even though you tried."

In another study, Dweck and her colleagues (1978) set up a classroom experiment. One group of boys and girls were told when they did poorly on an anagram test, "You didn't do very well that time; you didn't get it right." Another group of boys and girls were told that they did not do very well and that they did not write the answers neatly enough. This feedback led the boys and girls in this second group to believe that their poor performance was due to lack of effort. When the test was administered again, the first group of boys and girls gave up more easily after the initial failure, but the second group of boys and girls tried harder. In sum, if parents and teachers praise a child for working hard (*effort*) when he or she succeeds but question his or her (*ability*) when he or she fails, the child is less likely to persist at challenging tasks, thereby developing *learned helplessness*. Yet, if parents and teachers praise the child's *abilities* when he or she succeeds and emphasize lack of *effort* when he or she fails, the child is more likely to persist at challenging tasks, thereby developing *achievement motivation*. Thus, if adults treat children as if their mistakes can be remedied by their own actions, the children are likely to reflect this opinion of themselves and behave accordingly. The box titled "How Parents and Teachers Can Help Children Who Have Learned Helplessness" describes some methods parents and teachers can use.

Epilogue

Morality is the cornerstone of society. Without concepts of "good" and "bad" people could not live with one another. Cultural values, such as individualism and collectivism, influence moral behavior. For example, according to Bok (1989), pressure for success (achievement, power, wealth) as defined by individualistic societies can blur the line between "right" and "wrong". In the story, The Goose Girl, *the woman lied to better her life situation; in real life, Richard Nixon, Jimmy Swaggart,* *and Bill Clinton all lied to maintain theirs. In collectivistic societies, pressure to be loyal to one's family or peer group and/or to "save face" may be a motive to lie or to not reveal the truth. Even in the United States, recognizing the cohesiveness of family loyalties, spouses may not testify against each other in court.*

How morality, attitudes, and motives develop and are supported is influenced by significant others as well as by factors inherent in the individual. When microsystems work together and their efforts are supported by the macrosystem, positive outcomes for moral growth in children can occur.

SUMMARY

Values are qualities or beliefs that are viewed as desirable or important. They are outcomes of socialization, and provide the framework in which we think, feel, and act. Children construct and redefine their values as they get older. Certain values are basic to all civilized societies; others are basic to a particular society; still others are personal.

Morals encompass an individual's evaluation of what is right and wrong. They involve acceptance of rules and govern one's behavior toward others. Morality involves feeling, reasoning, and behavior.

One's moral code develops through social interaction and reflects one's level of intellectual development, as well as one's attitudes. It involves awareness of alternatives, ability to take another's perspective, ability to make judgments, as well as feelings about conformity and autonomy.

As children develop, their morality changes. Infants and toddlers do not distinguish right from wrong. Preschoolers and school-agers consider only the act, not the intent. Adolescents consider intent as well as situation. Piaget's developmental theory (heteronomous and autonomous morality) is discussed, as is Kohlberg's (preconventional, conventional, postconventional morality) and Gilligan's (morality of care versus morality of justice). In general, at the lower moral development levels, people act out of concern for personal consequences; at the middle levels, people act out of concern for what others think; at the higher levels, they act to avoid self-condemnation.

Influences on moral development are age, intelligence, social factors, situational contexts, temperament, self-control, and self-esteem. Also, parenting methods such as reasoning and modeling, peer experiences in social interaction and role taking, opportunities to democratically make rules, school group discussions on moral dilemmas, media portrayals of moral behavior, and community factors such as ideology, are influential.

Cultural ideology influencing moral development involves the degree of pluralism in a society. According to Bronfenbrenner and Garbarino, individuals who are exposed to many socializing agents are more likely to achieve a higher level of moral reasoning than those exposed to few socializing agents. Whether the culture stresses individualism or collectivism is also influential in internal or external moral orientations.

An individual's moral development is socially constructed and represents his or her scheme of personal and societal values that include a coordination of emotions, thoughts, and actions.

An attitude is a tendency to respond positively or negatively to certain persons, objects, or situations. Attitudes are composed of beliefs, feelings, and action tendencies. Attitudes guide behavior.

The development of attitudes is influenced by age, cognitive development, and social experiences. Parents and peers have a large impact on children's attitudes through instruction, modeling, reinforcement, and punishment.

The media, the community, and the school have the potential to change prejudicial and stereotypical attitudes.

A motive causes a person to act. Individuals are motivated to develop skills that help them understand and control their environment, whether or not they receive external enforcement. This motivation is exhibited in the need to achieve and the feeling of being in control of the outcomes of one's actions. When one is no longer motivated to master one's environment, overcome obstacles in solving problems, or do one's best, one is said to have learned helplessness.

The development of achievement motivation has been linked most often to parenting styles. In general, the child-rearing environment of children who show high achievement motivation includes warmth, developmentally appropriate timing of achievement demands, high confidence in child's abilities, a supportive affective family environment, and highly motivated role models.

Achievement is also related to one's expectancy for success and one's fear of failure as well as one's history of success and failure.

Locus of control relates to one's sense of personal responsibility. Individuals who believe they are in control of their world have an internal locus of control. Individuals who perceive that others or events have more control over them than they have over themselves have an external locus of control. Attribution factors include luck and powerful others (*external*) and ability and effort (*internal*).

Those who have an internal locus of control generally are more competent and effective than those with an external locus of control. Locus of control is related to age, gender, socioeconomic status, and performance attributes and outcomes.

When people are placed in situations where outcomes are unaffected by their behaviors, they become passive and unmotivated. They have learned helplessness. Learned helplessness is influenced by experience and interaction with others, such as the kind of feedback one gets for performing a task.

ACTIVITY

A. Purpose: To gain insight into personal values.

1. The eighteen values listed ("What values are important to you?") in the box titled "What Values Are Important to You?" are in alphabetical order. Select the value that is most important to you and write a *1* next to it in column I. Then choose your next most important value and write a *2* beside it in the same column. Continue until you have ranked all eighteen values in column I.

2. Now rank the eighteen values as you believe your parents, your spouse, or a very close friend would have ranked them. Put these numbers in column II.

What Values Are Important to You?

	I	II	III
A COMFORTABLE LIFE a prosperous life			
EQUALITY brotherhood, equal opportunity for all			
AN EXCITING LIFE a stimulating, active life			
FAMILY SECURITY taking care of loved ones			
FREEDOM independence, free choice			
HAPPINESS contentedness			
INNER HARMONY freedom from inner conflict			
MATURE LOVE sexual and spiritual intimacy			
NATIONAL SECURITY protection from attack			
PLEASURE an enjoyable, leisurely life			
SALVATION saved, eternal life			
SELF-RESPECT self-esteem			
A SENSE OF ACCOMPLISHMENT lasting contribution			
SOCIAL RECOGNITION respect, admiration			
TRUE FRIENDSHIP close companionship			
WISDOM a mature understanding of life			
A WORLD AT PEACE free of war and conflict			
A WORLD OF BEAUTY beauty of nature and the arts			

Source: *Copyright 1967, 1982 by Milton Rokeach. Permission to reprint Halgren Tests, 873 Persimmon Avenue, Sunnyvale, California 94087.*

3. Finally, rank the eighteen values as you believe a person with whom you have not been able to get along would have ranked them. Put these numbers in column III.

4. Compare the rankings of the values in the three columns. How do your values compare to those of the person you are close to? How do they compare to the person who is your adversary? Compare your rankings with others'. What is your relationship with them? Is there any correlation between similarity in values and closeness of relationship?

5. What values are important to you? Since values and morals involve making choices, do the forced choice exercise.

Instructions: Write your top 10 values from the list in any order. If you had to choose between #1 and #2, which would you choose. Circle your choice. #1 and #3? #1 and #4? and so on. If you had to choose between #2 and #3, which would you choose? #2 and #4, and so on. Continue making forced choices until you've completed (#9 or #10) the list. Now rank your values in order.

Forced Choice Exercise

1. _____

2. _____

3. _____

4. _____

5. _____

6. _____

7. _____

8. _____

9. _____

10. _____

```
1 1 1 1 1 1 1 1 1
2 3 4 5 6 7 8 9 10
  2 2 2 2 2 2 2 2
  3 4 5 6 7 8 9 10
    3 3 3 3 3 3 3
    4 5 6 7 8 9 10
      4 4 4 4 4 4
      5 6 7 8 9 10
        5 5 5 5 5
        6 7 8 9 10
          6 6 6 6
          7 8 9 10
            7 7 7
            8 9 10
              8 8
              9 10
                9
                10
```

B. Purpose: To discover to what extent you are guided by inner principles of right and wrong or by external constraints.

If you had at your command a genie who could grant you any wish without personal consequences, what would you request? Would your wishes benefit or harm others?

RESOURCES

American Civil Liberties Union
http://www.aclu.org/

Ethics Updates
http://ethics.acusd.edu/index.html

Institute for the Academic Advancement of Youth
http://www.jhu.edu/

RELATED READINGS

Aboud, F. (1988). *Children and prejudice.* Cambridge, MA: Basil Blackwell.

Bandura, A. (1994). *Self-efficacy: The exercise of control.* New York: Freeman.

Bok, S. (1989). *Lying: Moral choice in public and private life.* New York: Vintage.

Damon, W. (1988). *The moral child: Nurturing children's natural moral growth.* New York: Free Press.

Dinkmeyer, D., & McKay, G. (1973). *Raising a responsible child.* New York: Fireside.

Dunn, J. (1988). *The beginnings of social understanding.* Cambridge, MA: Harvard University Press.

Ekman, P. (1989). *Why kids lie: How parents can encourage truthfulness.* New York: Penguin.

Gilligan, C. (1982). *In a different voice: Psychological theory and women's development.* Cambridge, MA: Harvard University Press.

Lawrence-Lightfoot, S. (1999). *Respect: An exploration.* Boulder, CO: Perseus.

Lewis, H. (1990). *A question of values.* San Francisco: Harper & Row.

Lickona, T. (Ed.). (1976). *Moral development and behavior.* New York: Holt, Rinehart and Winston.

McClelland, D. C. (1961). *The achieving society.* New York: Van Nostrand.

McInerney, P. K., & Rainbolt, G. W. (1994). *Ethics.* New York: HarperCollins.

Piaget, J. (1965). *The moral judgment of the child.* (M. Gabain, Trans.). New York: Free Press.

Schulman, M., & Mekler, E. (1985). *Bringing up a moral child: A new approach for teaching your child to be kind, just, and responsible.* Reading, MA: Addison-Wesley.

Seligman, M. E. P. (1975). *Helplessness.* San Francisco: Freeman.

Seligman, M. E. P. (1990). *Learned optimism.* New York: Pocket Books.

Simon, S. B., Howe, L., & Kirschenbaum, H. (1972). *Values clarification: A practical handbook of strategies for teachers and students.* New York: Hart.

"All the world's a stage,
And all the men and women merely players:
They have their exits and their entrances;
And one man in his time plays many parts."

— William Shakespeare

EXPLICIT SOCIALIZATION OUTCOMES

Prologue

IDENTITY VERSUS IMAGE

Entering the teen years is a developmental milestone in establishing a self-concept. As was discussed in Chapter 2, according to Erik Erikson (1963), the developmental crisis is identity versus identity diffusion, or role confusion. Successful resolution of earlier crises (trust, autonomy, initiative, industry) is in turn influenced by significant socialization agents regarding attachment, self-control, motivation, and achievement. Anne Frank: The Diary of a Young Girl (originally published in 1947) exemplifies successful resolution of identity crisis. It is the story of a Jewish teenager who died during World War II at Bergen-Belsen, Germany in 1945.

Born in 1929, Anne received a blank diary for her thirteenth birthday. Soon afterward, when the Nazis occupied Amsterdam and began rounding up Jews to put in concentration camps, Anne, her family, and another family went into hiding in the "secret annex" of an old office building. Cut off from the outside world, Anne's vividly recorded impressions in her diary for two years record the claustrophobic, quarrelsome intimacy with her parents, sister, and the other family.

The diary is unique in that it describes the details of life during the war (constant fear of discovery; death, hunger, confinement, and boredom), yet universal in that it discusses typical adolescent emotions (Everyone criticizes me; No one knows "the real me"; Will I ever be loved?).

Anne represents the achievement of an identity even though, because of the circumstances of war, she was "at risk" for many of the psychological disorders plaguing today's teens (depression, anxiety, substance abuse, self-mutilation, eating disorders, and/or suicide). What enabled her to be resistant to such negative developmental outcomes?

Mary Pipher, a psychologist, observing various disorders in adolescent girls documented her findings about identity development in her book, Reviving Ophelia: Saving the Selves of Adolescent Girls (1994). The title was inspired by the character of Ophelia in William Shakespeare's play, "Hamlet." Ophelia loses her sense of self when she falls in love with Hamlet. Rather than have a direction in life, she does everything for the approval of her father and Hamlet. So torn apart by her efforts to please both, she commits suicide by drowning.

In Reviving Ophelia, Pipher describes the adolescent girls she sees in therapy because they have succumbed to the risk of identity diffusion and are confused.

> Girls become fragmented, their selves split into mysterious contradictions. They are sensitive and tenderhearted, mean and competitive, superficial and idealistic. They are confident in the morning and overwhelmed with anxiety by nightfall. . . . They try on new roles every week—this week the good student, next week the delinquent, and the next, the artist (Pipher, 1994, p. 20).

They are full of contradictions, elusive, and slow to trust adults. "Adolescent girls experience a conflict between their autonomous selves and their need to be feminine, between their status as human beings and their vocation as females" (pp. 21–22). In other words, they are confused in trying to achieve self-actualization while assuming their perceived cultural role as females.

According to William Pollack (1999), author of Real Boys: Rescuing Our Sons from the Myths of Boyhood, not only is Ophelia at risk for negative developmental problems, so is Hamlet. Hamlet hides *his feelings—he puts aside his love for Ophelia while pretending to be insane in order to avenge his uncle who has taken over the throne after killing his father. But Hamlet cannot bring himself to act on his anger. Meanwhile, Ophelia's brother, spurred by the king (Hamlet's uncle), challenges Hamlet to a duel and plans to use a poisoned sword. After both he and Hamlet get stabbed during the duel, Hamlet finally owns up to his feelings and actions ("This above all: To thine ownself be true . . .") killing the king before dying himself.*

Hamlet's pretense and vacillation to act represent the conflicts facing today's adolescent boys. According to Pollack, boys are at risk for violence, substance abuse, depression, or suicide. Pollack attributes this to "The Boy Code" (the pretense that everything is fine). The Boy Code dictates conformity to the cultural stereotype of the "real" male as silent, unemotional, tough, and independent. Society teaches that it is unacceptable for males to be fearful, uncertain, lonely, or in need of comfort or help. Pollack says that boys are encouraged to separate emotionally from their parents—particularly their mothers—too early and are shamed into hiding their fears and sorrows. The shaming process ("Don't be a wimp") is perpetuated unconsciously by parents, peers, teachers, coaches, and media stars and serves to enforce the code.

Why are today's adolescents at risk for identity diffusion, as described by Pipher and Pollack? How do they differ from the adolescents of the past? Is it that adults were more involved and protective of children then? Anne Frank's short life was experienced in a very close family and community. She lived and breathed their values. Today's children are exposed to a world of values via media that may conflict with those of family and religion. Parents are not always accessible to mediate all that the child is exposed to; parents may be working, divorced, and living their own lives. So then who are the children going to model? What messages do they get from society to develop a self-concept? Media messages and peers focus on image (the outer shell rather than the inner core—girls are supposed to be beautiful, sexy, charming, cooperative, submissive; boys are supposed to be strong, brave, competitive, independent, dominant. Apparently, these stereotypical gender roles are not adaptive—Ophelia and Hamlet both died.

- *How can the microsystems in society provide children with coping skills to be resilient to various risks?*
- *How can the microsystems in society cooperate to foster socialization outcomes that enable children to become self-confident, self-actualized, productive adults?*

SELF-CONTROL

Self-control refers to the ability to regulate one's impulses, behavior, and/or emotions until an appropriate time, place, or object is available for expression. As was discussed in Chapter 2, it is one of the aims of socialization.

Self-control begins to be observed in children at about age 2 (Berk, 1997) and increases with age (Logue, 1995). To behave appropriately, children have to have the cognitive maturity to understand they are separate, autonomous beings with the ability to control their own actions. They also have to have the language development to understand directives, the memory capabilities to store and retrieve a caregiver's instructions, and the information-processing strategies to apply them to the particular situation. In addition, children need to have some concept of the future, which expands as they get older ("If I don't tease my brother, Mommy said she would take me skating").

According to Vygotsky (1978), children cannot control their behavior until they incorporate into their own speech adult standards expressed in communication. This occurs when children transform adult standards (sanctions on behavior, stereotypical roles, and/or ideals for perfection), referred to as "social speech," into private, or "inner speech," to direct their own behavior.

Self-control includes the ability to delay gratification (waiting for an appropriate time to behave or achieve a desired result), instead of engaging in impulsive behavior (acting without much thought to consequences). The development of such ability is partially dependent upon the parenting practices and the child's temperament (Berk, 1997).

Temperament (*easy, slow to warm up, difficult*), as was discussed in Chapter 4, consists of genetically based characteristics that determine an individual's sensitivity to various experiences and responsiveness to patterns of social interaction. *"Easy"* children are more likely to comply with adult standards than those who are "slow to warm up" or "difficult" because, physiologically, they are more "relaxed." "Slow to warm up" children may need time, reasoning, repetition, and patience to comply. "Difficult" children need even more of the same because they are more "tense" and, therefore, resistant to change.

Parenting practices influence the development of self-control in that the motive for children to internalize adult standards, as was discussed in Chapter 2, is attachment. Children are willing to comply to parental demands because they want to please the individuals who love them; they try not to displease because they fear loss of that love. According to Damon (1988), this is the foundation for respect for authority and social order in society. *Authoritative* parenting practices in which there is extensive verbal give and take, reasoning, and nonpunitive adult control influence the development of self-control.

Self-control is a continuous process, an outcome of affective, cognitive, and social forces. In the beginning, the child responds emotionally to situations instinctively. These biological reactions are responded to accordingly by adults and redefined through social experience. Through continuous instruction, observation, participation, feedback, and interpretation, various levels of self-control are established (Damon, 1988).

Because emotional regulation, including the ability to control anger and exhibit empathy, is part of self-control, explored here is how these emotions are translated into antisocial behavior, *aggression,* and prosocial behavior, *altruism.*

Antisocial behavior includes any behavior that harms other people, such as aggression, violence, and crime. **Prosocial behavior** includes any behavior that benefits other people, such as altruism, sharing, and cooperation.

How do children learn behavior that is pro- rather than antisocial? While antisocial behavior—*aggression*—has been studied for many years, it is only relatively recently that attention has been given to prosocial behavior—*altruism.* **Aggression** includes an unprovoked attack, fight, or quarrel. **Altruism** encompasses voluntary actions that help or benefit another person or group of people without the actor's anticipation of external rewards. Such actions often entail some cost, self-sacrifice, or risk on the part of the actor (Eisenberg & Fabes, 1998.)

Figure 12.1   An Ecological Model of Human Development

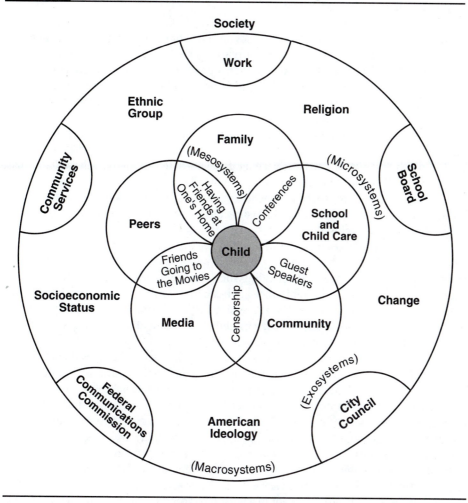

The child's antisocial or prosocial behavior, gender role, and self-esteem are outcomes of his or her socialization.

ANTISOCIAL BEHAVIOR: AGGRESSION

The development of antisocial behavior is examined here to better understand how socialization contributes to aggression and how it can then be prevented. Aggression in childhood often forecasts later maladaptive outcomes, such as delinquency and criminality (Coie & Dodge, 1998; Farrington, 1991).

Development of Aggressive Behavior: Theories

Some theories explaining the causes of aggression fall into the following general categories: (1) it is biologically influenced; (2) it is learned; (3) it is an information-processing impulsive response to frustration; (4) it is a result of social cognitive factors such as peer group pressure or the reduction of restraining socialization forces; and (5) it is socialized by interacting factors.

Biological Theories. Biological influences on behavior include *evolution* and *genetics.* Evolution encompasses passing on the survival and adaptive characteristics from one generation to the next; genetics refers to individual characteristics that are passed on.

Sigmund Freud (Freud, 1925; Hall, 1954) believed humans are born with two opposing biological instincts: a life instinct (Eros), which causes the person to grow and survive, and a death instinct (Thanatos), which works toward the individual's self-destruction. According to him, the death instinct is often redirected outward against the external world in the form of aggression toward others. Freud believed that the energy for the death instinct is constantly generated and if it cannot be released in small amounts in socially acceptable ways, it will eventually be released in an extreme and socially unacceptable form, such as violence against others or violence against the self. Thus, if the aggressive instinct can be redirected (crying, punching a doll, hammering nails), then it can be defused.

Konrad Lorenz (1966) held that the aggressive instinct is what has made the major contribution to the evolution and survival of animals. Such vital functions as protecting one's territory against invasion, defending the young, and engaging in fights to eliminate the weak so they will not reproduce are basic to the survival of the species. According to Lorenz, the expression of the aggressive instinct in most humans, especially in middle-class Western societies, has been inhibited; consequently, the drive will build up until it can be expressed, even if it is vicious.

However, the problem with Freud's and Lorenz's theories is that they do not explain the differences in levels of aggressiveness within a society and in various situations.

There is some evidence supporting a genetic basis for antisocial behavior. Behavioral tendencies that might be influenced genetically include impulse control, frustration tolerance, and activity level (Segal, 1997). There is a stability of aggressive and antisocial behavior over the life course (Coie & Dodge, 1998). To exemplify, in a large-scale study of adopted persons, it was found that deviant, criminal behavior was more common in those individuals whose biological parent was a criminal, regardless of the environment in the adoptive family (Mednick, Moffit, Gabrielli, & Hutchings, 1986). For another example, the level of certain hormones present in a person has been shown to be related to aggressive behavior (Olweus, 1986). In addition, males are more aggressive than females, not only physically but also verbally (Eley, Lichtenstein, & Stevenson, 1999; Maccoby & Jacklin, 1974, 1980).

In analyzing the research of the relationship of biological factors to aggressive behavior, Coie and Dodge (1998) conclude that aggression occurs indirectly through the interaction of biological processes and environmental events.

Learning Theories. According to Albert Bandura (1973, 1991), children learn through a series of experiences when it is appropriate to act aggressively, what forms of aggression are permissible, and to whom they can express aggression without disapproval or punishment. For example, children cannot hit mothers when they take a toy away because severe socialization consequences ensue. However, children can hit peers when they take a toy away without experiencing such consequences.

Children identify with role models and imitate behavior. The role models can be peers. For example, a child who has been attending school for a while may come home and display some new behavior never displayed before (such as biting when angry). The role models can be parents. For example, parents sometimes respond to aggressive acts by spanking. Punishing aggression with aggression is providing model behavior for the child to imitate.

The role models can also be other adults. In one classic study by Bandura, Ross, and Ross (1963), a group of preschool children watched a film of woman hitting a Bobo doll (a 5-foot, plastic inflated clown), while another group of children watched a model play with Tinkertoys. After watching the models, the children were left alone with a number of toys, including a Bobo doll and Tinkertoys, and were observed. The children who had watched the aggressive behavior on film acted more aggressively with the Bobo doll in the laboratory situation than did the other children. They punched, kicked, and hammered the doll. They even made the same aggressive comments the adult had.

Whether or not models will be imitated depends on their perceived status. Children have been found to imitate high-status dominant models (Bandura, 1989). Characteristics of the observer can also influence the incidence of imitation, such as motivation, ability to remember what is observed, and ability to perform the observed act (Bandura, 1989).

Whether or not aggressive acts will be imitated by the observer also depends on whether the aggressive model was rewarded or punished. In one experiment (Bandura, 1977), children were exposed to one of three conditions: they viewed a successful, aggressive model on film who was enjoying a victory, they viewed an aggressive model on film who was severely punished by the intended victim, or they did not see any film (this condition was provided as an experimental control). The children who saw the aggressive model rewarded for aggressive behavior exhibited more aggression on subsequent observation than the children who either saw the model punished or saw no model.

The explanation behind these results is that the consequences of the model's behavior may have served as cues to the kind of behavior that is permissible in a given social context. Responses that are rewarded tend to occur more frequently, because behavior that results in successful outcomes is likely to be repeated (Bandura, 1973, 1991). For example, if a child pushes another in order to get to the swing first and the other child acquiesces (does not resist or retaliate), it is likely that the aggressor will repeat the aggressive act the next time he or she pursues an activity that is being blocked by someone.

Responses that are rewarded intermittently resist extinction, or elimination. In other words, responses that are not rewarded every time they occur, but only sometimes, are very difficult to "unlearn." Aggressive acts are highly likely to be rewarded intermittently. For instance, they may be allowed to occur successfully by some children and not by others, and they may be punished by adults when noticed, which may not be every single occurrence.

That aggression can be learned through observation of an aggressive model causes attention to be turned to the content of television shows and their potential impact on children. As has been discussed, a number of studies (Comstock & Paik, 1991; Huston & Wright, 1998; Pearl, 1982) report that both children and adults are exposed to a lot of television violence. Many feel that watching a lot of aggression on television increases the tendency of the viewers, especially children, to behave aggressively. By watching, children may learn that aggression is acceptable, and may even learn aggressive techniques. Those who believe that the aggressive instinct is present in all humans believe that watching aggression is a catharsis or a way of releasing pent-up aggressive feelings.

This antisocial behavior, aggression, was probably learned by observation and modeling.

If one believes this, then one believes that watching aggression on television reduces potential aggressive behavior. Some believe that televised aggression has little effect on aggressive behavior, compared to direct rewards and models for aggression provided by parents, teachers, and friends.

Several factors have been found to moderate the effects of viewing television violence on aggressive behavior (Coie & Dodge, 1998). They include the child's repertoire of alternative behaviors, whether the child believes the violence on TV is real; whether the child identifies with the TV character; whether the parent watches and discusses the show with the child; and whether the aggressive acts viewed were punished, justified, or rewarded (the aggressor gets something or wins). An alternative behavior might be verbalization. Children who know how to verbalize their frustration ("I don't like it when you take my things"), as opposed to children who do not (when something is taken, the child just grabs it back, giving the transgressor a punch), are less likely to imitate aggressive behavior. Children who, due to cognitive immaturity, believe that what they see on TV is real, are more likely to imitate aggression, especially if they identify with the aggressor or if the aggressor is rewarded. Children whose parents mediate TV viewing are less likely to imitate aggression.

There is much documentation on the relationship between parenting practices and childhood aggression (Coie & Dodge, 1998; Kim, Hetherington, & Reiss, 1999; Patterson, 1982; Rubin, Stewart, & Chen, 1995). Coercive, hostile parenting is related to children's aggression. Thus, if parents want to discourage aggressive behavior in their children, they must not model it (spanking is aggressive behavior). They must also not reward it (let it succeed or go unnoticed). And they must teach alternative acceptable behaviors, such as talking about one's feelings.

Information-Processing Theories. *Information-processing* refers to the way an individual interprets situations or events. One who behaves impulsively acts without thinking ahead of the consequences. One who is frustrated views interfering factors preventing achieving a motive. Some believe impulsivity is a genetic temperamental trait that affects behavior (Buss & Plomin, 1975; Coie & Dodge, 1998; Kagan, 1994). For example, some researchers have found a link between low impulsivity and self-control (Kochanska, DeVet, Goldman, Murray, & Putnam, 1994). Thus, aggressive behavior can be a response to frustrating experiences, especially in impulsive individuals (Staub, 1986). An example would be "road rage," where people get involved in verbal or physical fights—or even shoot one another—when cut off in traffic. The strength of the frustrated motive, the degree of interference, and the number of motives blocked determine the intensity of the aggression exhibited (Grusec & Lytton, 1988). If a frustrated motive (for example, not getting a turn to ride the tricycle) is interfered with (the teacher calls "clean-up time"), and the motives blocking it are numerous (the other children tease and take extra long turns before putting the tricycles away), then the intensity of the aggression is likely to be increased (pushing a child off the tricycle or yelling).

Others (Coie & Dodge, 1998; Dodge, 1986; Dodge & Frame, 1982) believe that one's reaction to frustration depends not so much on the social cues (what *actually* happens) as on how one processes the information (one's *interpretation* of what happens). Dodge (1986) assumes that children enter each social situation with a memory of past experiences and a goal (making friends, for example). When an event occurs, such as being bumped into, the child must interpret its meaning. A child's past experiences with social interaction as well as his or her skills in processing information will influence whether the event will be interpreted as "accidental" or "purposeful." Aggressive children tend to interpret ambiguous events as hostile, whereas nonaggressive children tend to interpret such events as benign. Dodge's explanation of how such social information is processed cognitively will be discussed in more detail later.

Social Cognitive Theories.   People are influenced by the attitudes, values, and behavior patterns of those around them, particularly significant others. Aggression can be a result of peer group pressure. Studies (Coie & Dodge, 1998; Wall, Power, & Arbona, 1993) have shown that violence is much higher in some groups than in others. For example, in some parts of Italy violence is the acceptable reaction to personal affronts. If one wants to be part of the groups that subscribe to this norm, one must act as expected. For another example, low-socioeconomic-status adolescents who recently immigrated from Mexico were more susceptible to antisocial peer pressure than those who had been in the United States for a longer time.

Peers are thought to supply the individual with the attitudes, motivations, and rationalizations to support antisocial behavior as well as providing opportunities to engage in specific delinquent acts (Coie & Dodge, 1998; Patterson, DeBaryshe, & Ramsey, 1989). A study of children from first to sixth grade found the classroom context to be influential in increasing or reducing aggressive behavior (Kellam, Ling, Merisca, Brown, & Ialongo, 1999). Aggressive first-graders in classrooms with aggressive peers showed an increase in aggressive behavior by sixth grade; whereas aggressive first-graders in classrooms using preventive intervention strategies showed a decrease in aggressive behavior by sixth grade. Whether or not individuals succumb to group pressure depends on their personalities, the situation, and also the number of reference groups to which they belong. If they belong to several groups that use aggression as an acceptable means for revenge, then the tendency to behave aggressively increases. On the other hand, if they belong to one group that subscribes to this norm but also to other groups that do not, the likelihood of conforming to the aggressive behavior of the one group decreases. Thus, if one's peer group sanctions aggression, one is more likely to exhibit aggressive behavior.

Some believe when restraining socialization forces are reduced aggression is more likely. Restraining socialization forces can be external pressures, such as fear of consequences (punishment, criticism, opinion of others), or internal pressures (guilt, shame, moral development level).

Anonymity tends to reduce the restraining forces of external pressures. In other words, when people are anonymous, they are more likely to be aggressive than when not. Anonymity can result when a person is unknown to others (disguised, hidden by darkness) or is "lost in the crowd" (part of a uniformed group, or is with too many people to be noticed). When people are anonymous, they cannot be identified by others and therefore cannot be evaluated, criticized, judged, or punished by them.

Experiments (Baron, 1970; Deax & Wrightsman, 1988) have shown that when individuals are made to feel anonymous, their levels of aggression increase in a laboratory situation. In a naturalistic study (Diener, Frasier, Beaman, Kelem, 1976), 1,300 children were unobtrusively observed trick-or-treating on Halloween. They were given the opportunity to steal candy and money. When the children were anonymous (identities hidden by costumes), more stealing of extra candy and money was observed than was noted when they had been previously asked to reveal their identities to the adult host.

"Sanctions for evil" (Sanford & Comstock, 1971) provided by the group may reduce internal restraining pressures such as guilt. For example, members of the group may feel that what they are doing is morally required (Duster, 1971). War exemplifies this: In war, loyalty to the group (the army, for instance) obliterates individuality. Soldiers are trained to do as they are ordered; the responsibility for decisions rests with their superiors, not them. Another example of sanctions for evil is the famous Milgram (1963) experiment, in which subjects were told to inflict electric shocks (even though shocks were not actually given) on other subjects when they gave a wrong answer. Some subjects refused immediately, and some subjects quit the experiment after they heard the other subjects scream, yet 65% of the subjects did inflict the maximum level of shock possible when told to do so.

The community usually provides the restraining socialization forces for aggression through its members, its laws, and its police. Community members are a restraining force when they disapprove of aggression by another community member. The restraining force is the opinion of the group: "What will the neighbors say if I beat up Fred?" Anonymity or alienation reduces the force of that disapproval: "Why should I care what the neighbors think? They don't know me, so they'll never know who beat up Fred."

The laws of the community spell out what behavior is unacceptable and must be punished. The restraining force of the laws depends on how stringently they are enforced.

The police provide protection for community members. Parents and children living in neighborhoods characterized by high crime rates perceive their environments as unsafe (Fick, Osofsky, & Lewis, 1997). Adaptive behavior can result in fear, social isolation, and/or desensitization to violence.

Interaction Theories.   In a review of the literature, Patterson, DeBaryshe, and Ramsey (1989) have synthesized the findings on aggression in the hypothesis that the route to chronic delinquency is marked by a reliable developmental sequence of experiences: the first experience is ineffective parenting (influenced by such variables as the way the parents were parented, socioeconomic status, ethnicity, neighborhood, education); the second is behavioral conduct disorders that lead to academic failure and peer rejection, which, in turn, lead to increased risk of involvement in a deviant peer group; and the third, occurring in early adolescence, is chronic delinquent behavior.

Thus antisocial behavior appears to be a developmental trait that begins early in life (observable by age 4 to 5) and often continues into adolescence and adulthood. The socialization for aggression is bidirectional and interactional in that it includes poor parenting skills, which affect child behavior, and child behavior, which affects not only parenting, but school performance and peer relationships as well (Snyder & Patterson, 1995). The unintentional coercive training might begin with a parental demand that the child go to bed. The child refuses and the parent yells. The child whines complaining about always being picked on. The parent gives in, hence reinforcing in the child a coercive method to get his or her way.

Patterson and his colleagues (1989) believe that prevention of antisocial behavior is feasible if young children who are both antisocial and unskilled in peer interactions can be identified, if they receive social skills training (as discussed in Chapter 8) as well as academic remediation, and if their parents receive parenting training.

How can children at risk for conduct disorders be identified? A study by Dodge, Petit, and Bates (1994) identified such risk factors as harsh parental discipline, lack of maternal warmth, exposure to aggressive adult models, maternal aggressive values, family life stressors, mother's lack of social support, peer group instability, and lack of cognitive stimulation. The children, who were from the lowest socioeconomic status, were followed from preschool to grade three. The significance of these predictors is that they often accompany socioeconomic stress found in low-socioeconomic status or poor families. Thus it is not low socioeconomic status or poverty per se that influences aggressive behavior, but the socialization mediators that often accompany such socioeconomic stress (Coie & Dodge, 1998; Huston, McLoyd, & Coll, 1994). Socialization mediators have become the accepted way of studying aggression, as will be discussed next.

Ways of Studying Aggression

Social–Cognitive Model: A social–cognitive model for studying aggression has been developed by researchers drawing on earlier studies. Basically, the social–cognitive model attempts to identify mediating responses within the individual, such as an internal moral code and an ability to interpret social cues or behavioral responses from others. It also describes how these mediating responses may be predictive in various situations of an individual's aggressive behavior (Coie & Dodge, 1998; Parke & Slaby, 1983).

The social–cognitive model assumes that the developing child makes social interpretations about which interactions with others constitute aggressive provocation and require retaliation. As was said earlier, according to Kenneth Dodge (1986), children come to a particular social situation with a database (their memory store) and receive social cues as input from the interaction. Children's behavioral response to those cues is a function of certain cognitive processes: decoding the input, interpreting it, searching for potential responses, making a decision, and making a response.

For example, a child who is hit on the back by a peer must decode that action by searching for cues relevant to the peer's intention (was it on purpose or an accident?) and then focus on those cues. The child must also interpret those cues. (If the hit was intentional, was the peer trying to be friendly or mean?) The child's past experiences (memory store) aid in the interpretation. (If the peer runs away, then the action was intentionally mean; if the peer follows the hit with a comment such as "Let's go," then the action was intentionally friendly.) Once a situation is interpreted, the child has to search for possible behavioral responses (hit back, ignore, verbalize displeasure, and so on). The next step is to decide which response to execute. In choosing a response, the child must first assess the probable consequences of each response he or she has generated. ("If I hit back, I may get hit again.") Finally, the child must act out the chosen behavioral response. If, however, the choice is made to respond verbally, the child must possess the necessary language skills to do so.

Dodge and his colleagues (1984) generally found that aggressive children were more likely to attribute hostile intentions to their peers than were nonaggressive children. This biased way of thinking, then, increased the likelihood that they would retaliate aggressively, with behavior they thought was justified (although their peers did not).

Other researchers (Perry, Perry, & Rasmussen, 1986) found that not only do aggressive children often interpret provocation by others erroneously as hostility, they also respond aggressively because they expect their aggressiveness to be successful in eliminating their aversive state or to otherwise improve their plight. This supports Bandura's (1977, 1986) social cognitive theory: reinforced behavior, even behavior thought to be potentially reinforcing, will be repeated. The reinforcement, in this case, is the reduction of hostile (or perceived hostile) treatment by others.

Ecological Model: The development of aggression must also be viewed in an ecological context. The complex variables operating in aggressive behavior involve the child (personality, cognitive level, social skills), the family (parenting, interaction), the school (attitudes on handling aggressive behavior), the peer group (modeling, norms, acceptance/rejection), the media (modeling), and the community (socioeconomic stressors, attitudes on handling aggressive behavior, availability of support systems) (Coie & Dodge, 1998; Parke, 1982). Table 12.1 provides a summary of variables contributing to antisocial behavior.

The usefulness of the ecological model can be seen in Robert's case:

> Robert, age 8, was referred to the principal's office for the third time in two weeks for fighting in the playground. No consequence provided by the teacher seemed to be effective. The principal asked Robert's parents to come to school for a conference. Robert was very angry. He kept saying, "The other kids always start." He thought to himself, "I'll get them. I'll bring my brother's knife."

In order for the principal to deal with Robert's aggressiveness, she needs to know that Robert comes from a home where physical punishment is the means for dealing with misbehavior. Likewise, Robert resorts to physical means when he perceives others treating him badly. She also needs to understand that in Robert's neighborhood, gang fights are the primary means of settling disagreements; Robert's older brother belongs to a gang. Finally, she needs to be aware that Robert has been taught it is "unmanly" not to fight back when you have been challenged.

Table 12.1	Summary of Variables Contributing to Antisocial Behavior

CHILD	FAMILY	SCHOOL	PEERS	MEDIA	COMMUNITY
Biological influences (evolution, genetics)	Parenting style (authoritarian, coercive)	Teaching style (authoritarian)	Peer group pressure	Modeling	Modeling
Gender	Interaction	Modeling	Situation	Reinforcement/ punishment of model	Acceptance of and/or sanctions for violence
Hormones	Modeling	Reinforcement/ punishment for behavior	Aggressive norms	Mediation by adults	Anonymity/ alienation Safety
	Reinforcement/ punishment for behavior	Expectations	Modeling		Socioeconomic stressors
Temperament (impulsivity, frustration tolerance, activity level)	Attitudes		Acceptance/ rejection		Availability of informal/ formal support systems
Ability to delay gratification					
Information-processing ability					
Internally/ externally oriented conscience (guilt vs. fear of punishment)					
Cognitive developmental maturity					
Social skills					
Moral reasoning/ judgment					

Once the principal becomes cognizant of Robert's ecological background, she will be better equipped to try an approach that might reduce his aggressive behavior in school. Robert might need some intensive individual attention from an adult whom he respects and will model. Referring him to a Big Brother's program might help. Robert also needs to learn social skills that will enable him to deal with ambiguous and/or confrontational situations without resorting to fighting. Robert needs help to discover an ability that other children might admire (art, music, drama, or athletics). If the principal can get Robert's parents to support the school's attempts to help their son, there is a better chance the intervention will succeed in changing Robert's antisocial behavior.

The importance of early intervention in antisocial behavior is that aggression can be self-perpetuating. In a review of studies on antisocial children, Patterson and his colleagues (Patterson, DeBaryshe, & Ramsey, 1989; Snyder & Patterson, 1995) conclude that coercive, or harsh, parenting contributes to the development of children's defiant, aggressive behaviors and hostile interpretations of others' behavior, which in turn can cause these children to be rejected by normal peers as well as to do poorly in school. Moreover, the rejection experienced by aggressive children in early childhood may contribute to their attraction to deviant peers in adolescence who devalue school and engage in antisocial or delinquent acts (Dishion, Patterson, Stoolmiller, & Skinner, 1991).

Suggestions for early intervention on inhibiting aggressiveness in young children are given in the box titled "What Can Parents and Teachers Do to Inhibit Aggressiveness in Young Children?" (Caldwell & Crary, 1981; Slaby, Roedell, Arezzo, & Hendrix, 1995).

PROSOCIAL BEHAVIOR: ALTRUISM

One of the aims of socialization, as stated earlier, is to teach developmental skills, which include getting along with others. To participate in a group, one must cooperate, share, and help others when needed. As we all know, some people exhibit more of these behaviors than others. What is it that motivates someone to rescue a total stranger from a fire, to send money to someone whose story has been told in the newspaper, or to volunteer to work in a senior citizen center?

Altruism refers to behavior that is kind, considerate, generous, and helpful to others. Like aggression, it shows some consistency over time. Altruistic behavior begins to appear during the preschool years (in some children, it appears by age 2). Children's ability to take the perspective of others increases during this time, so they are more aware that others' feelings may differ from theirs and are more capable of experiencing empathy (Eisenberg & Fabes, 1998). Marion Radke-Yarrow and Carolyn Zahn-Waxler (1986), for example, observed consistent patterns of sharing, helping, and comforting behaviors among 3- to 7-year-olds at play.

What Can Parents and Teachers Do to Inhibit Aggressiveness in Young Children?

1. Organize the environment to minimize conflicts. Minimize crowding. Have plenty of stimulating and engaging developmentally appropriate materials. Have enough so children can play together with similar materials (bicycles, paint, toys, and so on).

2. Set standards, stick to them, and provide consequences for noncompliance. Let children know aggression is not sanctioned: "You hit Bobby on the playground; you must sit on the bench now for ten minutes." "You did not control your temper today. Since you disappointed me, I will have to disappoint you; you cannot stay up late, as you had wanted, to watch that program on television."

3. Stop aggression immediately. If possible, try not to let it carry to a successful completion. For example, if you see two children struggling over a toy, take the toy and ask both children to tell you their versions of the incident. Then ask them how you should resolve it. If they don't come up with a solution, say, "Well, you both think about it, and meanwhile I'll hold the toy."

4. Give children alternative ways of solving problems. Teach them how to verbalize their feelings and how to listen to others.

5. Anticipate possible situations for aggressive behavior to occur in, such as children playing together roughly or children complaining they have nothing to do, and redirect the children into an activity that interests them.

6. Provide opportunities for cooperative activities. Enable children to learn to listen to each other's ideas, to solve problems democratically, to compromise, and to respect each other.

7. Foster helpfulness and cooperation: "Could you help Daniel with that tower he's building?" "Could you help your sister put on her shoes while I make your lunch?"

8. Be a positive role model. Don't punish aggression with aggression; use alternative disciplinary methods.

9. Discuss rules and the reasons for them. Also discuss violence that children may be exposed to in the media or in their communities. Let children talk about their fears and feelings. Help children develop strategies for feeling protected by adults: "When you are scared, you can tell me." "Policeman Wilson is our friend."

10. Reward prosocial behavior. Give children attention when they share, are helpful or cooperative, or solve problems by discussion; don't allow them to get your attention only by being aggressive.

Altruistic behaviors in children age 10-, 15-, and 20-months were examined over a nine-month period (Zahn-Waxler, Radke-Yarrow, Wagner, & Chapman, 1992; Zahn-Waxler & Radke-Yarrow, 1990). It was found that between 10 and 12 months of age, incidents of emotional distress brought no significant altruistic responses. Over the next six to eight months, however, concern (exhibited by facial expression or crying) and positive initiations (exhibited by patting or touching the other person) began to be exhibited in response to the distress of others. Such responses, concerns, and positive interactions became increasingly differentiated and frequent by 18 and 24 months. For example, by age 2, children may bring objects to a person in distress, make suggestions about what to do, verbalize sympathy, bring someone else to help, aggressively protect the victim, and/or attempt to evoke a change in the feelings of the distressed person.

Children age 2 may also avoid the encounter, cry, or even behave aggressively. Thus by age 2 there are many individual differences in the exhibition of prosocial behaviors that can be classified as altruistic.

Prosocial responses, such as cooperating, sharing, giving comfort, and offering to help, become increasingly apparent throughout childhood as children develop cognitively and have more social interactions (Eisenberg & Fabes, 1998). For example, toddlers, age 2–3, exhibit some sharing and demonstrations of sympathy. They often react to others' distress by becoming distressed themselves (Zahn-Waxler, Radke-Yarrow, Wagner, & Chapman, 1992). Preschoolers, age 3–6, begin to become less egocentric and exhibit altruistic acts if they also benefit the self ("I'll share so you'll be my friend"). School-agers, age 6–12, who can take the role of others better understand legitimate needs ("I'll help because he can't do it himself"). Adolescents, age 13 and over, understand prosocial behavior in terms of more abstract social responsibility and may feel guilty for not acting altruistically when it is needed ("I should participate in the jog-a-thon to raise money for children with cancer") (Eisenberg & Fabes, 1998).

Whether or not a child will behave prosocially may depend on the individuals involved, the specific situation and how the child interprets it. Preschoolers, school-agers, and adolescents assist an individual more if that person had helped them (Eisenberg & Fabes, 1998). For example, children's moods at the time of the incident affects the motivation to be helpful (Carlson, Charlin, & Miller, 1988). Also, children are more likely to help those close to them rather than those who are unfamiliar (Eisenberg & Fabes, 1998).

Development of Altruistic Behavior: Theories

Some theories explaining the causes of altruistic behavior are: (1) biological (evolution and genetics, (2) learning (reinforcement, modeling, and instruction), (3) social cognitive, (4) interactional, and (5) cultural.

Biological Theories.   Freud (1938) believed children are born with innate sexual and aggressive impulses directed at self-gratification, which he labeled the *id*. Their experiences with reality cause them to develop an *ego,* which helps them delay gratification. Out of fear of parental hostility or loss of parental love, they develop a *superego,* or conscience, to regulate their impulses and behave accordingly to internalized parental standards. They may behave prosocially due to guilt. Thus children's adoption of prosocial values results from identification with parents.

Sociobiologists believe that evolution and genes account for certain complex human social behaviors. Children are believed to be genetically programmed to be kind and considerate as part of human nature. Altruism is regarded as behavior that promotes the genetic fitness of another at the expense of one's own fitness. Since altruism benefits the group's survival, natural selection favors those members of the species who have this characteristic (even though the altruistic member may die in performing the altruistic act). For example, protecting others is considered to be altruistic behavior. In the animal kingdom, the bee that protects the members of its species by stinging an intruder dies. Even though one member of the species dies, it is the altruistic action that enables the other members to live and reproduce. In the human species, the relationship of biology to sociology is explained by Richard Nalley (1983, p. 5) as follows:

This child is exhibiting prosocial behavior, altruism, by helping his friend tie his shoe.

As early human beings bonded together in social groups, perhaps for the purpose of cooperative hunting, selection pressures began to build for those traits that allowed them to adapt to community life. Genes promoting flexibility and conformity, for example, were probably passed on. Aggression had to be harnessed, social structure improvised and forms of communication developed. This acted as a kind of positive feedback loop: better communication led to reduced aggression, and vice versa.

The group, led by a dominant male, benefited each individual and his self-interested genes by providing protection, a ready supply of eligible mates and the ability to surround and bring down larger animals. From these cooperative dealings, sociobiologists say, culture arose: art, ethics, courtship rituals, and the rest. Humans came to reflect a mosaic of traits, each adaptive and not necessarily inherent in their old primate nature.

Martin Hoffman (1981, 1988, 1991) gives evidence supporting the idea that empathy, the various experiencing of another's emotions, is part of human nature in that it is an inherited biological predisposition. Empathy along with the internalization of society's moral norms and values, is the motive for altruism. One study (Martin & Clark, 1982) found that newborns became distressed by the cries of other newborns, thus indicating that humans are designed from birth to respond to the distress of their peers. Twin children (14 months old) were found to react similarly to simulation of distress in others at home and in the laboratory settings (Zahn-Waxler, Robinson, & Emde, 1992). Other studies (Eisenberg & Fabes, 1998; Rushton, Fulker, Neal, Nias, & Eysenck, 1986) found that identical twins (who have identical genes) were more similar to each other on questionnaires designed to assess altruism, empathy, and nurturance than were fraternal twins, who share about half of their genes. Thus differences in genetic composition among people have a considerable influence on differences in their tendencies to behave both prosocially and antisocially.

Learning Theories.   Despite the current uncertainty about how and when altruism begins, it is known that altruism can be encouraged by being directly reinforced or rewarded for an altruistic act and by observing someone else engaging in the act (modeling) and getting reinforced (Eisenberg & Murphy, 1995). One investigator, for example, found that children age 4 were more likely to share marbles with other children if, after sharing, they were rewarded with bubble gum (Fischer, 1963). However, the effect of giving tangible rewards for prosocial behavior lasts only briefly. Social reinforcement, or praise, has been shown to increase altruism in children for longer periods. For example, after having been prompted to share and then praised for doing so, children were found to give more to others (Bar-Tal, Raviv, & Lesser, 1980; Gelfand, Hartman, Cromer, Smith, & Page, 1975).

Although concrete rewards may induce altruism in the given context, the long-term effect of concrete rewards may be negative because it undermines intrinsic motivation (Lepper, 1983). Social rewards (praise) may induce altruism in the given context, but not in other contexts (Eisenberg & Fabes, 1998). It has been shown repeatedly that observing a helpful model encourages observers to be helpful themselves (Bandura, 1986; Eisenberg & Murphy, 1995). This modeling effect is found whether the model is another child or an adult, and whether the model is live or on film.

For example, children age 10–11 who had observed an adult donating to a charity were more likely to donate than children who had not seen the altruistic model. When children observed the adult model keeping the money instead of donating it to charity, they also imitated that behavior (Harris, 1970). Media models, as shown on *Mister Rogers Neighborhood* or *Sesame Street,* who exhibit prosocial behavior are likely to be imitated by their viewers especially when an adult reinforces the show's message by discussion (Coates, Pusser, & Goodman, 1976; Huston & Wright, 1998; Roberts & Maccoby, 1985).

Modeling altruism has generalizable effects. It has been shown that children who are taught to act helpfully in one situation will also act helpfully in others (Elliot & Vasta, 1970; Radke-Yarrow & Zahn-Waxler, 1986). It has also been shown that after having observed an altruistic model, children were still acting generously four months later (Radke-Yarrow & Zahn-Waxler, 1986; Rice & Grusec, 1975).

The peer group reinforces prosocial behavior, especially when it is directed at peers. Parkhurst and Asher (1992) found that among 12–14-year-olds, children who were actively rejected by peers were high in antisocial behavior whereas children who were popular among peers were high in prosocial behavior.

Children learn from each other. They model behaviors of admired peers. For example, children who witness the charitable acts of an altruistic model are more likely to donate toys or money, even anonymously (Radke-Yarrow, Zahn-Waxler, & Chapman, 1983). Thus, if a child has a group of friends who consistently exhibit prosocial behavior, it is likely that child will exhibit it also (Eisenberg & Fabes, 1998). If parents know who their child's friends are, they can predict fairly well how their child will behave in various situations. As was seen in the discussion of aggression, those who belong to groups that condone aggressive behavior are likely to exhibit aggression. It can likewise be concluded that those who belong to groups that disapprove of aggressive behavior are less likely to exhibit it.

Peers exert pressure to behave in certain ways. The desire to maintain a friendship sometimes motivates a person to behave altruistically. For example, it was found that people are more willing to donate blood if they believe their peers support such an action (Foss, 1983).

Since a good altruistic example is so effective, what about just instructing children to be kind, considerate, and helpful? Generally, observing an adult sharing is more effective than just telling a child to share (Eisenberg & Murphy, 1995). However, one experiment (Rice & Grusec, 1975) found that if the child is initially undecided about whether or not to act altruistically, being told to help is as effective as actually observing the adult helping. But if the child is resistant about sharing, then being told to share is less effective than actual observation.

Teaching altruism can be as effective as modeling it, especially if the instructions are strongly stated and reasons are given for sharing (Grusec, Saas-Korlsaak, & Simutis, 1978).

The *school* can train children to be prosocial by using the technique of role playing (Eisenberg & Mussen, 1989). For example, Staub (1971) worked with pairs of kindergarten children, asking one child to act the part of someone who needed help (carrying something too heavy) and the other child to act the part of a helping person (to think of actions to help). The children were then asked to change roles. A week after training, helpfulness was tested by giving the children the chance to help a crying child in the next room and the chance to share candy with another child. The trained children were compared to those who had not received training. The children who had undergone the reciprocal role training were more likely to be helpful to another child than the children who had not received this training.

Schools can also assign the responsibility to children to teach others to be helpful or to share (Eisenberg & Murphy, 1995). For example, Staub (1970) explicitly assigned responsibility to kindergarten and first-grade children. When the children were told they were "in charge" by a departing adult, there was an increase in the probability, especially among the first-graders, that they would go to the aid of another child who was heard crying in the next room. As children get older, the assigned prosocial task is generalized to other situations (Peterson, 1983). For example, children (over age 7) who are induced to donate to needy others in one context are more likely to behave similarly in another context several days later (Eisenberg & Murphy, 1995).

Thus prosocial behavior can be increased in children by experience. One way is to provide role-playing opportunities for them. When children take the place of a child who needs help, they know what it feels like to be in need; when they take the place of the helper, they learn what to do to be of assistance. Another way is to assign responsibility for a prosocial behavior. The child, then, experiences what it is like to be helpful and gets adult and peer approval as well.

In sum, parents who instruct children in altruistic acts, practice, or model, what they teach, and verbally reinforce children's helpful acts will foster prosocial behavior (Deax & Wrightsman, 1988; Eisenberg & Murphy, 1995).

Social Cognitive Theories.　Numerous theorists have hypothesized that sociocognitive skills, particularly perspective-taking and moral reasoning foster prosocial behavior (Eisenberg & Fabes, 1998). When one can put oneself in another's place, one is more likely to empathize and give comfort and help.

Kohlberg (1976) believed prosocial behavior to be a component of moral reasoning, which is a function of cognitive development. Kohlberg emphasized the contributions of social interactions and cognitions regarding the ability to take others' perspectives and understand consequences of behavior. Whether an individual is self-oriented or other-oriented influences moral reasoning and consequent selfish or altruistic behavior. Emotions, such as sympathy and guilt, may also play a role in moral judgment and behavior (Eisenberg & Fabes, 1998).

Interactional Theories. The *family* influences prosocial behavior bidirectionally. A team of researchers (Zahn-Waxler, Radke-Yarrow, & King, 1979) studied young children's altruism by asking mothers of a group of 15-month-olds and mothers of a group of 20-month-olds for careful reports of incidents occurring during the children's daily lives. The mothers were trained as observers, and the study lasted for nine months. The mothers tape-recorded descriptions of every incident in which someone in the child's presence expressed painful feelings (anger, fear, sorrow, pain, and/or fatigue). The mothers also described events preceding and following the incident, as well as both the child's and their own reactions.

> Today Jerry was kind of cranky; he just started completely bawling and he wouldn't stop. John kept coming over and handing Jerry toys, trying to cheer him up, so to speak. He'd say things like, "Here, Jerry," and I said to John, "Jerry's sad; he doesn't feel good; he had a shot today." John would look at me with his eyebrows kind of wrinkled together like he really understood that Jerry was crying because he was unhappy, not that he was just being a crybaby. He went over and rubbed Jerry's arm and said, "Nice Jerry," and continued to give him toys (pp. 321–322).

When the researchers found that the number of altruistic reactions varied greatly from child to child, they examined the individual mother's responses. They found that the way the mothers reprimanded their children was clearly related to the children's degree of altruism. The following exemplifies the various responses.

- Moralizing—"Look, you made Susie cry; it's not nice to pull hair."
- Prohibition with explanation or statement of principle—"You must never poke anyone's eyes! He won't be able to see!"
- Withdrawal of love—physical withdrawal from child when he or she attempts to get love, or verbal withdrawal ("I can't hug you when you've been mean").
- Neutral—"Russell is crying because you hurt him."
- Prohibitions without explanation—"Don't ever do that!"
- Physical restraint.
- Physical punishment.

Related to a high proportion of observed altruistic behaviors in children was the mother's use of moralizing and prohibitions, with explanations or statements of principle, when antisocial behavior was exhibited. Unexplained verbal prohibitions and physical punishment were associated with low degrees of altruism. Neutral explanations had little effect either way.

What other socializing techniques are related to prosocial behavior in children? A warm, nurturant, affectionate relationship between children and parents, in contrast to a cold, indifferent, distant relationship, seems to contribute to the development of prosocial tendencies (Eisenberg & Murphy, 1995; Staub, 1975).

The manner of execution of parental control influences the development of prosocial behavior—reasonable versus excessive or arbitrary (Eisenberg & Fabes, 1998). *Control* refers to the setting of certain standards and rules by parents and their insistence on adherence to them when deemed necessary. There is strong evidence that the frequent use of physical punishment by parents results in children's aggression, hostility, and resistance (Aronfreed, 1968; Coie & Dodge, 1998; Eron, Walder, & Lefkowitz, 1971; Patterson, DeBaryshe, & Ramsey, 1989). On the other hand, nurturing persons who do not exert control seem to have no effect on prosocial behavior (Radke-Yarrow & Zahn-Waxler, 1986; Rosenhan & White, 1967; Weissbrod, 1976). Baumrind (1967, 1971a), as was discussed in Chapter 4, found that firm enforcement of rules, combined with reasoning and warmth (authoritative parenting), was associated with positive and effective social behavior. Thus, when parents are affectionate and have certain firm standards that they explain, the child is likely to display prosocial behavior.

Cultural Theories.   Anthropological and psychological studies in non–Western cultures show that societies vary greatly in the degree to which prosocial and cooperative behaviors are expected (Eisenberg & Fabes, 1998). How does the society one grows up in influence prosocial behavior? It has been documented that some societies provide more opportunities for learning to behave prosocially than do others, particularly by involving older children in the care of younger ones (Graves & Graves, 1983; Whiting & Edwards, 1988). It has also been argued that the value a society puts on interdependence, cooperation, and social harmony (collectivistic orientation) versus independence, competition, and individual achievement (individualistic orientation) influences children accordingly (Bronfenbrenner, 1970; Eisenberg & Fabes, 1998; Garbarino, 1992). For example, Hindu Indian culture emphasizes more duty-based social responsibility than American culture, which emphasizes moral justice-based social responsibility (Miller & Bersoff, 1993). In other words, Hindus are more likely to respond prosocially out of duty or obligation; whereas Americans are more likely to do so because "it's the right or fair thing to do."

Cultural variations in children's tendencies to cooperate or compete have been investigated in a classic study by Madsen and Shapira (1970), that used various games that can be played cooperatively or competitively. One of these games is diagrammed in Figure 12.2.

The gameboard is 18 square inches and has an eyelet at each corner. A string passes through each of the eyelets and is attached to a metal weight that serves as a holder for a ball-point pen. A sheet of paper is placed on the gameboard for each trial so that the movement of the pen as the children pull their strings is recorded automatically.

In the cooperative condition, every time the pen crosses all four circles, all the players are rewarded. Thus, the more the children work together, the more they all win. In the competitive condition, each player is rewarded only when the pen crosses his or her circle. In this condition, if the children take turns helping one another, each child can win as often as any other. Some children never figure this out, however, and end up pulling the pen in their own direction, so no one wins.

Figure 12.2   Cooperation Board Game

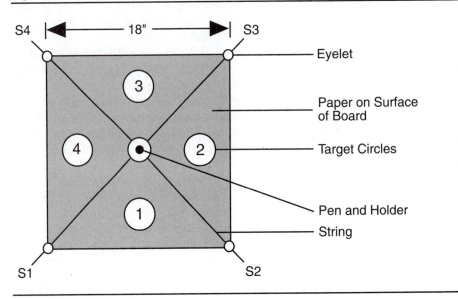

Source: M. C. Madsen & A. Shapira (1970). Cooperative and competitive behavior of urban Afro-American, Anglo-American, Mexican-American, and Mexican village children. *Developmental Psychology 3 (1),* p. 17. Copyright © 1970 by the American Psychological Association. Reprinted by permission of the publisher.

Children reared in traditional rural subcultures and small, semi-agricultural communal settlements cooperated more readily than children reared in modern urban subcultures. For example, schoolchildren in Mexican villages and small towns were found to be more cooperative than their urban middle-class Mexican, Mexican American, African American, or Anglo American peers (Madsen & Shapira, 1970). Similarly, Israeli children reared on a kibbutz and children from Arab villages were found to be more cooperative than Israeli urban children (Shapira & Lomranz, 1972; Shapira & Madsen, 1974).

In these studies, if cooperation with others on the various test situations was rewarded directly (group rewards to be shared by all), children from all cultures cooperated. If, however, only individual rewards were given for performance, cultural differences showed up. The Mexican village children and those from Israeli kibbutzim continued to cooperate with each other, even in an individual reward (competitive) situation. "Let's help each other." "Let's take turns." "Start here—go there—" were some comments. On the other hand, the urban African American, Anglo American, Mexican American, middle class, and Israeli children tended to compete ineffectively.

Apparently, children raised in traditional rural subcultures and small, semiagricultural communal settlements (collectivistic orientation) have been socialized to have *gemeinschaft* relationships (close personal ties, concern with community members' welfare, reciprocity, readiness to lend a helping hand); children raised in urban subcultures (individualistic orientation) have been socialized to have *gesellschaft* relationships (impersonal ties, competitiveness, obligations based on contracts, behavior for personal advantage). These two types of relationships were discussed in Chapter 10.

Cross-cultural comparisons by Beatrice and John Whiting (1973, 1975) illustrate in natural settings some of the laboratory findings. Working in small communities in Kenya, India, the Philippines, Okinawa, Mexico, and the United States, they observed children between the age of 3 and 6 and other children between the age of 6 and 10. The children were rated for exhibiting altruistic behavior spontaneously—offering help, which included feeding and assisting in carrying out a task; offering support, which included giving comfort and reassurance; and "suggest responsibility," which included making helpful suggestions. They were also rated for exhibiting egoistic behavior—seeking help, seeking attention, or dominating another.

The Whitings found that the cultural variable most closely associated with altruistic behavior was the extent to which children in the various cultures were given the responsibility to perform household tasks or chores related to the family's economic security. Most of the children in Kenyan, Mexican, and Philippine cultures were high above the median of the total sample in altruism; whereas most of the children in the other three cultures (Okinawan, Indian, and American) scored low in altruism. Presumably, in

. . . simpler kin-oriented societies, with economies based upon subsistence gardening, altruistic behavior is highly valued and individual egoistic achievement frowned upon. Women must work in the fields, and the children must help in order for the family to subsist. To offer help, to support others, and to be responsible are taught

Children from cultures that give them early responsibility in family functioning tend to exhibit spontaneous altruism.

both by precept and practice. Being helplessly dependent, showing off, boasting, and being egoistically dominant are incompatible with such a way of life.

On the other hand, in the more complex societies, where no child knows what he is going to be when he grows up, individual achievement and success must be positively valued. To help a friend sitting next to you in an examination is defined as cheating. To ask for help from specialists such as mechanics, dressmakers, shopkeepers, psychotherapists, priests, or servants is expected and paid for in cash rather than in reciprocal services (Whiting & Whiting, 1973, p. 64).

Thus, "children who . . . perform more domestic chores, help more with economic tasks and spend more time caring for their infant brothers, sisters, and cousins, score high on the altruistic versus egoistic dimension" (1973, p. 63).

Table 12.2 provides a summary of variables contributing to prosocial behavior.

Table 12.2 Summary of Variables Contributing to Prosocial Behavior

CHILD	FAMILY	SCHOOL	PEERS	MEDIA	COMMUNITY
Genetics	Parenting style (authoritative, warm)	Instruction/ set standards	Peer group pressure	Mediated discussion by adults	Simple social organization
Temperament	Communication of prosocial/antisocial instructions	Positive/ negative consequences	Learn by doing	Values cooperation	Traditional, rural
Age	Reinforcement/ punishment	Reinforcement/ punishment	Collaborative activities	Modeling	Extended family ties
Cognitive maturity	Modeling	Modeling	Modeling		Early assignment of tasks and responsibility to children
Perspective and role-taking ability	Assignment of responsibility	Assignment of responsibility			Individualistic/ collectivistic orientation
Empathy	Opportunities for role playing	Opportunities for role playing			Justice-based/ duty-based social responsibility
Moral reasoning/ judgment	Discussion	Discussion			
Situation					

How Can Prosocial Behavior Be Fostered in Young Children?

The school, as well as the family, can contribute to the socialization of prosocial behavior in children. The following are some suggestions for parents and teachers, based on research findings (Eisenberg & Murphy, 1995; Eisenberg & Mussen, 1989).

1. Be an example. Exhibit helping, cooperating, and sharing behavior.
2. Preach prosocial behavior, and give reasons. Take advantage of specific situations to instruct children how to share, how to be helpful, and how to cooperate.
3. Be warm and accepting.
4. Set firm standards of behavior that have consequences when not followed.
5. Provide role-playing opportunities for children, and discuss how one's actions may affect another's feelings.
6. Provide activities that require cooperation, such as group projects.
7. Suggest specific ways in which children can be cooperative and helpful.
8. Praise prosocial behavior.

GENDER ROLES

Do you remember the following English nursery rhyme (Gould & Gould, 1962)?

What are little boys made of?
    Frogs and snails
    And puppy dogs' tails
That's what little boys are made of.

What are little girls made of?
    Sugar and spice
    And all things nice
That's what little girls are made of.

This nursery rhyme, from the early 1800s, illustrates how children are socialized to acquire their appropriate gender roles. A **gender role**, or sex type, refers to the qualities an individual understands to characterize males and females in his or her culture. It is distinct from sex which refers to the biological aspects of being male or female.

DEVELOPMENT OF GENDER ROLES

Sex typing, or classification into gender roles based on biological sex, begins at birth (Maccoby, 1998; Ruble & Martin, 1998). The child is given what society considers to be a girl's name or a boy's name. (Woe to those whose names are ambiguous—they will have to cope with that for the rest of their lives. Jordan—is that a girl's name or a boy's name?) The child is then dressed according to that classification. Certain colors are generally worn by girls and certain ones by boys. Even though in the United States most children of both sexes wear shirts and pants, those worn by girls are decorated differently. And throughout childhood, the child is given certain toys to play with, also classified by sex. Girls' toys are generally related to nurturing or home activities (dolls, stuffed animals, dishes); boys' toys are generally related to action or work activities (cars, trucks, tools).

Theories of Gender-Role Development

There are four main theories explaining how children are socialized to assume gender roles.

1. *Psychoanalytic theory* deals with how one comes to *feel* like a male or female. According to Sigmund Freud (cited in Hall, 1954; Freud, 1925), children identify with the same-sex parent out of sexual love for the opposite-sex parent and fear of punishment from the same-sex parent for that love. In other words, a boy identifies with his father because he loves his mother (*Oedipus complex*) and is fearful that his father, who also loves his mother, will punish him for that love. A girl identifies with her mother because she loves her father (*Electra complex*) and is fearful that her mother, who also loves her father, will punish her for that love. In identifying with the same-sex parent, children unconsciously take on the characteristics of that parent. A boy becomes like his father so that his mother will love him as she loves his father; and a girl becomes like her mother so that her father will love her as he loves her mother. The process of gender identification occurs sometime between age 3 and 5, the phallic stage in Freud's sequence of personality development (where focus is on the genitals). After age 5 or 6, children enter Freud's latency stage, where they engage in normal play activities with same-sex peers and sexuality is dormant. At puberty, children enter Freud's genital stage, where they normally begin to be sexually attracted to the opposite gender.

2. *Social learning,* or *social cognitive, theory* deals with how one comes to *behave* as a male or female. According to theorists Walter Mischel (1970) and Albert Bandura (1989), children behave in what are considered to be gender-appropriate ways because they are reinforced or rewarded when they do so and punished when they do not by the various agents of socialization. Boys identify with male models (usually their fathers) because they are rewarded for doing so: "You are strong, just like your daddy." Girls identify with female models (usually their mothers) for the same reason: "You look pretty, just like your mommy." Children choose models with whom to identify on the basis of whether the model is perceived to be like themselves, is warm and affectionate, and has prestige in their eyes. When children identify with the same-sex parent, they incorporate that parent's behavior into their own.

3. *Cognitive developmental theory* deals with how one comes to *think* of oneself as a male or female. According to Lawrence Kohlberg (1966), the assumption of gender-role behavior is part of the child's total cognitive development. On the basis of their observations and interactions, children accommodate, or reconciliate, the differences

Stereotyped gender-role behavior is exemplified by these boys playing in the block corner and these girls playing in the housekeeping corner of a classroom.

between the categories of male and female. Once children know and understand the concepts of maleness and femaleness (about age 5 or 6), they then assimilate the appropriate gender behavior that matches their biological sex. In other words, a boy thinks, "I am a boy; therefore, I do boy things," and a girl thinks, "I am a girl; therefore, I do girl things." What children consider to be appropriate gender behavior depends on their experiences in their family, peer group, school, and community, and what they observe in the media.

4. *Gender schema theory* proposed by Sandra Bem (1981), as well as by Martin and Halverson (1981, 1987) deals with how one comes to *perceive* oneself as a male or female by processing gender-linked information. A *schema* is a conceptual framework of one's experiences and understandings. This theory explains how children code new information in terms of gender. The basis for coding information is first the recognition of males and females as distinct gender categories. Labeling occurs about age 2.5. As children develop, they observe male and female behavior around them. Consequently, they form a schema for what males do in their society as well as one for what females do. These gender schemata influence how new information gets processed in that they guide selective attention and imitation of same-sex models. For example, a girl observes her mother and her grandmother cooking. She also observes her father and other males doing repairs. About age 4–5 she can conceptualize that girls cook and boys fix things. Since she knows she is a girl, she chooses to engage in cooking activities rather than working with tools at preschool. Thus she gains information about cooking and rejects information about building or doing repairs. By age 7–8 gender behavior is fairly rigid. Gender schema

theory helps to explain why gender stereotypes are self-perpetuating and difficult to modify. It is as if one's earliest socialization experiences with gender set the path for later ones. This was demonstrated in a study with 5- to 10-year-olds who were asked to predict feminine or masculine interests of target children with certain characteristics. For example, "I know a child who likes to play with tool kits. How much would this child want to wear a dress?" Older children's responses were more gender stereotypic ("No way!") than those of younger children (Martin, Wood, & Little, 1990).

Gender schema theory also proposes that self-concept is associated with the degree to which children perceive themselves as congruent with their schemas of males or females. If their behavior matches what they interpret as appropriate to their gender, they feel positive about themselves; if they don't conform to the stereotype, they feel negative about themselves.

GENDER-ROLE RESEARCH

Regardless of which theory or theories one subscribes to as the explanation of gender-role socialization, the fact remains that males and females behave differently. This was documented in a classic review by Eleanor Maccoby and Carol Jacklin (1974), who made a comprehensive analysis of over 2,000 books and articles on possible psychological differences between males and females. They concluded that males are more aggressive than females, a difference that is apparent in infancy. They also concluded that girls have greater verbal ability than boys and that boys have greater visual–spatial ability than girls. These differences are more apparent in early adolescence. Maccoby and Jacklin discovered that some differences traditionally attributed to boys' and girls' behavior are myths. For example, girls are neither more "social" than boys, nor are they more suggestible. Boys do not have higher achievement motivation than girls, neither are they more "analytic." More recent reviews of research on gender differences have arrived at similar conclusions (Fagot, 1995; Ruble & Martin, 1998).

Maccoby and Jacklin's findings have implications for social and educational changes:

> We suggest that societies have the option of minimizing, rather than maximizing, sex differences through their socialization practices. . . . In our view, social institutions and social practices are not merely reflections of the biologically inevitable. A variety of social institutions are viable within the framework set by biology. It is up to human beings to select those that foster the lifestyles they most value (Maccoby & Jacklin, 1974, p. 374).

Additional research indicates that socialization practices maximize gender differences (Fagot, 1995; Ruble & Martin, 1998). For example, parents and significant others apply gender stereotypes to children as soon as they are born (or even in utero, if the sex is known). As a result, girls and boys are channeled into sex-typed behaviors that do not necessarily reflect the potential of their individual abilities (American Association of University Women [AAUW], 1991).

Jeanne Block (1984) reviewed the literature on psychological differences between the sexes in areas that included aggression, activity level, impulsivity, susceptibility to anxiety, achievement-related behaviors, self-concept, and social relationships. She

Girls usually play in small groups involving turn-taking.

concluded that differences in these areas arise from the different social contexts in which boys and girls grow up. In general, boys are given more opportunities for independent problem-solving and exploration, whereas girls are more closely supervised and restricted in their experiences. According to Block, such differential socialization causes boys and girls to think differently about the world around them and to use different strategies in dealing with the world. For example, boys are more curious and competitive; girls seek approval more often and are more affiliated.

By the time children reach preschool, they know which type of behavior is expected of their sex. Several years ago, a little boy in my preschool class who was pretending to iron in the housekeeping corner was told by his friend, "Daddies don't iron!" As children enter elementary school, their gender roles become more restrictive (Rubin & Martin, 1998). They play with children of the same sex, thus learning "gender-appropriate" games (the boys tend to play games involving running or throwing a ball at recess; the girls tend to stay close to the teacher, talking or playing games such as jump rope or hopscotch). Because of their cognitive development, they are also becoming more aware of potential models of their sex with whom to identify. These models will be examined to understand their influences on gender-role socialization.

INFLUENCES ON THE DEVELOPMENT OF GENDER ROLES

Influencing gender roles are family, peers, school, mass media, and the community. Each is examined in turn.

Family

Mothers and fathers treat sons and daughters differently (Fagot, 1995). Studies show that parents describe their newborn sons as stronger, more coordinated, and more alert than daughters; and their newborn daughters as smaller, softer, and more fragile than sons (Huston, 1983; Rubin, Provenzano, & Luria, 1974). Fathers, in particular, engage in more rough-and-tumble play with sons and more cuddly play with daughters (Lamb, 1977; Lytton & Romney, 1991). Parents buy different toys for their sons and daughters (O'Brien & Huston, 1985; Rheingold & Cook, 1975; Ruble & Martin, 1998). For example, males are given trucks, war toys, and sports equipment; girls are given dolls, dollhouses, and books. Mothers and fathers even communicate differently to sons and daughters, using more directive and supportive language with girls than with boys (Ruble & Martin, 1998).

Throughout childhood, parents encourage males in active, gross-motor, and manipulative play; females are encouraged in passive feminine role taking and fine-motor play, with fathers being more stereotypical than mothers (Huston, 1983). Males are also allowed to take risks (climb trees) and are left unsupervised more often and earlier than females (Basow, 1992; Huston, 1983). Finally, parents exert more achievement and independence demands on males while providing help more readily for females (Basow, 1992; Huston, 1983).

Through observed interactions of fathers and mothers with sons and daughters, it has repeatedly been demonstrated that fathers are the more influential gender-role socialization agent (Caldera, Huston, & O'Brien, 1989; Langlois & Downs, 1980; Ruble & Martin, 1998). For example, fathers' and mothers' reactions to preschool children's choice of toys were observed. Toys available were traditionally feminine (doll furniture, pots and pans) and masculine (cars, trucks, trains). Studies (Langlois & Downs, 1980; Lytton & Romney, 1991) found that fathers, more so than mothers, chose different kinds of toys for boys and girls and encouraged play that they considered gender-appropriate and discouraged play they considered gender-inappropriate. More specifically, the fathers rewarded their children by approving, helping, and joining in the play more often for play with gender-appropriate toys than for play with gender-inappropriate toys, and they discouraged play with gender-inappropriate toys more than play with gender-appropriate toys. Mothers encouraged both boys and girls to play with toys traditionally considered appropriate for girls. Mothers also tended to discourage both boys and girls from playing with "masculine" toys. The degree of differences in parental treatment of boys and girls may be influenced by age, socioeconomic status, and ethnicity (Fagot, 1995).

In addition, fathers engage in more physical play (tickling, chasing, playing ball) with both sons and daughters, whereas mothers spend more time in caretaking and nurturing activities (MacDonald & Parke, 1986). Apparently, this differential interaction with children enables mothers to become more, and fathers less, sensitive to individual needs of children (Lamb, 1986). Further, compared to mothers, fathers give more evaluative feedback of approval and disapproval (Fagot & Leinbach, 1987). Thus fathers generally appear to be the more playful, less sensitive, more critical parent in terms of gender-role socialization. Regarding relationships within the family, warm, positive father–son and mother–daughter relationships lead to the strongest gender-role identification (Huston, 1983). Sons model their father's behavior, and daughters model their mother's. In this regard, too, studies have found that the father has more influence on gender-role development of both boys and girls (Lamb, 1986).

When mothers are employed and fathers participate in child care, fathers' nontraditional activities influence their children's attitudes about gender-role stereotypes (Ruble & Martin, 1998). Although employed mothers still perform most child care and housekeeping chores, husbands of employed wives participate more than husbands of nonemployed wives (Hoffman, 1989). Thus children whose mothers are employed have less stereotypical role models than those whose fathers are "breadwinners" and mothers are "breadbakers" (Gardner & LeBrecque, 1986). They also receive more independent training, have generally higher career goals, and have somewhat higher achievement motivation. These results are particularly true for daughters (Basow, 1992). The most likely explanation is that the employed mother presents a positive role model for achievement, especially when she is satisfied with her job and gets support for household chores and child care.

Sibling sex constellation, sisters and brothers, and their birth order, influence children's gender-role socialization, especially in traditional families (McHale, Crouter, & Tucker, 1999). Not only do sisters and brothers model and reinforce gender-role behavior to their younger siblings, but the differential treatment due to their sex by their parents has an impact on younger children's gender schema.

In sum, individual differences in sex typing are influenced by paternal involvement, maternal work status, sex typing of parental roles within the home, and sibling sex constellation (Serbin, Powlishta, & Gulko, 1993).

Peers

Age mates, perhaps more so than parents, serve as influential gender-role socializing agents (Basow, 1992). Peers begin to exert influence during preschool and become increasingly important during elementary school and high school. For example, peers encouraged both boys and girls to play with gender-appropriate toys and actively punished (ridiculed and teased) play with toys considered appropriate for the opposite gender, especially among the boys (Fagot, 1977, 1984; Martin, 1989). Children and adolescents try to do what they perceive to be "cool" to gain acceptance and status among their peers. Preadolescent boys gain status on the basis of athletic ability and toughness, whereas girls' status relates to physical appearance and social skills (Basow & Rubin, 1999; Pollack, 1999; Ruble & Martin, 1998)

Sex segregation begins in the preschool years and intensifies during the school years. This can be observed in both boys and girls cross-culturally (Maccoby & Jacklin, 1987; Whiting & Edwards, 1988). Sex-segregated play groups value different behaviors for girls and boys (Maccoby, 1998). Girls tend to enjoy mutual play and use conflict mitigation strategies, whereas boys tend to play more roughly and use physical assertion to resolve conflicts.

One of the functions of the peer group, as discussed in Chapter 8, is to socialize children to learn appropriate sociocultural roles. Cognitively, since middle childhood is the age of concrete thought, it follows that children of this age have a rigid, rather than flexible, concept of gender roles. Since middle-years children are most susceptible to peer influence, it also follows that they will be likely to adopt via modeling, reinforcement, and punishment the gender roles expected by their peers. For example, boys will be socialized to be active, aggressive, and not to show emotion; girls will be socialized to be passive, dependent, and compassionate. Children whose activities are regarded as gender-appropriate by the peer group are rewarded by being included in the group. Children whose activities are regarded as gender-inappropriate by the peer group are either teased or left to play alone (Thorne, 1993). "Sissy" and "tomboy" are familiar jeers heard in childhood.

The result of sex segregation is that boys and girls tend to grow up in different peer environments—in other words, different subcultures (Maccoby, 1998; Maccoby & Jacklin, 1987). Sociologists Janet Lever (1978) and Barrie Thorne (1993), in separate studies, found significant differences in the play of boys' and girls' peer groups. Lever observed fifth-grade children, mostly Anglo and middle class, in three schools. She discovered that boys' play was more complex than girls' play on all of the following dimensions and criteria.

- Size of group—is it large or small?
- Role differentiation—do the players have the same role, as in checkers, or different roles, as in baseball?
- Player interdependence—does one player's move affect another's, as in chess or tennis, or not, as in darts or hopscotch?
- Explicitness of goals—is playing merely a cooperative venture with no winners or end point, as in "playing house," or is the purpose playing for a goal, scoring the most points, for example, or until a certain end point is reached—nine innings, for example?
- Number and specificity of rules—are there a few vague rules, as in tag, or many specific ones, as in baseball?
- Team formation—does the play require teams?

Lever (1978) observed that boys typically engaged in team sports with 10–25 players; girls typically played tag, jump rope, or hopscotch, usually involving two to six participants. Boys' play often involved multiple roles, whereas girls' play rarely involved role differentiation. (Girls commonly engaged in activities in which they all played the same role, as in skating, or two roles, as in jump rope—the jumper and the turner.) Boys' play involved more interdependence, which required decision making in regard to strategies. Girls' play tended to require less interdependence, but when it did, play was of a cooperative nature. Boys' games were found to have more elaborate rules—often, interpretations and discussions ensued. Finally, boys were involved in team play more often.

Thorne (1993), who observed kindergartners to sixth-graders, found that boys' play is generally characterized by larger groups, less proximity to adults, more public play, more fighting and physical contact, more dominance attempts, and the establishment of a hierarchical "pecking order." Girls' play generally is characterized by smaller, more intimate groups, closer proximity to adults, a strong convention of turn-taking, and more mutuality in play and conversation. Such patterns have been observed among African American children as well as Anglo (Coates, 1987).

The significance of peer group play is that it socializes individuals for adult roles in society, according to the particular skills that are reinforced. According to Lever (1978), boys' play reinforces the ability to deal with diverse actions simultaneously, coordinate actions in order to foster group cohesiveness and work for collective goals, engage in competition, cope with impersonal rules, and engage in strategic thinking. Girls' play, on the other hand, reinforces cooperation, spontaneity, imagination, flexibility, and empathy. What are socialization outcomes resulting from girls' participation in team sports? One study (Miller, Sabo, Farrell, Barnes, & Melnick, 1998) found that athletic participation influenced the status of girls and their relationships with boys. Specifically athletic participation was associated with lower frequency of heterosexual intercourse, fewer partners, and later onset.

School

> When I attended public school in the 1950s, there were two entrance doors, one marked "Girls" and one marked "Boys." At recess, the girls played jump rope, and the boys either ran around chasing and hitting each other or played ball. When the teacher blew the whistle, everyone lined up, the girls in one line, the boys in another; each line then entered the school building through the appropriate door. Why differentiate? We all knew which sex we were. Surprisingly, many school activities are still sex-segregated (Thorne, 1993).

Schools provide a number of gender-related messages to children, some intentional and some unintentional (Ruble & Martin, 1998). Schools have traditionally treated males and females differently—through portrayals of gender roles in textbooks, through different course requirements (for example, boys took shop and girls took home economics), through treatment by teachers and counselors, and even subtly, through the uneven sex distribution on the staff.

> Men hold a disproportionate number of positions in higher administration, whereas women are more often teachers particularly in the "early" grades. Only in older grades are children likely to have many male teachers, and these are often in classes such as mathematics and science (Ruble & Martin, 1998, p. 979).

The passage of federal legislation (Title IX Education Amendment) in 1972 outlawed discrimination on the basis of sex. As a result, textbooks are reviewed for sexual bias, courses are open to males and females, and teachers and counselors must channel students into higher educational programs or occupations on the basis of individual competencies rather than what was traditionally acceptable for the sexes.

One of the effects of Title IX has been the increased participation of girls in sports. In a longitudinal study of sports participation in a sample of public and private American high schools (Women's Sports Foundation, 1989), it was found that both boys and girls who participated in sports had better images of themselves. They were healthier, more energetic, and had more self-confidence. After high school, they were more likely to be involved in community groups. This was true of African Americans, Anglos, and Hispanic Americans.

Despite Title IX and the greater awareness of how children develop gender-role attitudes, it will be a while before teachers and school personnel can change any unconscious habitual behavior that interferes with children developing to their full potential. An example of such unconscious behavior is the finding that teachers respond differently to boys and girls. Lisa Serbin and her colleagues (Serbin, Powlishta, & Gulko, 1993; Serbin, 1973) found that teachers tend to respond negatively to the aggressive behavior of boys and positively to the proximity-seeking behavior of girls. Research in preschools (Fagot, 1984) confirmed that more teacher attention was given to boys for achievement-related behaviors and to girls for compliance.

Other studies (Sadker, Sadker, & Klein, 1991) revealed some differences in how elementary and high school teachers view male and female students. "Good" male students were described by the teachers as active, adventurous, aggressive, assertive, curious, energetic, enterprising, frank, independent, and inventive. "Good" female students were described as appreciative, calm, conscientious, considerate, cooperative, mannerly, poised, sensitive, dependable, efficient, mature, obliging, and thorough. Such attitudes may influence the way teachers interact with students and may even influence the way the students view their own gender roles. These stereotypical attitudes are similar to those found in Rosenthal and Jacobson's (1968) research on the effect of teachers' expectations on the achievement and behavior of their students (discussed in Chapter 6).

Sadker and Sadker (1986, 1994) report that from elementary to graduate school, boys are given more teacher attention and encouragement to learn. If a girl gave an incorrect answer when asked, the teacher called on someone else. If a boy gave an incorrect response, he was prompted to discover the right answer, then praised. When a girl gave a correct answer when asked, it was accepted with an OK. If a girl called out a correct answer without being asked, she was likely to be reprimanded for talking out of turn; if a boy did the same, his answer was likely to be accepted. Thus teachers tend to socialize boys to be active, assertive learners; and girls to be quiet, passive learners. Also, boys were more likely to be encouraged to take math and science classes, thereby becoming advantaged in competing for higher paying jobs; girls were more likely to be encouraged to take business classes, thereby becoming limited in their career options (AAUW, 1991).

Mass Media

The mass media affect gender-role development. Television and movies portray distinct male and female roles; so do books, magazines, and newspapers. For example, not only do males appear with greater frequency on TV than do females, they are also portrayed in a greater variety of occupations than are females and have higher-status jobs (Basow, 1992; Huston & Wright, 1998). To illustrate, most of the lawyers, ministers, store owners, and doctors on television are men; women are usually secretaries, nurses, entertainers, teachers, and journalists (Signorielli, 1989, 1993). However, women are shown as experts in ads for food products, laundry soap, and beauty aids (Basow, 1992).

In interactions between men and women on television, the men are ordinarily more dominant. Women are more passive and less involved in problem-solving. For men, the emphasis is on strength, performance, and skill; for women, it is on attractiveness and desirability. That television has the potential for influencing gender-role stereotyping was illustrated by several investigations (Condry, 1989) in which boys and girls were interviewed to determine how often they watched certain television programs and how they felt about males and females having certain occupational roles. Those who frequently watched programs in which women were portrayed in nontraditional female roles more often reported that they felt it was appropriate for women to have such occupations than did those who did not watch such programs very often.

Television has recently become more sensitive to how males and females are portrayed. For example, in a few of the programs that have appeared since the 1980s, women have difficult and daring jobs (Huston & Wright, 1998). However, according to Susan Isaacs (1999), author of *Brave Dames and Wimpettes: What Women Are Really Doing on Page and Screen,* too many "heroines" today are being portrayed as weak or ineffectual because they give in to the stereotypes imposed on them by their gender. For example, in *Thelma and Louise* (1991) the women were dominated and oppressed by their men. They fought back weakly rather than bravely—they were overemotional and ineffectual, going on a shooting spree for revenge and killing themselves rather than face the consequences. Unlike, "Wimpettes," "brave dames" take responsibility and don't give up; they stand up to injustice and meet challenges. Examples are Gail in *The River Wild* (1994) and Marge in *Fargo* (1996). Gail is a mother who takes her family on a rafting trip that turns dangerous—they encounter rough water and evil men along the way. She meets both the physical and moral challenges. Marge is police chief in the town of Fargo. Though very pregnant, she does her job with dignity, respect, and a sense of humor.

While TV and movies have some influence, children's prior attitudes about gender roles influence the impact of what they attend to. Children with highly stereotyped attitudes focus on traditional role portrayals, whereas children with more flexible attitudes attend equally well to both traditional and nontraditional role portrayals (List, Collins, & Westby, 1983; Signorielli, 1993).

That television impacts gender attitudes was demonstrated in Canada where television was introduced into several towns that had previously been unable to receive TV signals. Children in one town (Notel) had less traditional gender attitudes prior to TV introduction than children from a comparable town with access to multiple TV channels. After two years of television exposure, the children from Notel showed sharp increases in traditional gender attitudes (Kimball, 1986).

Gender-role stereotypes also appear in the print media. A research study by sociologist Janet Chafetz (1974) examined the Christmas toy catalogs of the two largest mail-order companies in the United States. Both of the catalogs had boys' and girls' sections. The boys' section featured athletic items and athletic hero dolls, building and technological toys (tractors, spaceships, cars), and war toys. The girls' section featured dolls, household items (dishes, appliances), and beauty aids. In my informal review of mail catalogs for toys from stores, I find this still generally holds true.

Studies of the Caldecott Medal picture books for preschool children, one from 1979 to 1982 (Collins, Ingoldsby, & Dellman, 1984) and another from 1989 to 1992 (Dellman-Jenkins, Florjancic, & Swadener, 1993), show an improvement in the representation of females as active, central characters. Males still dominate the world of picture books, however, and are generally presented in more independent, varied, and exciting roles, using productive items; whereas females are generally presented in more dependent, helping, and pleasing roles, using household objects (Turner-Bowker, 1996).

Stereotypes about men's and women's behavior are visible in rock music videos (Hansen & Hansen, 1988). Males are depicted as sexually aggressive, rational, demanding, and adventuresome. Females are portrayed as emotional, deceitful, illogical, frivolous, dependent, and passive. Rock music videos also show violence against women and women as sex objects (Basow, 1992; Huston & Wright, 1998).

Most of the action-packed interactive media software is male-dominated and attractive to boys. One study (Dietz, 1998) found nearly 80% of video games included aggression

This adolescent boy exhibits nonstereotyped gender-role behavior by reading to a group of preschool children.

or violence as part of the strategy or object. In 28% of the games, women were portrayed as sex objects. Females are in stereotypical dependent roles and often are portrayed as sexual objects (Provenzo, 1991). Thus children learn much from the media about what is culturally expected of males and females.

Community

The community influences gender-role development through its attitudes regarding what is appropriate behavior for males and females and the gender-role models it provides with whom children can identify. The community's attitudes on gender roles affect what behaviors it reinforces and punishes in children. Comments like "That's unladylike" or "Go and stick up for yourself like a man" make a big impression on children.

Sometimes community attitudes are expressed by the language used to describe males and females. Are females described by their appearance and men by their actions? Are occupational roles gender-free ("mail carrier," "salesperson")?

If the community has stereotypical attitudes—that women are nurturant and men are problem solvers, for example—the assignment of occupations to one or the other gender will be affected. One study (Arvey & Chapman, 1982) found that when identical applicants were compared, women received higher ratings for jobs as grocery clerks or telephone operators; whereas men were rated more favorably for auto or hardware clerk positions. Today, women still dominate occupations that involve service, nurturing, or teaching; men dominate such occupations as engineering, architecture, law, and medicine, which all involve problem-solving (U.S. Bureau of the Census, 1998). Such attitudes, together with the social visibility of men and women in their jobs, affect children's perceptions of and expectations for themselves. The U.S. government has enforced equal opportunity laws thereby opening up previously restricted fields to women; now, perhaps gender stereotypes in the world of work will gradually diminish.

Ethnicity influences children's perceptions and expectations for their gender, as does religion. For example, Asian females are expected to marry, carry on domestic duties, and bear children even if they work (Sue, 1989). Mexican American women are traditionally subordinant to men. However, as women increasingly become employed outside the home, they will have more equality in family decisions (Espin, 1993). Religious orientation was found to play an influential role in career choices of high school seniors in that those attending religious schools indicated a greater preference for traditional gender occupations than those attending public schools (Rich & Golan, 1992).

Not all communities differentiate male and female roles the way Americans do. Anthropologists Beatrice Whiting and Carolyn Edwards (1988) studied the interaction patterns of 2- to 10-year-olds in 12 communities around the world to clarify how children were socialized for their respective gender roles. Although they found that in most of the investigated societies boys were dominant and aggressive, and girls were dependent, compliant, and nurturant, there were cross-cultural differences in the tasks assigned to each gender. For example, in Nyansongo, an agricultural community in Kenya, as in many other East African communities, boys are categorized with girls and women until they reach puberty. Then the pubescent males are assigned "masculine" activities that, when accomplished, become part of the initiation rites into "manhood." Until that time, however, boys participate in caring for their younger siblings and help with domestic chores as needed. Girls, then, have some free time to play during those times when the boys assume their chores. Nyansongo men spend much of the day away from their families. Consequently, fathers have little impact on their children's development. Compared to children from other cultures, Nyansongo children display less stereotypical gender roles.

In the United States there are cultural variations in the gender-role expectations and gender stereotypes of individuals from diverse racial, ethnic, socioeconomic, and sexual orientations (Basow & Rubin, 1999). For example, in a study of sex-typing and gender-role attitudes it was found that African American women, compared to Anglo American women, were twice as likely to describe themselves as androgynous—having both active–instrumental and nurturant–expressive traits (Binion, 1996). Hispanic American women were found to be more submissive and dependent than Anglo American women in another study (Vasquez-Nutall, Romero-Garcia, & DeLeon, 1987). Similar findings held true for Asian American women (Uba, 1994).

In conclusion, to the extent that a child grows up in a restrictive gendered world with strong pressures toward conformity, that child will likely place importance on behaving accordingly. In contrast, to the extent that a child grows up in a flexible gendered world emphasizing individual choice, that child is less likely to conform to stereotypical gender behavior (Eccles & Bryan, 1994).

> ## How to Determine the Type of Gender Role Models Provided by the Community
>
> 1. In general, do mothers in the community stay home to raise their families, or are they employed outside the home?
> 2. In what activities do most fathers in the community engage?
> 3. Do children have an opportunity to observe people in their occupations?
> 4. Do men and women who have various occupations come to school and talk to the children?
> 5. Who occupies the positions of leadership in the community (government, church, service organizations, political organizations)?
> 6. In what kinds of activities do boys and girls participate in the community outside of school?

SELF-ESTEEM

In the beginning of this book, the socialized self was discussed in terms of a "looking glass," or mirrored self and a "generalized other." The book then dealt with the socializing influences on the self and specific outcomes of the socialization process. Now at the end of the book how the self is evaluated is examined.

DEFINITION OF SELF-ESTEEM

One's **self-concept** refers to one's idea of one's identity as distinct from others. **Self-esteem** refers to the value one places on that identity (Harter, 1998). Thus self-esteem can be described as high or low. One's *self-concept* emerges from the understanding of oneself as a being separate from others; one's *self-esteem* emerges from one's interactions with others. Some view self-esteem as a global perception of the self, whereas others view it as multidimensional consisting of: (1) scholastic competence, (2) athletic competence, (3) social competence, (4) physical appearance, and (5) behavioral conduct in addition to global self-worth (Harter, 1998). Occasionally, the terms "positive" or "negative self-concept" are used to describe self-esteem.

To exemplify these opposites are the following descriptions of Alice and Zelda. Alice displays the characteristics of *competent* children (discussed in Chapter 4) (Baumrind, 1967; White, 1975) in regard to parenting styles. She uses adults as resources after first determining that a job is too difficult. She is capable of expressing affection and mild annoyance to peers as well as adults. She can lead and follow peers. She can compete with peers and shows pride in personal accomplishments. She is able to communicate well. She has the ability to anticipate consequences, can deal with abstractions, and can understand other points of view. She can plan and carry out complicated activities. Finally, she is aware of others, even while working on her own projects. Zelda, on the other hand, displays the characteristics of *incompetent* children; she is deficient in the competencies discussed above.

Alice is in kindergarten this year. You notice her immediately because she is so enthusiastic. She is almost always the first to raise her hand when the teacher asks a question. Sometimes she just calls out excitedly, "I know, I know." She doesn't always know, however. Sometimes she makes mistakes and answers incorrectly. When that happens, she shrugs her shoulders and giggles along with her classmates. She approaches her assignments with equal enthusiasm. When one approach fails, she tries another. If her persistence doesn't work, she asks the teacher for help. The other children like her. She is often the leader of the group, but also doesn't seem to mind following. At home she is responsible for dressing herself and keeping her room tidy. She is proud she can tie her shoelaces and make her bed.

Zelda is in first grade this year. Her progress last year in kindergarten was below average. This year it's no better. Zelda's IQ is similar to Alice's, yet Zelda answers most questions with "I don't know." She never raises her hand or volunteers information. She approaches her assignments unenthusiastically and gives up at the first sign of difficulty. She never asks for help, and when the teacher approaches her, she says, "I can't do it." Zelda has few friends and rarely participates in group activities. At home, Zelda is more talkative. She has no responsibilities, and her mother still helps her to dress. She waits for others to do things for her because she "can't" do them for herself (Chance, 1982, p. 52).

Alice and Zelda, even though alike in natural intelligence, are as far apart as A and Z in competence. Alice likes herself and feels comfortable in her environment. She takes control of her actions and takes responsibility for them. In other words, she decides what she is going to do, does it, and takes pride in doing it. If she makes a mistake, she owns up to it and tries again. Zelda, on the other hand, is full of self-doubt. She thinks her environment is harsh and unfriendly. She feels helpless in controlling what happens to her, so she does not even try. Alice has high self-esteem. She has a sense of trust, autonomy, and initiative. Zelda has low self-esteem. She has a sense of mistrust, self-doubt, and inferiority. Each represents opposite poles in Erikson's (1963) psychosocial stages of development, discussed in Chapter 2. Why have these two young children developed such differing levels of self-esteem?

DEVELOPMENT OF SELF-ESTEEM

As children grow, they accumulate a personal complex set of evaluations about themselves. They know how they look; they know what they are good at doing and what they are poor at doing. They also know what they would like to look like ("I hope I grow taller than my dad") and what they would like to be doing ("I'm going to be a dancer when I grow up"). As children grow, they begin to understand how they are viewed by others. During the process of socialization, people internalize the values and attitudes expressed by their significant others and, as a result, express them as their own. This holds true for values and attitudes about oneself as well as about other people, objects, and experiences. Thus individuals come to respond to themselves in a way consistent with the way others have responded to them, thereby developing a concept of self. Self-esteem, or one's evaluation of one's self-concept, emerges from the success or failure at meeting one's internalized values and attitudes. As was pointed out, George Mead (1934) viewed self-esteem as being derived from the reflected appraisal of others. Simplistically, according to Mead, if one has been treated with concern and approval, one will have high self-esteem; if one has been rejected and criticized, one will have low self-esteem.

Alice and Zelda's differing levels of self-esteem have emerged as a result of cumulative experiences in their young lives with other people, places, and things.

Stanley Coopersmith (1967) has, in a classic extensive investigation, concluded that the following factors contribute to the development of self-esteem: "First and foremost is the amount of respectful, accepting, and concerned treatment that an individual receives from the significant others" (p. 37). Alice has a lot; Zelda has little. Second is the "history of successes and the status and position" an individual holds in the world. Alice has had many successes and is popular; Zelda has had few successes and few friends. Third, there is the individual's "manner of responding to devaluation." Alice is able to minimize or discount the teasing of others. Zelda is sensitive to others' judgments. She takes them as confirmation of her self-image of helplessness. Recent research concurs with Coopersmith's (1967) conclusions (Harter, 1998).

According to Dorothy Corkille Briggs (1975), author of *Your Child's Self-esteem,* "children value themselves to the degree that they have been valued (p. 14) . . . words are less important than the judgments that accompany them (p. 19) . . . and a positive identity hinges on positive life experiences" (p. 20). The differences in the experiences Alice and Zelda had growing up, illustrates how self-esteem can be enhanced through messages of acceptance and understanding, as well as by providing opportunities for mastery in order to develop feelings of competence.

When Alice was an infant, her mother most likely responded warmly and affectionately to her needs. When she fed Alice, her attention would be focused totally on her. After feeding, Alice's mother cuddled her and talked to her before putting her to bed. Zelda's mother probably was a bit cold and indifferent. She would use Zelda's feeding as a chance to catch up on her reading (she fed Zelda from a bottle). After feeding, Zelda's mother would bathe her and make sure her crib was immaculate, before putting her to bed.

By age 2, Alice was securely attached to her mother. She could be left with a babysitter without too much fuss, yet she was very happy when her mother returned. Zelda, at age 2, was insecurely attached. She would cling to her mother, screaming, when the babysitter came, yet when her mother returned, Zelda would ignore her.

When Alice entered school, she made friends easily. Her eager smile seemed to welcome other children. Even when she put her sweater on inside out and a few children laughed, she just laughed with them. When Zelda entered school, she approached no one. The only friends she made were the two children who sat on either side of her at her table. When Zelda had trouble using her scissors, she just gave up.

Coopersmith's classic study involved studying hundreds of fifth- and sixth-grade Anglo, middle-class, normal boys. He tested the level of self-esteem via an inventory, a sample of which is shown below (1967, pp. 265–266).

	Like me	Unlike me
I'm pretty sure of myself.	_____	_____
I often wish I were someone else.	_____	_____
I never worry about anything.	_____	_____
There are lots of things about myself I'd change if I could.	_____	_____
I can make up my mind without too much trouble.	_____	_____
I'm doing the best work that I can.	_____	_____
I give in very easily.	_____	_____
My parents expect too much of me.	_____	_____
Kids usually follow my ideas.	_____	_____

Coopersmith found the self-esteem of the children he tested to be relatively constant, even after retesting them three years later. He also asked their teachers to rate them on such behaviors as reactions to failure, self-confidence in new situations, sociability with peers, and need for encouragement and reassurance. He then classified the children on the basis of their scores on the Self-esteem Inventory and by teachers' ratings.

The children were further assessed through clinical tests and observations of their behavior in a variety of situations. For example, they were tested to determine how readily they would yield to group influence in a situation when their own judgment was actually superior. The children were also given tasks that were either very difficult or very easy in order to determine whether their interest in working on a task was sharpened or weakened by success or failure. They were tested for creativity and asked how they usually behaved in real-life situations that called for assertiveness. Finally, their classmates were asked to choose the other children in the class whom they would like to have for friends, and a record was kept of how often each child was chosen.

On the basis of this extensive study, Coopersmith concluded that there are "significant differences in the experiential worlds and social behaviors of persons who differ in self-esteem."

Persons high in their own estimation approach tasks and persons with the expectation that they will be well received and successful. They have confidence in their perceptions and judgments and believe that they can bring their efforts to a favorable resolution. Their favorable self-attitudes lead them to accept their own opinions and place credence and trust in their reactions and conclusions. This permits them to follow their own judgments when there is a difference of opinion and also permits them to consider novel ideas. The trust in self that accompanies feelings of worthiness is likely to provide the conviction that one is correct and the courage to express those convictions. The attitudes and expectations that lead the individual with high self-esteem to greater social independence and creativity also lead him to more assertive and vigorous social actions. They are more likely to be participants than listeners in group discussions, they report less difficulty in forming friendships, and they will express opinions even when they know these opinions may meet with a hostile reception. Among the factors that underlie and contribute to the actions are their lack of preoccupation with personal problems. Lack of self-consciousness permits them to present their ideas in a full and forthright fashion; lack of self-preoccupation permits them to consider and examine external issues.

The picture of the individual with low self-esteem that emerges from these results is markedly different. These persons lack trust in themselves and are apprehensive about expressing unpopular or unusual ideas. They do not wish to expose themselves, anger others, or perform deeds that would attract attention. They are likely to live in the shadows of a social group, listening rather than participating, and preferring the solitude of withdrawal above the interchange of participation. Among the factors that contribute to the withdrawal of those low in self-esteem are their marked self-consciousness and preoccupation with inner problems. This great awareness of themselves distracts them from attending to other persons and issues and is likely to result in a morbid preoccupation with their difficulties. The effect is to limit their social intercourse and thus decrease the possibilities of friendly and supportive relationships (Coopersmith, 1967, pp. 70–71).

(Reproduced by special permission of the publisher, Consulting Psychologists Press, Inc., Palo Alto, CA 94306.)

Coopersmith concluded that there are four criteria upon which self-esteem develops: significance (the way one perceives he or she is loved and cared about by significant others), competence (the way one performs tasks one considers important), virtue (how well one attains moral and ethical standards), and power (the extent to which one has control or influence over one's life and that of others).

Whereas Coopersmith measured overall self-esteem, Susan Harter (1990, 1998) measured the five specific areas of competence listed earlier, as well as general feelings of self-worth ("I am happy with myself") in *The Self-Perception Profile for Children*. Harter found that self-esteem is well established by middle childhood. Children can make global judgments of their worth as well as distinguish their competencies. For example, a child may perceive himself or herself as a poor athlete but good scholastically. Finally, children's perceptions of themselves accurately reflected how others perceived them. Thus, Cooley's term, "looking-glass self," and Mead's term, "generalized other," described in Chapter 2 have found their way into contemporary conceptions of the self.

INFLUENCES ON THE DEVELOPMENT OF SELF-ESTEEM

The significant socializing agents that influence the development of self-esteem are family, school, peers, media, and community. Each is discussed in turn.

Family

"There is a growing body of empirical evidence revealing that parental approval is particularly critical in determining the self-esteem of children, supporting the looking-glass self formulation" (Harter, 1998, p. 583).

Coopersmith (1967) investigated children's treatment by significant others, those whose attitudes matter most when children are forming their self-concepts. He did this by examining the parenting practices employed by his subjects' fathers and mothers. He administered a questionnaire to the mothers that required responses agreeing or disagreeing with statements having to do with parenting attitudes and practices. He

The self-esteem these boys feel is influenced by success in their performance.

also interviewed the mothers and the children. Coopersmith focused on acceptance of the child and affection exhibited, the kind and amount of punishment used, the level of achievement demands placed on the child, the strictness and consistency with which rules were enforced, the extent to which the child was allowed to participate in family decision making, the extent to which the child was listened to and consulted when rules were being set and enforced, and the extent to which the child was allowed independence. Interestingly, reviewing the many studies over the past 25 years that examined the relationship between parenting and child and adolescent outcomes, Holmbeck, Paikoff, and Brooks-Gunn (1995) conclude that those children exposed to authoritative parenting, the type described here by Coopersmith, are rated as more competent and higher in self-esteem, moral development, impulse control, and independence feelings than children from other types of parenting environments.

Coopersmith found some clear relationships between the parenting practices and self-esteem of sons. Parents of boys with high self-esteem were more often characterized as follows.

- *Warm* (accepting and affectionate). They frequently showed affection to their children, took an interest in their affairs, and became acquainted with their friends.

- *Strict,* but used noncoercive discipline. They enforced rules carefully and consistently. They believed it was important for children to meet high standards. They were firm and decisive in telling the child what he might or might not do. They disciplined their children by withdrawing privileges and by isolation. They tended to discuss the reasons behind the discipline with the children.

- *Democratic.* They allowed the children to participate in making family plans. The children were permitted to express their own opinions, even if it involved questioning the parents' point of view.

Diana Baumrind (1967) found similar results in the relationship between parenting styles and competent children. The children who were happy, self-reliant, and able to directly meet challenging situations had parents who exercised a good deal of control over their children and demanded responsible, independent behavior from them. These parents also explained, listened, and provided emotional support. Baumrind's (1991) later research investigating the relationship between authoritarian, authoritative, and permissive parenting styles and the behavior of children approaching adolescence, supported her original findings (1971b, 1973, 1977), as discussed in Chapter 4. Studies of competent adolescents found similar connections (Steinberg, 1993).

Why are parental warmth, strictness, and democracy associated with high self-esteem in children? If we view self-esteem in terms of Cooley's (1964) "looking-glass self," then parents become the child's first mirror, so to speak. If parents are affectionate and accepting, then children will look upon themselves as worthy of affection and acceptance.

According to various investigators (Baumrind, 1971b; Coopersmith, 1967; Holmbeck, Paikoff, & Brooks-Gunn, 1995), parental strictness helps the child develop firm inner controls. When parents give children a clear idea of how to behave, they are providing cues to maximize successful interaction and minimize conflict. Providing standards helps children judge their competence. When children experience a predictable, ordered social environment, it is easier for them to feel in control. Parental strictness combined with warmth demonstrates proof of parental concern for the child's welfare.

Democracy leads to confidence in the ability to express opinions and assert oneself. The opportunity to participate in family discussions enables children to better understand other people's views. Children whose parents respect their opinions and grant them concessions, if warranted, feel like contributing members of the family, and thus significant. It appears that the quality of the relationship with one's parents continues to influence self-esteem after the child becomes an adolescent (Harter, 1998; Walker & Greene, 1986).

School

Keeping in mind that the valued personality type in American culture is a responsible, self-reliant, autonomous, competent individual, the child who is reared to conform to these traits is likely to have high self-esteem. However, children who are raised in other cultures or in ethnic groups that are not dominant in American society do not necessarily have low self-esteem. Studies have shown that children from ethnic minorities generally enter American schools with strong, positive self-concepts, but that failure to conform to the majority group's expectations causes lower scores on measures of self-esteem (Phinney & Rotheram, 1987). More research is needed, especially on specific components of self-esteem such as Susan Harter's (1998) scale of global self-worth, scholastic competence, social acceptance, athletic competence, physical appearance, and behavioral conduct.

It probably could be predicted from the comparison of Alice and Zelda that Alice will go on to succeed in school, while Zelda will continue to fail. It has been found that students with higher self-esteem are more likely to be successful in school and achieve more than children with low self-esteem (Cole, 1991; Harter, 1998). This relationship shows up as early as the primary grades and becomes even stronger as the student gets older.

Apparently, then, the more positively children feel about their ability to succeed, the more likely they are to exert effort and feel a sense of accomplishment when they finish a task. Likewise, the more negatively children evaluate their ability to succeed, the more likely they are to avoid tasks in which there is an uncertainty of success, the less likely they are to exert effort, and the less likely they are to attribute any success or lack of it to themselves ("Oh, it was just luck").

People with low self-esteem tend to have a high fear of failure. This causes them to set easy goals or unrealistically difficult goals in tasks where goal-setting is required (Bednar, Wells, & Peterson, 1989). For example, in a ring-toss game where students could toss the rings at the goal from any distance they desired, those with low self-esteem stood either right next to the peg or too far away (Covington & Beery, 1976). Those who stood next to the peg avoided feelings of failure by ensuring success. Those who stood far away ensured failure, but the distance provided an excuse. Students with positive self-esteem were more likely to set goals of intermediate difficulty. In the ring-toss game they were more likely to choose a distance they thought reasonable for success. If they were given a chance to try the game again, they adjusted the distance according to how they performed on the first try. Those with low self-esteem did not make use of this information.

So far, the influence of self-esteem on achievement has been discussed, but what about the influence of achievement on self-esteem?

According to Benjamin Bloom,

[s]uccessful experiences in school are no guarantee of a generally positive self-concept, but they increase the probabilities that such will be the case. In contrast, unsuccessful experiences guarantee that the individual will develop a negative academic self-concept and increase the probabilities that he will have a generally negative self-concept (1973, p. 142).

Bloom's observation has been supported by research (Bednar, Wells, & Peterson, 1989). One study, for example, found that preadolescents with high self-concepts were rated by teachers as being more popular, cooperative, and persistent in class, showed greater leadership, were lower in anxiety, had more supportive families, and had higher teacher expectations for their future success than students with lower self-concepts (Hay, Ashman, Vankraayenoord, 1998). Similarly, other studies of school-agers found that achievement in school influenced students' estimations of their competence (Harter, 1998; Harter & Connell, 1984). This estimation of their competence, then, influenced their motivation to achieve.

How Parents and Teachers Can Enhance Children's Self-esteem

1. Enable children to feel accepted—understand and attend to their needs; be warm; accept their individuality; talk to them and listen to them.
2. Enable children to be autonomous—provide opportunities for them to do things themselves; give them choices; encourage curiosity; encourage pride in achievement; provide challenges.
3. Enable children to be successful—be an appropriate model; set clear limits; praise accomplishments and efforts; explain consequences and how to learn from mistakes.

4. Enable children to interact with others positively—provide opportunities to cooperate with others; enable them to work out differences dealing with feelings and others' perspectives.

5. Enable children to be responsible—encourage participation; provide opportunities for them to care for belongings, help with chores, and help others.

Peers

Children can be quite cruel to one another, as was discussed in Chapter 8. They tease and ostracize children who are different physically, intellectually, linguistically, and/or socially. Peer attitudes about "ideal" size, physique, and physical capabilities can influence children's self-esteem. Harter (1998) found that perceived physical appearance is consistently the most highly correlated domain with self-esteem from early childhood through adulthood with no gender differences.

It is generally agreed that there are three basic human body types: *endomorphy* (short, heavy build), *mesomorphy* (medium, muscular build), and *ectomorphy* (tall, lean build). Of course, in reality, most people are variations of these basic body types. Body type plays a role in self-esteem in cultures that emphasize a certain ideal type. In the United States, the ideal type for females is slim, well proportioned, and well toned; for males, it is the muscular type. Thus, short, fat adolescent girls and boys as well as tall, skinny adolescent boys are unhappy with their bodies (O'Dea, & Abraham, 1999; Phelps, Johnston, Jimenez, & Wilczenski, 1993).

Children discriminate among body types and know the cultural ideal quite early. One study (Johnson & Staffieri, 1971) demonstrated that by age 8, children distinguished among body types. Most of those children interviewed preferred the mesomorphic type over the other two. They rated endomorphy as socially unfavorable and associated ectomorphy with social submissiveness. It would follow, then, that children who do not conform to the ideal body type of their peers have lower self-esteem. This was found to be true in a study (Tucker, 1983) comparing the relationship between self-esteem and how close one's actual physical self conformed to one's ideal physical self. The larger the discrepancy, the greater tendency toward low self-esteem.

The rate at which one matures physically compared to one's peers affects self-concept. Studies have found that boys who mature early compared to their peers are more likely to have higher self-esteem than boys who are late maturers (Alsaker, 1992; Apter, Galatzer, Beth-Halachmi, & Laron, 1981; Clausen, 1975). Early maturers are better able to excel in sports, are more likely to get attention from girls, and are chosen more often for leadership roles. Girls who mature early (in elementary school), however, are likely to have low self-esteem because they feel awkward and "out of sync" with their peers. By junior high school, though, girls who mature earlier than their friends have prestige. Junior high school and high school girls who mature late experience a more negative self-concept than do their physically developed peers (Rice, 1996). In general, it can be concluded that children who differ from their peers, especially in appearance, tend to have lower self-esteem than those who are like their peers and who conform to their peers' ideal.

Not only does one's appearance compared to the perceived ideal of one's peers affect self-esteem, so does one's perceived status in relation to the rest of the group. Studies have found children's and adolescents' self-esteem dependent upon their perceived popularity among their friends (Cole, 1991; Harter, 1998; Walker & Greene, 1986). Another study found that the self-esteem of seventh- to twelfth-graders was related to the status of the peer group to which they belonged at their school. Generally, those who belonged to the "in" crowd exhibited higher self-esteem than outsiders (Brown & Lohr, 1987).

Mass Media

Where do children get their attitudes about ideal body and personality types? Advertising strategies on television and in magazines portray ideal physical stereotypes—handsome, mesomorphic, well-dressed men; beautiful, trim, well-dressed women. Advertising techniques often lead the viewer or reader to believe that the product advertised will produce or perpetuate ideal characteristics. For men, the TV emphasis is on strength, performance, and skill; for women, it is on attractiveness and desirability (Basow, 1992; Pipher, 1994; Wolf, 1991). Children's heroes and heroines in the media serve as models for the ideal type. According to Naomi Wolf (1991), author of *The Beauty Myth*, the self-serving interests of advertisers make the ideal unattainable, thereby influencing low self-esteem in order to motivate purchases of their product.

Community

The community may contribute to the differences found in the self-esteem of males and females. In a longitudinal study of the developmental change in self-esteem in males and females age 14 through age 23, Block and Robins (1993) found there was a tendency for males to increase in self-esteem and females to decrease. The investigators explain the differences in males and females as due to differences in gender-role socialization by society in general. Females are socialized to "get along," to connect and be mutually dependent; males are socialized to "get ahead," to achieve and be self-determinant (Block, 1973; Brown & Gilligan, 1990). Since, as one enters adulthood, especially the career world, achievement is rewarded more so than camaraderie, males socialized accordingly gain in self-esteem whereas females not socialized to compete lose in self-esteem. Thus the discrepancy between the values one is socialized as appropriate and what is valued in the "real world" may influence self-esteem. The self-esteem level of previously confident females drops in early adolescence (Rosner & Rierdan, 1994). This may be due to the realization that their socialization of emphasizing relationships rather than competition is not highly valued in American society, or it may be due to lack of encouragement from the school, as was discussed earlier in the chapter, or both.

It may be that some adolescent girls must wrestle with what it means to be a woman in American society (Basow & Rubin, 1999). Evidence from research suggests that girls are more negatively affected by failure than are boys. This sensitivity tends to limit their willingness to take risks for more challenging opportunities. Also, many young women may still believe there is an inherent conflict between feminine goals of interdependence and support with cultural goals of independence and competition. Belief in this conflict creates ambivalence and anxiety when these young women find themselves in competitive achievement settings (Eccles, Barber, Jozefowicz, Malenchuk, & Vida, 1999). Apparently, though females in minority ethnic groups do not generally experience such ambivalence, African American adult women are respected in their community for being strong, outspoken, and achievement-oriented as well as for being nurturant and caring, thereby influencing self-esteem. Asian American women subscribing to traditional gender roles were found to have lower self-esteem than those having nontraditional roles (Uba, 1994). For Hispanic American females, having a strong ethnic identity with group support contributed to high self-esteem (Phinney & Chavira, 1992).

According to Morris Rosenberg (1975) and others (Harter, 1998; Martinez & Dukes, 1991), difference or similarity of social identity (ethnicity, religion, social class) to that of the majority of the people in one's neighborhood affects one's self-esteem. For example, Rosenberg found that the Jewish children raised in Jewish neighborhoods were likely to have higher self-esteem than those raised in Catholic neighborhoods. He and others (Martinez & Dukes, 1991) also found that African American students in integrated schools were likely to have lower self-esteem than those in all-African American schools. Lower-class children attending a school where the majority of children were from higher social classes also had lower self-esteem than those attending a school where the majority of children were from lower-class environments. The same was true of upper-class children who were in the minority. Apparently, being socially different affects one's self-esteem, as has already been discussed in regard to appearance. Since we all cannot look like the ideal type of our peers, and since not everyone is of the majority ethnic, racial, or religious group, how can self-esteem be enhanced in those who are different from the majority?

Individuals with disabilities are examples of those who differ from the majority in appearance. These individuals often have low self-esteem, one reason being that they do not conform to the ideal body type of society (Koff, Rierdan, & Stubbs, 1990). Another reason is that others often step in to do things for them that they may be capable of doing themselves, if allowed to try. Many individuals with disabilities have developed learned helplessness.

In a project I directed to train college students with disabilities to work as teacher assistants in various special-needs facilities (Berns, 1981), the students with disabilities were given the Tennessee Self-Concept Test upon entering the project (pretest) and a year after participation (posttest). This test measures *identity* (feelings about what I am); *self-satisfaction* (feelings about how I act); *physical self* (feelings about appearance, skills, sexuality); *moral ethical self* (feelings of being a good or bad person); *personal self* (sense of adequacy as a person); *family self* (sense of adequacy as a family member); and *social self* (sense of adequacy in relations with others).

The purpose of measuring the students' levels of self-esteem before and after participation was to find out whether helping others like themselves would contribute to a rise in their self-esteem. A typical example of participation in the project was one student with multiple sclerosis who relied on a wheelchair for mobility and chose to work in a school for children with orthopedic impairments and children with multidisabilities.

On comparing pre- and posttest results, every project participant's total self-esteem score increased. Theoretically, the total self-esteem score reflects the overall level of self-esteem. Persons with high total scores tend to like themselves, feel they are persons of value and worth, have confidence in themselves, and act accordingly. When I asked the students, individually, for an explanation of the positive change in their self-concepts, the most frequent answer was "I realized I could do something worthwhile."

Thus the community can play a significant role in enhancing self-esteem, especially among community members who feel they are different, by providing opportunities for members to do worthwhile and responsible things. Children and youth can help younger children in school or in recreational programs; they can be of service to older citizens; they can be allowed to serve on advisory boards; they can help with community projects. Older community members can contribute their skills and expertise to younger members. Senior citizens can help in day care facilities, in schools, and in job-training programs. They, too, can serve on advisory boards and help with community projects. When many different people can have opportunities to work together, they learn that self-esteem comes from feeling proud of one's contribution, not from being like everyone else.

SUMMARY

Self-control refers to the ability to regulate one's impulses, behavior, and/or emotions until an appropriate time, place, or object is available for expression. It is a continuing process, an outcome of affecting cognitive and social forces exhibiting itself in antisocial and prosocial behavior. Antisocial behavior includes any behavior that harms other people, such as aggression, violence, and crime. *Prosocial behavior* includes any behavior that benefits other people, such as altruism, sharing, and cooperation

The theories explaining the causes of aggression are that it is biologically influenced; it is learned; it is an information-processing impulsive response to frustration; it is a result of social cognitive factors such as peer group pressure the reduction of restraining socialization forces; and it is socialized by interacting factors.

Aggression can be studied from a social–cognitive perspective (behavior is influenced by how one interprets social cues) and from an ecological perspective (behavior is influenced by the contexts of family, school, peer group, media, and community).

The theories explaining the causes of altruism are biological (evolution and genetics) learning (reinforcement, modeling, and instruction), cognitive developmental, interactional, and cultural.

The family influences altruistic behavior. An authoritative parenting style (warmth, firm control, and reasoning) seems to encourage altruistic behavior, whereas an authoritarian parenting style (coldness with physical punishment) seems to foster aggressive behavior. Moralizing and prohibitions with explanations as to why antisocial behavior is unacceptable increase prosocial behavior, as do role-taking opportunities.

The media provide role models for behavior and can influence altruism. Schools can train children to be prosocial through role playing. Peer groups provide real experiences in prosocial behavior ("learning by doing") and reinforcement for behaving in certain ways.

The community influences prosocial behavior through cultural values of cooperation and social harmony. Children from traditional, rural cultures who were given the responsibility to perform various household tasks related to the family's economic security exhibited more altruism than children from modern, urban cultures that tended to be more competitive and achievement oriented.

A gender role, or sex type, refers to the qualities that an individual understands as characterizing males and females in his or her culture.

The four main theories of gender-role development are psychoanalytic (feelings), social–learning, or social cognitive (behaving), cognitive–developmental (thinking), and gender schema (information processing).

Males and females behave differently. Research confirms that males are more aggressive and exhibit greater visual–spatial ability, and that females exhibit greater verbal ability. Additional research indicates that socialization practices maximize gender differences. As a result, girls and boys are channeled into gender-typed behaviors valued by society.

Warm, positive father–son and mother–daughter relationships lead to the strongest gender-role identification. Parenting practices influence the gender-role development of both boys and girls. Sibling sex constellation is another factor.

Peers exert strong pressure to conform to traditionally stereotypical gender roles via modeling, reinforcement, punishment, and sex-segregated activities.

The school, by its differential treatment of males and females, has maximized gender differences. This has occurred through teachers' responses to boys and girls as well as through gender-role models in textbooks.

The media still tend toward stereotypical portrayals of gender roles. The community's attitudes regarding gender roles and the models provided influence children's sex typing.

Self-esteem, the value one places on one's self-concept, is derived from the reflected appraisal of others. Simplistically, if one has been treated with concern and approval, one will have high self-esteem; if one has been rejected and criticized, one will have low self-esteem. Specific dimensions of self-esteem include scholastic competence, athletic competence, social competence, physical appearance, and behavioral conduct, as well as global self-worth.

The factors contributing to self-esteem are the amount of respectful, accepting, and concerned treatment an individual receives from significant others; an individual's history of successes and failures; his or her status among peers; and his or her manner of responding to devaluation or failure.

Parenting practices contribute to the development of self-esteem. The parenting styles of children with high self-esteem are described as warm, strict, and democratic. However, these results apply to American society. Parenting styles in diverse ethnic groups and children's self-esteem may differ.

Children with high self-esteem are more likely to be successful in school and are likely to achieve more than children with low self-esteem.

Peers influence self-esteem by their reinforcement of "ideal" types. Children who differ from the ideal tend to have lower self-esteem. Peers get their attitudes about ideal types from the media.

The community can contribute to the enhancement of self-esteem of its members by providing worthwhile, responsible activities in which to engage.

Epilogue

Adolescence is the time when prior socialization experiences show their influence in the formation of an identity, the "looking-glass self" or the "generalized other." Anne Frank showed impressive self-control to be able to live in such small quarters, having to get along with others under dire circumstances. She also was able to assume a feminine gender role, being compassionate and *interdependent as well as emotionally strong and assertive. Unlike Ophelia and Hamlet, Anne's socialization experiences and continued support of her family enabled her to have high self-esteem and provided her with coping skills to be resilient to negative developmental outcomes.*

ACTIVITY

Purpose: To evaluate conditions for development of self-esteem.

1. Observe three interactions between an adult and (a) a preschooler (age 2–5); (b) a schoolagr (age 6–12); and (c) a teenager (age 13–17).

2. Describe the setting, or environment, in which each interaction takes place.

3. Record five minutes of dialogue for each interaction.

4. For each interaction, analyze messages that you felt contributed to the child's high self-esteem, that you felt contributed to the child's low self-esteem, or that you felt were neutral.

5. Rewrite the basic message in each interaction to make it enhance high self-esteem.

RESOURCES

American Psychological Association
http://www.apa.org

National Clearinghouse for Alcohol and
Drug Information
http://www.health.org/

National Institute for Mental Health
http://www.nimh.nih.gov/

RELATED READINGS

Basow, S. A. (1992). *Gender stereotypes and roles* (3rd ed.). Pacific Grove, CA: Brooks/Cole.

Best, R. (1983). *We've all got scars: What boys and girls learn in elementary school.* Bloomington: Indiana University Press.

Briggs, D. C. (1975). *Your child's self esteem.* New York: Dolphin.

Coopersmith, S. (1967). *The antecedents of self-esteem.* San Francisco: Freeman.

Curry, N. E., & Johnson, C. N. (1990). *Beyond self-esteem: Developing a genuine sense of human value.* Washington, DC: National Association for Education of Young Children.

Damon, W. (1995). *Greater expectations: Overcoming the culture of indulgence in America's homes and schools.* Old Tappan, NJ: The Free Press.

Isaacs, S. (1999). *Brave dames and wimpettes: What women are really doing on page and screen.* New York: Ballantine.

James, M., & Jongeward, D. (1977). *Born to win.* Reading, MA: Addison-Wesley.

Maccoby, E. E. (1998). *The two sexes: Growing up apart, coming together.* Cambridge, MA: Harvard University Press.

Mussen, P. H., & Eisenberg-Berg, N. (1977). *Roots of caring, sharing, and helping: The development of prosocial behavior in children.* San Francisco: Freeman.

Olweus, D. (1993). *Bullying at school: What we know and what we can do.* Cambridge, MA: Blackwell.

Osofsky, J. D. (1997). *Children in a violent society.* York, PA: Guilford Press.

Pipher, M. (1994). *Reviving Ophelia: Saving the selves of adolescent girls.* New York: Ballantine.

Pollack, W. S. (1999). *Real boys: Rescuing our sons from the myths of boyhood.* New York: Henry Holt.

Sadker, M., & Sadker, D. (1994). *Failing at fairness: How America's schools cheat girls.* New York: Scribners.

Slaby, R. G., et al. (1995). *Early violence prevention: Tools for teachers of young children.* Washington, DC: National Association for Education of Young Children.

Staub, E. (1975). *The development of prosocial behavior in children.* Morristown, NJ: General Learning Press.

Thorne, B. (1993). *Gender play: Girls and boys in school.* New Brunswick, NJ: Rutgers University Press.

Developmental Tasks in Ten Categories of Behavior of the Individual from Birth to Death

	INFANCY (BIRTH TO 1 OR 2)	EARLY CHILDHOOD (2–3) TO 5–6/7	MIDDLE CHILDHOOD (5–6/7 TO PUBESCENCE)	EARLY ADOLESCENCE (PUBESCENCE TO PUBERTY)	LATE ADOLESCENCE (PUBERTY TO EARLY MATURITY)	MATURITY (EARLY TO MIDDLE ADULTHOOD)	LATE ADULT-HOOD (BEYOND FULL POWERS OF ADULTHOOD TO SENESCENCE)
I. Achieving an appropriate dependence/independence pattern	1. Establishing oneself as very dependent being 2. Beginning the establishment of self-awareness	1. Adjusting to less private attention; becoming independent physically (while remaining strongly dependent emotionally)	1. Freeing oneself from primary identification with adults	1. Establishing one's independence from adults in all areas of behavior	1. Establishing oneself as an independent individual in an adult manner	1. Learning to be interdependent—now leaning on, now succoring others, as need arises. 2. Assisting one's children to become gradually independent and autonomous beings	1. Accepting graciously and comfortably the help needed from others as powers fail and dependence becomes necessary.
II. Achieving an appropriate giving–receiving pattern of affection	1. Developing a feeling for affection	1. Developing the ability to give affection 2. Learning to share affection	1. Learning to give as much love as one receives; forming friendships with peers	1. Accepting oneself as a worthwhile person really worthy of love	1. Building a strong mutual affectional bond with a (possible) marriage partner	1. Building and maintaining a strong and mutually satisfying marriage relationship 2. Establishing a wholesome affectional bonds with one's children and grandchildren 3. Meeting wisely the new needs for affection of one's own aging parents 4. Cultivating meaningfully warm friendships with members of one's own generation	1. Facing loss of one's spouse and finding some satisfactory sources of affection previously received from mate 2. Learning new affectional roles with own children, now mature adults 3. Establishing ongoing, satisfying affectional patterns with grandchildren and other members of the extended family 4. Finding and preserving mutually satisfying friendships outside the family circle *(continued)*

continued

	INFANCY (BIRTH TO 1 OR 2)	EARLY CHILDHOOD (2–3 TO 5–6–7)	MIDDLE CHILDHOOD (5–6–7 TO PUBESCENCE)	EARLY ADOLESCENCE (PUBESCENCE TO PUBERTY)	LATE ADOLESCENCE (PUBERTY TO EARLY MATURITY)	MATURITY (EARLY TO MIDDLE ADULTHOOD)	LATE ADULT-HOOD (BEYOND FULL POWERS OF ADULTHOOD TO SENESCENCE)
III. Relating to changing social groups	1. Becoming aware of the alive as against the inanimate, and the familiar against the unfamiliar 2. Developing rudimentary social interaction	1. Beginning to develop the ability to interact with age mates 2. Adjusting in the family to expectations it has for the child as a member of the social unit	1. Clarifying the adult world as distinguished from the child's world 2. Establishing peer groups and learning to belong	1. Behaving according to a shifting peer code	1. Adopting an adult-patterned set of social values by learning a new peer code	1. Keeping in reasonable balance activities in the various social service, political, and community groups and causes that make demands on adults 2. Establishing and maintaining mutually satisfactory relationships with the in-law families of spouse and married children	1. Choosing and maintaining ongoing social activities and functions appropriate to health, energy, and interests
IV. Developing a conscience	1. Beginning to adjust to the expectations of others	1. Developing the ability to take directions and to be in the obedient presence of authority 2. Developing the ability to be obedient in the absence of authority where conscience substitutes for authority	1. Learning more about rules and developing true morality		1. Learning to verbalize contradictions in moral codes, as well as discrepancies between principle and practice, and resolving these problems in a responsible manner	1. Coming to terms with the violations of moral codes in the larger as well as in the more intimate social scene, and developing some constructive philosophy and method of operation 2. Helping children to adjust to the expectations of others and to conform to the moral demands of the culture	1. Maintaining a sense of moral integrity in the face of disappointments and disillusionments in life's hopes and dreams

(continued)

continued

	INFANCY (BIRTH TO 1 OR 2)	EARLY CHILDHOOD (2–3 TO 5-6-7)	MIDDLE CHILDHOOD (5-6-7 TO PUBESCENCE)	EARLY ADOLESCENCE (PUBESCENCE TO PUBERTY)	LATE ADOLESCENCE (PUBERTY TO EARLY MATURITY)	MATURITY (EARLY TO MIDDLE ADULTHOOD)	LATE ADULTHOOD (BEYOND FULL POWERS OF ADULTHOOD TO SENESCENCE)
V. Learning one's psychosociobiological gender role		1. Learning to identify with male adult and female adult roles	1. Beginning to identify with one's social contemporaries of the same gender	1. Strong identification with one's own gender mates 2. Learning one's role in heterosexual relationships	1. Exploring the possibilities for a future mate and acquiring "desirability" 2. Choosing an occupation 3. Preparing to accept one's future role in manhood or womanhood as a responsible citizen of the larger community	1. Learning to be a competent husband or wife, and building a good marriage 2. Carrying a socially adequate role as a citizen and worker in the community 3. Becoming a good parent and grandparent as children arrive and develop	1. Learning to live on a retirement income 2. Being a good companion to an aging spouse 3. Meeting bereavement of spouse adequately
VI. Accepting and adjusting to a changing body	1. Adjusting to adult feeding demands 2. Adjusting to adult cleanliness demands 3. Adjusting to adult attitudes toward genital manipulation	1. Adjusting to expectations resulting from one's improving muscular abilities 2. Developing sexual modesty		1. Reorganizing one's thoughts and feelings about oneself in the face of significant bodily changes and their concomitants 2. Accepting the reality of one's appearance 3. Controlling and using a "new" body	1. Learning appropriate outlets for sexual drives	1. Making a good sex adjustment within marriage 2. Establishing healthful routines of eating, resting, working, playing within the pressures of the adult world	1. Making a good adjustment to failing powers as aging diminishes strengths and abilities
VII. Managing a changing body and learning new motor patterns	1. Developing a physiological equilibrium 2. Developing eye–hand coordination 3. Establishing satisfactory rhythms of rest and activity	1. Developing large muscle control 2. Learning to coordinate large muscles and small muscles	1. Refining and elaborating skill in the use of small muscles			1. Learning the new motor skills involved in housekeeping, gardening, sports, and other activities expected of adults in the community	1. Adapting interests and activities to reserves of vitality and energy of an aging body

(continued)

continued

	INFANCY (BIRTH TO 1 OR 2)	EARLY CHILDHOOD (2–3) TO 5-6-7	MIDDLE CHILDHOOD (5-6–7 TO PUBESCENCE)	EARLY ADOLESCENCE (PUBESCENCE TO PUBERTY)	LATE ADOLESCENCE (PUBERTY TO EARLY MATURITY)	MATURITY (EARLY TO MIDDLE ADULTHOOD)	LATE ADULTHOOD (BEYOND FULL POWERS OF ADULTHOOD TO SENESCENCE)
VIII. Learning to understand and control the physical world	1. Exploring the physical world restrictive explo-	1. Meeting adult expectations for studying and conration and manipulation of an expanding environment	1. Learning more realistic ways of trolling the physical world			1. Gaining intelligent understanding of new horizons of medicine and science sufficient for personal well-being and social competence	1. Mastering new awareness and methods of dealing with physical surroundings as an individual with occasional or permanent disabilities
IX. Developing an appropriate symbol system and conceptual abilities	1. Developing preverbal communication 2. Developing verbal communication 3. Rudimentary concept formation	1. Improving one's use of the symbol system 2. Enormous elaboration of the concept pattern	1. Learning to use language actually to exchange ideas or to influence one's hearers 2. Beginning understanding of real causal relations 3. Making finer conceptual distinctions and thinking reflectively	1. Using language to express and to clarify more complex concepts 2. Moving from the concrete to the abstract and applying general principles to the particular	1. Achieving the level of reasoning of which one is capable	1. Mastering technical symbol systems involved in income tax, Social Security, complex financial dealings, and other contexts familiar to Western culture	1. Keeping mentally alert and effective as long as is possible through the later years
X. Relating oneself to the cosmos		1. Developing a genuine, though uncritical, notion about one's place in the cosmos	1. Developing a scientific approach		1. Formulating a workable belief and value system	1. Formulating and implementing a rational philosophy of life on the basis of adult experience 2. Cultivating a satisfactory religious climate in the home as the spiritual soil for development of family members	1. Preparing for eventual and inevitable cessation of life by building a set of beliefs that one can live and die with in peace

Source: Evelyn Millis Duvall & Brent C. Miller (1985, pp. 154–159). *Marriage and Family Development* (6th ed.). New York: Harper & Row. Copyright © by Harper & Row Publishers, Inc. Reprinted by permission of the publishers.

BASIC PARENTING STYLES

1. The *permissive* parent attempts to behave in a nonpunitive, acceptable, and affirmative manner towards the child's impulses, desires, and actions. He or she consults with him/her about policy decisions and gives explanations for family rules. He or she makes few demands for household responsibility and orderly behavior. He or she presents herself to the child as a resource for him/her to use as he/she wishes, not as an active agent responsible for shaping or altering his ongoing or future behavior. He or she allows the child to regulate his/her own activities as much as possible, avoids the exercise of control, and does not encourage him/her to obey externally defined standards. He or she attempts to use reason but not overt power to accomplish his/her ends (Baumrind, 1968, p. 256).

2. The *authoritarian* parent attempts to shape, control, and evaluate the behavior and attitudes of the child in accordance with a set standard of conduct, usually an absolute standard, theologically motivated and formulated by a higher authority. He or she values obedience as a virtue and favors punitive, forceful measures to curb self-will at points where the child's actions or beliefs conflict with what he or she thinks is right conduct. He or she believes in inculcating such instrumental values as respect for authority, respect for work, and respect for the preservation of order and traditional structure. He or she does not encourage verbal give and take, believing that the child should accept her word for what is right (Baumrind, 1968, p. 261).

3. The *authoritative* parent attempts to direct the child's activities but in a rational, issue-oriented manner. He or she encourages verbal give and take, and shares with the child the reasoning behind her policy. He or she values both expressive and instrumental attributes, both autonomous self-will and disciplined conformity. Therefore, he or she exerts firm control at points of parent-child divergence, but does not hem the child in with restrictions. He or she recognizes his/her own special rights as an adult, but also the child's individual interests and special ways. The authoritative parent affirms the child's present qualities, but also sets standards for future conduct. He or she uses reason as well as power to achieve his/her objectives. He or she does not base decisions on group consensus or the individual child's desires, but also does not regard himself/herself as infallible or divinely inspired (Baumrind, 1968, p. 261).

HOW TO CHOOSE A GOOD EARLY CHILDHOOD PROGRAM

A good early childhood program can benefit your child, your family, and your community. Your child's educational, physical, personal, and social development will be nurtured in a well-planned program. As a parent, you will feel more confident when your child is enrolled in a suitable program, and the time your family spends together will be more satisfying as a result. Early childhood education plays an important role in supporting families, and strong families are the basis of a thriving community.

If you are thinking about enrolling your child in an early childhood program, you probably have already decided upon some of your basic priorities, such as location, number of hours, cost, and type of care that best suits your child. If you feel that a group program is appropriate, you can obtain a list of licensed programs for young children from your local licensing agency. Then you can call several programs for further information, and arrange to visit the programs that seem best for you and your child so you can talk with teachers, directors, and other parents.

What should you look for in a good early childhood program? Professionals in early childhood education and child development have found several indicators of good quality care for preschool children. You will especially want to meet the adults who will care for your child—they are responsible for every aspect of the program's operation.

WHO WILL CARE FOR YOUR CHILD?

1. The adults enjoy and understand how young children learn and grow.

   - Are the staff members friendly and considerate to each child?

   - Do adult expectations vary appropriately for children of differing ages and interests?

   - Do the staff members consider themselves to be professionals? Do they read or attend meetings to continue to learn more about how young children grow and develop?

   - Does the staff work toward improving the quality of the program, obtaining better equipment, and making better use of the space?

2. The staff view themselves positively and therefore can continually foster children's emotional and social development.

   - Does the staff help children feel good about themselves, their activities, and other people?

   - Do the adults listen to children and talk with them?

- Are the adults gentle while being firm, consistent and yet flexible in their guidance of children?
- Do the staff members help children learn gradually how to consider others' rights and feelings, to take turns and share, yet also to stand up for personal rights when necessary?
- When children are angry or fearful, are they helped to deal with their feelings constructively?

3. There are enough adults to work with a group and to care for the individual needs of children.
   - Are infants in groups of no more than eight children with at least two adults?
   - Are two- and three-year-old children in groups of no more than fourteen children with at least two adults?
   - Are four- and five-year-olds in groups of no more than twenty children with at least two adults?

4. All staff members work together cooperatively.
   - Does the staff meet regularly to plan and evaluate the program?
   - Are they willing to adjust the daily activities for children's individual needs and interests?

5. Staff observe and record each child's progress and development.
   - Does the staff stress children's strengths and show pride in their accomplishments?
   - Are records used to help parents and staff better understand the child?
   - Are the staff responsible to parents' concerns about their child's development?

WHAT PROGRAM ACTIVITIES AND EQUIPMENT ARE OFFERED?

1. The environment fosters the growth and development of young children working and playing together.
   - Does the staff have realistic goals for children?
   - Are activities balanced between vigorous outdoor play and quiet indoor play? Are children given opportunities to select activities of interest to them?
   - Are children encouraged to work alone as well as in small groups?
   - Are self-help skills such as dressing, toileting, resting, washing, and eating encouraged as children are ready?
   - Are transition times approached as pleasant learning opportunities?

2. A good center provides appropriate and sufficient equipment and play materials and makes them readily available.

- Is there large climbing equipment? Is there an ample supply of blocks of all sizes, wheel toys, balls, and dramatic play props to foster physical development as well as imaginative play?
- Are there ample tools and hands-on materials such as sand, clay, water, wood, and paint to stimulate creativity?
- Is there a variety of sturdy puzzles, construction sets, and other small manipulative items available to children?
- Are children's picture books age-appropriate, attractive, and of good literary quality?
- Are there plants, animals, or other natural science objects for children to care for or observe?
- Are there opportunities for music and movement experiences?

3. Children are helped to increase their language skills and to expand their understanding of the world.
- Do the children freely talk with one another and with the adults?
- Do the adults provide positive language models in describing objects, feelings, and experiences?
- Does the staff plan for visitors or trips to broaden children's understanding through first-hand contacts with people and places?
- Are the children encouraged to solve their own problems, to think independently, and to respond to open-ended questions?

HOW DO THE STAFF RELATE TO YOUR FAMILY AND THE COMMUNITY?

1. A good program considers and supports the needs of the entire family.
- Are parents welcome to observe, discuss policies, make suggestions, and participate in the work of the center?
- Do the staff members share with parents the highlights of their child's experiences?
- Are the staff alert to matters affecting any member of the family that may also affect the child?
- Does the staff respect families from varying cultures or backgrounds?
- Does the center have written policies about fees, hours, holidays, illness, and other considerations?

2. Staff in a good center are aware of and contribute to community resources.
- Does the staff share information about community recreational and learning opportunities with families?
- Does the staff refer family members to a suitable agency when the need arises?

- Are volunteers from the community encouraged to participate in the center's activities?
- Does the center collaborate with other professional groups to provide the best care possible for children in the community?

ARE THE FACILITY AND PROGRAM DESIGNED TO MEET THE VARIED DEMANDS OF YOUNG CHILDREN, THEIR FAMILIES, AND THE STAFF?

1. The health of children, staff, and parents is protected and promoted.
   - Are the staff alert to the health and safety of each child and of themselves?
   - Are meals and snacks nutritious, varied, attractive, and served at appropriate times?
   - Does the staff wash hands with soap and water before handling food and after changing diapers? Are children's hands washed before eating and after toileting?
   - Are surfaces, equipment, and toys cleaned daily? Are they in good repair?
   - Does each child have an individual cot, mat, or crib?
   - Are current medical records and emergency information maintained for each child and staff member? Is adequate sick leave provided for staff so they can remain at home when they are ill?
   - Is at least one staff member trained in first aid? Does the center have a health consultant?
   - Is the building comfortably warm in cold weather? Are the rooms ventilated with fresh air daily?
2. The facility is safe for children and adults.
   - Are the building and grounds well-lighted and free of hazards?
   - Are furnishings, sinks, and toilets safely accessible to children?
   - Are toxic materials stored in a locked cabinet?
   - Are smoke detectors installed in appropriate locations?
   - Are indoor and outdoor surfaces cushioned with materials such as carpet or wood chips in areas with climbers, slides, or swings?
   - Does every staff member know what to do in an emergency? Are emergency numbers posted by the telephone?
3. The environment is spacious enough to accommodate a variety of activities and equipment.
   - Are there at least 35 square feet of usable playroom floor space indoors per child and 75 square feet of play space outdoors per child?

- Is there a place for each child's personal belongings such as a change of clothes?
- Is there enough space so that adults can walk between sleeping children's cots?

TEACHING STRATEGIES FOR YOUNG CHILDREN WHO HAVE SPECIFIC DIABILITIES

VISUAL DISABILITY

Arts and Crafts

1. Mark paint cans and brushes with some tactile code, for example, circle = red, triangle = yellow, and so on.
2. Use variety of textures in paint—for example, raw oatmeal.
3. Praise efforts of child to overcome distaste for touching wet or sticky substances.
4. Have child help make play dough from dry ingredients. It will help child accept the final product.

Music and Movement

1. Let child explore each instrument.
2. Use one-handed instruments first (maracas, clappers, bells, tambourine).
3. Use two-handed instruments later (sand blocks, sticks, drums, triangle).
4. Physically guide child in handling instruments.
5. Use peer as partner by having blind child place hand on partner's upper arm or shoulder.

Group or Circle Time

1. Have assigned places to help child learn classmates' voices and names.
2. At beginning of year, ask other children to identify themselves before speaking.

General Suggestions

1. Keep furniture stationary until child is familiar with room.
2. Warn child when changes are made.
3. When child loses toy, allow child time to retrieve; assist with verbal guidance.
4. Identify coat hook with some other object—for example, "next to the door."
5. Water play is usually a favorite; provide it often.
6. Cut out tactile shapes and attach to shelves for block storage.

Do

1. Provide many activities that use senses other than hearing.
2. Use short films in which story may be understood without seeing the action.

Avoid

1. Long films.
2. Activities that are primarily visual in nature.

PHYSICAL IMPAIRMENT

Arts and Crafts

1. Substitute large-handled brushes and large crayons or felt markers for small crayons.
2. Use training scissors if necessary.
3. Tilt surface for better visibility.
4. Outline fingerpaint paper with tape to help child with severe involuntary movements.

Music and Movement

1. Substitute "hands on knees" for walking and "hands on high" for running.
2. Stabilize instruments: tape or tie to hand or wrist or place between child's knees.
3. Substitute hand and arm circling for body turning.
4. When singing a "who's missing" song, move child instead of sending out of room.
5. Be creative! Think what you can substitute for actions a child cannot do.

Group or Circle Time

1. Use "sitting box" to replace wheelchair. Cut a box to simulate a seat. Cut holes for knit ties at hip level, and place a pillow between the knees.

General Suggestions

1. Use tray or shallow box to hold small objects; make back higher, front lower.
2. Use nonslip mat—for example, a towel under items to prevent slipping.
3. In listening center, pair with nonhandicapped child to turn pages of book while both use earphones.

Do

1. Put child's feet on a small stool when placing child at a table.
2. Move child to proximity of ongoing activities.
3. Place child with balancing difficulties behind others in a line.

Avoid

1. Allowing normal children to push wheelchair when in line. (Child may feel loss of control and become upset.)
2. Long periods of keeping child in same position (more than 20–30 minutes).

HEARING DISABILITY

Arts and Crafts

1. Provide multisensory experiences.
2. Provide vocabulary appropriate to activity.
3. Avoid complex verbal directions.
4. Demonstrate, if necessary.

Music and Movement

1. Have other children demonstrate movement or action.
2. Use items and individual flannel boards to illustrate songs. As children sing, have them hold up appropriate items or flannel cut-outs.

Group or Circle Time

1. Translate to group what child says, when possible.
2. Seat for best vision of teacher and other children.
3. Talk in natural tone of voice; avoid exaggerated or loud voice.

General Suggestions

1. Provide names of objects with which child is working.
2. Draw picture of fire drill and children in line; practice drill.
3. Practice use of commonly understood sign for "wait" and "stop" before field trips.
4. Pair child with a hearing child for field trips.

Do

1. Let child choose another activity when telling a story with no visual interest.
2. Encourage total communication—that is, lip-reading, signing, and pantomime.

Avoid

1. Playback equipment that requires removal of hearing aids.
2. Films with long dialogue not closely related to action.

DEVELOPMENTAL DELAY

Arts and Crafts

1. Use one-skill activities in the beginning.
2. Define edges of paper: use white glue or fold up edges.
3. Complete first two of a three-step activity others can do.
4. Send home written explanation of child's craft work.
5. Encourage independence: avoid doing for child.

Music and Movement

1. Use simple songs with strong rhythms.
2. Alternate quiet with active.
3. Use recordings that have a slower than normal tempo.
4. Pace speed of songs to children.
5. Provide many activities for walking, running, jumping, and so on.
6. Use wall or back of chair for support in activity.

Group or Circle Time

1. Keep group small when possible.
2. Give praise for sitting and attending several times during session.
3. Make realistic expectations for attention span.
4. If sharing time is part of your program, ask parents to provide items from home (for example, kitchen utensils).

General Suggestions

1. If necessary, teach and use consistent verbal clues or signals for bathroom.
2. Have extra set of clothes available and plastic bag for soiled clothes.
3. Use velcro instead of buttons and snaps.
4. Model appropriate play.

Do

1. Pair child with a capable child who likes to help.
2. Be aware of length of time child has been present at an activity.

Avoid

1. Long films: 8–10 minutes are enough, especially at the beginning of the year.
2. Long periods of keeping the child in the same position (more than 20–30 minutes).

Source: J. A. Schickedanz, M. E. York, I. S. Stewart, & D. A. White (1990). *Strategies for Teaching Young Children* (3rd ed.) pp. 108–111. Reprinted by permission of Prentice-Hall, Inc., Englewood Cliffs, N.J.

TEACHER OBSERVATION FORM
FOR IDENTIFYING PRESCHOOL CHILDREN
WHO MAY REQUIRE ADDITIONAL SERVICES

Child's Name _____ Birth Date _____

Date _____ Teacher's Name _____

Language	Yes	No	Sometimes
1. Does the child use two- and three-word phrases to ask for what he wants?			
2. Does the child use complete sentences to tell you want happened?			
3. When the child is asked to describe something, does he or she use at least two or more sentences to talk about it?*			
4. Does the child ask questions?			
5. Does the child seem to have difficulty following directions?			
6. Does the child respond to questions with the right answers?			
7. Does the child seem to talk too softly or too loudly?			
8. Are you able to understand the child?			

Learning	Yes	No	Sometimes
9. Does the child seem to take at least twice as long as the other children to learn pre-academic concepts?			
10. Does the child seem to take half the time needed by other children to learn pre-academic concepts?			
11. Does the child have difficulty attending to group activities for more than five minutes at a time?			
12. Does the child appear extremely shy in group activities—for instance, not volunteering answers or answering questions he or she is asked, even though you think he or she knows the answers?			

Motor	Yes	No	Sometimes
13. Does the child continuously switch a crayon back and forth from one hand to the other when he or she is coloring?			
14. Do the child's hands appear clumsy or shaky when he/she is using them?			
15. When the child is coloring with a crayon, does the hand that he or she is not using appear tense (for instance, clenched into a fist)?			
16. When the child walks or runs, does one side of his or her body seem to move differently from the other side? For instance, does the child seem to have better control of the leg and arm on one side than on the other?			
17. Does the child seem to fear or not be able to use stairs, climbing equipment, or tricycles?			
18. Does the child stumble often or appear awkward when he or she moves?			
19. Is the child capable of dressing himself or herself except for tying his or her shoes?*			
Social	**Yes**	**No**	**Sometimes**
20. Does the child engage in at least two disruptive behaviors a day (tantrums, fighting, screaming, etc.)?			
21. Does the child appear withdrawn from the outside world (fiddling with pieces of string, staring into space, rocking his or her body, banding his or her head, talking to himself, etc.)?			
22. Does the child play alone and seldom talk to the other children?			
23. Does the child spend most of the time trying to get attention from adults?			
24. Does the child have toileting problems at least once a week (wet or soiled)?			

Visual or Hearing	Yes	No	Sometimes
25. Do the child's eye movements appear jerky or not coordinated?			
26. Does the child seem to have difficulty seeing objects?			
For instance, does he or she:			
tilt his or her head to look at things?			
hold objects close to his or her eyes?			
squint?			
show sensitivity to bright lights?			
have uncontrolled eye-rolling?			
complain that his or her eyes hurt?			
27. Does the child appear awkward in tasks requiring eye–hand coordination such as pegs, puzzles, or coloring?			
28. Does the child seem to have difficulty hearing?			
For instance, does he or she:			
consistently favor one ear by turning the same side of his or head in the direction of the sound?			
ignore, confuse, or not follow directions?			
complain of head noises or dizziness?			
have very high or very low monotonous tone of voice?			

General Health	Yes	No	Sometimes
29. Does the child seem to have an excessive number of colds?			
30. Does he or she have frequent absences because of illness?			
31. Do his or her eyes water?			
32. Does he or she have discharge from: his or her eyes? his or her ears?			
33. Does the child have sores on his or her body or head?			
34. Does the child have periods of unusual movements (like rapid eye blinking) or "blank spells" that seem to appear and disappear without relationship to the social situation?			
35. Does he or she have hives or rashes? Does he or she wheeze?			
36. Does he or she have a persistent cough?			
37. Is he or she excessively thirsty? Ravenously hungry?			
38. Have you noticed any of the following conditions: constant fatigue? irritability? restlessness? feverish cheeks or forehead?			
39. Is the child overweight?			
40. Is he or she physically or mentally lethargic?			
41. Has he or she lost weight without being on a diet?			

* Question applies if child is four years or older.

Source: Model Preschool Center for Children with Disabilities, Seattle, Washington.

GLOSSARY

Abuse. Maltreatment, including physical abuse, sexual abuse, psychological or emotional abuse.

Accommodation. A Piagetian term for mental adaptation to one's environment by reconciling differences of experiences.

Achieved status. Status, class, rank, or position determined by education, occupation, income, and place of residence.

Achievement motivation. The motivation to be competent and the tendency to approach challenging tasks with confidence of mastery.

Active listening. Involves trying to understand what is being said as well as what is really meant by listening and checking on the accuracy of comprehension of the message received.

Adoption. A legal process of taking a child into one's own family and treating him or her as one's own.

Advocacy. The process of supporting a person, a group, or a cause.

Affective. Having to do with feelings or emotions.

Aggression. Unproved attacks, fight, or quarrel.

Alcoholism. A chronic, progressive, and potentially fatal disease characterized by tolerance and physical dependence or pathologic organ changes, or both all the direct or indirect consequences of the alcohol ingested.

Altruism. Voluntary actions that help or benefit another person or group of people without the actor's anticipation of external rewards. Such actions often entail some cost, self-sacrifice, or risk on the part of the actor.

Americanization. Assimilation of cultural minority groups into the U.S. majority culture.

Antisocial behavior. Includes any behavior that harms other people, such as aggression, violence, and crime.

Ascribed status. Status, class, rank, or position determined by family lineage, gender, birth order, or skin color.

Assessment. An evaluation according to certain specified criteria.

Assimilation. A Piagetian term for mental adaptation to one's environment by incorporating experiences.

Attachment. An affectional tie that one person forms to another person binding them together in space and enduring over time.

Attitude. A tendency to respond positively (favorably) or negatively (unfavorably) to certain persons, objects, or situations.

Attribution. An explantion for performance.

Authoritarian. A style of parent-centered parenting characterized by the belief in and enforcement of unquestioning obedience to authority.

Authoritative. A style of democratic parenting characterized by the belief in authority that is based on competence or expertise.

Autism. A severe behavior disorder usually characterized by extreme withdrawal and lack of language and communication skills.

Autocracy. Society in which one person has unlimited power over others.

Autonomous morality. Children at Piaget's stage of moral development when they realize that rules are arbitrary agreements that can be changed by those who have to follow them.

Behaviorism. The doctrine that observed behavior, rather than what exists in the mind, provides the only valid data for psychology.

Bilingual/multicultural education. Education in the student's native language as well as in English; respect for the student's culture and ethnicity; and enhancement of the student's self-concept.

Binuclear family. Children are part of two family homes and two family groups.

Caldecott Medal. Award given yearly for the most distinguished picture book for children.

Care moral perspective. Sees people in terms of their connectedness with others; other's welfare is intrinsically connected to one's own welfare.

Catharsis. The relief of fears, conflicts, aggressive feelings, and problems by bringing them into consciousness.

Classism. The differential treatment of people because of their class background and the reinforcing of these differences through values and practices of societal institutions.

Cognitive. Having to do with the process of knowing or perceiving.

Cognitive conceit. Elkind's term for children in Piaget's stage of concrete operations who put too much faith in their reasoning ability and cleverness.

Cognitively Oriented Curriculum. A curriculum that attempts to blend the virtues of purposeful teaching with open-ended, child-initiated activities.

Community. A group of people living in the same geographic area (neighborhood, town, or city) under common laws; it is also a group of people having fellowship, a friendly association, a mutual sharing, and common interests.

Community ecology. Comprises the psychological and practical relationships between humans and their social, as well as physical, environments.

Competence. Involves behavior that is socially responsible, independent, friendly, cooperative, dominant, achievement-oriented, and purposeful.

Competitive goal structure. Students work against each other to achieve goals that only a few students can attain.

Concrete operations. The third stage in Piaget's theory of cognitive development applying to children between the ages of 7 and 11. It is characterized by the ability to apply logical, systematic principles to specific experiences, but the inability to distinguish between assumptions or hypotheses and facts or reality.

Conformity. The condition of being similar or in agreement with others; action in accordance with the rules or customs of a group.

Conscience. The internal structure of one's socially learned standards of right and wrong by which an individual judges his or her behavior.

Contagion. The phenomenon in which an individual exposed to a suggestion will act on it.

Conventional level. Kohlberg's term to describe moral reasoning wherein the individual can look beyond personal consequences and consider other's perspectives.

Cooperative goal structure. Students work together to accomplish shared goals.

Cottage industry. One in which work takes place in the home.

Cultural pluralism. Mutual appreciation and understanding of various cultures in society; cooperation of diverse groups; co-existence of different languages, religious beliefs, and lifestyles; autonomy for each group to work out its own social purposes and future without interfering with the rights of other groups.

Culture. The knowledge, beliefs, art, morals, law, customs, and traditions acquired by humans as members of society.

Curriculum. Includes the goals and objections of the program, the teacher's role, the equipment and materials, the space arrangement, the kinds of activities and the way they are scheduled.

Daycare. Refers to the care given to children by persons other than parents during the parts of the day that parents are absent.

Deductive reasoning. Reasoning from a known principle to an unknown; from the general to the specific; from a premise to a logical conclusion.

Delinquency. Failure or neglect to do what the law requires; a misdeed.

Democracy. Societies in which those ruled have equal power to those who rule.

Democratic. Characterized by the acceptance and practice of the principles of equality of rights, opportunity, and treatment.

Desensitization. The gradual reduction in response to a stimulus due to repeated exposure.

Developmental appropriateness. Involves knowledge of children's normal growth patterns and individual differences.

Developmental Interaction Curriculum. A curriculum which is individualized in relation to each child's stage of development, while providing many opportunities for children to interact and become involved with peers and adults.

Developmental task. A task that lies between an individual need and a societal demand.

Direct Instruction Curriculum (DISTAR). A curriculum based on behaviorist principles.

Disability. Reduction in the functioning of a particular body part of organ, or its absence.

Discrimination. Perception of distinctions; difference or favoritism in treatment of others.

Eclectic. Gathered from various sources, systems, theories, and so on.

Ecology. The distribution of human groups with reference to material resources, and the consequent social and cultural patterns.

Egocentric. The cognitive inability to take another's point of view and consequent belief that everyone else looks at things the way one does.

Emancipation. Being set free from servitude or slavery.

Empowered. When individuals are enabled to have control over resources affecting them.

Equalitarian (egalitarian) family. Family in which both father and mother have equal authority and dominance.

Equilibrium. A Piagetian term for the state of balance between assimilation and accommodation, thereby allowing knowledge to be incorporated.

Ethnicity. An attribute of membership in a group in which members continue to identify themselves by national origin, culture, race, or religion.

Ethnographic study. A systematic recording of the distribution and characteristics of different cultures for the purpose of comparison.

Etiology. The cause(s) of a condition or disease, including genetic, physiological, and psychological or environmental factors.

Exosystem. A setting in which children do not actually participate, but which affects them in one of their microsystems (for example, parents' jobs, the school board, the city council).

Extended daycare. Care provided for children before or after school hours or during vacations.

Extended family. A family consisting of kin related to the nuclear family that lives nearby and is economically and emotionally dependent on each other.

External locus of control. Perception that others or events are responsible for one's fate.

Extinction. The gradual disappearance of a learned behavior, due to the removal of the reinforcement.

Fable. A fictitious story meant to teach a moral lesson. The characters are usually animals.

Family. Any two or more related people living in one household.

Family of orientation. The family into which one is born.

Family of procreation. The family that develops when one marries and has children.

Feedback. Valuative information about one's behavior.

Fixation. A Freudian term referring to arrested development.

Folk tale. A legendary or mythical story originating and handed down among the common people.

Formal operations. The fourth stage in Piaget's theory of cognitive development applying to children over the age of 11. It is characterized by the ability to think logically about abstract ideas and hypotheses as well as concrete facts.

Foster care. Parental care afforded someone not related by blood.

Gangs. Group of people who form an alliance for a common purpose and engage in unlawful or criminal activity.

Gemeinschaft. Communal, cooperative, close, intimate interpersonal informal relationships.

Gender role. Refers to the of qualities an individual understands to characterize males and females in his or her culture.

Generativity. Interest in establishing and guiding the next generation.

Gesellschaft. Associative, practical, objective, interpersonal formal relationships.

Goodness-of-fit. Accomodation of parenting styles to children's temperaments.

Handicap. Something that hampers a person; a disadvantage, a hindrance.

Handicapism. Assumptions and practices that promote the deferential and unequal treatment of people because they are different physically, mentally, or behaviorally.

Head Start. A federally funded comprehensive preschool program providing educational, health, and social services for qualified families in order to compensate for the effects of poverty, ethnic minority status, disability, and intended to enable children to enter school ready to learn.

Heterogenous. Composed of unrelated or unlike elements or parts.

Heteronomous morality. Children at Piaget's stage of moral development when they think of rules as moral absolutes that cannot be changed.

High-context macrosystem. Culture generally characterized by intuitiveness, emotionality, cooperation, group identity, and tradition.

Home Start. A federally funded project which extended the support services of Head Start by sending trained visitors to the homes of qualified families to teach parents how to work with their children.

Homogeneous. Composed of similar or identical elements or parts.

Humanism. A system of beliefs concerned with the interests and ideals of humans rather than those of the natural or spiritual world.

Impairment. Physical damage or deterioration.

Imaginary audience. The beliefs that others are as concerned with one's behavior and appearance as one is oneself.

Incest. Sexual relations between persons closely related.

Inclusion. The educational philosophy of being part of the whole, that all children are entitled to fully participate in their school and community.

Individualized Educational Program (IEP). A form of communication between school and family, developed by the group of people responsible for a handicapped child's education (teacher, parent, and other involved personnel).

Individualized goal structure. One student's achievement of the goal is unrelated to other students' achievement of that goal.

Inductive reasoning. Reasoning from particular facts or individual cases to a general conclusion.

Inner-directed person. One whose guidance comes from within.

Integration. The organization of various minority groups into one harmonious group.

Internalization. The process by which externally controlled behavior shifts to internally, or self-controlled, behavior.

Internal locus of control. Perception that one is responsible for one's own fate.

Intervention. The process of mediating as an influencing or protecting force.

Justice moral perspective. Emphasizes the rights of the individual; equitable rules of justice must prevail.

Kibbutz. Hebrew word for group; a collective where work and profits are shared.

Kinesthetic. Sensations from nerve endings in skin of muscles resulting from touch or movement.

Laissez faire. A policy of letting people do as they please; permissive.

Latchkey children. Children who carry their own key and let themselves into their homes.

Learner-directed curriculum. One in which the learning activities emerge from individual interests and teacher guidance.

Learned helplessness. A phenomenon exhibited by people who no longer perform effectively in a number of situations (they have learned to be helpless, as opposed to competent). This occurs when they feel their actions no longer provide control over outcomes.

Learning style. A consistent pattern of behavior and performance by which an individual approaches educational experiences. It results from the interaction of biological and contextual influences.

Locus of control. One's attribution of performance, or perception of responsibility for one's actions; may be internal or external.

Logical consequence. Natural outcome of misbehavior in which parents do not interfere.

Low-context microsystem. Culture generally characterized by rationality, practicality, competition, individuality, and progress.

Macrosystem. The child's society and the ideology in which he or she grows up (e.g., the United States, the middle class, Spanish ancestry, the Roman Catholic church).

Mainstreaming. A system for integrating disabled students into regular classes.

Maltreatment. Intentional harm to or endangerment of a child.

Mass media. Newspapers, magazines, books, radio, television, videos, and other means of communication that reach large audiences via an impersonal medium between the sender and the receiver.

Matriarchal family. Family in which the mother has formal authority and dominance.

Mediate. To interpose, come between, intervene.

Mesosystem. Interrelationships between two or more of a person's microsystems (for example, home and school, school and community).

Microsystem. The immediate setting where a child is at a particular time (the family, the school, the neighborhood, and so on).

Modeling. A form of imitative learning that occurs by observing the behavior of another person (the model).

Modern or open schools. Child-, or learner-, centered in that the curriculum emerges from child's interest with support from the teacher; value developing from the whole child.

Modern society. One that looks to the present for ways to behave, thereby being responsive to change.

Montessori curriculum. A curriculum involving different-aged children with materials designed for exercises in daily living, sensory development and academic development; the teacher facilitates individual learning via observation and encouragement.

Morality of constraint. Consists of behavior based on respect for persons in authority.

Morality of cooperation. Consists of behavior based on mutual understanding between equals.

Morals. An individual's evaluation of what is right and wrong. Morals involve acceptance of rules and govern one's behavior toward others.

Myth. A traditional story of unknown authorship, usually explaining some phenomenon of nature, the origin of man, or the customs, institutions, or religious rites of a people.

Negative reinforcement. The termination of an unpleasant condition following a desired response.

Neglect. Maltreatment involving abandonment, lack of supervision, improper feeding, lack of adequate medical or dental care, inappropriate dress, uncleanliness, lack of safety.

Neighborhood. A community composed of people living near one another having friendly relations.

Networking. A system of parallel involvement or communication connections that foster operation as a unit.

Newbery Medal. Award given for the most distinguished contribution to American literature for children.

Norms. Rules, patterns, or standards that express cultural values and reflect how individuals are supposed to behave.

Nuclear family. A family consisting of a husband and wife and their children.

On-task. Doing what one is supposed to do.

Operant. Producing an effect.

Other-directed person. One who cues his or her behavior from others.

Parenting. The implementation of a series of decisions about the socialization of children.

Passive listening. Listening without interrupting.

Patriarchal family. Family in which the father has formal authority and dominance.

Pedophilia. An adult's preference for, or addiction to, sexual relationships with children.

Peers. Individuals who are of approximately the same gender, age, and social status and who share interests.

Permissive. A style of child-centered parenting characterized by giving permission rather than forbidding.

Physical abuse. Maltreatment involving deliberate harm to the child's body.

Play. Behavior enjoyed for its own sake.

Pluralism. The existence of more than one belief system.

Positive reinforcement. Reward, or pleasant consequence, given for desired behavior.

Postconventional level. Kohlberg's term to describe moral reasoning wherein the individual considers and weighs the values behind various consequences from different points of view.

Preconventional level. Kohlberg's term to describe moral reasoning wherein the individual considers and weighs the personal consequences of the behavior.

Prejudice. An attitude involving prejudgment; the application of a previously formed judgment to some person, object, or situation.

Preoperational. The second stage in Piaget's theory of cognitive development applying to children from about ages 2 to 7. It is characterized by the use of symbols to represent objects, by judgment based on how things look, and by the belief that everyone has the same viewpoint as he or she.

Preventive services. Those which attempt to lessen the stresses and strains of life resulting from social and technological changes and to avert problems.

Primogeniture. The right of the eldest son to inherit his father's estate.

Professional. One who is engaged in an occupation requiring advanced training, usually involving intellectual work.

Project Follow Through. A federally funded project which extended the support services of Head Start to third grade.

Prosocial behavior. Includes only behavior that benefits other people, such as altruism, sharing, and cooperation.

Protestant Ethic. Belief in individualism, thrift, self-sacrifice, efficiency, personal responsibility, and productivity.

Psychological or emotional abuse. Maltreatment involving a destructive pattern of continual attack by an adult on a child's development of self and social competence, taking the forms of rejecting, isolating, terrorizing, ignoring, corrupting.

Punishment. Physical or psychologically painful stimuli or the temporary withdrawal of pleasant stimuli when undesirable behavior occurs.

Pygmalion. In Greek legend, a king of Cyprus, a sculptor, who fell in love with his statue of a maiden, Galatea. He prayed to Aphrodite to have his statue brought to life.

Reason. An explanation, or cause, for an act.

Rehabilitation. Restoring to a state of physical, mental, or moral health through treatment and training.

Rehabilitative services. Those that enable people to participate in the community.

Reinforcement. An object or event that is presented following a behavior, serving to increase the likelihood that it will occur again. Reinforcement can be positive or negative.

Religion. A unified system of beliefs and practices relative to sacred things.

Resilience. Refers to the ability to recover from, or adjust easily, to misfortune or change.

Ritual. A set form or system of rites; a ceremony.

Segregation. Separation of minority group from the majority group.

Selective attention. Choosing stimuli from one's environment to notice, observe, and consider.

Self-concept. The understanding of one's self as being separate from others.

Self-control. The ability to regulate one's impulses, behavior, and/or emotions until an appropriate time, place, or object is available for expression..

Self-esteem. One's regard, value, or favorable opinion of one's self.

Sensorimotor. The first stage of Piaget's theory of cognitive development applying to children from birth to about age 1 1/2 or 2. It is characterized by the use of one's senses and motor abilities to interact with the environment and the understanding of only the here and now.

Sexual abuse. Maltreatment whenever any person forces, tricks, or threatens a child in order to have sexual contact with him or her.

Shaping. The systematic immediate reinforcement of successive approximations of the desired behavior until the desired behavior occurs and is maintained.

Social cognition. Refers to conceptions and reasoning about people, the self, relations between people, social group's roles and rules, and relation of such conceptions to social behavior.

Socialization. The processes by which individuals acquire the knowledge, skills, and dispositions that enable them to participate as more or less effective members of groups and society.

Social support. Refers to the resources (tangible, intellectual, social, emotional) provided by others, usually in times of need.

Socioeconomic status. Rank or position within a system of society, based on social and economic factors.

Sociogram. A diagram showing preferences among group members for each other.

Sociometry. Techniques to measure patterns of acceptance, neglect, rejection among members of a group.

Sociotherapy. An intervention to enable children who have trouble making and keeping friends learn to relate to others.

Standard. A level or grade of excellence regarded as a goal or measure of adequacy.

Standardized tests. Tests in which an individual is compared to a norm on scientifically selected items.

Stereotype. An oversimplified, fixed attitude or set of beliefs about members of a particular group.

Stress. Any demand that exceeds the person's ability to cope.

Supportive services. Those which maintain the health, education, and welfare of society.

Symbols. Acts or objects that have come to be generally accepted as standing for something else.

Tabula Rasa. Refers to the mind before impressions are recorded upon it by experience (blank slate).

Teacher-directed curriculum. One in which the learning activities are planned by the teacher for all the children.

Temperament. The innate characteristics that determine an individual's sensitivity to various experiences and responsiveness to patterns of social interaction.

Therapy. The process of healing or curing.

Tradition. Stories, beliefs, customs, and so on, handed down from generation to generation.

Tradition-directed person. One who looks to tradition or the past for guidance and models of behavior.

Traditional school. Teacher-centered in that the curriculum is predetermined by the teacher and evaluation is based on success in mastering the learning objectives that value factual knowledge and preserving American cultural heritage.

Traditional society. One that relies on customs handed down from past generations as ways to behave.

Transductive reasoning. Reasoning from one particular fact or case to another similar fact or case.

Values. Qualities or beliefs that are viewed as desirable or important.

Values clarification. The process of discovering what things are most important or valuable to one.

Violence. The overt expression of physical force against one's will under threat of being hurt or killed; actually hurting or killing.

Zone of proximal development (ZPD). Vygotsky's term for the space between what one is capable of learning independently and the potential of what one can learn by participating with more capable others.

REFERENCES

Aaronfreed, J. (1968). *Conduct and conscience: The socialization of internalized control over behavior.* New York: Academic Press.

Aaronson, L. S., & MacNee, C. L. (1989). Tobacco, alcohol and caffeine use during pregnancy. *Journal of Obstetrics, Gynecology and Neonatal Nursing, 18,* 279–287.

Aboud, F. (1988). *Children and prejudice.* Cambridge, MA: Basil Blackwell.

Adams, G. R., & Crane, P. (1980). Assessment of parents' and teachers' expectations of preschool children's social preferences for attractive or unattractive children and adults. *Child Development, 51,* 224–231.

Adams, G. R., Gullotta, T. P., & Markstrom-Adams, C. (1994). *Adolescent life experiences* (3rd ed.). Pacific Grove, CA: Brooks/Cole.

Adler, J. (1998, November 2). Tomorrow's child. *Newsweek, 18,* pp. 54–64.

Adler, P. A., & Adler, P. (1998) *Peer power: Preadolescent culture and identity.* New Brunswick, NJ: Rutgers University Press.

Agne, K. J. (1992). Caring: The expert teacher's edge. *Educational Horizons, 70*(3), 120–124.

Aidman, A. (1995, December). Advertising in the schools. *ERIC Digest.* (No. ED389473)

Ainsworth, M. D. S. (1973). The development of infant–mother attachment. In B. M. Caldwell & H. N. Ricciuti (Eds.), *Review of child development research* (Vol. 3). Chicago: University of Chicago Press.

Ainsworth, M. D. S. (1979). Infant–mother attachment. *American Psychologist, 34,* 932–937.

Ainsworth, M. D. S. (1982). Attachment: Retrospect and prospect. In C. M. Parkes & J. Stevenson-Hinde (Eds.), *The place of attachment in human behavior.* New York: Basic Books.

Ainsworth, M. D. S., & Bell, S. M. (1970). Attachment, exploration, and separation: Illustrated by the behavior of one-year-olds in a strange situation. *Child Development, 41,* 49–67.

Ainsworth, M. D. S., Bell, S. M., & Stayton, D. J. (1971). Individual differences in strange-situation behavior of one-year-olds. In H. R. Shaffer (Ed.), *The origins of human social relations.* London: Academic Press.

Ainsworth, M. D. S. (1978). *Patterns of attachment: A psychological study of the strange situation.* Hillsdale, NJ: Lawrence Erlbaum.

Alsaker, F. D. (1992). Pubertal timing, overweight, and psychological adjustment. *Journal of Early Adolescence, 12,* 396–419.

Amato, P. (1998). More than money? Men's contributions to their children's lives. In A. Booth & A. C. Crouter (Eds.), *Men in families. When do they get involved? What difference does it make?* Mahwah, NJ: Lawrence Erlbaum.

American Academy of Child and Adolescent Psychiatry. (1997). *Facts for families: Children of alcoholics.* (No. 17). http://www.aacap.org/publications/factsfam/

American Academy of Child and Adolescent Psychiatry. (1997). *The influence of music and rock videos.* (No. 40). http://www.aacap.org/publications/factsfam/

American Academy of Pediatrics (1996). The impact of music lyrics and music videos on children and youth. Policy Statement. *Pediatrics, 98*(6), 1219-1221.

American Association of University Women. (1991). *How schools shortchange girls.* Washington, DC: American Association of University Women Educational Foundation.

Anastasiow. N.J. (1973). *Educational psychology: A contemporary view.* New York: Random House.

Apter, A., Galatzer, A., Beth-Halachmi, N. & Laron, Z. (1981). Self-image in adolescents with delayed puberty and growth retardation. *Journal of Youth and Adolescence, 10,* 501–505.

Archambault, R. D. (Ed.). (1969). *John Dewey on education: Selected writings.* New York: Random House.

Arenas, S. (1978). Bilingual/bicultural programs for preschool children. *Children Today, 7*(4), 2–6.

Arensberg, C. M., & Niehoff, A. H. (1975). American cultural values. In J. P. Spradley & M. A. Rynkiewich (Eds.), *The Nacirema: Reading on American culture.* Boston: Little, Brown.

Aries, P. (1962). *Centuries of childhood: A social history of family life.* New York: Knopf.

Aristotle. *Nicomachean ethics.* (Book II, Chapter 1). Author.

Arnett, J. (1991). Adolescents and heavy metal music: From the mouths of metal heads. *Youth and Society, 33*(1), 76–98.

Aronfreed, J. (1968). *Conduct and conscience.* New York: Academic Press.

Aronson, E., & Patenoe, S. (1996). *The jigsaw classroom: Building cooperation in the classroom.* Reading, MA: Addison-Wesley.

Arvey, R. D., & Chapman, J. E. (1982). The employment interview. *Personnel Psychology, 25,* 281–290.

Asch, S. E. (1958). Effects of group pressure upon the modification and distortion of judgments. In E. E. Maccoby, T. M. Newcomb, & E. L. Hartley (Eds.), *Readings in social psychology.* New York: Holt, Rinehart & Winston.

Asendorpf, J. B., & Baudoniere, P. (1993). Self-awareness and other-awareness: Mirror self-recognition and synchronic imitation among unfamiliar peers. *Developmental Psychology, 29,* 88–95.

Asher, S. R. (1982). Some kids are nobody's best friend. *Today's Education, 71*(1), 23.

Asher, S. R., & Coie, J. D. (1990). *Peer rejection in childhood.* New York: Cambridge University Press.

Asher, S. R., Gottman, J. M., & Oden, S. L. (1977). Children's friendships in school settings. In E. M. Hetherington & R. D. Parke (Eds.), *Contemporary readings in child psychology.* New York: McGraw-Hill.

Atkin, C., & Gibson, W. (1978). *Children's nutrition learning from television advertising.* Unpublished manuscript: Michigan State University.

Atkinson, A. H., & Green, V. P. (1990). Cooperative learning: The teacher's role. *Childhood Education, 67*(1), 8–11.

Ausubel, D. P. (1957). *Theory and problems of child development.* New York: Grune & Stratton.

Avery, C. D. (1971). A psychologist looks at the issue of public versus residential school placement for the blind. In R. L. Jones (Ed.), *Problems and issues in the education of exceptional children.* Boston: Houghton Mifflin.

Bachman, J. G. (1970). *Youth in transition* (Vol. 2). Ann Arbor: University of Michigan, Institute for Social Research.

Bain, S., Holliman, B., & McCallum, R. S. (1989). Children's self-predictions and teachers' predictions of basic concept mastery: Effects of socioeconomic status, locus of control, and achievement. *Journal of Psychoeducational Assessment, 7,* 235–245.

Baker, A. K., Barthelemy, K. J., & Kurdek, L. A. (1993). The relation between fifth and sixth graders' peer-rated classroom social status and their perceptions of family and neighborhood factors. *Journal of Applied Developmental Psychology, 14,* 547–556.

Baker, C. H., & Young, P. (1960). Feedback during training and retention of motor skills. *Canadian Journal of Psychology, 14,* 257–264.

Balk, D. E. (1995). *Adolescent development.* Pacific Grove, CA: Brooks/Cole.

Ball, S. J., & Bogatz, G. (1970). *The first year of Sesame Street: An evaluation.* Princeton, NJ: Educational Testing Service.

Bandura, A. (1965). Influence of models' reinforcement contingencies on the acquisition of imitative responses. *Journal of Personality and Social Psychology, 1,* 589–595.

Bandura, A. (1973). *Aggression: A social learning analysis.* Englewood Cliffs, NJ: Prentice-Hall.

Bandura, A. (1974). Behavior theory and the models of man. *American Psychologist, 29,* 859–869.

Bandura, A. (1977). *Social learning theory.* Englewood Cliffs, NJ: Prentice-Hall.

Bandura, A. (1986). *Social foundations of thought and action: A social cognitive theory.* Englewood Cliffs, NJ: Prentice-Hall.

Bandura, A. (1989). Social cognitive theory. In R. Vasta (Ed.), *Annals of child development. Vol. 6. Six theories of child development: Revised formulations and current issues.* Greenwich, CT: JAI Press.

Bandura, A. (1991). Social cognitive theory of moral thought and action. In W. M. Kurtines & J. L. Gewirtz (Eds.), *Handbook of moral behavior and development* (Vol. 1). Hillsdale, NJ: Lawrence Erlbaum.

Bandura, A., Ross, D., & Ross, S. (1963). Imitation of film-mediated aggressive models. *Journal of Abnormal and Social Psychology, 66,* 3–11.

Bandura, A., Ross, D., & Ross, S. (1965). A comparative test of status, envy, social power, and secondary reinforcement theories of identificatory learning. *Journal of Abnormal and Social Psychology, 67,* 527–534.

Bandura, A., & Walters, R. H. (1963). *Social learning and personality development.* New York: Holt, Rinehart & Winston.

Bangert-Drowns, R. L., Kulik, C. C., Kulik, J. A., & Morgan, M. (1991). The instructional effect of feedback in test-like events. *Review of Educational Research, 61,* 213–238.

Banks, J. A. (1994). *Multiethnic education: Theory and practice* (3rd ed.). Boston, MA: Allyn & Bacon.

Bannerman, A. (1899). *The story of little black Sambo.* Philadelphia: J.B. Lippincott.

Barclay, K., Benelli, C., & Curtis, A. (1995). Literacy begins at birth: What caregivers can learn from parents of children who read early. *Young Children, 50*(4), 24–28.

Barker, R. G., & Gump, P. G. (1964). *Big school, small school: High school size and student behavior.* Stanford, CA: Stanford University Press.

Barnett, D., Manley, J., & Cicchetti, D. (1993). Defining child maltreatment: The interface between policy and research. In D. Cicchetti & S. Toth (Eds.), *Child abuse, child development, and social policy.* Norwood, NJ: Ablex.

Baron, R. (1970). *Anonymity, deindividuation and aggression.* Unpublished Ph.D. dissertation. University of Minnesota.

Barry, H., Child, I. L., & Bacon, M. K. (1957). Relation of child training to subsistence economy. *American Anthropologist, 61,* 51–63.

Bar-Tal, D., Raviv, A., & Lesser, T. (1980). The development of altruistic behavior: Empirical evidence. *Developmental Psychology, 16,* 516–524.

Basow, S. A. (1992). *Gender stereotypes and roles* (3rd ed.). Pacific Grove, CA: Brooks/Cole.

Basow, S. A., & Rubin, L. R. (1999). Gender influence on adolescent development. In N. G. Johnson, M. C. Roberts, & J. Worell (Eds.), *Beyond appearance: A new look at adolescent girls*. Washington, DC: American Psychological Association.

Baumrind, D. (1966). Effects of authoritative parental control on child behavior. *Child Development, 37*, 887–907.

Baumrind, D. (1967). Child care practices anteceding three patterns of preschool behavior. *Genetic Psychology Monographs, 74*, 43–88.

Baumrind, D. (1971a). Current patterns of parental authority. *Developmental Psychology, 4*, 1–101.

Baumrind, D. (1971b). Current patterns of parental authority. *Developmental Psychology Monographs, 4*(1). (Part 2)

Baumrind, D. (1973). The development of instrumental competence through socialization. In A. Pick (Ed.), *Minnesota symposium on child psychology* (Vol. 7). Minneapolis: University of Minnesota Press.

Baumrind, D. (1977, April). *Socialization determinants of personal agency*. Paper presented at the biennial meeting of the Society for Research in Child Development, New Orleans, LA.

Baumrind, D. (1989). Rearing competent children. In W. Damon (Ed.), *Child development today and tomorrow*. San Francisco: Jossey-Bass.

Baumrind, D. (1991). Effective parenting during the early adolescent transition. In P. A. Cowan & E. M. Hetherington (Eds.), *Family transitions*. Hillsdale, NJ: Lawrence Erlbaum.

Baydar, N., & Brooks-Gunn, J. (1991). Effects of maternal employment and child care arrangements on preschoolers' cognitive and behavioral outcomes. Evidence from the children of the National Longitudinal Survey of Youth. *Developmental Psychology, 27*(6), 932–945.

Beane, J. A. (1991). Sorting out the self-esteem controversy. *Educational Leadership, 49*(1), 25–30.

Beatty, B. (1995). *Preschool education in America. The culture of young children from the colonial era to the present*. New Haven: Yale University Press.

Bednar, R. L., Wells, M. G., & Peterson, S. R. (1989). *Self-esteem*. Washington, DC: American Psychological Association.

Beez, W. V. (1968). Influence of biased psychological reports on teacher behavior and pupil performance. *Proceedings of the 75th APA Annual Convention*. Washington, DC: American Psychological Association.

Begley, S. (1997, Spring/Summer). How to build a baby's brain. *Newsweek*, 28–32.

Behrman. R. E. (Ed.). (1997a, Spring). Executive summary: Welfare to work. *The Future of Children, 7*(1).

Behrman, R. E. (Ed.). (1997b, Summer/Fall). Executive summary: Children and poverty. *The Future of Children, 7*(2).

Behrman, R. E. (1999 Fall). Executive-summary: When school is out. *The Future of Children, 7*(1).

Bell, P.A., Greene, T.C., Fisher, J.D., & Baum, A. (1996). *Environmental psychology* (4th ed.). Fort Worth, TX: Harcourt Brace.

Belle, D. (1989). Studying children's social networks and social supports. In D. Belle (Ed.), *Children's social networks and social supports*. New York: John Wiley & Sons.

Belle, D. (1999). *The after-school lives of children: Alone and with others while parents work*. Mahwah, NJ: Lawrence Erlbaum.

Belsky, J. (1988). The "effects" of infant day care reconsidered. *Early Childhood Research Quarterly, 3*, 235–272.

Belsky, J. (1992). Consequences of child care for children's development: A deconstructionist view. In A. Booth (Ed.), *Childcare in the 1990s: Trends and consequences*. Hillsdale, NJ: Lawrence Erlbaum.

Belsky, J. (1993). Etiology of child maltreatment: A developmental–ecological analysis. *Psychological Bulletin, 114*, 413–434.

Belsky, J., & Rovine, M. (1988). Nonmaternal care in the first year of life and infant–parent attachment security. *Child Development, 59*, 157–167.

Bem, S. L. (1981). Gender schema theory: A cognitive account of sex-typing. *Psychological Review, 88*, 354–364.

Bennett, C. I. (1998). *Comprehensive multicultural education: Theory and practice* (4th ed.). Boston: Allyn & Bacon.

Bennett, W. J. (1993). *The book of virtues: A treasury of great moral stories*. New York: Simon & Schuster.

Bereiter, C., & Engelmann, S. (1966). *Teaching disadvantaged children in the preschool*. Englewood Cliffs, NJ: Prentice-Hall.

Berenda, R. (1950). *The influence of the group on the judgment of children*. New York: King's Crown Press.

Berg, M., & Medrich, E. A. (1980). Children in four neighborhoods: The physical environment and its effects on play and play patterns. *Environment and Behavior, 12*(3), 320–346.

Berger, E. H. (1995). *Parents as partners in education: Families and schools working together* (4th ed.). Columbus, OH: Merrill.

Berk, L. E. (1997). *Child development* (4th ed.). Needham Heights: Allyn & Bacon.

Berk, L. E., & Winsler, A. (1995). *Scaffolding children's learning: Vygotsky and early childhood education*. Washington, DC: National Association for the Education of Young Children.

Berndt, T. J. (1979). Developmental changes in conformity to peers and parents. *Developmental Psychology, 15,* 608–616.

Berndt, T. J. (1983). Correlates and causes of sociometric status in childhood: A commentary on six current studies of popular, rejected and neglected children. *Merrill-Palmer Quarterly, 29,* 439–448.

Berndt, T. J., & Ladd, G. W. (1989). *Peer relationships in child development.* New York: John Wiley & Sons.

Bernhard, J. K., Lefebvre, M.L., Kilbride, K.M., Chud, G., & Lange, R. (1998). Troubled relationships in early childhood education: Parent–teacher interactions in ethnoculturally diverse childcare settings. *Early Education and Development, 9,* 5–28.

Berns, R. (1981). *When handicaps come in handy.* Washington, DC: Department of Health, Education and Welfare, National Institute of Education, Educational Resources Information Center. (ED 208621)

Bernstein, A. (1984, September). *Parents,* pp. 40–44, 48–49.

Bernstein, B. (1961). Social class and linguistic development: A theory of social learning. In A. H. Halsey, J. Floud, & C. A. Anderson (Eds.), *Education, economy and society.* New York: Free Press.

Berreth, D., & Berman, S. (1997, May). The moral dimensions of schools. *Educational Leadership,* 24–27.

Best, R. (1983). *We've all got scars: What boys and girls learn in elementary school.* Bloomington: Indiana University Press.

Bettelheim, B. (1976). *The uses of enchantment. The meaning and importance of fairy tales.* New York: Random House.

Bhavnagri, N. P. (1997). The cultural context of caregiving. *Childhood Education, 74*(1), 2–7.

Bigler, R. S., & Liben, L. S. (1990). The role of attitudes and interventions in gender-schematic processing. *Child Development, 61,* 1440–1452.

Bigner, J. (1979). *Parent-child relations.* New York: Macmillan.

Biklen, D., & Bogdan, R. (1977). Media portrayals of disabled people: A study in stereotypes. *Interracial Books for Children Bulletin, 6, 7, 8,* 4–9.

Biller, H. B. (1993). *Fathers and families: Paternal factors in child development.* Wesport, CT: Auburn House.

Binion, V. J. (1990). Psychological androgyny: A black female perspective. *Sex roles, 22,* 487–507.

Biskind, P. (1983). *Seeing is believing. How Hollywood taught us to stop worrying and love the fifties.* New York: Pantheon Books.

Bjorklund, D. F. (1994). *Children's thinking* (2nd ed.). Pacific Grove, CA: Brooks/Cole.

Black, C. (1991). *It will never happen to me!* (reissue ed.). Denver: M.A.C.

Black, E. I., & Roberts, J. (1992, September/October). Rituals for our times. *New Age Journal,* 70–23.

Blake, J. (1989). *Family size and achievement.* Berkeley, CA: University of California Press.

Block, J. H. (1973). Conceptions of sex role: Some cross-cultural and longitudinal perspectives. *American Psychologist, 28,* 512.

Block, J. H. (1984). The influence of differential socialization on the personality development of males and females. In A. Pines & C. Maslach (Eds.), *Experiencing social psychology* (2nd ed.). New York: Knopf.

Block, J. H., & Robins, R. W. (1993). A longitudinal study of consistency and change in self-esteem from early adolescence to early adulthood. *Child Development, 64,* 909–923.

Bloom, B. S. (1964). *Stability and change in human characteristics.* New York: John Wiley & Sons.

Bloom, B. S. (1973). Individual differences in achievement. In L. J. Rubin (Ed.), *Facts and feelings in the classroom.* New York: Viking.

Blume, J. (1970). *Are you there, God? It's me, Margaret.* New York: Dell.

Blume, J. (1974). *Blubber.* New York: Dell.

Bogenschneider, K., Wu, M., Raffaelli, M., & Tsay, J. C. (1998). Parental influences on adolescent peer orientation and substance use: The interface of parenting practices and values. *Child Development, 69,* 1672–1688.

Bok, S. (1989). *Lying: Moral choice in public and private life.* NewYork: Vintage.

Bornstein, M. H. (1995). Parenting infants. In M. H. Bornstein (Ed.), *Handbook of parenting* (Vol. 1). Hillsdale, NJ: Lawrence Erlbaum.

Bossard, J. H. S., & Boll, E. S. (1954). The status of children in society. In J. H. S. Bossard & E. S. Boll (Eds.), *The society of child development.* New York: Harper & Row.

Bossard, J. H. S., & Boll, E. S. (1956). *The large family system.* Philadelphia: University of Pennsylvania Press.

Boswell, D. A., & Williams, J. E. (1975). Correlates of race and color bias among preschool children. *Psychological Reports, 36,* 147–154.

Bowlby, J. (1966). *Maternal care and mental health* (2nd ed.). New York: Schocken. (Orig. publication by World Health Organization of the United Nations, Geneva, 1952)

Bowlby, J. (1969). *Attachment* (Vol. 1). New York: Basic Books.

Bowlby, J. (1973). *Loss.* (Vol. 2). New York: Basic Books.

Bowlby, J. (1988). *A secure base: Parent–child attachment and healthy human development.* New York: Basic Books.

Bowman, H. E., & Ahrons, C. R. (1985). Impact of legal custody status on fathers' parenting postdivorce. *Journal of Marriage and the Family, 47,* 481–488.

Boyd, B. J. (1997). Teacher response to superhero play: To ban or not to ban? *Childhood Education, 74*(1), 23–28.

Boyer, E. L. (1991). *Ready to learn: A mandate for the nation.* Princeton, NJ: Carnegie Foundation for the Advancement of Technology.

Boyer, P. J. (1983, March 15). TV grants kids a short shrift. *Los Angeles Times* (Part VI), p. 1.

Bradley, R. H, Caldwell, B. M., & Rock, S. L. (1990). Home environment classification system: A model for assessing the home environments of developing children. *Early Education and Development, 1,* 237–265.

Bray, S. H. (1988). Children's development during early remarriage. In E. M. Hetherington & J. D. Arasteh (Eds.), *Impact of divorce, single parenting and stepparenting on children.* Hillsdale, NJ: Lawrence Erlbaum.

Brazelton, T. B. (1984, February 13). Working parents. *Newsweek,* 66-70.

Bredekamp, S. (Ed.). (1986). *Developmentally appropriate practice.* Washington, DC: National Association for the Education of Young Children.

Bredekamp, S. (Ed.). (1993). *Developmentally appropriate practice in early childhood programs serving children from birth through age eight.* Washington, DC: National Association for the Education of Young Children.

Bredekamp, S., & Copple, C. (Eds.). (1997). *Developmentally appropriate practice in early childhood programs* (rev. ed.). Washington, DC: National Association for the Education of Young Children.

Bria, G. (1998). *The art of family.* New York: Dell.

Bridges, K. B. (1933). A study of social development in early infancy. *Child Development, 4,* 36–49.

Bridges, L. J., & Grolnick, W. S. (1995). The development of emotional self-regulation in infancy and early childhood. In N. Eisenberg (Ed.), *Review of personality and psychology.* Newbury Park, CA: Sage.

Briggs, D. C. (1975). *Your child's self-esteem.* New York: Dolphin.

Brim, O. G. (1966). Socialization through the life cycle. In O. G. Brim & S. Wheeler (Eds.), *Socialization after childhood: Two essays.* New York: John Wiley & Sons.

Britton, G., & Limpkin, M. (1983). Basal readers: Paltry progress pervades. *Interracial Books for Children Bulletin, 14*(6), 4–7.

Brody, G. H., & Flor, D. L. (1998). Maternal resources, parenting practices, and child competence in rural, single-parent African American families. *Child Development, 69*(3), 803–816.

Bromer, J. (1999). Cultural variations in child care: Values and action. *Young Children, 54*(6), 72–75.

Bronfenbrenner, U. (1970a). *Two worlds of childhood: U.S. and U.S.S.R.* New York: Russell Sage.

Bronfenbrenner, U. (1970b). Reaction to social pressure from adults versus peers of Soviet day-school and boarding-school pupils in the perspective of an American sample. *Journal of Personality and Social Psychology, 15,* 179–189.

Bronfenbrenner, U. (1970c, November). *Who cares for American's children?* Address presented at the National Association of Educators of Young Children Conference, Boston, MA..

Bronfenbrenner, U. (1977). Is early intervention effective? In S. Cohen & T. J. Comiskey (Eds.), *Child development: Contemporary perspectives.* Itasca, IL: Peacock.

Bronfenbrenner, U. (1979). *The ecology of human development.* Cambridge MA: Harvard University Press.

Bronfenbrenner, U. (1980). Reunification with our children. In P. Mussen, J. Conger, & J. Kagan (Eds.), *Readings in child and adolescent psychology: Contemporary perspectives.* New York: Harper & Row.

Bronfenbrenner, U. (1989). Ecological systems theory. In R. Vasta (Ed.), *Annals of child development* (Vol. 6). Greenwich, CT: JAI Press.

Bronfenbrenner, U. (1995). Developmental ecology through space and time: A future perspective. In P. Moen, G. H. Elder Jr., & K. Luscher (Eds.), *Examining lives in context: Perspectives on the ecology of human development.* Washington, DC: American Psychological Association.

Bronfenbrenner, U. (Ed.). (1974). *A report on longitudinal evaluations of preschool programs. Vol. 2: Is early intervention effective?* Washington, DC: U.S. Department of Health and Human Services.

Bronfenbrenner, U., & Crouter, A. (1982). Work and family through time and space. In S. B. Kammerman & C. D. Hayes (Eds.), *Families that work: Children in a changing world.* Washington, DC: National Academy Press.

Bronfenbrenner, U., & Garbarino, J. (1976). The socialization of moral judgment and behavior in cross-cultural perspective. In T. Lickona (Ed.), *Moral development and behavior.* New York: Holt, Rinehart & Winston.

Bronfenbrenner, U., & Morris, P. A. (1998). The ecology of developmental processeses. In W. Damon (Ed.), *Handbook of child psychology* (5th ed., Vol. 1). New York: John Wiley & Sons.

Brook, J. S., & Cohen, P. (1990). The psychological etiology of adolescent drug use: A family interactional approach. *Genetic Psychology Monographs, 116*(2).

Brooks-Gunn, J., & Furstenberg, F. F., Jr. (1989). Adolescent sexual behavior. *American Psychologist, 44*(2), 249–257.

Brophy, B. (1989, August 7). Spock had it right: Studies suggest that kids thrive when parents set firm limits. *U.S. News & World Report*, 49–51.

Brophy, J. E. (1986). Teacher influences on student achievement. *American Psychologist, 41*, 1069–1077.

Brophy, J. E. (1992). Probing the subtleties of subject matter teaching. *Educational Leadership, 49*(7), 4–8.

Brophy, J. E., & Good, T. L. (1986). Teacher behavior and student achievement. In M. Wittrock (Ed.), *Handbook of research on teaching* (3rd ed.). New York: Macmillan.

Brown, B. B., & Lohr, M. J. (1987). Peer group affiliation, adolescent self-esteem, and integration of ego-identity and symbolic-interaction theories. *Journal of Personality and Social Psychology, 52*(1), 47–57.

Brown, B. B., Clasen, D. R., & Eicher, S. A. (1986). Perceptions of peer pressure, peer conformity dispositions and self-reported behavior among adolescents. *Developmental Psychology, 22*, 521–530.

Brown, L. M., & Gilligan, C. (1990, March). *The psychology of women and the development of girls*. Paper presented at the meeting of the Society for Research on Adolescence, Atlanta, GA.

Brown, L. S., & Zimmer, D. (1986). An introduction to therapy issues of lesbian and gay male couples. In N. S. Jacobson & A. S. Gurman (Eds.), *Clinical handbook of marital therapy*. New York: Guilford.

Brown, M. W. (1947). *Goodnight moon*. New York: Harper & Row.

Bruner, J. (1981). The art of discovery. In M. Kaplan-Sangoff & R. Y. Magid (Eds.), *Exploring early childhood*. New York: Macmillan.

Bryant, J., & Rockwell, S. C. (1994). Effects of massive exposure to sexually oriented prime-time television programming on adolescents' moral judgment. In D. Zillman, J. Bryant, & A. C. Huston (Eds.), *Media, children, and the family: Social, scientific, psychodynamic, and clinical perspectives*. Hillsdale, NJ: Lawrence Erlbaum.

Bugental, D. B., & Goodenow, J. J. (1998). Socialization processes. In W. Damon (Ed.), *Handbook of child psychology* (5th ed., Vol. 3). New York: John Wiley & Sons.

Bullock, J. R. (1992, Winter). Children without friends: Who are they and how can teachers help? *Childhood Education*, 92–96.

Burhans, K. K., & Dweck, C. S. (1995). Helplessness in early childhood. The role of contingent worth. *Child Development, 66*, 1719–1738.

Burton, C. B. (1985). Children's peer relationships. *ERIC Digest*.

Buss, A. H., & Plomin, R. (1994) *Temperament: Early developing personality traits*. Hillsdale, NJ: Lawrence Erlbaum.

Byrnes, D. A. (1996). Addressing race, ethnicity and culture in the classroom. In D. A. Byrnes & G. Kiger (Eds.), *Common bonds: Anti-bias teaching in a diverse society* (2nd ed.). Wheaton, MD: Association for Childhood Education International.

Cain, K. M., & Dweck, C. J. (1995). The relation between motivational patterns and achievement cognitions through the elementary school years. *Merrill Palmer Quartery, 41*, 25–52.

Caldera, Y. M., Huston, A. C., & O'Brien, M. (1989). Social interactions and play patterns of parents and toddlers with feminine, masculine, and neutral toys. *Child Development, 60*, 70–76.

Caldwell, B. M. (1986). Education of families for parenting. In M. W. Yogman & T. B. Brazelton (Eds.), *In support of families*. Cambridge, MA: Harvard University Press.

Caldwell, B. M., & Bradley, R. H. (1984). *Manual for the home observation for measurement of the environment*. Little Rock: University of Arkansas Press.

Caldwell, B. M., & Crary, D. (1981). Why are kids so darned aggressive? *Parents, 56*(2), 52–56.

California State Department of Education [CSDE]. (1987). *Handbook for teaching Japanese-speaking students*. Sacramento, CA: Author.

CSDE. (1986). *Handbook for teaching Filipino-speaking students*. Sacramento, CA: Author.

CSDE. (1989). *Handbook for teaching Cantonese-speaking students*. Sacramento, CA: Author.

CSDE. (1992). *Handbook for teaching Korean-American students*. Sacramento, CA: Author.

CSDE. (1994). *Handbook for teaching Vietnamese-speaking students*. Sacramento, CA: Author.

Campbell, J. D. (1964). Peer relations in childhood. In M. Hoffman & L. Hoffman (Eds.), *Review of child development research* (Vol. 1). New York: Russell Sage.

Cantor, J. (1998). *"Mommy, I'm scared": How TV and movies frighten children and what we can do to protect them*. San Diego, CA: Harcourt Brace.

Carle, E. (1986). *The very hungry caterpillar*. New York: Putnam.

Carlsen, G. R. (1980). *Books and the teenage reader*. New York: Harper & Row.

Carlson, M., Charlin, V., & Miller, N. (1988). Positive mood and helping behavior: A test of six hypotheses. *Psychological Bulletin, 55*, 211–229.

Carpenter, C. J. (1983). Activity, structure, and play: Implications for socialization. In M. B. Liss (Ed.), *Social and cognitive skills: Sex roles and children's play*. New York: Academic Press.

Carpenter, C. J., Huston, A. C., & Hart, W. (1986). Modification of preschool sex-typed behaviors by participation in adult-structured activities, *Sex Roles, 4,* 603–615.

Carr, M., Borkowski, J. G., & Maxwell, S. E. (1991). Motivational components of underachievement. *Developmental Psychology, 27*(1), 108–118.

Cashdan, S. (1999). *The witch must die: How fairy tales shape our lives.* New York: Basic Books.

Caudill, W. (1988). Tiny dramas: Vocal communication between mother and infant in Japanese and American families. In G. Handel (Ed.), *Childhood socialization.* New York: Aldine de Gruyter.

Caudill, W., & Weinstein, H. (1969). Maternal care and infant behavior in Japan and America. *Psychiatry, 32,* 12–43.

Center for Media and Public Affairs. (1999). *I'm okay, you're dead! TV and movies suggest violence is harmless.* http://www.cmpa.com/pressrel/

Centers for Disease Control and Prevention. (1994). *Preventing tobacco use among young people: A report of the Surgeon General.* Atlanta, GA: U.S. Department of Health and Human Services.

Cesarone, B. (1994, January). Video games and children, *ERIC Digest.* (ED-PS-94-3)

Cetron, M. J. (1988, November/December). Class of 2000. *The Futurist,* 9–15.

Chafel, J. A. (1997). Schooling, the hidden curriculum, and children's conceptions of poverty. Social Policy Report. *Society for Research in Child Development, 11*(1).

Chafetz, J. S. (1974). *Masculine/feminine or human? An overview of the sociology of sex roles.* Itasca, IL: Peacock.

Chance, P. (1982). Your child's self-esteem. *Parents, 57,* 54–59.

Chao, R. (1994). Beyond parent control and authoritarian parenting style: Understanding Chinese parenting through the culture notion of training. *Child Development, 65,* 1111–1119.

Char, C. A., & Meringoff, L. K. (1981, January). The role of story illustrations: Children's story comprehension in three different media. *Harvard Project Zero Technical Report.* (No. 22)

Chase-Lansdale, P. L., & Hetherington, E. M. (1990). The impact of divorce on life-span development: Short and long-term effects. In D. Featherman & R. M. Lerner (Eds.), *Lifespan development and behavior* (Vol. 6). Orlando, FL: Academic Press.

Cherian, V. I. (1989). Academic achievement of children of divorced parents. *Psychological Reports, 64,* 355–358.

Chess, S., & Thomas, A. (1987). *Know your child.* New York: Basic Books.

Child Welfare League of America. (1987). *The children's presidential campaign '88.* New York: Author.

Children Now. (May, 1998). *A different world: Children's perceptions of race and class in media.* Oakland, CA: Author.

Children's Defense Fund [CDF]. (1990). *Children, 1990: A report briefing book and activity primer.* Washington, DC: Author

CDF. (1994). *The state of America's children: Yearbook 1994.* Washington, DC: Author.

CDF. (1998). *The state of America's children: Yearbook 1998.* Washington, DC: Author.

Chomsky, N. (1972). Stages in language development and reading exposure. *Harvard Educational Review, 42,* 1–33.

Christenson, P. G., & Roberts, D. F. (1990). *Popular music in early adolescence.* Washington, DC: The Carnegie Council on Adolescent Development.

Cicchetti, D., & Lynch, M. (1993). Toward an ecological transactional model of community violence and child maltreatment: Consequences for children's development. *Psychiatry, 56,* 96–118.

Clarke-Stewart, K. A. (1987). Predicting child development from day care forms and features: The Chicago study. In D. A. Phillips (Ed.), *Quality in childcare. What does research tell us? Research Monographs of the National Association for the Education of Young Children* (Vol. 1). Washington, DC: National Association for the Education of Young Children.

Clarke-Stewart, K. A. (1988). The "effects" of infant day care reconsidered: Risks for parents, children, and researchers. *Early Childhood Research Quarterly, 3,* 293–318.

Clarke-Stewart, K. A. (1989). Infant day care: Maligned or malignant? *American Psychologist, 44*(2), 266–273.

Clarke-Stewart, K. A. (1992). Consequences of child care for children's development. In A. Booth (Ed.), *Childcare in the 1990s: Trends and consequences.* Hillsdale, NJ: Lawrence Erlbaum.

Clarke-Stewart, K. A. (1993). *Daycare* (rev. ed.). Cambridge, MA: Harvard University Press.

Clarke-Stewart, K. A., Allhusen, V. D., & Clements, D. C. (1995). Nonparenting caregiving. In M. H. Bornstein (Ed.), *Handbook of parenting* (Vol. 3). Mahwah, NJ: Lawrence Erlbaum.

Clausen, J. A. (1975). The social meaning of differential physical and sexual maturation. In S. E. Dragastin & G. H. Elder (Eds.), *Adolescence in the life cycle.* New York: John Wiley & Sons.

Coates, B., Pusser, H. E., & Goodman, I. (1976). The influence of "Sesame Street" and "Mister Rogers' Neighborhood" on children's social behavior in the preschool. *Child Development, 47,* 138–144.

Coates, D. L. (1987). Gender differences in the structure and support characteristics of black adolescents' social networks. *Sex Roles, 17,* 719–736.

Cochran, M. (1993). Parenting and personal social networks. In T. Luster & L. Okagaki (Eds.), *Parenting: An ecological perspective*. Hillsdale, NJ: Lawrence Erlbaum.

Cochran, M., & Henderson, C. R. Jr. (1986). *Family matters: Evaluation of the parental empowerment program*. Ithaca, NY: Cornell University. (ED 262862)

Cocks, J. (1985, September 30). Rock is a four-letter word. *Time*, pp. 70–71.

Cohen, D., Pettigrew, T., & Riley, R. (1972). Race and the outcoming of schooling. In R. Mosteller & D. P. Moynihan (Eds.), *On equality of educational opportunity*. New York: Random House.

Cohen, R., Bornstein, R., & Sherman, R. C. (1973). Conformity behavior of children as a function of group make-up and task ambiguity. *Developmental Psychology, 9*, 124–131.

Cohen, S., Glass, D. C., & Singer, J. E. (1973). Apartment noise, auditory discrimination, and reading ability in children. *Journal of Experimental Social Psychology, 9*, 407–422.

Coie, J. D., Dodge, K. A., & Kupersmidt, J. B. (1990). Peer group behavior and social status. In S. R. Asher & J. D. Coie (Eds.), *Peer rejection in childhood*. New York: Cambridge University Press.

Coie, J. J., & Cilleson. A. (1993). Peer rejection: Origins and effects on children's development. *Current Directions in Psychological Science, 2*, 89–92.

Colby, A., Kohlberg, L., Gibbs, J., & Lieberman, M. A. (1983). A longitudinal study of moral judgment. *Monographs of the Society for Research in Child Development, 48*, 1–2. (Serial No. 200)

Cole, D. A. (1991). Change in self-perceived competence as a function of peer and teacher evaluation. *Developmental Psychology, 27*, 682–688.

Cole, E., & Duva, J. (1990). *Family preservation: An orientation for administrators and practitioners*. Washington, DC: Child Welfare League of America.

Coleman, J. (1961). *The adolescent society*. New York: Macmillan.

Coleman, J. (1966). *Equality of educational opportunity*. Washington, DC: U.S. Government Printing Office.

Coleman, J. S. (1990). *Foundations of social theory*. Englewood Cliffs, NJ: Prentice-Hall.

Coletta, A. J. (1977). *Working together, a guide to parent involvement*. Atlanta: Humanics Limited.

Collins, J. D. (1981). Recognition of the body and its parts during adolescence. *Journal of Youth and Adolescence, 10*, 243–254.

Collins, L. J., Ingoldsby, B. B., & Dellman, M. M. (1984). Sex-role stereotyping in children's literature: A change from the past. *Childhood Education, 60*(4), 278–285.

Collins, W. A., Harris, M. L., & Susman, A. (1995). Parenting during middle childhood. In M. H. Bornstein (Ed.), *Handbook of parenting* (Vol. 1). Mahwah, NJ: Lawrence Erlbaum.

Collodi, C. (1972). Pinocchio. In *The new Walt Disney treasury*. New York: Garden Press.

Comer, I. P. (1988) Educating poor minority children. *Scientific American, 259*(5), 42–48.

Comstock, G., Ghaffee, S., Katzman, N., Maxwell, M. & Roberts, D. (1978). *Television and human behavior*. New York: Columbia University Press.

Comstock, G., & Paik, H. (1991). *Television and the American child*. San Diego, CA: Academic Press.

Comstock, G., & Sharrer, E. (1999). *Television: What's on, who's watching and what it means*. San Diego, CA: Academic Press.

Condry, J. (1989). *The psychology of television*. Hillsdale, NJ: Lawrence Erlbaum.

Condry, J. C., & Simon, M. L. (1974). Characteristics of peer- and adult-oriented children. *Journal of Marriage and the Family, 36*, 543–546.

Condry, J., Bence, P., & Scheibe, C. (1988). Nonprogram content of children's television. *Journal of Broadcasting and Electronic Media, 32*(3), 255–270.

Conger, R. D., Xiaojia, G., Elder, G. H. Jr. , Lorenz, F. O., Simons, R. L., & Whitebeck, L. B. (1994). Economic stress, coercive family process, and developmental problems of adolescents. *Child Development, 65*(2), 541–561.

Connors, L. J., & Epstein, J. L. (1995). Parent and school partnerships. In M. H. Bornstein (Ed.), *Handbook of parenting* (Vol. 4). Mahwah, NJ: Lawrence Erlbaum.

Cooley, C. (1909/1964). *Human nature and the social order*. New York: Schocken.

Coontz, S. (1997). *The way we really are: Coming to terms with America's changing families*. New York: Basic Books.

Cooper, J., & Mackie, D. (1986). Video games and aggression in children. *Journal of Applied Social Psychology, 16*, 726–744.

Coopersmith, S. (1967). *The antecedents of self-esteem*. San Francisco: Freeman.

Corcoran, M. E., & Chandry, A. (1997). The dynamics of childhood poverty. *The Future of Children, 7*(2), 40–54.

Corder-Bolz, C. R. (1980). Mediation: The role of significant others. *Journal of Communication, 30*(3), 108–118.

Corsaro, W. A. (1981). Friendship in the nursery school: Social organization in a peer environment. In S. R. Asher & J. M. Gottman (Eds.), *The development of children's friendships*. Cambridge: Cambridge University Press.

Cost, Quality & Child Outcomes Study Team. (1995). *Cost, quality, and child outcomes in child care centers, executive summary* (2nd ed.). Denver: Economics Department, University of Colorado at Denver.

Cotterell, J. L. (1986). Work and community influences on the quality of child rearing. *Child Development, 57*, 362–374.

Cottle, T. S., & Edelman, M. (1975). What every parent should know about our country's neglected children. *Parents, 50*(12), 36–37.

Council of Better Business Bureaus. (2000). *The children's advertising review unit. Self-regulatory guidelines for children's advertising.* http://www.bbb.org/advertising/caruguid.asp

Covington, M. V., & Beery, R. G. (1976). *Self-worth and school learning.* New York: Holt, Rinehart & Winston.

Cowan, P. A., Powell, D., & Cowan, C. P. (1998). In W. Damon (Ed.), *Handbook of child psychology* (5th ed., Vol. 4). New York: John Wiley & Sons.

Cox, M. J., Owen, M.T., Henderson, V.K., & Margand, N. A. (1992). Prediction of infant–father and infant–mother attachment. *Developmental Psychology, 28*(3), 474–483.

Crick, N. R., Casas, J. F., & Ku, Hyon-Chin. (1999). Relation of physical forms of peer victimization in preschool. *Developmental Psychology, 35*, 376–385.

Crime Prevention Center. (1988). *Child abuse prevention handbook.* Sacramento, CA: California Department of Justice.

Crook, C. (1992). Cultural artifacts in social development: The case of computers. In H. McGurk (Ed.), *Childhood social development: Contemporary perspectives.* Hove, England: Lawrence Erlbaum.

Crouter, A. C., & McHale, S. M. (1993). The long arm of the job: Influences of parental work on childrearing. In T. Luster & L. Okagaki (Eds.), *Parenting: An ecological perspective.* Hillsdale, NJ: Lawrence Erlbaum.

Cubberley, E. P. (1919). *Public education in the United States.* Boston: Houghton Mifflin.

Curran, D. (1985). *Stress and the healthy family.* Minneapolis, MN: Winston Press.

Dahl, R. (1964). *Charlie and the chocolate factory.* New York: Knopf.

Daiute, C. (1983). Writing, creativity and change. *Childhood Education, 59*(4), 227–231.

Damon, W. (1988). *The moral child: Nurturing children's natural moral growth.* New York: Free Press.

Damon, W. D. (1999). The moral development of children. *Scientific American, 281*(2), 72–78.

Darlington, R., & Lazar, I. (1977). *Lasting effects after preschool.* Washington, DC: U.S. Department of Health and Human Services.

Daugherty, W. J., Kouneski, E. F., & Erickson, M. F. (1998). Responsible fathering: An overview and conceptual framework. *Journal of Marriage and the Family, 60*, 277–292.

Davidson, E., & Schiederwind, N. (1992). Class differences: Economic inequality in the classroom. In D. A. Byrnes & G. Kiger (Eds.), *Common bonds: Anti-bias teaching in a diverse society.* Wheaton, MD: Association for Childhood International.

Davidson, P., & Youniss, J. (1995). Moral development and social construction. In W. M. Kurtines & J. L. Gewirtz (Eds.), *Moral development: An introduction.* Boston: Allyn & Bacon.

Dean, C. (1984). Parental empowerment through family resource programs. *Human Ecology Forum, 14*(1), 17-22.

Deax, K., & Wrightsman, L. J. (1988). *Social psychology* (5th ed.). Pacific Grove, CA: Brooks/Cole.

Deci, E. L., & Ryan, R. M. (1985). *Intrinsic motivation and self-determination in human behavior.* New York: Plenum.

Dellman-Jenkins, M., Florjancic, L., & Swadener, E. B. (1993). Sex roles and cultural diversity in recent award-winning picture books for young children. *Journal of Research in Childhood Education, 7*(2), 74–82.

Deno, E. (1979). Special education as developmental capital. *Exceptional Children, 37*, 229–237.

Derman-Sparks, L. (1989). *Anti-bias curriculum: Tools for empowering young children.* Washington, DC: National Association for the Education of Young Children.

DeSilva, A. D. (1983). The Spanish reading process and Spanish-speaking Mexican American children. In T. H. Escobedo (Ed.), *Early childhood bilingual education: A Hispanic perspective.* New York: Teachers College Press.

Desmond, R. J., Singer, J. L., & Singer, D. G. (1990). Family mediation: Parental communication patterns and the influences of television on children. In J. Bryant (Ed.), *Television and the American family.* Hillsdale, NJ: Lawrence Erlbaum.

DeToledo, S., & Brown, D. E. (1994). *Grandparents as parents.* New York: Guilford.

Devereaux, E. C. (1970). The role of peer group experience in moral development. In J. P. Hill (Ed.), *Minnesota Symposia on Child Psychology* (Vol. 4). Minneapolis: University of Minnesota Press.

Dewey, J. (1944). *Democracy and education.* New York: Macmillan.

Diener, E., Frasier, S. C., Beaman, A. L., & Kelem, R. T. (1976). Effects of deindividuation variables on stealing among Halloween trick-or-treaters. *Journal of Personality and Social Psychology, 33*, 178–183.

Dietz, T. L. (1998). An examination of violence and gender-role portrayals in video games:

Implications for gender socialization and aggressive behavior. *Sex Roles, 38,* 425–442.

Dishion, T. J., Patterson, G. R., Stoolmiller, M., & Skinner, M. L. (1991). Family, school, and behavioral antecedents to early adolescent involvement with antisocial peers. *Developmental Psychology, 27,* 172–180.

Dishion, T. J., McCord, J., & Poulin, F. (1999). When interventions harm: Peer groups and problem behavior. *American Psychologist, 54*(8), 755–764.

Dobkin, P. L., Tremblay, R. E., Masse, L. C., & Vitaro, F. (1995). Individual and peer characteristics in predicting boys' early onset of substance abuse: A seven-year longitudinal study. *Child Development, 66,* 1198–1214.

Dobson, J. (1970). *Dare to discipline.* Wheaton, IL: Tyndale House.

Dodge, K. A., (1981, April). *Behavior antecedents of peer rejection and isolation.* Paper presented at the meeting of the Society for Research in Child Development, Boston, MA.

Dodge, K. A. (1983). Behavioral antecedents of peer social status. *Child Development, 54,* 1386–1399.

Dodge, K. A. (1986). A social information processing model of social competence in children. In M. Perlmutter (Ed.), *Minnesota symposia on child psychology* (Vol. 18). Hillsdale, NJ: Lawrence Erlbaum.

Dodge, K. A., Bates, J. E., & Petit, G. S. (1990). Mechanisms in the cycle of violence. *Science, 250,* 1678–1683.

Dodge, K. A., & Frame, C. L. (1982). Social cognitive biases and deficits in aggressive boys. *Child Development, 53,* 620–635.

Dodge, K.A., Petit, G. S., & Bates, J. E. (1994). Socialization mediators of the relation between socioeconomic status and child conduct problems. *Child Development, 65,* 649–665.

Dorr, A. (1982). Television and the socialization of the minority child. In G. L. Berry & C. Mitchell-Kerman (Eds.), *Television and the socialization of the minority child.* New York: Academic Press.

Dorr, A. (1986). *Television and children: A special medium for a special audience.* Beverly Hills, CA: Sage.

Dorr, A., & Rabin, B. E. (1995). Parents, children, and television. In M. H. Bornstein (Ed.), *Handbook of parenting* (Vol. 4). Mahwah, NJ: Lawrence Erlbaum.

Dougherty, W. H., & Engle, R. E. (1987). An 80's look for sex equality in Caldecott winners and Honor books. *Reading Teacher, 40*(4), 394–398.

Downey, D. B., & Powell, B. (1993). Do children in single-parent households fare better with same-sex parents? *Journal of Marriage and the Family, 55,* 55–76.

Dreikurs, R., & Grey, L. (1968). *A new approach to discipline: Logical consequences.* New York: Hawthorn.

Dreman, S. (Ed.). (1997). *The family on the threshold of the 21st century: Trends and implications.* Mahwah, NJ: Lawrence Erlbaum.

Dresser, N. (1996). *Multicultural manners: New rules of etiquette for a changing society.* New York: John Wiley & Sons.

Drucker, P. (1992). *The age of discontinuity: Guidelines to our changing society.* New Brunswick, NJ: Transaction Publishers.

Dunlop, K. H. (1977). Mainstreaming: Valuing diversity in children. *Young Children, 32*(4), 26–32.

Dunn, J. (1988). *The beginnings of social understanding.* Cambridge, MA: Harvard University Press.

Dunn, J. (1992). Siblings and development. *Current Directions in Psychological Science, 1*(1), 6–9.

Dunn, L. M. (1968). Special education for the mildly retarded—Is much of it justified? *Exceptional Children, 35*(24), 5–22.

Durkheim, E. (1947). *The elementary forms of the religious life.* Glencoe, IL: Free Press.

Duska, R., & Whelan, M. (1975). *Moral development: A guide to Piaget and Kohlberg.* New York: Paulist Press.

Duster, T. (1971). Conditions for guilt-free massacre. In N. Sanford & C. Comstock (Eds.), *Sanctions for evil.* San Francisco: Jossey-Bass.

Duvall, E. M., & Miller, B. C. (1985). *Marriage and family development* (6th ed.). New York: Harper & Row.

Dweck, C. S. (1975). The role of expectations and attributions in the alleviation of learned helplessness. *Journal of Personality and Social Psychology, 31,* 674–685.

Dweck, C. S. (1981). Social-cognitive processes in children's friendships. In S. R. Asher & J. M. Gottman (Eds.), *The development of children's friendships.* Cambridge: Cambridge University Press.

Dweck, C. S. (1990). Self-theories and goals: Their roles in motivation, personality, and development. In R. Dienstbier (Ed.), *Nebraska Symposium on Motivation* (Vol. 36). Lincoln: University of Nebraska Press.

Dweck, C. S., & Bush, E. S. (1976). Sex differences in learned helplessness: I. Differential debilitation with peer and adult evaluators. *Journal of Personality and Social Psychology, 12,* 147–156.

Dweck, C. S., Davidson, W., Nelson, S., & Enna, B. (1978). Sex differences in learned helplessness: II. The contingencies of evaluative feedback in the classroom: III. An experimental analysis. *Developmental Psychology, 14,* 268–276.

Dweck, C. S., & Gillard, D. (1975). Expectancy statements as determinants of reactions to failure: Sex differences in persistence and expectancy change. *Journal of Personality and Social Psychology, 32*, 1077–1084.

Dweck, C. S., & Leggett, E. L. (1988). A social-cognitive approach to motivation and personality. *Psychological Review, 95*, 256–273.

Dweck, C. S., & Reppucci, N. D. (1973). Learned helplessness and reinforcement responsibility in children. *Journal of Personality and Social Psychology, 25*, 109–116.

Eccles, J. (1983). Expectancies, values, and academic behaviors. In J. T. Spence (Ed.), *Achievement and achievement motives: Psychological and sociological Approaches*. San Francisco: Freeman.

Eccles, J. S., & Bryan, J. (1994). Adolescence and gender-role transcendence. In M. Stevenson (Ed.), *Gender roles across the life span*. Muncie, IN: Ball State University Press.

Eccles, J. S., Wigfield, A., & Schiefele, U. (1998). Motivation to succeed. In W. Damon (Ed.), *Handbook of child psychology* (5th ed., Vol. 3). New York: John Wiley & Sons.

Eccles, J., Barber, B., Jozefowicz, D., Malenchuk, O., & Vida, M. (1999). Self-evaluation of competence, task values, and self-esteem. In N. G. Johnson, M. C. Roberts, & J. Worell (Eds.), *Beyond appearance: A new look at adolescent girls*. Washington, DC: American Psychological Association.

Eder, D. (1995). *School talk. Gender and adolescent school culture*. New Brunswick, NJ: Rutgers University Press.

Edwards, C. P., & Whiting, B. B. (1980). Differential socialization of girls and boys in light of cross-cultural research. *New Directions for Child Development, 8*, 88–111.

Eisenberg, N. (1998). Introduction. In W. Damon (Ed.), *Handbook of child psychology* (5th ed., Vol. 3). New York: John Wiley & Sons.

Eisenberg, N., & Fabes, R. A. (1998). Prosocial development. In W. Damon (Ed.), *Handbook of child psychology* (5th ed., Vol. 4). New York: John Wiley & Sons.

Eisenberg, N. (1986). *Altruistic emotion, cognition and behavior*. Hillsdale, NJ: Lawrence Erlbaum.

Eisenberg, N., & Murphy, B. (1995). Parenting and children's moral development. In M. H. Bornstein (Ed.), *Handbook of parenting* (Vol. 4). Mahwah, NJ: Lawrence Erlbaum.

Eisenberg, N., & Mussen, P. (1989). *The roots of prosocial behavior in children*. Cambridge, England: Cambridge University Press.

Elder, G. H. Jr. (1963). Parental power legitimation and its effect on the adolescent. *Sociometry, 26*, 50–65.

Elder, G. H. Jr. (1974). *Children of the Great Depression: Social change in life experience*. Chicago: University of Chicago Press.

Elder, G. H. Jr. (1979). Historical change in life patterns and personality. In P. Baltes & O. Brim (Eds.), *Life-span development and behavior* (Vol. 2). New York: Academic Press.

Elder, G. H. Jr. (1998). The life course and human development. In W. Damon (Ed.), *Handbook of child psychology* (5th ed., Vol. 1). New York: John Wiley & Sons.

Elder, G. H. Jr., & Bowerman, C. E. (1963). Family structure and child-rearing patterns: The effect of family size and sex composition. *American Sociological Review, 30*, 81–96.

Elder, G. H. Jr., & Hareven, T. K. (1993). Rising above life's disadvantage: From the Great Depression to war. In G. H. Elder Jr., J. Modell, & R.D. Parke (Eds.), *Children in time and space: Development and historical insights*. New York: Cambridge University Press.

Elder, G. H. Jr., Van Nguyen, T. V., & Casper, A. (1985). Linking family hardship to children's lives. *Child Development, 56*, 361–375.

Elders, J. (1994). Violence as a public health issue for children. *Childhood Education, 70*(5), 260–262.

Eley, T. C., Lichtenstein, P., & Stevenson, J. (1999). Sex differences in the etiology of aggressive and nonaggressive antisocial behavior: Results from two twin studies. *Child Development, 70*, 155–168.

Elkin, F., & Handel, G. (1989). *The child and society* (5th ed.). New York: Random House.

Elkind, D. (1981a). Egocentrism in children and adolescents. In D. Elkind (Ed.), *Children and adolescents: Interpretive essays on Jean Piaget* (3rd ed.). New York: Oxford University Press.

Elkind, D. (1981b). How grown-ups help children learn. *Education Digest, 80*(3), 20–24.

Elkind, D. (1984). *All grown up and no place to go: Teenagers in crisis*. Reading, MA: Addison-Wesley.

Elkind, D. (1986). Formal education and early childhood education: An essential difference. *Phi Delta Kappan, 67*, 631–636.

Elkind, D. (1988). *The hurried child: Growing up too fast too soon* (rev. ed.). Reading, MA: Addison-Wesley.

Elkind, D. (1994). *Ties that stress: The new family imbalance*. Cambridge, MA: Harvard University Press.

Elkind, D. (1998). *Reinventing childhood: Raising and educating children in a changing world*. Rosemont, NJ: Modern Learning Press.

Elliot, E. S., & Dweck, C. S. (1988). Goals: An approach to motivation and achievement. *Journal of Personality and Social Psychology, 54*, 5–12.

Elliot, R., & Vasta, P. (1970). The modeling of sharing: Effects associated with vicarious reinforcement, symbolization, age, and generalization. *Journal of Experimental Child Psychology, 10,* 8–15.

Ellis, J. B. (1994). Children's sex-role development: Implications for working mothers. *Social Behavior and Personality, 22,* 131–136.

Ellis, S., Rogoff, B., & Cromer, C. C. (1981). Age segregation in children's social interactions. *Developmental Psychology, 17,* 399–407.

Emery, R. E. (1988). *Marriage, divorce, and children's adjustment.* Newbury Park, CA: Sage.

Emery, R. E. (1989). Family violence. *American Psychologist, 44,* 321–332.

Epstein, J. L. (1983). Longitudinal effects of family-school-person interactions on student outcomes. In J. L. Epstein (Ed.), *Research in sociology of education and socialization* (Vol. 4). Greenwich, CT: JAI Press.

Epstein, J. L. (1995). School/family/community partnerships. *Phi Delta Kappan, 76*(9), 701–712.

Epstein, J. L., & Dauber, S. L. (1991). School programs and teacher practices of parent involvement in inner-city elementary and middle schools. *The Elementary School Journal, 91*(3), 288–305.

Erikson, E. H. (1963). *Childhood and society.* New York: Norton.

Erikson, E. H. (1980). *Identity and the life cycle.* New York: Norton.

Eron, L., Walder, L. O., & Lefkowitz, M. M. (1971). *Learning of aggression in children.* Boston: Little, Brown.

Escobedo, T. H., & Huggans, J. H. (1983). Field dependence-independence: A theoretical framework for Mexican American cultural variables? In T. H. Escobedo (Ed.), *Early childhood bilingual education: A Hispanic perspective.* New York: Teachers College Press.

Espin, O. M. (1993). Psychological impact of migration on Latinos. In D. R. Atkinson, G. Morten, & D. W. Sue (Eds.), *Counseling American minorities* (4th ed.). Dubuque, IA: Brown & Benchmark.

Esslin, M. (1982). *The age of television.* San Francisco: Freeman.

Estes, E. (1944). *The hundred dresses.* New York: Harcourt Brace Jovanovich.

Etzioni, A. (1993*). The spirit of community: The reinvention of American Society.* New York: Touchstone.

Evans, E. D., & McCandless, B. R. (1978). *Children and youth: Psychosocial development.* New York: Holt, Rinehart & Winston.

Evans, E. D., Rutberg, J., Sather, C., & Turner, C. (1991). Content analysis of contemporary teen magazines for adolescent females. *Youth Society, 23*(1), 99–120.

Evans, G. W., Palsane, M. N., Lepore, S. J., & Martin, J. (1989). Residential density and psychological wealth: The mediating effects of social support. *Journal of Personality and Social Psychology, 57*(6), 994–999.

Evans, G. W., Hygges, S., & Bullinger, M. (1993). *Psychology and the environment.* Unpublished manuscript. Ithaca, NY: Cornell University.

Fagan, J. (1993). Drug selling and illicit income in distressed neighborhoods. The economic lives of street-level drug users and dealers. In G. Peterson & A. H. Washington (Eds.), *Drugs, crime, and social isolation.* Washington, DC: Urban Institute Press.

Fagot, B. I. (1977). Consequences of moderate cross-gender behavior in preschool children. *Child Development, 48,* 902–907.

Fagot, B. I. (1984). Teacher and peer reactions to boys' and girls' play styles. *Sex Roles, 11,* 691–702.

Fagot, B. I. (1985). Beyond the reinforcement principle: Another step toward understanding sex-role development. *Developmental Psychology, 21,* 1097–1104.

Fagot, B. I. (1995). Parenting boys and girls. In M. H. Bornstein (Ed.), *Handbook of parenting* (Vol. 1). Mahwah, NJ: Lawrence Erlbaum.

Fagot, B. I., & Leinbach, M. D. (1987). Socialization of sex roles within the family. In B. Carter (Ed.), *Current conceptions of sex roles and sex typing: Theory and research.* New York: Praeger.

Falbo, T., & Polit, D. (1986). A quantitative review of the only child literature: Research evidence and theory development. *Psychological Bulletin, 100,* 176–189.

Fantz, R. L. (1965). Visual perception from birth as shown by pattern selectivity. *Annals of the New York Academy of Sciences, 118,* 793–814.

Farmer, S. (1989). *Adult children of abusive parents.* New York: Ballantine.

Farrington, D. P. (1991). Childhood aggression and adult violence: Early precursors and later life outcomes. In D. J. Pepler & K. H. Rubin (Eds.), *The development and treatment of childhood aggression.* Hillsdale, NJ: Lawrence Erlbaum.

Federal Interagency Forum on Child and Family Statistics (1998). *America's children: Key National indicators of well-being.* Washington, DC: Author.

Feld, S. C. (1967). Longitudinal study of the origins of achievement strivings. *Journal of Personality and Social Psychology, 7,* 408–414.

Feldman, F. L., & Scherz, F. (1987). *Family social welfare.* New York: Atherton Press.

Feldstein, B. (1989). Selection as a means of diffusing censorship. In M. K. Rudman (Ed.), *Children's literature: Resources for the classroom.* Norwood, MA: Christopher Gordon.

Feshbach, N. D., & Feshbach, S. (1998). Aggression in the schools: Toward reducing ethnic conflict and enhancing ethnic understanding. In P. K. Trickett & C. J. Schelienbach (Eds.), *Violence against children in the family and the community*. Washington, DC: American Psychological Association.

Feurstein, R. (1980). *Instrumental enrichment*. Baltimore, MD: University Park Press.

Fick, A. L., Osofsky, J. D., & Lewis, M. L. (1997). Perceptions of violence: Children, parents, and police officers. In J. D. Osofsky (Ed.), *Children in a violent society*. New York: Guilford Press.

Field, T., Masi, W., Goldstein, S., & Perry, S. (1988). Infant day care facilitates preschool social behavior. *Early Childhood Research Quarterly, 3*, 341–359.

Fiese, B. H., Sameroff, A. J., Grotevant, H. D., Wamboldt, F. S., Dickenstein, S., & Fravel, D. H. (1999). The stories that families tell: Narrative coherence, narrative interaction, and relationship beliefs. *Monographs of the Society for Research in Child Development, 64*, 2 (Serial No. 257).

Fincham, F. D., & Cain, K. (1986). Learned helplessness in humans: A developmental analysis. *Developmental Review, 6*, 301–333.

Findley, M. S., & Cooper, H. N. (1983). Locus of control and academic achievement: A literature review. *Journal of Personality and Social Psychology, 44*, 419–427.

Finkelhor, D. (1984). *Child sexual abuse: New theory and research*. New York: Free Press.

Finn, J. D., & Achilles, C. M. (1990). Answers and questions about class size: A statewide experiment. *American Association Research Journal, 27*(3), 557–577.

Fischer, W. (1963). Sharing in preschool children as a function of amount and type of reinforcements. *Genetic Psychological Monographs, 68*, 215–245.

Fiske, E. B. (1980). School vs. television. *Parents, 55*(1), 54–59.

Fiske, E. B. (1992). *Smart schools, smart kids*. New York: Touchstone.

Flavell, J. (1986). The development of children's knowledge about the appearance-reality distinction. *American Psychologist, 41*, 418–425.

Flavell, J. H., Miller, P. H., & Miller, S. A. (1993). *Cognitive development* (3rd ed.). Englewood Cliffs, NJ: Prentice-Hall.

Fletcher, A. C., Darling, N. E., Steinberg, L., & Dornbusch, S. M. (1995). The company they keep: Relation of adolescents' adjustment and behavior to their friends' perceptions of authoritative parenting in the social network. *Developomental Psychology, 31*, 300–310.

Fodor, E. (1971). Resistance to social influence among adolescents as a function of level of moral development. *Journal of Social Psychology, 85*, 121–126.

Fontana, D. J. (1992) *Save the family, save the child; What we can do to help children at risk*. New York: Dutton.

Footlick, J. K. (1990). What happened to the family? *Newsweek, 94*(27), 14–23.

Foss, R. D. (1983). Community norms and blood donation. *Journal of Applied Social Psychology, 13*, 281–290.

Foster-Clark, F. S., & Blyth, D. A. (1991). Peer relations and influences. In R. M. Lerner, A. C. Petersen, & J. Brooks-Gunn (Eds.), *Encyclopedia of adolescence* (Vol. 2). New York: Garland.

Fraiberg, S. (1977). *Every child's birthright: In defense of mothering*. New York: Basic Books.

Francese, P. (1995). America at mid-decade. *American Demographics, 17*(2), 23–29.

Frank, A. (1993). *Anne Frank: The diary of a young girl* (B. M. Mooyaart, Trans.). New York: Bantam. (Orig. work published 1947)

Francke, L. B. (1983). *Growing up divorced*. New York: Fawcett/Crest.

Frede, E. C. (1995). The role of program quality in producing early childhood program benefits. *The Future of Children, 5*(3), 115–132.

Freedman, D. P. (1986, February). Yearning for community. *Cornell Alumni News, 14*, 16.

Freud, A. (1968). *The psychoanalytical treatment of children*. New York: International Universities Press.

Freud, S. (1925). Some psychical consequences of the anatomical distinction between the sexes. In J. Strachey (Ed. and Trans.), *The standard edition of the complete psychological works of Sigmund Freud*. London: Hogarth Press.

Freud, S. (1938). *The basic writings of Sigmund Freud*. New York: Random House.

Friedrich, L. K., & Stein, S. H. (1973). Aggressive and prosocial television programs and the national behavior of preschool children. *Monographs of the Society for Research in Child Development, 38*. (Serial No. 151)

Fuligni, A. J., & Eccles, J. S. (1993). Perceived parent-child relationships and early adolescents' orientation toward peers. *Developmental Psychology, 29*, 622–632.

Fulgini, A. J., Tseng, V., & Lam, M. (1999). Attitudes toward family obligations among American adolescents with Asian, Latin American, and European backgrounds. *Child Development, 70*(4), 1030–1044.

Fulton, L. (1994). Peer education partners: A program for learning and working together. *Teaching Exceptional Children, 26*(4), 6–8, 10–11.

Funkel, K. A., & Bates, J. E. (1990). Mother-toddler problem solving: Antecedents in attachment, home behavior, and temperament. *Child Development, 61*, 810–819.

Furman, W. (1995). Parenting siblings. In M. H. Bornstein (Ed.), *Handbook of parenting* (Vol. 1). Mahwah, NJ: Lawrence Erlbaum.

Furman, W., & Masters, J. C. (1980). Affective consequences of social reinforcement, punishment, and neutral behavior. *Developmental Psychology, 16*, 100–104.

Furstenberg, F. (1976). *Unplanned parenthood: The social consequences of teenage childbearing.* New York: Free Press.

Furstenburg, F. F., & Cherlin, A. J. (1991). *Divided families: What happens to children when parents part.* Cambridge, MA: Harvard University Press.

Galinsky, E. (1981). *Between generations: The six stages of parenthood.* New York: Times Books..

Galinsky, E. (1992). The impact of child care on parents. In A. Booth (Ed.), *Childcare in the 1990s: Trends and consequences.* Hillsdale, NJ: Lawrence Erlbaum.

Galton, L. (1980). *Your child in sports.* New York: Watts.

Gandini, L. (1993). Fundamentals of the Reggio Emilia approach to early childhood education. *Young Children, 49*(1), 4-8.

Garbarino, J. (1977). The human ecology of child maltreatment: A conceptual model for research. *Journal of Marriage and the Family, 39*, 721–736.

Garbarino, J. (1985). Habitats for children: An ecological perspective. In J. F. Wohlwill & W. Van Vliet (Eds.), *Habitats for children: The impact of density.* Hillsdale, NJ: Lawrence Erlbaum.

Garbarino, J. (1986). Can American families afford the luxury of childhood? *Child Welfare, 65*(2), 119–128.

Garbarino, J. (1992). *Children and families in the social environment* (2nd ed.). New York: Aldine de Gruyter.

Garbarino, J. (1995a). *Raising children in a socially toxic society.* San Francisco: Jossey-Bass.

Garbarino, J. (1995b). *Building a socially nourishing environment with children.* San Francisco: Jossey-Bass.

Garbarino, J., & Barry, F. D. (1997). *Understanding abusive families: An ecological approach to theory and practice.* New York: Jossey-Bass.

Garbarino, J., & Gilliam, G. (1980). *Understanding abusive families.* Lexington, MA: Heath.

Garbarino, J., Guttman, E., & Seely, J. W. (1986). *The psychologically battered child: Strategies for identification, assessment and intervention.* San Francisco: Jossey-Bass.

Garber, H. L. (1988). *The Milwaukee project: Preventing mental retardation in children at risk.* Washington, DC: American Association of Mental Retardation.

Garcia, E. E. (1992). Hispanic children: Theoretical, empirical, and related policy issues. *Educational Psychology Review, 4*, 69–94.

Garcia, R. L. (1998). *Teaching for diversity.* Bloomington, ID: Phi Delta Kappa Educational Foundation.

Garcia-Coll, C. T. (1990). Developmental outcome of minority infants: A process-oriented look into our beginnings. *Child Development, 61*, 270–289.

Garcia-Coll, C. T., Meyer, E. C., & Britton, L. (1995). Ethnic and minority parenting. In M. H. Bornstein (Ed.), *Handbook of parenting* (Vol. 2). Mahwah, NJ: Lawrence Erlbaum.

Gardner, H. (1993). *Frames of mind: The theory of multiple intelligences.* New York: Basic Books.

Gardner, H. (1999). *Intelligence reframed: Multiple intelligences for the 21st century.* New York: Basic Books.

Gardner, K. E., & LaBrecque, S. V. (1986). Effects of maternal employment on sex-role orientation of adolescents. *Adolescence, 21*(84), 875–885.

Gargiulo, R. M., & Graves, J. B. (1991). Parental feelings. *Childhood Education, 67*(3), 176–178.

Gatz, I. L. (1975). On children and television. *Elementary School Journal, 75*(7), 415–418.

Gay, L. (1998). *The history of rock music.* http://orpheus.la.utk.edu/music

Geen, R. G. (1994). Television and aggression: Recent development in research and theory. In D. Zillman, J. Bryant, & A. C. Huston (Eds.), *Media, children and the family: Social scientific, psychodynamic and clinical perspectives.* Hillsdale, NJ: Lawrence Erlbaum.

Gelfand, D., Hartman, D. P., Cromer, C. C., Smith, C. L., & Page, B. C. (1975). The effects of instructional prompts and praise on children's donation rates. *Child Development, 46*, 980–983.

Gellene, D. (1996, August 7). Scaring up lots of young readers. *Los Angeles Times*, pp. A1, 18–19.

Gelles, R. J., & Lancaster, J. B. (1987). *Child abuse and neglect.* New York: Aldine de Gruyter.

Gerbner, G., Gross, L., Jackson-Beck, N., Jeffries-Fox, S., & Signorielli, N. (1978). *Violence profile* (No. 9). Philadelphia: University of Pennsylvania Press.

Gesell, A., & Ilg, F. (1943). *Infant and child in the culture of today.* New York: Harper & Row.

Gibbs, J. C. (1995). The cognitive developmental perspective. In W. M. Kurtines & J. L. Gewirtz (Eds.), *Moral development: An introduction.* Boston, MA: Allyn & Bacon.

Gilkeson, E. C., & Bowman, G. W. (1976). *The focus is on children.* New York: Bank Street Publications.

Gilligan, C. (1982). *In a different voice*. Cambridge, MA: Harvard University Press.

Gilligan, C. (1985, April). *Response to critics*. Paper presented at the biennial meeting of the Society for Research in Child Development, Toronto.

Ginsberg, G. S., & Bronstein, D. (1993). Family factors related to children's intrinsic/extrinsic motivational orientation and academic performance. *Child Development, 64*, 1461–1474.

Goff, B. G., & Goddard, H. W. (1999). Terminal core values with adolescent problem behaviors. *Adolescence, 34*, 47–60.

Goffin, S. G., & Lombardi, J. (1988). *Speaking out: Early childhood advocacy*. Washington, DC: National Association for Education of Young Children.

Golden, H. (1962). *You're entitled*. New York: Crest.

Golding, W. (1954). *Lord of the flies*. New York: Putnam.

Goldman, J. (1994, January 23). Rose Kennedy, 104, dies; matriarch of a dynasty. *Los Angeles Times*, pp. A1, 20.

Goldstein, A. P. (1991). *Delinquent gangs: A psychological perspective*. Champaign, IL: Research Press.

Goleman, D. (1995). *Emotional intelligence*. New York; Bantam.

Gollnick, D. M., & Chinn, P. C. (1998). *Multicultural education in a pluralistic society* (5th ed.). Upper Saddle River, NJ: Merrill/Prentice-Hall.

Good, T. C., & Brophy, J. E. (1986). *Educational psychology* (3d ed.). New York: Longman.

Good, T. L., & Brophy, J. E. (1991). *Looking in classrooms* (5th ed.). New York: HarperCollins.

Good, T. L., & Brophy, J. E. (1997). *Looking in classrooms* (7th ed.). New York: Longman.

Goode, W. J. (1982). *The family* (2nd ed.). Englewood Cliffs, NJ: Prentice-Hall.

Goodlad, J. I. (1984). *A place called school: Prospects for the future*. New York: McGraw-Hill.

Goodman, G. S., Emery, R. E., & Haugaard, J. J. (1998). Developmental psychology and law: divorce, child maltreatment, foster care, and adoption. In W. Damon (Ed.), *Handbook of child psychology* (5th ed., Vol. 4). New York: John Wiley & Sons.

Goodman, G. S., Emery, R. E., & Haugaard, J. F. (1998). Developmental psychology and law: Divorce, child maltreatment, foster care, and adoption. In W. Damon (Ed.), *Handbook of child psychology* (5th ed., Vol. 4). New York: John Wiley & Sons.

Goodman, M. E. (1964). *Race awareness in young children* (rev. ed.). New York: Collier Books.

Gordon, I. J. (1971). *Parental involvement in compensatory education*. Urbana, IL: Research Press.

Gore, T. (1987). *Raising PG kids in an X-rated society*. Nashville, TN: Abington Press.

Gorn, G. J., & Goldberg, M. E. (1982). Behavioral evidence of the effect of televised food message on children. *Journal of Consumer Research, 9*, 200–205.

Gorsuch, R. L. (1976). Religion as a major prediction of significant human behavior. In W. J. Donaldson Jr. (Ed.), *Research in mental health and religious behavior*. Atlanta, GA: Psychological Studies Institute.

Gottfried, A. E., & Gottfried, A. W. (1988). *Maternal employment and children's development*. Longitudinal research. New York: Plenum.

Gottman, J., Gonso, J., & Rasmussen, B. (1975). Social interaction, social competence, and friendship in children. *Child Development, 46*, 709–718.

Gould, W. S., & Gould, C. B. (1962). *Annotated Mother Goose*. New York: Clarkson N. Potter.

Gozali, H., Cleary, T. A., Walster, G. W., & Gozali, J. (1973). Relationship between the internal-external control construct and achievement. *Journal of Educational Psychology, 64*, 9–14.

Graves, N. B., & Graves, T. O. (1983). The cultural context of prosocial development: An ecological model. In D. L. Bridgeman (Ed.), *The nature of prosocial development: Interdisciplinary theories and strategies*. New York: Academic Press.

Green, F. (1990, June 13). Officials say schools aren't prepared for first wave of crack babies. *San Diego Union*, pp. A1, A14, A15.

Greenberg, B. S. (1994). Content trends in media sex. In D. Zillman, J. Bryant, & A. C. Huston (Eds.), *Media, children and the family: Social scientific, psychodynamic, and clinical perspectives*. Hillsdale, NJ: Lawrence Erlbaum.

Greenberger, E., & Goldberg, W. A. (1989). Work, parenting, and the socialization of children. *Developmental Psychology, 25*(1), 22–35.

Greenberger, E., O'Neil, R., & Nagel, S. K. (1994). Linking workplace and homeplace; Relations between the nature of adults' work and their parenting behaviors. *Developmental Psychology, 30*, 990–1002.

Greenfield, L. A., (Ed.). (1998, March). *Violence by intimates: Analysis of data on crimes by current or former spouses, boyfriends, and girlfriends*. Washington, DC: U.S. Department of Justice.

Greenfield, P. M. (1984). *Mind and media: The effects of television, video games and computers*. Cambridge, MA: Harvard University Press.

Greenfield, P. M., Yut, E., Chung, M., & Land, D. (1990). The program-length commercial: A study of the effects of television on toy tie-ins on imaginative play. *Psychology and Marketing, 7*(4), 237–255.

Greenfield, P. M., & Suzuki, L. K. (1998). Culture and human development: Implications for parenting, education, pediatrics, and mental health. In W. Damon (Ed.), *Handbook of child psychology* (5th ed., Vol. 4). New York: John Wiley & Sons.

Griffiths, M. D. (1991). Amusement machine playing in childhood and adolescence: A comparative analysis of video games and food machines. *Journal of Adolescence, 14*, 53–74.

Grinder, R. E. (1964). Relations between behavior and cognitive dimensions of conscience in middle childhood. *Child Development, 34*, 881–891.

Groos, K. (1901). *The play of man*. New York: Appleton.

Grotevant, H. D. (1998). Adolescent development in family contexts. In W. Damon (Ed.), *Handbook of child psychology* (5th ed., Vol. 3). New York: John Wiley & Sons.

Grusec, J. E., & Lytton, H. (1988). *Social development: History, theory, and research*. New York: Springer-Verlag.

Grusec, J. E., Saas-Korlsaak, P., & Simutis, Z. M. (1978). The role of example and moral exhortation in the training of altruism. *Child Development, 49*, 920–923.

Gunnar, M. R. (1980). Contingent stimulation: A review of its role in early development. In S. Levine & H. Ursin (Eds.), *Coping and health*. New York: Plenum.

Haan, N., Smith, M. B., & Block, J. (1968). Moral reasoning of young adults: Political–social behavior, family background, and personality correlates. *Journal of Personality and Social Psychology, 10*(3), 183–201.

Haefner, M. J., & Wartella, E. A. (1987). Effects of sibling coviewing on children's interpretations of television programs. *Journal of Broadcasting and Electronic Media, 31*, 153–168.

Haith, M. M. (1966). The response of the human newborn to visual movement. *Journal of Experimental Child Psychology, 3*, 235–243.

Hale, J. (1991). The transmission of cultural values to young African American children. *Young Children, 46*(6), 7–15.

Hale-Benson, J. E. (1986). *Black children: Their roots, culture, and learning styles* (rev. ed.). Baltimore, MD: Johns Hopkins University Press.

Haley, G. E. (1989). Cited in J. Trelease, *The new read-aloud handbook*. New York: Penguin.

Hall, C. S. (1954). *A primer of Freudian psychology*. New York: New American Library.

Hall, E. T. (1964). *The silent language*. New York: Doubleday.

Hall, E. T. (1966). *The hidden dimension*. New York: Doubleday.

Hall, E. T. (1976). *Beyond culture*. New York: Doubleday.

Hallahan, D. P., & Kauffman, J. S. (1998). *Exceptional children* (7th ed.). Boston: Allyn & Bacon.

Hansen, C. H., & Hansen, R. D. (1988). How rock music videos can change what is seen when boy meets girl: Priming stereotypic appraisal of social interactions. *Sex Roles, 19*, 287–316.

Hardman, M., Drew, C. J., & Egan, M. W. (1999). *Human exceptionality: Society, school, and family* (6th ed.). Boston: Allyn & Bacon.

Hareven, T. K. (1989). Historical changes in children: Networks in the family and community. In D. Belle (Ed.), *Children's social networks and social support*. New York: John Wiley & Sons.

Harms, T., & Clifford, R. M. (1980). *Early childhood environment rating scale*. New York: Teachers College Press.

Harris, J. R. (1998). *The nurture assumption: Why children turn out the way they do*. New York: Free Press.

Harris, M. (1970). Reciprocity and generosity: Some determinants of sharing in children. *Child Development, 41*, 313–328.

Harris, M. B., & Turner, P. (1986). Gay and lesbian parents. *Journal of Homosexuality, 12*, 101–113.

Harrison, A., Serafica, F., & McAdoo, H. (1984). Ethnic families of color. In R. D. Parke (Ed.), *Review of child development research. Vol. 7: The family*. Chicago: University of Chicago Press.

Harrison, A. O., Wilson, M. N., Pine, C. J., Chan, S., & Buriel, R. (1990). Family ecologies of ethnic minority children. *Child Development, 61*, 347–362.

Hart, B., & Risley, T. R. (1995). *Meaningful differences in the everyday experiences of young American children*. Baltimore: Brookes.

Hart, C. H., DeWolf, D. M., & Burts, D. C. (1992). Linkages among preschoolers' playground behavior, outcome expectations, and parental disciplinary strategies. *Early Education and Development, 3*, 265–283.

Harter, S. (1990). Issues in the assessment of the self-concept of children and adolescents. In A. M. La-Greco (Ed.), *Through the eyes of the child: Obtaining self-reports from children and adolescents*. Boston: Allyn & Bacon.

Harter, S. (1998). The development of self-representations. In W. Damon (Ed.), *Handbook of child psychology* (5th ed., Vol. 3). New York: John Wiley & Sons.

Harter, S., & Connell, J. P. (1984). A model of children's achievement and related self-perceptions of competence, control, and motivational orientations. In J. Nicholls (Ed.), *The development of achievement-related cognition and behavior*. Greenwich, CT: JAI Press.

Hartshorne, H., & May, M. (1978). *Studies in the nature of character, Vol. I: Studies in deceit*. New York: Macmillan.

Hartup, W. W. (1964). Friendship status and the effectiveness of peers as reinforcing agents. *Journal of Experimental Child Psychology, 1*, 154–162.

Hartup, W. W. (1983). Peer relations. In P. H. Mussen (Ed.), *Handbook of child psychology* (4th ed., Vol. 4). New York: John Wiley & Sons.

Hartup, W. W. (1989). Social relationships and their developmental significance. *American Psychologist, 44*(2), 120–126.

Hartup, W. W. (1996). The company they keep: Friendships and their developmental significance. *Child Development, 67*, 1–13.

Hassett, J. (1981). But that would be wrong. *Psychology Today, 15*(11), 34.

Hatcher, B., & Beck, S. S. (1997). *Learning opportunities beyond the school* (2nd ed.). Olney, MD: Association for Childhood Education International.

Haugland, S. W., & Wright, J. L. (1997). *Young children and technology*. Boston, MA: Allyn & Bacon.

Havighurst, R. (1972). *Human development and education* (3rd ed.). New York: McKay.

Hay, D. F. (1985). Learning to form relationships in infancy: Parallel attainments with parents and peers. *Developmental Review, 5*, 122–161.

Hay, I., Ashman, A. F., & Van Kraayenoord, C. E. (1998). Educational characteristics of students with high or low self-concepts. *Psychology in the Schools, 35*, 391–400.

Hayes, J. W., & Lipset, S. M. (1993/1994, Winter). Individualism: A double-edged sword. *The Responsive Community*, 69–80.

Hayward, D. G., Rothenberg, M., & Beasley, R. R. (1974). Children's play in urban playground environments: A comparison of traditional, contemporary and adventure playground types. *Environment and Behavior, 6*(2), 131–168.

Healy, J. (1991). *Endangered minds: Why children don't think and what to do about it*. New York: Touchstone Books.

Healy, J. (1998). *Failure to connect: How computers affect our children's minds and what we can do about it*. New York: Touchstone.

Heath, S. B. (1983). *Ways with words: Language, life and work in communities and classrooms*. Cambridge, MA: Cambridge University Press.

Heath, S. B. (1989). Oral and literate traditions among black Americans living in poverty. *American Psychologist, 44*(2), 367–373.

Helburn, S. W., & Howes, C. (1996, Summer/Fall). Child care cost and quality. *The Future of Children, 6*(2), 62–82.

Helfer, R., & Kempe, C. H. (1989). *The battered child* (4th ed.). Chicago: University of Chicago Press

Henderson, A. T., & Berla, N. (Eds.). (1994). *A new generation of evidence: The family is critical to student achievement*. Washington, DC: National Committee for Citizens in Education.

Henderson, Z. P. (1990, Summer). Short reports. *Human Ecology Forum, 18*(4), 37.

Hermans, H. J. M., Terlaak, J. J. F., & Maes, P. C. J. M. (1972). Achievement and fear of failure in family and school. *Developmental Psychology, 6*, 520–528.

Hernandez, D. J. (1995, winter). Changing demographics: Past and future for early childhood programs. *The future of children, 5* (3), 145–160.

Hess, R. D., & Holloway, S. D. (1984). Family and school as educational institutions. In R. D. Parke (Ed.), *Review of child development research. Vol. 7: The Family*. Chicago: University of Chicago Press.

Hess, R. D. (1986). Family influences on school readiness and achievement in Japan and the United States: An overview of a longitudinal study. In H. Stevenson, H. Azuma, & K. Hakuta (Eds.), *Child development and education in Japan*. New York: W. H. Freeman.

Hetherington, E. M. (1972). The effects of father absence on personality development in adolescent daughters. *Developmental Psychology, 7*, 313–326.

Hetherington, E. M. (1988). Parents, children, and siblings six years after divorce. In R. A. Hinde & J. Stevenson-Hinde (Eds.), *Relationships within families*. Oxford: Oxford University Press.

Hetherington, E. M. (1989). Coping with family transitions: Winners, losers, and survivors. *Child Development, 60*, 1–4.

Hetherington, E. M. (1993). A review of the Virginia longitudinal study of divorce and remarriage: A focus on early adolescence. *Journal of Family Psychology, 7*, 39–56.

Hetherington, E. M., Cox, M., & Cox, R. (1982). Effects of divorce on parents and children. In M. Lamb (Ed.), *Nontraditional families*. Hillsdale, NJ: Lawrence Erlbaum.

Hetherington, E. M., & Camara, K. A. (1984). Families in tradition: The processes of dissolution and reconstitution. In R. D. Parke (Ed.), *Review of child development research. Vol. 7: The family*. Chicago: University of Chicago Press.

Hetherington, E. M., & Clingempeel, W. G. (1992). Coping with marital transitions. *Monographs of the Society for Research in Child Development, 57*(2–3), (Serial No. 227).

Hetherington, E. M., Stanley-Hagan, M., & Anderson, E. R. (1989). Marital transitions. *American Psychologist, 44*(2), 303–312.

Heward, W. L. (1996). *Exceptional children: An introduction to special education* (5th ed.). Englewood Cliffs, NJ: Prentice-Hall.

Heward, W. L., & Orlansky, M. D. (1988). *Exceptional children* (3rd ed.). Columbus, OH: Merrill.

Hewitt, J. P. (1994). *Self and society: A symbolic interactionist social psychology*. Boston: Allyn & Bacon.

Hewlett, S. A., & West, C. (1998). *The war against parents*. Boston: Houghton Mifflin.

Higgins, A. (1995). Educating for justice and community: Lawrence Kohlberg's vision of moral education. In W. M. Kurtines & J. L. Gewirtz (Eds.), *Moral development: An introduction*. Boston: Allyn & Bacon.

Hilliard, A. (1992, Summer). Behavioral style, culture, and teaching and learning. *Journal of Negro Education, 61*(3), 370–371.

Hochschild, A. R (1989). *The second shift*. New York: Avon.

Hochschild, A. R. (1997). *The time bind*. New York: Metropolitan Books.

Hofferth, S. (1992). The demand for and supply of child care in the 1990s. In A. Booth (Ed.), *Child care in the 1990s: Trends and consequences*. Hillsdale, NJ: Lawrence Erlbaum.

Hofferth, S. L. (1996, Summer/Fall). Child care in the United States today. *The Future of Children, 6*(2), 41–61.

Hoffman, L. W. (1989). Effects of maternal employment in the two-parent family. *American Psychologist, 44*(2), 283–292.

Hoffman, M. L. (1970). Moral development. In P. H. Mussen (Ed.), *Carmichael's manual of child psychology* (Vol. 2). New York: John Wiley & Sons.

Hoffman, M. L. (1976). Empathy, role taking, guilt, and development of altruistic motives. In T. Lickona (Ed.), *Moral development and behavior*. New York: Holt, Rinehart & Winston.

Hoffman, M. L. (1981). Is altruism part of human nature? *Journal of Personality and Social Psychology, 70*, 237–241.

Hoffman, M. L. (1982). Development of prosocial motivation. In N. Eisenberg-Berg (Ed.), *The development of prosocial behavior*. New York: Academic Press.

Hoffman, M. L. (1983). Affective and cognitive processes in moral internalization. In E. T. Higgins, D. N. Ruble, & W. W. Hartup (Eds.), *Social cognition and social development*. Cambridge, England: Cambridge University Press.

Hoffman, M. L. (1988). Moral development. In M. H. Bornstein & M. E. Lamb (Eds.), *Developmental psychology: An advanced textbook* (2nd ed.). Hillsdale, NJ: Lawrence Erlbaum.

Hoffman, M. L. (1991). Empathy, social cognition, and moral actions. In W. M. Kurtines & J. L. Gewirtz (Eds.), *Handbook of moral behavior and development. Vol. 1. Theory*. Hillsdale, NJ: Lawrence Erlbaum.

Hoffman, M. L., & Saltzstein, H. D. (1967). Parent discipline and the child's moral development. *Journal of Personality and Social Psychology, 5*, 45–57.

Hogan, R., & Emler, N. (1995). Personality and moral development. In W. M. Kurtines & J. L. Gewirtz (Eds.), *Moral development: An introduction*. Boston, MA: Allyn & Bacon.

Hohmann, M., Banet, B., & Weikart, D. P. (1979). *Young children in action: A manual for preschool teaching*. Ypsilanti, MI: High/Scope Press.

Hohmann, M., & Weikart, D. P. (1995). *Educating young children: Active learning practices for preschool educators and child care programs*. Ypsilanti, MI: High/ScopePress.

Holmbeck, G. N., Paikoff, R. L., & Brooks-Gunn, J. (1995). Parenting adolescents. In M. H. Bornstein (Ed.), *Handbook of parenting* (Vol. 1). Mahwah, NJ: Lawrence Erlbaum.

Holtzman, W. H. (1982). Cross-cultural comparisons of personality development in Mexico and the United States. In D. A. Wagner & H. W. Stevenson (Eds.), *Cultural perspectives on child development*. San Francisco: W. H. Freeman.

Honig, A. S. (1986). Stress and coping in children (Part I). *Young Children, 41*(4), 50–63.

Honig, A. S. (1993). Mental health for babies: What do theory and research teach us? *Young Children, 48*(3), 69–76.

Honig, A. S. (1995). Choosing child care for young children. In M. H. Bornstein (Ed.), *Handbook of parenting* (Vol. 4). Mahwah, NJ: Lawrence Erlbaum.

Honig, B. (1988). *Here they come ready or not! Report of the school readiness task force*. Sacramento, CA: State Department of Education.

Hopkins, H. R., & Klein, H. A. (1994). Multidimension self-perception: Linkages to parental nurturance. *The Journal of Genetic Psychology, 154*, 465–473.

Horowitz, F. D., & Paden, L. Y. (1973). The effectiveness of environmental intervention programs. In B. M. Caldwell & H. N. Riccuiti (Eds.), *Review of child development research* (Vol. 3). Chicago: University of Chicago Press.

Horwitz, R. (1979). Psychological effects of the "open classroom." *Review of Educational Research, 49*, 71–86.

Howes, C. (1988). Peer interaction of young children. *Monographs of the Society for Research in Child Development, 43*(1). (Serial No. 217)

Howes, C., & Matheson, C. C. (1992). Sequences in the development of competent play with peers; Social and social pretend play. *Developmental Psychology, 28*, 961–974.

Howes, C., Matheson, C. C., & Hamilton, C. E. (1994). Maternal, teacher, and child care history correlates of children's relationships with peers. *Child Development, 65*, 264–273.

Huck, C. S., & Helper, S. (Eds.). (1996). *Children's literature in the elementary school* (6th ed.). New York: WCB/McGraw-Hill.

Huesmann, L. R. (1986). Psychological processes promoting the relation between exposure to media violence and aggressive behavior by the viewer. *Journal of Social Issues, 42,* 125–139.

Huesmann, L. R., Eron, L. D., Klein, R., Brice, P., & Fisher, P. (1983). Mitigating the imitation of aggressive behavior by changing children's attitudes about media violence. *Journal of Personality and Social Psychology, 44,* 899–910.

Hughes, F. P. (1998). *Children, play, and development* (3rd ed.). Boston: Allyn & Bacon.

Hugo, V. (1992). *Les miserables.* New York: Modern Library. (Orig. work published 1862)

Humphrey, J. H. (1993). *Sports for children: A guide for adults.* Springfield, IL: Charles Thomas.

Hunt, J. McV. (1961). *Intelligence and experience.* New York: Ronald Press.

Hunt, M. (Trans.). (1944). *The complete Grimm's fairy tales.* New York: Pantheon Books.

Hurd, T. L., Lerner, R. M., & Barton, C. E. (1999). Integrated services. Expanding partnerships to meet the needs of today's children and families. *Young Children, 54*(2), 74–80.

Huston, A. C. (1983). Sex-typing. In P. H. Mussen (Ed.), *Handbook of child psychology* (4th ed., Vol. 4). New York: John Wiley & Sons.

Huston, A. C., Carpenter, C. J., Atwater, J. B., & Johnson, L. M. (1986). Gender, adult structuring of activities, and social behavior in middle childhood. *Child Development, 57,* 200–209.

Huston, A. C. (1992). *Big world, small screen: The role of television in American society.* Lincoln: University of Nebraska Press.

Huston, A. C., McLoyd, V. C., & Coll, C. G. (1994). Children and poverty: Issues in contemporary research. *Child Development, 65,* 275–282.

Huston, A. C., Watkins, B. A., & Kunkel, D. (1989). Public policy and children's television. *American Psychologist, 44*(2), 424–433.

Huston, A. C., & Wright, J. C. (1998). Mass media and children's development. In W. Damon (Ed.), *Handbook of child psychology* (5th ed., Vol. 4). New York: John Wiley & Sons.

Huston, A. C., Zillman, D., & Bryant, J. (1994). Media influence, public policy, and the family. In D. Zillman, J. Bryant, & A. C. Huston (Eds.), *Media, children, and the family: Social scientific, psychodynamic, and clinical perspectives.* Hillsdale, NJ: Lawrence Erlbaum.

Hutchison, R. (1987). Ethnicity and urban recreation: Whites, blacks and Hispanics in Chicago's public parks. *Journal of Leisure Research, 19,* 205–222.

Hyde, D. (1992). School–parent collaboration results in academic achievement. *NASSP Bulletin, 76*(543), 39–42.

Hymel, S., Bowker, A., & Woody, E. (1993). Aggressive versus withdrawn unpopular children: Variations in peer and self-perceptions in multiple domains. *Child Development, 64,* 879–896.

Inhelder, B., & Piaget, J. (1958). *The growth of logical thinking from childhood to adolescence.* New York: Basic Books.

Inkeles, A. (1969). Social structure and socialization. In D. A. Goslin (Ed.), *Handbook of socialization theory and research.* Chicago: Rand McNally.

Isaacs, S. (1999). *Brave dames and wimpettes: What women are really doing on page and screen.* New York: Ballantine.

Iverson, T. J., & Segal, M. (1990). *Child abuse and neglect: An information and reference guide.* New York: Garland Publishing.

Jacklin, C. N. (1989). Female and male: Issues of gender. *American Psychologist, 44*(2), 127–133.

Jackson, R. K., & McBride, W. D. (1985). *Understanding street gangs.* Sacramento, CA: Custom.

Jacobs, J. S., & Tunnell, M. O. (1996). *Children's literature, briefly.* Englewood Cliffs, NJ: Prentice-Hall.

Jacobson, J. L., & Wille, D. E. (1986). The influence of attachment pattern on developmental changes in peer interaction from the toddler to the preschool period. *Child Development, 57,* 338–347.

Jaffe, M. L. (1998). *Adolescence.* New York: John Wiley & Sons.

James, M., & Jongeward, D. (1971). *Born to win.* Reading, MA: Addison-Wesley.

Jensen, A. R. (1969). How much can we boost IQ and scholastic achievement? *Harvard Educational Review, 39,* 1–123.

Jensen, A. R. (1988). Speed of information processing and population differences. In S. H. Irvine & J. W. Berry (Eds.), *Human abilities in cultural context.* New York: Cambridge University Press.

Jensen, E. (1999, November 18). Study finds TV still prime source of kids' media time. *Los Angeles Times,* pp. A1, A31.

Johnson, D. W., & Johnson, R. T. (1989). *Cooperation and competition: Theory and research.* Edina, MN: Interaction Book.

Johnson, D. W., & Johnson, R. T. (1999). *Learning together and alone: Cooperative, competitive, and individualistic learning* (5th ed.). Boston: Allyn & Bacon.

Johnson, D. W., Johnson, R. T., & Maruyama, G. (1983). Interdependence and interpersonal attraction among heterogeneous and homogeneous individuals: A theoretical formulation and a meta-analysis of the research. *Review of Education Research, 53,* 5–54.

Johnson, J. A., Dupuis, V. L., Musial, D., & Hall, G. E. (1999). *Introduction to the foundations of American education* (11th ed.). Needham Heights: Allyn & Bacon.

Johnson, P. A., & Staffieri, J. R. (1971). Stereotype affective properties of personal names and somatotypes in children. *Developmental Psychology, 5*(1), 176.

Johnson, W. B., & Packer, A. E. (Eds.). (1987). *Work force 2000*. Indianapolis, IN: Hudson Institute.

Johnston, J. R., Kline, M., & Tschann, J. M. (1989). Ongoing post-divorce conflict: Effects on children of joint custody and frequent access. *Journal of Orthopsychiatry, 59*(4), 576–592.

Johnston, J., & Ettema, J. S. (1982). *Positive images: Breaking stereotypes with children's television.* Newbury Park, CA: Sage.

Jones, K. L., Smith, D. W., Ulleland, C. L., & Streissguth, P. (1973). Patterns of malformation in offspring of chronic alcoholic mothers. *Lancet,* 1, 1267–1271.

Jose, P. E. (1990). Just world reasoning in children's immanent justice judgments. *Child Development,* 61, 1024–1033.

Jowett, G., & Linton, J. M. (1989). *Movies as mass communication* (2nd ed.). Newbury Park, CA: Sage.

Jung, C. G. (1938). *Psychology and religion.* New Haven, CT: Yale University Press.

Kagan, J. (1964). Acquisition and significance of sex typing and sex-role identity. *Review of child development research* (Vol. 1). New York: Russell Sage.

Kagan, J. (1971). *Personality development.* New York: Harcourt Brace Jovanovich.

Kagan, J. (1975, September 22). The parent gap. *Newsweek.* (Reprinted *in Annual Editions: Readings in Human Development 76/77.* Guilford, CT: Dushkin)

Kagan, J. (1984). *The nature of the child.* New York: Basic Books.

Kagan, J. (1994). *Galen's Prophecy: Temperament in human nature.* New York: Basic Books.

Kagan, J., Reznick, S., Davies, J., Smith, J., Sigal, H., & Miyake, K. (1986). Selective memory and belief: A methodological suggestion. *International Journal of Behavioral Development,* 9, 205–218.

Kagan, J., & Moss, H. (1959). Stability and validity of achievement fantasy. *Journal of Abnormal and Social Psychology,* 58, 357–364.

Kagan, J., Reznick, J. S., & Gibbons, J. (1989). Inhibited and uninhibited types of children. *Child Development,* 60, 838–845.

Kagitcibasi, C. (1996). *Family and human development across cultures: A view from the other side.* Mahwah, NJ: Lawrence Erlbaum.

Kaiser Family Foundation. (1999). *Kids and media and the new millennium.* Menlo Park, CA: Author.

Kallen, H. M. (1956). *Cultural pluralism and the American ideal.* Philadelphia: University of Pennsylvania Press.

Kantrowitz, B. (1996). Gay families come out. *Newsweek,* 128(19), 50–57.

Kantrowitz, B., & Wingert, P. (1990). Step by step. *Newsweek,* 94(27), 24–4.

Kantrowitz, B., & Wingert, P. (1998). Learning at home: Does it pass the final test? *Newsweek,* 132(14), 64–71.

Karoly, L. A. (Ed.) (1998). *Investing in our children: What we know and don't know about the costs and benefits of early childhood interventions.* Santa Monica, CA: Rand.

Katchadourian, H. (1990). Sexuality. In S. S. Feldman & G. R. Elliot (Eds.), *At the threshold: The developing adolescent.* Cambridge, MA: Harvard University Press.

Katz, P., & Zalk, S. (1978). Modification of children's racial attitudes. *Developmental Psychology, 14*(5), 447–461.

Katz, P. A. (Ed.). (1975). *Toward the elimination of racism.* New York: Pergamon Press.

Kaufman, J. (1989). The regular education policy. A trickle-down theory of education of the hard to teach. *Journal of Special Education,* 23, 256–278.

Kearny, M. (1999). The role of teachers in helping children of domestic violence. *Childhood Education, 75*(5), 290–296.

Keats, E. J. (1967). *Peter's chair.* New York: Harper & Row.

Kellam, S. G., Ling, X., Merisca, R., Brown, C. H., & Ialongo, N. (1999). The effect of the level of aggression in the 1st grade classroom on the course and malleability of aggressive behavior into middle school. *Development and Psychopathology, 10*, 165–185.

Keltikangas-Jarvinen, L., Terav, T., & Pakaslati, L. (1999). Moral reasoning among Estonian and Finnish adolescents: A comparison of collectivist and individual settings. *Journal of Cross-Cultural Psychology, 30*, 257–290.

Kempe, R. S., & Kempe, C. H. (1978). *Child abuse.* Cambridge, MA: Harvard University Press.

Kemple, K. M. (1991). Research in review: Preschool children's peer acceptance and social interaction. *Young Children, 46*(5), 47–54.

Keniston, K. (1977). *All our children: The American family under pressure.* New York: Harcourt Brace Jovanovich.

Kennell, J., Voos, D., & Klaus, M. (1976). Parent–infant bonding. In R. Helfer & C. H. Kempe (Eds.), *Child abuse and neglect: The family and the community.* Cambridge, MA: Ballinger.

Keogh, B. K. (1988). Perspectives on the regular education initiative. *Learning Disabilities Focus*, *4*, 3–5.

Kerkman, D. D. , Kunkel, D., Huston, A. C., Wright, J. C., & Pinon, M. F. (1990). Children's television programming and the "free market" solution. *Journalism Quarterly*, *67*(1), 147–156.

Killen, M., & Nucci, L. P. (1995). Morality, autonomy, and social conflict. In M. Killen & D. Hart (Eds.), *Morality in everyday life: Developmental perspectives*. Cambridge, England: Cambridge University Press.

Kim, J. E., Hetherington, E. M., & Reiss, D. (1999). Associations among family relationships, antisocial peers, and adolescents' externalizing behaviors: Gender and family type differences. *Child Development, 70*, 1209–1230.

Kimball, M. M. (1986). Television and sex-role attitudes. In T. M. Williams (Ed.), *The impact of television: A natural experiment in three communities*. Orlando, FL: Academic Press.

Kinman, J. R., & Henderson, D. L. (1985). An analysis of sexism in Newberry Medal award books from 1977 to 1984. *The Reading Teacher*, *38*(9), 885–889.

Kinney, D. A. (1993). From nerds to normals. *Sociology of Education*, *66*(1), 21–40.

Kirk, S., Gallagher, J. J., & Anastasiow, N. J. (1997). *Educating exceptional children* (7th ed.). Boston: Houghton Mifflin.

Kluckhohn, F. (1961). Dominant and variant value orientation. In C. Kluckhohn & H. Murray (Eds.), *Personality in nature and society*. New York: Knopf.

Kluckhohn, F., & Strodbeck, F. (1961). *Variations in value orientations*. Evanston, IL: Row Peterson.

Koblinsky, S., & Behana, N. (1984). Child sexual abuse: The educator's role in prevention, detection, and intervention. *Young Children, 39*(6), 3–15.

Kochanska, G. (1991). Socialization and temperament in the development of guilt and conscience. *Child Development, 62*, 1379–1392.

Kochanska, G. (1993). Toward a synthesis of parental socialization and child temperament in early development of conscience. *Child Development*, 64, 325–347.

Kochanska, G. (1995). Children's temperament, mothers' discipline, and security of attachment: Multiple pathways to emerging internalization. *Child Development*, 66, 597–615.

Kochanska, G., DeVet, K., Goldman, M., Murray, K., & Putnam, S.P. (1994). Maternal reports of conscience development and temperament in young children. *Child Development*, *65*, 852–868.

Koff, E., Rierdan, J., & Stubbs, M. L. (1990). Gender, body image, and self-concept in early adolescence. *Journal of Early Adolescence*, *10*, 56–68.

Kohl, H. (1967). *36 children*. New York: New American Library.

Kohl, H. (1984). *Growing minds: On becoming a teacher*. New York: Harper & Row.

Kohlberg, L. (1966). A cognitive developmental analysis of children's sex-role concepts and attitudes. In E. E. Maccoby (Ed.), *The development of sex differences*. Stanford, CA: Stanford University Press.

Kohlberg, L. (1969). Stage and sequence: The cognitive developmental approach to socialization. In D. A. Goslin (Ed.), *Handbook of socialization theory and research*. Chicago: Rand McNally.

Kohlberg, L. (1976). Moral stages and moralization. In T. Lickona (Ed.), *Moral development and behavior*. New York: Holt, Rinehart & Winston.

Kohlberg, L. (Ed.). (1980). *Recent research in moral development*. New York: Holt, Rinehart & Winston.

Kohlberg, L. (1985). The just community approach to moral education in theory and practice. In M. W. Berkowitz & F. Oser (Eds.), *Moral education: Theory and application*. Hillsdale, NJ: Lawrence Erlbaum.

Kohlberg, L. (1986). A current statement on some theoretical issues. In S. Modgil & C. Modgil (Eds.), *Lawrence Kohlberg*. Philadelphia: Folmer.

Kohn, M. L. (1977). *Class and conformity: A study in values* (2nd ed.). Chicago: University of Chicago University Press.

Kohn, M. L., Naoi, A., Schoenbach, V., Schooler, C., & Slomczynski, K. M. (1990). Position in the class structure and psychological functioning in the United States, Japan, and Poland. *American Journal of Sociology*, *95*(4), 864–1008.

Korbin, F. E. (1978). The fall in household size and the rise of the primary individual in the United States. In M. Gordon (Ed.), *The American family in social historical perspective*. New York: St. Martin's Press.

Kostelnik, M. J., Whiren, A. P., & Stein, L. C. (1986). Living with He-Man. *Young Children, 41*(4), 3–9.

Kounin, J. (1970). *Discipline and group management in the classroom*. New York: Holt, Rinehart & Winston.

Kozol, J. (1991). *Savage inequalities: Children in America's schools*. New York: Crown.

Krebs, R. (1967). *Some relations between moral judgment, attention and resistance to temptation*. Unpublished doctorate dissertation. Chicago: University of Chicago.

Krononberger, L. (1966). Uncivilized and uncivilizing. *TV Guide*, 14(9),15.

Krug, M. (1976). *The melting of the ethnics*. Bloomington, IN: Phi Delta Kappa.

Kuczen, B. (1987). *Childhood stress*. New York: Dell.

Kuczynski, L., Kochanska, G., Radke-Yarrow, M., & Girnius-Brown, O. (1987). A developmental interpretation of young children's noncompliance. *Developmental Psychology, 23,* 799–806.

Kunkel, D., & Roberts, D. (1991). Young minds and marketplace values: Issues in children's television advertising. *Journal of Social Issues, 47,* 57–72.

Kupersmidt, J. B., Coie, J. D., & Dodge, K. A. (1990). The role of poor peer relationships in the development of disorder. In S. R. Asher & J. D. Coie (Eds.), *Peer rejection in childhood.* New York: Cambridge University Press.

Kurtines, W., & Greif, E. B. (1974). The development of moral thought: Review and evaluation of Kohlberg's approach. *Psychological Bulletin, 81,* 453–470.

Kurtines, W. M., & Gewirtz, J. (Eds.). (1991). *Handbook of moral behavior and development.* Hillsdale, NJ: Lawrence Erlbaum.

Ladd, G. W. (1990). Having friends, keeping friends, making friends, and being liked by peers in the classroom: Predictions of children's early school adjustment. *Child Development, 61,* 1081–1100.

Ladd, G. W., & LeSieur, K. D. (1995). Parents and peer relationships. In M. H. Bornstein (Ed.), *Handbook of parenting* (Vol. 4). Mahwah, NJ: Lawrence Erlbaum.

Lamb, M. E. (1977). The development of mother–infant and father–infant attachment in the second year of life. *Developmental Psychology, 13*(6), 637–648.

Lamb, M. E. (1981). Fathers and child development: An integrated overview. In M. E. Lamb (Ed.), *The father's role in child development.* New York: John Wiley & Sons.

Lamb, M. E. (1986). The changing roles of fathers. In M. E. Lamb (Ed.), *The father's role: Applied perspectives.* New York: John Wiley & Sons.

Lamb, M. E. (1997). *The role of the father in child development* (3rd ed.). New York: John Wiley & Sons.

Lamb, M. E. (1998). Nonparental child care: Context, quality, correlates, and consequences. In W. Damon (Ed.), *Handbook of Child Psychology* (5th ed., Vol. 4). New York: John Wiley & Sons.

Lamble, D. Z., Bond, J. T., & Weikart, D. P. (1974). *Home teaching with mothers and infants.* Ypsilanti, MI: High/Scope Educational Research Foundation.

Lamborn, S. D. , Mounts, N. S., Steinberg, L., & Dornbusch, S. (1991). Patterns of competence and adjustment among adolescents from authoritative, authoritarian, indulgent, and neglectful families. *Child Development, 62,* 1049–1065.

Landre, R., Miller, M., & Porter, D. (1997). *Gangs: A handbook for community awareness.* New York: Facts on File.

Langlois, J. H. (1986). From the eye of the beholder to behavioral reality: Development of social behavior and social relations as a function of physical attractiveness. In C. P. Herman, M. P. Zanna, & E. T. Higgins (Eds.), *Physical behavior: The Ontario Symposium* (Vol. 3). Hillsdale, NJ: Lawrence Erlbaum.

Langlois, J. H., & Downs, A. C. (1980). Mothers, fathers, and peers as socialization agents of sex-typed behaviors in young children. *Child Development, 51,* 1217–1247.

Larrick, N. (1975). Children of television. *Teacher Magazine, 93,* 75–77.

Larson, R. (1995) Secrets in the bedroom: Adolescents' private use of media. *Journal of Youth and Adolescence, 24*(5), 535–550.

Larson, R., Kubey, R., & Colletti, J. (1989). Changing channels: Early adolescent media choices and shifting investments in family and friends. *Journal of Youth and Adolescence, 18*(16), 583–599.

Larson, T. (1992). Understanding stepfamilies. *American Demographics, 14,* 360.

Lasker, J. (1972). *Mothers can do anything.* Chicago: Albert Whitman.

Lazar, I. (1977). The persistence of preschool effects: A long-term follow-up on fourteen infant and preschool experiments. *Final report to the administration on children, youth and families.* Washington, DC: Office of Human Services, U.S. Department of Health, Education, and Welfare.

Lazar, I., & Darlington, R. B. (1982). Lasting effect of early education: A report from the consortium for longitudinal studies. *Monographs of the Society for Research in Child Development, 47,* 2–3. (Serial No. 195)

Leach, P. (1994). *Children first.* New York: Knopf.

Leaf, M. (1936). *The story of Ferdinand.* New York: Viking/Penguin.

Leershen, C., & Namuth, T. (1988), *Alcohol and the family.* 111(3), 62–68.

LeFlore, L. (1988). Delinquent youths and family. *Adolescence, 23,* 629–642.

Leibert, R. M., Neil, M., & Davidson, E. S. (1973). *The early window: Effects of television on children and youth.* New York: Pergamon Press.

Leibert, R., & Poulos, R. W. (1976). Television as a moral teacher. In T. Lickona (Ed.), *Moral development and behavior.* New York: Holt, Rinehart & Winston.

Leibert, R. M., & Sprafkin, J. (1988). *The early window: Effects of television on children and youth* (3rd ed.). New York: Pergamon Press.

LeMasters, E. E. (1988). Blue-collar aristocrats and their children. In G. Handel (Ed.), *Childhood socialization.* New York: Aldine de Gruyer.

Lenski, G. (1961). *The religious factor: A sociological study of religious impact on politics, economic, and family life*. Garden City, NY: Doubleday.

Lepper, M. R. (1983). Social-control processes and the internalization of social values: An attributional perspective. In E. T. Higgins, D. N. Ruble, & W. W. Hartup (Eds.), *Social cognition and social development: A sociocultural perspective*. Cambridge, England: Cambridge University Press.

Lepper, M. R., & Gurtner, J. (1989). Children and computers: Approaching the twenty-first century. *American Psychologist, 44*, 170–178.

Lerner, J. V. (1993). The influence of child temperamental characteristics on parent behaviors. In T. Luster & L. Okagaki (Eds.), *Parenting: An ecological perspective*. Hillsdale, NJ: Lawrence Erlbaum.

Lerner, R. M. (1998). Theories of human development: Contemporary perspectives. In W. Damon (Ed.), *Handbook of child psychology* (5th ed., Vol. 1.). New York: John Wiley & Sons

Lerner, R. M., & Karabeneck, S. (1974). Physical attractiveness, body attitudes, and self-concept in late adolescents. *Journal of Youth and Adolescence, 3*, 307–316..

Levenstein, P. (1988). *Messages from home: The mother–child home program and the prevention of school disadvantage*. Columbus: Ohio University Press.

Lever, J. (1976). Sex differences in the games children play. *Social Problems, 23*, 478–487.

Lever, J. (1978). Sex differences in the complexity of children's play. *American Sociological Review, 43*, 471–482.

Levin, D. E. (1994). *Teaching young children in violent times: Building a peaceable classroom*. Cambridge, MA: Educators for Social Responsibility.

Levin, D. E. (1998). *Remote control childhood? Combating the hazards of media culture*. Washington, DC: National Association for Education of Young Children.

Levin, D. E., & Carlsson-Paige, N. (1995). The Mightly Morphin Power Rangers: Teachers voice concern. *Young Children, 50*(6), 67–72.

Levine, D. U., & Levine, R. F. (1996). *Society and education* (9th ed.). Needham Heights, MA: Allyn & Bacon.

LeVine, R. A. (1977). Child rearing as a cultural adaptation. In P. H. Leiderman, S. R. Tulken, & A. Rosenfeld (Eds.), *Culture and Infancy*. New York: Academic Press.

LeVine, R. A. (1988). Human parental care: Universal goals, cultural strategies, individual behavior. In R. A. LeVine, P. M. Miller, & M. M. West (Eds.), *Parental behavior in diverse societies*. San Francisco: Jossey-Bass.

Lewin, K., Lippitt, R., & White, R. (1939). Patterns of aggressive behavior in experimentally created social climates. *Journal of Social Psychology, 10*, 271–299.

Lewis, J. M. (1976). *No single thread: Psychological health in family systems*. New York: Brunner/Mazel.

Lewit, E. M., & Baker, L. S. (1995). School readiness. *The Future of Children: Critical Issues for Children and Youths, 5*(2), 128–139.

Lickona, T. (1977). How to encourage moral development. *Learning, 5*(7), 36–43.

Lickona, T. (1991). *Educating for character*. New York: Bantam.

Limber, S. P., & Nation, M. A. (1998). Violence within the neighborhood and community. In P. K. Trickett & C. J. Schellenbach (Eds.), *Violence against children in the family and the community*. Washington, DC: American Psychological Association.

Linney, J. A., & Seidman, E. (1989). The future of schooling. *American Psychologist, 44*(2), 336–340.

Lionni, L. (1968). *The biggest house in the world*. New York: Pantheon.

Lippitt, R., & White, R. K. (1943). The social climate of children's groups. In R. G. Barker, J. S. Korinen, & H. F. Wright (Eds.), *Child behavior and development*. New York: McGraw-Hill.

Lipsky, D., & Gartner, H. (1989). *Beyond separate education*. Baltimore: Paul H. Brooks.

List, J. A., Collins, W. A., & Westby, S. D. (1983). Comprehension and inferences from traditional and nontraditional sex-role portrayals on television. *Child Development, 54*, 1579–1587.

Logue, A. W. (1995). *Self-control: Waiting until tomorrow for what you want today*. Englewood Cliffs, NJ: Prentice-Hall.

Lohr, J. M., & Staats, A. (1973). Attitude conditioning in Sino-Tibetan languages. *Journal of Personality and Social Psychology, 26*, 196–200.

Long, L., & Long, T. (1982). The unspoken fears of latchkey kids. *Working Mother, 5*(76), 88–90.

Long, L., & Long, T. (1983). *The handbook for latchkey children and their parents*. New York: Arbor House.

Lorenz, K. (1966). *On aggression*. New York: Harcourt, Brace & World.

Love, J. M., Schochet, P. Z., & Meckstroth. A. L. (1996). Are they in any real danger? What research doesn't tell us about child care quality and children's well-being. *Child Care and Research Policy Papers*. ERIC Digest. (ED415030)

Lowry, B. (1999, August 20). Networks face a bumpy ride. *Los Angeles Times*, p. F1.

Lull, J. (1980). The social uses of television. *Human Communication Research, 6*, 197–209.

Luster, T., & Okagaki, L. (1993). Multiple influences on parenting: Ecological and life-course perspectives. In T. Luster & L. Okagaki (Eds.), *Parenting: An ecological perspective*. Hillsdale, NJ: Lawrence Erlbaum.

Lytton, H., & Romney, D. M. (1991). Parents' differential socialization of boys and girls: A meta-analysis. *Psychological Bulletin, 109*, 267–296.

Maccoby, E. E. (1980). *Social development: Psychological growth and the parent–child relationship*. New York: Harcourt Brace Jovanovich.

Maccoby, E. E. (1990). Gender and relationships: A developmental account. *American Psychologist, 45*, 513–520.

Maccoby, E. E. (1998). *The two sexes: Growing up apart, coming together*. Cambridge, MA: Harvard University Press.

Maccoby, E. E., & Jacklin, C. N. (1974). *The psychology of sex differences*. Stanford, CA: Stanford University Press.

Maccoby, E. E., & Jacklin, C. N. (1980). Sex differences in aggression: A rejoinder and reprise. *Child Development, 51*, 964–980.

Maccoby, E. E., & Jacklin, C. N. (1987). Gender segregation in childhood. *Advances in Child Development and Behavior, 20*, 239–287.

Maccoby, E. E., & Martin, J. (1983). Socialization in the context of family: Parent–child interaction. In P. H. Mussen (Ed.), *Handbook of child psychology* (4th ed., Vol. 4). New York: John Wiley & Sons.

MacDonald, K., & Parke, R. D. (1986). Parent–child physical play: The effects of sex and age of children and parents. *Sex Roles, 15*(7/8), 367–378.

MacLeod, A. S. (1994). *American childhood*. Athens: University of Georgia Press.

Madsen, M. C., & Shapira, A. (1970). Cooperative and competitive behavior of urban Afro-American, Anglo-American, and Mexican-American and Mexican village children. *Developmental Psychology, 3*, 16–20.

Maehr, M. L. (1974). *Sociocultural origins of achievement*. Monterey, CA: Brooks/Cole.

Maidman, F. (Ed.). (1984). *Child welfare: A sourcebook of knowledge and practice*. New York: Child Welfare League of America.

Mann, J. (1982). What is TV doing to America? *U.S. News & World Report, 93*(5), 27–30.

Marcossen, M., & Fleming, V. (Eds.). (1978, November). *The children's political checklist*. Washington, DC: Coalition for Children and Youth.

Margolin, G. (1998). Effects of domestic violence on children. In P. K. Trickett & C. J. Schellenbach (Eds.), *Violence against children in the family and the community*. Washington, DC: American Psychological Association.

Margolis, C. (1971). The black student in political strife. *Proceedings of the 79th Annual Convention of the American Psychological Association, 10*, 395–396.

Martin, A. (1985). Back to kindergarten basics. *Harvard Educational Review, 55*, 318–320.

Martin, C. L. (1989). Children's use of gender-related information in making social judgments. *Developmental Psychology, 25*, 80–88.

Martin, C. L., & Halverson, C. F. (1981). A schematic processing model of sex-typing and stereotyping in children. *Child Development 52*, 1119–1134.

Martin, C. L., & Halverson, C. F. Jr. (1987). The roles of cognition in sex-roles and sex-typing. In D. B. Carter (Ed.), *Current conceptions of sex roles and sex-typing: Theory and research*. New York: Praeger.

Martin, C. L., Wood, C. H., & Little, J. K. (1990). The development of gender stereotype components. *Child Development, 61*, 1891–1904.

Martin, G., & Pear, J. (1996). *Behavior modification: What it is and how to do it* (5th ed.). Upper Saddle River, NJ: Prentice-Hall.

Martin, G. B., & Clark, R. D. (1982). III. Distress crying in neonates: Species and peer specificity. *Developmental Psychology, 18*, 3–9.

Martin, J. B. (1998). *Snowflake Bentley*. Boston: Houghton Mifflin.

Martin, J. R. (1995, January). A philosophy of education for the year 2000. *Phi Delta Kappan*, 355–359.

Martin, M., & Waltman-Greenwood, C. (Eds.) (1995). *Solve your child's school-related problems*. New York: HarperCollins.

Martin, R. (1999). "Shake your bon bon." Sony/Columbia.

Martinez, R., & Dukes, R. L. (1991). Ethnic and gender differences and self-esteem. *Youth and Society, 3*, 318–338.

Mason, K. O., & Duberstein, L. (1992). Consequences of child-care practices and arrangements for the well-being of parents and providers. In A. Booth (Ed.), *Child care in the 1990s: Trends and consequences*. Hillsdale, NJ: Lawrence Erlbaum.

Mason, M. A. (1998). *The custody wars: Why children are losing the legal battle—and what we can do about it*. New York: Basic Books.

McAdoo, H. P. (1993). Ethnic families: Strengths that are found in diversity. In H. P. McAdoo (Ed.), *Ethnic families: Strength in diversity*. Newbury Park, CA: Sage.

McCartney, K., & Galanopoulos, A. (1988). Child care and attachment: A new frontier the second time around. *American Journal of Orthopsychiatry, 58*(1), 16–24.

McClelland, D. C. (1961). *The achieving society*. New York: Van Nostrand.

McClelland, D. C., Atkinson, J. W., Clark, R. A., & Lowell, E. L. (1953). *The achievement motive*. New York: Appleton-Century-Crofts.

McClelland, D. C., & Pilon, D. A. (1983). Sources of adult motives in patterns of parent behavior in early childhood. *Journal of Personality and Social Psychology, 44*, 564–574.

McCloskey, R. (1948). *Blueberries for Sal*. New York: Viking Press.

McCormick, L., & Holden, R. (1992). Homeless children: A special challenge. *Young Children, 47* (6), 61–67.

McGuffey, W. H. (1879). *McGuffey's third eclectic reader*. New York: American Book.

McGuire, W. J. (1985). Attitudes and attitude change. In G. Lindzey & E. Aronson (Eds.), *Handbook of social psychology* (3rd ed., Vol. 2). New York: Random House.

McHale, J. P. (1995). Coparenting and triadic interactions during infancy: The roles of marital distress and child gender. *Developmental Psychology, 31*, 985–996.

McHale, S. M., Crouter, A. C., & Tucker, C. J. (1998). Family context and gender-role socialization in middle childhood: Comparing girls to boys and sisters to brothers. *Child Development, 70*, 990–1004.

McIntyre, T. (1992, Summer). The culturally sensitive disciplinarian. *Monographs in Behavioral Disorders: Severe Behavior Disorders of Children and Youth, 15*, 107–115.

McLane, J. B., & McNamee, G. D. (1990). *Early literacy*. Cambridge, MA: Harvard University Press.

McLoyd, V. C. (1990). The impact of economic hardship on black families and children. Psychological distress, parenting, and socioemotional development. *Child Development, 61*, 311–346.

McLoyd, V. C. (1998). Children in poverty: Development, public policy, and practice. In W. Damon (Ed.), *Handbook of child psychology* (5th ed., Vol. 4). New York: John Wiley & Sons.

McLoyd, V. C., & Wilson, L. (1990). *Maternal behavior, social support and economic conditions and predictors of distress in children*. In V. C. McLoyd & C. A. Flanagan (Eds.), *Economic stress: Effects on family life and child development*. San Francisco: Jossey-Bass.

McLuhan, M. (1974). *Understanding media: The extension of man*. New York: McGraw-Hill.

McLuhan, M. (1989). A McLuhan mosaic. In G. Sanderson & F. Macdonald (Eds.), *Marshall McLuhan: The man and his message*. Golden, CO: Fulcrum.

McNally, L., Eisenberg, J., & Harris, J. D. (1991). Consistency and change in maternal child-rearing practices and values: A longitudinal study. *Child Development, 62*, 190–198.

McNeal, J. (1987). *Children as consumers*. Lexington, MA: Lexington Books.

Mead, G. H. (1934). *Mind, self, and society*. Chicago: University of Chicago Press.

Meadow-Orlans, K. P. (1995). Parenting with a sensory or physical disability. In M. H. Bornstein (Ed.), *Handbook of parenting* (Vol. 4). Mahwah, NJ: Lawrence Erlbaum.

Mediascope Inc. (1996). *National television violence study*. Studio City, CA: Author.

Mednick, S. A., Moffit, M., Gabrielli, W. Jr., & Hutchings, B. (1986). Genetic factors incriminal behavior: A review. In D. Olweus, J. Block, & M. Radke-Yarrow (Eds.), *Development of antisocial and prosocial behavior: Research, theories, and issues*. Orlando: Academic Press.

Medrich, E. A., Roizen, J. Rubin, V., & Buckley, S. (1981). *The serious business of growing up: A study of children's lives outside of school*. Berkeley: University of California Press.

Meisels, S. J., & Provence, S. (1989). *Screening and assessment: Guidelines for identifying young disabled and developmentally vulnerable children and their families*. Washington, DC: National Center for Clinical Infant Programs.

Meisels, S. J., & Wasik, B. A. (1990). Who should be served? Identifying children in need of early intervention. In S. J. Meisels & J. P. Shonkoff (Eds.), *Handbook of early childhood intervention*. New York: Cambridge University Press.

Melendez, D., Cole-Melendez, D., & Molina, A. (1989). Pluralism and the Hispanic student: Challenge to educators. *Theory into Practice, 20*(8), 89.

Melson, G. F., Ladd, G. W., & Hsu, H. L. (1993). Maternal support networks, maternal cognitions and young children's cognitive development. *Child Development, 64*, 1401–1417.

Mercer, J. (1973). *Labeling the mentally retarded: Clinical and social system perspectives on mental retardation*. Berkeley: University of California Press.

Meringoff, L. K. (1980). Influence of the medium on children's story apprehension. *Journal of Educational Psychology, 72*, 240–249.

Milgram, S. (1963). Behavioral study of obedience. *Journal of Abnormal and Social Psychology, 67*, 371–378.

Miller, B. C., Christopherson, C. R., & King, P. K. (1993). Sexual behavior in adolescence. In T. P. Gullotta, G. R. Adams, & R. Montemayor (Eds.), *Adolescent sexuality*. Newbury Park, CA: Sage.

Miller, D. F. (1989). *First steps toward cultural differences: Socialization in infant/toddler day care*. Washington, DC: Child Welfare League of America.

Miller, D. R., & Swanson, G. E. (1958). *The changing American parent*. New York: John Wiley & Sons.

Miller, J. G. (1995, March). *Culture, context, and personal agency: The cultural grounding of self and morality*. Paper presented at the biennial meeting of the Society for Research in Child Development, Indianapolis, IN.

Miller, J. G., & Bersoff, D. M. (1992). Culture and moral judgment: Resolved? *Journal of Personality and Social Psychology, 62*, 541–554.

Miller, J. G., & Bersoff, D. M. (1993, March). *Culture and affective closeness in the morality of caring.* Paper presented at the biennial meeting of the Society for Research in Child Development, New Orleans, LA.

Miller, K. E., Sabo, D. F., Farrell, M. P., Barnes, G. M., & Melnick, M.J. (1998). Athletic participation and sexual behavior in adolescents: The different worlds of boys and girls. *Journal of Health and Social Behavior, 39*, 108–123.

Miller, K. S., Forehand, R., & Kotchick, B. A. (1999). Adolescent behavior in two ethnic minority samples: The role of family variables. *Journal of Marriage and the Family, 61*, 85–98.

Miller, L. B., & Dyer, J. L. (1975). Four preschool programs: Their dimensions and effects. *Monographs of the Society for Research in Child Development, 40* (5–6). (Serial No. 162).

Minkler, M., & Roe, K. (1993). *Grandmothers as caregivers.* Newbury Park, CA: Sage.

Mintz, S. (1998). From patriarchy to androgeny and other myths. Placing men's family roles in historical perspectives. In A. Booth & A. C. Crouter (Eds.), *Men in families.* Mahwah, NJ: Lawrence Erlbaum.

Minuchin, P. M. (1977). *The middle years of childhood.* Monterey, CA: Brooks/Cole.

Minuchin, P. M., & Shapiro, E. K. (1983). The school as a context for social development. In P. H. Mussen (Ed.), *Handbook of Child Psychology* (4th ed., Vol. 4). New York: John Wiley & Sons.

Mischel, W. (1970). Sex typing and socialization. In P. H. Mussen (Ed.), *Carmichael's manual of child psychology* (Vol. 1). New York: John Wiley & Sons.

Mischel, W. (1974). Processes in the delay of gratification. In L. Berkowitz (Ed.), *Advances in experimental social psychology* (Vol. 7). Orlando, FL: Academic Press.

Mischel, W., Shoda, Y., & Peake, P. K. (1988). The nature of adolescent competencies predicted by preschool delay of gratification. *Journal of Personality and Social Psychology, 54*, 687–696.

Mize, J., & Ladd, G. W. (1990). A cognitive social learning approach to social skill training with low-status preschool children. *Developmental Psychology, 26*, 388–397.

Montessori, M. (1965). *Montessori's own handbook.* New York: Schocken Books.

Montessori, M. (1967). *The absorbent mind.* New York: Holt, Rinehart & Winston.

Moore, S. G., & Bulbulian, K. N. (1976). The effects of contrasting styles of adult–children interaction on children's curiosity. *Developmental Psychology, 12*(2), 171–72.

Morrison, A., & McIntyre, D. (1971). *Schools and socialization.* Hammondsworth, Middlesex, England: Penguin Books.

Murdock, G. P. (1962). Structures and functions of the family. In R. F. Winch, R. M. McGinnis, & H. R. Barringer (Eds.), *Selected studies in marriage and the family.* New York: Holt, Rinehart & Winston.

Murphy, S. (1999). *The cheers and the tears: A healthy alternative to the dark side of youth sports today.* San Francisco, CA: Jossey-Bass.

Mussen, P. H., & Eisenberg-Berg, N. (1977). *Roots of caring, sharing, and helping: The development of prosocial behavior in children.* San Francisco: Freeman.

Naisbitt, J. (1982). *Megatrends.* New York: Warner.

Naisbitt, J. (1994). *Global paradox.* New York: Avon.

Naisbitt, J., & Auberdene, P. (1990). *Megatrends 2000.* New York: William Morrison.

Nalley, R. (1973). Sociobiology: A new view of human nature. In H. E. Fitzgerald & T. H. Carr (Eds.), *Human development 83/84.* Guilford, CT: Dushkin.

Nardi, P. M. (1981). Children of alcoholics: A role theoretical perspective. *Journal of Social Psychology, 115*, 237–245.

National Association for the Education of Young Children [NAEYC]. (1984). *Accreditation criteria and procedures of the national academy of early childhood programs.* Washington, DC: Author.

NAEYC. (1986). Position statement on developmentally appropriate practice in early childhood programs serving children from birth through age 8. *Young Children, 41*(6), 3–19.

NAEYC. (1988). NAEYC Position statement on standardized testing of young children 3 through 8 years of age. *Young Children, 43*(3), 42–47.

NAEYC. (1996a). NAEYC position statement: Responding to linguistic and cultural diversity—recommendations for effective early childhood education. *Young Children, 51*(2), 4–12.

NAEYC. (1996b). Public policy report: Be a children's champion. *Young Children, 51*(2), 58–60.

National Cable Television Association. (1994, April). *Cable television developments.*

National Center for Health Statistics [NCHS]. (1998). *U.S. Department of Health and Human Services.*

National Clearinghouse for Alcohol Information. (1985, October). *Children of alcoholics.* Rockville, MD: Author.

National Coalition against Domestic Violence. (1999). *The Violence against Women Act of 1999.*

National Commission on Children. (1991). *Beyond rhetoric: A new American agenda for children and families.* Washington, DC: U.S. Government Printing Office.

National Commission on Excellence in Education [NCEE]. (1983). *A nation at risk: The imperative for educational reform*. Washington, DC: U.S. Government Printing Office.

National Council on Alcoholism. (1986, March). *National council on alcoholism fact sheet: Children of alcoholics*. Santa Ana, CA: Author.

National Institute of Child Health and Human Development [NICHD]. Early Child Care Research Network. (1996). Characteristics of infant child care: Factors contributing to positive caregiving. *Early Childhood Research Quarterly, 11*, 269–306.

NICHD. Early Child Care Research Network. (1997). The effects of infant child care or infant–mother attachment security: Results of the NICHD study of early child care. *Child Development, 68*, 860–879.

NICHD. Early Child Care Research Network. (1998). Early child care and self-control, compliance, and problem behavior at twenty-four and thirty-six months. *Child Development, 69*, 1145–1170.

National Research Council. (1993). *Losing generations: Adolescents in high-risk settings*. Washington, DC: National Academy Press.

National Science Foundation. (1994). *Investing in human resources: A strategic plan for the human capital initiative: Executive summary*. Washington, DC: Author.

Nazario, T. A. (1988). *In defense of children: Understanding the rights, needs, and interests of the child*. New York: Charles Scribner's Sons.

Neill, A. (1977). *Summerhill: A radical approach to child rearing*. New York: Pocket Books.

Nettles, S. M. (1990). *Community involvement and disadvantaged students: A review*. Baltimore: Johns Hopkins Center for Research on Effective Schooling for Disadvantaged Students.

Neuman, S. G. (1991). *Literacy in the television age: The myth of the TV effect*. Norwood, NJ: Ablex.

Newcomb, M. D., & Bentler, P. M. (1989). Substance use and abuse among children and teenagers. *American Psychologist, 44*, 247–248.

New Testament, Timothy 3:5.

Nielson, A. C. (1998). *Nielson media research*. New York: Author.

Nieting, P. (1974). School-age child care. *Childhood Education, 60*(1), 6–11.

Niles, F. S. (1981). The youth culture controversy: An evaluation. *Journal of Early Adolescence, 1*(3), 265–271.

Noll, R. B., Zucker, R. A., Fitzgerald, H. E., & Curtis, W. J. (1992). Cognitive and motor functioning of sons of alcoholic fathers and controls: The early childhood years. *Developmental Psychology, 28*, 665–675.

Norton, D. E. (1999). *Through the eyes of a child: An introduction to children's literature* (5th ed.). Upper Saddle River, NJ: Prentice-Hall.

Nowicki, S., & Segal, W. (1974). Perceived parental characteristics, locus of control orientation, and behavioral correlates of locus of control. *Developmental Psychology, 10*, 33–37.

O'Brien, M., & Huston, A. C. (1985). Activity level and sex-stereotyped toy choice in toddler boys and girls. *Journal of Genetic Psychology, 146*, 527–534.

O'Brien, S. J. (1991). Finding a way to serve. *Childhood Education, 67*(5), 320–321.

O'Dea, J. A. & Abraham, S. (1999). Association between self-concept and body weight, gender, and pubertal development among male and female adolescents. *Adolescence, 34*, 64–79.

Oden, S., & Asher, S. (1977). Coaching children in social skills for friendship making. *Child Development, 48*, 495–506.

Ogburn, W. F. (1962). The changing functions of the family. In R. F. Winch, R. M. McGinnis, & H. R. Barringer (Eds.), *Selected studies in marriage and the family*. New York: Holt, Rinehart & Winston.

Oguntari, J. T. (1985). Somatic deviation in adolescence. Reactions and adjustment. *Adolescence, 20*, 179–183.

Old Testament. Proverbs 23:13,14; Proverbs 13:24; Proverbs 22:6.

Olweus, D. (1986). Aggression and hormones: Behavioral relationship with testosterone and adrenaline. In D. Olweus, J. Block, & M. Radke-Yarrow (Eds.), *Development of antisocial and prosocial behavior: Research, theories, and issues*. Orlando, FL: Academic Press.

Olweus, D. (1993). *Bullying at school: What we know and what we can do*. Cambridge, MA: Blackwell.

Oppenheimer, T. (1997, July). The computer delusion. *The Atlantic Monthly*, pp. 45–48, 50–56, 61–62.

Ornstein, A. C., & Levine, D. U. (1982). Multicultural education: Trends and issues. *Childhood Education, 58*(4), 245.

Ornstein, A. C., & Levine, D. U. (1989, September/October). Social class, race and school achievement: Problems and prospects. *Journal of Teacher Education, 40*(4), 17–23.

Orwell, G. (1946). *Animal farm*. New York: Harcourt Brace.

Osler, S. F., & Kofsky, E. (1965). Stimulus uncertainty as a variable in the development of conceptual ability. *Journal of Experimental Child Psychology, 2*, 264–279.

Pagano, A. I. (1982). Total community support for children's development. *Childhood Education, 59*(2), 95–99.

Pagano. A. I. (1997). Community service groups enhance learning. In B. Hatcher & S. S. Beck (Eds.), *Learning opportunities beyond the school* (2nd ed.). Olney, MD: Association for Childhood Education International.

Pagelow, M. D. (1982). Children in violent families. Direct and indirect victims. In S. B. Hill & B. J. Barnes (Eds.), *Young children and their families*. Lexington, MA: D.C. Heath.

Palladrino, G. (1996). *Teenagers: An American history*. New York: Basic Books.

Papert, S. (1993). *The children's machine: Rethinking school in the age of the computer*. New York: Basic Books.

Papert, S. (1999). *Mindstorms: Children, computers, and powerful ideas* (2nd ed.). New York: Basic Books.

Park, H., & Comstock, G. (1994). The effects of television violence on antisocial behavior: A meta-analysis. *Communication Research*, *21*, 516–546.

Park, K. A., & Waters, E. (1989). Security of attachment and preschool friendships. *Child Development*, *60*, 1076–1080.

Parke, R. D. (1982). On prediction of child abuse: Theoretical considerations. In R. Starr (Ed.), *Prediction of abuse: Policy implications*. Philadelphia: Ballinger.

Parke, R. D. (1990, Fall). Family-peer systems: In search of a linking process. *Newsletter: Developmental Psychology*. Washington, DC: American Psychological Association. (Division 7)

Parke, R. D. (1995). Fathers and families. In M.H. Bornstein (Ed.), *Handbook of parenting* (Vol. 3). Mahwah, NJ: Lawrence Erlbaum.

Parke, R. D., & Buriel, R. (1998). Socialization in the family: Ethnic and ecological perspectives. In W. Damon (Ed.), *Handbook of child psychology* (5th ed., Vol. 3). New York: John Wiley & Sons.

Parke, R. D., & Slaby, R. B. (1983). The development of aggression. In P. H. Mussen (Ed.), *Handbook of child psychology* (4th ed., Vol. 4). New York: John Wiley & Sons.

Parker, J. G., & Asher, S. R. (1987). Peer relations and later adjustment: Are low-accepted children "at risk"? *Psychological Bulletin*, *102*, 357–389.

Parker, J. G., & Gottman, I. M. (1989). Social and emotional development in a relational context: Friendship interaction from early childhood to adolescence. In T. J. Berndt & G. W. Ladd (Eds.), *Peer relations in child development*. New York: John Wiley & Sons.

Parker, S. T. (1984). Playing for keeps: An evolutionary perspective on human games. In P. K. Smith (Ed.), *Play in animals and humans*. Oxford: Basil Blackwell.

Parkhurst, J. T., & Asher, S. R. (1992). Peer rejection in middle school: Subgroup differences in behavior, loneliness, and interpersonal concerns. *Developmental Psychology*, *28*, 231–241.

Parsons, J. E., Adler, T. F., & Kaczala, C. M. (1982). Socialization of achievement attitudes and beliefs: Parental influences. *Child Development*, *53*, 310–321.

Parten, M. (1932). Social play among preschool children. *Journal of Abnormal and Social Psychology*, *27*, 243–269.

Pate-Bain, H., Achilles, C. M., Boyd-Zaharias, J., & McKenna, B. (1992). Class size does make a difference. *Phi Delta Kappan*, *74*(30), 253–256.

Patterson, C. J., Kupersmidt, J. B., & Vaden, N. A. (1990). Income level, gender, ethnicity, and household composition as predictors of children's school-based competence. *Child Development*, *61*, 485–494.

Patterson, G. R. (1982). *Coercive family processes*. Eugene, OR: Castilia Press.

Patterson, G. R., & Capaldi, D. (1991). Antisocial parents: Unskilled and vulnerable. In P. A. Cowan & M. E. Hetherington (Eds.), *Family transitions: Advances in family research* (Vol. 2). Hillsdale, NJ: Lawrence Erlbaum.

Patterson, G. R., DeBaryshe, D., & Ramsey, E. (1989). A developmental perspective on antisocial behavior. *American Psychologist*, *44*(2), 329–335.

Patterson, G. R., & Dishion, T. J. (1988). Multilevel family process models: Traits, interactions, and relationships. In R. A. Hinde & J. Hinde-Stevenson (Eds.), *Relationships within families*. Oxford: Oxford University Press.

Patterson, G. R., Littman, R. A., & Bricker, W. (1976). Assertive behavior in children: A step toward a theory of aggression. *Monographs of the Society for Research in Child Development*, *32*. (Whole no. 113)

Patterson, G. R., Reid, J. B., & Dishion, T. J. (1992). *Antisocial boys*. Eugene, OR: Castilia.

Pearce, M. L. (1978). *Child advocacy in 10 easy steps: A resource guide*. Sacramento, CA: California Association for the Education of Young Children.

Pearl, D. (Ed.). (1982). *Television and behavior: Ten years of scientific progress and implication for the eighties: Vol. 1. Summary report*. Washington, DC: U.S. Government Printing Office.

Pearl, D. (1984). Violence and aggression. *Society*, *21*(6), 17–22.

Pease-Alvarez, L., Garcia, E. E., & Espinosa, P. (1991). Effective instruction for language-minority students: An early childhood case study. *Early Childhood Research Quarterly*, *6*(3), 347–361.

Peaslee, M. W. (1976). The development of competency in two-year-old infants in day care and home-reared environments. Published doctoral dissertation, Florida State University. Cited in K. A. Clarke-Stewart (1982), *Daycare*. Cambridge, MA: Harvard University Press.

Perry, D. G., Perry, L. C., & Rasmussen, P. (1986). Cognitive social learning mediators of aggression. *Child Development*, *57*, 700–711.

Perry, N. J. (1991, October 21). Where we go from here. *Fortune*, pp. 114–115, 118, 122, 124, 129.

Peters, T. J., & Waterman, R. H. (1982). *In search of excellence*. New York: Warner.

Peterson, L. (1983). Influence of age, task competence, and responsibility focus on children's altruism. *Developmental Psychology, 19*, 141–148.

Petit, G. S., & Mize, J. (1993). Substance and style: Understanding the ways in which parents teach children about social relationships. In S. Duck (Ed.), *Learning about relationships*. Newbury Park, CA: Sage.

Phelps, L. A., Johnston, L. S., Jimenez, D. P., & Wilczenski, F. L. (1993). Figure preference, body dissatisfaction, and body distortion in adolescence. *Journal of Adolescent Research, 28*, 297–310.

Phillips, D. A. (1987a). Socialization of perceived academic competence among highly competent children. *Child Development, 58*, 1308–1320.

Phillips, D. A. (Ed.). (1987b). *Quality in child care: What does research tell us?* Washington, DC: National Association for the Education of Young Children.

Phillips, D. A. (1992). Child care and parental well-being: Bringing quality of care into the picture. In A. Booth (Ed.), *Child care in the 1990s: Trends and consequences*. Hillsdale, NJ: Lawrence Erlbaum.

Phillips, D. A,. & Howes, C. (1987). Indicators of quality in child care: Review of research. In D. A. Phillips (Ed.), *Quality in child care. What does research tell us?* Washington, DC: National Association for Education of Young Children.

Phillips, M. (Ed.). (1981). *Statement on child advocacy*. New York: Child Welfare League of America.

Phillips, S. U. (1983). *The invisible culture: Communication in classroom and community on the Warm Springs Indian Reservation*. New York: Longman.

Phinney, J. S., & Chavira, V. (1992). Ethnic identity and self-esteem: An exploratory longitudinal study. *Journal of Adolescence 13*, 171–183.

Phinney, J. S., & Rotheram, M. J. (Eds.). (1987). *Children's ethnic socialization: Pluralism and development*. Newbury Park, CA: Sage.

Piaget, J. (1952). *The origins of intelligence in children* (M. Cook, Trans.). New York: New American Library.

Piaget, J. (1962). *Play, dreams, and imitation in childhood* (C. Gattegno & F. M. Hodgson, Trans.). New York: Norton.

Piaget, J. (1965). *The moral judgment of the child* (M. Gabain, Trans.). New York: Free Press.

Piaget, J. (1974). *The language and thought of the child*. (M. Gabain, Trans.). New York: New American Library.

Pineus, C., Elliot, L., & Schlachter, T. (1980). *The roots of success*. Englewood Cliffs, NJ: Prentice–Hall.

Pipher, M. (1994). *Reviving Ophelia: Saving the selves of adolescent girls*. NY: Ballantine.

Pitcher, E. G., & Schultz, L. H. (1983). *Boys and girls at play: The development of sex roles*. New York: Bergin & Garvey.

Plummer, J. T. (1989, January/February). Changing values. *The Futurist*, 8–13.

Podhoretz, J. (1987). Metallic rock that's designed to shock. *U.S. News & World Report*, 103 (10), 50–51.

Poinsett, A. (1997, March). *The role of sports in youth development*. Report of Carnegie Corporation Meeting, New York: Carnegie Corporation.

Polk, K., & Schafer, W. (1972). *Schools and delinquency*. Englewood Cliffs, NJ: Prentice-Hall.

Pollack, W. S. (1999). *Real boys: Rescuing our sons from the myths of boyhood*. New York: Henry Holt.

Popenoe, D. (1993). Parental androgeny. *Society, 30*(6), 6–11.

Porter, J. D. R. (1971). *Black child, white child: The development of racial attitudes*. Cambridge, MA: Harvard University Press.

Postman, N. (1981). TV's disastrous impact on children. *U.S. News & World Report*, 90(2), 43–45

Postman, N. (1982). *The disappearance of childhood*. New York: Dell.

Postman, N. (1985). The disappearance of childhood. *Childhood Education, 61*(4), 288–293.

Postman, N. (1986). *Amusing ourselves to death*. New York: Penguin Books.

Postman, N. (1992). *Technopoly: The surrender of culture to technology*. New York: Vintage.

Power, T. G. (1987). Parents as socializers: Maternal and paternal views. *Journal of Youth and Adolescence, 18*, 203–220.

Powlista, K. K., Serbin, L. A., & Moller, L. C. (1993). The stability of individual differences in gender typing: Implications for understanding gender segregation. *Sex Roles, 239*(11/12), 723–737.

Prinsky, L. E., & Rosenbaum, J. L. (1987). Leerics or lyrics? *Youth and Society, 18*, 384–394.

Proctor, P. C. (1984, March). Teacher expectations: A model for school improvement. *Elementary School Journal, 84*(4), 469–481.

Provenzo, E. F. (1991). *Video kids: Making sense of Nintendo*. Cambridge, MA: Harvard University Press.

Putnam, L. (1986). Reading program decisions: The connection between philosophy and practice. *Childhood Education, 62*(5), 330–336.

Putnam, P. C. (1983, February). *A descriptive study of two philosophically different approaches to reading readiness, as they were used in six inner-city kindergartens*. Washington, DC: George Washington University. (ERIC Document Reproduction Service. ED 220 807/808)

Radke-Yarrow, M., & Zahn-Waxler, C. (1970). Dimension and correlates of prosocial behavior in young children. *Child Development, 47,* 118–125.

Radke-Yarrow, M., & Zahn-Waxler, C. (1986). The role of familial factors in the development of prosocial behavior: Research findings and questions. In D. Olweus, J. Block, & M. Radke-Yarrow (Eds.), *Development of antisocial and prosocial behavior: Research, theories, and issues.* Orlando, FL: Academic Press.

Radke-Yarrow, M., Zahn-Waxler, C., & Chapman, H. (1983). Prosocial dispositions and behavior. In P. H. Mussen (Ed.), *Handbook of child psychology* (4th ed., Vol. 4). New York: John Wiley & Sons.

Ramirez, M., & Castaneda, A. (1974). *A cultural democracy, bicognitive development and education.* New York: Academic Press.

Ramsey, P. (1998). *Teaching and learning in a diverse world: Multicultural education for young children* (2nd ed.). New York: Teachers' College Press.

Ramsey, P. G. (1987). Young children's thinking about ethnic differences. In J. S. Phinney & M. J. Rotheram (Eds.), *Children's ethnic socialization: Pluralism and development.* Newbury Park, CA: Sage.

Rawlings, M. K. (1938). *The yearling.* New York: Scribner's.

Reed, S., & Sautter, R. C. (1990, June). Children of poverty. *Phi Delta Kappan,* pp. 1–12.

Reggio Children. (Eds.). (1987). *The hundred languages of children.* Reggio Emilia: Department of Education.

Reiss, A. J. Jr., & Roth, J. A. (Eds.). (1993). *Understanding and preventing violence.* Washington, DC: National Academy Press.

Reynolds, J., & Gerstein, M. (1992). Learning style characteristics: An introductory workshop. *The Clearing House, 66*(2), 122–126.

Rheingold, H. L., & Cook, K. V. (1975). The content of boys' and girls' rooms as an index of parent behavior. *Child Development, 46,* 459–463.

Rice, F. P. (1996). *The adolescent: Development, relationships, and culture* (8th ed.). Needham Heights, MA: Allyn & Bacon.

Rice, M. L., Huston, A. C., Truglio, R., & Wright, J. C. (1990). Words from "Sesame Street": Learning vocabulary while viewing. *Developmental Psychology, 26,* 421–428.

Rice, M., & Grusec, J. (1975). Saying and doing: Effects on observer performance. *Journal of Personality and Social Psychology, 32,* 584–593.

Rich, D. (1992). *Megaskills* (rev. ed.). Boston: Houghton Mifflin.

Rich, M., Woods, E. R., Goodman, E., Emans, S. J., & DuRant, R. H. (1998, April). Aggressors or victims: Gender and race in music video violence. *Pediatrics, 101*(4, Pt.1), 669–674.

Rich, Y., & Golan, R. (1992). Career plans for male-dominated occupations and female seniors in religious and secular high schools. *Adolescence, 27,* 73–86.

Richman, A. L., LeVine, R. A., New, R. S., & Howrigan, G. A. (1988). Maternal behavior to infants in five cultures. In R. A. Levine, P. M. Miller, & M. M. West (Eds.), *Parental behavior in diverse societies.* San Francisco: Jossey-Bass.

Rickel, A. U., & Becker, E. (1997). *Keeping children from harm's way: How national policy affects psychological development.* Washington. DC: American Psychological Association.

Ritts, V., Patterson, M. L., & Tubbs, M. E. (1992). Expectations, impressions, and judgments of physically attractive students: A review. *Review of Educational Research, 62,* 413–426.

Rivkin, M. S. (1995). *The great outdoors: Restoring children's right to play outside.* Washington, DC: National Association for Education of Young Children.

Robbins, W. (1974). The educational needs of Native Americans. In A. Castaneda, R. L. James, & W. Robbins (Eds.), *The educational needs of minority groups.* Lincoln, NE: Professional Educators.

Roberts, D. E., & Maccoby, E. E. (1985). Effects of mass communication. In G. Lindsey & E. Aronson (Eds.), *Handbook of social psychology* (3rd ed., Vol. 2). New York: Random House.

Rodin, J. (1976). Crowding, perceived choice and response to controllable and uncontrollable outcomes. *Journal of Experimental Social Psychology, 12,* 564–578.

Rogers, G. (1957). The necessary and sufficient conditions of therapeutic personality change. *Journal of Consulting Psychology, 21,* 95–103.

Rogoff, B. (1990). *Apprenticeship in thinking: Cognitive development in social context.* New York: Oxford University Press.

Rogosch, F. A., Cicchetti, D., Shields, A., & Toth, S. L. (1995). Parenting dysfunction in child maltreatment. In M. H. Bornstein (Ed.), *Handbook of parenting* (Vol. 4). Mahwah, NJ: Lawrence Erlbaum.

Rose, A. (1986, May 20). Breaking down cultural barriers. *Los Angeles Times,* pp. 1, 6. (Orange County Edition, Part II)

Rosen, B. C., & D'Andrade, R. G. (1959). The psychosocial origins of achievement motivation. *Sociometry, 22,* 185–218.

Rosenberg, M. (1975). The dissonant context and the adolescent self-concept. In S. E. Dragastin & G. H. Elder Jr. (Eds.), *Adolescence in the life cycle: Psychological change and social context.* New York: John Wiley & Sons.

Rosenberg, M. (1979). *Conceiving the self.* New York: Basic Books.

Rosenfeld, A. H. (1985). Music, the beautiful disturber. *Psychology Today, 19*(12), 48–56.

Rosenhan, D., & White, G. (1967). Observation and rehearsal as determinants of prosocial behavior. *Journal of Personality and Social Psychology, 5,* 424–431.

Rosenkoetter, L. I., Huston, A. C., & Wright, J. C. (1990). Television and the moral judgment of the young child. *Journal of Applied Developmental Psychology, 11,* 123–127.

Rosenthal, R., & Jacobson, L. (1968). *Pygmalion in the classroom.* New York: Holt, Rinehart & Winston.

Rosner, B. A., & Rierdan, J. (1994, February). *Adolescent girls' self-esteem: Variations in developmental trajectories.* Paper presented at the meeting of the Society for Research on Adolescence, San Diego, CA.

Ross, H., & Sawhill, I. (1975). *Time of transition: The growth of families headed by women.* Washington, DC: The Urban Institute.

Ross, J. L. (1988). Challenging boundaries: An adolescent in a homosexual family. *Journal of Family Psychology, 2*(2), 227–240.

Ross, R. P., Campbell, T., Wright, J. C., Huston, A. C., Rice, M. L., & Turk, P. (1984). When celebrities talk, children listen: An experimental analysis of children's responses to TV ads with celebrity endorsement. *Journal of Applied Developmental Psychology, 5,* 185–202.

Rotherdam, M. J., & Phinney, J. S. (1987). Ethnic behavior patterns as an aspect of identity. In J. S. Phinney, & M. J. Rotherdam (Eds.), *Children's ethnic socialization: Pluralism and development.* Newbury Park, CA: Sage.

Rothman, J. (1973). *I can be anything you can be.* New York: Scroll Press.

Rothman, S. (1996, January/February). The decline of bourgeois America. *Society, 976.*

Rotter, J. B. (1966). Generalized expectancies for internal versus external control of reinforcement. *Psychological Monographs, 80.* (Whole No. 609)

Rotter, J. B. (1971). Who rules you? External control and internal control. *Psychology Today, 5,* 37–42.

Rubenstein, E. A. (1988). Television and the young viewer. *American Scientist, 65*(6), 685–693.

Rubenstein, J., & Howes, C. (1976). The effects of peers on toddler interaction with mothers and toys. *Child Development, 47,* 597–605.

Rubin, J. Z., Provenzano, F. J., & Luria, A. (1974). The eye of the beholder: Parents' views on sex of newborns. *American Journal of Orthopsychiatry, 43,* 720–731.

Rubin, K. H., Bukowski, W., and Parker, J. G. (1998). Peer interactions, relationships, and groups. In W. Damon (Ed.), *Handbook of child psychology* (5th ed., Vol. 3). New York: John Wiley & Sons.

Rubin, K. H., & Coplan, R. J. (1992). Peer relationships in childhood. In M. H. Bornstein & M. E. Lamb (Eds.), *Developmental psychology: An advanced textbook* (3rd ed.). Hillsdale, NJ: Lawrence Erlbaum.

Rubin, K. H., Stewart, S. L., & Chen, X. (1995). Parents of aggressive and withdrawn children. In M. H. Bornstein (Ed.), *Handbook of parenting* (Vol. 1). Mahwah, NJ: Lawrence Erlbaum.

Ruble, D., & Martin, C. L. (1998). Gender development. In W. Damon (Ed.), *Handbook of child psychology* (5th ed., Vol. 3). New York: John Wiley & Sons.

Ruopp, R., Travers, J., Glantz, F., & Coclen, G. (1974). *Children at the center: Final results of the national day care study.* Cambridge, MA: Abt Associates.

Rushton, J. P., Fulker, D. W., Neal, M. C., Nias, D. K. B., & Eysenck, H. J. (1986). Altruism and aggression: The heritability of individual differences. *Journal of Personality and Social Psychology, 50,* 1192–1198.

Rutter, M. (1971). Parent–child separation: Psychological effects on the children. *Journal of Child Psychology and Psychiatry, 12,* 233–256.

Rutter, M., Giller, H., & Hagell, A. (1998). *Antisocial behavior by young people.* Cambridge, England: Cambridge University Press.

Rutter, V. (1994, May/June). Lessons from step families. *Psychology Today,* pp. 30–33, 60, 62, 64, 66, 68–69.

Saarni, C., Mumme, D. L., & Campos, J. J. (1998). Emotional development: Action, communication, and understanding. In W. Damon (Ed.), *Handbook of child psychology* (5th ed., Vol. 3). New York: John Wiley & Sons.

Sadker, M., & Sadker, D. (1986, March). Sexism in the classroom: From grade school to graduate school. *Phi Delta Kappan, 67,* 512–515.

Sadker, M., & Sadker, D. (1994). *Failing at fairness: How America's schools cheat girls.* New York: Scribner's.

Sadker, M., Sadker, D., & Klein, S. (1991). The issue of gender in elementary and secondary education. *Review of Research in Education, 17,* 269–334.

Saltzstein, H. D. (1975, April). Role taking as a method of facilitating moral development. *Symposium on Role-Taking and Moral Development.* Paper presented at the meeting of the Eastern Psychological Association, New York.

Saltzstein, H. D. (1976). Social influence and moral development: A perspective on the role of parents and peers. In T. Lickona (Ed.), *Moral develop-*

ment and behavior. New York: Holt, Rinehart & Winston.

Sameroff, A. J. (1983). Developmental systems: Contexts and evolution. In P. H. Mussen (Ed.), *Handbook of child psychology* (4th ed., Vol. 4). New York: John Wiley & Sons.

Sameroff, A. J. (1987). The social content of development, In N. Eisenberg (Ed.), *Contemporary topics in developmental psychology*. New York: John Wiley & Sons.

Sameroff. A. J. (1994). Developmental systems and family functioning. In R. D. Parke & S. G. Kellan (Eds.), *Exploring family relationships with other social contexts*. Hillsdale, NJ: Lawrence Erlbaum.

Sampson, R. J. (1983). Structural density and criminal victimization. *Criminology, 21*, 276–293.

Sampson, R. J., & Laub, J. H. (1994). Urban poverty and the family context of delinquency: A new look at structure and process in a classic study. *Child Development, 65*, 523–540.

Sandler, I. N., Miller, P., & Short, J., & Wolchik, S. A. (1989). Social support as a protective factor for children in stress. In D. Belle (Ed.), *Children's social networks and social supports*. New York: John Wiley & Sons.

Sandler, I. N., Tein, J. Y., & West, S. G. (1994). Coping, stress, and the psychological symptoms of children of divorce: A cross-sectional and longitudinal study. *Child Development, 64*, 1744–1763.

Sandrstom, M. J., & Coie, J. D. (1999). A developmental perspective on peer rejection: Mechanisms of stability and change. *Child Development, 70*, 955–966.

Sanford, N., & Comstock, C. (Eds.). (1971). *Sanctions for evil*. San Francisco: Jossey-Bass.

Santrock, J. W. (1996). *Adolescence: An introduction*. Dubuque, IA: Brown /Benchmark.

Santrock, J. W., & Sitterle, K. A. (1987). Parent-child relationships: Stepmother families. In K. Pasley & M. Ihinger-Tallman (Eds.), *Remarriage and stepparenting: Current research and theory*. New York: Guilford Press.

Santrock, J. W., & Warshak, R. A. (1979). Father custody and social development in boys and girls. *Journal of Social Issues, 35*, 112–125.

Santrock, J. W., Warshak, R. A., & Eliot, G. (1982). Social development and parent–child interaction in father-custody and stepmother families. In M. E. Lamb (Ed.), *Nontraditional families*. Hillsdale, NJ: Lawrence Erlbaum.

Satir, V. (1988). *The new people making*. Mountain View, CA: Science and Behavior Books.

Savage, D. G. (1983, February 15). Freeway noise linked to poorer test scores. *Los Angeles Times*, p. 1. (Part I)

Saxton, L. (1983). *The individual, marriage, and the family*. Belmont, CA: Wadsworth.

Scarr, S. (1984). *Mother care/other care*. New York: Basic Books.

Scarr, S. (1992). Theories for the 1990s: Developmental and individual differences. *Child Development, 63*, 1–19.

Scarr, S., Caparulo, B., Fernman, M., Tower, R. B., & Caplan J. (1983). Developmental status and school achievement of minority and nonminority children from birth to 18 years in a British Midlands town. *British Journal of Developmental Psychology, 1*, 31–48.

Scarr, S., & McCartney, K. (1983). How people make their own environments: A theory of genotype-environment effects. *Child Development, 54*, 424–435.

Schaefer, E. S. (1991). Goals for parent and future-parent education. *The Elementary School Journal, 91*(3), 239–247.

Scheibe, C. (1989). Character portrayal and values in network TV commercials. Unpublished Master's thesis, Cornell University, Ithaca, NY. Cited in J. Condry, *The psychology of television*. Hillsdale, NJ: Lawrence Erlbaum.

Schickedanz, J. (1986). *More than the ABCs: The early stages of reading and writing*. Washington, DC: National Association for the Education of Young Children.

Schickedanz, J. (1990). Preschoolers and academics: Some thoughts. *Young Children, 46*(1), 4–13.

Schoonover, S. (1959). The relationship of intelligence and achievement to birth order, sex of sibling, and age interval. *Journal of Educational Psychology, 50*, 143–146.

Schorr, L. B. (1997). *Common purpose: Strengthening families and neighborhoods to rebuild America*. New York: Anchor Books.

Schorr, L. B., Both, D., & Copple, C. (Eds.). (1991). *Effective services for young children: Report of a workshop*. Washington, DC: National Academy Press.

Schorr, L. B., with D. Schorr (1988). *Within our reach: Breaking the cycle of disadvantage*. New York: Doubleday/Anchor Press.

Schweinhart, L. J., & Weikart, D. P. (1993). Success by empowerment: The High/Scope Perry Preschool study through age 27. *Young Children, 49*(1), 54–58.

Schweinhart, L. J., Weikart, D. P., & Larner, M. B. (1986a). Child-initiated activities in early childhood programs may help prevent delinquency. *Early Childhood Research Quarterly, 1*(3), 303–312.

Schweinhart, L. J., Weikart, D. P., & Larner, M. B. (1986b). Consequences of three preschool curriculum models through age 15. *Early Childhood Research Quarterly, 1*(1), 15–45.

Seaver, W. B. (1973). Effects of naturally induced teacher expectancies. *Journal of Personality and Social Psychology, 28*, 333–342.

Sebald, H. (1986). Adolescents' shifting orientation toward parents and peers: A curvilinear trend over recent decades. *Journal of Marriage and the Family, 48*, 5–13.

Sebald, H. (1989). Adolescent peer orientation: Changes in the support system during the last three decades. *Adolescence, 24*, 937–945.

Sebald, H. (1992). *Adolescence: A social psychological analysis* (4th ed.). Englewood Cliffs, NJ: Prentice-Hall.

Segal, N. L. (1997). Genetic bases of behavior: Contributions to psychological research. In N. L. Segal, G. E. Weisfeld, & C. C. Weisfeld (Eds.), *Uniting psychology and biology*. Washington, DC: American Psychological Association.

Seligman, M. E. P. (1975). *Helplessness*. San Francisco: Freeman.

Seligman, M. E. P. (1990). *Learned optimism*. New York: Pocket Books.

Selman, R. L. (1980). *The growth of interpersonal understanding*. New York: Academic Press.

Selman, R. L., & Selman, A. P. (1979). Children's ideas about friendship: A new theory. *Psychology Today, 12*(4), 71–80.

Sendak, M. (1963). *Where the wild things are*. New York: HarperCollins.

Sendak, M. (1970). *In the night kitchen*. New York: Harper & Row.

Serbin, L. A., O'Leary, K. D., Kent, R. N., & Tonick, I. J.(1973). A comparison of teacher response to the preacademic and problem behavior of boys and girls. *Child Development, 44*, 796–804.

Serbin, L. A., Powlishta, K. K., & Gulko, J. (1993). The development of sex typing in middle childhood. *Monographs of the Society for Research in Child Development* 58(2). (Serial No. 232)

Sexton, D., Snyder, P., Sharpton, W. R., & Strickin, S. (1993). Infants and toddlers with special needs and their families. *Childhood Education, 69*(5), 278–286.

Selye, H. (1956). *The stress of life*. New York: McGraw-Hill.

Shantz, C. U. (1983). Social cognition. In P. H. Mussen (Eds.), *Handbook of child psychology* (4th ed., Vol. 3). New York: John Wiley & Sons.

Shapira, A., & Lomranz, J. (1972). Cooperative and competitive behavior of rural Arab children in Israel. *Journal of Cross-Cultural Psychology, 3*, 353–359.

Shapira, A., & Madsen, M. C. (1974). Between- and within-group cooperation and competition among kibbutz and non-kibbutz children. *Developmental Psychology, 10*, 140–145.

Shepard, L. A., & Smith, M. L. (1986). Synthesis of research on school readiness and kindergarten retention. *Educational Leadership, 44*, 78–86.

Sherif, M. (1956). Experiments in group conflict. *Scientific American, 195*(2), 54–58.

Sherif, M., Harvey, O. J., White, B. J., Hood, W. R., & Sherif, C. W. (1961). *Intergroup conflict and cooperation: The robber's cave experiment*. Norman: Institute of Group Relations, University of Oklahoma.

Sigman, M., Neumann, C., Carter, E., & Cattle, D. J. (1988). Home interactions and the development of Embu toddlers in Kenya. *Child Development, 57*, 1251–1261.

Signorella, M. L., Bigler, R. S., & Liben, L. S. (1993). Developmental differences in children's gender schemata about others: A meta-analytic review. *Developmental Review, 13*, 147–183.

Signorielli, N. (1989). Television and conceptions about sex roles: Maintaining conventionality and the status quo. *Sex Roles, 21*(5/6), 341–360.

Signorielli, N. (1993). Television, the portrayal of women and children's attitudes. In C. L. Berry & J. K. Samen (Eds.), *Children and television: Images in a changing sociocultural world*. Newbury Park, CA: Sage.

Silberman, C. (1970). *Crisis in the classroom: The remaking of American education*. New York: Random House.

Simeonsson, R. J., & Bailey, D. B. (1986). Siblings of the handicapped child. In J. J. Gallager & W. Vietze (Eds.), *Families of handicapped persons*. Baltimore, MD: Brookes.

Simon, R. I. (1996). *Bad men do what good men dream: A forensic psychiatrist illuminates the darker side of human behavior*. Washington, DC: American Psychiatric Press.

Simpson, E. (1974). Moral development research: A case study of scientific cultural bias. *Human Development, 17*, 81–106.

Singer, D. G., & Singer, J. L. (1976). Family television viewing habits and the spontaneous play of preschool children. *American Journal of Orthopsychiatry, 46*, 496–502.

Singer, D. G., & Singer, J. L. (1990). *House of make-believe*. Cambridge, MA: Harvard University Press.

Singer, D. G., & Singer, J. L. (1994). Evaluating the classroom viewing of a televised series: "Degrassi Junior High." In D. Zillman, J. Bryant, & A. C. Huston (Eds.), *Media, children, and the family: Social scientific, psychodynamic, and clinical perspectives*. Hillsdale, NJ: Lawrence Erlbaum.

Singer, D. G., Singer, J. L., & Zuckerman, D. M. (1990). *The parent's guide: Use TV to your child's advantage*. Reston, VA: Acropolis Books.

Skalka, P. (1983). Take control of your TV. *Friendly Exchange, 3*(1), 26–27.

Skeels, H. M. (1966). Adult status of children with contrasting early life experiences. *Monographs of the Society for Research in Child Development, 31*(3). (Whole No. 105)

Skill, T. (1994). Family images and family actions as presented in the media: Where we've been and what we've found. In D. Zillman, J. Bryant, & A. C. Huston (Eds.), *Media, children, and the family*. Hillsdale, NJ: Lawrence Erlbaum.

Skinner, B. F. (1948). *Walden two*. New York: Macmillan.

Skinner, B. F. (1954). The science of learning and the art of teaching. *Harvard Educational Review, 25*, 86–97.

Skinner, E. A. (1995). *Perceived control, motivation, and coping*. Thousand Oaks, CA: Sage.

Skolnick, A. (1987). *The intimate environment: Exploring marriage and the family* (4th ed.). Boston: Little, Brown.

Skolnick, A. (1991). *Embattled paradise: The American family in an age of uncertainty*. New York: Basic Books.

Slaby, R. G., Roedell, W. C., Arezzo, D., & Hendrix, K. (1995). *Early violence prevention: Tools for teachers of young children*. Washington, DC: National Association for the Education of Young Children.

Slavin, R. E. (1991, February). Synthesis of research on cooperative learning. *Educational Leadership*, pp. 71–77, 79–82.

Slavin, R. E., Devries, D. L., & Hutten, B. H. (1975). *Individual vs. team competition: The interpersonal consequences of academic performance*. Baltimore, MD: Johns Hopkins University Center for Social Organization of Schools. (Report No. 188)

Sleek, S. (1998). Isolation increases with internet use. *APA Monitor, 29*(9), 1, 30-31.

Small, J. (Ed.). (1987). *Children of alcoholics: A special report*. Washington, DC: National Institute on Alcohol Abuse and Alcoholism.

Small, S., & Luster, T. (1994). Adolescent sexual activity: An ecological risk-factor approach. *Journal of Marriage and the Family, 56*, 181–192.

Smetana, J. (1981). Preschool children's conceptions of moral and social rules. *Child Development, 52*, 1333–1336.

Smetana, J. G. (1985). Preschool children's conceptions of transgressions: Effects of varying moral and conventional domain-related attributes. *Developmental Psychology, 21*, 18–29.

Smetana, J. G. (1989). Toddlers' social interactions in the context of moral and conventional transgressions in the home. *Developmental Psychology, 25*, 499–508.

Smith, A. B., Dannison, L. L., & Vach-Hasse, T. (1998, Fall). When "grandma" is "mom." *Childhood Education, 75*(1), 12–16.

Smith, C. P. (1969). The origin and expression of achievement-related motives in children. In C. P. Smith (Ed.), *Achievement related motives in children*. New York: Russell Sage Foundation.

Smith, D. D., & Bassett, D. (1991). The REI debate: A time for a systematic research agenda. In J. Lloyd, A. C. Repp, & N. N. Sing (Eds.), *Perspectives on integration of atypical learners in regular education settings*. Sycamore, IL: Sycamore Press.

Smith, J. W. (1963). *Outdoor education*. Englewood Cliffs, NJ: Prentice-Hall.

Smith, P. K., & Dutton, S. (1979). Play and training indirect and innovative problem solving. *Child Development, 60*, 830–836.

Snow, M. E., Jacklin, C. N., & Maccoby, E. E. (1981). Birth order differences in peer sociability at thirty-three months. *Child Development, 52*, 589–596.

Snyder, J. J., & Patterson, G. R. (1995). Individual differences in social aggression: A test of a reinforcement model of socialization in the natural environment. *Behavior Therapy, 26*, 371–391.

Soldier, L. L. (1985). To soar with the eagles: Enculturation and acculturation of Indian children. *Childhood Education, 61*(3), 185–191.

Solomon, C. (1999, October 2). The Gen-P gold mine. *Los Angeles Times*, pp. F1, F18.

Spinelli, J. (1997). *Wringer*. New York: HarperCollins.

Spinetta, J., & Rigler, D. (1972). The child abusing parent: A psychological review. *Psychological Bulletin, 77*, 296.

Spitz, E. H. (1999). *Inside picture books*. New Haven, CT: Yale University Press.

Spitz, H. R. (1992). Early childhood intervention. In T. G. Sticht; M. J. Beeler; & B. A. McDonald (Eds.), *The intergenerational transfer of cognitive skills*. Norwood, NJ: Ablex.

Spitz, R. (1946). Hospitalism: An inquiry into the genesis of psychiatric conditioning in early childhood. In A. Freud (Ed.), *Psychoanalytic studies of the child* (Vol. 1). New York: International Universities Press.

Spock, B. (1946). *The common sense book of baby and child care*. New York: Duell Sloan Pearce.

Spock, B. (1957). *The pocket book of baby and child care*. New York: Pocket Books.

Spock, B. (1968). *Baby and child care*. New York: Pocket Books.

Spock, B. (1985). *Raising children in a difficult time* (2nd ed.). New York: Pocket Books.

Sprafkin, J. M., Leibert, R. M., & Poulos, R. W. (1975). Effects of a prosocial example on children's helping. *Journal of Experimental Child Psychology*, *20*, 119–126.

Sroufe, L. (1978). Attachment and the roots of competence. *Human Nature*, *1*, 50–57.

Sroufe, L. A. (1996). *Emotional development*. Cambridge University, England: Cambridge University Press.

Sroufe, L. A., & Fleeson, J. (1986). Attachment and the construction of relationships. In W. W. Hartup & Z. Rubin (Eds.), *Relationships and development*. Hillsdale, NJ: Lawrence Erlbaum.

St. Peters, M., Marguerite, F., Huston, A. C., Wright, J. C., & Eakins, D. J. (1991). Television and families: What do young children watch with their parents? *Child Development*, *62*, 1409–1413.

Stabiner, K. (1993, August). Get 'em while they're young. *Los Angeles Times Magazine*, pp. 15, 12, 14, 16, 38.

Staffieri, J. R. (1967). A study of social stereotype of body image in children. *Journal of Personality and Social Psychology*, *7*, 101–104.

Stainback, S., Stainback, W., East, K., & Sapon-Shevin, M. (1994). A commentary on inclusion and the development of a positive self-identity by people with disabilities. *Exceptional Children*, *60*(6), 486–490.

Stallings, J. (1974). *Follow through classroom observation evaluation, 1972–1973: Executive summary*. Menlo Park, CA: Stanford Research Institute.

Starr, R. H. Jr. (1990, June). The lasting effects of child maltreatment. *The Word and I*, 484–499.

Staub, E. (1970). A child in distress: The effect of focusing responsibility on children on their attempts to help. *Developmental Psychology*, *2*, 152–153.

Staub, E. (1971). The use of role playing and induction in children's learning of helping and sharing behavior. *Child Development*, *42*, 805–816.

Staub, E. (1975). *The development of prosocial behavior in children*. Morristown, NJ: General Learning Press.

Staub, E. (1978). Socialization by parents and peers and experimental learning of prosocial behavior. In J. H. Stevens Jr. & M. Matthews (Eds.), *Mother/child father/child relationships*. Washington, DC: National Association for Education for Young Children.

Staub, E. (1986). A conception of the determinants and development of altruism and aggression: Motives, the self, and the environment. In C. Zahn-Waxler, E. M. Cummings, & R. Iannotti (Eds.), *Altruism and aggression: Biological and social origins*. Cambridge, England: Cambridge University Press.

Stein, A. H., & Bailey, M. M. (1973). The socialization of achievement orientation in females. *Psychological Bulletin*, *80*, 345–365.

Stein, L. C., & Kostelnick, M. J. (1984). A practical problem-solving model for conflict resolution in the classroom. *Childcare Quarterly*, *13*, 5–20.

Steinberg, L. (1986). Latchkey children and susceptibility to peer pressure: An ecological analysis. *Developmental Psychology*, *22*, 433–439.

Steinberg, L. (1987). Single parents, step parents, and the susceptibility of adolescents to antisocial peer pressure. *Child Development*, *58*, 269–275.

Steinberg. L. (1993). *Adolescence*. New York: McGraw-Hill.

Steinberg, L. (1996). *Beyond the classroom: Why school reform has failed and what parents need to do*. New York: Touchstone.

Steinberg, L., Elmen, J. D., & Mounts, N. S. (1989). Authoritative parenting, psychosocial maturity, and academic success among adolescents. *Child Development*, *60*, 1424–1436.

Steinberg, L., Mounts, N. S., Lambourn, S. D., & Dornbusch, S. M. (1991). Authoritative parenting and adolescent adjustment across various ecological niches. *Journal of Research on Adolescence*, *1*, 19–36.

Steinberg, L., Lamborn, S. D., Darling, N., Mounts, N., & Dornbusch, S. M. (1994). Over-time changes in adjustment and competence among adolescents from authoritative, authoritarian, indulgent, and neglectful families. *Child Development*, *65*, 754–770.

Steinman, S. B., Zimmelman, S. E., & Knoblauch, T. M. (1985). A study of parents who sought joint custody following divorce. Who reaches agreement and sustains joint custody and who returns to court. *Journal of the American Academy of Child Psychiatry*, *24*, 554–563.

Stendler, C. B. (1950). Sixty years of child training practices. *Journal of Pediatrics*, *36*, 122–134.

Stephens, M. W., & Delys, P. (1973). External control expectancies among disadvantaged children at preschool age. *Child Development*, *44*, 670–674.

Stevenson, H., Stigler, J. W., Lee, S., Kitamura, S., & Kato, T. (1986). Achievement in mathematics. In H. Stevenson, H. Azuma, & K. Hakuta (Eds.), *Child development and education in Japan*. New York: W. H. Freeman.

Stevenson, H. W. (1972). *Children's learning*. New York: Appleton-Century-Crofts.

Stevenson, H. W., & Lee, S. Y. (1990). Contents of achievement: A study of American, Chinese, and Japanese children. *Monographs of the Society for Research in Child Development*, *55*(1–2). (Serial No. 221)

Stewart, E. C., & Bennett, M. J. (1991). *American cultural patterns: A cross-cultural perspective* (rev. ed.). Yarmouth, ME: Intercultural Press.

Stewart, I. S. (1982). The larger question: Bilingual education, family and society. In J. D. Quisenberry (Ed.), *Changing a family lifestyle*. Washington, DC: Association for Childhood Educational International.

Stiles, D. A., Gibbons, J. L., & Schnellmann, J. D. L. G. (1990). Opposite-sex ideal in the U.S.A. and Mexico as perceived by young adolescents. *Journal of Cross-Cultural Psychology, 211*, 180–199.

Stinnett, N., & Birdsong, C. W. (1978). *The family and alternate life styles*. Chicago: Nelson Hall.

Stinnett, N., & Defrain, J. (1985). *Secrets of strong families*. Boston: Little, Brown.

Stomfay-Stitz, A. M. (1994). Pathways to safer schools. *Childhood Education, 70*(5), 279–282.

Straus, M. A. (1992). Children as witness to marital violence: A risk factor for lifelong problems among a nationally representative sample of American men and women. In D. F. Schwarz (Ed.), *Children and violence: Report of the twenty-third Ross Roundtable on Critical Approaches to Common Pediatric Problems*. Columbus, OH: Ross Laboratories.

Streitmatter, J. (1994). *Toward gender equity in the classroom: Everyday teachers' beliefs and practices*. New York: State University of New York Press.

Strouse, J. S., Buerkel-Rothfuss, N., & Long, E. C. J. (1995). Gender and family as moderators of the relationship between music video exposure and adolescent sexual permissiveness, *Adolescence, 30*(119), 505–522.

Suchara, H. (1982). Parents and teachers: A partnership. *Childhood Education, 58*(3), 130.

Sue, D. W. (1989). Ethnic identity: The impact of two cultures on the psychological development of Asians in America. In D. R. Atkinson, G. Morten, & D. W. Sue (Eds.), *Counseling American minorities* (3rd ed.). Dubuque, IA: Wm. C. Brown.

Suls, J., Gutken, D., & Kalle, R. (1979). The role of intentions, damage, and social consequences in the moral judgment of children. *Child Development, 50*, 874–877.

Sunley, R. (1955). Early nineteenth-century American literature on child rearing. In M. Mead & M. Wolfenstein (Eds.), *Childhood in contemporary cultures*. Chicago: University of Chicago Press.

Sutton-Smith, B. (1971). Children at play. *Natural History, 80*, 54–59.

Sutton-Smith, B. (1972). *The folkgames of children*. Austin: University of Texas Press.

Sutton-Smith, B. (1982). Birth order and sibling status effects. In M. E. Lamb (Ed.), *Sibling relationships: Their nature and significance over the lifespan*. Hillsdale, NJ: Lawrence Erlbaum.

Swick, K. J. (1986). Locus of control and interpersonal support as related to parenting. *Childhood Education, 62*, 41–50.

Swick, K. J. (1997). Learning about work; Extending learning through an ecological approach. In B. Hatcher & S. S. Beck (Eds.), *Learning opportunities beyond the school* (2nd ed.). Olney, MD: Association for Childhood Education International.

Taishido Study Group. (1984/1985). Generations of play in Taishido. *Childrens' Environment Quarterly, 1*(4), 19–28.

Tamis-LeMonda, C. S., & Cabrera, N. (1999). Perspectives on father involvement: Research and policy: *Society for Research in Child Development*, XII(2). (Social policy report)

Teale, W. H. (1984). Reading to young children: Its significance for literary development. In H. Coleman, A. Oberg, & F. Smith (Eds.), *Awakening and literacy*. Portsmouth, NH: Heinemann.

Teasley, S. D., & Parker, J. G. (1995, March). *The effects of gender, friendship, and popularity on the targets and topics of adolescent gossip*. Paper presented at the Bienniel Meeting of the Society for Research in Child Development, Indianapolis, IN.

Tharp, R. G. (1989). Psychocultural variables and constraints: Effects on teaching and learning in schools. *American Psychologist, 44*(2), 349–359.

Thiederman, S. (1991). *Bridging cultural barriers for success: How to manage the cultural work force*. New York: Lexington Books.

Thomas, A., & Chess, S. (1977). *Temperament and development*. New York: Brunner/Mazel.

Thomas, A., & Chess, S. (1980). *The dynamics of psychological development*. New York: Brunner/Mazel.

Thomas, A., Chess, S., & Birch, H. S. (1970). The origin of personality. *Scientific American, 223*, 102–109.

Thompson, K. P. (1993). Media, music, and adolescents. In R. M. Lerner (Ed.), *Early adolescents: Perspectives on research, policy, and intervention*. Hillsdale, NJ: Lawrence Erlbaum.

Thompson, R. A. (1994). Social support and the prevention of child maltreatment. In G. B. Melton & F. Barry (Eds.), *Safe neighborhoods: Foundations for a new national strategy on child abuse and neglect*. New York: Guilford.

Thompson, R. L., & Larson, R. (1995). Social context and the subjective experience of different types of rock music. *Journal of Youth and Adolescence, 24*(6), 731–744.

Thompson, R. S. (1998). Early sociopersonality development. In W. Damon (Ed.), *Handbook of child psycholgy* (5th ed., Vol 3). New York: John Wiley & Sons.

Thompson, S. H. (1998). Working with children of substance-abusing parents. *Young Children, 53*(1), 34–37.

Thompson, W. E., & Dodder, R. A. (1986). Containment theory and juvenile delinquency: A reevaluation through factor analysis. *Adolescence, 21,* 365–376.

Thornburg, H. D. (1975). Sources in adolescence of initial sex information. In H. D. Thornburg (Ed.), *Contemporary adolescence: Readings* (2nd ed.). Monterey, CA: Brooks/Cole.

Thornburg, H. D. (1981). The amount of sex information learning obtained during early adolescence. *Journal of Early Adolescence, 1,* 171–183.

Thorne, B. (1993). *Gender play: Girls and boys in school.* New Brunswick, NJ: Rutgers University Press.

Thuy, V. G. (1983). The Indochinese in America: Who are they and how are they doing? In D. T. Nakanishi & M. Huano-Nakanishi (Eds.), *The education of Asian and Pacific Americans: Historical perspectives and prescriptions for the future.* Phoenix, AZ: Oryx Press.

Tittle, C. K. (1986). Gender research in education. *American Psychologist, 41*(10), 1161–1168.

Tizard, J., Schofield, W. N., & Hewison, J. (1982). Collaboration between teachers and parents in assisting children's reading. *British Journal of Education, 52,* 1–15.

Tobin, J. J., Wu, D. Y. H., & Davidson, D. H. (1989, April). How three key countries shape their children. *World Monitor,* 36–45.

Toch, T. (1996, October 7). Schools that work. *U.S. News & World Report,* pp. 58–64.

Toffler, A. (Ed.). (1974). *Learning for tomorrow: The role of the future in education.* New York: Random House.

Toffler, A. (1980). *The third wave.* New York: Knopf.

Toffler, A. (1990). *Powershift.* New York: Bantam Books.

Toffler, A. (1994). A magna carta for the knowledge age. *New Perspective Quarterly, 11*(4), 26.

Tonnies, F. (1957). *Community and society* (Gemeinshaft und Geseillshaft) (C. P. Loomis, Trans.). East Lansing, MI: Michigan State University.

Took, K. J., & Weiss, D. S. (1994). The relationship between heavy metal and rap music and adolescent turmoil. Real or abstract? *Adolescence, 29*(115), 613–623.

Toufexis, A. (1991). Innocent victims. *Time,* 137(19), 56–60.

Trelease, J. (1995). *The read-aloud handbook* (4th ed.). New York: Viking.

Troy, M., & Sroufe, L. A. (1987). Victimization among preschoolers: Role of attachment relationship history. *Journal of the American Academy of Child and Adolescent Psychiatry, 26,* 166–172.

Tubman, J. G. (1993). Family risk factors, parental alcohol use, and problem behaviors among school-age children. *Family Relations, 42,* 81–86.

Tucker, L. A. (1983). Self-concept: A function of self-perceived somatotype. *Journal of Psychology, 14,* 123–133.

Turiel, E. (1966). An experimental test of the sequentiality of developmental stages in the child's moral judgments. *Journal of Personality and Social Psychology, 3,* 611–618.

Turiel, E. (1983). *The development of social knowledge: Morality and convention.* Cambridge, England: Cambridge University Press.

Turiel, E. (1998). The development of morality. In W. Damon (Ed.), *Handbook of child psychology* (5th ed., Vol. 3). New York: John Wiley & Sons.

Turnbull, A. P., & Turnbull, H. R. III. (1997). *Families, professionals, and exceptionality* (3rd ed.). Columbus, OH: Merrill.

Turner-Bowker, D. M. (1996). Gender stereotyped descriptors inchildren's picture books: Does "Curious Jane" exist in the literature? *Sex Roles,* 35, 461-488.

Tushscherer, P. (1988). *TV interactive toys: The new high tech threat to children.* Bend, OR: Pinnaroo.

Twain, M. (1999). *The adventures of Tom Sawyer.* New York; Random House. (Original work published 1876)

Tyler, R. (1992, May). Prenatal drug exposure: An overview of associated problems and intervention strategies. *Phi Delta Kappan,* 705–708.

Uba, L. (1999). *Asian Americans: Personality patterns, identity, and mental health.* New York: Guilford Press.

U.S. Bureau of the Census. (1990). Current population reports series P-70, No. 2. *Who's minding the kids? Child care arrangements, 1986–1987.* Washington, DC: U.S. Government Printing Office.

U.S. Department of Education [USDE]. (1991a). *America 2000: An education strategy.* Washington, DC: Author.

USDE. (1991b). *Preparing children for success: Guideposts for achieving our first national goal.* Washington, DC: Author.

USDE. (1994). *Strong families, strong schools: Building community partnerships for learning.* Washington, DC: Author.

U.S. Department of Health and Human Services [USDHHS]. (1980). *Head Start in the 1980s: Review and recommendations.* Washington, DC: U.S. Government Printing Office.

USDHHS. (1992). Project No. OEI 09-91-00651. Washington, DC: Office of Evaluations and Inspections.

Vandell, D. L., Henderson, V. K., & Wilson, K. S. (1988). A longitudinal study of children with daycare experiences of varying quality. *Child Development, 49,* 1286–1292.

Vandell, D. L., & Mueller, E. C. (1995). Peer play and friendship during the play years. In H. C. Foot,

A. J. Chapman, & J. R. Smith (Eds.), *Friendship and social relations in children*. New Brunswick, NJ: Transaction.

Vandell, D. L., & Su, Hsiu-Chih. (1999). Child care and school-age children. *Young Children, 54*(6), 62–71.

Vander Voort, T. H. A., & Valkenburg, P. M. (1994). Television's impact on fantasy play: A review of research. *Developmental Review, 14*, 27–51.

Vander Zanden, J. W. (1995). *Sociology: The core* (3rd ed.). New York: McGraw-Hill.

Vanderslice, V. J. (1984). Empowerment: A definition of process. *Human Ecology Forum, 14*(1), 2–3.

Vasquez, J. A. (1990). Teaching to the distinctive traits of minority students. *The Clearing House, 63*, 299–304.

Vasquez-Nutall, E., Romers-Garcia, I., & DeLeon, B. (1987). Sex roles and perceptions of femininity and masculinity of Hispanic women: A review of the literature. *Psychology of Women Quarterly, 11*, 409–425.

Vaughn, S., Bos, C. S., & Schumm, J. S. (1997). *Teaching mainstreamed, diverse, and at-risk students in the general education classroom.* Boston: Allyn & Bacon.

Verdugo, R., Kuttner, A., Seidel, S., Wallace, C., Sosa, M., & Faber, M. (1990). *Safe schools manual: A resource on making schools, communities, and families safe for children.* Washington, DC: National Education Association.

Vigil, J. D. (1980). *From Indians to Chicanos: The dynamics of Mexican-American culture.* Prospect Heights, IL: Wavel Press.

Vincze, M. (1971). The social contacts of infants and young children reared together. *Early Child Development and Care, 1*, 99–109.

Vorrath, H. H., & Brendtro, L. K. (1985). *Positive peer culture* (2nd ed.). New York: Aldine.

Vygotsky, L. S. (1978). *Mind and society: The development of higher psychological processes* (Edited by M. Cole, V. John-Steiner, S. Scribner, & E. Souberman). Cambridge, MA: Harvard University Press.

Walker, L. J. (1991). Sex differences in moral development. In W. M. Kurtines & J. Gewirtz (Eds.), *Handbook of moral behavior and development* (Vol. 2). Hillsdale, NJ: Lawrence Erlbaum.

Walker, L. J., & Taylor, J. H. (1991). Family interaction and the development of moral reasoning. *Child Development, 62*, 264–283.

Walker, L. S., & Greene, J. W. (1986). The social context of adolescent self-esteem. *Journal of Youth and Adolescence, 15*(4), 315–323.

Wall, J. A., Power, T. G., & Arbona, C. (1993). Susceptibility to antisocial peer pressure and its relation to acculturation in Mexican-American adolescents. *Journal of Adolescent Research, 8*, 403–418.

Wallach, L. B. (1993). Helping children cope with violence. *Young Children, 48*(4), 4–11.

Wallerstein, J. S., & Kelly, J. B. (1996). *Surviving the breakup. How parents and children cope with divorce.* New York: Basic Books.

Wallerstein, J. S., Corbin, S. B., & Lewis, J. H. (1988). Children of divorce: A ten-year study. In E. M. Hetherington & J. D. Arasteh (Eds.), *Impact of divorce, single parenting and stepparenting on children.* Hillsdale, NJ: Lawrence Erlbaum.

Wang. A. Y. (1994). Pride and prejudice in high school gang members. *Adolescence, 29*, 279–291.

Ward, C. (1978). *The child in the city.* New York: Pantheon.

Warren, R. (1983). The community in America. In R. L. Warren & L. Lyon (Eds.), *New perspectives on the American community.* Homewood, IL: Dorsey Press.

Wasserman, S. (1982). Interacting with your students. *Childhood Education, 58*(5), 281–286.

Waters, E., Posada, G., Crowell, J., & Keng-ling, L. (1993). Is attachment theory ready to contribute to our understanding of disruptive behavior problems? *Development and Psychopathology, 5*, 215–224.

Weber, M. (1930). *The Protestant ethic and the spirit of capitalism.* London: Allen.

Wegscheider, S. (1981). *Another chance: Hope and health for the alcoholic family.* Palo Alto, CA: Science and Behavior Books.

Weikart, D. P. (1989). *Quality preschool programs: A long-term social investment.* New York: Ford Foundation.

Weinberg, M. (1977). *A chance to learn.* New York: Cambridge University Press.

Weiner, B. (1992). *Human motivation: Metaphors, theories, and research.* Newbury Park, CA: Sage.

Weiner, M., & Wright, F. (1973). Effects of undergoing arbitrary discrimination upon subsequent attitudes toward a minority group. *Journal of Applied Social Psychology, 3*, 94–102.

Weinstein, C. S. (1991). The classroom as a social context for learning. *Annual Review of Psychology, 42*, 493–525.

Weiss, M. F. (1994). Children's attitudes toward the mentally ill: An eight-year longitudinal follow-up. *Psychological Reports, 74*, 51–56.

Weissbourd, R. (1996). *The vulnerable child: What really hurts America's children and what we can do about it.* Reading, MA: Addison-Wesley.

Weissbrod, C. (1976). Noncontingent warmth, induction, cognitive style, and children's imitative donation and rescue effort behaviors. *Journal of Personality and Social Psychology, 34*, 274–281.

Weitzman, L. J. (1972). Sex-role socialization in picture books for preschool children. *American Journal of Sociology, 77*, 1125–1150.

Weitzman, L. J. (1985). *The divorce revolution*. New York: Free Press.

Welborn, S. N. (1981, September 14). When school kids come home to an empty house. *U.S. News & World Report*, pp. 42–47.

Wentzel, K. A., & Erdley, C. A. (1993). Strategies for making friends: Relations to social behavior and peer acceptance in early adolescence. *Developmental Psychology, 29*, 819–826.

Werner, E. E. (1993). Risk, resilience, and recovery: Perspectives from Kauai longitudinal study. *Development and Psychopathology, 5*, 503–515.

Werner, E. E., & Smith, R. S. (1992). *Overcoming the odds: High risk children from birth to adulthood*. Ithaca, New York: Cornell University Press.

West, M. M. (1988). Parental values and behavior in the outer Fiji Islands. In R. A. Levine, P. M. Miller, & M. M. West (Eds.), *Parental behavior in diverse societies*. San Francisco: Jossey-Bass.

White, B. L. (1971, October). *Fundamental early environmental influences on the development of competence*. Paper presented at Third Western Symposium on Learning: Cognitive Learning. Western Washington State College, Bellingham, WA.

White, B. L. (1995). *The new first three years of life*. New York: Simon & Schuster.

White, B. L., & Watts, J. C. (1973). *Experience and environment: Major influences on the development of the young child* (Vol. 1). Englewood Cliffs, NJ: Prentice-Hall.

White, L. (1960). Symbol, the basis of language and culture. In W. Goldschmidt (Ed.), *Exploring the ways of mankind*. New York: Holt, Rinehart & Winston.

White, R. W. (1959). Motivation reconsidered: The concept of competence. *Psychology Review, 66*, 297–333.

White, S., & Tharp, R. G. (1988, April). *Questioning and wait-time: A cross-cultural analysis*. Paper presented at the annual meeting of the American Educational Research Association, New Orleans.

Whitebook, M., Howes, C., & Phillips, D. (1989). *Who cares? Child care teachers and the quality of care in America: Final report, National Child Care Staffing Study*. Oakland, CA: Child Care Employee Project.

Whitehead, B. F. (1998). *The divorce culture: Rethinking our commitment to marriage and family*. New York: Vintage Books.

Whiting, B. B., & Edwards, C. P. (1988). *Children of different worlds: The formation of social behavior*. Cambridge, MA: Harvard University Press.

Whiting, B. B., & Whiting, J. W. M. (1973). Altruistic and egoistic behavior in six cultures. In L. Nader & T. W. Maretski (Eds.), *Cultural illness and health: Essays in human adaptation*. Washington, DC: American Anthropological Association.

Whiting, B. B., & Whiting, J. W. M. (1975). *Children of six cultures: A psychoanalysis*. Cambridge, MA: Harvard University Press.

Whittaker, J. K. (1983). Social support networks in child welfare. In J. K. Whittaker & J. Garbarino (Eds.), *Social support networks: Informal helping in the human services*. New York: Aldine.

Whyte, W. H. (1957). *The organization man*. New York: Doubleday.

Willer, B. (1992). An overview of the demand and supply of child care in 1990. *Young Children, 47*(2), 19–22.

Willer, B., Hofferth, S. L., Kisker, E. E., Divine-Hawkins, P., Farquhar, E., & Glantz, F. B. (1991). *The demand and supply of child care in 1990*. Washington, DC: National Association for the Education of Young Children.

Williams, G. (1982). *The rabbit's wedding*. New York: HarperCollins.

Williams, R. M. (1960a). *American society: A sociological interpretation*. New York: Knopf.

Williams, R. M. (1960b). Generic American values. In W. Goldschmidt (Ed.), *Exploring the ways of mankind*. New York: Holt, Rinehart & Winston.

Williams, T. M. (Ed.). (1986). *The impact of television: A natural experiment in three communities*. New York: Academic Press.

Wilson, B. J., & Gottman, J. M. (1995). Marital interaction and parenting. In M. H. Bornstein (Ed.), *Handbook of parenting* (Vol. 4). Hillsdale, NJ: Lawrence Erlbaum.

Wilson, B. J., & Weiss, A. J. (1993). The effects of sibling coviewing on preschoolers' reactions to a suspenseful movie scene. *Communication Research, 20*, 214–248.

Wilson, S., & Mishra, R. (1999, April 28). In high school, groups provide identity. *Washington Post*, p. A1.

Wilson, W. J. (1987). *The truly disadvantaged: The underclass and public policy*. Chicago: University of Chicago Press.

Wilson, W. J. (1995). Jobless ghettos and the social outcome of youngsters. In P. Moen, G. H. Elder, & K. Luscher (Eds.), *Examining lives in context: perspectives on the ecology of human development*. Washington, DC: American Psychological Association.

Winn, M. (1977). *The plug-in drug*. New York: Bantam.

Woititz, J. G. (1990). *Adult children of alcoholics: Common characteristics* (Expanded ed.). Hollywood, FL: Heath Communications.

Wolery, M., & Wilbers, J. S. (1994). Introduction to the inclusion of young children with special needs in early childhood programs. In M. Wolery & J. S. Wilbers (Eds.), *Including children with special needs in early childhood programs*.

Washington, DC: National Association for the Education of Young Children.

Wolf, N. (1991). *The beauty myth: How images of beauty are used against women.* New York: Anchor.

Wolfe, D. A. (1994). The role of intervention and treatment services in the prevention of child abuse and neglect. In G. B. Melton & F. Barry (Eds.), *Safe neighborhoods: Foundations for a new national strategy on child abuse and neglect.* New York: Guilford.

Wolfenstein, M. (1953). Trends in infant care. *American Journal of Orthopsychiatry, 23,* 120–130.

Women on Words and Images. (1975). *Dick and Jane as victims: Sex stereotyping in children's readers.* Princeton, NJ: Author.

Women's Sports Foundation. (1989). *Minorities in sports.* New York: Author.

Wright, J. C., Huston, A. C., Reitz, A. L., & Piemymat, S. (1994). Young children's perceptions of television reality: Determinants and developmental differences. *Developmental Psychology, 30*(2), 229–239.

Wright, J. C., St. Peters, M., & Huston, A. C. (1990). Family television use and its relation to children's cognitive skills and social behavior. In J. Bryant (Ed.), *Television and the American family.* Hillsdale, NJ: Lawrence Erlbaum.

Yafai, S. (1992). *Individualism vs. collectivism: What to do?* Unpublished paper. Los Angeles: University of California, Department of Psychology.

Yarrow, M. R., Scott, P. M., & Waxler, C. Z. (1973). Learning concern for others. *Developmental Psychology, 8,* 240–260.

Yearbook of American and Canadian Churches. (1998). Nashville, TN: Abington Press.

Yogman, M. W., & Brazelton, T. B. (1986). The family: Stressed yet protected. In M. W. Yogman & T. B. Brazelton (Eds.), *In support of families.* Cambridge, MA: Harvard University Press.

Young, B. A., & Smith, T. M. (1997). *The condition of education, 1997.* Washington, DC: U.S. Department of Education.

Young, E. (1992). *Seven blind mice.* New York: Putnam.

Young, K. T. (1994). *Starting points.* New York: Carnegie Corporation.

Young, M., & Willmott, P. (1962). *Family and kinship in East London* (rev. ed.). Baltimore, MD: Penguin.

Young, T. W., & Shorr, D. N. (1986). Factors affecting locus of control in school children. *Genetic, Social, and General Psychology Monographs, 112*(4).

Youniss, J. (1981). Moral development through a theory of social construction: An analysis. *Merrill-Palmer Quarterly, 27,* 385–403.

Youniss, J., & Volpe, J. (1978). A relational analysis of children's friendship. In W. Damon (Ed.), *Social cognition.* San Francisco: Jossey-Bass.

Zahn-Waxler, C., & Radke-Yarrow, M. (1990). The origin of empathetic concern. *Motivation and Emotion, 14,* 107–130.

Zahn-Waxler, C., Radke-Yarrow, M., & King, R. A. (1979). Child-rearing and children's prosocial initiations toward victims of distress. *Child Development, 50,* 319–330.

Zahn-Waxler, C., Radke-Yarrow, M., Wagner, E., & Chapman, M.(1992). Development of concern for others. *Developmental Psychology, 28,* 126–136.

Zahn-Waxler, C., Robinson, J., & Emde, R. (1992). The development of empathy in twins. *Developmental Psychology, 28,* 1038–1047.

Zajonc, R. B. (1976). Family configuration and intelligence. *Science, 912,* 227–236.

Zajonc, R. B., Markus, H., & Markus, G. B. (1979). The birth order puzzle. *Journal of Personality and Social Psychology, 37,* 1325–1341.

Zarbatany, L., Hartmann, D. P., & Rankin, D. B. (1990). The psychological functions of preadolescent peer activities. *Child Development, 61,* 1067–1080.

Zaslow, M., Tout, K., Smith, S., & Moore, K. (1998). Implications of the 1996 welfare legislation for children: A research perspective. *Social Policy Report, 12*(3). Society for Research in Child Development.

Zill, N., & Schoenbom, C. (1990). Developmental, learning, and emotional problems. *Advance data.* National Center for Health Statistics. Washington, DC: U.S. Department of Health and Human Services. (No. 190)

Zion, G. (1956). *Harry the dirty dog.* New York: Harper & Row.

Zober, E. (1982). The socialization of adolescents into juvenile delinquency. *Adolescence, 16,* 321–330.

Zussman, J. U. (1980). Situational determinants of parental behavior: Effects of competing cognitive activity. *Child Development, 51,* 792–800.

ACKNOWLEDGMENTS

Figure 1.1: An Ecological Model of Human Development, based on concepts from U. Bronfenbrenner (1989). Ecological systems theory in R. Vasta (Ed.) *Annals of Child Development* (Vol. 6). Reprinted by permission of JAI Press.

Figure 2.2: The Processes and Outcomes of Socialization, adapted from *Human Socialization* by E. B. McNeil. Copyright © 1969 by Wadsworth Publishing Company, Inc. Reprinted with permission of Wadsworth Publishing, a division of Thomson Learning. FAX: 800-730-2215.

Figure 3.5: Social Class Structure in the United States from *Society and Education*, 8/e by D. U. Levine and R. J. Havighurst. Copyright © 1992 by Allyn & Bacon. Reprinted/adapted by permission.

Box: "How to Choose a Good Early Childhood Program" Copyright © 1990 by the National Association for the Education of Young Children. Reprinted by permission.

Figure 5.3: High/Scope Perry Preschool Project: Major Findings at Age 27 from "Success by Empowerment: High/Scope Perry Preschool Project: Major Findings at Age 27," by L. J. Sweinhart and D. P. Weikart in *Young Children*, 49 (1), p. 54. Copyright © 1993 by High/Scope Press.

Figure 5.4: Who's Watching the Children? from *The State of America's Children, Yearbook 1998.* Copyright © 1998 by the Children's Defense Fund, Washington, DC.

Figure 6.3: Meeting the Special Socialization Needs of Children with Disabilities from "Special Education as Developmental Capital" by E. Deno, in *Exceptional Children*, 37, pp. 229-237. Copyright © 1979 by the Council for Exceptional Children. Reprinted by permission.

Table 7.2: Suggestions for Working with Young Children who have Specific Impairments from *Strategies for Teaching Young Children* 3/e by J. A. Schickedanz, M. E. York, I. S. Stewart, and D. A. White. Copyright © 1990 by Prentice-Hall, Inc.

Box: Leadership Power and Punishment excerpt from *Blubber* by Judy Blume. Copyright © 1974 by Judy Blume, Reprinted with the permission of Simon & Schuster Books for Young Readers, an imprint of Simon & Schuster Children's Publishing Division.

Empowering Families to Help Themselves from *The State of America's Children, Yearbook 1994.*

Copyright © 1994 by the Children's Defense Fund, Washington, DC.

Table 10.3: Moments in America for Children from *The State of America's Children, Yearbook 1998.* Copyright © 1998 by the Children's Defense Fund, Washington, DC

Table 11.1: Stages of Moral Development from "Moral Stages and Moralization" by Lawrence Kohlberg in *Moral Development and Behavior*, edited by T. Lickona. Copyright © 1976 by Holt, Rinehart & Winston, Inc. Reprinted by permission.

Table 11.2: Types of Moral Judgments Made in Heinz's Dilemma from *Educational Psychology: A Contemporary View*, by Nicholas J. Anastasion, et al. Copyright © 1973 by Random House, Inc. Reprinted by permission.

Box: Suggestions for Promoting Moral Growth in the Classroom by Ronald Duska and Mariellen Whelan, from *Moral Development:* A guide to Piaget and Kohlberg (New York: Paulist Press). Copyright © 1975 by The Missionary Society of St. Paul the Apostle in the State of New York. Used by permission of Paulist Press.

Box: "Stages in the Development of Prejudice" from *Roots & Wings:* Affirming Culture in Early Childhood Programs by S. York. Reproduced by permission. Copyright © 1991 Redleaf Press, St. Paul, Minnesota. 800-423-8309

Box: Creating an Anti-Bias Environment from *Anti-bias curriculum:* Tools for empowering young children by L. Derman Sparks & the Anti-bias Task Force. Copyright © 1989 by the National Association for the Education of Young Children. Reprinted by permission.

Box: Measuring Locus of Control from "Who Rules You? External Control and Internal Control" by J. B. Rotter in *Psychology Today*, 5, 37-42. Reprinted from Psychology Today. Copyright © 1971 by the American Psychological Association.

Table A.1: "Developmental Tasks in Ten Categories of Behavior of the Individual from Birth to Death" from *Marriage and Family Development* 6/e by Evelyn Mills Duvall and Brent C. Miller. Copyright © 1985 by Harper and Row Publishers, Inc. Reprinted by permission of Addison-Wesley Educational Publishers.

PHOTO CREDITS

INDEX

Culture: altruism, 549–552; described, 78, 368; developmental skills, 55; families, 91; games, 338–339; gender roles, 565; high-context, 29–31; lifestyles, 127; mass, 371; media stereotyping, 403–404; morality, 489, 498–499; parenting, 146–147; self-concept, 572; symbolism, 287; youth, 407
Curran, Dolores, 102
Curriculum, 204–211, 288
Custody arrangements, 104, 108, 165
Custody Wars (Mason), 110
Customs, 432

D

Dahl, Roald, 366
D'Amato, Alfonse, 346
Day care, 184, 185. *See also* Child care
De La Hoya, Oscar, 272, 305
Death instinct, 534
Decentralization, 15
Decisions, 479–481
Deductive reasoning, 77
Delayed gratification, 123, 125, 532, 544
Delinquency, 351–352, 538–539
Democracy, 28–29, 141, 571, 572
Democracy and Education (Dewey), 234
Democratic leadership, 248–249, 357, 358
Democratic parenting, 153–155, 316, 318
Dependent-dominant behavior, 147–149
Depression, 21, 193
Deregulation, 371
Deschooling, 226
Desensitization, 380–381, 497
Developmental appropriateness, 189–190, 514
Developmental delay, 262–263
Developmental interaction curriculum, 210–211
Developmental skills, 53–55, 72–73
Developmental task, 54
Developmentally appropriate practice, 189
Dewey, John, 145, 210, 231–232, 234
Diana, Princess of England, 88, 369
Direct instruction curriculum, 207–208, 289
Disabilities: defined, 260; effect on parenting style, 162–163; learned helplessness, 576; maltreatment associated with, 176; portrayed in media, 404; prejudice towards, 502, 504
Discipline, 144, 492, 492
Discrimination, 255, 293, 507
Disengagment, 113
Diversity, 55, 213–214
Divorce, 100, 104–107; effect on children, 107–108; effect on parenting style, 165–166; rate, 103, 104; remarriages, 114
The Divorce Revolution (Weitzman), 104
Doctor-patient relationship, 7
Dodge, Kenneth, 539–540

Domestic partnerships, 90, 115
Domestic violence, 172, 173, 297–298
Donne, John, 420
Drucker, Peter, 7
Drug abuse. *See* Substance abuse
Drug addiction, 294
Dual-earner families, 19, 116–118, 152
Dubroff, Jessica, 5–6, 36–37
Dunn, Judy, 164, 329
Dunn, Lloyd, 262

E

Early childhood: education, 185; friends, 343; peer relationships, 316; play activity, 337; psychosocial development, 49; self-concept, 317; stages, 342
Early Childhood Environment Rating Scale, 188
Early Intervention Program, 289
Eating disorders, 21
Ecological model, 25–26, 540
Ecology, 4, 25–33
Economic assistance, 439, 447–451
Economic fluctuations, 22
Economic Opportunity Act, 185, 235
Economy: global, 13–14; industrial- to information-based, 8–12; interconnectedness, 6–7; neighborhood, 64, 427–429; status indicators, 35
Ectomorphy, 574
Education: for adaptability, 60; alternative, 434; attitude development, 504; bilingual, 235–236, 258–260; compensatory, 123; compulsory, 20; early childhood, 185, 186; family's role, 95; goals, 22f; learner-directed, 229–232; lifetime, 14; moral, 13, 491; multicultural, 258–260; occupation and income determinant, 58; status indicators, 35; teacher-directed, 229–231; value, 13
Education Excellence for All Children Act, 237
Education for All Handicapped Children Act, 235, 262
Education reform, 236, 434
Educational television (ET), 394
Edward, Prince of England, 88
Edwards, Carolyn, 565
Egalitarian attitude, 59
Egalitarian family, 91
Ego, 544
Egocentrism, 61, 76
Elder, Glen, 31–33, 429
Electra complex, 554
Elementary and Secondary Education Act, 235, 449
Elizabeth II, 91
Elkind, David, 22, 66, 322
Elliott, Jane, 509
E-mail, 100–101, 238
Emile (Rousseau), 226, 231